The L/L Research Channeling Archives

Transcripts of the Meditation Sessions

Volume 6
September 26, 1982 to June 3, 1984

| Don Elkins | Jim McCarty | Carla L. Rueckert |

Copyright © 2009 L/L Research

All rights reserved. No part of this book may be reproduced or used in any form or by any means—graphic, electronic or mechanical, including photocopying or information storage and retrieval systems—without written permission from the copyright holder.

ISBN: 978-0-945007-80-7

Published by L/L Research
Box 5195
Louisville, Kentucky 40255-0195

E-mail: contact@llresearch.org
www.llresearch.org

About the cover photo: *This photograph of Jim McCarty and Carla L. Rueckert was taken during an L/L Research channeling session on August 4, 2009, in the living room of their Louisville, Kentucky home. Jim always holds hands with Carla when she channels, following the Ra group's advice on how she can avoid any possibility of astral travel.*

Dedication

These archive volumes are dedicated to Hal and Jo Price, who faithfully and lovingly hosted this group's weekly meditation meetings from 1962 to 1975,

to Walt Rogers, whose work with the research group Man, Consciousness and Understanding of Detroit offered the information needed to begin this ongoing channeling experiment,

and to the Confederation of Angels and Planets in the Service of the Infinite Creator, for sharing their love and wisdom with us so generously through the years.

Table of Contents

Introduction 6
Year 1982 8
    September 26, 1982 9
    October 3, 1982 17
    October 17, 1982 25
    October 24, 1982 29
    October 28, 1982 36
    November 7, 1982 41
    November 14, 1982 49
    November 18, 1982 56
    November 18, 1982 59
    November 21, 1982 62
    November 28, 1982 69
    November 29, 1982 74
    November 29, 1982 77
    December 5, 1982 79
    December 11, 1982 83
    December 12, 1982 96
    December 12, 1982 102
    December 21, 1982 106
    December 21, 1982 113
    December 25, 1982 118
    December 26, 1982 121
Year 1983 129
    January 2, 1983 130
    January 13, 1983 140
    January 16, 1983 142
    January 23, 1983 147
    January 30, 1983 152
    February 13, 1983 156
    February 20, 1983 162
    February 27, 1983 166
    March 6, 1983 169
    March 13, 1983 175
    March 20, 1983 181
    March 22, 1983 186
    March 27, 1983 191
    April 3, 1983 201
    April 10, 1983 208

April 17, 1983	212
April 25, 1983	217
May 1, 1983	223
May 8, 1983	229
May 15, 1983	234
May 22, 1983	242
May 29, 1983	249
June 5, 1983	257
June 10, 1983	263
June 10, 1983	266
June 12, 1983	269
June 19, 1983	277
June 26, 1983	279
July 3, 1983	285
July 27, 1983	290
July 31, 1983	295
August 8, 1983	301
August 14, 1983	302
August 21, 1983	307
August 28, 1983	315
September 3, 1983	321
September 18, 1983	327
October 2, 1983	331
October 16, 1983	339
October 19, 1983	342
October 23, 1983	348
October 30, 1983	352
Year 1984	**357**
March 15, 1984	358
April 15, 1984	367
April 22, 1984, Easter	373
April 29, 1984	378
May 13, 1984	384
May 20, 1984	388
June 3, 1984	394

Introduction

Welcome to this volume of the *L/L Research Channeling Archives*. This series of publications represents the collection of channeling sessions recorded by L/L Research during the period from the early seventies to the present day. The sessions are also available on the L/L Research website, www.llresearch.org.

Starting in the mid-1950s, Don Elkins, a professor of physics and engineering at Speed Scientific School, had begun researching the paranormal in general and UFOs in particular. Elkins was a pilot as well as a professor and he flew his small plane to meet with many of the UFO contactees of the period.

Hal Price had been a part of a UFO-contactee channeling circle in Detroit called "The Detroit Group." When Price was transferred from Detroit's Ford plant to its Louisville truck plant, mutual friends discovered that Price also was a UFO researcher and put the two men together. Hal introduced Elkins to material called *The Brown Notebook* which contained instructions on how to create a group and receive UFO contactee information. In January of 1962 they decided to put the instructions to use and began holding silent meditation meetings on Sunday nights just across the Ohio River in the southern Indiana home of Hal and his wife, Jo. This was the beginning of what was called the "Louisville Group."

I was an original member of that group, along with a dozen of Elkins' physics students. However, I did not learn to channel until 1974. Before that date, almost none of our weekly channeling sessions were recorded or transcribed. After I began improving as a channel, Elkins decided for the first time to record all the sessions and transcribe them.

During the first eighteen months or so of my studying channeling and producing material, we tended to reuse the tapes as soon as the transcriptions were finished. Since those were typewriter days, we had no record of the work that could be reopened and used again, as we do now with computers. And I used up the original and the carbon copy of my transcriptions putting together a manuscript, *Voices of the Gods*, which has not yet been published. It remains as almost the only record of Don Elkins' and my channeling of that period.

We learned from this experience to retain the original tapes of all of our sessions, and during the remainder of the seventies and through the eighties, our "Louisville Group" was prolific. The "Louisville Group" became "L/L Research" after Elkins and I published a book in 1976, *Secrets of the UFO*, using that publishing name. At first we met almost every night. In later years, we met gradually less often, and the number of sessions recorded by our group in a year accordingly went down. Eventually, the group began taking three months off from channeling during the summer. And after 2000, we began having channeling meditations only twice a month. The volume of sessions dropped to its present output of eighteen or so each year.

These sessions feature channeling from sources which call themselves members of the Confederation of Planets in the Service of the Infinite Creator. At first we enjoyed hearing from many different voices: Hatonn, Laitos, Oxal, L/Leema and Yadda being just a few of them. As I improved my tuning techniques, and became the sole senior channel in L/L Research, the number of contacts dwindled. When I began asking for "the highest and best contact which I can receive of Jesus the Christ's vibration of unconditional love in a conscious and stable manner," the entity offering its thoughts through our group was almost always Q'uo. This remains true as our group continues to channel on an ongoing basis.

The channelings are always about love and unity, enunciating "The Law of One" in one aspect or another. Seekers who are working with spiritual principles often find the material a good resource. We hope that you will as well. As time has gone on the questions have shifted somewhat, but in general the content of the channeling is metaphysical and focused on helping seekers find the love in the moment and the Creator in the love.

At first, I transcribed our channeling sessions. I got busier, as our little group became more widely known, and got hopelessly behind on transcribing. Two early transcribers who took that job off my hands were Kim

Howard and Judy Dunn, both of whom masterfully transcribed literally hundreds of sessions through the eighties and early nineties.

Then Ian Jaffray volunteered to create a web site for these transcriptions, and single-handedly unified the many different formats that the transcripts were in at that time and made them available online. This additional exposure prompted more volunteers to join the ranks of our transcribers, and now there are a dozen or so who help with this. Our thanks go out to all of these kind volunteers, early and late, who have made it possible for our webguy to make these archives available.

Around the turn of the millennium, I decided to commit to editing each session after it had been transcribed. So the later transcripts have fewer errata than the earlier ones, which are quite imperfect in places. One day, perhaps, those earlier sessions will be revisited and corrections will be made to the transcripts. It would be a large task, since there are well over 1500 channeling sessions as of this date, and counting. We apologize for the imperfections in those transcripts, and trust that you can ascertain the sense of them regardless of a mistake here and there.

Blessings, dear reader! Enjoy these "humble thoughts" from the Confederation of Planets. May they prove good companions to your spiritual seeking. ☙

For all of us at L/L Research,

Carla L. Rueckert

Louisville, Kentucky

July 16, 2009

Year 1982

September 26, 1982 to December 26, 1982

L/L Research is a subsidiary of Rock Creek Research & Development Laboratories, Inc.

P.O. Box 5195
Louisville, KY 40255-0195

L/L Research

www.llresearch.org

Rock Creek is a non-profit corporation dedicated to discovering and sharing information which may aid in the spiritual evolution of humankind.

ABOUT THE CONTENTS OF THIS TRANSCRIPT: This telepathic channeling has been taken from transcriptions of the weekly study and meditation meetings of the Rock Creek Research & Development Laboratories and L/L Research. It is offered in the hope that it may be useful to you. As the Confederation entities always make a point of saying, please use your discrimination and judgment in assessing this material. If something rings true to you, fine. If something does not resonate, please leave it behind, for neither we nor those of the Confederation would wish to be a stumbling block for any.

CAVEAT: This transcript is being published by L/L Research in a not yet final form. It has, however, been edited and any obvious errors have been corrected. When it is in a final form, this caveat will be removed.

© 2009 L/L Research

Sunday Meditation
September 26, 1982

(Carla channeling)

[I am Hatonn,] and I greet you, my friends, in the love and the light of the one infinite Creator. May we thank and bless each within this circle at this time for the privilege of being able to share our lives and our thoughts with you. The service that you render us by requesting our humble opinions is very great. We find in this group a request which is unusual for this group, and that is for a specific instrument to speak our words for some of the time, and as this instrument is willing, we are happy to comply, but would suggest to you that each instrument is equally capable of offering, each in his or her own way, the message of the one original Thought.

You see, my friends, we have so little to tell you. It is extremely helpful for us to have a variety of instruments through whom we may share our thoughts, for each instrument brings to the task of speaking on a very simple subject memories, thoughts and vocabulary peculiar to that particular entity. Therefore, cherish you each other as you channel, each in your own way, for all of you are channels, if not in the service of this particular vocal channeling, then, my friends, in whatever you do are you the channels for the infinite Creator.

My friends, it behooves us to bring before your attention at this time the great amount of excess involved in the accepted ways of your peoples. More specifically, the excess of supply, the excess of interpersonal politeness, and the excess of spiritual hypocrisy. How much, my friends, do you need to give you that diaphanous, unshaped and inchoate thing called happiness? What of this world's belongings are necessary to the establishment and the perfection of your being and your seeking? How soft and how many must be your beds? How redundant your raiment? How filled your rooms within your dwellings and indeed how many rooms do you find necessary within them? Look you to the society with which you have commerce. What do you require of those to whom you have said, "I shall love you"?

Look again, and this time with the most careful eye at those efforts, specifically spiritual, and bring upon them the blinding light of honesty. Is there any variance at all between who you are and how you act? My friends, we are not suggesting that you give up civility, that you toss out furniture and live in smaller dwellings or that you are in any way lacking because there is some distance yet to go in learning the lessons of love. Far from it. What we are attempting to do is give to you a perspective from which to see that the Creator does provide all that is necessary. This, however, does not necessarily include large dwelling places, a multitude of friends trained to speak well of you, or your own good opinion of yourself at all times.

No, my friends. The Creator has provided you with that which you may call manna. You know the word from the holy book you call your Old Testament, and you may understand it to mean that supply without which you would no longer be able to inhabit this particular density, given that it is still your desire and your purpose to learn the lessons that you have come here to learn. The Creator has offered you an unlimited amount of love and with it you may choose the most miraculous lesson.

Yes, my friends, you may choose to love. This is the manna of the heart. Beyond this blessing there is no provision, for this blessing is what you may call an end in itself, working by the Law of Reflection within your spiritual life, and this is indeed always the most difficult to penetrate. The Creator has provided discrimination and this is the manna of the spirit. It is to be used against yourself. It is to be used with the understanding that all events which cause you to query your capacity for the penetration of understanding of love involve yourself and spiritual manna is most abundant. You may work upon yourself as much as you desire and that, my friends, is the important word. What do you desire? Do you desire physical manna? The manna of the heart, the manna of the spirit? Very well, then, your path shall be made plain. With every difficulty there shall come manna, and your will and your faith shall bring you into pleasant places where the heart may rest and the soul may bide. Do you desire other? Very well, then, you shall have to disentangle yourself periodically from the added and unnecessary enjoyments that the Creator has made available for each.

There is no lack of virtue in a great house, in many friends, or in expanded ministry as you see fit to aid others. If you may see your life as a tabernacle, we ask you to understand that your life may be as capacious as you wish to make it, as complicated as you wish to make it, as busy as you wish to make it, and in no case shall any portion or detail of your life be upon anything but holy ground. Great confusions among your people come from the belief that anything except manna is worth love. Enjoy those things which you have, but, boring as it may be, look at what the Creator has offered day by day, year by year. Always the same, my friends. You are one with the Father. Your body has its safekeeping, your heart, the gift of love that you may radiate with that one great original Thought of love to the ends of the Earth, if so you burn. It is your choice. You may progress as quickly as you desire. Encourage that desire, and let the tangles out of your light periodically through the practice of the presence of that manna. Be it a fleeting instant of awareness or a long meditation, the duration does not matter nearly so much as your desire to feel that presence, to touch the source that created in love and in light all that there is.

Hear you then, the clock strike. Say to yourself, "I have a choice, for the Creator is with me." See you the insignificant and petty detail of living, the unwashed dish, the unraked leaf? Go about that task knowing for a moment that you are the Creator, and that all that you see is the Creator. Look at the beauty of the shining plate, the sunlit window, the pleasant smell of cleanliness. Or as you rake, observe the creation of the Father. How can any creation be so filled with wonder, and yet you are one with all that is. Within you each leaf a miracle, and you the observer and the extension. And the one who says, "Praise and thanksgiving be to you, Creator." My friends, we know there are challenges within your lives. That is why we are here. We wish to let you know that that is cause for rejoicing and for work and again for rejoicing.

I am Hatonn. We have enjoyed speaking through this channel, and would like to defer now to the use of one or two others in order that each, as we have said, may offer the precious coloration of his or her being to our very simple thoughts. I now transfer this contact. I am Hatonn.

(K channeling)

I am Hatonn, and again I greet you, my friends, in the love and the light of the infinite Creator. As we contemplate the words, "of the light of the infinite Creator," our mind seems to stand still momentarily because these thoughts are more than we can grasp. As you listen to the news day by day and the confusion that your planet is in, it is difficult indeed to keep the faith, to use an expression of yours. But, my friends, the power to live the good life is a matter of your own choice because the power of the Creator is all about you. It is like the air you breathe. It is like the silence we feel at times. Indeed, the psalmist is right when he said, "Be still and know." The moments that are about you oftentimes make it difficult to be still, but again I repeat, the power to live the good life, the joyful life, the peaceful life, the compassionate life is yours for the choosing. And to repeat in closing, the power is available. I am Hatonn and I now leave this instrument.

(Carla channeling)

I am Hatonn. We speak briefly through this instrument in love and in light to note for the confirmation of the one known as M1 that we were indeed attempting to close through him. We shall again attempt this contact. I am Hatonn.

(M1 channeling)

I am Hatonn, and I am with this instrument. This instrument was a reluctant channel this evening because of desire that other channels may have their opportunity to share with you our words. We are pleased to have had the opportunity to share with each of you this evening our thoughts, our philosophies, and most of all, our love. It is a great service you do us by calling upon us, and a great honor indeed not only to speak to those who are quite familiar with our teachings, [but] especially this evening to those who are new to us. We take this opportunity to remind and to stress to you that we of Hatonn are sharing with you our understanding that we as a planet have assimilated over a great period of what you would call time. They are our perceptions, our concepts, and is the truth to the best of our understanding. But, my friends, we are certainly fallible. We are continuing on a path of learning. So take each morsel of teaching that we offer as food for thought. If we inspire you to think about your spiritual growth and the path you have chosen, we are honored. But take each thought, each concept, as only that, for of course it is up to each entity to choose for themselves what is truth, what is right, what is wrong, and not teacher or prophet can dictate for you your truth. For the Creator has given each of you the opportunity to choose for yourselves your path, to exercise your free will, to learn your lessons as you will, to experience the opportunities for learning you wish. And we are pleased to have the opportunity to give you a fresh insight from another point of view. We leave you now in the love and the light of the infinite Creator. I am Hatonn.

(Jim channeling)

I am Latwii, and I greet you, my friends, in the love and in the light of the one infinite Creator. It is our privilege once again to be able to join your group in the capacity of attempting to answer your queries. We thank each for extending to us this opportunity. It is a joyful privilege which we always look forward to. May we ask then if there might be a question we might attempt to answer?

Carla: Well, everybody's got questions. I hope you'll say for the instrument when the instrument's worn out. But I have one. First of all, I'd like to thank you very much for your presence on my walk the other day, and ask if you were aware that I was being greeted by a fifth-density negative friend, and was therefore attempting to either protect, or whether you were simply with me?

I am Latwii. As we perceive the heart of your query, my sister, may we say it was our privilege to join you at that time—and others as well—in response to your petition in the form of what you call prayer. For we of Latwii have the honor of serving as what you might call a comforter to various of your peoples who seek our service and our comfort.

May we answer you further, my sister?

Carla: No. Thank you very much, Latwii.

I am Latwii. May we thank you, my sister, as well. Is there another question at this time?

S: Yes. Would you please address or enlarge upon the concept that we label with the word "lazy"?

I am Latwii, and find that we have been given a rather large area upon which to expound. We shall attempt to respond as best we can. Each word which your peoples use has some type of connotation according to its use. Within your illusion the activities of busyness and accomplishing one task and then another and then another, seemingly without end, are given great value. And in such tasks there does indeed reside the lessons that teach love in some form or another. Yet, to those who do not choose to behave in the manner of busying themselves as proscribed by the culture in which they reside is given a variety of terms, one of which you have classed that of laziness. To laze about and to relax into the essence of one's being is frequently not valued among your people. But we ask you, my friends, is there not value in your very essence, and does that value not reside there of its own accord? Need you labor at one task or another in order to store up some form of chit that represents …

(Side one of tape ends.)

(Jim channeling)

I am Latwii, and am again with this instrument. To continue our thought—to those who labor without end at tasks of one sort or another would seem to fall the great value, but can the value or worth of an entity be measured in such a fashion? If such attempt is made, then what is the value of the one Creator which resides within each particle of your illusion which then does not accomplish work? Are the trees without value? Are the rivers which only flow and nourish by their beingness without value? Is the soil which does not move of its own accord without value? Is the Creator, which rejoices in Its beingness, within your beingness, without movement, therefore without value?

May we answer you further, my sister?

S: Thank you.

I am Latwii. We are most grateful to you, my sister. Is there another query at this time?

E: I have a question in regards to the last question, and that is, why is it then that most of our people have organized their lives so they have practically no time to spend peacefully, lazily?

I am Latwii, and am aware of your query, my brother. We find within your illusion that there has been of necessity a great forgetting. To forget the essence of one's being, though of an infinite value, is to allow the possibility of the increase of that beingness through the gaining of the experience which comes from what you call doing or acting. Entities then by such activity express the nature of the Creator in one form or another. By this expression is distilled the essence of the Creator. This essence then feeds that beingness so that there is completed a cycle of doing and being, each balancing the other.

Within your illusion it is most common to concentrate on that which is apparent, the seeming separation of all beings, and the ability to act in an infinite variety of ways because of this seeming separation. This then allows the Creator within each entity to know Itself more fully. It then becomes the task of each individual to balance the activity with the being. It is not easy within such an intense illusion to penetrate even the most simple mysteries of being. Seldom does an entity within your illusion truly ponder the reason for its being, the purpose for its life. Yet at some time, each does this, and whether the decision is made upon a conscious or upon a subconscious level, yet each decides to act, to be, and to balance as determined before the incarnation.

May we answer you further, my brother?

E: No, thank you. But I'd just like to see if I have it straight. In other words, if one proceeds through life and doesn't make any mistakes, one learns. And if one proceeds through life and makes a lot of mistakes, one learns more quickly?

I am Latwii, and am aware of your query, my brother. We would not choose the term "mistake," but would rather see all activities as the Creator knowing Itself. For indeed, if there is only the Creator which is acting and being, can there be a mistake?

May we answer you further, my brother?

E: No, thank you.

I am Latwii. We thank you. Is there another query at this time?

A1: Yes, Latwii. I have a question for a woman who is not here. Her name is A2. She was wondering—she understood that normally answers were not offered if the question was not directly asked. So therefore, if the question was asked mentally without words, could there be any answer?

I am Latwii, and am aware of your query, my sister. Normally this is also seen as an infringement. For to answer the query which has not been verbalized is to tread quite closely to infringing upon the free will which has not chosen to freely express itself.

May we answer you further, my sister?

A1: No, thank you.

I am Latwii. We thank you. Is there another query at this time?

J: Yes, Latwii. I have another question from A2 also. I believe the question that she would like answered is this. Is it possible that an entity would choose a third-density experience that would be lived in a state of mental pathology for the purpose of using this experience to learn about love and light, and also that this experience of living with the illness continue pretty much throughout life partly also for the benefit of those others who might learn from her in the way that she handles this?

I am Latwii. We believe that we perceive the heart of your query, and can respond by suggesting that indeed all things are most possible. We do not mean to sound simplistic, but look about you, my sister. Within your illusion, is there not an infinite variety of beingness exhibited within each entity? Is there not that which you call insanity, poverty, hunger, confusion, wealth, power, fame? Look about you. Recognize that each life pattern was chosen. There are no mistakes. Within your illusion is the lesson to be learned called love. Though the lesson be simple, the means of learning it are infinite.

It may indeed be such that an entity would choose to spend an entire life mute, crippled or in any other configuration of mind, body and spirit that can be imagined so that love might be learned in such and such a fashion. Each entity now incarnate upon your planet is living but a small portion of its total beingness at this time. The inertia, the accumulated experience of each entity determines the next lesson to be learned. The great variety contained within all of the infinite creation, therefore, suggests a great variety of biases to be gained and a great variety of biases to be the balances to be experienced for these biases in each incarnation.

May we answer you further, my sister?

J: Thank you, I believe that answers that one. Now I would like to ask for myself. Could you give me any understanding about the nature of the mental illness that is known as borderline personality?

I am Latwii, and am aware of your query, my sister. Those of your peoples who study the personality, as you have called it, have many descriptions for its expression. Such descriptions are utilized because they are convenient, and allow the entities to place in certain compartments, shall we say, those variations of the personality which they study. That type of personality which has most recently been called the borderline personality is a personality which is not well understood among your peoples, and therefore the termination of this personality, or that which is more correctly called the naming of this personality is most accurate, but regards those who name rather than those who are named.

We do not by this description mean to suggest that those who study and name are in any way to be denigrated or looked down upon, but mean to suggest that the term they have chosen describes more their inability to describe. The personality which is viewed as borderline is simply one which expresses in such a fashion as to be somewhat incomprehensible to the normal way of description. A personality which does not always reside within the normal bounds of your illusion then steps over the border or the line, shall we say, and expresses in a fashion which is comprehensible only to the deeper self of the entity so expressing.

There is not, to our knowledge, a personality or expression of personality which does not allow the entity so expressing the opportunity to learn the lessons of love. It may not be understandable in any ordinary fashion to those who view such an entity as to how such an entity might be benefiting either itself or any other by such expression which crosses the border, shall we say. Yet, within the one Creation there are no borders. Each entity is free to travel however it chooses. Most within your illusion travel in such and such a fashion and this fashion by the inertia, shall we say, and the numbers of its travelers, creates the parameters of normalcy. Yet, if each entity were closely studied, there would be found within each a portion of the personality which was not within these parameters and which had indeed crossed the border. For each entity has in its being a great variety of expression, and from time to time this expression becomes that which is not considered normal. Thus, [for] those entities which express in this non-normal fashion a greater percentage of their lives then is given a term such as this term of borderline personality.

May we answer you further, my sister?

J: Yes, let me just try to sort that out a little more. So this, then, is unusual and perhaps not ordinary, but it seems from what you've said that it's not necessarily pathological either. And from that point then, does it necessarily need to be corrected or made ordinary in the sense of being "not-different," or "not-pathological"?

I am Latwii, and am aware of your query, my sister. In responding most accurately, we must suggest that yes and no both be used. To an entity which is that known as pathological, it is both a service to experience in that mode, and to have others attempt to serve it by responding to it in one fashion or another. The interaction between the two serves as catalyst to teach each. Whether the entity becomes that known as normal or remains that known as pathological is of no importance. The dynamic interrelationship between such an entity and all entities surrounding it is that experience which offers the opportunity to each to learn love.

May we answer you further, my sister?

J: No. I guess I'm beginning to see that this is a difference just like any other disease. It offers catalyst and that's all right. Is that about it?

I am Latwii. This is correct, and indeed your entire illusion may be viewed in this manner.

May we answer you further, my sister?

J: Thank you, no. That's fine.

I am Latwii. We thank you. Is there another query at this time?

K: Yes, let me just see if I can ask this a little bit different. Then we can assume that any kind of an aberration or anything that we perceive as an aberration offers an opportunity for some to express love and others—offers the opportunity for both to learn love. Is that right? I don't think I said that very well. Any kind of an aberration gives each one the opportunity to learn to love? Is that right?

I am Latwii. This is quite correct, my sister. May we answer you further?

K: So then what we see going on in the Middle East, such as the massacre, can be seen in the same light? Is that right also?

I am Latwii. This is also quite correct, my sister. May we answer you further?

K: Well, I think that answers that. But I'd like to ask a question about dreams. Can one choose one's own dreams, or do we just pick up a lot of stuff that goes on about us in our dreams, and sometimes we can do nothing about it, we just simply do pick up what goes on about us? I didn't make that very clear either, I don't guess. Can we choose what we dream about?

I am Latwii, and am aware of your query, my sister. It is only for those which you might call the adept to choose the dream which shall be experienced, for the dream, though it has a great variety of uses, has the primary use of reflecting in symbolic form the catalyst that the entity faces in its daily life so that the entity might once again review and utilize that catalyst. To choose the dream assumes a great efficiency in the use of the catalyst. It assumes the conscious recognition upon the part of the entity so choosing that it does indeed reside within an illusion which provides a means of progress in evolution through the catalyst of daily experiences. To program, shall we say, a dream is quite like the entity programming the incarnation before entering the incarnation. This requires much ability, which does not normally begin to be recognized or accumulated by an entity while in the incarnation, but is possible.

May we answer you further, my sister?

K: No, I don't believe so, thank you.

I am Latwii. We thank you. Is there another query at this time?

Carla: Following up on K there, I'm intrigued. There are two kinds of dreams that I have frequently enough to be noticeable. The one kind really common with everybody—I'm either teaching somebody or somebody's teaching me, and the other one, I'm somewhere else going through Raiders of the Lost Ark kind of things, the good guys against the bad guys, or whatever, on another planet, though. I've never been able to tie these two particular kinds of dreams to catalyst, and the only other kind of dream that I have that doesn't seem to be tied to catalyst is dreams where I see something happening in the future, which I've done a couple of times, and it has happened. So, are there also other uses for dreams besides working through the catalyst on a deeper level? And are these uses far less important?

I am Latwii, and am aware of your query, my sister. There are indeed a great variety of uses for dreams, none to be considered more or less valuable. The varieties which you have mentioned are examples of a perspective upon the life experience. For example, might not a life be looked at as a teaching and a learning? And does not each teach each? Look into that which is being taught for the catalyst. And as you journey through your life, might it not be seen as a great adventure? Look then to the kind of adventure you experience for the catalyst. And it is true that from time to time an entity may see that which is called the future. Indeed, there are many futures, as you may call them, and when an entity in the dreaming state experiences that experience which does then occur in what you call your future, there is a special connection which has been made between the entity and a deeper portion of itself. And the deeper mind has made available to the conscious mind an experience which shall be of especial value to this entity.

May we answer you further, my sister?

Carla: Yes, on another subject, but first I wanted to share a terrible joke that just occurred to me. What would be another term for a bill of lading on a boxcar full of bulls? A catal-lyst.

(Giggles and groans.)

Carla: The other question I have … Sorry about that! I thought Latwii would like it. Latwii, you're not laughing.

I am Latwii. We find ourselves convulsing in laughter.

Carla: Thank you.

We appreciate your humor, as you know. Please continue.

Carla: The other question that I had, I really wanted to pursue it a little further. Just so I could get it. I really want to get this. I understand how a healer—even if a healer fails—is learning the lessons of love by trying, by trying to heal, by offering itself in service. But, because of the fact my mother happens to be a psychologist, I hear some really wild things about real psychopaths. And, one simple example. There's a lady that speaks only Spanish who came into Central State Hospital five days before my mother told me the story. She was on her way out of town to a spiritual retreat, and looked a bit drawn. In that five days, this hundred and sixty pound Spanish-speaking woman, whom everybody calls C because she does nothing except dance and sing when she is not attacking people, had attacked nineteen people, and put several of them in the hospital. She had not gotten around to my mother yet. There is no way, either in Spanish or in English, that anyone can cause her to focus her attention. There is no medication except megadoses of tranquilizer that will cause her to stop dancing, singing and attacking people, which she does seemingly without any anger. She simply attacks them and attempts to kill them until someone subdues her, still singing and dancing. There is no connection.

Now, we're not talking about people that are seeing life a little differently, we're talking about somebody who sees life a lot differently, who is not able to communicate across the boundary in any way. How is this person learning the lesson of love? If you can't answer this, I understand.

I am Latwii, and am aware of your query, my sister. To begin, may we suggest that the healer never fails, but may exert an effort which has results which are different than those intended. May we also suggest that an entity such as the one you have described may indeed learn those lessons of love in such behavior as you have described over what might be called the longer span of its beingness. For its current life experience has accumulated a certain bias which is being expressed in that behavior which is seen as quite erratic, and this bias, when viewed between what you call the incarnations by this entity in time/space, this then as a bias will teach that entity a certain lesson. This entity shall determine to take one path or another in continuing its learning of love according to the bias gained in this incarnation. Sometimes the lessons of love come quite slowly. Yet, the progress is always made, and one incarnation might be as the grain of sand upon the beach.

May we answer you further, my sister?

Carla: You mean even when there is apparently no motion, there is absolutely flat affect, nothing from the outside in and from the inside out, a person is learning from the experiences that it is apparently not experiencing? To some degree, in some way? A yes will do—I've taken up too much time.

I am Latwii: Our sister, though "yes" is our response, may we also suggest that the entity which acts within the incarnation is but a portion of itself. And though, as that portion, may have difficulty in learning from the great variety of its experiences, yet those experiences do teach love. You may look at each incarnation as containing a great abundance of useless detail, in that the detail itself does not have value, but the detail upon detail upon detail creates a bias. The bias expands experience and experience teaches love.

May we answer you further, my sister?

Carla: No, thank you, Latwii.

I am Latwii. We thank you, my sister. Is there another query at this time?

M: Yes, I have one. While Hatonn was with us, I had this weird feeling of floating on a cloud and looking down and looking down, and floating for a long time, and finally looking down and seeing this rather violent scene of a deserted street with either wolves or dogs growling and fighting. Does that have any meaning?

I am Latwii. My sister, we are quite pleased to see that you have pulled yourself from the hole which you inhabited upon our previous meeting.

(Laughter)

L: It was hole-arious!

Indeed, each experience then does have a meaning, but the meaning of such must be determined by the entity so experiencing the sensation.

May we answer you further, my sister?

M: No, but I don't think I'll ever understand it.

I am Latwii. Do not underestimate yourself, my sister. Last week you were quite despairing of ever climbing from the hole. Next week may bring further miracles.

May we answer you further?

M: No, that's sufficient.

I am Latwii. Is there another query at this time?

J: Yes, Latwii. Let me try an observation, and ask you to comment on it. Now, ordinarily in third-density illusion we see people as being successful in, say, their personal evolution as we see it in third density who are healthy, organized, successful and they've got it all together. Now I'm beginning to see that on a more transcendent basis there's no real way of being able to evaluate the real personal evolution that may be going on. It is possible for a person to be experiencing a great deal of catalyst, for instance, economic misfortune, or mental illness or physical illness or depression or confusion, and be at a more advanced level of evolution, or progressing, making a lot of progress or not. Is there any … well, could you comment?

I am Latwii, and am aware of your query, my sister. Indeed it does not matter which distortion an entity chooses. There are lessons to learn. Entities, as you are aware, are quite unique, and each does not learn in the same manner. You may view any entity's position in your social, political, economic or other arenas, and yet be unable to determine where upon the path of evolution that entity treads. There are, of course, the various accepted means within your culture by which an entity might be measured. It is as though the children were gathered upon the playground …

(Tape ends.)

L/L Research

L/L Research is a subsidiary of Rock Creek Research & Development Laboratories, Inc.

P.O. Box 5195
Louisville, KY 40255-0195

www.llresearch.org

Rock Creek is a non-profit corporation dedicated to discovering and sharing information which may aid in the spiritual evolution of humankind.

ABOUT THE CONTENTS OF THIS TRANSCRIPT: This telepathic channeling has been taken from transcriptions of the weekly study and meditation meetings of the Rock Creek Research & Development Laboratories and L/L Research. It is offered in the hope that it may be useful to you. As the Confederation entities always make a point of saying, please use your discrimination and judgment in assessing this material. If something rings true to you, fine. If something does not resonate, please leave it behind, for neither we nor those of the Confederation would wish to be a stumbling block for any.

CAVEAT: This transcript is being published by L/L Research in a not yet final form. It has, however, been edited and any obvious errors have been corrected. When it is in a final form, this caveat will be removed.

© 2009 L/L Research

Sunday Meditation
October 3, 1982

(M1 channeling)

[I am Hatonn.] I am now with this instrument. We greet you with the love and the light of the one infinite Creator. If you need an example of something that is at peace with its environment, think of a cloud floating along on gentle breezes, blown by every wind, rained on, made fresh again, gets where its going, at peace with its environment. When you seem to be scurrying and at odds with the things around you, think of yourself as a floating cloud. This will help you see that there is meant to be harmony in all things. Try to feel in your harmony in harmony with your God. Problems will not seem as acute, more as an ongoing thing, as weeds in a flower garden, as rain in the sky. Get the feeling of oneness. This will help you, people and animals around you, feel your serenity. It will not solve your problems but it will give you a harmony with them. I am Hatonn. I leave this instrument.

(Carla channeling)

I am Hatonn, and greet you once again through this instrument in the love and the light of the infinite Creator. It is our joy to speak through each instrument, and we respect the always courteous portion of the one known as A, and the one known as M2 as they each wish to allow others the opportunity to exercise their channel. At the risk of sounding repetitious, we would point out to each the ultimate difficulty of such an overwhelming courtesy. However, we are inclined to allow these developing channels the opportunity to feel with more and more certainty when we wish to speak through one or the other. It is very seldom that we shift our communication to more than one instrument at a time, and when the parallel activation is done, it is for the purpose of confirmation. Therefore, we will leave this instrument for a time and once again offer to one but not both of these instruments an opportunity which may be taken at this time to speak a few words. We will then gladly confirm through this instrument the intention which we had. I am Hatonn.

(M2 channeling)

I am Hatonn. I am at last with this instrument. We are pleased at an opportunity to work briefly with this instrument as we are pleased at the opportunity to share this time with each that is here tonight. We would speak on a topic we have spoken on many times in your gatherings, the topic of love, which is essentially intertwined in everything that we bring to share with you. Love for one another, love of a country, for your world, and of course, an important love you must have for yourself. When we speak of a love for oneself, we wish to express the importance of one appreciating themselves, their essence, as being one with the Creator, for if one cannot fully appreciate their true essence, are they not handicapped in their desires to spread the Creator's love to all that is around them? For without that appreciation by which you value the self can one have the strong faith that in turn accounts for the strong will which is so important a driving force in spreading that love you wish to share with those around you?

My friends, each of you are indeed the Creator. We have spoken this to you many times before and yet it seems to be a concept which you hear but do not fully believe. You seem to look at yourself as all too often an insignificant, unable, weak, small factor in the things that go on around you. My friends, the things, the events, the experience that occurs around you is truly your own creation. From the smallest grain of sand on the seaside to the multitudes, it is all your creation, certainly not the work of an insignificant [entity] or another faceless soul, just one among the masses. Recognize, my friends, the gift the Creator has bestowed upon you. Be one with the essence of unlimited abilities the Creator has bestowed upon you; at the same time, the opportunity to limit yourself. Each of you are truly a treasure, a masterpiece, a consummation of all the greatness of your imaginations and beyond. A difficult concept for you in the confines of this illusion, but all the same, a very real opportunity for each who struggles by themselves.

We will transfer this contact. I am Hatonn.

(Carla channeling)

I am Hatonn, and greet you once again in love and light, speaking briefly through this instrument only, and to use this instrument as vehicle for confirmation both of the direction of our intention and of the subject matter. We are pleased that the confidence of the instruments begins to become set in ways of a realization of service, for in truth, as we move about the group with its several channels, the normal courtesy of awaiting a turn and of listening for others should be laid aside so that the tuning may be more and more precise. Then when the signal comes to you, each channel may pick it up and receive it. Thus, each indeed will take the turn but the flow of communication will be unfettered and much stronger for this confidence.

We would proceed, using other channels at this time, and again we ask, as you feel our contact, please feel free to speak, knowing that we speak through only one at a time, and do not, shall we say, put our contact up for grabs, but rather attempt to move from instrument to instrument in such a way that our very simple message may be given the most beautiful and rich interpretation of which we are capable.

We would now transfer this contact. I am Hatonn.

(A channeling)

I am Hatonn. I greet you once again, and we shall speak briefly through this instrument, for that is her desire. To continue on our previous message, we shall add these few words. Desire to find peace with yourself while you are walking along the path. For when you are at peace, you will be at your center where you can see your own light so that you might bring forth to others more fully.

We shall now leave this instrument. I am Hatonn.

(K channeling)

I am Hatonn. I am now with this instrument, and again greet you in the light and the love of the infinite Creator. It has been a joy to listen to your animated conversations tonight. However, we would add one bit of warning which all of you know can't be repeated too often. As has been indicated through the one known [as] M2, you are all creators. And as you very well know, negative thoughts create, just the same as the positive ones. And when you find yourselves dwelling on the negative thoughts of yourself or others, it would be well to remember that you are the Creator. Just stopping long enough to remember that we are creators reminds us again of the path we should follow. Indeed, my friends, life can be beautiful. It can be harmonious as you learn how to create your own harmony and beauty. However, we would add one further word. The essence of each of us is harmony and beauty and peace, but your illusion makes it difficult for you to keep this in mind at all times.

Again may we say it has been a pleasure and a joy for us to be with you, and I leave you now in the light and the love of the infinite Creator. I am Hatonn.

(Carla channeling)

I am Latwii. First our brother Hatonn speaks soberly through this instrument about reluctant channels, and then this channel is reluctant. Well, my friends, we still greet you most joyously in the love and the light of the one infinite Creator. How joyful, how wonderful, how lovely it is to be with you. We are so pleased to be able to use this instrument for a word or two before receiving questions. We sense, my friends, that there is a point which wisdom seeks within you this evening. Therefore, we are called in a general way, and so we shall share our humble thoughts with you, reminding you that we are but poor fools and our mummery is but the shabbiest of words covering the nakedness of our ignorance of the ultimate truth. However, what little we know we share with the utmost pleasure.

We are aware, my friends, that each of you has desired to know what it is that you shall do in response to your great and precious knowledge. How shall you be the givers of yourselves? How shall you share? Well, my friends, if we were speaking of your money, we could simply say give such and such an amount, give such and such a percentage. For in your world, is it not easy to think in terms of quantity, and in your life, do you not often judge yourself by the quantity of your actions? Let us examine, my friends, what it is that you have to share. It is written in your holy works that that which you have is like a tiny bit of yeast, which put in a large amount of grain leavened the whole. It was not a great quantity that the one known as Jesus discussed in his teaching. It was a very small amount. But it was a very small amount of the proper quality.

What you have to share is a quality, not a quantity. Those who love want to do much but they must first understand that the work of love is infinite. You cannot do a great deal of infinite work or a small amount of infinite work. You do infinite work. Now, my friends, to business, then! How do you do infinite work of a certain quality? You are not all alike. This, our brothers and sisters of Hatonn have spoken of. Each has a totally unique radiance, and that is the quality that you have to give. You do not all have equal gifts. Yet each gift is most blessed, and that gift, whatever it may be, is the quality that you have to give. Therefore, my friends, before you share that leaven of hope, of praise, of joy, of faith, of light, of love, allow that second of silent opening within, that prayer which is so simple, my friends. Not my will, but My will, O Creator, the will of me as You, be done. Not the little self, but the great Self. Open me, use me. This is the prayer, this is the hope, this is the faith.

It only takes a fraction of a second, my friends, and in that fraction of a second, you may well exchange quantity for quality. Your people hurry and scurry. Our brother, Hatonn, points us to the clouds of your planet. What quality of radiance awaits you in the center of your effortless perfect being? And under what bushel of busyness and quantity do you hide that radiance? Much has been given you, my brothers and my sisters. You are very close to the kingdom you desire. All that is precious lies just beyond the illusion of the door. Meditation is a key, prayer another. Now may you rejoice and shine forth your light in a dark world that all who come unto you may feel the healing. But let it not be effortful or burdensome or difficult. Let it be that which is done so that no one shall know. Let your light shine so that the kingdom is revealed, not you. Perhaps the most difficult thing for a pilgrim to do is to discover how to get out of the way of that great and abiding flame of love. Let it burn through you, never from you.

We shall now put you atop the clouds of our brothers and sisters of Hatonn, and let you float merrily there, thinking your thoughts and perhaps asking a few questions if you would. To this end, we thank this instrument, reluctant though she was, and would at this time transfer to one who does us great service, for which we are forever grateful. I am Latwii.

(Jim channeling)

I am Latwii, and greet you once again in love and light. We are now honored to offer our humble selves in the capacity of attempting response to your queries. May we ask then if there might be a query?

M1: I have one, Latwii. What is the principle behind identical twins or identical triplets?

I am Latwii, and am aware of your query, my sister. In the case of the births of entities of what you would call the identical nature there is the incarnation of entities of the exact vibrational frequency which have chosen to play out certain patterns of interrelationships which have developed over great periods of what you call time and through many of what you call the incarnations …

(Side one of tape ends.)

(Jim channeling)

I am Latwii, and am with this instrument once again. Such entities have experienced a great portion of their existence in a shared manner so that it becomes appropriate at a certain time, so to speak, to make that shared experience complete. In such a situation it is then determined that what is called the birth of twins, triplets and so forth of an identical nature might be appropriate and is then undertaken. The underlying reason for this, to summarize, is the completion of a pattern of existence which has been chosen by free will by entities which have found a mutual comradeship and learning possible in an intensified manner with an other or others. And this journey is then manifested in such and such a manner.

May we answer you further, my sister?

M1: Thank you. I do have another question. What causes people to go to excesses, whether it's overeating or drinking or drugs or overworking or any other form of excesses?

I am Latwii, and am aware of your query, my sister. To reply most accurately to such a query, we find that our response may seem much too simplistic. But it might be said that any entity which exhibits the great distortion in any direction is either attempting to balance the opposite bias or is attempting to develop a certain bias which then may itself be balanced. This is the plan of the Creator for the gathering of experience. It might also be suggested that for some entities there is the momentary difficulty in developing the desired bias, and what might be called an overreaction to the halting of progress might then also be developed as a bias which was not the primary intention. Nevertheless, each bias provides the opportunity for balance and each balance the opportunity for experience.

May we answer you further, my sister?

M1: I'm not exactly sure. Do you mean that they deliberately go in a certain direction or that their personality is out of sync at that particular time and they are not entirely aware of what they are doing?

I am Latwii, and to clarify our previous response, may we suggest that before the incarnation, certain lessons, which might be called biases, are determined appropriate for that incarnation. These biases may appear during the incarnation to be in excess. There might also be the free will choice of the entity during the incarnation, unaware of the preincarnative choice, to respond to the developing bias in yet another overblown fashion, shall we say. Each action, whether determined before the incarnation or during the incarnation provides a bias, whether great or small, which then must needs be balanced by its opposite bias. Such balancing then aids in the gathering of experience, and this experience is the reason for the incarnation itself.

May we answer you further, my sister?

M1: No, I think you've answered it, but it seems like I have a lot of questions. I've got a third one. When test tube babies are formed, does that interfere with their normal progression?

I am Latwii, and am aware of your query, my sister. Within the bounds of your illusion, such would seem the case, for the great majority of entities which enter your illusion do so in a manner which is quite unlike that you have described, and would seem then to be quite homogeneous. In some respects, of course, this is quite correct. But we might also note that each entity's entrance into the illusion which you now inhabit is quite unique. Some who enter your illusion do not actually inhabit the physical vehicle of the fetus for some period of what you call time, choosing to enter at the last moment, shall we say, when birth has occurred, and some even after that event, as well. If an entity should, therefore, decide to enter your illusion, a method for its entering shall be made available. This method might include what has recently been developed by your scientists, that being the test tube entrance. This does provide a certain framework within which the new entity then begins the incarnation. That it is different from most others is undeniably correct. That most others are homogeneous is not correct, for all are quite unique. Each entity is provided the precise requirements to proceed with the incarnation before it.

May we answer you further, my sister?

M1: No, I think you've answered that question, but it's brought up a fourth one. When babies are aborted, are they usually inhabited by an entity or are they babies which no entity has inhabited?

I am Latwii. To speak again to the heart of this query, we must again note that there cannot be a general statement which is adequate. Some entities need only the briefest of experiences of a certain nature within your illusion, and are with the vehicle which has been, as you have described, aborted. A larger majority, shall we say, of these aborted physical vehicles are not inhabited, for it is known that they shall not reach your illusion, shall we say.

May we answer you further, my sister?

M1: No, that's fine. You've given me a lot of good answers.

I am Latwii. We thank you, my sister, for your excellent queries. May we ask if there might be another query at this time?

K: I'd like to follow up on the last question just a little bit. Are you saying then that although a fetus is beginning to grow, it is not really alive with the soul yet in some cases?

I am Latwii, and am aware of your query, my sister. This is not a simple query with which a response can easily be matched. In one sense the entire creation is alive and sings with the spirit of the one Creator. There is no portion that does not have this spirit. And it is also true in another sense that when an entity known as a fetus is housed within its mother's womb, there is often the absence of the enlivening mind/body/spirit complex which is common among your peoples, and without which the fetus would not appear to be human, as you call it, but without which, in rare instances, the physical vehicle of the orange ray may yet function. In some cases this fetus does indeed contain the mind/body/spirit complex which gives its coloration of humanity, as you call it, for it has been determined by the incarnatinq entity that an early, as you might call it, entrance into this fetus is useful for the beginning of the lessons of this incarnation.

May we answer you further, my sister?

K: Is a child ever born without that whole complex, and receives it afterwards?

I am Latwii. This is correct, my sister. May we answer you further?

K: No, thank you, that's fine.

I am Latwii. We thank you. Is there another question at this time?

Carla: Are there ever borderline cases where a mother and a child may have an agreement before the incarnation of both to have a life together, and then the mother finds herself in a position where the public ethic is not useful to her, and the private ethic is basically unknown, and so she wavers a great deal and finally ends up aborting—so that the fetus is occupied—and then when it is observed that birth is not going to be possible, the mind/body/spirit complex simply leaves and awaits another opportunity. Is that ever possible so that it's sort of yes and no sometimes instead of just sometimes yes and sometimes no?

I am Latwii, and am aware of your query, my sister. You have correctly surmised that before each incarnation agreements are made. The agreements made, shall we say, are not ironclad. There are in many cases contingency plans, as you might call them, which recognize the ever changing nature of what you call your future as free will exerts its force within your illusion. If certain boundaries or parameters of the incarnation in its beginning are met, then it is begun as planned. If there is a significant change in such boundaries, then there might be the decision to take an alternative route for entry into the illusion, and an alternative means of joining the relationship with the one already within the illusion. Though this is somewhat unusual, it is ever possible.

May we answer you further, my sister?

Carla: Yes, I'm very interested in this subject. Along with almost everybody, I suppose, I have instinctive feelings about whether abortion is right or not. The debate runs high on that one and discarding the concept of sin, I would take up the concept of karma. Is it ever possible that by aborting a child with whom one has made a very careful agreement, one may—a mother may collect the karma which is simply the promise for future—so it's missed this time, but there will be another lifetime in which that relationship will be worked out. Is it ever that inevitable or is it freer than that?

I am Latwii, and am aware of your query, my sister. To speak of that known as karma is to use a term which has among many of your peoples an emotional impact which we do not desire to invoke. We would, however, suggest that entities which engage in an agreement which is then altered by the activity known as abortion will at some point within that incarnation or another complete that agreement which has been made. The ability of entities upon your planet to utilize what you have called abortion adds yet another variable to entities which are deciding upon the means of relating one to another and of beginning the incarnation. Within your illusion are an infinite variety of such considerations which must be taken into account by each entity before the incarnation. Thus, the addition of one more variable does have its effect, and this effect may or may not be profound. It is, however, considered by each entity before the incarnation is begun and does, as does each consideration, have certain repercussions which then must be balanced.

May we answer you further, my sister?

Carla: Only to confirm that this would be the answer which you would also give to questions about voluntary birth control and voluntary sterilization?

I am Latwii. My sister, this is quite correct, as would such items within your illusion as the transportation by your various vehicles and their likelihood of collision and subsequent passing from the incarnation, as would the various chemicals and drugs utilized by those whom you call healers, as would the great variety of means of interacting which your game sports provide, as indeed would each activity which is available within your illusion provide the need for an entity entering your illusion to consider its impact upon the incarnation.

May we answer you further, my sister?

Carla: Yes, because that last, although general, didn't get to what I wanted to find out. There are many more women, I think, that are simply very careful not to have children for one reason or another than have abortions. My question was whether there was a possibility that the same karma, to use a non-emotional form of this word, might be caused by being voluntarily sterilized or using voluntary birth control when a woman had forgotten that she had agreed before incarnation to be in a mother and child relationship with another entity who is then unable to enter. What I'm trying to do is get to the heart of all of the nonsense that has been spoken on both sides about—not just abortion but birth control, so I'd like to find out if there is an actual amount of, shall we say, delay or damage that one can do by birth control or sterilization to an entity with whom you've had the agreement or whether birth control is simply something that person does because that person is inwardly aware that no such agreements have been made for this period or at all. Can you get anything out of that question?

I am Latwii, and indeed, my sister, we believe we feel the heart of your query has been well expressed. We would once again respond by suggesting that there are no mistakes within your illusion. When an entity chooses to enter within your third-density illusion, it is well aware of the parameters within which it shall move, of the resources which to it shall be available. The agreements made before the incarnation are agreements made in the light of this knowledge. Therefore, there is, in truth, no action which can be undertaken by any during the incarnation which were not seen as possibilities before the incarnation began. Thus, each activity which is engaged in during the illusion does have its effect, yet each activity was also known to be a possibility before the incarnation was begun. Therefore, such actions are not undertaken in a willy-nilly fashion, shall we say. Though their effects shall be felt by those in their vicinity, these effects have also been chosen.

May we answer you further, my sister?

Carla: So there isn't the case where there is a child waiting and hoping to be born to a certain mother, and then it comes as a big surprise because sterilization has occurred or birth control is consistently used. You're saying that to a certain extent this is—enough is known about the incarnations of both that this situation just doesn't occur?

I am Latwii, and am aware of your query, my sister. This in general is quite correct, though it is also a possibility that an entity awaiting the incarnation shall await that incarnation somewhat longer than originally intended. This is also a possibility which is seen by each entity which attempts to enter that illusion which you now inhabit. The great range of sight, shall we say, or the far-seeing ability which is denied to those within your illusion is that factor which resolves the great complex difficulty which an entity has in attempting to clarify just how this illusion operates. Before the incarnation, the range of sight is quite without time or space and an entity might view into what you call the future with a great degree of clarity, and therefore make the necessary choices for the upcoming, as you would say, incarnation.

May we answer you further, my sister?

Carla: I'd like to ask one more short question. I think I've dragged this line of questioning out long enough. Is it possible that a person could have to reincarnate instead of graduating in order to complete an agreement? In other words, stay in third density instead of going on with graduation because of a missed agreement?

I am Latwii, and am aware of your query, my sister. As we have said many times, all things are quite possible, though most activities are very difficult to generalize and to predict with certainty. All things are indeed quite possible.

May we answer you further, my sister?

Carla: No, thank you, Latwii.

I am Latwii. We thank you. May we ask if there might be another question at this time?

K: Yes. Regarding the free will of the woman who chooses to abort or not to have children, is the woman exercising the same free will that she exercises when she decides to marry or not to marry or when she decides to work or not to work? Is it a matter of exercising the free will? What I'm trying to say, she's exercising her free will in each instance in whether to abort or whether not to abort, and is there any difference in the degrees of exercising her free will?

I am Latwii, and am aware of your query, my sister. Each choice, no matter what the subject, is an exercise of will, freely made. As the mind is configured by its very nature of being, and as it gathers the experiences of your illusion, it becomes biased either in the service-to-self sense or in the service-to-others sense. With this general coloration, then does the individual entity begin to increase its polarization so that each choice which is made adds in some fashion to that polarization. Each choice, no matter what the subject of the choice, then might be seen as adding or subtracting from the polarization which is the general character, shall we say, of the entity. The various choices available within the illusion are simply means by which an entity adds to the polarization which it has chosen.

May we answer you further, my sister?

K: No, I think that answers the question. Just one other brief question. The planet is rapidly becoming overpopulated, and I think in the last session I remember that you said that people were—entities were choosing to come here at this point in time, as we call time, in order to go through the harvest. Now my question is—if I've got that much of it right—my question is: Are entities coming here choosing to live in poverty, because many of them are living in poverty, are they literally choosing to live in poverty until the time of harvest?

I am Latwii, and am aware of your query, my sister. Indeed, you have stated the situation quite correctly. It is a paradox within your illusion to consider those elements of your illusion—such as the poverty, hunger, disease, pain, warfare—delicacies. Yet such existences provide an entity with the greatest of opportunities in which to learn love in the shortest of what you call periods of time.

Therefore, as your cycle grows to an end, you will see the varieties of experience increase in all fashions, including those which within your illusion are normally seen as quite undesirable, yet within the greater framework of the progression through the densities such characteristics offer great opportunities for evolution of mind and body and spirit.

May we answer you further, my sister?

K: So then, some may have come here at this point just to get blown up with an atomic bomb? Is that stretching it a little too far?

I am Latwii, and am aware of your query, my sister. It is somewhat, shall we say, the case that entities would seek the traumatic experience up to a certain point. For beyond that point which you have described, there is seen the trauma to the mind/body/spirit complex which tends to break apart that complex and reduce its ability to assimilate experience, and therefore require a great period of what you would call time to be undergone in the healing and reintegration of those complexes. Therefore, it is the desire of entities entering your illusion at this time to experience as intensely as possible the opportunities for learning the lessons of love without damaging the complexes which enable that learning to continue.

May we answer you further, my sister?

K: No, that makes sense. Thank you very much.

I am Latwii. We thank you very much as well. Is there another query at this time?

Carla: Yes, I have one more because I'm sort of riveted on this point here. I always thought when I was a young woman that I was destined to have children, about six of them, as a matter of fact, and I never had children. The one child I ever conceived, I lost spontaneously, and I'm now sterilized voluntarily. Reluctantly, but voluntarily. And I have spent much time actually thinking about what children wanted me for their mother. And although I realized that it was completely necessary within the way I look at things now that I not have children, so that I can do the work that we're doing, I think about those children, and I wonder how they're doing and if I have in some way incurred some karma because of the forgotten agreements that I made possibly with them. I feel sure that this is true of other women as well. Is there some way to communicate with these souls in such a way as to ask their forgiveness? And so stop the wheel of karma?

I am Latwii, and am aware of your query, my sister. To begin, may we suggest that you presume much that is not necessarily as you have presumed it to be. It is the case with most entities entering your illusion that parallel, if we may call them, programs of incarnation are seen as possibilities. If one choice is not taken, then another presents itself so that those lessons to be learned are available. It is quite difficult to describe to entities within your illusion the freedom and fluidity with which these choices are made and pursued. Within your illusion it is generally the case that a plan is made and undertaken and then, if an alteration is made, the changes in the outcome are easily attributable. However, before the incarnation, the range and freedom of choice is such that level upon level of agreement is made, therefore allowing for changes to occur. For though there is the ability to see into what is called your future, this ability also sees that nothing can be known for sure, that there shall be changes, that therefore, there needs to be plans for the changes. If one event occurs, then this allows another, but may disallow yet another, and so forth in an endless progression of cause and effect. Therefore, there cannot truly be said to be mistakes within any incarnation, for each has been …

(Tape ends.)

Sunday Meditation
October 17, 1982

(Unknown channeling)

I am Hatonn, and I greet you, my brothers and sisters, in the love and the light of the infinite Creator. My friends, it is, as always, a great pleasure to be able to speak to those present, for, although we are frequently called upon by yourselves in your efforts to understand or accept those experiences of your daily lives, it is more rare for us to have the opportunity to communicate in this manner, and for this opportunity we are grateful. It is our desire at this time to exercise the instruments present that we may have the opportunity to fine tune those same instruments, if you will, and if they are willing to allow this. Therefore, it is our desire to progress from instrument to instrument and speak a few words through each that this might be accomplished. We will now leave this instrument. I am known to you as Hatonn.

(Unknown channeling)

I am Hatonn, and am now with this instrument. We greet you once more, my friends, in the love and the light of the one Creator. We are pleased to be with you again this evening so as to share a few of our thoughts with you, simple as they may be. We have spoken many times on the concept of learning to love, learning to be one with the Creator. We now wish to continue this *(inaudible)* through another instrument. I am Hatonn.

(Unknown channeling)

I am Hatonn, and am now with this instrument. Again, we greet you in the light and the love of the infinite Creator. Each of you has had and will have concerns about progress on your spiritual path, but let me assure each of you that you are making progress. You do not see the small baby growing moment-by-moment, but over a period of time the growth is very obvious. You have a tendency to become impatient, and you want to see things happen quickly, but if you will think back you will recall experiences and dreams that have fit together and have guided you on the path. So may we say do not be impatient, but be joyful and cheerful as you *(inaudible)* continue day-by-day as you think of time. And may we remind you again that we shall be with you upon request.

I now leave this instrument and transfer the contact to another.

(Unknown channeling)

I am Hatonn. I am now with this instrument. I greet you in the love and the light of the infinite Creator. When you look back on your past, you look at it as a different person. You are not as *(inaudible)* involved.

Your highs and lows do not seem as *(inaudible)*. Sometimes, when the present seems too intense, if you can stand apart from yourself, you will see that the intensity is not necessary. As the great philosopher, *(inaudible)* once said, "And this too will pass." Both the good and the bad will pass. You need the positive and the negative to [get a] proper perspective. Then you *(inaudible)* the learning experience a success.

Often, when you do not have *(inaudible)* work, you can study your objectives. Sometimes, this will turn you in a different direction. If you have too much success, you become so involved in the [world] that some of your learning stops, and you lose track of your overall *(inaudible)*. Rejoice in your problems. Overcoming them can give you great joy, more joy than if you never had them. Treat your trouble as something that will pass and something that is very educational. Even great failure sometimes gives you much *(inaudible)*. It makes it possible for you to understand great philosophies.

Do not become too involved in your world because all of you must leave it. And, when you look down on your life, you will not see its *(inaudible)* and mountains as you presume them to be; just ripples and hills and great courage and interesting experiences. Take great interest in your failures as well as your successes. They are important to the total picture.

I am Hatonn, and I leave this instrument.

(Unknown channeling)

I am Hatonn. I greet you once again in the love and in the light of our infinite Creator. We had intended to contact the one known as [C] but *(inaudible)* the request that we allow this instrument to listen for this period of time. This we are most happy to do, and we thank this instrument for all the many times that he has served and all the times that he intends to serve again as a vocal channel.

Each of you needs to know that at any time, though we may be fairly insistent in knocking upon the door *(inaudible)*, you may simply repeatedly request that we move on, and we shall do so when we are convinced that it's your desire. Not to speak is greater than your desire to learn better how to serve in this manner. It is a delicate point, but be assured that we never intend to break the law of free will that binds us and all creation in the freedom of service.

The light and the dark together, my friends, day and night, make each round, each somehow the same and each somehow different. You observe your many cycles, and your memory causes you to reflect upon the sameness, and yet each experience is a new one. Attempt to remember the difficulties that you had as the leaves turned to jewel tones and fell upon the fading grass in the last of the years, for many of those same problems have you now. Look back two and three and five years and again reflect upon the incessant changes that make up the seeming monotony of a life spent day-by-day, light and dark, light and dark.

If, indeed, you may locate one or more difficulty that has remained with you over the period of the years, cause this difficulty to attain its rightful place in your attentions. For any difficulty that remains for that long of a period is part of that because of [that for] which you came here. Attend to your difficulties with a loving and balanced hand of one who is not at enmity with the self.

There is in your ear the seeming repetition of so many events, dates, characters, situations and opportunities. You, my friends, are the being who each day sees for the first time the miraculous creation of [thought]. It is in your mind to see creation in all its glory, each rising sun. It is within your mind to greet each entity with the joy *(inaudible)*. It is within your mind to be aware of the new vibrations that enfold and surround and caress your planet at this time.

However, my friends, it is not within your mind *(inaudible)*. Seek, therefore, the caravans of the righteous, the pure and what your holy books call the "poor in spirit." Join this glad train, this retinue, and make of your pilgrimage [the thing ever new]. Yes, my friends, you may indeed concentrate upon the petty details of the mundane existence; you may also invest each moment with the spirit of adventure that will bring you laughter and shared joy and the peace that this world truly does not know.

We leave you through this instrument, rejoicing with you in the opportunities *(inaudible)*. We are ever with you. I am known to you as Hatonn. I leave you in the love and in the light of our infinite Creator. Adonai vasu *(inaudible)*.

Sunday Meditation, October 17, 1982

I am Maitreya. I greet you, my friends, in the love and the light of the one fair Creator. Please pardon the slowness of this contact. Ours is broadband, and we normally do not have a call to speak to a group such as this one but rather are called to those groups whose vision of the one divine light is centered upon the figure of that teacher whom you know as Jesus. We find in this instrument both the devotion to this teacher and the opened consciousness which allows us to speak more purely than is our usual privilege.

We find those in this group who seek the Christ Consciousness. My friends, let the gentle drops of dew *(inaudible)* upon your consciousness as you become still, so still that night and day may pass and naught has been moved. There is the Christ Consciousness. We have been frequently identified as being a ray, a portion of the entity, Jesus. This is incorrect. The vibration Maitreya is that vibration from which the one known as Jesus sprang, but that entity's incarnation was the incarnation of one entity, not of the vibration or group from which those whom you call wanderers have been sent.

We are, rather, that group being of the Confederation of Planets in the Service of the Infinite Creator. It has pleased your peoples to invent worship of many entities. Thus do many such as Jesus feel that they have failed to communicate. For the desire of such teachers is for the seeker to seek the Father. We thank this group for calling this vibration. It may be truly spoken that those comforters which each seeker must needs have are with each seeker as the direct result of the deep prayer or conscious calling of the one known as Jesus. This entity did indeed cause a great distortion, as we find this instrument would call it, within your time/space world. We are borrowing this instrument's vocabulary, and we thank this instrument.

We find the call this day to be for us to speak directly to one point, that is that no matter what you must do to follow the light and the love which you seek, the thing left undone shall be greater. Shall you change your mind in one opinion in order to be a better *(inaudible)*? Shall you love deeply and serve us? Shall you covet nothing, give all, preserve justice and peace? Very well then, my friends, you have only begun.

Not for one moment, then, allow the feeling of a plateau to [comfort] you. If you seek, then you do not seek comfort, for seeking is uncomfortable. Joyful it may be; loving it may be; but comfortable, never, my friends, not if you keep moving. We come to you as those who have offered themselves as martyrs, and thus we may not blush at the thought of discomfort among your peoples, for the martyr's physical demise is seldom comfortable. We do not suggest the life of the martyr, but we answer a call, a calling which has come to us, and our answer is take up your pilgrimage. Take the next step, and do not seek comfort. Because you are spiritual, seek only to seek.

You must know, and we shall repeat it to you, that in your own way you shall be judged not by this seeking of yours. Be thankful for the support of each other, but carry on. For, as you love, so shall you be given the next lesson, and the next, and the next. And, as you seek more and more, so shall more and more of the creation move with you, seek with you, blend with you, feel with you and be transformed with you. The teacher known as Jesus said, "You shall all take up your crosses if you wish to follow me." Remove all that which is surrounding those words. Remove all …

(Side one of tape ends.)

(Unknown channeling)

You have asked yourselves, do you wish to be perfect? Do you wish to be so serious? Consider well, my friends, the potential of each perfect being, and find within yourselves tears and reconciliation upon that most inner plane where you set your face toward the rising sun and never again glance away. Fear you then the failure, the glancing away, the dropping of the glass, the mishap? Do not fear. Someone stands beside your world ready to *(inaudible)* with your own evolution. That someone, whatever its manifestation, is you.

May we thank you, and may we thank this instrument. We do not expect to be called to this group, for this group is not that group which is focused upon Jesus the Christ but upon the grand unity of the Divine Father. So be it and amen. It has been a great blessing to be with you. *(Inaudible)*. May blessings be with you in each of your lifetimes, and may your rest be gentle as you come always, again and again to see the face of the one infinite Creator. Only *(inaudible)*.

Carla: Does anyone sense the presence of entities?

Questioner: Yes.

Carla: We shall *(inaudible)*.

(Unknown channeling)

I am Latwii. I am now with this instrument only to say a few words to the group, partly to exercise the instrument but also so say that the group has felt such powerful vibrations tonight, and there has been such peace and joy that we do not feel a question and answer period is needed tonight. Therefore, we leave you in the light and in the love of the infinite Creator. May we assure you that we it has been *(inaudible)* to be with you and remind you that a request is all we need, and we shall be with you in your meditations. Again we repeat, we leave you in the love and the light of the infinite Creator. Adonai vasu *(inaudible)*. ♣

L/L Research

Sunday Meditation
October 24, 1982

(C channeling)

I am Hatonn, and I am now with this instrument. We greet you, my friends, as always, in the love and in the light of the one infinite Creator. Tonight we will exercise all those wishing for practice as vocal channels speaking a few words, a thought to each. We are indeed privileged to have so many who wish to serve in this fashion. We of Hatonn wish to … We are having a slight bit of difficulty with our contact. This instrument has not been practiced for a while and we would pause for a moment to strengthen our contact …

I am Hatonn and now feel that our contact has been improved if this instrument would but relax and speak freely. Time upon your planet has begun to come into the time of your seasons known to you as autumn. The warmth of your summer gives way to the coolness and the winding down of your year. Each of the various species on your planet prepare themselves to face the coldness of your winter. A time of testing, for all things that give life become harder to find. Nourishment is hard to find. My friends, the times in which you feel alone, lost, unsure of your path, can be likened unto your winter. You will experience times when it may seem that things, events, are destined to go against you. My friends, if you can but remember that each thing faced is an opportunity, a chance to learn, that in each the love can be found, is there to nourish so that you shall not starve yourself. When one begins to see with love and with the light, they are prepared for the times of difficulty and can weather the storm, the cold, and the seeming darkness. We shall now transfer this contact. I am Hatonn.

(M channeling)

I am Hatonn. I am with this instrument. I greet you with the love and the light of the infinite Creator. I would like to say a few words on the subject of laughter and humor. Next to love, nothing will lighten your burden as much as laughter and humor. It is similar to sunshine. When you are dreary and have grave thoughts, laughter can brighten your outlook. It will help you not to be so tense. If you can laugh about yourself and your situation, you will not become so serious that you could even be depressed. It is a good gauge for judging your balance. People who can laugh never become too depressed. In retrospect people can laugh about their problems, but if they laugh at the time they are happening, they are able to see that the problem is not as serious as they might take it. Laughter changes your whole being. It sets you on an even keel and makes everything about you work well. Laughter is as good as vitamins. It tunes and tones up your whole system. Laughter is next to love. I am Hatonn. I leave this instrument.

Sunday Meditation, October 24, 1982

(A channeling)

I am Hatonn. We greet you once again in the love and the light of the one infinite Creator. We pause for a second to readjust this instrument to us … I am Hatonn. We shall now continue. We have spoken many times to you of the concepts of sharing and giving and we wish to approach this subject once again in a new light. Many on your planet give of themselves wholeheartedly. They spend their whole life sharing with others but putting themselves last in the line of receivers. This is by their choice, for they feel that it is more important for the others to be first. They forget, however, the need that the self feels, the need for the soul to be given something from the self. But your society is one that does not always promote this idea and therefore one soon believes this to be true, that the self should stand last in the line. It is important that this self is not last, but is one of the many who receives all that is given from the individual. It doesn't take much to please oneself. But it does take initial effort of first giving to the self. We are all one, therefore, do not leave anyone out when you are giving love and light. We shall now transfer to another instrument. I am Hatonn.

Carla: This is Carla. There is a, in my opinion, slight overtone of a Hatonn that is not Hatonn and I would like to address our love and our light to the Hatonn that is not Hatonn. I ask this entity to be nameless and I realize that this entity has only tiny vestiges due to the opening in the group when the instrument, C, was inadvertently hypnotized. Dear friend, we are not of your polarity. We send you love, we send you light, we bless you and we bid you farewell. Be gone forever from our circle and know that we will recognize you and always ask you to go. You shall not make us uncomfortable for we shall simply love you. Goodbye, in the name of Christ.

Let's envision a little light before anybody else channels.

(Carla channeling):

I am Hatonn. We greet you, my friends, in the love and in the light of our infinite Creator. May we apologize to each instrument which we allowed to continue and indeed encouraged to continue channeling. We may foresee the possibility that this group shall function without the instrument which we presently use and we wish to, although it takes great patience from you, give each of you enough experience with our vibration that you may, as this instrument has done, discriminate to a nicety. It is extremely unlikely that any further difficulties shall occur due to the fact that this instrument will not use the relaxation technique which was so disastrous at any future session. But should you sense discomfort that does not remove itself at your request, we always request that you not channel rather than detune your instrument. We may say with gratitude that each was channeling a great portion of our material with only the smallest twist which might be seen to be leading in the direction of the service-to-self polarity. Each opinion is equal. It is for you to choose. We may also say that the one known as M had no trace of this overtone in her communication and, except for some collaboration with herself, was channeling us. We thank you all and we thank the one known as S who sensed enough to be silent. We consider in this particular circumstance that this was a very sound decision. We are aware that each would care to hear some message. And indeed there have been several different avenues whereby this message has been attempted this evening. We shall attempt another one due to this instrument's unique personality and talk to you upon the subject of love.

There was once a young man who wished to know the truth. One sentence stood before this young man. Of this one thing he was sure. That truth is love and love is truth. And he asked a friend, "What is love?" And the friend said, "How much of it do you wish to have?" He said, "I wish to have all of it." And the friend said, "I don't know if you can have all of it, but come with me next Saturday night and I will see that you get some of it." "Oh, no," said the young man, "I don't think that's what I'm seeking." "Do you not like pleasure," replied his friend. "Why, yes I do," answered the young man, "but I seek something else."

And he went to another friend. He said, "What is love?" And his friend said, "Love is relationships. Love is personal communication. From yourself to another and from another to yourself. Love is understanding what the other fellow has in mind and knowing whether or not what you need and what he needs will work out." The young man thought about this for some time, for surely a great deal of life, as he had observed it, was involved in relationships. And it did seem indeed like most personal relationships took on some of the echoes of the business view. And indeed he would not like to disappoint one with whom he had a relationship, nor would he wish to be disappointed. So he said to his friend, there is much in what you say, but I believe I shall continue seeking.

And to another friend he went, and he said, "What is love?" And his friend said, well many people think that the only love is sexual love or personal love, but I tell you it is the love of ideas that move nations, the love of great thoughts for which you might die and because of whose truth you might live that is truly important. And again the young man thought long and hard for he had been inspired by many speeches and had seen the failure of love, the failure of ideals and the failure of truth lead to no end of human error. But his heart was not satisfied and he said to his friend, "I believe I shall seek further."

And he found another friend and said, "What is love?" And the friend said, "I have a theory about that. The truth is, love is laying down your life for others, loving with your whole heart, casting all your gifts upon the waters and never looking back. In this way lies the greatest sense of love that you can ever feel." And the young man was thrilled for it seemed that he had finally gotten an answer that might suit him. And so he began casting his love upon the waters. Waters that often seemed muddy. He aided his fellow man even when his fellow man didn't seem to want to be aided. Finally he said to himself, "I think I'm looking for more."

He was running out of friends and he sought a wise stranger, a spiritual man, much revered by seekers. And he said, "Sir, I have been searching with diligence and determination to find the nature of love, for only in love will I discover the truth." And the sage said, "Interesting that you should say that. In fact, anything that you say with feeling is lovely. Love is communication; with yourself, with the Creator, with all those about you." "Aha!" said the young man, who by this time was not so young, "I have been giving love but I have not been speaking." And so he began loving and communicating. And many were his friends and much was he beloved. And yet. And yet. He had not found the truth.

And having no one to turn to, he sat in silence and he asked himself, "What is love? It is not in the body. It is not in my relationships. It is not in society. It is not in loving everyone the same. It is not in communicating. What is the heart? Where have I missed the truth?" And a golden sun burst within the darkness of his inner mind and love rained down upon him, not from above, but from within. And as he opened his eyes, that golden sun gleamed and shone in his heart and he knew the world as himself, light and shadow knew he both. Much he forgave; much he gave. But always, he found the source within.

My friends, each of you is seeking. And each of you is indeed seeking love. But what answer that you receive depends upon what question you ask. If you ask a question in general, you shall be given a general concept in meditation. Therefore, seek ye and seek ye again and again, for with each seeking you refine the question. And with each refinement you learn more and more of the truth. A truth that does not lie in the illusion except when seen with eyes that shine with the light of the inner sun. Without that light, my friends, you seek that which is outward in vain. Without that source, my friends, you have only your own resources upon which to draw. And, my friends, they are not infinite. Yet you are given the pathways to infinity. How are you blind? How are you lame? Seek and seek and seek again. This seeking for the original Thought is that which we have come to offer you as a method of enhancing your evolution. All the actions flowing therefrom may well be again and again washed and refreshed by turning once again to the source. We send you that of love and of light which comes through us from the Creator and leave you bathed in that inner …

(Side one of tape ends.)

(Carla channeling)

I am known to you as Hatonn. Again we apologize for putting each through the experience of an uncomfortable channeling. But in case the group consists of members without this instrument and the one known as Jim, we very much wish that you have confidence in yourselves to discriminate. Adonai, my friends. Adonai vasu.

(M channeling)

I am Hatonn. I am now with this instrument. I greet you with the love and the light of the infinite Creator. The people of your planet have many rules against touching, taboos. Yet it is one way that you can communicate with your other self. It is a very healing thing. Yet on your planet, people do not spontaneously hug one another. It would have more meaning than many words. Many people on your planet commit suicide because they feel no one cares. If your people could form the habit of showing affection even between men and women which is taboo on your planet except under certain circumstances, if they could spontaneously love one another, people would not feel as alone.

When you are extremely close to a person, you tend to see the good in them rather than their faults. When you step back, you view them coldly. There is not a lot of hugging and touching and kissing on your planet. I know you people do feel love for one another, but why don't you show it? You refer to the art of healing, the touch of healing, but the touch of love is very valuable too. Even in your tuning, holding hands when you say the Lord's prayer has more meaning. Hugging one another is a very good form of tuning. Let the people around you know that you are with them. People who hug one another with genuine feeling can usually adjust to their differences. All people sometimes feel very lonely because no one hugs them. Little children feel unwanted because they are not hugged as often as necessary. And men and women should hug each other with sheer affection, but on your planet it is almost taboo.

We realize that a valuable tool, the sense of touch, is not enjoyed by your people. If possible in any situation, try to encourage people to touch one another. But you do have to be careful. There are a few people who feel so isolated they do not want anyone to touch them. And it would be an intrusion to their personality for you to touch them. But there are many people who are starved for affection. And there are many people who feel no one cares. If it is possible, try to hug someone each day. Try to make it a pattern in your life of hugging. The beauty of living will be enhanced by the number of people you hug. I am Hatonn. I leave this instrument.

(Jim channeling)

I am Latwii, and I greet you, my friends, in the love and in the light of the one infinite Creator and thank you for requesting our presence. As always, we present ourselves only in an attempt to be of service by answering those queries which hold importance in your seeking. May we then ask if there might be a query with which we might begin?

C: I'm concerned because it seems that through me a disturbing influence has found its way into the group and I want to know what I can do to strengthen myself to prevent this happening again.

I am Latwii, and feel the heart of your query, my brother. Firstly may we say that it might be useful to step back from your experience of the evening and see that it was not only through your instrument that this influence was experienced. The nature of the work which is undertaken by those within this group has attracted an unusual presence. The contact with the social memory complex which you have come to know as Ra has the effect of drawing unto this group in its various efforts this presence which seeks to disrupt in whatever way possible the experience of this group. Secondly, the use of the relaxation technique some of your time ago as a tuning device was an accident, shall we say, which was not beneficial to your instrument in particular and others as well. Therefore, my brother, do not take upon yourself the responsibility for permitting this influence within the group. What you might do to insure positive contact in future sessions is precisely the same as what any instrument might do, that is, the challenging of any contact by whatever means has meaning to you, whether it be in the name of Jesus Christ, in the name of the Christ consciousness, in the name of the service-to-others polarity, or by whatever means carries weight within your perception. Therefore, let this means be used so that each instrument at each sensing of contact might then challenge that contact and continue the challenging until a firm response in the positive polarity has been received. This may take some small portion of what you call time, but if you will pursue this general suggestion, you may rest assured that only the positive polarity entities will remain to use your instrument.

May we answer you further, my brother?

C: Yes. Tonight the original contact was comfortable, was smooth, and then it came to an abrupt stop. And then it continued after a period of time comfortably again. Was I at that time, or was I receiving a mixture of contact during the course of the channeling?

I am Latwii, and am aware of your query, my brother. Your contact became what is called mixed upon the cessation of the initial contact. The addition of the negative influence is one which is not easily perceived, therefore whenever doubt is encountered within your mind, then challenge the contact for its purely positive polarity.

May we answer you further, my brother?

C: No, thank you. Not at this time.

I am Latwii. We thank you. Is there another question at this time?

Questioner: I have a question and that is, aside from the possibility of channeling this negative entity, are there any other inconveniences that we might be aware of? In relation to the entity?

I am Latwii. My brother, to state this in general terms, we might say that indeed such an entity when it has made its presence felt among a group such as this may attempt in the future to intensify those experiences which the members of this [group] encounter as catalyst in the daily round of activities. Each entity as the path of seeking is traveled encounters those experiences in which discomfort, anger, frustration, depression, jealousy, etc. are felt. This is the normal means by which an entity learns to balance those distortions with their opposite and to see within each opportunity love and the one Creator. The process by which this is done varies with each entity. It may take more or less time; the catalyst may be used with more or less efficiency.

Negative entities of any source, whether this entity or another, always stand at the ready, shall we say, in the wings of your consciousness and your perception. So that when by your own free will [you call] to center stage the negative response to catalyst within your own being, these entities then may don the costume and the mask of negativity and intensify this experience. This is what you might call a gamble; for an entity, such as yourself, which is able to see the love and the light and the one Creator even in such an intensified moment, [may] therefore progress more purely and positively upon its path. And the forces of darkness have then aided the positive pursuit of the seeker. However, there is also the possibility that such an intensification might for the moment become too great and for that moment [and] perhaps additional moments after that, the seeker might be moved from the purely positive path and might seek to serve the self for some portion of what you call time. In this case the forces of darkness have for that moment achieved an increase in their own means of seeking and serving.

May we answer you further, my brother?

Questioner: No, thank you.

I am Latwii. We thank you. Is there another question at this time?

A: Yes, Latwii, why did you refer to the service to self as a force of darkness?

I am Latwii and am aware of your query, my sister. There are many descriptions for the negative polarity. The darkness as a means of describing negative refers to what has been recently described by the one known by the one known as Don as a flux ratio, that is, entities of negative polarity draw within themselves the love and the light of the one Creator, keep it for themselves, and therefore remove from their vicinity the potential for the radiating of that light to others. Therefore, the darkness in the sense of love and light is experienced.

May we answer you further, my sister?

A: Yes, just to clarify something I'm a little confused on. For myself, I feel that it is unfair to the service of self to continually refer to them always in such a not-nice of a fashion and it … and I guess I'm confused because if all are one in the Creator, the splitting seems to be a little, oh, just, it might cause some biases in people too quickly. Is there anything wrong with having different biases toward service to self and service to others?

I am Latwii, and am aware of your query, my sister. Indeed, there is nothing wrong when we speak with your words to describe either path, whether it be positive or negative. We do not mean to judge. We do not mean to say that one is good, the other bad. There is nothing wrong with darkness. For within the great depths of the primeval darkness of the spirit is the love and the light of the one Creator potentiated into being. Thus one cannot exist without the other within your creation. All is indeed one. To describe any portion of that oneness with any term is indeed to distort through the description.

May we answer you further, my sister?

A: No, thank you. You've clarified a lot of terminology.

I am Latwii. We thank you, my sister. Is there another question at this time?

M: Yes, Latwii. I was wondering if a person was worried about negative influences entering in their channeling, if they channeled for shorter periods of time in the beginning, would there be less chance for the negative influence to invade them?

I am Latwii. My sister, we might suggest that this would not be effective as a means of reducing the possibility of that influence. To reduce that possibility, one might begin by removing the worry. To respond to such a potential with fear or worry is to open the door yet wider. Rejoice in your positive choice. Praise the one Creator. Give thanks for each opportunity to serve. Seek within the heart of your being to serve others with every fiber of your being. And then when the opportunity to serve as vocal instruments approaches, challenge that contact which approaches and persist until the feeling of confidence grows within your being. Then speak to the best of your ability.

May we answer you further, my sister?

M: No, I think that answers it very well.

I am Latwii. We thank you, my sister. Is there another query at this time?

K: Yes. Let me try to clear up something that A has asked. We read in the Bible that Jesus said, "Love others as you love yourself," and I'm assuming that Jesus said that. And that seems to [be] psychologically [sound] because, as I worked in the hospital, it seemed that the people who hated themselves, also hated others, and that it's psychologically sound that one must love oneself before one can love others. And yet we read about denying self, and it does seem a little incongruent. So could you comment on Jesus' statement: "Love others as you love yourself"?

I am Latwii, and am aware of your query, my sister. To serve others and to choose the positive path is to love all the creation and to see all as one. This includes the self, for all is one. To serve the self is to love the self, yet to exclude the love for others and to seek instead to have others serve you and bring their love to you, their treasures to you. One path excludes others. One path includes all.

May we answer you further, my sister?

K: No, I think that's … I see the difference. Thank you.

I am Latwii. We thank you, my sister. May we attempt another query at this time?

Carla: Well, I recently had a mystical experience, I guess you'd call it, in a church service. And for some few minutes, I was no longer consciously in the church, but was consciously seated beside Jesus at the last supper at a wooden table. I could smell and feel and see everything that was going on, although it was very hazy, and I think the thing I remember the most was Jesus' sleeve, big, kind of like a burlap material, reaching across me to offer bread and he was saying, "This is my body," and I was very puzzled, whoever I was at that point, I was very puzzled that he wanted me to think of this bread as his body. It didn't make any sense. But I decided I would do it because he said so. I was his disciple. And then after awhile I was back in myself, and, the thing that I'm asking is, I'm sure that I'm not the only one who's had this sort of mystical experience, because that and many other places in the Bible where fairly careful description is given of what Jesus did, that they create in the imagination of a person who is attempting to follow his teachings the possibility of that kind of mystical experience, given that you're prey to them. Were the people that were actually there that night overlaid and overlaid and overlaid again by all these people from the future who have visited that spot? Should I ask that another way?

I am Latwii. We shall attempt what response we can without infringing upon your free will for such an experience has great potential for unlocking within your being the continued experience of love. Such an experience has within its potential those characteristics which many throughout what you call recorded history have built within the system of belief surrounding the one known as Jesus, the Christ. To one such as yourself who reveres this master there is then available a great reservoir of potential meaning in this experience. This framework, shall we say, has been constructed throughout the many years which have elapsed since this entity walked your planet by those who also have revered this entity. The master known as Jesus chose twelve disciples, each representing a facet of the one Creator expressed in a manner much likened unto the facets of a jewel. You have within your group studied that known as the Logos, the archetypical mind of which has facets. The twelve disciples, therefore, represented facets of a jewel of the one Creator. Each entity on your planet has certain tendencies, preferences, biases, means of seeking which may find a harmonic resonance with at least one of these facets. When the seeking has reached a certain intensity along its path, experiences of this nature are available to the beliefs which the entity holds and through which the entity seeks. Your experience was likened unto viewing the one Creator in the distortion called Christianity from yet a finer distortion, one of those disciples. Thus was opened unto you the ability to experience that which was experienced as a means by which you might more fully find love blooming within your life.

May we answer you further, my sister?

Carla: Well, I'm reluctant to say this, because that was a beautiful answer, but what I was wondering was, did the roots of that experience go back to a physical reality? Or was this a thought form reality which I experienced, as shared by others of my faith?

I am Latwii, and am aware of your query, my sister. Either might be the case; for any entity so experiencing this phenomenon, to specifically describe your experience in this regard, would be an infringement, therefore we may suggest your meditation upon this query.

May we answer you further, my sister?

Carla: Yes. I really don't care at all whether it was a flesh and blood experience or whether it was a thought form, it was all one. To me, what interested me was the possibility that these very human people might have from the future, from all the people, the possibility of bearing, sort of, on their shoulders, around them the casting back of so many faithful that there weren't just twelve people in the room; there were many, many, many people in the room. Whether it is I or someone else, makes no difference to me, just whether it was possible or not was really what I wondered.

I am Latwii. My sister, it is so that it is quite possible. Such occurs, not only within this realm of experience, but also within each experience of each entity upon your planet in all times, for each entity being the one Creator and all time being simultaneous, therefore these two requirements, shall we say, for the experiencing of the one Creator make it possible for each entity to create a pattern or a framework or a distillation of learning that might be utilized at any future, past or present time by any other entity. Thus the Creator learns from the Creator.

May we answer you further, my sister?

Carla: No, thanks, Latwii, that's fantastic.

I am Latwii. We thank you, my sister. Is there another query at this time?

K: Yes. I don't know if I can put this into words very well, but Carl Jung talked about the collective unconscious which I am assuming is what Ra talks about in the social memory bank. And recently after my meditation as I'm going about my business, thoughts will come to mind and my query is, when I'm tuned in, so to speak, do I pick up these thoughts from the collective unconscious, or do we … I'm sure all of us have the same thing happen, do we pick up these thoughts from the collective unconscious or the social memory bank, or where do they come from?

I am Latwii, and am aware of your query, my sister. Each entity within your illusion has access to that which you have called the collective unconscious. Each entity by engaging in what might be called the exercise of intuition receives messages from that collective mind. Such messages are also received in meditation, in dreams and other experiences of an inspirational nature, such as visions. Within your illusion the unconscious mind of your race and of your planet awaits the penetration of the veil which separates your conscious from your unconscious mind so that each entity upon our planet has an increasingly large reservoir of information, experience and illumination available to it which seeking might make more available as the seeking serves to penetrate the veil which withholds, shall we say, the full brilliance of being of the one Creator from each entity within your illusion.

May we answer you further, my sister?

K: So then in meditation or tuning, as I think of it sometimes, is really just a calming or a putting aside of the conscious thoughts that go through our minds all the time so that the unconscious can penetrate the veil. Is that what you're saying?

I am Latwii. To clarify our statement, perhaps it would be useful to look at an entity as being similar to a tree. Look at the limbs as your conscious mind. See the att …

(Tape ends.)

L/L Research

L/L Research is a subsidiary of Rock Creek Research & Development Laboratories, Inc.

P.O. Box 5195
Louisville, KY 40255-0195

www.llresearch.org

Rock Creek is a non-profit corporation dedicated to discovering and sharing information which may aid in the spiritual evolution of humankind.

ABOUT THE CONTENTS OF THIS TRANSCRIPT: This telepathic channeling has been taken from transcriptions of the weekly study and meditation meetings of the Rock Creek Research & Development Laboratories and L/L Research. It is offered in the hope that it may be useful to you. As the Confederation entities always make a point of saying, please use your discrimination and judgment in assessing this material. If something rings true to you, fine. If something does not resonate, please leave it behind, for neither we nor those of the Confederation would wish to be a stumbling block for any.

CAVEAT: This transcript is being published by L/L Research in a not yet final form. It has, however, been edited and any obvious errors have been corrected. When it is in a final form, this caveat will be removed.

© 2009 L/L Research

Intensive Meditation
October 28, 1982

(A channeling)

I am Hatonn, and greet you this evening in the love and in the light of the one infinite Creator. We are pleased this instrument did finally initiate our contact, for it is in hopes to rebuild her confidence in channeling. We are aware and appreciate the effort made to keep the contact pure. We wish to work with each instrument present tonight so as to give further practice in channeling our thoughts and so as to become more familiar with our vibration. We would at this time transfer to another instrument. I am Hatonn.

(Carla channeling)

I am Hatonn, and I greet this assemblage once again in the love and light of the infinite Creator. As we observe the vibratory complexes of each of you, it occurs to us that perhaps the most helpful form of aiding each instrument in building its own skills at this chosen service at this particular time would be the technique of the telling of a story through all instruments, each telling only a small portion, knowing neither beginning nor end. This is a technique which is reserved for more experienced channels due to the infinite possibilities of panic upon the part of [the] new instrument which does not yet have the confidence to simply speak without analysis of those thoughts which are brought before it. However, it is through techniques such as this that we may offer to the more practiced instruments a means of observing the way our contact does indeed work. Thus it is a confidence builder. Therefore we shall begin a story through this instrument and cease before the story is well begun to transfer to another, then another, then another, then another, and so forth until the story is well told and each has both given and received the love and the light of the infinite Creator.

There once [was], my friends, a young prince who strode out one day with a quiver full of arrows and a strong bow. It was this mellow youth's wish to practice the marksmanship of the arrow until he could hit the mark. He began his journey in the bright light of morning. The earth seemed young about him although it was early autumn. The dew was still upon the grass and the air seemed full of promise, vague and unspoken, yet very real. We now transfer to another instrument.

(S channeling)

I am Hatonn, and would go on with our story through this instrument. As the youth walked through the forest, examining closely the many beautiful and wondrous details that nature has provided for your eyes to see, the nose to smell, the ears to hear, he stumbled upon a small patch of openness within the heart of the forest and in this open place there arose before his wondering eyes a beautiful and bright entity that spoke of love to the youth. He was astounded and amazed and at first would not believe he was seeing or hearing what his senses told him was to be. We will now transfer this contact.

(A channeling)

I am Hatonn, and shall continue. The prince's first thoughts after listening were to run, to leave, for this entity indeed must be a mad man for it spoke of words not commonly spoken and indeed he was a prince and therefore he must not be influenced by such a man. But the prince did not run but paused and listened and felt all that was spoken. He stayed, not knowing exactly why, for any sane person would flee from the opening to avoid this confrontation. We shall transfer.

(M channeling)

I am Hatonn, and we will continue the story. The prince and the most fair entity communed in the forest during which time our fair entity shared many truths with the prince, unfolded many a mystery that had puzzled the young man, much as a mentor would. The boy at the end of some time of shared conversation looked to the fair entity and asked, "Who might you be? How is it that you know all of these wondrous things? Who is it that taught you and where might I go to learn more of these things? How is it that you can be?" Our fair entity looked at the prince and explained that surely all these things the prince had learned this day he had inside known all along, nor had he taught the prince anything that the prince was not capable of learning himself. Then the fair entity turned the question upon the prince. "Since you, my young prince, have in truth known these seeming secrets I have shared with you this day, I ask you, who am I? For this too you know." The prince, puzzled by the question from such a seemingly wise and mysterious entity looked back, puzzled, and looked in the eyes of this fair one, and in the locked stare seemed to be able to almost look within this other soul. And what he saw when he looked within was himself. We transfer this contact. I am Hatonn.

(Jim channeling)

I am Hatonn. To continue. The young prince had begun that day hoping to learn a skill with bow and arrow and had found the mark he sought was himself. My friends, so it is with each seeker. You travel the path of your seeking using the implements of your choice to penetrate the mystery of your being. It may seem that the mystery of being would need a special tool and only that tool would do for such a search. But, my friends, we say to you, the outer manifestation is meaningless. For the desire comes from within your being. To seek the truth is all that counts. You may use whatever tools are at your disposal and of your choosing, for each will find that catalyst most appropriate for its personal journey of seeking. To fire the self with the desire to know the truth of what it is you seek, and who indeed you are as you seek is the ingredient that might find any manifestation appropriate within your journey.

We have enjoyed this means of exercising instruments which find a greater challenge helpful at this time in their experience of this means of serving. We thank each present for partaking with us in the bounty of oneness and in the abundance of love. We would now leave this group, as always, in love and light. I am known to you as Hatonn. Adonai, my friends. Adonai vasu borragus.

(Jim channeling)

I am Latwii, and I greet you, my friends, in the love and the light of the one infinite Creator. We are honored once again to be asked to join your group in our capacity of attempting answers to your queries. It is always an honor and a pleasure to join with this group. May we ask then if there might be a question with which we may begin?

M: Yes, Latwii. It's not a question, but it's a request for comment. A moral question and comment. Let's take an example of a weapon. A gun in a soldier's hand or anyone's hand may be used to kill another person, take their life. And there are certain karmic consequences or balances that have to be made when someone takes another's life. What I'm interested in is not so much the individual that pulls the trigger, for certainly he is responsible for his actions, but take, for example, the individual who created the instrument of death. While he did not pull the trigger, is he not as responsible? Certainly the weapon may never be used unless someone is willing to pick it up and use it for destruction, but the entity that developed the weapon, is he not as much at fault for its destruction and chaos? How does that entity that created the weapon figure in from a moral point of view? That's all.

I am Latwii and am aware of your query, my brother. To begin, may we suggest that our comments might be seen more clearly not within the moral framework of good and evil or any type of judging action, but from the realm of oneness where each entity is truly one with each other, so that each entity might be seen to be the Creator gathering the experience of your illusion that evolution might occur. Then whatever the action, we might fruitfully look to the motivation for that action. This is true also with thoughts. Why does the entity think and act as it does? Does it wish in the action or the thought to be of service to another or does it wish to be of service to the self? Or, is it aware of either choice? These are the possibilities which each entity faces as evolution is completed through your illusion. The entity creating that implement called a weapon, whether upon the assembly line or the designing board or whether creating the, shall we say, literature which shall feature the saleable points is an entity which is either motivated by a desire to be of service to the self, to others, or is unaware that either choice exists and only subconsciously vacillates, shall we say, between the two choices. It may be that an entity is firmly committed to the idea of the preservation of what it conceives to be truth, beauty and goodness that exists within the boundaries of what you call a country and is further committed to the defense of these ideas and seeks therefore to serve those others within that boundary by its work upon the weapon. The motivation, then, is of service to others. There are, of course, ramifications in that there is a price, shall we say, that is paid when the weapons are used. The taking of life that does not wish to be taken is an infringement upon that life. And in such a fashion may somewhat reduce the positive choice. This is true with all actions and thoughts. For it is most difficult within your illusion to pursue a very purely polarized path, either positive or negative. For there are many who are affected by each action. Of course, it is also possible that the entity wishes to be of service to self by this activity of making the weapon and may indeed polarize in that direction by its actions and yet find there is some reduction of its polarity when it partakes with others and aids their efforts as a part of it own in the producing of the weapon. Insomuch as others are served is its negative polarity reduced. Those unaware of the need for conscious choice in either direction then are randomly affected according to whatever motivation is present within their mind as they carry out their activities.

May we answer you further, my brother?

M: No, thank you. You answered me better than I expected. Thank you.

I am Latwii. We are grateful to you, my brother. May we ask if there is another question at this time?

Carla: I have a series of questions which may take a very short amount of time, because they are questions that I would normally be asking Ra, but we can't talk to Ra for awhile and I'm very curious about some matters. First of all, I'm taking a chemical called Erythrocin and I seem to have observed in addition to the expected side effects a general debilitation or weakness of all the muscle tissue and energy level which is connected with the continued taking of this medication. Is this a correct observation or can you speak?

I am Latwii, and feel that we may speak upon this query. The chemical of which you speak does have some effect upon your musculature and energy level, but this is also a function of the lack of what you call the exercising. One then accelerating the action of the other so that in general you experience a lower level of energy and a reduced musculature tone. There is also the consideration that other physical distortions have been energized so that your energy levels have from time to time been reduced as the variety of distortions present in your physical vehicle have at times crossed paths, shall we say, so that there is an intensification of the reduced energy.

May we answer you further, my sister?

Carla: Yes, please. Is there a limit to the amount of exercise that I may attempt now that the problem which was the reason for taking this chemical has been seemingly almost entirely removed and is there any other method whereby I might work with my body to combat the unfortunate side effects of this heavy chemical?

I am Latwii, and am aware of your query, my sister. There is the need to use the normal caution in accelerating your program of exercise. This we have observed to be a practice which is well known to you, the increasing gradually so that the muscles which have not received the normal amount of exercise might slowly regain their tone. The general level of pain within your physical vehicle might be reduced by the beginning and continued use of the swirling waters. We observe this in your near future. To continue in praise and thanksgiving is most helpful, for the mind is the great motivator of the body. Those about you send you their love as do those which are beyond your senses at this time.

May we answer you further, my sister?

Carla: Yes, but thank you for that response. For saying all this I observed two items which occurred before a rather horrendous allergy attack and an out-of-season menstrual period. One was a good deal of emotional stress and strain …

(Side one of tape ends.)

Carla: … comment on the nature of the allergy especially as to whether it is primarily a function of the mind and the emotions and if that is so, could you comment on methods for those who are dealing with allergic reactions which are already in progress to attempt to be of more service to self and to others by helping the mind. Otherwise, I'd just be interested in finding out if it's a combination of mind and body. If that made any sense?

I am Latwii, and feel that we have a good grasp upon your query, my sister. As you are aware, the body is truly a creature of the mind, for the mind creates it. Yet, while the body is the creation of the mind, it does have its own biases, abilities and distortions which are available. As the body is able to express the will of the mind and gather about it its own experience, it also is able then to feed back to the mind the fruits of its experience. The allergies of which you speak, as you have recently discovered, are within the deep portions of the mind a rejection of the environment or some portion of the environment in which the body moves. The illusion which you inhabit is most intense in providing catalyst. Many there are who experience various forms of alienation or rejection of the catalyst of your illusion and the framework of various portions of your illusion. These express, then, within the complex of the physical vehicle as the allergic reaction, so that when contact with that portion of the illusion which has been rejected or contact with a symbolic representation of that portion is experienced by the entity, then within the deep portion of the mind the entity reacts to that rejected portion of the illusion in such a way that its physical vehicle expresses that rejection. It is not an easily understood or explained phenomenon. For each entity has its own variety of responses and reasons for the rejection or the difficulty with a portion of the illusion. In general, as we are forced therefore to speak, the ability of the entity to find the core of the rejection beyond the symbol, beyond the outer manifestation, and then to accept through the process of balancing that portion which has been rejected, is most helpful in alleviating the reaction which your peoples call the allergy.

May we answer you further, my sister?

Carla: Yes. Just one quick one, cause this is a little difficult to get pounded into my brain. One allergy which was quite obvious was to mashed potatoes. The next morning I could hardly open my eyes at all after eating this innocent substance. What you're saying then, is that this is the outer manifestation which is a symbol of a rejection, that my deeper self has done, has rejected that which the food is the symbol of. So what I would have to do in order to be working with my allergies more and more, and I guess what anybody would have to do, would be to try to discern what something like mashed potatoes symbolizes. Right? I eat food and *(inaudible)* having to eat? Does one go along that track? Is that right?

I am Latwii, and am aware of your query, my sister. This is, in general, once again, correct. To look at the meaning behind the manifestation is most helpful in alleviating that which you have called the allergic reaction. But again, we must repeat that to speak in general is most difficult, for each entity is quite unique and each rejection doubly unique. It may be that the reason for the rejection is most helpful in allowing the entity to proceed with a certain portion of its mission or learning, shall we say. It may be on the other hand that the entity might find it more useful to attempt to alleviate the allergic reaction so that service and learning might proceed more efficiently. Therefore, what might be true for one entity may not be true for another. And further, what might be true for one entity's response to one allergic reaction may not be true for another response to another allergic reaction. It is most difficult, as we have mentioned, to attempt to speak with clarity upon this subject, for the allergic reaction and the rejection of the environment which the reaction implies is a subject which has great depth and breadth. We hope we have been of some small service in attempting clarity.

May we speak further, my sister?

Carla: No, thank you, you have been a great help and it's very intriguing.

I am Latwii, and we thank you, my sister, and agree that indeed the creation is most intriguing. May we answer yet another query?

(Pause)

I am Latwii. We hope that our responses to your queries have not made you allergic to further queries. We are most honored, my friends, to have been able to speak with your group this evening and to blend our vibrations with yours. It is an honor which we cannot thank you enough for extending to us once again. We shall be with you upon request and remind you that in the silence of your meditations do we linger at the fringes waiting for the opportunity to be of that service. We are known to you as those of Latwii. We leave you now in love and in light. Adonai vasu borragus. ❧

Sunday Meditation
November 7, 1982

(S channeling)

I am Hatonn, and I greet you, my brothers and sisters, in the love and the light of the one infinite Creator. Again, my friends, we are pleased to be with you, for to share in so large a group is indeed a pleasure for us. We would only speak a few words through this instrument as there are other instruments that are very willing this evening to serve us as we would serve you in sharing our simple message. It is one of love and peace and sharing that we bring to you. It is one of many hearts combining into one, striving to attain the togetherness, the like mind of serving the Creator, of being one with your brothers and sisters, of seeing that in each is the Creator, is the love. The truth, my friends, is seeing that in each is you.

At this time we would transfer to another instrument. I am Hatonn.

(C channeling)

I am Hatonn, and am with this instrument. We greet you again in the love and the light. As you journey, there will be times when you may very well meet obstacles from which you may back up. As you journey and meet such obstacles do not stop at them but take them as a lesson, learn from them and continue, for to grow, to continue your journey, you need be persistent. You need not rush, and always try to do that which you may.

We shall now transfer. I am Hatonn.

(Carla channeling)

I am Hatonn, and I greet you once again through this instrument. We are pleased to speak through this instrument as there is some calling for channeling which this instrument may do. May we take this opportunity to welcome in voice those who are not always with this group as they sit in this domicile. May we assure each who consider themselves a visitor that you are not any longer visitors, but have indeed become an integral part of this family of souls. It is a great privilege to spend this small amount of your time sharing community with you.

My friends, we are taking our time with this instrument for she is somewhat fatigued and we are aware that there is a calling for some information and some inspiration which this instrument is capable of channeling given the slow method of communication, for what we have to say is not what this instrument expects. Indeed, we are often a "Johnny-One-Note," as this instrument would call us, sounding ever the theme of meditation, for only through meditation or a parallel resource of being can you find that original Thought which each of you seeks.

This evening, however, we would speak to you of several seemingly disconnected items: of mirrors, of families, and of the definition of home. Each of you is aware that each is a mirror for another. This can sometimes be discomfiting, perplexing and painful. Within your daily framework of activities it is usual for each within a family to be absent for a long enough time, as you would call it, that the mirroring effect is diluted. It is quite unusual to have an extremely strong reaction to one with whom your acquaintance is somewhat shallow. Therefore, the definition of family is one that may be seen in many ways to be etched in pain, for it is in the pain of realization that transformation occurs. And because each of you insulates yourself from most of the mirrors around you, it is only in the family that that which is truly painful may occur. It is also the only place where there is the resource of comfort from those about you, and this occurs, of course, through clear communication.

Therefore, the definition of home is quite simply that place where any family dwells. Blood ties may be quite properly in place, yet the place not be a home. If there is no work done upon the mirroring, the transformations, and the support, each of the other, there is no home. If those resources are there, there is a home, regardless of those ties which may or not be offered as—known among the peoples as—the kinship of the family.

Going beyond this, my friends, we have a mirroring effect which begins to occur when the student applies himself to the point where he becomes the mirror for himself. This is more advanced work and it is more subtle work. You cannot fool your family. They will call you out. It is possible, however, to fool yourself. It is this point which we wish to dwell upon briefly.

Many of you in this group are at the point at which you have no need of a family. You have only the need to give to be of service, unless you are within families. Your true work has become internalized. At this stage the methods of causing yourself to be confused are myriad. You as an observer may distort your observation of yourself in any way that you choose if you choose to avoid any iota of the pain of the further, more subtle, and more defined transformations that you seek at this level of being.

How do you perceive yourselves, my friends? Let us sound a great challenge to you. See yourselves within the perspective of those whom you might call saints, enlightened beings, angels or oversouls, and then do not spare yourself as you analyze those things which you have done which you wish you had not, those things you wish you had done that you have not. We do not ask you to be so hard upon yourself for the sake of some masochistic pleasure. We ask you to do this in order that you may grow, be nourished, and thrive. We ask you to do this that you may be at peace. We ask you to do this because it is time for you to do this.

Each of you begins each day as a newborn and yet each of you brings to that newborn day the baggage of your yesterdays, unless, my friends, you have unpacked those bags, you have removed your luggage, you have shed your skin. Do you wish to miss today? Do you wish to miss tomorrow? Very well, then, you have eternity. Your family will continue to aid you and you will continue to make some progress. But the great fire that refines is within you, and each of you at this point is capable of choosing to turn to that fire, not only for warmth, but for growth and strength. This path, my friends, can be said over and over to be one of love, of warmth, of joy, and of caring. But turn the card, my friends, and demand of yourself as you can that last great honesty that will bring you peace that the world indeed cannot give you, but more, that no other person can give you. In the end, the great mirror is within. We welcome and accept each glance away from that mirror.

We remember and have within our being the memory of not knowing oneness. We remember the feeling of being totally unredeemed. We do not disparage any days, weeks, or years in your incarnation in which you have done less than that which is spiritually strenuous. There is a joy in testing yourself. The athlete strives to do that which he does one instant better or quicker. The scholar strives to seek for one more piece of the great circle of intellectual knowledge that has not been discovered, and those of your orthodox spirituality strive to know to the last echo the feelings and the experience of the mystic.

And what we say to you is: In the cold look you give yourself, in the honest appraisal and in the surrender to that which is most truly you, there is the satisfaction of having been just that much faster, just that much more careful, just that much more curious. Never doubt that we are with you, and never doubt that you shall succeed, and that the joy which balances cold introspection shall come upon you most unexpectedly and most frequently. But we know that this group desires more than comfortable inspiration, and so we say to you, take the hard road. It is the quick road and you shall be fleet of foot, for this is what you came here to be.

We would close through another. I am Hatonn.

(Carla channeling)

We apparently shall not close through another, as the one known as M1 desires to listen. We thank this group for calling us. We thank you for all that you have experienced in recent times in learning the discrimination of channeling. We thank each channeler. We thank each present for the privilege of being with you. In greatest humility may we beg you not to take our words as anything but what they are, the conversation of brothers and sisters. Take what you can use and discard the rest. We send you visions of lilies and roses and hyacinths and jonquils. We send you the blue skies, the warm breezes, and the sweet scents that at this time are not with you in your season. We send you the knowledge so often forgotten that all of these things are long in [the] making. The earth must nurture long the seeds of being before springtime blazes forth in its pastel symphony.

As you look in your mirror, my friends, do not forget the lesson of the seasons, and do not look upon an occasional winter as a disaster. It is absolutely necessary for a butterfly to have been in a cocoon. It is mandatory that the flowers be nurtured in the ground. We leave you, my friends, in whatever season of being may be yours. Please know always that the kingdom which you may call summer is all about you and within you, and that the illusion that so powerfully affects you is merely that which teaches you not to inhabit summer, but to be that great season of brightness and blooming. We leave you in the love and in the light of the infinite Creator. I am known to you as one of Hatonn. Adonai, my friends. Adonai vasu.

(Jim channeling)

I am Latwii, and I greet you, my friends, in the love and in the light of the one infinite Creator. It is our privilege once again to be asked to join your group this evening. We are filled with joy at this opportunity to be of service in our attempt to answer your queries. We feel there are many queries present this evening, therefore, without further ado, may we ask for the first query?

Carla: Well, I'll jump in. I've been having several people giving me lectures about these contacts, as a matter of fact, especially the one with Ra, and connecting them with the concept of Satan. I don't really have a lot of trouble with what they are saying because I know it is because they are very concerned and care about me. But I just wonder if you could comment on the use and misuse of judgment, especially as it applies to Christianity?

I am Latwii, and am aware of your query, my sister. Each entity within your illusion attempts to sort through the confusion of its own being, the confusion which surrounds it in its daily life. It is known from within each that there is the ability within the being to find, shall we say, the proper path for the moment. Many are the means of journeying. Each has the dictates, shall we say, as to how the path might best be traveled. In an attempt to aid the seeker, each means of seeking has the rules, shall we say, for it is known through experience that some techniques work better than others. Therefore, it is easy for the eager seeker who has found some means of clarifying the confusion for itself to feel that this is the means by which all might progress.

Within the heart of love, therefore, is born the desire to share this means. But within your illusion, confusion still exists for each in greater or lesser degree, and adds the factor of distortion so that when any seeker attempts to share its means with another by condemning other means, there is the distortion …

(Side one of tape ends.)

(Jim channeling)

I am Latwii. To continue. These within the distortion which you have called Christianity are no more liable to exercise the faculty of judgment than are any others upon your planet, for even within this distortion of Oneness it is plainly stated that to judge not that the entity be not judged itself is proper. Yet, in the fervor of a moment of seeking and attempting to share the love that has been found in whatever degree it has been found is often borne the distortion of judgment. Know, my friends, that such entities have at the core of their being love which seeks to be expressed, however distorted it might finally be manifested.

May we answer you further, my sister?

Carla: Yeah. I guess, just one more thing. I accept Jesus as my personal savior, and yet I have never had the slightest desire to inflict this on anyone who thought it was an infliction instead of a joy, because—I don't know, I just didn't expect anybody else to fall in line with me just because of what I thought. Is there something missing in my makeup or what? That's what I haven't been able to figure out is, what is it that I'm missing that causes other people who are also Christians to do this thing and I never have any desire to do it—called judgment?

I am Latwii, and am aware of your query, my sister. Each path attempts to aid the seeker in learning the lessons of your illusion. All lessons have love and acceptance, compassion and understanding as their heart. Whatever the seeker, whatever the path, love and acceptance are those goals which are sought. Some have achieved a greater reward for their efforts than others, and reflect the love and acceptance they have found by truly loving and accepting others no matter what their manifestations of seeking.

Love and acceptance have as their polar opposites judgment and separation. It is a continuum, a path, a journey. Those who express the judgment are at the beginning of this journey, however their means of journeying. Those who refuse to judge and who instead love and accept have traveled further this path.

May we answer you further, my sister?

Carla: One more thing. Everything involved with judgment that can be found in the same book as the words, "Judge not that you be not judges," all the things about, "Accept me or you'll really be gnashing your teeth," and all that, it's all in the same book. There was an inspired reason for this book to be collected and saved over so many thousands of years, and for such mutually exclusive material to be in the same book. What was it?

I am Latwii, and am aware of your query, my sister. The reason, my sister, is that this book, for those on your planet, for a great majority of them, reflects that which is sought. It has been called for in such and such a manner, And it has, therefore, been collected, and contains, as you are aware, a mixture of the positive and negative polarities, as both have been called for, and does therefore present the confusions and the riddles which the pure seeker might find strength of spirit in solving. This is true for each of what you have called religions, for it is true of the peoples of your planet.

May we answer you further, my sister?

Carla: No, Latwii. That bunch of answers really smoothes everything out. Thank you so much.

I am Latwii. We are most grateful to you, my sister, for [without] your sincere queries we would be silent. May we attempt another query?

L: I'd like to ask a question on G's behalf. A couple of weeks ago she heard a television or radio report that several instances had occurred, I believe in Germany, in which a hitchhiker was picked up on the road at night, after traveling with the driver of the auto for a period of time and told the driver that the hitchhiker was the archangel Gabriel, and had appeared for the purpose of issuing a warning that the world was to come to an end, I believe, in the year 1984. And as the story went, the hitchhiker promptly disappeared from there within the car. To reiterate, this supposedly happened on a number of occasions within apparently a few days. Would you like to comment on this?

I am Latwii, and am aware of your query, my brother. We find that there are among your peoples at this time many such occurrences such as this of which you speak. Not only do entities of your planet receive the messages in what might be called the first person presence of another self, but also through instruments using the telepathic and trance channeling. And by other means as well, for as you know, there are those of negative polarity which speak the words of doom in order that the fear which is generated by them might be gathered and used to gain the mastery and power over others which will lend efficiency in the negative polarization.

May we answer you further, my brother?

L: Yes, if you are capable of answering this. The entity which I described, do you have any knowledge as to whether this entity was of a service-to-self or service-to-others polarity, and second, if you're capable of answering, again, either way, was there any significance to the date 1984, as it has certain emotional connotations to most of the Western world?

I am Latwii. To answer the latter portion of your query first, the significance is as you mentioned. It has the proper connotative qualities to promote the emotions of fear. The entities upon your planet hearing this type of information may then discern for themselves the polarity, for where there is the speaking of doom, of fear, of doubt, then there is the negative coloration. Where there is the speaking purely of joy, of peace, of love, of brotherhood, then there is the evidence of positive polarity.

May we answer you further, my brother?

L: Yes, one more question on a more philosophical vein. To paraphrase another speaker, "By their words you shall know them," it's fairly obvious by the content of a person's message what their orientation is as far as their polarity. Yet, it puzzles me that although some messages appear to be originating from a service-to-others source that often appears to be Confederation, very often the Confederation seems reluctant to admit being the originator of such communications, and it seems that there must be more than modesty involved in this. Could you speak on that topic please?

I am Latwii, and am aware of your query, my brother. The reason for such modesty, shall we say, is that free will must be maintained. Many entities begin to receive a positive contact of Confederation origin and then attract the temptations of negative entities as a balance. When such entities are unaware of the necessity for maintaining what you have called the tuning in the positive sense, and fall prey to the temptations to glorify the self or the organization in any way, then the inroads might be made by the negative entities in polluting the contact. Even when this occurs, the negative entities find it necessary to utilize a major portion of positively-oriented information, putting the twist of service-to-self polarity here and there, so that little by little the positive message becomes tainted and the organization becomes less and less able to share in the service-to-others sense.

When this occurs, it is usually not recognized by the entities to which it has occurred. Therefore, their confusion must be maintained and no clear speaking by entities of the Confederation may be allowed, for the confusion presents the opportunity to grow and such opportunities are treasures for those experiencing the surrounding confusion, and must be preserved for the growth of such entities.

May we answer you further, my brother?

L: No, thank you, that very greatly clarified it. Thank you very much.

I am Latwii. We thank you, my brother, as well. Is there another query at this time?

Carla: Yeah. I've got a question, now that you mention it, now that L mentioned it. Was our group about 1975—you can just confirm this or tell me that you can't answer it—I have the feeling that all of 1975 or so, our group was getting pretty polluted information. We went through a whole year or so of getting fairly specific information. And then again about, somewhere in 1980, we went through a few months of that. Did we go through those seasons and then just survive by persevering? Is that true?

I am Latwii, and am aware of your query, my sister. We find that there is some limit to what we might say in this regard. It has been the case that in your more distant past there have been instances where there have been momentary lapses, shall we say, in the polarity of service to others. The temptations were offered and the interests turned from philosophy and the evolution of the soul to the specific and glamorous, shall we say, gathering of information concerning dates and catastrophes.

In other cases, there has been the straining to the limits of acceptability of the contact of the Confederation which has been asked query upon query concerning this same general type of information. Confederation contacts are able to respond to a certain degree to this type of query, always adding the notation of its unimportance so that the questioners might reevaluate their desires. When such queries do not contain such notations of unimportance, one may then be aware that the possibility exists that the contact is no longer of Confederation origin.

May we answer you further, my sister?

Carla: No, thank you. I believe I perceive the heart of your reply.

I am Latwii. We thank you, my sister, for your query and your perception. Is there another query at this time?

M2: Yes, Latwii. Why is it some people are so frightened of death and other people are so accepting?

I am Latwii, and am aware of your query, my sister. For each entity there is the reason. To reply in broad terms for the masses of peoples upon your planet would be a great distortion, for each entity is quite aware of the phenomenon of death, and has either a general type of acceptance or avoidance of that concept. Some fear the death only because it is a great mystery and the unknown often causes entities to find fear within themselves. Some fear the death because they have not yet learned to live, and have not yet learned what they came to live for, and are aware that the death shall come surely and perhaps they shall not be ready. Some gladly accept their own physical departure from your illusion, for its catalyst weighs heavily upon their shoulders and they yearn only for rest. Some welcome the death because they seek another adventure and feel certain that death shall bring it. For each within your illusion there is some response to life and to death. Each is unique.

May we answer you further, my sister?

M2: Yes. Is there correlation between the way a person lives and the way they die? What I mean is, if a person dies, say, accidentally, is there any correlation between the way they lived and the accidental death?

I am Latwii, and am aware of your query, my sister. To begin, may we suggest that there are no accidents. Many deaths appear accidentally, as many experiences appear random. This is because the grand design of your life patterns is greatly hidden from your view. Within your illusion this is necessary so that lessons might be learned with greater efficiency, for in truth all are one and love is the heart of each. Yet to learn these lessons there must be the forgetting and the limiting of the view. The means of the passing from this illusion is chosen by each with variations also chosen should certain circumstances come to pass in such and such a fashion. Therefore, the correlation between the life and the death is most clearly seen when it is seen that both are chosen as means for learning the lessons of love.

May we answer you further, my sister?

M2: No, thank you. That's very helpful.

I am Latwii. We thank you, my sister. Is there another query at this time?

L: I have another question. I have recently read a couple of books that are autobiographical accounts of a Tibetan lama's life. There are parts in it that interest me very much concerning previous history on our planet. I also realized, though, that it may not be possible for you to answer whether those parts are true or not, because it may cast same doubt upon the accuracy of the rest of the individual's statements if I am told that he is not telling the truth. Is it at all possible for you to verify whether certain segments in the text are true or not?

I am Latwii, and am aware of your query, my brother. May we suggest that such recapitulations of the history of your planet are frequently in some degree of what you might call error, for it is most difficult for entities both within your illusion and without your illusion to see clearly the great panorama of events which have pieced the puzzles of your existence together in what seem to be a linear progression of evolution. Many see the basic fabric of the evolution of your peoples, the cultures which have grown and flourished and died, the experiences which have been shared by entities throughout the various countries and times, but then in the specific rendering of this or that instances, especially concerning famous personalities, may find that the clear description is quite difficult to render, for to look into what you call your distant past to discover an event might require the discernment of whether the event finally discovered occurred within the space/time or time/space continuum, or whether the entities involved truly interacted in the manner which is viewed, for there are multiple planes of interaction that are called into activation whenever any activity is undertaken, and when viewed from certain levels of existence, the events became somewhat blurred as to their place or plane of origin.

To speak as to the accuracy of these particular books would not be proper, in our estimation. Therefore, we share with you these general thoughts.

May we answer you further, my brother?

L: There were two specific locations he described, one being a large city for the most part encased in a glacier, the second being a large cave which contained machinery and a device which acted as a mental dome projector, if you will, showing the creation of that cave and the purpose of its creation as a storage facility. Would it be possible for you to verify whether those two things exist or not? A "yes" or "no" will be fine.

I am Latwii, and am aware of your query, my brother. That such exists is quite possible; since they have been described, they must therefore exist within some realm of being.

May we answer you further, my brother?

L: No. Simply thank you for allowing me to try your patience.

I am Latwii. We thank you, my brother, and our patience is endless. May we answer yet another query?

J: I have a question concerning something that I've experienced ever since I was a child, and in talking with a friend I have discovered that she has also experienced this: a sort of energy discharge, a sense of electrical impulse almost, traveling sometimes through the back of my head or through my whole body, and it has the sense of a kind of release with it. Sometimes it happens during stress or during fatigue, and I'm wondering if it means something, or what it is. Can you just talk to me about this?

I am Latwii, and am aware of your query, my sister. Again we must speak in general terms, for such an experience as you describe does have its significance in your seeking and your being. Each entity has an unique configuration or pattern of beingness which is expressed in equally unique manners. As you travel through this illusion, you gather an energy or momentum which might be equated to the processing of catalyst into experience so that your seeking becomes more refined. There is in this process the necessity of discharging, shall we say, certain accumulated energies which are a natural by-product of the seeking, the processing, and the manifesting of experience, and this is necessary so that the channels of perceptions might be kept clear and might efficiently function.

Would it then be possible for the entity to continue the seeking were the energies not discharged? This would be difficult. Therefore, each entity has an unique means of clearing the channels of perception so that further learning might occur.

May we answer you further, my sister?

J: Would I be incorrect in guessing that this may have something to do with unblocking energy centers?

I am Latwii. My sister, this is in quite general terms correct, for the unblocking of the energy centers is equal to the process of evolution and the purpose for each incarnation.

May we answer you further, my sister?

J: Yes, on a different topic. Is it possible that there are people living now, entities in separate bodies, living separate experiences, who at one time shared a single life, a single body?

I am Latwii, and am aware of your query, my sister. This is possible, for some entities are the children, shall we say, of the same higher self or oversoul, as others have described this great being to which each is connected. Some entities join portions of what might be seen as their own self in various incarnational patterns so that experience might be gained in yet another manner that is deemed proper by the higher self.

May we answer you further, my sister?

J: No. I can't think of another question I can ask about it, but—so, I'll have to think about that. Thank you.

I am Latwii. We thank you, my sister. This instrument has some depletion of energies at this time. Therefore, might we suggest a final query before we depart this group.

Carla: If two parallel portions of an oversoul were one once, would the events and the death of one affect the events and the death of another incarnation?

I am Latwii, and am aware of your query, my sister. In such an event, it is most usual for the entities of parallel existence to also exist within different planes, or shall we say, universes. Were they to exist within the same universe, as is possible, the events in one's incarnation world have definite correlations to the events in the other's incarnation, yet the correlation would not always be identical but might be complimentary. For example, the experiencing of great personal loss by one entity might generate the catalyst of extreme sorrow in one entity while in the other there might be seen the birth of great hope.

May we answer this query in any further detail?

(Tape ends.) ❧

L/L Research

L/L Research is a subsidiary of Rock Creek Research & Development Laboratories, Inc.

P.O. Box 5195
Louisville, KY 40255-0195

www.llresearch.org

Rock Creek is a non-profit corporation dedicated to discovering and sharing information which may aid in the spiritual evolution of humankind.

ABOUT THE CONTENTS OF THIS TRANSCRIPT: This telepathic channeling has been taken from transcriptions of the weekly study and meditation meetings of the Rock Creek Research & Development Laboratories and L/L Research. It is offered in the hope that it may be useful to you. As the Confederation entities always make a point of saying, please use your discrimination and judgment in assessing this material. If something rings true to you, fine. If something does not resonate, please leave it behind, for neither we nor those of the Confederation would wish to be a stumbling block for any.

CAVEAT: This transcript is being published by L/L Research in a not yet final form. It has, however, been edited and any obvious errors have been corrected. When it is in a final form, this caveat will be removed.

© 2009 L/L Research

Sunday Meditation
November 14, 1982

(C1 channeling)

We are now with this instrument. I greet you with the love and the light of the infinite Creator. Tonight I would like to say something about the little things that people could do. One of your holy leaders said, "Sell your goods and give it to the poor." But there are so many little things that people could do—a smile, a handshake, a compliment, picking someone [up] in your car and taking them somewhere, giving your *(inaudible)* clothes or material things to someone who needs them. If every person would do the little things, it's amazing how much better the giver and receiver would feel. You really don't have to sell everything and give it to the poor to do a great deal of good. Have you ever thought how many times you saw something nice and didn't say it? Or someone you love and didn't tell them? Many times the big things will take care of themselves. Sometimes the little things have more meaning for the person who receives them. A compliment at the right time could save a life if the person was severely depressed and felt worthless. Try to make a point of giving the little things. In proportion they will do more good than a few big gifts.

I am Hatonn, and I leave this instrument.

(Carla channeling)

I am Hatonn, and I also greet you through this instrument in the love and in the light of our infinite Creator. We shall continue speaking through this instrument and we shall speak to two subjects. Firstly the one which is called by some this evening and secondly quite a different one which is called specifically by the one known as M and the one known as C2 and the one known as A.

In fact, to this subject perhaps we shall speak first in order that we may remove from this evening all traces of that which in itself may color the contact by the pale shade of fear. We are aware that due to an unusual instance within this group in which the one known as C2 inadvertently brought very close to trance a channel of less than purely Confederation association, the concern of the group has been that the message be true. We have spoken upon this subject several times in the past, and not only we, but perhaps more helpfully those of Latwii. We shall be eager to continue speaking upon this subject until all doubts and fears are put to rest. That which is most central to a confidence about positivity of contact is the proper unification and tuning of the group. This group seeks to know the truth, seeks inspiration, and seeks to serve others. There is in each a spirit of what many would call Christ

Consciousness, a desire to know the love and light of the one infinite Creator.

There is at this time very little desire within this present gathering to know specific events of the future, for to request specific information which would interfere with the free will which is yours. Therefore, this group is not an hospitable place for one which is not oriented towards service to others. In fact, it would indeed be very difficult for any entity to be able to contact anyone in this group. We are not saying that such entities might not be attracted to the light which burns as a lighthouse when a group is united in prayer and seeking. It is only to say that those who have sought to be of service as channels having once tuned and then having tuned personally by prayer while awaiting contact simply do not offer an opportunity for negative contact.

We wish that we could comfort you more, but we are aware that we must leave to your own discrimination any doubts between that which is positive and negative as each of you in your own hearts may discriminate. We would not wish to have more authority than we do, for we are your brothers and your sisters—not greater that you, only those who care and thus come to you as comforters, as strengtheners, and hopefully as those who may offer some inspiration that your own life within may be somehow aided by our humble drifts. We know we have little to offer but we are so grateful that you allow us that small *(inaudible)* which is ours, for we are only messengers. The love and the light is the Father's. The kingdom that we all seek is His. And so we say, especially to those three named, fear not but be of good faith and good cheer. All that is yours awaits you. We would at this time return to our original consideration and focus the attention of those present on being of service.

Our friends, each of you is aware of many ways to be of service which the society in which you live also recognizes. There is hunger in the world and it is recognized that you are of service if you attempt to feed those who have no food. There is great poverty, loneliness and solitude unwanted and forced upon some and to those unfortunates, so called, your culture deems it charitable to aid by a helping hand. Some political movements and social issues seem to be full of service and so those who wish to be of service become active and this is service.

There are those, great leaders, whose careers are known and whose lives are great examples of service. Selfless men and women who have given all that they have to a profession, or a belief, and have spent a lifetime in creating a very visible form of service. To such people go public praise and great recognition. But let us focus now upon each here. My friends, do you know how great your opportunities for service are? There are so many things that the culture in which you live requires you to do that sometimes your sense of yourself seems to be lost and you are in effect the one who is doing, the one functioning, the one coping—neither positively nor negatively. But let us take a step back.

What time have you spent this day in meditation? What time in prayer? What time in contemplation? If you have spent no time in these activities your instinctive ability to sense the needs of others will have been greatly impaired. Your instinctive sense of yourself as a being created in love, placed in this environment here and now to offer a channeling, a witness, will be greatly impaired. Therefore *(inaudible)* we encourage each of you to begin with that which is basic: the seeking of the original Thought. For if you do not experience truth then you are not truth, or [rotten] you will have removed yourself from clarity, for the truth is within you just as the Creator is within you. Your source is within you. Your comforter awaits within you. The doors you wish to open to the outside world of service must first be opened from the inside, for your truth awaits the opening of that door. That truth cannot come to you. You must come to it, or at least open the door to it. It takes a mere moment to mentally open the door within. It takes one gentle thought to open a universe of love within you. And with a universe of love within you, my friends, what service can you help but be? Then you will not miss the chance to smile, and oh, my friends, what a lovely dance a smile makes. You will not miss a chance to reach and touch those who may need it. Indeed, my friends, there are many times when you feel that you are being of no service whatever because someone is aiding you and you feel that you are on the receiving end and cannot possibly be of service. My friends, when with a grateful heart you receive, you have greeted the Creator in manifestation.

And what of those times, my friends, that you do not pray, nor meditate, nor contemplate, nor even speak civilly, but rather attempt to survive because your world has become turned upside down for some reason? What of those times? May we say to you that even then you are of service, for those about you will learn by those things which you offer. They may not learn great feelings of warmth and smiles and hugs, and may instead learn toughness and integrity and unselfishness. You cannot help but be of service. Is that not a great lesson, my friends? Undoubtedly you wish to be of somewhat more service than we have just described. When those days occur—and in any incarnation those days will occur, if you are pursuing a path of growth—try to learn that toughness, that integrity, and that unselfishness yourself that will accept your self. By accepting yourself as you change, as you fight and struggle to learn, you greatly speed the process of your own learning, and incidentally shorten the period of your own discomfort.

We greet each of you. With you we meditate. With you we praise the infinite Creator. And with you, with many thanks, we have shared a few meager thoughts. We ask *(inaudible)* greet and welcome the one known as [S] who has not been with this group for some time.

We would, if the one known as C1 would accept it, enjoy closing this particular message through her and at this time would transfer the contact. I am Hatonn.

(C1 channeling)

I am Hatonn. Again I greet you, my friends, in the love and the light of the infinite Creator. Again may we express our great joy at being with you tonight. We have observed in some of your meditations experiences of growth and joy. We have been aware of the love that you send to each other. Perhaps you are not aware that in sending this love to each other the entire group benefits and as you send out love and light to others that is strengthened also. What we are trying to say, my friends, is that it's difficult for you to be aware of the strength that each of you gain from a group and from the experiences you share together. The one known as M and C1 will soon be leaving the group and you can make their transition much easier by continuing to send love and light to them. May we repeat again it has been our pleasure to be with the group tonight and we leave you now in the love and the light of the infinite Creator, knowing that you are always safe in that love and light, and you have but to be aware of it and you will know for yourself that it does provide safety. We take our leave now of the group and leave you in the love and the light of the infinite Creator. I am Hatonn.

(Jim channeling)

I am Latwii, and I greet you, my friends, in the love and the light of the one infinite Creator. We have been eagerly awaiting our opportunity to join your group this evening and to once again attempt to answer those queries which you have brought with you. May we then ask if there is a query with which we might begin?

C1: Yes. We've been talking about doing little things by way of serving our fellow man. Will you comment on what Jesus said when he said, "If a cup of cold water is given in my name it will not go unrewarded." What does it mean by "given in my name"?

I am Latwii, and am aware of your query, my sister. The one known as Jesus was the teacher whose purpose for incarnation was to teach the lesson of love—unconditional love for all of creation. This entity was love, love this entity had attained through its seeking of the one Creator. Therefore, this entity's name could be said to be vibrating in resonance with that known as love and compassion. Therefore, when he said that to give the cup of cold water in his name would be an action rewarded he was in fact saying that to give even the smallest gift in love for the one to whom it is given is not only to share love but also to know and to be love and to be rewarded with the knowledge of that love.

May we answer you further my sister?

C1: Well, yes, just one little bit more about that. I am reminded of … I had charge of a service years ago in the jail speaking to the women and one night after the service I tried to find a woman three stories up in a dark hallway that about scared me to death, but she had great need and I took her twenty dollars and gave it to her and I was trying to live up to that "give a cup of cold water in my name," and I said, "I give you this in the name of Jesus." And I felt like a fool and she looked at me like a fool and so I felt like I was trying to live up to the letter of the law, and yet I was doing it the best I could. That's what I was trying to get at. Are we to say or indicate that we are doing this in the name of Jesus or [do] we just do it? I didn't try that anymore, by the way.

(Laughter)

I am Latwii, and am aware of your query, my sister. When one attempts to share the love that is within the heart, open the heart without premeditation so that that love which is within may be expressed freely and naturally if such words as you have spoken come easily to your lips, then speak them freely. Do not worry with concerns about how you shall accompany the love with words or actions, simply seek within the heart of your being to give freely and the words and clothing of the action shall naturally be made clear to you, or should we say through you.

May we answer you further, my sister?

C1: No that helps me to understand. I think I must have been trying to live up to the letter of the law. Thank you, I understand better.

I am Latwii. We thank you, my sister. Is there another query at this time?

Carla: I'd just like to pursue it a little further. Of course, having just come off a Christian weekend I am probably really oriented toward this question, but it does seem to me that a lot of people are ready to hear the name of Jesus.

(Side one of tape ends.)

Carla: … equally powerful whereas there's something to that particular vibration—Jesus—that makes a difference. Is it within me, as I in my heart believe, or is it in a name that the bulk of the power would reside?

I am Latwii, and am aware or your query, my sister. We see that the one known as C1 has once again generated within your being the seeking for similar understanding and we greatly appreciate the combination of your efforts. To speak to your query may we suggest that it is the heart of your being which gives the force, shall we say, to any words which emanate from your lips, for the words are the attempts to clothe the great feeling of love from your heart in understandable concepts so that the mind of another may receive the understanding which emanates from heart to heart. Yet it is also true, as you have surmised, that many within your culture especially yearn to hear the name of the master known as Jesus. For within your culture this entity is equated, correctly so, with the vibration of Love. Yet this yearning to hear the name exists not because of any name but because of what the name expresses.

Speak yea then your heart, my sister, in the way which has meaning for you, for each entity's ability to be of service to others is unique and to be fully expressed must be so in the way which is natural, shall we say, for that entity.

May we answer you further my sister?

Carla: No. I think that that's really clear. Thank you.

I am Latwii. We thank you, my sister. Is there another query at this time?

Carla: I have a query. Something that has occurred to me several times recently because I've been talking to people and just have these things occur to me several times. We've been talking to Ra off and on about polarity for some time. I noticed with the women friends that I have that are really strong friends of mine that it is almost as if we were of one body. It's a different relationship than I have with my man friends, although no less close, simply a different feeling and it seems to me probably, I'm guessing, to be related to our similar polarity so that consequently rather than being attracted to each other in a polarized fashion we are one identity basically in polarity and are able simply to merge. Does this reading of polarity and its effects on human relationships have any merit?

I am Latwii, and am aware of your query, my sister. Those who seek with a like mind and heart shall attract to themselves the experiences which will blend their seeking and their being. This is basically the situation which you find yourself within. As you seek the love and light of the one Creator you attract to yourself those who also seek in a similar fashion so that in the larger sense you become more in unity with those who seek as you seek. To reduce this phenomenon further, those of the female gender who are together with you seeking are, with you, realizing the potential of their gender. This is a portion of your seeking. As you seek together you utilize those faculties of your being on all levels which are available to you. Some are available because you are the gender you are. To be more, shall we say, intuitive and inspirational therefore becomes a factor of unification according to gender and you do indeed become of one beingness or body as you have described it with those of your gender.

May we answer you further my sister?

Carla: Just the balancing question. I have very close male friends also and consider those relationships as close as relationships with my women friends. It is simply that I have observed that there is the potential for misuse of the polarity between two spiritual seekers who are male and female, regardless of age or attractiveness, simply that the polarity exists and because of the intense seeking on both. Consequently, that being dealt with in a mature manner, that is to say, being accepted for what it is, as polarity, as proper and appropriate, that same intimate relationship can exist between man and woman in their spiritual search. It's simply that the polarity is there instead of the identity and after that point we're all capable, it seems to me, of helping each other, male or female, it doesn't matter. But I do think it seems that polarity is something to be dealt with simply by recognizing it and not being bemused by it or taken away from the track of mutual spiritual seeking. Is this also a fair reading of polarity, as it applies to spiritual seekers?

I am Latwii, and am aware of your query, my sister. We find that you have made a quite acceptable explanation of this phenomenon. May we answer you further?

Carla: No, thanks.

I am Latwii. We thank you, my sister. Is there another query at this time?

Questioner: Yes. For the last couple of weeks—last week or the week before—I was in this general vicinity visited by a thought form of the Confederation. It's kind of a specific question—not terribly important but I ask it for someone who was interested and it was on the night of a meditation.

I am Latwii, and am aware of your query, my brother. We find in scanning the recent memory of your friend that it is necessary to refrain from the direct answer so that free will shall not be abridged. Phenomena of this variety must present a riddle, shall we say, to such participants and observers so that through the strength of their own inner seeking the answers of value might be found.

May we be of further service, my brother?

Questioner: I think your answer was the desired answer. Thanks.

I am Latwii. We thank you, my brother. Is there another query at this time?

C1: I have a puzzle. I normally keep my eyes closed during meditation but I opened them to look at the sofa beside me and no one was sitting there and mentally I felt I was sitting on this sofa alone. Why would I get that weird impression when I know this girl is sitting here with me?

I am Latwii, and am aware of your query, my sister. Again we find that the experiences that one such as yourself observes have meaning according to the unique configuration of seeking and perception which is yours. To express in simple and clear terms those characteristics which cause you to experience one or another sensation is to give you information which we feel is best sought within your own meditative being.

May we be of further service, my sister?

C1: No I guess someday I'll figure it out myself.

I am Latwii. My sister, this illusion which you inhabit is full of mysteries. The one Creator is hidden in each. To find the face of the Creator is the goal which each seeks and so shall ye find as ye seek.

Is there another query at this time?

C1: Yes, one more. I don't want to hog this thing, but one more question. It's certainly not profound, but it has been interesting to me. I've had a *(inaudible)* because of where I was born and raised I guess, the experiences I've had in church and all, I've had … it's been an obsession to me to seek what I call the truth and get rid of as much ignorance as possible. And at the risk of making a nuisance out of myself much of my life, and *(inaudible)* going into bookstore, I have literally found books on bookshelves I did not know existed, had no idea of knowing they were existed, but it just seemed to me that that book was just what I needed at that point in time. Was I guided to that book or did I just stumble onto it or a … would you comment on that?

I am Latwii, and am aware of your query, my sister. As the strength of the seeking increases, for each entity each shall find seeming coincidences crossing the path of the seeking so that a book, a friend, a stranger, an event may lend yet one more piece to the puzzle of the mystery of being and make more sense, shall we say, out of what was confusion. When you seek you are as the magnet attracting the filings of iron. Never forget you are one with all of creation. Therefore, when you seek that which you seek is a portion of yourself and as you seek that portion of yourself it, being yourself, is aware of that seeking and shall reveal itself unto you through whatever means is understandable to you at that time, be it a book, a song, a sign in the sky, a conversation, a chance encounter. There are many, many ways by which the mystery of your being is revealed to you each moment in which you seek. Truly it has been said there are no accidents.

May we answer you further, my sister?

C1: Well, let me just summarize what I think I heard. For instance, when I would go to the bookstore and find a book, which I didn't know existed and I would be just tremendously inspired and just mark this book all up, you mean I found a part of me, truth with me … I found something within me … now is that what your saying? Or I discovered a part of me that I did not know was me. Is that what I heard?

I am Latwii, my sister, and this is correct. It might be that at that moment this was the means by which you would most clearly understand that portion of your being which you were seeking to understand. It might also be that at another moment the seeking which you were engaged in would reveal to you through meditation that which was sought. It might be as is generally the case that some experience in your life would reveal to you the general nature of that which you were seeking so that event upon event would present itself to you so that you might see through the power of your seeking the core of truth both in the event and in yourself which you have been seeking and so the path of evolution of the mind, the body, and the spirit continues endlessly within your illusion. The seeking and the finding. The seeking and the finding.

May we answer you further, my sister?

C1: The seeking carries with it a certain amount of frustration and pain but the finding is like the light or the joy that I experience then and I don't want to ask you to talk a long time on that. It seems that the seeking is frustrating, but the finding is very joyous so the joy almost outweighs the seeking. Is that a pretty good evaluation of this seeking and finding and seeking and finding?

I am Latwii, and am aware of your query, my sister. So it is within your illusion that there must be the motivation for the seeking, for the effort to be made.

For if you had no need to increase your understanding, how would understanding increase? Must you not then feel the pain, the frustration, of your ignorance so that this might draw you forward, shall we say, and provide the means by which your journey continues and the finding of that which was lost within your being brings the joy of the reunion and the union on the conscious level within yourself with all that is. To not be aware of that unity creates the pain of the ignorance. The pain of the ignorance drives one forward so that the unity might be further revealed.

May we answer you further, my sister?

C1: No, that's fantastic. A lot of things make sense now. Thank you very much.

I am Latwii. We thank you, my sister. Is there another query at this time?

Carla: A quick one, I hope. I'm considering for personal reasons changing the day of the week we hold our weekly meditations. I'm concerned that the level of my own service will be maintained. Could you comment?

I am Latwii, and am aware of your query, my sister. We find some limits surrounding our potential response due to our unwillingness to infringe upon your free will, but might suggest that when the desire of the group is focused upon the meeting and those present desire the meditation for increasing inspiration and understanding then it is possible to conduct such a meeting no matter the day.

May we answer you further, my sister?

Carla: No, thank you *(inaudible)*.

I am Latwii. Is there another query at this time?

(No further queries.)

I am Latwii. As we observe the great peace and joy of the silence within this group we feel that we have exhausted the queries for the evening. It is always our honor to be asked to join your group. We thank each of you. We remind each as well that we would be most happy to join you in your private meditations should you but request our presence. Peace be with each. We leave this group at this time rejoicing in the peace and the power of the one infinite Creator. We are known to you as Latwii. Adonai vasu borragus.

(Carla channeling)

I am Nona. I come in the love and in the light of the infinite Creator. We are those of healing and offer to you our song.

(Carla channels a song from Nona.) ❦

L/L Research

L/L Research is a subsidiary of Rock Creek Research & Development Laboratories, Inc.

P.O. Box 5195
Louisville, KY 40255-0195

www.llresearch.org

Rock Creek is a non-profit corporation dedicated to discovering and sharing information which may aid in the spiritual evolution of humankind.

ABOUT THE CONTENTS OF THIS TRANSCRIPT: This telepathic channeling has been taken from transcriptions of the weekly study and meditation meetings of the Rock Creek Research & Development Laboratories and L/L Research. It is offered in the hope that it may be useful to you. As the Confederation entities always make a point of saying, please use your discrimination and judgment in assessing this material. If something rings true to you, fine. If something does not resonate, please leave it behind, for neither we nor those of the Confederation would wish to be a stumbling block for any.

© 2009 L/L Research

The Law of One, Book IV, Session 99
November 18, 1982

Ra: I am Ra. I greet you in the love and in the light of the one infinite Creator. We communicate now.

Questioner: Would you please give me the condition of the instrument?

Ra: I am Ra. This instrument's physical deficit continues but has the potential for the lessening due to the removal in your probable future of foodstuffs to which the instrument has significant allergy. The vital energy levels are somewhat lessened than the last asking but remain strong. The change in the mental/emotional energy level is towards the distortion of the weakening of this complex.

Questioner: We now have an additional set of tarot images. Which of these two sets are closer to Ra's original intention?

Ra: I am Ra. The principle which moves in accordance with the dynamics of teach/learning with most efficiency is constancy. We could explore the archetypical mind using that set of images produced by the one known as Fathman or we could use those which have been used.

In point of fact, those which are being used have some subtleties which enrich the questioning. As we have said, this set of images is not that which we gave. This is not material. We could use any of a multitude of devised tarot sets. Although this must be at the discretion of the questioner, we suggest the maintaining of one and only one set of distorted images to be used for the querying and note that the images you now use are good.

Questioner: The wings above Card Five, I am guessing, have to do with a protection over the Significator of the Mind. I am guessing that they are a symbol of protection. Is this in any way correct?

Ra: I am Ra. Let us say that you are not incorrect but rather less than correct. The Significator owns a covenant with the spirit which it shall in some cases manifest through the thought and action of the adept. If there is protection in a promise, then you have chosen the correct sound vibration, for the outstretched wings of spirit, high above manifestation, yet draw the caged mind onward.

Questioner: Thank you. In Card Number Six I see the Transformation of the Mind, the male with crossed arms, representing transformation. The transformation is possible either toward the left or the right-hand path. The path is beckoned or led by the female, the Potentiator. The one on the right has the serpent of wisdom at the brow and is fully clothed, the one on the left having less clothing and indicating that the Potentiator is more concerned or attracted to the physical as the left-hand path is chosen and more concerned and attracted to the mental as the right-hand path is chosen.

The creature above points an arrow at the left-hand path indicating that if this path is chosen the chips, shall we say, will fall where they may, the path being unprotected as far as the activity of catalyst. The intellectual abilities of the chooser of the left-hand path would be the main guardian rather than the designed or built-in protection of the Logos for the right-hand path. The entity firing the arrow seems to be a second density entity which indicates that this catalyst could be produced by a lesser evolved source, you might say. Would Ra comment on these observations?

Ra: I am Ra. We shall speak upon several aspects seriatim. Firstly, let us examine the crossed arms of the male who is to be transformed. What, O student, do you make of the crossing? What see you in this tangle? There is a creative point to be found in this element which was not discussed overmuch by the questioner.

Let us now observe the evaluation of the two females. The observation that to the left-hand path moves the roughly physical and to the right-hand path the mental has a shallow correctness. There are deeper observations to be made concerning the relationship of the great sea of the unconscious mind to the conscious mind which may fruitfully be pursued. Remember, O student, that these images are not literal. They haunt rather than explicate.

Many use the trunk and roots of mind as if that portion of mind were a badly used, prostituted entity. Then this entity gains from this great storehouse that which is rough, prostituted, and without great virtue. Those who turn to the deep mind, seeing it in the guise of the maiden, go forth to court it. The courtship has nothing of plunder in its semblance and may be protracted, yet the treasure gained by such careful courtship is great. The right-hand and left-hand transformations of the mind may be seen to differ by the attitude of the conscious mind towards its own resources as well as the resources of other-selves.

We now speak of that genie, or elemental, or mythic figure, culturally determined, which sends the arrow to the left-hand transformation. This arrow is not the arrow which kills but rather that which, in its own way, protects. Those who choose separation, that being the quality most indicative of the left-hand path, are protected from other-selves by a strength and sharpness equivalent to the degree of transformation which the mind has experienced in the negative sense. Those upon the right-hand path have no such protection against other-selves for upon that path the doughty seeker shall find many mirrors for reflection in each other-self it encounters.

Questioner: In the previous session you mentioned the use of the forty-five minute interval of the tape recorders as a signal for the end of the session. Is this still the appropriate time?

Ra: I am Ra. This is, of course, at the discretion of the questioner for this instrument has some transferred energy and remains open as it has unfailingly done. However, the fragility of the instrument has been more and more appreciated by us. We, in the initial observations, saw the strength of will and overestimated greatly the recuperative abilities of the physical complex of this entity.

Therefore, we may say that ending a working at approximately this amount of energy expenditure; that is, some point soon following upon the sound vibration of which you speak, would be appropriate and, insofar as we may determine, may well extend the incarnational amount of your space/time which this instrument shall be able to offer to this contact.

Questioner: In that case I will just ask this short question as we terminate this session. I want to know if the Logos of this system planned for the mating process as possibly depicted in Card Six—I don't know if this is related to some type of DNA imprinting. In many second-density creatures there seems to be some sort of imprinting that creates a lifetime mating relationship and I was wondering if this was also carried into third density?

Ra: I am Ra. There are some of your second-density fauna which have instinctually imprinted monogamous mating processes. The third-density physical vehicle which is the basic incarnational tool of manifestation upon your planet arose from entities thusly imprinted, all the aforesaid being designed by the Logos.

The free will of third-density entities is far stronger than the rather mild carryover from second-density DNA encoding and it is not part of the conscious nature of many of your mind/body/spirit complexes to be monogamous due to the exercise of free will. However, as has been noted there are many signposts in the deep mind indicating to the alert adept the more efficient use of catalyst. As we have said, the Logos of your peoples has a bias towards kindness.

Questioner: Thank you. In closing I will ask if there is anything that we can do to make the instrument more comfortable or to improve the contact?

Ra: I am Ra. We note the relative discomfort of this group at this space/time and offer those previous statements made by Ra as possible aids to the regaining of the extraordinary harmony which this group has the capability of experiencing in a stable manner.

We find the addition of the swirling waters to be helpful. The appurtenances are conscientiously aligned.

We encourage the conscious strengthening of those invisible ribbands which fly from the wrists of those who go forward to seek what you may call the Grail. All is well, my friends. We leave you in hopes that each may find true colors to fly in that great metaphysical quest and urge each to urge each other in love, praise, and thanksgiving.

I am Ra. We leave you in the love and light of the one infinite Creator. Go forth rejoicing in the power and in the peace of the one glorious infinite Creator. Adonai.

L/L Research

L/L Research is a subsidiary of Rock Creek Research & Development Laboratories, Inc.

P.O. Box 5195
Louisville, KY 40255-0195

www.llresearch.org

Rock Creek is a non-profit corporation dedicated to discovering and sharing information which may aid in the spiritual evolution of humankind.

ABOUT THE CONTENTS OF THIS TRANSCRIPT: This telepathic channeling has been taken from transcriptions of the weekly study and meditation meetings of the Rock Creek Research & Development Laboratories and L/L Research. It is offered in the hope that it may be useful to you. As the Confederation entities always make a point of saying, please use your discrimination and judgment in assessing this material. If something rings true to you, fine. If something does not resonate, please leave it behind, for neither we nor those of the Confederation would wish to be a stumbling block for any.

© 2009 L/L Research

The Law of One, Book V, Session 99, Fragment 49
November 18, 1982

Jim: Most people would probably not have described the feeling of not quite being whole and in harmony which our group experienced during the fall of 1982 as true disharmony. Yet as one moves further along the path of seeking light and begins to stand closer to it, as we were privileged to do in the Ra contact, even the smallest of lapses of harmony, when left unresolved, can become targets of opportunity for those such as our friend of negative polarity to intensify. These psychic greetings can become great opportunities to heal those lapses of harmony and to move even further and faster upon the evolutionary journey because what such a negative entity is actually doing when it intensifies one's disharmonious choices is pointing out to you weak points which you might have missed in your own conscious seeking. But one must take quick and thorough action in order to unravel these distortions in one's beingness or further confusion and difficulty may ensue, again due to, first, your original free will choice, second, the intensification of that choice by the negative entity, and third, by lack of attention on your part in finally resolving the distortion and balancing it. Fortunately, most people do not have to deal with the magical abilities of a fifth-density entity but with the lesser abilities of the fourth-density minions who are usually quite effective on their own.

Thus as Carla was finally getting rid of the effects of the intensification of her blue-ray blockage concerning renting and then cleaning the house next to the airport in Atlanta, I began to notice an increase in my pre-incarnatively chosen distortion of anger/frustration. Notice the fundamental principle in Ra's first sentence in response to my question. All of our distortions and thus all of our learning are the result of the limitation of the viewpoint. We limit our points of view consciously or unconsciously, pre-incarnatively or during the incarnation, in order to gain a certain bias that may then draw unto it the opposite bias and offer us the opportunity for balance. By being able to see each bias as an opportunity for the Creator to know Itself and for us to know ourselves as the Creator, we more and more become able to accept ourselves. We become able to find love and acceptance not only in ourselves but in others who share our characteristics, and our viewpoint is widened by our efforts to learn and to serve. Such growth is not possible without biases or distortions, and these biases and distortions are not possible without the choice to limit the viewpoint in one way or another. So we determine what lessons and services we shall attempt during any incarnation by the way in which we limit our viewpoint.

Another interesting point to note here is that whatever one's basic nature is, whether it be love, wisdom, power, or some blend of these three, one does well to express that nature in a regularized fashion. So does one become a channel for it, not by holding on to it, but by giving it away.

Again, we see another purpose of anger, or opportunity that it might present to one expressing it. Being the polar opposite of love, it may attract that love and compassion to the person feeling it. Remorse and sorrow often attract love and compassion to a positive seeker who has experienced a great deal of anger. Anger may also be seen as the negative expression of power; that is, destruction and separation, with the positive side being construction and unification. So it is not necessary to repress or overcome qualities in our being which seem negative and hurtful but, rather, to see them as potentials for achieving balance. When these negative qualities are followed to their source, they can enable the seeker to take advantage of the opportunities for knowing the self, the Creator, and the creation as portions of a complete unity. Ra's last sentence underscores this point.

Carla: I have thought that this particular fragment is perhaps the best example in this present volume of why Ra can be so helpful. We three humans were doing our level best to stay totally harmonized in movement and rhythm, but we often erred, as do all of us, no matter what, if not today then tomorrow. This is the human estate. Working on this catalyst between us with an intensity born of wishing to remain clear enough to contact Ra, we developed questions for Ra, trying to get more of a bead on what our distortions were, and how to approach seating these incoming catalysts. But no question, however cleverly phrased, could expect to garner a piece of advice like: "as in all distortions, the source is the limit of the viewpoint." In terms of the old saw about a choice between giving a man a fish and giving him a pole and teaching him fishing, Ra always went for the fishing pole, plus bait. And all without infringement on free will: an impressive task, and appreciated by us. We pored over these little comments a lot. They really did help us focus.

I've already talked about the buttermilk/penicillin cure. The principle Ra followed in OK'ing my wearing of a little cross in sessions seems very telling for a lot of questions we have about should we do something or not. They said it wasn't the greatest in terms of what complications it would cause, but it was OK because it was a symbol which strengthened me in a real way. This concept of balance and the strength of being as flowing into a pattern which is read as metaphysical rather than physical is a real help to people who want to be less allergic or depressed or whatever: do what feels right, letting the mystical meaning have as much importance as the physical. Find the balance.

Ra's advice to Jim struck home both to Jim and to Don and me. After we read this, we decided to encourage Jim to take the afternoon for solitude. He really enjoyed, and still enjoys, this routine, going out into the gardens for whatever needs doing after lunch and finishing up at eventide with a bath. I am often out there with him, but I do leave him in solitude unless I have a gardening question. To watch Jim work is to understand the power and purpose of ritual and magic.

My dear Mick (I call him that to distinguish him from my brother and also from my first husband, both named Jim) still has an amazingly bright and fiery temper. I stand in awe, quite literally, and watch it sweep through him like a tornado. He has, through the years, found ways to behave less angrily, but that core imbalance for him runs very deep, rather like my wanting to do too much. Some things about all of us are far from smart, but when you try to eradicate them, they just snicker! Nope—we're part of the package, they seem to say. I have worked my way through the substantial catalyst this has been for me, and give Mick thanks for such excellent catalyst. I have never been hurt physically, mind you. This is a solo act. I now simply observe and accept. I know it only seems that way. I affirm perfection. That is what I have learned to do so far, both to my own humanity and other people's. Meanwhile, he has had to learn to tend me rather like a shepherd, walking along and picking up the things I drip behind me as I go absent-mindedly on. No one gets away free!

I can only say that meditation, and a daily offering each day as a beginning, help for me. They are the basis of my day, and I think Jim would also say that. So I encourage any who might have had trouble doing that to try again. This time, adapt the practice to your life. It is a routine that has served us well. Perhaps that is too much for you, but you see how to build a time for you and the Creator to meet. You can't just remake your life around a newly discovered devotional or mystic aspect of yourself; you have to practice a rule of life that gives you time to do your necessaries. I think that one quick drink is a powerful thing. So please try again, if you have given up. For those who want to read about meditation, I recommend Joel Goldsmith's little book, The Art Of Meditation.

Session 99, November 18, 1982

Questioner: What are the foodstuffs that are creating this allergic reaction?

Ra: I am Ra. That which you call the buttermilk, though appropriately used in the healing work undertaken for the throat and chest areas, is the substance to which the entity has allergy.

Questioner: The instrument asked if she could keep the small gold cross on while she is in one of these sessions. Will that cause any distortion in these workings?

Ra: I am Ra. We scan the mental distortions of the instrument. Although the presence of the metallic substance is, in general, not recommended, in this instance, as we find those distortions weakening the mental/emotional complex of the instrument due to its empathic distortions, the figure is specifically recommended for use by this instrument. We would request that should any strengthening be done to the chain, as we find intended by this instrument, the strengthening links which symbolize eternity to this instrument be as high in purity or higher than the remainder of the device.

In this nexus that which this device represents to this instrument is a much-needed strengthener of the mental/emotional patterns which have been much disrupted from the usual configuration of distortions.

Questioner: Is there anything further that needs to be done by or for the instrument to remove the magical working, or any of its after-effects, in her throat area by our fifth-density, negative companion?

Ra: I am Ra. No.

Questioner: Finally, I have a question from Jim stating: "For the last two weeks I have often found myself on the edge of anger and frustration, have had a nearly constant dull pain in the area of my indigo-ray center, and have felt quite drained of energy. Would Ra comment on the source of these experiences and any thoughts or actions that might alleviate them?"

Ra: I am Ra. As in all distortions, the source is the limit of the viewpoint. We may, without serious infringement, suggest three courses of behavior which shall operate upon the distortion expressed.

Firstly, it would be well for the scribe to engage, if not daily then as nearly so as possible, in a solitary strenuous activity which brings this entity to the true physical weariness. Further, although any activity may suffice, an activity chosen for its intended service to the harmony of the group would be quite efficacious.

The second activity is some of your space/time and time/space taken by the entity, directly or as nearly so as possible to the strenuous activity, for solitary contemplation.

Thirdly, the enthusiastic pursuit of the balancing and silent meditations cannot be deleted from the list of helpful activities for this entity.

We may note that the great forte of the scribe is summed in the inadequate sound vibration complex, power. The flow of power, just as the flow of love or wisdom, is enabled not by the chary[1] conserver of its use but by the constant user. The physical manifestation of power being either constructive or destructive strenuous activity, the power-filled entity must needs exercise that manifestation. This entity experiences a distortion in the direction of an excess of stored energy. It is well to know the self and to guard and use those attributes which the self has provided for its learning and its service.

---

[1] chary: cautious, careful, wary; fastidious; particular; sparing, frugal; stingy [< OE *cearig* sorrowful, sad < *cearu* care]

Sunday Meditation
November 21, 1982

(L channeling)

I am Hatonn, and I greet you, my brothers and sisters, in the love and the light of the infinite Creator. My friends, it is with great pleasure that we receive your request that our vibration be joined with your own, for, as always, it is our desire to be of service in whatever manner possible. Tonight we would share with you some thoughts concerning your desires for your brothers and sisters, for those who seek to follow the path of service to others by nature attempt to envision that which would benefit their other selves. My friends, regard for a moment the possibilities open to those whose lives involve selection. For example, if one desires an object, it is possible that the possession of that object might be beneficial to the individual. It is also possible that the inability to possess that same object might also be of benefit to that individual in that they may learn the lack of value in possessing that which is finite and thus of a very temporary nature. When one regards this situation, one might be reluctant to select a wish, if you will, for this other self, for it is not readily apparent which would benefit the individual more.

Obviously, my brothers and sisters, this is a very simplistic rendition of the situations you encounter daily as your desires for your brothers and sisters are expressed. How then may one possessing the ability to create, to alter the universe within one—correction—within which one exists, best serve in this manner? My friends, might we suggest that rather than expending your energies confounding yourselves in attempting to decipher the lessons of another, rather we would suggest the expression that the will of the Creator be manifested through the perception by the other self of that selection most effective in continuation of their progress upon their chosen path.

My friends, it is often difficult for those upon your path to desire that opportunities for service to self be manifested for one's other selves who have selected that path. Yet, my friends, are not both paths to finally achieve the same objective? Therefore, our suggestion would be that one avoid the temptation to define for another self that which one regards as best for that other self, and instead exert one's energies in the direction of desiring for any other self that which would best assist that other self in the progression along their chosen path.

At this time, it is our desire to transfer our contact to another instrument. I am known to you as Hatonn.

(M1 channeling)

I am now with this instrument. I greet you with the love and the light of the infinite Creator. What you really possess are not the things around you but the things to which you give your attention. If every morning you see a beautiful tree in your neighbor's yard and it brightens your breakfast, in a real sense you own it. If the tree in your yard gives you no attention and you pay no attention to it, it really isn't yours. The same is true of friendship. You may meet a person that you only see a few times, and yet the feeling between you is so intense in depth, and the attention which you give to each other is so bright that if that person should leave the Earth, even though you had seen her only a few times, you would feel a real loss. It is important to give attention to things rather than go blindly through life. Somehow a man's first house, which he lovingly put together and saved his money to buy the furniture, remains with him forever and if he becomes a rich man and has many houses and could not describe the rooms in the houses or what is on the table or what is on the shelf, they don't really belong to him.

If you really want to acquire possessions, notice things. You had a poet who talked about daffodils, and when the season was gone he still possessed them. Do not go blindly through life not noticing things. The only things you really own are the things to which you give your attention either lovingly or with hate. If you dislike something intensely, you own it. If you love it intensely you own it. But if you can't remember it, even though in your world you possess it, it does not belong to you. Do not go blindly through life. Be aware of people. Be aware of things. Live intensely. I am Hatonn. I leave this instrument.

(Carla channeling)

I am Hatonn, and again I greet you in the love and in the light of our infinite Creator. We may rename this instrument, "Wait-A-While," for every time we contact her when the newer channels are present she says, "Wait a while." But we say to you, my sister, we must exercise you as well. There are varying degrees of newness, but there is no oldness. We shall continue through this instrument. And so as you strive for excellence in being, my friend, as you strive to serve others, to serve the Creator, you come up against a formidable difficulty and that, my brothers and sisters, is your own sensibility. You know what you would do to be kind and good and helpful. But there are many cases in which, not having expected telepathy between yourselves, you do not know what will truly be kind, good or helpful for one to whom

you wish only good. And in many cases that other self will not be able to tell you what he or she may need. For your density is a complex one, and if you are dealing with it in all of its illusory splendor, your feelings grow complex and difficult to discern amidst the grit and grime that gets into the machinery of complexity.

There is, however, one way which cannot fail to aid an other self, and we present it to you in all of its stark simplicity, knowing that it is the simple things that are the hardest to grasp and attain. If you can be who you are clearly and lucidly, with each petal of your own bloom open to the world, you are then by your presence manifesting your totally unique and utterly personal love. Who you are may be cranky, judgmental, difficult or angry, but if that is who you are, and if that is what you show, then you are living; and as you open, those angers, those uncomfortable configurations of mind and emotions are flicked away by the clean waters of experience. Very few people, my friends, feel free to be, and yet only out of that being, that which you see as imperfect and possibly implausible to love, can come the spontaneity in which you catch a moment for love as a dewdrop catches the sun.

Yes, my friends, it is very difficult to do anything for another, and do it in total harmony with the desires of another. But can you give yourself to the world about you? If you can, my friends, the Creator's manifestation shall never be more nearly perfect in your illusion than at that very moment. Much has been written in your holy works about trust. Trust in the Creator. Abide in the Creator. Shelter yourself under His wings. But Who is the Creator, and how far away are those beings? We say to you, my friends, you dwell in the tabernacle. Your feet are upon holy ground. The Creator is with you at this moment without reservation, without holding back. He is not only among you, He is you. This infinite invisible presence of love is you. We dwell with you. The creation dwells with you. And to come to a more everyday ethic, your other selves dwell with you in that tabernacle, and only you can open the gates that let them in.

Why is it that some seem to offer a blessing? Is it not, my friends, because they have opened to you that which is their own self? Thus begin always by loving the Creator that is you. And then go forward proudly, and love what you are manifesting this very day, this very moment. Whatever you consider imperfect of God, take time to love it. Good or bad, however you judge, remember to put aside and love, and open and open and again until the universe is beloved within you. And the next time that you attempt to say the right thing, to make the right gesture, to give the right gift, to show the right consideration, and fall completely flat upon your nose, arise from this in the knowledge that you have done something, and what you have done has not had the outcome you thought would be helpful. But how do you know how your being affects those whose lives you touch, touch now and will touch? This, my friends, shall always in your illusion be a mystery.

We would close, if we may, through another instrument. I am known to you as Hatonn.

(M1 channeling)

I am Hatonn. I am now with this instrument. I greet you with the love and the light of the infinite Creator. Continuing my theme on your attention. Not everyone can be a famous painter as Rembrandt. His attention could concentrate so much that he saw the inner soul of the people, the inner meaning of a tree or the animal. You may not have the hands to put this intensity on paper but you can have the eyes of a Rembrandt. When you see a tree do you feel the struggle that made the growth? Do you feel the sun and the light and the stars through which it weathered? When you meet a human being do you see only the surface or do you look to their soul? When you see a beautiful object, does it have an inner meaning? You may not have the hands of a Rembrandt, but try to cultivate the eyes of a Rembrandt.

I am Hatonn. I leave this instrument.

(M2 channeling)

I am Hatonn. We greet you through this instrument. We were going to close through the one known as K, but find this instrument does not wish to channel at this time. Just a brief word of closing, my friends. It is a great service you offer us by letting us share our humble thoughts with you and share this joyous fellowship with you. For as we share with you the morsels of understanding, we once again have the opportunity to review those concepts and thoughts and learn even as we teach. What a joy to learn and teach and share with other selves such as you. Our blessings are with you. We leave you in the love and the light of the one infinite Creator. We are known to you as Hatonn.

(Jim channeling)

I am Latwii, and I greet you, my friends, in the love and in the light of our infinite Creator. Once again it is our honor to be asked to join your group in the capacity of attempting to answer those queries which are upon your minds. May we then begin with the first query?

K: I have a question. It came to mind last week when we were ending the meditation. We always end by sending light to someone who is either sick or going through some problems and I noticed what happens then—and what happens often when I'm, say, reading about someone in a newspaper or hearing about it or on TV—that I think about what they're going through and pray for them to have strength, but I also imagine what they're feeling, and when I do I feel an overwhelming sorrow to the point of tears sometimes, imagining what they are feeling. My question is, am I spending more energy on feeling what they're going through—is that taking away from the energy that I could be sending to them to give them strength?

I am Latwii, and am aware of your query, my sister. Quite the contrary, my sister. The feelings which you feel might be termed the motivating factor which makes the healing vibrations you send such entities most effective, for what you feel is compassion. Compassion which is felt deeply enough, the tear is an outer manifestation of the great desire and ability to love which resides within your and every being. And, my sister, what greater healing power than love?

May we answer you further, my sister?

K: No, thank you.

I am Latwii. We thank you. Is there another query at this time?

S: Yes. Latwii, can you give me any information on—about the unusual physical sensation I experienced this evening?

I am Latwii, and am aware of your query, my sister. We find there is some limit to that which we might describe, for we do not wish to infringe upon your free will, but may suggest that in part the sensation which you are experiencing is the re-contact with those entities gathered about you who for, shall we say, a family of seekers—that you have felt the presence of fellow seekers is a manifestation of your own desire to seek, which has blended or harmonized, shall we say, with a kindred vibration of others.

May we answer you further, my sister?

S: No, thank you, Latwii.

I am Latwii. We thank you. Is there another query at this time?

Carla: Is there anything that you can tell me about why …

(Side one of tape ends.)

(Jim channeling)

I am Latwii, and we are once again with this instrument. Please continue.

Carla: Okay. Is there any comment that you can make about why my singing voice seemed to change quite a bit when I went to sing on my brother's record album in Washington a couple of weeks ago. I've pondered this a bit, and all of the ideas that I first had about getting used to the microphone—it was different than any I'd any used before, and what not—don't really wash, and I wondered if there was some sort of subliminal guidance involved. I certainly prayed for it, and we consciously all prayed each night as we began our recording.

I am Latwii, and am aware of your query, my sister. To begin, may we say that your great desire to be of service in the recording of the music which you and your brother created was the overriding factor which permitted your voice to become a more finely tuned instrument of praise for the one Creator. As you refined this desire each moment by focusing upon each note, powered by the prayer, of those about you, your voice then became transformed, shall we say. The vibrations of sound which emanated then from your vehicle were stepped up so that the love and the light which you desired to share would have clearer access and expression through your voice. We find that this experience was also tinted, shall we say, with an underlying concern which was somewhat deleterious, and times—and at times was responsible for the relapse, shall we say, of the voice into less than desirable patterns. This concern which was at that time felt has been, as we notice, dealt with in your daily pattern of existence. Therefore we may speak as we have spoken.

May we answer you further, my sister?

Carla: No, I guess not, although I haven't a clue as to what it is I solved in my daily existence that allowed you to speak. I'm glad I did something. Thank you very much. I'm still puzzled, I think. I think I liked my old voice better. I was really disturbed by listening to the changes. Perhaps I'm not the one to judge. Is it possible that the softer voice, more transparent voice, gets across the words better for people to listen to? Is that possible?

I am Latwii. My sister, as we have stated many times …

Carla: Anything is possible.

This is correct. May we also suggest that that vibration which emanates from the heart and is felt to the core of the being is the most effective vehicle for transmitting the concepts which you wish to share. It is not just the ear which hears, but also the heart.

May we answer you further, my sister?

Carla: [Not] unless you know how to make me sound more like Carly Simon.

I am Latwii. My sister, our limits are quite evident.

Carla: Right. Me too. Thank you very much.

I am Latwii. We thank you. Is there another query at this time?

K: Well, yes. I guess I know the answer, and yet let me ask anyway. I listened to the—I think it was, "Face The Nation," at twelve o'clock today and there was a man. I forgot his name right now, but he was the one that helped bring New York out of financial mess five years ago, and the statement went something like this, that the whole world is in a mess, and that if the United States and Europe … Western Europe and Japan, if they cannot cooperate for the good of the world, he sees nothing but ruin ahead of us, and he also said that before this can be done there must be a Congress and a Executive Branch that will be absolutely bipartisan in their decisions, so it really sounded very bad. Would you comment on that?

I am Latwii, and am aware of your query, my sister. If we might borrow the message which our brothers and sisters of Hatonn have shared with your group this evening, it is not easy to determine what is of value and what shall be of service to another. As you look about you, you see the world in which you live transforming itself in ways quite confusing. That there are problems is agreed. The solutions are many and in doubt. What it—we correct this instrument—what is it that is lacking? Above what level shall entities upon your planet find the love which they seek, yet which is so little found. Can it be legislated? As you look about you and see pain, sorrow, poverty, suffering, confusion, illness, violence, death intensified beyond all imagination, what then can there be to hope for? Can love be found in such surroundings? Have your peoples traveled this path to such an extent that love is unavailable? Can some elected official change the course, my friends?

Consider that what you seek is a portion of [the] one original Thought. That Thought is unity. That Thought of the one Creator has allowed each portion of Itself to travel through free will within the creation of the one original Thought. The journey takes many turns. Yet within each moment, love exists. Within each moment, the Creator resides in full at all times. That this is not recognized does not diminish its truth. Such difficulties provide the stimulus for the inner seeking as the outer world begins to fade, for it becomes apparent to the seeker that love may best be found within the heart of the being. Love then found there might be radiated, as a beacon shines light in the darkest portion of the night. Sorrow and suffering then motivate those feeling the suffering to seek more and more within, more and more in that portion of your illusion which love inhabits purely and always readily available.

May we answer you further, my sister?

K: Well, to summarize just a bit, when the distress of the world—and to use his expression—the mess that it's in really does then cause or bring about greater seeking. In other words, that the mess gets worse, we seek more to find this love, or we seek more as a result. That's what I'm asking.

I am Latwii. This is correct, my sister. To use a simple analogy, the students taking a class know there is that which you call the final exam. If the work is done as the course proceeds, the final exam presents but nominal difficulty. If on the other hand, the work is done imperfectly, perhaps ignored, the final exam becomes a challenge, yet each knows there is the exam and shall then make the greater effort to pass it. Each entity upon your planet within the depths of the being knows that the incarnations now enacted are what might be called the last opportunity of this master cycle to pass the exam upon your planet. Therefore each subconsciously seeks the greatest means of making available those lessons whose learning shall allow the passing. The lessons may be many. The catalyst may be great. Yet the opportunities also are infinite and each seeks the one Creator within the being as the catalyst grows more and more intense.

May we answer you further, my sister?

K: No, I guess not, except I guess then we should rejoice and weep at the same time. Is that about where we are?

I am Latwii. My sister, in truth there is only joy, for the Creator within each always rejoices at the experience each brings to each and to the Creator. Each is a treasure. Rejoice then in your being.

May we answer you further?

K: No, thank you very much.

I am Latwii. We thank you. Is there another query at this time?

S: Yes, Latwii. Along the same lines, can imagery aid our people and our planet in any way?

I am Latwii, and am aware of your query, my sister. For those with the desire to be of service in this manner, the sending of love and light, whether by prayer or imagery or ritual is most effective, for as you are in truth one being, as any portion of that being bids love and light to another portion, it bids it to itself, and as it is bid so it is felt, and so its work is done.

May we answer you further, my sister?

S: No, thank you.

I am Latwii. We thank you. Is there another query at this time?

Carla: There is a person that is not ill in a life-threatening sense, but has a very critical injury which will affect his future, and I asked Nona, and I called for Nona all through the—when I wasn't actually channeling I was asking for her to come, but there is no Nona around. Why?

I am Latwii, and am aware of your query, my sister. Again, may we borrow from the message of the brothers and sisters of Hatonn. It is most difficult, my sister to know how to serve another well. What may seem to one to be a great difficulty in need of removal may in truth be to the one suffering such difficulty the appropriate [means] of learning a certain lesson or of experiencing a certain event that will in turn lead to the learning that is desired. Upon the deeper levels of the being, the entity itself may consciously wish that every waking moment to be rid of the difficulty yet be unaware of its deeper significance which serves it far better than the removal would serve it. Therefore, the entities which serve as guardians to such an entity protect in a certain manner the learning for that entity, and this protection may include the healing of the distortion or the continuation of the distortion so that the wishes of the entity upon its deepest level of being might be respected.

May we answer you further, my sister?

Carla: So when Nona comes, it's because the person for whom help is desired also in free will would accept help. Is this correct? In other words, I was coming up against the Law of Free Will.

I am Latwii. This is correct, my sister. May we answer you further?

Carla: Is it beyond the bounds of free will to send light to the person?

I am Latwii. To send the love and the light is that which may always be done without the infringement upon free will, for each entity has the free will as to how or whether to use such love and light.

May we answer you further, my sister?

Carla: That's a very clear answer. Thank you.

I am Latwii. We thank you. Is there another query at this time?

R: Yes. The more exposure I get to the new age, the more it's turning into a kind of a zoo. Levels and dimensions and planets, channels, and I've lost any attempt to come up with a score card for sorting them all out, or trying to reconcile one point or another. At least they don't seem to be fighting each other like in centuries past, but there still seems to be room for a lot of tolerance of contradictions or limited viewpoints, no matter where they come from, what level who's revealing, even some of the so-called highest sources that only a decade or two ago we were hearing [from] about the hierarchy and stuff. Hardly a week passes in my life without some channeler, some source trying to correct some job that some other channel or source seems to have been inadequate on, and I'm just wondering how long we're going to have to put up with this. Are we ever going to find an age when this kind of work, when there's a lot of corroboration, and it's really getting together, or are we going to go through a lot more confusion yet, even in the higher levels?

I am Latwii, and am aware of your query, my brother. Within your illusion it is most important that each entity seek for the truth of its being within the heart of its being. To have information which reveals the truth of the being given from, shall we say, outside of the being's own seeking is what we of the Confederation of Planets in the Service of the Infinite Creator determine as an infringement of free will, for if entities of other dimensions were able to give information which was without doubt the truth then the people of your planet would not have the impetus to seek from within. If, for example, what you call the UFOs were to land, speak openly to your peoples so that all could see the great feats and miracles possible in performance by such entities, then undue weight would be given to their words and inner seeking upon the part of each of your peoples would suffer.

The confusion that exists upon your planet at this time is most important, for it then requires that each seeker attempt to sort through that confusion, to take that which has value within its seeking in meditation, and to enlarge there upon it using it as a signpost and to discard that information which has no value. In this way, the seeker's strength of being is exercised and the seeker grows spiritually. If the seeker did not use the discrimination which confusion necessitates, the seeking would be less effective. The truth exists within each entity no matter what source is information. No channeled information can match the truth which lies within each being. Therefore, when we speak to groups such as this one, we always advise each to take whatever we say as our offering of service, yet our opinion only, to take that which has meaning, to discard that which has none, for we are not infallible, and seek only to serve as what may be called the guide. We cannot give the truth to any. The truth is already within each and awaits the seeking.

May we answer you further, my brother?

R: No, thank you.

I am Latwii. We thank you. Is there another query at this time?

K: Yes, one brief question. I have in the past had some of my best friends believe in the literal interpretation of the Bible, and our friendship has naturally grown apart even though that's not the way I want it, but does taking the Bible literally prevent one from seeking and finding out who one really is?

I am Latwii, and am aware of your query, my sister. To use an analogy of a simplified nature, might we suggest that each means of seeking and each method utilizing it might be seen as a rung upon a ladder or a step upon a journey. No step prevents the next, yet each step is preceded by another, and shall eventually be followed by another.

May we answer you further, my sister?

K: No, thank you.

I am Latwii. We thank you. Is there another query at this time?

L: Yes, would you briefly discuss the subject of competition? I'm kind of puzzled by the apparent paradox. The concept of competing against one's other selves while at the same time doing it as a form of sharing with one's other selves. Could you speak briefly on that subject?

I am Latwii, and am aware of your query, my brother. As with each activity which is undertaken by the seeker, the motivation for the activity is most important. If one wishes to be of service with another by sharing a game which contains competitive elements of entity against entity, there are then many avenues of expression available. If it is desired in truth that the other self be defeated, then there is the expression of the orange-ray energy center which is, as we have mentioned, but a step upon the path. If others are joined with in the competition so that a unit confronts another unit and the groupings compete for victory, then the yellow ray of the group efforts has been expressed. If any entity within the gaming competition wishes to express its love for any other entity by simply joining in whatever activity is desired by the other entity, then the green-ray energy center is activated. If the experience can be used to inspire love or wisdom within another, then the blue-ray energy center has been utilized. The possibilities of any activity are endless. The desire of those undertaking such activities is most important in determining what expression is experienced.

May we answer you further, my brother?

L: No, thank you.

I am Latwii. We thank you. We find at this time there is enough energy within this instrument for one brief query before we leave this group. May we then ask if there is another query?

Questioner: Will it never stop getting worse before it gets better?

I am Latwii. My brother, it is the viewpoint which determines the degree of worse or better. To one a certain situation may be quite unbearable. To another, the same situation compared to its own may be bliss. Within each situation is love. Within each is the Creator. To find the love and the Creator is your honor and your privilege and is a pearl of great price.

May we answer you further?

Questioner: No, thank you.

I am Latwii. We are most honored to have been able to blend our vibrations with yours this evening, my brothers and sisters. We thank you for this service which is a treasure to us and a joy which sings throughout the creation. We remind each that a simple request for our presence in your meditations is all that is necessary for our joining you there at the throne of the infinite Creator. We leave you now, rejoicing in love and in light. We are known to you as those of Latwii. Adonai vasu borragus. ❧

Sunday Meditation
November 28, 1982

(Unknown channeling)

I am Hatonn, and I am now with this instrument. We greet you, my friends, in the love and in the light of the one infinite Creator. There's a very *(inaudible)* calm present tonight, an aura of peace is with you. Peace is stemmed from *(inaudible)* of the love and the light that is you and surrounds you. Peace instills your mind as you sit in meditation and open yourself to the love and light. A new world of peace, it comes [in new ways]. This gives many of the people of your planet … Many search and try to find physical signs *(inaudible)* but find it not, for they have not taken the time to go within and look and see that peace is not an external thing; it comes from within. As you look around, and as you become aware, you will see, feel the struggles *(inaudible)*. Learn from them. As you meditate tonight, *(inaudible)*.

I am Hatonn. We will now transfer this contact to another instrument.

(Unknown channeling)

I am Hatonn, and I greet you again, my brothers and sisters, in the love and the light of our infinite Creator. My friends, it is often hard to understand how one might attain that which we call peace, for in many of the situations that you experience it seems *(inaudible)*. Indeed, there are times in your lives when that which you know as peace seems even inappropriate for the situation within which one finds oneself. For, as you well know, there are many situations in which your expected behavior patterns do not include a display of peaceful acceptance as an option.

My friends, we understand that in your illusion there are times when such a display of calm, relaxed acceptance might be offensive to those other selves in your presence who have expectations of you. My friends, it is not the display that is significant but rather the inner awareness that one chooses to accept and make a part of oneself. It is not necessary, my friends, in feeling peace to make your acceptance of that state obvious to those around you. For consideration of one's other selves is important. Yet, my friends, do not let this requirement for reticence prevent you from accepting within your soul the calmness, the tranquility for which you strive.

By accepting this vibration, my friends, without displaying its manifestations, you may find yourself availed of the opportunity to be of service to your brothers and sisters, for you will be capable of extending that vibration to the participants in your small drama while not distracting or fighting them with a more obvious denotation by your facial expression or verbal expression. It is sufficient in the situation to consciously elect to accept peace within yourself, and, in accepting that vibration for yourself, the same vibration is made more available to those nearby you who are able, either consciously or subconsciously, to detect the comfort of that vibration. We will now transfer our contact to another instrument. I am Hatonn.

(Unknown channeling)

I am Hatonn. I am now with this instrument and greet you with the love and the light of the infinite Creator. If only you would see the peace which you can allow to fly and bloom and radiate. There could be a whole room of individuals, each radiating their own peace. But, if one person leaves his own space and tries to control another either by undue praise, by criticism, by judgment, by turning the other person from his designated path, peace is no longer in the room. Respect inner peace in each person. Give them understanding to allow them to *(inaudible)*. Love is allowing the other person to be themselves. *(Inaudible)* self in some people. You are [inhuman], but they are [inhuman], and, when you [improve] on their destiny, you're creating chaos. If you want to have peace, let other individuals find their way. If you are in it, *(inaudible)*. If you are not in it, they would be more *(inaudible)*, you will find peace, and they will find peace.

I am Hatonn, and I leave this instrument.

(Carla channeling)

I am Hatonn. I greet you once again in the love and the light of the infinite Creator and shall continue *(inaudible)*. When one speaks or thinks of peace in connection with what you call relationships, there is a temptation to think about that peace which is the absence of [strife]. This definition of peace, negative though it is, has sufficed for your peoples and what you call your nations for many generations. And yet, when we speak of peace, we do not speak of the absence of anything but the presence of something that is very much alive.

This instrument has had occasion within this past week to contemplate the structure of the ring, the circle that so often is given *(inaudible)* one to another as a symbol of a relationship. The symbol itself is that of endlessness or eternity *(inaudible)* having no end will continue *(inaudible)*. But, the two rings are not the same diameter. They are made for different hands, and they will not roll side-by-side at the same speed naturally.

No, this symbol is a symbol of our inner covenant, an inner relationship, something which all that is counter to the relationship is only symptomatic. *(Inaudible)* a living relationship between any of two entities, there are two eternal beings, separated and joined by the Creator. The relationship is the Creator's. Each of you within this circle *(inaudible)* in an environment called the creation. That is all that there is. You will not ever be *(inaudible)*. You will have change in perceptions from reincarnation to reincarnation and from density to density, but you will always be in and of the creation.

You are a completely integral part of all that there is. You are the completion of all that there is, and so is each other entity with whom you come in contact. Therefore, the ring, that great symbol which touches your peoples' hearts *(inaudible)* may be seen far more nearly to be a spiral. For those whom you contact in love reflect back to you love a hundredfold, and you learn, in disappointment and in joy, by all reflections as you move every onward in an endless relationship.

It may seem to be a relationship with *(inaudible)*, with a friend, with a stranger, or that strangest of all concepts, *(inaudible)*. But we say to you that it is a relationship with the Creator. It was written that the one known as Jesus said, "My peace I give unto you, not as the world gives do I give unto you. My peace is [not understood]." As you gaze about you, you will find a considerable amount of the absence of strife. You will find those who have accepted the cooperative silence of the *(inaudible)*. We ask you to look further; we ask you to begin with yourself; we ask you to encounter a storm so great and so powerful that it changes that personality that is capable of indifference. We ask you to encounter your own caring self, that first great ring of eternity, for only in full conscience—we correct this instrument—*(inaudible)* of your self can you become [aware] of the [course] of relationships with others. And when that storm has left you, you will find [effective] peace, a finely-tuned *(inaudible)*, a means of perception which includes both discrimination and sympathy.

Above all, my friends, be aware that that which joins each spiraling life path is the Creator. You may feel separated; you may feel that there is the possibility of union through finding special entities; you may dream of the drama of what this instrument would call star-crossed love *(inaudible)* that each relationship is both separated and connected by the Creator. You are all one, and all that you need will come to you. [For in] the spiral of your being is all that there is.

As always, we ask firstly that you *(inaudible)*, secondly, that you choose wisely those words of ours that you find helpful and discard the remainder, for we are your very fallible brothers and sisters and have little more knowledge than you. What we do have is a clearer understanding of love. We would at this time close to *(inaudible)*.

(Unknown channeling)

I am Hatonn. I am now with this instrument, and we will say one final word about peace. My friends, the word, peace, or the concept of peace may be compared to the anchor that holds the ship as the waves beat against it, or the concept of peace may be compared to the eye of the storm. In your illusion, there are plenty of storms, but the eye is always, the calm is always at the center of the storm. And, without the anchor, the ship would be utterly helpless as it tries to make the landing. And, my friends, this kind of peace can be shared, and this kind of peace is *(inaudible)* to *(inaudible)*. And it is well to remember, again, the words of Jesus, when he said, "My peace I give unto you." Therefore, it is worth seeking this kind of peace, not only for the individual who seeks it, but for every other individual.

Again, may we say it has been a joy to be with this group tonight, and we leave you now rejoicing in the love and the light of the infinite Creator. I am Hatonn.

(Unknown channeling)

I am Hatonn. I am now with this instrument. I greet you in the love and light [of the infinite Creator]. *(Inaudible)* peace is love. *(Inaudible)*, give love to someone. It is the fertilizer of the soul. Love requires nothing in return; it is a free gift; it does not control another person and does not have to be returned with interest. At any time you give this free love to another human being, you have reached the greatest form of peace. Not only is it peace for your soul, but you bring peace to other selves. If you can say *(inaudible)* that you gave free love to another self, you will find *(inaudible)*. It might be a good idea before you rest at night to think about how much free love you're getting. And, if you did not see another human being, did you think good thoughts about other people. This too will bring you together. Love, undemanding, is the highest form of peace. I am Hatonn, and I leave this instrument.

(Carla channeling)

I am Hatonn. I speak through this instrument [only]. Too often *(inaudible)* to this group, *(inaudible)*. We leave you in the love and the light of the infinite Creator. Adonai. Adonai vasu *(inaudible)*.

(Jim channeling)

I am Latwii, and I greet you, my friends, in the love and in the light of the one infinite Creator. We are most pleased to be able once again to speak to this group. We hope that we shall be able to provide answers to those queries which have meaning to you. We remind each present that our efforts *(inaudible)* of this nature are as fallible as our brothers and sisters of Hatonn, and we offer our words that perhaps another aspect of your concerns might be uncovered so that you yourselves might find the answers which you seek. May we at this time, therefore, ask if there is a query with which we might begin?

Questioner: Yes, Latwii. Why does your presence cause such an uplifting experience?

I am Latwii …

(Side one of tape ends.)

(Jim channeling)

I am Latwii, and am again with this instrument. To continue, you have experienced a contact which corresponds to the energy center which you know as the heart chakra. The vibration of love is the vibration of our brothers and sisters of Hatonn, and therefore, when we follow those of Hatonn, you may experience a resonating harmony between the two energy centers which you may then interpret in any number of ways, the term, uplifting, being such a description.

May we answer you further, my sister?

Questioner: No, I just wanted to let you know it's wonderful. Thank you.

I am Latwii. We are pleased that our presence is pleasing. May we ask if there is another question at this time?

Questioner: Yes, right along that line. I have one chair that I sit in for my meditation, the same place all the time, and, when I sit in that chair to dress, I feel nothing, but, when I sit in that chair to meditate, there's something happens. Would you comment on that?

I am Latwii, and am aware of your query, my sister. The chair used for meditation builds an energy which surrounds it. The vibration of this energy corresponds to your desire to seek the truth. When you use this chair for meditation, you open a door, shall we say, within your being that allows this energy to be tapped and for you to become aware of its presence. This is energy which you have built yourself which you yourself then call upon and experience.

When you use this chair for another purpose, you may consider the door to that energy closed. For then you seek it not. It is often helpful to reserve such locations or implements used in meditation for meditation alone in order that the energy which you store in that location might not be mixed with vibrations of a lesser nature.

May we answer you further, my sister?

Questioner: No, thank you. That helped. One other question. I have a friend who lives on the same floor of the condo where I do, and she is suicidal. This is about the third bout she's had of depression. She tells me that she does not want [any help], and yet I feel that she's reaching out to me, and I have to confess I have some mixed feelings about whether I should do anything, or … I'm not sure. Would you comment on that?

I am Latwii. My sister, to serve another is most difficult. For to serve most perfectly is to provide the service for which the other seeks without infringing upon that entity's free will. Often among your peoples entities do not know what they wish without great searching within. Many worries may be spoken as to this or that desire. Oftentimes, the desires conflict so that another hearing the speaking may find confusion and not know the heart of the other's desires. This confusion is of the mind. Seek ye then to be of service by knowing your heart. In your meditation, open your being to the desire to serve the one Creator however the opportunity may arise. In this state of openness, then ask within if you may serve another. Await the response. If the response is yes, ask how. Again, await the response. At the depths of your being, you are one with those whom you seek to serve. When you query in this manner, you touch that point of unity and might then find more clearly the path opened before you of service to the other.

May we answer further, my sister?

Questioner: No, thanks. That helped.

I am Latwii. Is there another query at this time?

Carla: *(Inaudible).*

I am Latwii, and am aware of your query, my sister. We find some difficulty in responding in full to this query, for the affliction of the throat region and the chest region of the one known as L is symbolic and has as source a catalyst which seeks efficient use. And the communication of one being is most necessary for entities upon your planet at this time. For to share the heart of being is to share love. At these gatherings, the focus is refined so that the manifestations which accompany this desire of each entity are also intensified for each, each in a unique manner.

May we be of further service, my sister?

Carla: Yes, first I grasp that there is much unsaid which [falls in the "out-of-bounds" realm]. Second, I believe I heard in there that there's a possibility that that was part but not all of the problem, that part of the problem if he's allergic to cats by any chance, should I be doing something like putting the cats in another room [that I'm not doing]?

I am Latwii and am aware of your query, my sister. We find no such difficulty with the one known as *(inaudible).* May we answer further, my sister?

Carla: No, thanks.

I am Latwii. We thank you, my sister, for your concern. Is there another query at this time?

Questioner: Hatonn, can you feel the peace within everyone in this room to the point where it overflows into love?

I am Latwii, and can even feel the love within the ones known as Hatonn. Although we are of one being, we have different sound vibrations. To answer your query, we may say that the love within all creation is available to each entity whose sense of seeking love has been opened wide by the desire to know love. Therefore, it is our joy to know the love within this group, upon this planet, and throughout the universe of this octave of beingness.

May we answer you further, my sister?

Questioner: No, thank you.

I am Latwii. We thank you, my sister. Is there another query at this time?

Questioner: I have one more question. We have some people leaving this group who are very much a part of this group. Is there any way on Sunday night that we can *(inaudible)* how much we feel for them to the area in which they will be?

I am Latwii, and am aware of your query, my sister. The ways in which this might be done are numerous. You could *(inaudible)* at a certain time, complete a ritual of your own description which would personify and send on its way the love which each feels for those who shall soon be departing this group. You may also at any time in your meditative state [dive deep] to the heart of your being which is the heart of their being as well and reach in love and know that there it is felt for them as well.

May we answer you further, my sister?

Questioner: Yes, could we set a time? I know there is a *(inaudible)* difference in time where they're going to be, but could we set a time for a few minutes so that they know that we're going to send them love at that particular time. Would that be helpful?

I am Latwii. This would be most helpful, indeed. May we answer you further?

Questioner: No, thank you. That was very helpful.

I am Latwii. We are pleased to be of service. Is there another query at this time?

(No further queries.)

I am Latwii. We find that we have exhausted the queries for the evening. The pleasure which we take in this endeavor is of great dimension. We thank each present for offering this service to us that we might more fully appreciate the endless love within each and within the one Creator. We find each opportunity to join this group a treasure, and we cherish each opportunity. Remember, my friends, a simple request for our presence is all that is necessary in your meditations, and we shall join you to aid in the deepening that each might find the peace that is the foundation of each being and the peace which binds all into one great being.

We are known to you as Latwii. We leave you now, my friends, rejoicing in love and light and in the great peace of the one glorious infinite Creator. Adonai vasu borragus. ☥

The Law of One, Book IV, Session 100
November 29, 1982

Ra: I am Ra. I greet you, my friends, in the love and in the light of the one infinite Creator. We communicate now.

Questioner: Could you first please give me the condition of the instrument?

Ra: I am Ra. It is as previously stated with the exception of the vital energy distortion which leans more towards strength/weakness than the last asking.

Questioner: Thank you. To continue with the tarot, I would like to make the additional observation with respect to Card Number Six that with the male's arms being crossed, if the female to his right pulls on his left hand it would turn his entire body and the same is true for the female on the left pulling on his right hand from the other side. This is my interpretation of what is meant by the tangle of the arms. The transformation, then, occurs by the pull which tends to turn the entity toward the left or the right-hand path. Would Ra comment on that observation?

Ra: I am Ra. We shall. The concept of the pull towards mental polarity may well be examined in the light of what the student has already accreted concerning the nature of the conscious, exemplified by the male, and the unconscious, exemplified by the female. Indeed, both the prostituted and the virginal deep mind invite and await the reaching.

In this image of Transformation of Mind, then, each of the females points the way it would go, but is not able to move, nor are the two female entities striving to do so. They are at rest. The conscious entity holds both and will turn itself one way or the other or, potentially, backwards and forwards, rocking first one way then the other and not achieving the transformation. In order for the Transformation of Mind to occur, one principle governing the use of the deep mind must be abandoned.

It is to be noted that the triangular shape formed by the shoulders and crossed elbows of consciousness is a shape to be associated with transformation. Indeed, you may see this shape echoed twice more in the image, each echo having its own riches to add to the impact of this complex of concepts.

Questioner: Thank you. We will probably return to this card in the next session with more observations after we consider Ra's comments. To make efficient use of our time at this time I will make some notes with respect to Card Seven.

First, the veil between the conscious and unconscious mind is removed. The veil, I assume, is the curtain at the top and is lifted. Even though this veil has been removed the perception of intelligent infinity is still distorted by the beliefs and means of seeking of the seeker. Would Ra comment on that?

Ra: I am Ra. As one observes the veil of the image of the Great Way of Mind it may be helpful to ideate using the framework of environment. The Great Way of Mind, Body, or Spirit is intended to limn the milieu within which the work of mind, body, or spirit shall be placed.

Thusly, the veil is shown both somewhat lifted and still present, since the work of mind and its transformation involves progressive lifting of the great veil betwixt the conscious and deep minds. The complete success of this attempt is not properly a portion of third-density work and, more especially, third-density mental processes.

Questioner: The fact that the veil is raised higher on the right-hand side indicates to me that the adept choosing the positive polarity would have greater success in penetrating the veil. Would Ra comment?

Ra: I am Ra. This is a true statement if it is realized that the questioner speaks of potential success. Indeed, your third-density experience is distorted or skewed so that the positive orientation has more aid than the so-called negative.

Questioner: It would also seem to me that, since Ra stated in the last session that the limit of the viewpoint is the source of all distortions[2], the very nature of the service-to-self distortions that create the left-hand path are a function of the veil. Therefore, they are dependent, you might say, to some degree on at least a partial continued veiling. Does this make any sense?

Ra: I am Ra. There is the thread of logic in what you suppose.

The polarities are both dependent upon a limited viewpoint. However, the negative polarity depends more heavily upon the illusory separation betwixt the self and all other mind/body/spirit complexes. The positive polarity attempts to see through the illusion to the Creator in each mind/body/spirit complex, but for the greater part is concerned with behaviors and thoughts directed towards other-selves in order to be of service. This attitude, in itself, is full of the stuff of your third-density illusion.

Questioner: The crown of three stars, we are guessing, would represent the balancing of the mind, body, and spirit. Is this in any way correct?

Ra: I am Ra. This device is astrological in origin and the interpretation given somewhat confusing. We deal, in this image, with the environment of mind. It is perhaps appropriate to release the starry crown from its stricture.

Questioner: The small black-or russet-and white entities have changed so that they now appear to be sphinxes which we are assuming means that the catalyst has been mastered. I am also assuming that they act as the power that moves the chariot depicted here so this mastery enables the mind in its transformation to become mobile unlike it was prior to this mastery, locked as it was within the illusion. Would Ra comment?

Ra: I am Ra. Firstly, we ask that the student consider the Great Way not as the culmination of a series of seven activities or functions but as a far more clearly delineated image of the environment within which the mind, body, or spirit shall function. Therefore, the culturally determined creatures called sphinxes do not indicate mastery over catalyst.

The second supposition, that of placing the creatures as the movers of the chariot of mind, has far more virtue. You may connote the concept of time to the image of the sphinx. The mental and mental/emotional complex ripens and moves and is transformed in time.

Questioner: There is the forty-five minute signal. Does Ra suggest a termination of this session, taking into consideration the instrument's condition?

Ra: I am Ra. Information pertinent to this query has been previously covered. The choice of termination time, as you call it, is solely that of the questioner until the point at which we perceive the instrument beginning to use its vital resources due to the absence of transferred or native physical energy. The instrument remains open, as always.

Questioner: In that case I will ask only one more question and that will have to do with the sword and the scepter. It seems that the sword would represent the power of the negative adept in controlling other-selves and the scepter would indicate the power of the positive adept operating in the unity of the mind, body, and spirit. However, they seem to be in the opposite hands than I would have guessed. Would Ra comment on these observations?

---

[2] Ra made this statement in response to a personal question which, along with its answer, was removed from the last session.

Ra: I am Ra. These symbols are astrological in origin. The shapes, therefore, may be released from their stricture.

We may note that there is an overriding spiritual environment and protection for the environment of the mind. We may further note that the negatively polarized adept will attempt to fashion that covenant for its own use whereas the positively polarized entity may hold forth that which is exemplified by the astrological sword; that is, light and truth.

Questioner: Would there be two more appropriate objects or symbols to have the entity in Card Seven holding other than the ones shown?

Ra: I am Ra. We leave this consideration to you, O student, and shall comment upon any observation which you may make.

Questioner: Is there anything that we can do to make the instrument more comfortable or to improve the contact?

Ra: I am Ra. All is well. The appurtenances are most conscientiously placed. We thank this diligent group. There is much greater distortion towards harmony at this asking and we join you in praise and thanksgiving. This is always the greatest boon to improvement of the contact, for it is the harmony of the group which supports this contact.

I am Ra. I leave you in the love and the light of the One. Go forth, therefore, rejoicing in the power and in the peace of the one infinite Creator. Adonai.

(RA, Session #101, December 21, 1982, and RA, Session #102, April 22, 1983, contain only personal material—pertaining to the illnesses of the instrument and the scribe which delayed the Ra contact during the winter—and were, for that reason, removed.)

L/L Research is a subsidiary of Rock Creek Research & Development Laboratories, Inc.

P.O. Box 5195
Louisville, KY 40255-0195

L/L Research

www.llresearch.org

Rock Creek is a non-profit corporation dedicated to discovering and sharing information which may aid in the spiritual evolution of humankind.

ABOUT THE CONTENTS OF THIS TRANSCRIPT: This telepathic channeling has been taken from transcriptions of the weekly study and meditation meetings of the Rock Creek Research & Development Laboratories and L/L Research. It is offered in the hope that it may be useful to you. As the Confederation entities always make a point of saying, please use your discrimination and judgment in assessing this material. If something rings true to you, fine. If something does not resonate, please leave it behind, for neither we nor those of the Confederation would wish to be a stumbling block for any.

© 2009 L/L Research

The Law of One, Book V, Session 100, Fragment 50
November 29, 1982

Jim: In the material from Session 100 note how the limit of the viewpoint changes the nature of the answer. Carla's tendency towards martyrdom, seen from the time/space or metaphysical point of view, is quite helpful in her own evolutionary process. But that same tendency, seen from the space/time or physical point of view, is seen as a tendency which may present difficulties for the services which one wishes to offer during the incarnation.

Carla: *I had a very hard time with the "swirling waters" from the start. Immersed in that high tub, just big enough to fold myself into, I had to tolerate levels up around my mouth in order for the water to beat on my upper back and neck, which were where the worst of the joints of my spine were. All the claustrophobia I had ever felt was squared by this exercise. It was as much an act of will and faith as a physical practice. I did find it very comforting. At the time, I was so small, wearing pre-teen sizes and weighing around 80-85, that I had to wear a weight to hold myself down on the floor of the specially made tub; otherwise I floated around. I would have no such trouble now, as change of life has rendered me a larger and more mature looking being. Jim says I used to be a little angel, and now I am a cherub. So I could probably endure this better now. But I find that Jim's massages are the best thing. Water is wonderful, but the healing power of touch cannot be overrated.*

Shortly after we acquired this therapy tub, I was struck with a sudden and dramatic frenzy of fear. I bolted out of the tub and found myself cowering on the back of one of the sofas, growling at Jim and Don. At the time I thought it was a psychic greeting, but later Ra confirmed that Don and I had just made a deleterious and complete unity/exchange of our mental and emotional natures, and I was experiencing for the first time the degree of alienation and real fear with which he saw this quarrelsome world. He really, really had trouble living on this earth, although one would never have known it from gazing at him. Don was always infinitely cool. But beneath that calm surface was a really difficult and challenging amount of imbalance. How he managed to live here as long as he did is perhaps beyond me to know.

Session 100, November 29, 1982

Questioner: The instrument asks if there is some problem with the swirling waters since she feels very dizzy after each application. Could Ra comment on that, please?

Ra: I am Ra. Yes.

Questioner: Would Ra please comment?

Ra: I am Ra. As has been previously noted, the instrument has the propensity for attempting to exceed its limits. If one considers the metaphysical or time/space aspect of an incarnation, this is a fortunate and efficient use of catalyst as the will is constantly being strengthened and, further, if the limitations are exceeded in the service of others the polarization is also most efficient.

However, we perceive the query to speak to the space/time portion of incarnational experience and in that framework would again ask the instrument to consider the value of martyrdom. The instrument may examine its range of reactions to this swirling waters. It will discover a correlation between it and other activity. When the so-called aerobic exercise is pursued no less than three of your hours, and preferably five of your hours, should pass betwixt it and the swirling waters. When the walking has been accomplished a period of no less than, we believe, forty of your minutes must needs transpire before the swirling waters and preferably twice that amount of your space/time.

It is true that some greeting has encouraged the dizziness felt by the instrument. However, its source is largely the determination of the instrument to remain immersed in swirling waters past the period of space/time it may abide therein without exceeding its physical limits. ☙

Sunday Meditation
December 5, 1982

(Carla channeling)

[I am Hatonn,] and we greet you in the love and in the light of the infinite Creator. Now [is] the time of forgetfulness *(inaudible)* [as you sit in this circle], you struggle against the pressures of the illusion. Now are the dark and dismal days, the *(inaudible)*, [cloud-filled hours]. Now is the time of each pilgrim resting quietly under the skeleton of a once-leafy tree, *(inaudible)* the dusty miles behind and pondering the bend in the road ahead and which turn should be taken when two roads converge. Now is the time when the weary pilgrim may learn the lesson *(inaudible)*, for upon its surface is nothing of comfort. It is a creature forged in fire and left to [weather] the millennia. As the weather moves, so moves the *(inaudible)*. It may be shaped by water *(inaudible)*, but it must be; it has no nimble feet, nor shall it ever, a *(inaudible)* unto itself [more of itself].

(Inaudible) with light and laughter, and yet, my friends, upon the rock [the] pilgrim may gaze to see moss and lichen growing green and vivid [evermore], sharing light and laughter and [growth] so that even the bare rock finds companionship, finds that which draws upon it, finds that which very slowly brings the great elements which [compose it] towards the *(inaudible)* to grow, to turn towards the light and to seek laughter that is the harvest of growth.

It is not within us, as those who offer our humble words to you, to speak easy words about difficult matters. Far more is it like us to speak in many different ways about that which is easy [to us], for when we speak of love, when we speak of light and when we speak of the original Thought, we speak of the most simple [union] of all that there is and the seeking of it in meditation. But there is a great desire in this group, as we perceive, to put forth into manifestation [a] not-so-hazy picture of spirituality, [not] some motto upon a wall, some words easily spoken and more easily forgotten, but rather a desire to learn to be a clear and lucid manifestation of the love and the light of the infinite Creator.

And, when we begin to speak of the manifestation of that inward grace which comes to those who seek, we then must speak as simply as possible, in parable and description, of the great complexity which you face as you face the illusion. It is our thanksgiving and our joy to greet each other within and beyond that illusion, yet we know also that you are the pilgrims of the rock and that there are many, many times, as you would say, when your [cane] shall fail you, when your legs grow weary with working, and when your mind can no longer hear the silence of that truth which you seek. Sit you down *(inaudible)* and know that there is no need for you to carry those difficulties, confusions and burdens which are yours by using your own resources. It is to be expected that you shall not be able to carry what load it is that you face, for it is only in working with the difficulties that seem to limit your time, your space, and your peace that you learn at last to turn and seek for the infinity of strength, love and light which lies within you.

If you are a rock, if you must nakedly face your burdens, how is it then that you are temporarily unaware of that which is alive, miraculously and impossibly alive: moss upon stone. Does the moss gain its food from the air itself? Does is feed upon the stone? Neither of these is true, my friend, and yet moss does grow.

You are never without comfort, although you may choose to avoid embracing that comfort. You may wish to push on with your cane and your weary legs to handle those relationships which are difficult, to do your duty, to ponder your *(inaudible)* and to forge your way ahead, saying sternly to yourself that you shall be equal to your task. But, my friends, the serenity of the great surrendering of that point of view is one of the great initiations into pilgrimage. As you face that which comes to you, rejoice when it comes to you, but, when it comes to you to be driven to rest upon your stone and gaze from *(inaudible)* difficulty, remember, inasmuch as you can, that your desire to seek the truth may best be manifested in your illusion by a surrendering, a giving up of the [hardness] of your nature. For, when there is that surrender, you become a thing able to manifest growth and light and laughter where there was only stone.

It is not for us to be bold and say to this assemblage that you must do this or do that, but, as we know that you seek, we can only recommend, as we always do, that meditation is the greatest tool which you possess for lifting that stoniness from your countenance and from your inner character. Do you make a fist? Relax your hand. Do you set your face against a wind? Bow to it. Do you attempt to speak? Listen. Do you want to serve? Be silent. For that consciousness which serves will serve through you, not from you, and you cannot be clear while you [yourself] are very, very sure that you know how to serve.

We would like to close through the instrument known as *(inaudible)*. If this instrument would find that acceptable, we shall now transfer this contact. I am Hatonn.

(Unknown channeling)

I am Hatonn. I am now with this instrument. I greet you in the love and the light of the Creator. I could not bring any difficult thoughts to this instrument, she is much too joyful. So, if you will bear with me, we will discuss *(inaudible)*. Do you glory in the fact that you can see, or are you uncomfortable because of the things you see? There are many unpleasant things *(inaudible)*, but, if you do not look *(inaudible)*, you do not glory in the fact that you can see, and every beautiful thing you see makes the world more beautiful. Do you glory in the fact that [you] can hear? Truly, there are harsh *(inaudible)*, but it is remarkable that you can hear them. Do you have any idea of what stillness *(inaudible)*? Even harsh sounds are better than [none]. Do you glory in the fact that you can [taste]? Maybe things are not seasoned, but you can taste them. Are you thankful that you can smell? Some things are unpleasant, but they're better than [nothing]. Do you make a point of smelling the fresh air, smelling the clean baby, smelling the [infinite] smells of the *(inaudible)*? Do you glory in this? Do you glory in the fact that you can feel? Your hands may be rough, they may be calloused, but you can feel. Do you glorify *(inaudible)* by seeing and feeling beautiful things? Do you glory in the fact that you have feelings and people to love? Do you spend your time loving, or do you do the reverse, do you spend it hating?

The choice is yours. You can make the world beautiful and loving, or you can not appreciate these things. The Mona Lisa was just a painting until someone said it was beautiful. And, every time another person says it is beautiful, it becomes more beautiful. Spend your time going around the world seeing beauty, feeling beauty, touching beauty, smelling beauty, loving. These very acts will change the world.

I apologize for the cheerfulness of this instrument, but she has gone through a dark tunnel and she has seen the light, and no other thoughts will come to her. I am Hatonn, and I leave this instrument.

(Carla channeling)

I am Latwii. I greet you in the love and the light of the one infinite Creator. It is a great pleasure to speak briefly through this instrument, since we normally cannot use this instrument due to its prohibition against using the question and answer format. We could, of course, give the answers and leave off the questions, but this might not serve the interests of the group as well. Or, we could pose the questions, and leave you to answer later. Again, that might not serve the group.

We do wish to express to you our great joy that we are incorporated with you in the great body of creation. Can any consolation be greater than the knowledge that such an infinity called love lies in the hearts of those friends along the way? We do not think so. We had [entered into] contact [with the one] known as A for the questions and answers; however, we were sadly rejected. We shall adapt once again in our most meek guise to contact this extremely helpful instrument. *(Inaudible)* sharing this instrument *(inaudible)*, there is no need to *(inaudible)* unless it is [freely] desired at this particular time. For all questions shall truly be answered. It is only a matter of time. Each of you knows your own questions, but, more than that, my friends, each of you knows your own answers. We merely facilitate the process from time to time and, in other cases, we fear, sadly confuse you.

What a joy it is to use this instrument. We would now leave it in love and light in hopes of transferring to the instrument known as A, if this instrument would be willing to accept the contact. I am Latwii.

(A channeling)

I am Latwii, and we are now with this instrument. We greet you all once again, and we come in hopes of answering your queries. So, without further ado, are there any questions?

Questioner: I have a question … Is [M] with us in spirit tonight?

I am Latwii, and am aware of your question. My dear, we would just like to say that, indeed, the one known as [M] is with you all always, and the thought is all that is needed to send your love to him also, for indeed his love can be felt here.

May we answer you further?

Questioner: No, thank you, Latwii.

I am Latwii. We thank you. Is there another question we might answer at this time?

Carla: We're practicing a piece called *Magnificat*, which is what Mary, mother of Christ, was supposed to have said when the angel gave her the bad news, or good news, whatever, about being pregnant, and I had pondered to myself without coming to a conclusion whether or not the historical Mary, mother of the historical person Jesus, was called upon when so many people concentrated upon words like this and also the *Ave Maria* in other prayers to that saint or whether those prayers were given over to a, shall we say, an angelic presence that took on the vibration of her function in life.

I am Latwii, and, my sister, we are aware of your query. To answer this we would have to say that, indeed, when the call is made, or when the prayers and the words you have mentioned are spoken, this, indeed, is heard by the original one you know as Mary. For this was the desire and therefore other *(inaudible)* you call angelic souls do not [—we correct this instrument.] The other souls have not been requested to answer the calling.

May we answer you further?

Carla: Yes. When I think about either Mary or Jesus or any of those figures so centrally in that great story, I think about the intensity or the degree of prayer that is offered up. And I wonder whether or not if these incarnated entities are those ones, those single entities to whom these prayers are offered whether or not they might be in some way parts of the kind of the social memory complex that *(inaudible)* are, for instance so that the entire social memory complex could have that vibration of Mary, for instance. This may run really close to the Law of Confusion, so I understand if you can't answer that.

I am Latwii, and, my sister, we would like to say that, in some respects, it might be difficult to comprehend the meaning of one soul listening to the calls and prayers, for it might seem overwhelming, but it is less overwhelming to think that one group which acts as one would have or would be less overwhelmed. Therefore, we shall allow you to decide if the one of Mary is the same or different than the one of a group and the possibilities of … if the one of Mary is a single or a single group.

May we answer you further?

Carla: No, I think I have it sorted out, thank you.

I am Latwii, and we thank you. Is there another question at this …

(Side one of tape ends.)

(A channeling)

… and the small task that Mary accomplished would seem so simple in some respects; yet, by some very, very difficult … yet, the outcome was one such that there was an inspiration, or there was an individual that could be pondered, and, during the glorification, there was and there still is this pondering which is the seeking.

My sister, may we answer you further on this *(inaudible)*?

Carla: No, thank you.

I am Latwii, and we thank you, once again. Is there another query that we may answer?

(No further queries.)

I am Latwii, and we shall now be leaving this group once again. It indeed has been a pleasure to be with you and to share our thoughts with you. We shall be always near, and a call is all that is needed. Adonai, my friends. W are known to you as Latwii. ☙

L/L Research

L/L Research is a subsidiary of Rock Creek Research & Development Laboratories, Inc.

P.O. Box 5195
Louisville, KY 40255-0195

www.llresearch.org

Rock Creek is a non-profit corporation dedicated to discovering and sharing information which may aid in the spiritual evolution of humankind.

ABOUT THE CONTENTS OF THIS TRANSCRIPT: This telepathic channeling has been taken from transcriptions of the weekly study and meditation meetings of the Rock Creek Research & Development Laboratories and L/L Research. It is offered in the hope that it may be useful to you. As the Confederation entities always make a point of saying, please use your discrimination and judgment in assessing this material. If something rings true to you, fine. If something does not resonate, please leave it behind, for neither we nor those of the Confederation would wish to be a stumbling block for any.

CAVEAT: This transcript is being published by L/L Research in a not yet final form. It has, however, been edited and any obvious errors have been corrected. When it is in a final form, this caveat will be removed.

© 2009 L/L Research

Saturday Meditation
December 11, 1982

(L1 channeling)

I am Hatonn, and I greet you, my brothers and sisters, in the love and the light of the infinite Creator. My friends, we are grateful for the opportunity to join with you in your meditation and we thank you for requesting our presence, for it is our desire to be of service, yet our service is contingent upon your request, for we have no wish to press upon you our vibration or services if they are not desired. My friends, we of Hatonn are that which is referred to as a social memory complex, which might be interpreted as a unified mind consisting of the total population of our world, directed toward the service of the Creator by following the path of serving others.

At this time brothers and sisters of the entity Laitos desire to pass among you and share their vibrations with those of you who request this service. If you desire that this service be extended to you we ask that you mentally request the presence and vibration of our brothers and sisters of Laitos, for as with ourselves, it is not their desire to infringe upon your free will.

At this time we shall pause that this opportunity might be made available. I am Hatonn.

(Pause)

(S1 channeling)

I am Laitos. I am now with this instrument. We would like, my brothers and sisters, to greet you in the love and light of the one infinite Creator. We are very pleased to be called among your group to share our conditioning vibration with you. This vibration, my friends, will help if you wish to deepen your meditation to possibly tune the group into a more of a oneness. All that is necessary to receive this conditioning love is to request it. Again, we wish to thank you for this opportunity to be of service to you. I am Laitos.

(L1 channeling)

I am Hatonn, and I am once again with this instrument. My friends, you exist within a world of illusion, a school in which there are many lessons to be learned, often requiring the individual entity many lifetimes in which to accomplish this task. This is as it should be, for it is the desire of the Creator that each of His children experience the totality, the fullness of creation. You currently exist within that which [is] described as the third density, and are for the most part occupying the middle ground between two selections of polarization, that of service to self and that of service to others.

Although we of the Confederation are dedicated toward the service to others and have followed that path, we would emphasize that both paths lead to the Creator, for in serving oneself, one also serves a facet of the totality, and therefore serves the Creator. This is in accordance with the will of the Creator, and is greatly misunderstood upon your planet. We do not wish to infringe upon your right to select your personal path or polarity, as it is commonly termed, for this is your right and yours alone. However, we would strongly encourage those of your planet to endeavor intensely in the direction of either polarity, for the refusal to select a path during this lifetime will result in another lifetime and another and another and yet another until the individual entity has selected his or her own path of service and dedicated themselves sufficiently towards its pursuit.

Because we of Hatonn have elected to follow the path of service to others, we offer our services to those of your planet, assistance in the forms which we are able to provide. We are unable, due to our desire to avoid infringing upon one's free will, to prove physically our existence to any or all comers, for, my friends, would not this bear heavily on your decision of which path to follow? For this same reason, my friends, we are quite reticent in the discussion of specific information due—correction—specific information concerning your planet's future due to the fact that such information, if proven true, would weigh heavily in your willingness to believe or disbelieve in our existence or assistance.

We of Hatonn are able to advise and extend our own vibration to any individual or group that should request this assistance. And, my friends, please believe that we are literally at your beck and call to accomplish service of this nature. Therefore, if at any time you should desire our presence, if at any time you wish to be made aware of our advice, to receive our comfort, you need only ask, my friends, but be aware that it is not ours to make decisions that are yours to make. And we would further caution that one distinction between those of service to others and those of service to themselves can be perceived in the willingness to make specific statements or judgments …

(Side one of tape ends.)

(L1 channeling)

I am Hatonn. I am again with this instrument. At this time, we shall relinquish our use of this instrument so that our brothers and sisters of Latwii might perform their specific service of answering those questions which you may desire to pose. In the love and the light of the infinite Creator we bid you farewell. We are known to you as Hatonn.

(L1 channeling)

I am Latwii, and I greet you, my brothers and sisters, in the love and the light of the infinite Creator, and we would desire to express to you at this time our great pleasure at being invited to join this group, for as we have watched the events leading to this assembly, we have enjoyed the companionship and love that has been shared among those assembled, and we're quite anxious to be able to throw in our two bits as well. At this time, are there any questions that we might attempt to answer?

S2: Yes, I'd like to leap right in. Welcome. We are glad to have you with us. Could you please speak about the phenomenon that occurs if an entity who is actually seeking to serve the self pretends to be serving others, or an entity who is actually serving others pretends to be serving itself.

I am Latwii, and we thank you for your generous welcome. In reference to your question let us first state that the members of the Confederation who are all in service to others will not attempt to portray themselves as in service to self at any time, for in doing so, they deprive the recipient of their contact, of the opportunity to select between the two polarities by in effect removing one of the polarities. As it is our desire that the opportunity to elect to serve others rather than oneself be made available, one can understand our reluctance to provide a situation in which there is but one selection available, that is, the service to self alone.

In reference to the portrayal of a service-to-others role by those entities who sincerely desire to serve themselves, we would state that in this action they first of all sincerely desire to be of service. When an individual such as yourselves exerts a force upon the creation or universe, in effect a metaphysical shout for greater knowledge or assistance, this desire for aid is always responded to, and will be responded to by those of both polarities to the best of their abilities. As we have stated before, the polarity of service to others will portray themselves as such, for in this manner, they can best be of service. However, those of service to self may, in perceiving the desire of the summoning entity as a desire leaning strongly toward service to others may attempt to dilute or diffuse the entity's intensity of summons or dedication by masquerading as an entity dedicated toward the service to others, yet supplying information or advice which is in opposition to that particular path.

An example, briefly, would be the suggestion implanted that the entity or other entities of the group contacted are in some [way] special, unique or different from their brothers or sisters. For, my friends, there are no elite; the people of your planet are one.

May we answer you further?

S2: Yes. Do you have any advice or suggestions for those of us who live in this confusion to understand our own leanings toward either polarity?

I am Latwii. My sister, we would first suggest that one be grateful for the confusion, for its value lies in the fact that your lack of surety enables you to make a choice rather than to follow such obvious signals that your choice would be meaningless. The tendency toward both polarities is quite natural, for both polarities exist within the Creator's universe within your planet, and you find yourself often torn between your simultaneous desire to be of service to others or to yourself. It is not our role to make the decision for you or to advise you to select one polarity over the other. However, we would suggest that those of you who strive to became more closely allied with your Creator would consider strongly the value of selecting a polarity and advancing it to the next stage of your education, for, my friends, to graduate you have to pass the test.

Is there another question?

A1: Yes, I have one, Latwii. I feel you already know that I felt like giggling. It felt like I met you and what kept going through my mind is how cute you felt. I never have felt this when reading and it is a neat feeling. I would like to ask you please, if you could give me—us—your understanding of what basic trust is in the third density.

I am Latwii. First of all, my sister, we have evaluated carefully this statement prior to its utterance, and may without affecting your polarity state that your recognition is quite accurate. And we welcome your vibration again as well, my sister. To undertake to define the subject of trust within your density is a difficult task, for the word trust is symbolic, and is often interpreted in various manners by your people. However, we would in an effort to respond to your question offer the following for consideration. Trust can be regarded as a bridge that gaps the crevasse separating one from one's other selves or brothers and sisters. The power lies within either to destroy the bridge, and, my sister, to rebuild upon an old foundation, as you are aware, is an act that, if we may borrow a phrase, that will try men's souls.

Trust, however, must not be regarded as a contract in which one exchanges a commodity for a like commodity, for the requirement for return does not exist within trust. One cannot control trust on the basis of trade for trade. It must be as a form of love, given freely and without desire for recompense. It is often quite trying to maintain the stability of that bridge in difficult situations or circumstances. But, my sister, is it not but a bridge between one and oneself? And if so, is it truly within the desire of your heart for any reason to destroy the bridge? To disrupt the love that ties you to your brothers and sisters? One might say, "I no longer trust this person for what he or she has done to me." Yet in doing so, my sister, they place a price upon their trust, and in so demeaning it, draw a clear delineation of the limited extent of their willingness to love, for trust as a form of love must be given unconditionally. One does not say, "I will trust you if you will trust me," and seriously expect to be able to trust. The absurdity is obviously apparent.

To trust another, my sister, is to say, "I will love you, and that love will not be discontinued, will not be disrupted, for I trust you to be as myself. I recognize that you are myself. For we are of the Creator whom we mirror."

May we answer you further?

A1: No, thank you, Latwii. Thank you for your loving answer.

S2: I'd like to explore that just a little further. When one trusts someone who has betrayed a trust before, there is a tendency to have some fear along with the new trust. Are you saying that trust without fear that you will be betrayed is understanding how you yourself don't mean to hurt others when you accidentally betray their trust?

I am Latwii. My sister, there is none who may hurt you but yourself. There is none who may cause you joy, who may cause you pain, envy, guilt, but yourself. If another's actions are regarded as betraying a trust, is it not a situation resulting from your desire to define the limits of another's behavior, and finding this did not occur, and if so, is it your right to make decisions that infringe upon the freedom of another?

My sister, one of the most difficult and misunderstood benefits of your density, of your particular planetary experience, is the presence and intensity of emotions, for they are tools and as such may be used or abused. There is but one person in your life who can bring love into your life and that is yourself. There is one person who may decide for you to love or not to love another. Is it therefore possible for another person to force you against your will to experience emotional hurt? Or is it more correct to say to oneself, "I expected this behavior of another person, and in failing to perceive the required behavior I elected to feel emotional pain as a response." My sister, to trust is to trust, not to exchange.

May we answer you further?

S2: No, thank you. You not only answered my question but my unspoken question as well.

A1: Latwii, may I continue something on that, please? Is it also true what you say about—is what you have just said about another entity not giving you love, but you accepting the love and I'm not sure—I'm not confused on that—is this also true, say for a newborn infant, of a child up to the age where their mental processes begin working?

I am Latwii. My sister, consider for a moment the existence of the young child. The veil of forgetting has been quite recently drawn across their consciousness, and in a state of mind similar to the amnesiac, who would upon waking discover not only a lack of awareness of identity or purpose in being in a specific location, the young child suddenly realizes the quite uncomfortable sensation of being within an unfamiliar body on an unfamiliar planet. It is quite difficult for the entity in this condition to either receive or express love in your density, for this involves the use of various tools to which the newborn entity is not accustomed. For example, the physical expressions of love on your planet, the kissing, the hug, the handshake, the wave, are all quite obviously gibberish to the newborn infant, and are tools of expression which must be learned. In like manner, the difficulty experienced by the infant with language is quite obvious.

However, the expression of love that is universal is that of extending one's proximity in a beneficial attitude to reach and overlap that of another's. When the parent holds or cuddles the young child, the vibration of the parent is perceived by the young child, and if the vibration is that of love, this love will be received and appreciated. The child, in return, will extend its own vibration, and as you are aware, this is also perceivable. The major difficulty, however, for the young child is the education through which the symbolic expressions are learned, and the many distortions that are acquired during this learning process hobble the young person's ability to extend love during the rest of their life.

May we answer you further?

S2: What about the neglected infant?

I am Latwii. My sister, if we might answer your question by posing a question in return. Consider your reaction to being placed in a hostile environment at a point in your life in which you are physically incapacitated and are simply abandoned. There is no hatred. There is simply nothing. Consider, if you will, a flowering plant which is very carefully uprooted from its pot by a loving gardener who very cautiously washes away the soil with great care not to damage the roots and then places this same flower in all of its beauty upon a mound of hot sand and leaves it to survive on its own. My sister, this is the effect that you describe. The plant, the incapacitated person, may survive. But the survival will result in many opportunities being lost, many nutrients not being provided will not be incorporated into the plant, nutrients that would enable the plant to grow tall, to bloom, to be what the gardener had prepared.

May we answer you further?

S2: I don't think so, thank you.

We thank you. Is there another question?

L2: I have a question. What is the—two questions. What are the visions? And what are they for?

I am Latwii. My sister, the visions are exactly that. The brain with which you accomplish the interpretation of the world which surrounds, attempts to modify or interpret sensory input into preestablished channels. When this same tool is used to sort and define information from previously unused or infrequently used sensory apparatus, the result is an attempt by this instrument, the brain, to assemble the sensory input into an understandable form. In your case, the vibrations which you experience are transformed into visual patterns which are more readily organized for perception. The purpose is that of your brain and not ours, for it is your instrument, your brain, which seeks to provide a logical format for that which it receives. This is not an uncommon occurrence and should not be regarded as an effort on our part to do more than simply extend to you our own vibration in a manner which you will find acceptable. If the vibratory intensity is uncomfortable or presenting difficulty, we ask only that you request that it be lessened or cease, and we will respond to your request.

Is there another question?

L2: That takes care of visions here. Are there—is there a purpose in seeing things to come?

I am Latwii. My sister, the universe, as you are aware, is not limited by that which you call time, for that which exists at this moment has always existed, will always exist. The individual who desires may attune themselves to the perception of that which one might describe as prerecorded information, in that time is a facet of your illusion, describes that which already exists which you call your future. The ability to perceive that which does occur is the attunement to these recordings, so to speak. The ability to perceive that which is likely to occur is the ability to attune oneself to another entity's evaluation of that which is most likely to occur, for at this point we simultaneously describe that which will occur, yet that which is only likely to occur on the basis of probability, for as you know, the freedom of choice always exists.

May we answer you further?

L2: Thank you. I sense a great deal of loving in the presence that's very nice. Thank you.

My sister, we of Latwii also sense a great deal of loving. We thank you. Is there another question?

D: Yes, I have a question concerning free will. There have been many discussions by many, many arguments by many different people concerning what free will is and how one goes about preserving it. Some of those arguments would suggest that the mere contact that you have now is an interference in our free will. There are other arguments that suggest just the opposite, that without information, without knowledge, without a full set of information, free will cannot be exercised. It appears as though you have struck a middle ground between those two arguments that is uncommon among those who seriously consider the two sides of the coin. Most of the time individuals, philosophers who deal with this subject, will either go on one side or go on the other, and typically do not find a middle ground. Usually the difference, the reason they go to one side or another, lies in their definition of free will. I was wondering if you could elaborate on your definition of free will.

I am Latwii. My brother, we would precede such an elaboration with an analogy. Consider if you will, the student who undertakes that which is involved—correction—that which is termed homework. The student has the choice of perhaps guessing at the answers. The student has the option of, through diligent work, arriving at the difficult answer by himself or herself without the influence of any outside support. The student also might seek the assistance, however limited, of a tutor. If we were to elect to characterize our own participation in your free will, we would describe ourselves as a loving friend, brother or sister who desires to see those of this planet be successful in attaining that for which they came, yet are cautious that we do not supply the answers, but rather provide information through which the individual's efforts might lead to the individual discovering the answer for themselves.

The subject of free will is generally referred to as the Law of Confusion. To define in your language would be quite difficult because the act of defining immediately requires …

(Side two of tape ends.)

(L1 channeling)

The act of defining requires additional clarification immediately, for the weakness of spoken language is its lack of function in communication. If we might offer a second analogy, consider the statement of a law such as, "Thou shall not steal." Superficially this is a clearly stated, tersely defined rule. Yet, my friends, it is obvious to all present that in certain situations the act of stealing is more than just appropriate. The individual who steals food to survive would be condemned under such a rule yet all here recognize the unfairness of that application. Let us therefore state that the Law of Confusion, as we call it, is written within your heart, and your inability to clearly and tersely define it by the use of word symbols does not bear upon your ability to understand it.

May we answer you further?

D: Yes. Given that you can't define free will, and apparently do not feel that the contact that you are making interferes with free will, I would ask if there are others among you that feel that what you are doing is an interference with free will. Certainly this question has been raised among our own societies and our relations with, as an example, with primitive cultures. To what extent do we, when we find these cultures, interfere with their activities, are we interfering with their free will, and the arguments run the full spectrum. The question, therefore is, is this also the case among yourselves?

I am Latwii. My brother, the defining of that which you term free will is accomplished not through word symbols, but through one's actions and intentions. The manipulation of any other self is a violation of that which you term free will. It is the desire of all members of the Confederation to avoid this type of activity. For this reason, specific members are selected for the purpose of contacting those such as yourselves, and we would also emphasize that as you speak you address not an individual, but rather the massed awareness of the population of what one might term a planet. The answers that you receive are those resulting from the deliberation of this communal awareness or social memory complex.

May we answer you further?

D: No, thank you.

We thank you, my brother. Is there another question?

J: I'm curious about the people who took A2's battery. A2 had said the robe of light prayer for her car in which she stated and asked that any persons coming in contact with the car be drawn to God and healed. So I'm thinking about the scenario. Is this in fact taking place?

I am Latwii. My sister, we would suggest the examination of the specific terminology used, for being of God, one can hardly be drawn closer. However, there are, as you are aware, there are two paths of polarity which simultaneously are directed toward identification with the Creator and the pursuit of either path will accomplish that which—correction—that to which you refer. May we answer you further?

J: No, thank you.

Is there another question?

L2: Latwii, I am delighted to hear your wisdom, and I recognize the wisdom that I so love in Emerson and Shakespeare and many others in literature. Surely you were among them. And perhaps, they now among you?

I am Latwii. My sister, we thank you for the compliment you offer. We would, however, suggest that although we are unable to define the specific location of the entities to whom you refer in relation to placement within the universe, we can assure that although not among our own social memory complex, their efforts have been enjoyed by those of our complex.

L2: Thank you.

We thank you as well as them, my sister. Is there another question?

J: In reading *The Prophet*, by Kahlil Gibran, the prophet speaks of himself as, "we who are wanderers." Is he speaking of himself as a wanderer in the sense you speak of in the Confederation of Planets? Is he a wanderer? Was he?

My sister, we sincerely regret our inability to answer your question, for to do so would be to define or—correction—to define a specific status for the poet if we were to respond in the affirmative, and to potentially detract from the efforts by the same entity should we respond to the negative. As you are familiar with our reluctance to inflict judgment or evaluation of one's self or one's other self, you may understand our reluctance to respond to your question.

May we answer you further?

J: No, thank you. I appreciate your respect for my free will. Thank you.

Is there another question?

L2: I have a question that's a poetic question that I thought you might like. Where is the best place to plant the tree for it to flourish?

I am Latwii. My sister, the tree will always flourish. Is there another question?

L2: Thank you.

S2: I have a question. As we live out our lives in this plane and in this lifetime, each entity has a set of attributes that seem to come along with the entity from birth. Attributes such as a cheery disposition or a certain level of intelligence, or a certain ability for endurance or stamina, that is, I'm thinking specifically of attributes that are not developed within this lifetime but seem to come intact from some previous somewhere or were chosen. And that is my question. Does an entity choose, pick and choose, the attributes of this lifetime or does the entity carry along from previous lifetimes levels of attainment that continue from lifetime to lifetime to lifetime, growing perhaps somewhat each lifetime?

I am Latwii. My sister, consider the individual to whom you refer as a plumber. The individual arrives at your home and proceeds to accomplish a specific task that is required for his own attainment as well as your own, and with his arrival he brings certain tools with which to assist him in the accomplishment of his efforts. The fact that be brings the tools does not imply success, but rather facility to success. One can understand the plumber's failure to bring such items as a calligraphy set or nuclear reactor, for these tools are not particularly well adapted for the accomplishment of his task. Yet, when the plumber completes his daily rounds and returns to his home, he does not bear with him his wrenches, his hammers, to the dinner table and to bed that night, for in completing his task, he sheds his tools. The potential for tools is infinite and they are not borne from lifetime to lifetime in the manner of a set of cosmic Samsonite.

May we answer you further, my sister?

S2: Yes. Are attributes such as wisdom and compassion for others or the capability for compassion for others, are these also in the same category as tools, or are they a central part of the entity itself?

I am Latwii. My sister, the compassion is the individual's willingness to extend love and empathy. This potential exists for all at any time and is more a facet of the Godness within us all than a learned attribute or skill. Wisdom in your illusion may generally be defined as one of two types: the type which is acquired through the manipulation of the specific tool referred to as the brain, which we regard as a rather limited form of wisdom, in the manner of card tricks; the true wisdom lies not in the talent or skill of any entity, but rather in that entity's willingness to open himself or herself to the awareness that pervades the universe. The presence of that knowledge which is real, which is lasting, is everywhere and is available only to those who choose to listen for it.

May we answer you further, my sister?

S2: No, thank you.

Is there another question?

A2: Yes. Latwii, I have a rather trivia question that kind of sparked from the last question and the last answer. From my understanding, there is the mind/body/spirit, okay, and somewhere along the way you have the brain. Is the brain part of the body or is it part of the mind?

I am Latwii. My sister, consider your hand. Is this physical composition part of your body or part of your spirit? Is it not true that the physical shell is but a tool, a physical form which is controlled by the essence of that which is you? We distinguish between the mind and the brain in that the mind is that which is borne with you from lifetime to lifetime, and is a portion of your total composition, while your brain is a physical device designed to perform and accomplish limited tasks. It is not rechargeable and requires no deposit.

May we answer you further?

(Chuckles from the group.)

A2: The first thing I thought of was someone stealing my battery and then stealing my mind. Well, okay, so, how about going into the aspect of the mind/spirit, like it kind of seems to me that the brain is the mind/body link?

I am Latwii. The brain performs two tasks. First it takes care of that which one might regard as the more menial or undemanding tasks concerned with existence, such as reminding the physical carriage to breathe and the heart to continue beating, thereby avoiding the necessity for reacquiring a different vehicle at an inopportune moment. The mind/body/spirit complex, being expressed in verbal symbols, is misleading in terminology, for each blends into the other while it is simultaneously discernible from the other. Briefly, the spirit might be referred to as the individualized awareness of the individual unit. This is the basic structure of the social memory complex. The mind is that portion of oneself which learns, records and serves as a link in both directions—to the cosmic awareness in one direction and to the awareness of the physical envelope through the brain in the other direction. However, it, unlike the brain, is not a simple tool, but a major descriptive term or many facets of existence which cannot be expressed in your words. We are aware that the interpretation of this answer is quite difficult, yet we would remind the entity posing the question that it was a trivial question.

May we answer you further?

A2: No, thank you.

We thank you, my sister. Is there another question?

P: I have a question, Latwii. How may one most effectively open oneself and listen for the wisdom and the guidance which you say pervades the universe?

I am Latwii. My brother, your world is created to distract you, for it is created by those who populate it. Its various characteristics are the result of eons of effort on the part of its occupants to avoid that which you describe. Therefore, my brother, the first step that we would suggest is the attempt to remove oneself as much as possible from sources of distraction. When this has been accomplished, the act of that which you call meditation is that which we recommend, highly, for meditation is the tool with which the major and final distracter may be brought under control, that being your own brain. The experience of most on your planet to shut off, so to speak, the brain so as to listen is that this is a quite difficult undertaking, for the brain has been raised in the manner of an unruly dog which clamors constantly for attention and affection and will respond to the act of being ignored by redoubling its efforts to bring itself once again to your attention.

Therefore, my brother, if we were to recommend an effort for those of either polarity to undertake in their desire to progress, we would recommend the setting aside of a specific period of the day at the same time daily for the disciplining of this unruly child through meditation, that in its silence one might listen to that which is available.

May we answer you further?

P: Yes. How does one—how may one develop that confidence or assurance that one is not simply conjuring or hearing chatter from one's own brain, but is in fact receiving wisdom and guidance from beyond oneself?

I am Latwii. My brother, there is no beyond oneself, for all are one. However, we would in response to your question remind you that there is a time in your life in which you have said to yourself, "I am in love. I love this person," and recognized that this was hardly idle chatter. My brother, the voice of your heart will not lie to you. If you desire, if you knock, the door will be opened to you, and that for which you ask, you will receive.

May we answer you further?

P: There is that within me which rejoices as you remind me of what I've heard before and I thank you.

We thank you, too, my brother, for that which you share is that which we all must share to be one in our awareness. There is no distinction between us except that which we ourselves construct, and we are grateful, my brothers and sisters, that at this moment so little distinction exists within this room.

Is there another question?

P: I have a question on another subject. Earlier this afternoon I was engaged in a conversation with a man with whom I've spoken before and whose wisdom I value. In the course of the conversation, as he was engaged in conversation with another, I began to experience a view of the man I had not seen before. I began to hear within myself what I cannot refer to except to call a voice that was saying, "I have seen you before. You have been my father before." What was happening?

I am Latwii. My brother, we regret that there is very little that we can offer in response to your question, for there is a lesson within this subject for you. For this reason, we elect to respond no further to your question.

Is there another question?

A1: Yes, Latwii. I am experiencing something right here not only with the unity of the group and with you that I am aware, when I think of it, it feels like I experienced before I even knew words. A sense of God within me, of unity, a sense of oneness always, and no matter how discordant, it is always as though it has always been as though God's not only had His arms tight around me, but I had mine tight around Him in that unity, and I've been aware that it has, that I have felt this with other people, sometimes even when I was angry and feeling great negativity, there was still that sense of, I guess, being in their shoes. I became aware, just a little bit ago, of thinking of the times when I've been tired, when I've been angry, and I wanted to get away from it all, and I'd always experienced this as my stiff-arming God—this is the way I worded it in my head—and I've had a new awareness that it was not God that I was stiff-arming, that it was me. May I just ask you a question after this discourse—I started to say statement, but I realize that it's gone on. Can you just answer me with a yes or no if you of the Confederation have always been with me as I feel you have?

I am Latwii. If it is permissible, we would extend our answer beyond yes or no. My sister, we have always been with you just as each in this room have always been with you. Just as the Creator whom we strive to serve, whom we strive toward oneness with, has always been with you. For in truth, my sister, there is no you, there is no he or she. There is simply a oneness that may be recognized or refused. We find it preferable to recognize that oneness.

May we answer you further?

A1: Latwii, it's been a mad scramble. It's been a mad scramble. I don't know if I can hold more. I thank you for everything. I thank you.

I am Latwii. My sister, quite often one forgets the pleasure and the love that awaits one and when finally reminded, the pleasure is overwhelming, both for the one who returns home and for those who wait at home.

Is there another question?

R: I have a question. How does one recognize and discover the God within and believe in that when the going gets tough?

I am Latwii. My sister, we might rephrase your question as, "How does one successfully accomplish the major task undertaken while in this density?" Our response, my sister, would be quite limited, yet it is our belief that it is more than sufficient. We would suggest that you choose to love one another, for in this is encompassed the entirety of your struggle during your sojourn on this planet.

We are aware that our answer seems overly simple for the complex problems to which you refer. But my sister, the answer is simple, and it is the solution. May we answer you further?

R: No, thank you.

Is there another question?

L2: Latwii, in the laboratory where I work we deal with radiation, and I wondered if I am to be particularly careful …

(Side three of tape ends.)

(L1 channeling)

I am Latwii. My sister, in the laboratory within which you are learning there are many who work with that which you term radiation. The likelihood is high that the laboratory may not survive the conclusion of your education, for there are many on your planet who have small regard for this laboratory we term the Earth. We would recommend that extreme care be undertaken both by yourself within your employment and by those of your planet who seek to conclude their education in its due course without interruption.

May we answer you further?

L2: Yes. Shall I leave and go elsewhere then, and not continue working at that lab?

My sister, that decision must be your own. We would offer in passing the observation that that which exists in your life does so as a result of your own desire for experience, and one must carefully select which experiences one draws to oneself.

May we answer you further?

L2: I strongly wish to find a course that is best for the ethereal plane and the Earth plane. Do you have any special directions? Therein is my question.

My sister, we cannot answer your question, for to do so would be to simply return your question to you. Is there another question?

L2: I think I'll follow that thinking. Thank you.

We thank you for the opportunity to be of service, my sister. Is there another question?

S2: Yes. I'm sorry that I had to leave but glad to return. Could you—this is actually a two-fold question—could you address the difference between altruism and service to others, and secondly, does service to others deny in any way, and I'm thinking here of our misunderstanding of self, does service to others deny service to others in any way?

I am Latwii. With your permission, we will address the latter portion of your question initially. We would like to offer again a small analogy in which the mother of a small child has spent a large period of time during a morning involved in various conflicts with various selves, the result of which left the mother of the child quite distraught and short-tempered. The same mother had previously promised to take the child on a recreational outing, yet found herself reluctant to do so because of her emotional state. The mother's strongest desire at the moment in question was to take some time for herself away from the child or any other individual that she might reestablish her emotional balance. We would place before you the question, "Does the mother serve the child in doing so?" The mother is obviously acting in a manner interpreted as serving herself, yet is not her action beneficial also to her offspring who, if taken upon the recreational outing at such a time as described, would likely experience what this instrument would refer to as getting the hell beat out of them?

The act of service superficially is an act of service to the self, yet may be undertaken so as to best serve another. The topic, altruism, is quite synonymous with service to others, yet is somewhat limited in that it is generally interpreted as a description of action performed or a superficial evaluation of action performed as opposed to the awareness of the intent. The large corporation which generously endows a museum or orphanage may be regarded as altruistic even though their intention was to reduce a substantial tax responsibility. The core of service, be it to another, is the intention with which the service was undertaken.

May we answer you further?

S2: You have addressed the phenomenon that serving oneself does not deny service to others. Could you more directly address the phenomenon of whether serving others involves serving yourself?

I am Latwii. The core of that which you seek to distinguish, my sister, again is intention, for although the results of service, be it to others or oneself, may benefit the other party, the intention is the diamond that refracts the light and, if we might humorously offer the suggestion, shows one's true colors.

May we answer you further?

S2: Yes. I hear you saying that the choice to serve oneself in no way restrains the individual from behaving exactly as if that individual had chosen to serve others?

My sister, the desire to serve, be it others or oneself is in no manner a restraint. There is no restraint upon service except the refusal to perform that service. The appearance of serving others while serving oneself occurs quite frequently. If we might offer an example, there are many entities which would quite happily attempt to identify themselves as our brothers and sisters of Hatonn so as to, in the guise of performing service to such as this group, serve themselves in misleading the same. It is not the appearance that is significant, my sister, but intention that brings the reward.

May we answer you further, my sister?

S2: I am aware that I am straying very deeply into specifics here. However, I would like to pursue this if the instrument is capable of it.

I am Latwii. We evaluate the instrument as being capable and willing.

S2: Okay, knowing full well that I am straying far into the area of great specificness, I personally have a strong leaning towards service of self because I feel that since that all others are myself, the only way I can give meaning to serving them is by serving myself. At the same time, it is very important to me to serve the other portions as myself as honestly as I wish to serve myself. It is not my intent to mislead others, as you are suggesting may be occurring with other groups who represent themselves as some of the group Hatonn, but at the same time, I am honestly aware that my intent is to serve myself, or at least, currently, and the service to others being primary only in the sense that they are also myself. Do you have any response to this statement?

I am Latwii. My sister, we are confident at this point that you are aware of our inability to respond to specifics. We would offer, however, the following commentary on the general subject of service, that being the desire to serve oneself has no connotation on a scale or range of good or evil, for the action is simply the action. So also, the action of serving one's other selves. If we were to assist one, however, in selecting one path or the other, we would offer the observation that to successfully graduate, one would need a service-to-others score, if you will, in excess of fifty percent or a service-to-self score in excess of ninety percent. This is because service to others is significantly more difficult to undertake with sincerity and without expectation of recompense in some form, while the service of oneself is quite easily and frequently accomplished. We therefore suggest that those who desire to leave this density should examine the percentage of service—correction—the percentage of their life spent in service to others or service to self against these scales so as to successfully accomplish their objective.

Is there another question?

S2: I hate to do this to you, but I want to pursue this just a little further. I don't hate to do this to you, I teeny-eeny-eeny bit regret, but I will do it anyway. It seems to be that in the final analysis after graduation from the highest level, so to speak, that a score of one hundred percent on service to self and a score of one hundred percent on service to others is necessary and at that point an entity has reached exactly the same place, whether using one path or the other. Is that accurate? And that they are the same?

I am Latwii. My sister, we regret our inability to answer your question, due not to reticence but lack of knowledge, having acquired neither a one hundred percent rating in either polarity. However, we are still kicking.

Is there another question?

S2: You've given me a lot to think about. Thank you for your help.

We thank you, my sister. Is there another question?

S2: Yes. Is there any way that we may be of service to you?

I am Latwii. My sister, we have been somewhat at a loss in our efforts to serve those of your planet, due to their overall lack of interest in the service which we desire to extend. My sister, in extending us your patience and attention you have been of service to us, and we thank you.

Is there another question?

J: I know we've gone on for a long time, so I'd like to phrase this briefly and ask for a brief response. I've been aware of a lot of sadness lately in people and a lot of depression, and I'm wondering if there's a correlation. Is there a correlation between depression and the beginning of consciousness or the awareness of one's place in the cosmic plan, as if people who are becoming aware of who they are experience depression in the confusion of this growing knowledge?

I am Latwii. We would precede our comments with the statement that what we offer is a generalized observation and not applicable to specific individuals that may occur to the questioner. The observation you have offered is to some extent correct in that one who elects to climb a ladder might be appalled both by the number of rungs and the angle of incline which faces them. We would also add that the time available to those of your planet to arrive at a conclusion to their studies is quite limited, and for that reason substantial amounts of catalyst are being introduced into your existence which accelerate the frequency of those events occurring which assist one in accomplishing alteration of oneself.

May we answer you further?

J: No, thank you.

Is there another question?

A1: May I ask a very brief question with a very brief answer? Are there entities born in which the veil of forgetting—I guess I'm feeling some resistance to my own asking the question. I can't think of the words I want to use. Are there individuals, are there entities born in which the veil of forgetting is not solid, in other words, it is penetrable by them, and therefore it is as though the catalyst comes from not only external but internal?

I am Latwii. The observation that you have offered is correct in that a number of—correction—in that among the number of tools brought into a specific incarnation by an individual entity, memories or partial memories or the later access to either may be a portion of the tool kit. For example, an entity who intended to accomplish the actions necessary to establish peaceful relationships with neighbors during a feudal existence, yet experienced a cessation of physical life prior to the accomplishment might in a new incarnation recall a strong drive toward that same objective and extend those efforts in an establishment such as that which you call the United Nations. The memories, as you describe them, may be quite detailed and accurate, or might be simply a vaguely defined drive or impulse to strive in a specific direction. The clarity is dependent upon the nature and use of the tool.

May we answer you further?

A1: No, thank you.

We thank you. Is there another question?

S2: I would like to compliment you on your growing facility in conveying what you want to say using our words and grammatical structure.

I am Latwii. We thank you, my sister, and must confess no small amount of self-esteem at our efforts to make heads or tails of some of your more difficult idioms. Is there another question?

J: Latwii, if the opportunity presented itself, would you like to participate and come to a group in Dayton?

I am Latwii. My sister, [whatever] the location—Dayton or any other—the request for our presence will always be answered. May we answer you further?

J: No, thank you.

S2: Yeah, I'd like to press that. At this point, the entity known to you as A2 is the only channel available to those of us who reside in Dayton. Is she sufficiently tuned to, as we say, go it on her own?

I am Latwii. My sister, we regard the instrument to whom you refer as being more than merely competent in the area of channeling our communications. The difficulty quite often lies not in the instrument, but in the group within which the instrument attempts to function, for the actual control of the signal, its intensity and clarity as delivered to the channel is maintained or disrupted by the direct efforts of the members of the group. For example, in a large group the effect of an individual falling asleep or daydreaming is noticeable, but not overwhelming upon our signal, for it is your group attunement that enables us to focus. The smaller in size the—correction—the smaller-sized group results in an emphasized accuracy or distortion, depending upon the efforts of the individuals involved.

The tendency of each individual participating to distort that which they believe themselves to be on the verge of hearing is also intensified in the group of smaller numbers, for each individual who has a strong bias toward the subject under discussion contributes to its reception inadvertently when they are in agreement and distorts the reception when a conflict between their own beliefs and that of the—correction—and that information being received from the channel. The purpose of our discussion at length of this subject is not to discourage the effort which you have in mind, but rather to explore the ramifications of what you consider undertaking.

Finally, we would suggest that a major part of your evaluation be the consultation with the instrument known to you as A2, for a reluctance or unwillingness to perform this service would result in a high amount of distortion.

May we answer you further?

S2: Thank you, you've been very helpful.

Thank you, my sister. Is there another question?

A2: Yes, Latwii. Have we tired the instrument?

I am Latwii. We would regard the instrument as capable of fielding a few more pop flies, but would advise transfer of contact to another instrument if any overtime innings are expected.

A2: Well, I was just asking for, if the instrument was tired, as to what would be best for the instrument once the meditation session was over, what would be in order or if he was just going to spring back to his normal, jubilant, punning self.

Our evaluation of the instrument's physical capacity is that the life force is quite strong, although a slight muscular stiffness is beginning to be evident, as well as a quite nearly filled bladder. May we answer you further on this subject?

A2: So I take it a back rub and a bathroom would be all he needs?

I am Latwii. The instrument has expressed to us a substantial amount of gratitude for either, but not necessarily in random succession.

A2: Thank you, Latwii.

Is there another question?

A1: Latwii, I don't have a question, I just want to say again what joy I am feeling. What joy I am feeling! And I thank you for being a part of it.

I am Latwii. My sister, we share your joy as you share ours.

Is there another question?

(Pause)

I am Latwii. As there are no more questions, we will relinquish our use of this instrument with our sincere gratitude for the patience and willingness to listen without prejudice to those present. In the love and the light of the infinite Creator, we bid you adieu. I am known to you as Latwii. ✡

Sunday Meditation (Louisville)
December 12, 1982

(Carla channeling)

[I am Hatonn.] I greet you, my friends, in the love and the light of our infinite Creator. "In Memoriam." "In the memory of." How many times have your hearts been touched by the memory of one whose courage, bravery or goodness was so outstanding that your attention is commended and your heart is drawn up in an emotion of love and admiration for the memory of someone, some brave act, some heroic deed. It is written that the one known as Jesus looked past his own physical death and offered to his disciples a proper memorial, for this teacher knew well that those seeds which he had planted during his incarnation, if they were good, would bloom long after that passage which confronted him when he offered bread and wine to his brothers.

As you look about your own memories you may find yourself realizing that due to the exigencies of your third-density illusion, the difficulties and problems of living, you are not able to crystallize and bring into an orderly form your appreciation for those whose lives you touch until they have departed from you. When they have gone, you evaluate an incarnation and say, "There is a great loss. There was a fine person."

Let us turn the eye of the seeker upon this common misconception of the ways of love. It is always helpful to the one who loves to offer that love, even if it is only to a memory. But far more lively does that love become when it is offered to one who lives in his or her imperfect way, within the framework of your observation. How difficult it is to love the living person in motion, in change, in transit. You are fortunate if you can achieve that love for any great percentage of your experience, for to many among your peoples experiencing that love within the illusion while faced with the waking face of another is utterly unknown and will not ever be experienced.

For you see, my friends, entities do not seem to be perfect. One may watch a tree flower and exclaim over the lovely blooms and cherish the fruit in its season and glory, in the radiance of the autumnal leaf, and stand in admiration of the sturdy skeleton the winter tree gives us, unafraid, unbowed and utterly without pretense. In reality, people are just as the tree. They flower, they bear fruit, they have their moments of dazzling radiance, they have their births, they have their deaths and they have those moments when they stand naked to the world, caught in an instant of being precisely who they are.

But how can each of us see each other as perfect without waiting for each other to become memories?

We must always move within when we seek the truth of love, for that which is love begins with each entity in the circle, each of Hatonn who speaks to you. The original Thought is each of you. So it is to yourself you must apply for wisdom upon the matter of how to love the ever-changing people about you. And the first person whom you encounter as you seek the heart of that truth is yourself. How many times today have you experienced yourself as perfect? How many times today have you experienced yourself as utterly without pretense and totally open to view? If your answer is in the negative, or is in the low numbers, do not feel that you are one of few who have missed noticing the perfection of their own beings. No, my friends, few there are indeed who are willing even to consider the possibility of themselves as sparks of that divine fire, that original Thought, that Logos, the Creator.

As you meditate, my friends, look for yourself. You are perfect. The place whereon you stand is holy ground. You cannot separate yourself from the sanctity of the truth which you seek. In all humility, may we suggest that you experience surrendering yourself to that divine Creator within you. The offshoots of this surrender are many, and you will find that you do not need to be touched only by memories, for life will begin to fill itself with the beauty, the joy, and the completion of the one Creator as it is shown to you in the ever-changing faces of all those who surround you and of yourself.

It was written in your holy works, "Lift up your heads, oh ye gates." Imagine that those great portals are the eyes of your inner being and lift up those everlasting doors within, that the King of Glory who waits may fill your being.

We ask that you hear our words, knowing that we are full of mistakes and errors and only wish to share with you those things which have inspired us as we go upon our own pilgrimage. To speak with you is an enormous aid for us and we thank you with all our hearts while reminding you to let no word of ours influence your thinking if it does not seem comfortable and appropriate to your seeking at this time.

We would like to exercise the other instruments and close through others. We will transfer now if the one known as M would accept our contact. I am Hatonn.

(M channeling)

I am Hatonn. I am now with this instrument. I greet you with the love and the light of the infinite Creator. Your attention at this time is focused on the birth of a child and how he changed the world. But do you realize the beauty of the birth of any child? All are similar and yet every one is different. You are aware of the effect of this miraculous child on the world, but do you realize that each child born changes the world? Some people change many people. Some people change things. But everyone has some effect. If you would see the miraculous things that a life can do and appreciate it, taking your hand, reaching over, picking up something is truly miraculous. If you are aware of all the things that had to go right for you to perform this single simple act, you would see the whole universe and consider it a miracle.

You see many miracles every day, but because they happen often you don't think on these miracles. You don't see the entire creation when you reach your hand to pick up something. Nothing is born that is not a miracle. A little animal, a plant, and the world will never be the same because that animal and that plant and that human are different than every other plant, animal and human. They are truly miracles. You would [find it] difficult to be depressed if you realized all the miracles that are around you. Even a cake baking in the oven if you had never seen a cake baked would be truly miraculous. People who have never seen snow falling are speechless when they see it. To them it is a miracle. Everything, my friends, is a miracle if you see the infinite Creator in all things.

As you go through your life and as you go through your everything else, do you see the Creator in everything? Do you realize that you personally truly are miraculous? How much it took for you to be born, to grow, and even to die and make place for another? All things are miraculous. And yet some people see none of them. The only miracle they see is the first time they see something. But if you see something for the thousandth time and still think of it as a miracle, you have a link with eternity. And if you can see a miracle for ten thousand times and still see it as a miracle, you are close to truth.

I am Hatonn. I leave this instrument.

(K channeling)

I am Hatonn. I am now with this instrument, and again I greet you with the love and the light of the infinite Creator. We will close with one final thought about creation. Everything that is manifest is just another aspect of the infinite Creator. Nothing is manifest without the power and the presence of the one infinite Creator. These concepts are difficult for those of you of the third density and yet if one ponders for a short time, the truth of it becomes evident.

It has been great pleasure and joy for us to be here with you in meditation and I now leave you in the love and the light of the infinite Creator. I am Hatonn.

(Jim channeling)

I am Latwii, and I greet you, my friends, in the love and in the light of the one infinite Creator. We are especially pleased to be able to greet this group this evening, for we have an honor and a duty—that is growing greater and greater as time passes—to this group; that is, our attempt to answer your queries in a way which may be of service to each of you. We thank each for requesting our presence. May we now begin with the first query?

Carla: I challenge you. [Speak] you in the name of Christ? Are you truly Latwii and do you come in the name of Christ?

I am Latwii. We do indeed come and greet you in the name of the Christ whom you know as Jesus. We speak more deliberately this evening as a result of the request of this instrument that it be more purely able to communicate our thoughts. Therefore, a portion of this process must include the increase of what your group knows as the conditioning vibration. This is not necessarily true for another instrument, but true for this instrument so that it might be reassured that it is operating more purely without the inclusion of its own thoughts in a conscious manner to the message which we share.

May we answer you further, my sister?

Carla: Not on that point. I'm satisfied. Thank you very much. You're right, it was the difference in the rate of delivery that concerned me. On the same bent, though, I would like to ask another question. Donnie told me that Friday there was very strong conditioning that came to several instruments in the group that they were not able to distinguish the signal and my suspicion, merely from experience with this particular contact, was that it may well have been Oxal, which is a fairly narrowband contact and, while very strong in the conditioning, is difficult to get clearly. I was wondering if you could confirm this and if it were indeed a pure contact, that is, purely positive?

I am Latwii, and am aware of your query, my sister. We find in this instance the opportunity being offered to these two entities to channel an entity which is less than purely positive. You are familiar with the greetings which the work of this group has produced from the entities which enjoy the darker portion of the one infinite Creator. It is not an easy task to purely channel entities which are beyond your ken. It is a task which requires great vigilance, for you may look upon each instrument as likened unto a crystal of your precious stones. Each instrument in the configuration of mind presents a structure or latticework which transmits that similar to light that is the thoughts of another of Confederation origin according to the tuning. Be there thoughts of separation—such as anger, frustration, jealousy—then there is the break in the regularity of the crystalline structure which causes a distortion in that structure and allows an opening for other entities to utilize.

This is not a great problem for this group at this time, for in general each is quite aware of the necessity for the proper tuning as a group. The utilization of the individual tuning has been less than desired in some cases. That is to say, as each potential instrument enters the meditative state after the tuning for the group has been accomplished, there is the further need to purify the desire of the entity to serve as an instrument in the positive sense of service to others. This may take any form, as we have mentioned. Then the challenging of any contact which is received is necessary in order that the final phase of tuning might be accomplished.

This instrument, for example, took longer than was its means or method usually in speaking our words, for it was in the process of accomplishing this challenge. Then if any within the group feels uncomfortable with the contact as it is transmitted, then let that entity challenge the contact as did the one known as Carla this evening.

May we answer you further, my sister?

Carla: No, thank you.

I am Latwii. We thank you. Is there another query at this time?

K: Yes. I really don't know how to ask this question, but I'm going to make a try. After my meditation this morning, the thoughts occurred to me that, well, these thoughts occurred to me, I guess, as a result of having had backache again because I did too much at Thanksgiving time and I've had to pay the heavy price again, but the thought occurred to me after the meditation that, one, that we can request a healer to help in the healing process in the body and the second thought was that we can visualize healing energies in the body that does the same thing for the body that the oil does for the moving parts of my automobile. And I've been able to get through the day without pain as a result of those thoughts that came to after my meditation.

Now my question is, did my thoughts relieve the pain, or … well, can you comment on that?

I am Latwii. My sister, we can comment by suggesting that whatever the means used by the entity seeking healing, the healing occurs as a result of the efforts of the one Creator which is at the heart of your being. There are various means by which this might be accomplished. Whatever the means, it is only necessary that the entity seeking healing at some portion within itself realize that it is whole and perfect and that healing has been accomplished. Some seek the aid of your orthodox healers who may be of assistance simply by giving their attention to the one seeking healing. Therefore, many symptoms disappear in the waiting room. Some seek the blessing of a sacred place or thought …

(Side one of tape ends.)

(Jim channeling)

I am Latwii. To continue … and allow this blessing to connect the conscious mind with the deep portion of mind that is one with the Creator and thereby allow the healing to occur. Whatever means is used, the more conscious the entity is of the reality of unity of self with all, the more effective the means of healing is.

May we answer you further, my sister?

K: Your comment about tuning in was interesting because the thought had also come two or three days previously that my radio is powerless until I plug it into the wall, connect it to the power. And as I had the pain, I thought, why can't I tune into power like that? So it seems like the thoughts all were sort of connected and had the same meaning. Now is this—and I hadn't really been asking for healing—if this is true for one's own self, then can this be extended to others, this kind of healing extended to others or given to others?

I am Latwii, and am aware of your query, my sister. The process of healing, as we have mentioned, is the process of realizing that the self at the heart of self is one with all, therefore, is whole, perfect and healed of any distortion. You inhabit an illusion that allows great distortions in many directions that you might experience the variety and depth of meaning of the one Creator. As you bring these distortions into balance you create the process of healing for yourself, for in that process of balancing polarities of distortion, you emphasize within your deep mind the unity that binds all of creation.

As this process of balancing continues within your own being, this growth then acts as a healing process to your own complex of mind, body and spirit. The process of growth and the process of healing, therefore, are one process. As you proceed upon this journey you became able to offer a service to others which has been likened unto shining a light in the darkness. The minds and hearts of others are touched, inspiration is delivered and received. You may further refine this process by offering to the physical vehicle of another the catalyst, shall we say, that allows that entity to complete the process of healing within itself in a certain distortion if that entity so requests it to the depths of its being. Then you function as what you may call a healer upon the levels of mind, body and spirit.

May we answer you further, my sister?

K: No, that makes a lot of sense and I understand my own thoughts better. But just let me make one little summary statement. Then the pain that I had served as a catalyst for my own growth and understanding. Is that right?

I am Latwii. This is correct, my sister, when you realize that the pain is one among many catalysts, though a quite efficient one.

May we answer you further?

K: I agree it's pretty efficient! It has been for me. No, thank you.

M: Well, I have the reverse situation, Latwii. I never have a pain. Am I missing something? Am I missing an opportunity to grow? Or is there some particular reason why I never have a pain? Almost everybody I know have got aches and pains and something's wrong with them. And I never take an aspirin and I never have any pain. Am I missing something?

I am Latwii, and am aware of your query, my sister. The concept of "missing something" is correct, although one might more fruitfully state the situation as the experiencing of that which is necessary for growth of mind, body and spirit. Some entities do not utilize all forms of catalyst, for their lessons do not require all forms of catalyst. Therefore, you may indeed be missing something, but the something may not be necessary for your growth as you have designed it.

May we answer you further, my sister?

M: No. I guess it doesn't matter, then, that I'm missing it. I do have another question, though. How could we have made the birth of Christ which was in a stable and was a very simple thing into a very expensive, complicated, disappointing, annoying holiday?

I am Latwii, and am aware of your query, my sister. The birth of the one known as Jesus has occurred within the previous two millennia of your planet's history. The entity accomplished its mission with great love and profound effect upon the minds and the spirits of the people of your planet. Through these many years the various perceptions of this entity's purpose have grown and flowered in many directions. Each perceives in a certain manner the value of the entity's life stream.

The people of your planet at this time, and especially of your country at this time, have the means of communication which allows many to experience the perceptions of a few concerning this event. Therefore, the perceptions of the few have been combined with the, shall we say, economic realities of your illusion so that there is an effect which may be likened unto looking at a picture buried in a pool of muddy water. Therefore, it is the case that each within your illusion to see most clearly the purpose of the life of the one known as Jesus of Nazareth must look within the heart, for there the illusion of profit and loss falls away so that the message of love radiates throughout the being.

May we answer you further, my sister?

M: I'm still not sure how all this bustle and shopping and shopping and losing their temper and buying gifts to exchange them, how that came into being in connection with a child born in a stable. It seems like we would have a simple meal and maybe sleep on straw pallets to give us some of the feeling of Christmas. Instead we just reversed Jesus' birth. And I can't figure out how we accomplished that.

I am Latwii. Perhaps we may use a simple analogy, well known to some within this group. Imagine a row of people, as you call them, each sitting upon a chair. Many are the numbers. A thought is spoken into the ear of one at the end of the row. This entity then leans to his right and speaks the thought to the next entity who in turn does the same and so forth down the line of entities until at the end there is the speaking of a thought which began at the far end and traveled the course being spoken and distorted at each speaking so that when it arrives at the other end it is very different than when it began.

Imagine also that the surroundings of these entities changes greatly as the thought is spoken towards the far end and there is great noise, confusion and distraction. The thought at its final destination appears greatly distorted from when it began. In this manner the simplicity of the message of love has been distorted by the years, the perceptions of mind, and the surrounding cultures in which the perception has been nurtured, however distorted.

May we answer you further?

M: No. I think you've explained it. Thank you.

We thank you, my sister. Is there another question at this time?

Carla: If the instrument is not too fatigued, I have a question. I have a friend who has experienced a good deal of swelling in the limbs, water weight, apparently, and it seems to have been in connection with some sort of an insect bite to which he was allergic, we're not sure. I was wondering if you could comment, and if you could, if you would comment on any of four points. The physical cause of this, the metaphysical cause or implications, what I can do for this entity, and what this entity can do for himself.

I am Latwii, and am aware of your query, my sister. We find that though this information may be spoken of in some general sense, that the relationship of this instrument to the entity to which you speak has a distorting factor which we cannot penetrate at this time, for there are extenuating circumstances, as you may call them, concerning the process of relaying our thoughts.

Carla: In that case I take it back.

I am Latwii. We appreciate your concern and thoughtfulness. Is there another question at this time?

K: Yes, I don't want this to be a long answer and wear out the instrument, so it can be answered briefly. When Jesus, according to the scripture, when Jesus left this planet, or he told the disciples that it was necessary for him to leave and that he could do a greater work by leaving because he was going to send the comforter, or as the holy spirit, is this a vibration that we can tune into sort of like tuning into the radio or TV?

I am Latwii, and am aware of your query, my sister. This is indeed as you have surmised. There is a characteristic vibration with each seeker which attracts to the seeker entities who serve that particular calling, so that when the seeker calls in meditation, in contemplation, in the conscious thinking process during the daily round of activities, then the seeker is answered by the entity or group of entities which serves as comforter to that seeker.

May we answer you further, my sister?

K: Then I assume that those who follow the teaching of Buddha, I'm assuming that Buddha left some kind of vibration that seekers of that faith can tune in to also. Is that true?

I am Latwii. This is correct, my sister, though we add that the comforter for those whose distortions correspond to the teachings of the one known as the Buddha may also correspond to entities seeking according to the teachings of the one known as Jesus or the teachings of the one known as Mohammed or according to the teachings of any teacher, for the vibration is the key, the means of its reflection is unimportant.

May we answer you further?

K: No, that's fine. Thank you very much.

I am Latwii. We thank you. Is there another query at this time?

M: I have a very short one. How important are dreams in helping a person fulfill their destiny?

I am Latwii. That state of being which you know of as the dream state is most efficient for those consciously seeking to accelerate the evolution of mind, body and spirit. The dream is the symbolic representation of the catalyst which the entity is attempting to process. The dream presents this symbolic picture in a means which is oftentimes more easily recognized than the entity may find catalyst to be in its daily round of activities. Therefore, one may see the dream as a reminder and a crystallization of that which is the entity's next opportunity for growth.

May we answer you further, my sister?

M: Just a little bit. If a person doesn't remember their dream, is that at all helpful? Does the dream in itself accomplish anything if it's not remembered?

I am Latwii, and am aware of your query, my sister. Many are the varieties of dreams. Some work their purpose when unrecalled by the entity experiencing them. These, in general, are of a healing nature, and it is not always the case that the entity shall remember dreams of this nature.

May we answer you further?

M: Just one short question. If a person tries to remember their dreams, is this good or bad?

I am Latwii. We refrain from using either term, for there is no judgment of this nature that is helpful, in our humble opinion. We would instead suggest that the attempt to remember and utilize the dream is an efficient means of processing catalyst and accelerating growth.

May we answer you further?

M: No, thank you, that answers it very well. I knew I shouldn't have said good or bad, after I said it.

I am Latwii. Is there another question at this time?

(Pause)

I am Latwii. We thank you, my friends, for allowing us to join you this evening. It has been an honor which we treasure. We remind each, as always, that a simple request for our presence shall bring us rejoicing to you at any time that you call. We shall leave this group now rejoicing in that love and that light of the one infinite Creator. I am Latwii. Adonai vasu borragus.

Sunday Meditation (Dayton)
December 12, 1982

(S1 channeling)

I am Hatonn, and am now with this instrument. My friends, we greet you in the love and the light of the one infinite Creator. We are greatly pleased to be called once again to be among you, to share with you in this time of love and peace and sharing upon your planet. In this season which you call Christmas there is more than ever a sense of oneness upon your planet. A sense of wishing to share with your brothers and sisters what in a small way you have found, the joy you have felt, helping people open their hearts and their minds to the love of the Creator, of wanting to share this love. My friends, this love is in truth all you are seeking on your paths, whatever path you may choose to walk, you will in the end be at the same place. There are hurdles. There may seem to be times of darkness, times in which it will be and seem to be very distressing, times that may seem so terribly hard in their lessons that you may seem to be lost for a while. But, my friends, at the end of the path there is the light. Along the path there is ever the light, my friends. All you must do is open your hearts, your minds, your souls to that light, ever striving onward [toward] the oneness of the Creator, striving to maintain that openness, to maintain that feeling of joy that so often accompanies the first awareness of the light. Ah, my friends, how beautiful is that awareness. And that awareness will grow, will become ever stronger, the light will grow much brighter, my friends. We have seen the striving of each of you, the lessons that have been undertaken, and can say that the light will became much brighter, and much joy is felt.

At this time we would transfer this contact to another instrument. I am Hatonn.

(S1 channeling)

I am Hatonn, and am again with this instrument. We were attempting to transfer this contact but the door was not opened to us so we will continue through this instrument. Our message will continue. It is a simple message, my friends, as all of our messages, and we would wish to stress again that we are a very fallible source of information for your peoples. We would not at any time, my friends, wish you to think we do not make mistakes, for we are in our way learning ever more also. The simple messages that we bring you through these instruments, we would want you to discern for yourselves what seems right for you, to discard the rest. We have stated many times in the past and will state this fact again. It is very important for us for you to know that if any information you receive from any source, to discern that information that may be of importance to you, to meditate, to contemplate that information and to receive any benefit you may from it.

Meditation, my friends, is extremely important. To go within yourselves, to see the beauty of the oneness of the creation within yourselves. For within you, my friends, is a part of the wholeness of the universe and within you is the love of the universe, the truth. Within you, my friends, is all you would ever wish to know. Through meditation you may tap into this source, the true source. For in you is the Creator. This is the truth we all seek on our paths, and this may seem very simplistic and yet very difficult.

My friends, the original Thought is quite simple itself. Love, becoming one, truth, these are the things we seek, these are the things, my brothers, my sisters, that you will find if you will but seek within yourselves. There is much peace within this room this evening, much joy at sharing a little of yourselves with your brothers and sisters. We delight in the vibrations we have felt within this room this evening. There is indeed much love among you.

We would take our leave at this time, leaving you surrounded in peace and love. Adonai, my friends. Adonai vasu borragus. I am Hatonn.

(A1 channeling)

I am Latwii, and greet you, my brothers and sisters, in the love and in the light of the one infinite Creator. We too are pleased to be called back among you, and have come to answer what questions we may. At this time are there any questions?

S2: Yes. Would you ask your brothers and sisters of Hatonn who they were attempting to channel through?

I am Latwii, and we are aware of your question, my sister. My sister, we will answer this because the instrument who declined does not mind answering this question for you, and those of Hatonn also do not feel it will go against free will. The instrument known as A1 was indeed approached but due to this instrument's slight fatigue and soreness of the throat chose to decline the opportunity to channel the thoughts of Hatonn.

May we answer you further?

S2: If the instrument, A1, is fatigued, will you let us know as soon as she may wish for you to transfer?

I am Latwii, and, my sister, we thank you for your concern and indeed we shall, my sister.

S2: Thank you.

We thank you, my sister, and the instrument asked us to add her gratitude also.

Is there another question at this time that we might answer?

L: Yes, Latwii. S1 mentioned to me earlier this week that at one point when she was channeling, she was under the impression that an entity whom she could not identify might have been trying to contact her. Can you shed any light on this?

I am Latwii. My brother, the group that the one known as S1 was in was putting out a calling to a group which is very commonly called upon at this time of your season, and this group was attempting to speak through this instrument, and we feel that for the instrument known as S1, we would prefer not to disclose the identity of the group, for they were, as you would say, on the tip of her tongue, and we feel that she herself might receive more enjoyment out of allowing—we correct this instrument—that she would be happier to solve this small riddle for herself, but we leave it to her discretion, for, indeed, frustration can do more harm sometimes than good in learning a lesson.

May we answer you further?

L: Yes, of what polarity was this group?

I am Latwii. My brother, an answer to this is that if a pure contact is one of a polarity of service to others, and at this point would like to remind those instruments of the need to challenge any new contact they might be receiving and trying to challenge, and we feel that great effort was made toward this.

May we answer you further?

L: Yes, one more question. Is the instrument growing fatigued?

I am Latwii, and this instrument is doing quite well, and is, as you know, relishing in the vibration. May we answer you further?

L: No, thank you.

I am Latwii. Is there another question at this time we might answer?

A2: Latwii, I'm happy to be with you again. I wish to know if the light entity at the end of my hospital bed in 1955 was one of my original teachers.

I am Latwii. And first of all, my sister, we would like to greet you once again. My sister, to answer your question, the light form which you saw could have been many possibilities, and we wish to expand upon this. One possibility is as you have said. It could have been a teacher. The form could have been yourself. The form could have been just a friend. There is the possibility of the guardian which is always watching. But, my sister, we feel indeed that this life form was a part of you; the loving part that is you and is always with you, but at that time was very clear and seen by you.

May we answer you further?

A2: Yes, please. Oh dear, I think you're going to tell me that I have a lesson to understand and I don't think that's really what I want to hear. I still—I partially understand your answer, but I still hear a small voice in me wanting to ask, needing to ask, of what density is this life-form?

I am Latwii, and my sister, this indeed is a difficult question to answer, for there is that of free will, but there is the overall answer to all questions that the image was a part of you, therefore had no true density, for being one, there was no separation, and indeed there is the lesson to be learned, and if we may say in generalities, the points to be considered are what was felt, what was the experience, what do you wish to continue to learn, and there are endless other small queries which could be thought upon. But, my sister, we hope you respect that we wish to decline in giving a specific answer to this query of yours, but if possible wish to expand more if you desire.

A2: You're offering me a choice. Yes, I would like for you to expand, please.

I am Latwii. My sister, we would first ask if there is a certain point which we might expand upon or we might be here for some time.

A2: Yes. The incident, as I'm sure you well know, was one where I was close to death. I was not afraid other than I could not contact help because the buzzer on my hospital bed was broken, and when help finally came, I was aware as the help came that I was in the position of slipping from this life, and I recall clearly seeing the light form, the hand extended, and I recall absolute peace. Later on when I became well again I was aware of recalling this, at first thinking that I had been called to come to the other side, to death, to die, which I wasn't afraid of, but it didn't make sense, and then I realized finally that the outstretched hand really was a choice, but it was more telling me that I was not alone. It's difficult for me still to comprehend that I was there reaching out to myself saying that I wasn't alone.

I am Latwii, and, my sister, indeed it is difficult to consider and to grasp and to think of, but we wish to pose a question to you. Did or do you remember recognizing the light form, or was the light form one of love and unity and light? Or was it both of these? You felt great peace and you remembered the incident and we feel you are aware of the possibilities of the meaning and therefore we ask one more time in a gentle manner if you have still a definite question to ask or if you have many thoughts that you are wanting to meditate on?

A2: I appreciate your answer. I feel some clarity. I feel comfortable with it. Thank you. Thank you very much.

I am Latwii. My sister, we thank you, and hope that if any confusion is caused that you do not hesitate to ask us once again or do not hesitate to seek us out in your meditation.

A2: Thank you, Latwii.

I am Latwii. Is there another question at this time that we might answer?

J: Latwii, an acquaintance of ours died just a week ago. What is it like for a person at the point where they die? What is the experience that happens to them at that point and then onward?

I am Latwii, and we are aware of your question. This is a difficult question to answer because of the free will, and we hesitate in giving concrete answers that diminish your chances and opportunities to make the decisions yourself. But to speak generally, when an individual dies the physical body is left and there is this change from going out of the physical body and into a state of either preparing to enter another physical body of need or to continue on. My sister, we apologize for the small answer to this large question, for there is—we correct this instrument—for there are many experiences that occur when one, as you say, dies. But we ask if more information is wanted, then we would transfer this contact, for the instrument is now slowly fatiguing and is having some difficulty in fully grasping the concepts.

So, may we answer you further?

J: No, thank you, Latwii.

I am Latwii. If there are other queries to be asked, we would like a nod from the group and we shall then transfer to another.

L: Are there any more questions?

(Pause)

L: Looks like a clean slate, Latwii.

I am Latwii. Thank you. We shall be leaving you now, in so many words, but shall be around listening for our name and shall come when asked. We leave you in great joy and peace. Adonai, my friends. We are known to you as Latwii.

Tuesday Meditation (Dayton)
December 21, 1982

(A1 channeling)

I am Hatonn, and I greet you, my friends, in the love and the light of the one infinite Creator. We are so pleased to be called back to your group again, to share in your joy and to listen to your joyous sounds. It is so peaceful here. There is contentment and ease about you. My friends, remember this peace you feel. The ease as it goes through your body. The calmness that is felt. The tension of your daily lives slowly slips away as you seek silence, seek the quietness. The quietness when the thoughts of your illusion have faded. When times are busy, as you make plans and gather friends around, take the time to find the peace in the solitude of being yourself, for when you are at peace with yourself you are able to be at peace with others.

This sounds very simple, and indeed is quite simple, but it takes a small effort. It takes the wanting to have peace. Otherwise, confusion that surrounds you will slowly slip in and will mingle with the peace. At times, my friends, when it is difficult to slow the mind down, stop and think of something simple which has meaning, such as a flower or a sunset or the smile of a child, and focus upon this thought and allow the other thoughts to slowly slide away, and then with this thought, slowly allow it also to slide away. And at this point you shall find great silence, and it shall be calm and peaceful and you shall be one with yourself. Do this, my friends, when you are anxious or worried for there is no need to have fear from the illusion, for you have yourself whom you love. You will always have yourself to be there, to be a friend to give you love. Just take time to listen to your silence and feel the joy of your peace.

My friends, this is just a small reminder of something you know deep inside. We hope they are a few words you may ponder on and [have] to remember during those times when the rushing seems so great and confusion seems to be so engulfing. And please remember that we are always there also, and in your time of meditation we shall hear your calling. We are always listening to those who ask for help. We shall leave your group now, as we found it, with a great love and a great peace that surrounds you. Adonai, my friends. We are known to you as Hatonn.

(A1 channeling)

I am Latwii, and we also greet you in the love and in the light of the one infinite Creator. We so enjoyed listening to your songs. They are so soft and soothing, and we too feel the peace within the group. And without further praise we shall ask if there are any questions which you have to ask?

S: I have a question. It's a little complicated, so bear with me please. I have a friend who seeks very much to serve others. However, her service is rather difficult to bear. Can you speak to that phenomenon both from the point of view of the entity who forces service on another and to the entity who is the recipient?

I am Latwii. Indeed, we are aware of your question. First of all we shall address the individual who is giving the service, for this is the more difficult of the two to understand. In dealing with certain others it is most difficult to know when it is the proper time to serve someone or to help and to assist. Many, however, have no regard for a proper time, and seem to just serve and to serve and to serve, for they truly believe this is what is wanted. We realize that many times individuals try to explain to the server that there might be more appropriate means of serving, but the server feels that deep down they know the most appropriate way, and therefore continue on with their desires. This phenomenon is one of where the individual in the past might have received service from no one, and therefore to retaliate will seek to serve everyone, or possibly the individual desires attention and sees this as a means of receiving a great deal of attention. For one who is always busy is always moving and not idle. And the moving object such as a ball is more noticeable than the floor it rolls on.

We know that that small comparison is indeed hardly comparative to the situation, but in a small way represents how one object can be more noticeable than another. Also, an individual who is desiring to just serve with no regard to the self may not be at ease with the self, and therefore is covering this up with a great deal of service to others, and will not listen to the requests of others because this might cause reflection upon the self.

This brings us to the point of dealing with such an individual, for those who work with them try many different facets of relating to the person and all seem fruitless. So, my friends, there is the point of learning patience, and seeing beyond the service to the root of the situation, and then dealing with this point. This reflects back to those few points we mentioned earlier as to why one would wish to serve so greatly. So in seeking to solve the original or to deal with the original point of interest, indeed there is a great deal of patience needed because at times it is difficult to be served in a manner which is not desirable. But then again, one might best serve another by being served in a way which is not comfortable, but it is important to remember not to neglect the self, for all things should be in balance. My friend, we wish to leave the analyzing of the different points to you and those in the group, for we feel the most can be learned from this.

May we answer you further?

S: No, thank you.

I am Latwii. We thank you. Is there another question we may answer at this time?

A2: Yes, Latwii. I'm glad to be with you again. Along this same line, I don't understand the phenomenon of being of service to others and being unaware of doing so. I don't know if I'm making myself clear. Do you understand what I'm saying?

I am Latwii, and, my sister, we feel we have the gist of your question. When being of service to others, in many ways it can be very subtle, and when being in service to others in a way which is not desirable, is not always seen by the individual. For when there is great intent of wanting to help, to aid another friend or individual, this intent sometimes overshadows the actual good will which is intended and may impose a barrier so that the individual serving does not realize the service is not needed. Many will never know that their services are desired or not. One of the important points to remember is to listen to yourself and other individuals when trying to be of service, for if this is accomplished, there is no need to worry about being a burden to another.

May we answer you further?

A2: No, I don't believe so, thank you.

I am Latwii. We thank you. Is there another question at this time we may answer?

J: I have difficulty understanding how it can be retaliatory in nature for a person who has experienced a lack of service from others to want to be of service to others. It seems to me that it would rise out of a raised sensitivity to the need of service, and that seems to me to be a more positive response than a retaliatory response. Could you clarify that for me, please?

I am Latwii, and we are aware of your query. My sister, at times people will retaliate by doing good deeds. This may sound a little contradictory, but to the individual it will serve their purpose. It is like saying, "Well, I'll show you; I'll be good."

May we answer you further?

J: So, then, as a person progresses in the evolution of their understanding, it seems that they would be able to give up serving in a sort of retaliatory way and be able to serve by not serving sometimes. Do I have the general idea?

My sister, indeed, all things are possible, so we may add that what you have said is possible and an option. There is also a possibility that an individual who is desiring to serve completely and wholeheartedly might forget the reason why he is doing this, but will then become so engrossed with the idea, [that he] will continue more and more to have this as the only idea and, [if one were to] use a term or label on this, it would be an obsession.

May we answer you further?

J: Just a little bit. Last week we heard that it is the intention behind the service that is the crux of the matter. Then, are you saying that the intention behind obsessive serving is not positive?

I am Latwii. My sister, there is some confusion in using the words of positive and negative. When seeking the center of the reason of service, there are many points to be considered. One with an obsession might be trying to serve the self by serving others or may wholeheartedly want to just serve other individuals without any bias to anyone except the self, and feels that the self should be left out of those being served. This way of serving with a bias to not serving the self is hardly positive or negative, but just rather confusing, and leaves the individual slightly unbalanced, for there will seem to be something missing, and therefore the individual will try to serve more but will forget to serve the self and feel that that is not necessary, and then the confusion will be increased so they will try to serve even more. Therefore there is an imbalance which causes the person to have the confusion continue until the realization is made to serve the self in the same manner.

May we answer you further?

J: I'm wondering if one of the confusing aspects of that situation you described would be where a person is forgetting the principle of free will and imposing service or imposing lack of concern for the self. Does free will have anything to do with that whole situation?

I am Latwii. And indeed, my sister, free will does. One problem which will arise is the individual wishing to serve feels something is missing and then will disregard other individuals so as to serve them more. They will disregard their free will of choice and practically demand the individual to receive their serving. This causes great problems, for the individual being served does not wish the service, and this causes an ill feeling toward the server, whereas the server does not realize the problem that is being caused by their service, and does not understand why there is an ill feeling towards him. Also it leads back into the vicious circle of wanting to serve as many as possible, and this sometimes overshadows the remembrance of free will.

May we answer you further?

J: That was very helpful. Thank you, Latwii.

I am Latwii. We thank you. Is there another question at this time?

A2: Yes, Latwii. Could you say something about walking the line between giving energy? When to give energy to people who drain your energy and when not to? When is it too much of a drain, and not? And how you can tell.

I am Latwii. And, my sister, first of all, there is always listening to yourself, because if you just go ahead and blunder through and just try to give energy, it is defeating the purpose, for you may not help them at all, and you may use up all your energy trying. Therefore, when giving energy to another, there is the mental thought of sending it out, and there will be either an open door or a closed door. If you find you slam up against a wall, then it is not an appropriate time. There is also just having the open conversation with any individual or any entity which you wish to give energy in asking them if they desire being served in this manner, then if there is the go-ahead, use your own judgment as to how much is helpful to all parties considered. For it is important to remember that if you deplete your own energies then you are of no service at all.

May we answer you further?

A2: No, that was very nice, thank you.

I am Latwii, and we thank you. Are there any other questions that we may answer?

A2: May I go back just a little bit to the serving of others and being served by others. May I ask for a yes or a no if this is correct? Are you saying in essence that there is conscious recognition of being served, and a conscious recognition of serving at the time that either receiving service or giving service is valid and useful?

I am Latwii, and, my sister, we regretfully have to say yes, but we regretfully have to say no. Take your pick. If we may expand on this, we would have to say that sometimes there are those who are aware they are serving, and are very conscious indeed of free will, but they realize that other individuals are not conscious of their serving. Therefore, there is the fine line of knowing when to serve and when not to. But if there are individuals who communicate well, there is a very conscious awareness between both the server and the servee. We pardon that word. Then the awareness is very beneficial in dealing with free will. It is difficult for the one being served to be conscious of it and the one serving to not be conscious of it, but this also can be the case where one is just very natural at serving without infringing upon free will because of the sensitivity of the server to those the individual is wishing to serve.

May we answer you further?

A2: No, thank you.

I am Latwii, and we thank you for your patience in listening. Is there another question?

S: Yes, Latwii. Could you speak on the topic, "tradition"?

I am Latwii. My sister, this is a very, very broad subject, for tradition is something that individuals love to cling to and feel great security in it. Traditions are symbolic events or objects used in events which are handed down from generation to generation. Some feel that it is very important to continue exactly with the tradition, whereas some desire to add small changes to their tradition to hand down to the next generation, whereas some would rather forget the whole thing. This is where the subject gets very broad and we wish to speak generally on each.

When an individual desires to keep to the letter of a tradition they are desiring to not change and to keep in the security of the past. Therefore there is no pressure on them to worry about what the next generation has to work with, for it will not be their fault. The tradition has been set. It is very simple and very easy.

The next group wishes to make a small change. It can be either deleting a part or adding a part. Deleting could signify something which is uncomfortable which does not seem to fit with the basic general thought of the present day or adding could be wanting to give of the self to make it better or to add a little spice, so to say.

The last group is one of those desiring to alleviate the whole situation, for they see no use of the tradition but in some instances there might be great benefits from having traditions, for many traditions draw people together and allow new friendships to be made or rekindle the old, and if this is the outcome then the tradition has fulfilled its purpose of continuing through the generations and bringing those in each generation together.

May we answer you further?

S: No, thank you, I enjoyed that.

I am Latwii. We thank you. Is there another question we may answer?

J: Yes, Latwii. We're at the season of the year when we are celebrating the tradition of Christmas, and I know there are quite a few people who are learning new insights and understandings through the meditations, and finding it sometimes difficult to integrate new understandings with the old understandings, the understandings we've grown up with as children, especially some taught by our church about Jesus the Savior, and the only Savior. Could you give us some enlightenment, some blending of the truths?

I am Latwii, and first of all, my sister, it is good to remember that whenever there is a change involved it may always be quite difficult, for, as you say, there is the wingwalker's rule and it is hard to let go of that wire. It is hard to let go of that which is taught to you. Then again sometimes it is not necessary to let go of what is taught, but to add on and to build upon. This indeed is very useful, for in building a foundation it is best to start from the bottom and to work up.

My sister, at this time of your season there are many thoughts centered around the one known as Jesus. There are many beliefs, there are many stories, and there are many things which you are supposed to think. But indeed it is up to your own imagination, your own thought, as to who Jesus was, and what this individual was, and the purpose of the individual, for there are many truths to this spoken by many, and they are all right, while they may all be wrong. This may sound like the easy way out, but if some thought is given, it can be realized that to some it is most important that Jesus be the only Savior. This is a starting point. It is something to believe in. While another individual may feel there are many saviors throughout history. This is just as important as the first, but many problems arise when one wishes to force their thought and opinion on another. This goes against the free will of having your own thoughts and your own imagination.

For, my sister, what is important? Is it important to know the exact answer to this, or to think about what the individual accomplished, or what other saviors might have accomplished? Also, who is to say what a savior is? At this time we would prefer not to put words in this definition, for it is a very, very personal word to many which has great significance to the individual, or we should say, to any specific individual.

We realize that we have sort of danced around the bush in answering your question, but the subject you have chosen is one which has been discussed many, many times, and there are many, many beliefs to what is the answer. We wish to just add a few words as thoughts to be pondered as to how to find the only answer that is best fitting to yourself. Also, we would like to address the point of trying to add in new thoughts which might come from this group to those thoughts which are so impressed upon by the church. We just would like to add this to clarify that it is indeed that all things are possible, and that the one known as Jesus indeed was of great service in helping others to seek, and there are those present who help individuals in their seeking. Therefore, it can be known that maybe all individuals are saviors, for there is the thought that all are one.

May we answer you further?

J: No, thank you. That was very nice, Latwii.

I am Latwii. We thank you, my sister. Is there another question we may answer?

A2: May I ask how the instrument is doing?

I am Latwii. The instrument is doing well. We thank you for your concern. Is there another question we may answer?

R: Latwii, I'd like to ask a question. It might be many questions, but the area that I would like to address is very broad, and as a beginning would you address, say something about creation, about why there was a creation, why there is you, why there is me?

I am Latwii, and, my sister, we are aware of your query. My sister, indeed this is a very broad question, and if limited to what you know as time, it might be very difficult to answer your question, but we shall stick to the generals of the question. What you see as creation is an illusion designed to provide different experiences for the purpose of learning. That of learning is to seek and become aware of the one infinite Creator, and become aware of the oneness. There are many different facets to the oneness, and you are a part of it as is the Confederation, and as we are. My sister, as we have said before, we are those desiring to serve by coming to those who call upon our services. We desire to help with those seeking and those wishing to learn.

(Side one of tape ends. Some minutes are not recorded.)

(A1 channeling)

… is very hard to give, for we do not wish to give a concrete answer because, my sister, this is what you are seeking to learn. You are seeking to learn what the creation is, and it might take the fun out of it if we tell you the whole story.

May we answer you further?

R: Well, just on your last comment, may I ask. Do you know the whole story?

My sister, no. We, indeed, are also seeking and learning. That is why it is difficult to answer the question.

R: Will this seeking and learning ever cease to be?

I am Latwii. My sister, we have a great deal of difficulty answering this, but we would wish to give our one belief, and we are sorry to say this. All things are possible. My sister, we would also like to add that at times you know as much as we do, for we all know the answers.

May we answer you further?

R: No, thank you.

I am Latwii, and we thank you for your desire to learn. Is there another question we may answer at this time?

S: Yes. As part of our tuning we say the Lord's prayer which is a prayer to our God. Do you also have a God?

I am Latwii, and, my sister, there is the technicality of words. We choose to think of the one infinite Creator. May we answer you further?

S: No, thank you.

Is there another question we may answer?

A2: Yes, Latwii, I have one. In private meditation when I call upon you, can you help me learn to distinguish, or is there a way that I can distinguish with some better degree of certainty whether I am in actual contact with you or whether it's my own imagination running wild and having fun?

I am Latwii, and, my sister, first of all, there is just having the trust in your wild imagination, for indeed it is difficult to believe in something you cannot see, for we will not come and knock at your door and walk in your house. My sister, therefore we visit you in meditation, and we first of all would say that in calling us it might be of a good point to challenge the contact. The challenging is one where you would ask for service in the love and in the light of the one infinite Creator or where you ask for our service specifically by name in one of love, and, indeed, we shall come if desired with all barrels, and, as this instrument says, with the two-by-four effect. This is not always needed, but if this is so desired, we shall serve as asked. My sister, all that is needed is time to become familiar with our vibration, for we like to think we have a different vibration than that of Hatonn, while indeed it is rather similar, but we all have our own uniqueness and our own identity, for although you are a human being you have the loveliness of your own individual, and this is what you need to seek when desiring our service. So when we come knocking, become familiar with our vibration.

May we answer you further?

A2: Goodness, no. Thank you, thank you. That was more than I expected. Thank you.

I am Latwii, and we thank you. Is there another question we may answer?

J: Latwii, are you aware of whether or not there are a number or many, or some other social memory complexes such as yourselves and Hatonn and Laitos and Nona—those are the ones I know of—from the Confederation who would be of service to us if we knew of them and asked them?

My sister, when desiring a service, all that is needed is the mental thought of what type of service is desired, and the group which can best serve you in this manner shall answer the calling, and as in the past, to the group, many times Hatonn has done all of what you know of as a session, for their calling was more important, and was stressed more than was the calling for our service, and therefore we, in our gracious manner, allow them to have the full glory. My sister, you need not call us by name, for this is difficult for those unaware of the actual calling being made, for we are at times with groups and individuals when they are not aware of our presence, but they have made the calling.

May we answer you further?

J: No, thank you. I have a whole bunch of questions, but I can't seem to sort out one just right now.

I am Latwii and we have great patience.

S: I would like to restate J's question. Are there other social memory complexes known to you but not known to us?

I am Latwii. My sister, we apologize for not making this answer clearer. Indeed, there are other groups which are present in the Confederation which you do not know by name which indeed are serving individuals such as yourself and this group.

May we answer you further?

S: Yes, but not at this moment. Thank you.

I am Latwii. We thank you. Is there another question we may answer at this time?

J: Yes, I've thought of another question. When I get ready to drop off to sleep, I suggest to myself that I will dream, and that I will remember my dreams, and I also mention your name and Hatonn's. And I do have neat dreams, and I remember many of them. Is it true that I have an experience of being with you at some point of consciousness as I'm sleeping?

I am Latwii, and we shall not say, "All things are possible," for indeed you are already aware of this point. However, my sister, the point of dreams is one where the individual is experiencing other levels of awareness, and indeed more points are possible, for the individual is not encompassed in such a strong illusion.

May we answer you further?

J: Then it would be likely and be possible that I can be in touch with my higher self and my own teacher as the source of wisdom coming through my dreams? Is this true?

I am Latwii. My sister, you are very perceptive. May we answer you further?

J: No, thank you. I appreciate that.

I am Latwii, and we thank you once again. Is there another question at this time we may answer?

A2: Yes, Latwii. I have just had some clarification. As a very small child I was told that I was driving people crazy with my questions. You come to answer questions. You also stated that there are other social memory complexes, and they're there when we ask for them. I've been sensing throughout my body overwhelming verification and knowledge of where the integration that I have managed to hold on to is all *(inaudible)* without even any knowledge that you all existed consciously. I sense that I'm simply not just speaking to you, Latwii, but to all those who helped. I want to say, "Thank you very much."

I am Latwii, and, my sister, we realize you have no question to ask, but indeed you have many friends who are watching over you, who are helping you with questions, and there are many who you are not at this time fully aware of, and, my sister, we thank you.

I am Latwii. Is there another question we may answer?

(Pause)

I am Latwii, and with the silence we shall leave this group, for we are aware there are many, many questions left unspoken, but we shall be taking our leaving until called upon once again. We are with you always in the love and in the light of the one infinite Creator. We are known to you as Latwii. Adonai vasu borragus.

L/L Research

L/L Research is a subsidiary of Rock Creek Research & Development Laboratories, Inc.

P.O. Box 5195
Louisville, KY 40255-0195

www.llresearch.org

Rock Creek is a non-profit corporation dedicated to discovering and sharing information which may aid in the spiritual evolution of humankind.

ABOUT THE CONTENTS OF THIS TRANSCRIPT: This telepathic channeling has been taken from transcriptions of the weekly study and meditation meetings of the Rock Creek Research & Development Laboratories and L/L Research. It is offered in the hope that it may be useful to you. As the Confederation entities always make a point of saying, please use your discrimination and judgment in assessing this material. If something rings true to you, fine. If something does not resonate, please leave it behind, for neither we nor those of the Confederation would wish to be a stumbling block for any.

© 2009 L/L Research

The Law of One, Book V, Session 101, Fragment 51
December 21, 1982

Jim: In Session 101 I got an excellent opportunity to work on my anger/frustration distortion again. This time, however, it was not pointed only at myself. This "negative wisdom" was pointed at Don over a period of two days when it was time to have Books Two and Three reprinted. Don wanted to put all of the books—one, two and three—into one book instead. It didn't matter that that was impossible due to lack of money to do it the way Don wanted to do it—typeset and hardback. What mattered was that I allowed a disharmony to result that went unresolved for two days. This became an excellent opportunity for our friend of negative fifth density to magnify the difficulty, and the means by which this was done proved to be quite interesting, especially to me, when I developed a rare kidney disease. It was called lipoid nephritis or minimal change syndrome, and soon I had gained about thirty pounds of water weight as a result of it. The last sentence in the first paragraph of Ra's response seems to us to be the key concept in this particular incident. The last two sentences in that response are interesting in their general application to all seekers.

You will note toward the middle of this session that another house in Atlanta is mentioned as a possible location for our group. We were still hoping to get closer to Don's work so that there would be less strain on him in getting to his job. Later, we found a third house which will be mentioned in Session 105, and it was this house that we eventually moved to in November of 1983.

The next to the last question concerns another instrument who had reported difficulties with her body swelling much as mine had done. Don asked if there were any way that we could give her information about her condition since we had just talked to her on the phone to compare the swelling in the ranks of our two groups. The first paragraph of Ra's response lays out the general principle which affects all individuals and groups doing work of a more intensive service-to-others nature. The second paragraph of Ra's response refers to the situation in which that particular instrument worked, but the general application of those concepts is obvious.

The combination of healing approaches found my condition in remission within six months.

Carla: I wish you could have seen the look on Dr. Stewart Graves' face when that worthy reviewed Ra's diagnosis. He carefully looked up the known causes of Jim's variety of kidney disease, and found that insect bites and the allergic reaction to them were a rarely found but duly noted cause of the condition. In the absence of any other possible cause, it was recorded an allergic reaction. Oddly, when I experienced kidney failure as a teenager, allergic reaction was also the doctor's best guess as to cause.

By this time, it may seem to you that psychic greetings were really occupying our time. You would be right. As Jim and Ra both say, it is easier to be noticed when you're standing in a spotlight. Metaphysically, the contact with those of Ra was a blinding cynosure. Although we continued to be obscure and completely anonymous in any earthly sense, we had become very noticeable to "the loyal opposition."

To my mind, the fatal weakness of our group was its humanity, in dealing with three-ness. Although in fact our consciously known energies were in perfect harmony and agreement, there were human distortions from below the level of conscious control, that allowed a wedge to be driven in between Don and me, so he lost faith in "us." When he began experiencing this profound depression which seemed to overtake him at a crawling, yet inexorable pace, his utter disdain for any opinion but his own did not stand him in good stead. This was the beginning of a pattern that in the end turned fatal and ended my beloved companion's life, and dear Ra's contact with our group.

Does this constitute a suggestion that a group should not work unless the energies are two-by-two, and only couples can join in? Not specifically, I do not think, but it is certainly something to ponder. Could we have done better? After years of the Joyceian "agenbite of inwit," I still do not think we could have. Our behavior was at all times a true manifestation of ourselves. In no wise did either Jim or myself ever even think to change the relationship with each other, or with Donald. And Don had ever kept his own counsel, and there was no hope that he would come to me or Jim and tell us what worries he had in his mind and heart.

Further, when any group works and lives together, regardless of whether the number is paired or singles are mixed in, there will always be human error in the manifested life of each, and to the extent that people's distortions and fears have a dynamic, there will be misunderstandings and confusion, pulling back and apart from total trust. So it behooves all those working with the light, hoping to be a positive influence on the planetary consciousness to communicate at once those fears and doubts that might pile up inside. If we had ever been able to talk with total openness, Don and I, I think I could have set his mind at ease. But Don would not have been himself if he had done so. Nor would I have been myself if I had somehow known Don was doubting my fidelity. Being within my self, I cannot imagine, either then or now, anyone thinking that I would be disloyal or untrue to any agreement. I have never done that in this incarnation.

Ultimately, one looks at such a pickle as we got into, and knows its utter perfection and inevitability. I have and will always think of Don, my B.C., every hour of every day, and his suffering is ever before me. But I no longer feel the keen sorrow that laid me low for the first few years after his death. All is well, nothing is lost. And I can feel the sun on my face this day, without the urge I used to have to stay in the shade and mourn my losses. Time has restored my broken spirit, and let my being flow sweetly and rhythmically again. And Donald is right here, within. Interestingly enough, we often get mail saying that Don has helped them, either with something from his work, or in an actual visitation. Don's great generosity of spirit, freed from the constrictive hold he had on it when alive, has overflowed into timelessness, and I think his service will continue as long as there are those who need his special brand of wisdom and depth of soul.

Ra's statement that the source of catalyst is the self, especially the higher self, is profound, I think. We always relate to the pain of new catalyst by relating to the other person as bringer of catalyst. In doing so we forget that the other is ourselves. Not LIKE ourselves, but our very hearts and souls. In this way of seeing, we can look at the fullness of tragedy in Don's and my illness and his death as the Creator serving the creator with exactly the catalyst needed for the utmost polarization in consciousness and the greatest growth of spirit. In opening his heart, Don fell ill and died, in the tradition of lost love and desperate romance that has moved us since the beginning of history. And that death was an utter giving away of self. It was as though Don finished everything else he wished to do in life, and then took on the personal reason he had come to earth's physical plane: the opening of his heart. He was so very wise—and with the sacrifice of self in the most brutal, literal sense, that wisdom was balanced fully with compassion and open-hearted love.

As for me, I cannot fault the path that stubbornly sent my soul to batter against the walls of self until I at last began struggling to express wisdom as well as love in my life. Such were our gifts to each other; such are the currents between us all.

Since Ra gave us the cleansing ritual referred to in this session, I've seen it used several times by those who have come to L/L Research, and in every case it seems to have *been quite useful. I think that doing some sort of cleansing of a new place is a good metaphysical habit, for people do leave behind the thought forms' traces imprinted on the aura of the places they have been, especially those they've stayed in for considerable time. And even when the vibrations are basically good, they might not harmonize completely with your own. So it is good to magnetize the place for your own uses, even if all you do is burn sage, or say a prayer of dedication. The world of spirit has much to do with us, though we cannot in most ways know or see such influence. Offering that part of things respect is wise.*

Session 101, December 21, 1982

Ra: I am Ra. I greet you in the love and in the light of the one infinite Creator. We communicate now.

Questioner: Could you first please give me the condition of the instrument?

Ra: I am Ra. All energy levels of the instrument are somewhat diminished due to the distortions of physical pain and recent mental/emotional catalyst. However, the energy levels appear to be very liable to be improved in what you call your immediate future.

Questioner: Thank you. What has caused the swelling in Jim's body, and what can be done to heal it?

Ra: I am Ra. For the answer to this query we must begin with the consideration of the serpent, signifying wisdom. This symbol has the value of the ease of viewing the two faces of the one who is wise. Positive wisdom adorns the brow indicating indigo-ray work. Negative wisdom, by which we intend to signify expressions which effectually separate the self from the other-self, may be symbolized by poison of the fangs. To use that which a mind/body/spirit complex has gained of wisdom for the uses of separation is to invite the fatal bite of that wisdom's darker side.

The entity has a mental/emotional tendency, which has been lessening in distortion for some of your space/time, towards negative wisdom. The entity's being already aware of this causes us not to dwell upon this point but merely to specifically draw the boundaries of the metaphysical background for the energizing of a series of bites from one of your second-density species. In this case the bite was no more than that of one of the arachnids, sometimes called the wood spider. However, it is possible that were enough work done to test the origin of the pathology of the entity, it is within possibility/probability limits that the testing would show the bite of the cottonmouth rather than the bite of the common wood spider.

The energizing took its place within the lymphatic system of the entity's yellow-ray, physical body. Therefore, the working continues. There is increasing strain upon the spleen, the supra-renal glands, the renal complex, and some possibility/probability of difficulty with the liver. Further, the lymphatic difficulties have begun to strain the entity's bronchial system. This is some general information upon what is to be noted as a somewhat efficient working.

The removal of these distortions has several portions. Firstly, it is well to seek the good offices of the one known as Stuart so that harsh chemical means may be taken to reawaken the histaminic reflexes of the entity and to aid in the removal of edema.

Secondly, we suggest that which has already begun; that is, the request of the one known now to this group as Bob that this entity may focus its aid upon the metaphysical connections with the yellow-ray body.

Thirdly, the entity must take note of its physical vehicle's need for potassium. The ingesting of the fruit of the banana palm is recommended.

Fourthly, the link between the swelling of contumely[3] and the apparent present situation is helpful. As always the support of the harmonious group is an aid, as is meditation. It is to be noted that this entity requires some discipline in the meditation which the others of the group do not find necessary in the same manner. Therefore, the entity may continue with its forms of meditation knowing that each in the group supports it entirely although the instinct to share in the discipline is not always present. Each entity has its ways of viewing and learning from the illusion, and each processes catalyst using unique circuitry. Thus all need not be the same to be equal in will and faith.

Questioner: Thank you. I will make a statement about the way I see the action in this instance and would request Ra's comment on it. I see the present

---

[3] contumely: insulting rudeness in speech or manner; scornful insolence; an insult, or an insulting act [< OF *contumelie* < L *contumelia* reproach]

situation as the Creator knowing Itself by using the concept of polarization. We seem to accentuate or to produce catalyst to increase the desired polarization whether the desired mechanism be random, through what we call the higher self, or through utilizing the services of an oppositely polarized entity acting upon us. All of these seem to produce the same effect which is more intense polarization in the desired direction once that direction has been definitely chosen. I see the catalyst of the second-density insect bite being a function of either or any of the sources of which I have spoken, from random to the higher self or polarized services of negative entities who monitor our activities, all of which have roughly the same ultimate effect. Would Ra comment on my observation?

Ra: I am Ra. We find your observations unexceptional and, in the large, correct.

Questioner: In this particular case, which avenue was the one that produced the catalyst of the bite?

Ra: I am Ra. The nature of catalyst is such that there is only one source, for the catalyst and experience are further attempts at specificity in dealing with the architecture of the unconscious mind of the self. Therefore, in an incarnational experience the self as Creator, especially the higher self, is the base from which catalyst stands to offer its service to the mind, body, or spirit.

In the sense which we feel you intend, the source was the fifth-density, negative friend which had noted the gradual falling away of the inharmonious patterns of the distortion called anger/frustration in the entity. The insect was easily led to an attack, and the physical vehicle, which had long-standing allergies and sensitivities, was also easily led into the mechanisms of the failure of the lymphatic function and the greatly diminished ability of the immune system to remove from the yellow-ray body that which distorted it.

Questioner: Something occurred to me. I am going to make a guess that my illness over the past week was a function of an action by my higher self to eliminate the possibility of a residence in the proximity of a large number of bees that I observed. Would Ra comment on my statement?

Ra: I am Ra. We can comment, not upon the questioner's physical distortions but upon the indubitable truth of second-density hive creatures; that is, that a hive mentality as a whole can be influenced by one strong metaphysical impulse. Both the instrument and the scribe have the capacity for great distortions toward nonviability, given such an attack by a great number of the stinging insects.

Questioner: Are the thought-form parameters and the general parameters of the 893 Oakdale Road address in Atlanta such that no cleansing would be necessary, if Ra has this information?

Ra: I am Ra. No.

Questioner: Would cleansing of the nature suggested for the other house just south of the airport in Atlanta be advisable for the 893 Oakdale Road address?

Ra: I am Ra. We note that any residence, whether previously benign, as is the one of which you speak, or previously of malignant character, needs the basic cleansing of the salt, water, and broom. The benign nature of the aforementioned domicile is such that the cleansing could be done in two portions; that is, no egress or entrance through any but one opening for one cleansing. Then egress and entrance from all other places while the remaining portal is properly sealed. The placing of salt may be done at the place which is not being sealed during the first of the cleansings, and the salt may be requested to act as seal and yet allow the passage of gentle spirits such as yourselves. We suggest that you speak to this substance and name each entity for which permission is needed in order to pass. Let no person pass without permission being asked of the salt. This is the case in the residence of which you speak.

Questioner: Thank you. Could Ra give information on any way that we could give information to (name) as to how to alleviate her present condition of swelling?

Ra: I am Ra. We may only suggest that the honor of propinquity to light carries with it the Law of Responsibility. The duty to refrain from contumely and discord in all things, which, when unresolved within, makes way for workings, lies before the instrument of which you speak. This entity may, if it is desired by the scribe, share our comments upon the working of the latter entity.

The entity which is given constant and unremitting approval by those surrounding it suffers from the loss of the mirroring effect of those which reflect truthfully rather than unquestioningly. This is not a suggestion to reinstate judgment but merely a suggestion for all those supporting instruments; that is, support, be harmonious, share in love, joy, and thanksgiving, but find love within truth, for each instrument benefits from this support more than from the total admiration which overcomes discrimination.

Questioner: Thank you. That was the forty-five minute signal, so I will ask if there is anything that we can do to make the instrument more comfortable or to improve the contact?

Ra: I am Ra. We find that this instrument has used all the transferred energy and has been speaking using its vital energy reserve. We do suggest using the transferred sexual energy to the total exclusion of vital reserves if possible.

The alignments are as they must be for all to continue well. We are grateful for the conscientiousness of the support group.

I am Ra. I leave this group glorying in the love and in the light of the one infinite Creator. Go forth rejoicing, therefore, in the power and in the peace of the Creator. Adonai.

Saturday Meditation
December 25, 1982

(Unknown channeling)

[I am Hatonn.] I greet this group in the love and in the light of the infinite Creator. We thank you for the privilege of requesting our words and we thank each for the care taken to tune to our vibrations, so that we may speak as clearly as possible *(inaudible)* one original Thought.

We had wished to speak through the one known as Don, as this instrument is fatigued. But [we] find that this instrument is also fatigued and *(inaudible)*.

As this instrument opens its inner ears to our thoughts it discovers the beating of wings and the experience of clouds of *(inaudible)*. When we speak of love, we speak of something exceedingly simplistic. That is, one thing from which all depends. The one original Thought of the infinite Creator has been called logos and love and we say to you that you may find it in diverse places, in all manner of situations *(inaudible)* in the sanctity and peace of your conscience or in the noisy humdrum of the daily routine.

Within that daily routine there are many, many chances for the seeker to feel isolated and alienated in the illusion which surrounds [him]. How many times on this holyday, as you call this day, have you felt in full strength the power and the inevitability of the one original Thought? How many times have you centered yourself within the Creator? It is difficult to imagine turning yourself towards the Creator, as you may find the Creator in any quarter within, without, north and south, east and west, in the faces of strangers and of the most dearly beloved. And yet the Creator's original Thought is most often missed even upon the feast celebrating the growth of the spirit, a spirit new within you, new, indeed, each day as each day you turn towards that Creator, that original Thought of love, and offer that day, that moment, to the service of the Creator, to the service of the Creator in others and in yourself.

Your lips have moved many times this day. How many times when they moved has the intention been to aid in the spiritual evolution of yourself or another?

We ask these questions to strip away a veneer of old and tarnished myth and legend and destructive distortion surrounding that which is needed to nurture your own evolution of mind, body and spirit. What you seek in rock or star or word or sign may far more fruitfully be sought within the confines of the meditation and within the recesses of *(inaudible)* heart that *(inaudible)* the channeling of that one great Thought of love through the self to those about you.

In order to set about the business of seeking and to continue when the way seems steep and *(inaudible)*, you have provided yourselves with a host of angelic presences, with those of light vibration who support each loving thought and each caring action. You may be solitary from men, but you shall never be solitary from the grace and the consolation of those messengers who serve the Creator by caring, in sympathy and in like mind, for all those who desire to become a transparent being full of the light and the love of the Creator. In your meditations, in your actions, you are not alone, unless you choose to shut the door upon many and many who love in the name of the Father.

Due to the fatigue of this instrument we shall allow this contact to be relatively brief. We thank this instrument for making itself available.

You know us as those of Hatonn. We are always available to aid you in the deepening of your meditative state. Please remember that we are but fallible brothers and sisters. Our thoughts are shared freely [but only] with the understanding that we have no claim to infallibility. Therefore, take what you can, take what is of aid and dismiss the rest, for we wish to aid you, not confuse you; to inspire you, not cause you a stumbling block.

We leave this instrument in the love and in the light of the one infinite Creator. Adonai vasu borragus.

(Pause)

(Unknown channeling)

I am Latwii, my friends, and I greet you in the love and in the light of our one infinite Creator. It is once again our great privilege to be asked to join this group. It is our humble hope that we might once again be of some small service by attempting to answer those queries which you have this evening. Therefore, may we ask for the first query?

Questioner: I would like to know if I am doing the right thing by starting this church, and if it will go through as I am hoping?

I am Latwii, and am aware of your query, my brother. We find in a query of this nature that we must be general in responding for were we to give information of a specific nature which affected your future, then we would be removing the doubt which has the valuable service of preparing your will for that task which you propose.

As a general response, therefore, let us say that to look within the heart for the deepest service possible and to meditate upon the carrying out of those heart's desires is that which is the most helpful to the seeker of truth. If you look within your being and ask what can be done, and wait then for that portion of yourself which has all answers, then it shall be revealed unto you the path which is most helpful to tread. Remove from your being fear that you shall fail and go forth in the glorious light and love of the one Creator that exists at the center of your being.

You may not accomplish those things which you set before yourself in precisely the manner which you have arranged them. This is not to say that you shall fail, for there is not such concept to one who seeks the truth. The will of the one Creator moves in ways which are most mysterious to those upon your planet, for you exist within a veil of forgetting. But know ye that ever do you glorify the one Creator when you seek to know the truth and to serve in the purest manner possible.

May we answer you further, my brother?

Questioner: Should I change in what … in my striving, in the direction I am going? Is there any reason why I should change in what I am trying to do?

I am Latwii. My brother, once again we find the necessity for speaking in general terms. For us to advise a change in the path which you tread would be exercise an undue influence upon your free will. We ask only that those such as yourself who seek to be of service be ever aware that service is ever present. Your journey shall be full of change but always shall it contain service, for there is only one being of which you are a part. Therefore, there can only be service to that one being who is the Creator within.

May we answer you further, my brother?

Questioner: Thank you, Latwii.

I am Latwii. We are most grateful to you, my brother. You do us a great honor by asking our humble service. In such a manner do we learn more of the light and the love of the one Creator.

May we ask at this time if there might be another question?

Questioner: *(Inaudible)*.

I am Latwii. We thank each present for allowing us to join our vibrations with yours this evening. An evening which is most holy among your peoples. An evening which expresses and experiences the love of the one Creator in a way which is most joyful upon your planet. We remind each that a simple request for our presence in your meditative state is all that is necessary for us to join our vibrations with yours and to deepen your meditative state.

We shall now leave this group and this instrument, rejoicing in that love and light and that unity of the one infinite Creator. Blessings and peace. I am Latwii. Adonai vasu borragus. ✣

L/L Research

L/L Research is a subsidiary of Rock Creek Research & Development Laboratories, Inc.

P.O. Box 5195
Louisville, KY 40255-0195

www.llresearch.org

Rock Creek is a non-profit corporation dedicated to discovering and sharing information which may aid in the spiritual evolution of humankind.

ABOUT THE CONTENTS OF THIS TRANSCRIPT: This telepathic channeling has been taken from transcriptions of the weekly study and meditation meetings of the Rock Creek Research & Development Laboratories and L/L Research. It is offered in the hope that it may be useful to you. As the Confederation entities always make a point of saying, please use your discrimination and judgment in assessing this material. If something rings true to you, fine. If something does not resonate, please leave it behind, for neither we nor those of the Confederation would wish to be a stumbling block for any.

CAVEAT: This transcript is being published by L/L Research in a not yet final form. It has, however, been edited and any obvious errors have been corrected. When it is in a final form, this caveat will be removed.

© 2009 L/L Research

Sunday Meditation
December 26, 1982

(S channeling)

I am Hatonn, and am now with this instrument. We greet you, our friends, in the love and light of the one infinite Creator and are greatly pleased to be called to you this evening to be of what small service we may be. We have been enjoying your friendship, the love you have shared. We have been watching at this time of year you call Christmas. The love that has been shown upon your planet is great indeed. For as the time of harvest grows nearer, my friends, more and more of your people will come to know of the love and light of the infinite Creator. It is ones such as yourselves that dare to let the light shine that is within you and to draw others to the light, to what we believe is the path, the shortest path to the final goal of the one original Thought. There is much upon your planet at this time which may cause disturbance among you should you dwell on those things. But, my friends, there is also much, much happening that should cause great joy in your hearts and your souls and your minds. Look about you, my friends, at the love that has been displayed, that has been showered upon you, with a heartfelt hug from a friend, with a glance that is full of love and sharing of two souls. My friend, these are the things that should occupy your minds, for when one loves, that love can do nothing but grow and grow. At this time we would transfer this contact. I am Hatonn.

(C channeling)

I am Hatonn, and I am now with this instrument. We greet you again. The love during this time of your year is at a level rarely reached. Many at this time feel that special need to quietly give of themselves without thought of reward or of the return of love. The shining of your light, the giving of your love does not need an audience or conditions, for as you celebrate the birth of the one that your peoples see as the ideal of love and light, never—correction—the one known as Jesus, that many use as their ideal, refrained from showmanship, came quietly and humbly into your world and reached and touched in silence and gave [up] the thought of reward for himself. Each time that you reached out and gave of yourself the light shone that much brighter. My friends, your light, the light of your fellow beings, glows warmly at this time. Your planet feels the healing love and responds. It would be well if the feelings of love could continue at this level. For at this time in your illusion there is much need for love and light. Much healing needs doing and can be done. So if you would, allow your light to shine and reach out quietly to those around you. A quiet touch, the gentle hug, the loving look, the acceptance, all aids your peoples and your planet. We join with you and pray. I am Hatonn. I leave you now in the love and the light of the one infinite Creator. Adonai.

(M channeling)

I am Hatonn, and am now with this instrument. I greet you with the love and the light of the infinite Creator. At the time of year on your planet when your people think of the Christ who rose, realize that you too can rise. Second-density entities are earthly. They think mainly of their immediate environment. Think how wonderful it is that you can see the sky and the sun and the moon and realize that in no sense are you bound to the earth. Your soul and your mind can soar. Many people who think they are free are in prison and some people in prison are free because their soul and their mind is not limited. Open the gates and all eternity is within your grasp. Then you will be able to leave this third density. Prepare yourself to expand your soul and your mind and see the beauty of eternity. Think how sad it would be if you always had a roof over you and could never see beyond the earth. When you become too involved in earthly things, go out and look at the sky. Look at the sun come up; watch the sun go down. Look at the moonlit night. If you appreciate these things, you will never be in prison. Your soul will soar forever. I am Hatonn. I leave this instrument.

(Carla channeling)

I am Oxal, and I greet you, my friends, in the love and in the light of our infinite Creator. We thank you for the privilege of sharing with you concepts related to those subjects so familiar to you having to do with the birth of the one you call Jesus. We would like you to consider the passage from your holy book, the Bible, which speaks of the Word which was made flesh and dwelt among you. It then compared that happening to the light that shines in darkness. The darkness does not know the light, but it cannot overcome the light. There is much to consider in these phrases concerning each entity's spiritual birth within incarnational experience. Each at some point within the incarnation consciously chose to be born in spirit or each would not be within this circle. For we are called by a harmonious and unified circle of those who seek. In the same sense that the light came into the darkness does the spiritual self consciously come into being within, that manifestation of being which is each entity within the illusion. And so each of you experienced the conscious acceptance of a portion of the self being born that was not there before and that is to the remainder of the conscious self as a light in the darkness. Further, the incarnational experience within the illusion is designed to challenge that light. Growth of the light does not occur except by intent. It may not be the conscious intent to grow spiritually. It may simply be the dogged intent to survive without harming another. Many are the souls that have been harvested whose concept of the truth was never articulated, yet whose lives became radiant because the light shone in the darkness and the darkness could not overcome it. When each period or portion or phase of the spiritual or metaphysical journey commences, turn again to the experience of the one known as Mary, the mother of Jesus. Each mother physically experiences the nurturing of that in darkness which will be delivered forth into the light. However, when viewed in the spiritual or metaphysical sense, you may see this deliverance as one which is pondered, as it is written in the same holy work, in the heart as you nurture your own infant spirits, and indeed, each new phase of our journey renders you an infant again, it is well to ponder all things in your heart. For yours is the responsibility for your spirit and some care may well be taken, therefore. It has been written, although mythically rather than literally, that the one known as Jesus was forced to flee to the desert as a young child to escape death at the hand of that which may be called a negative influence. Have you given yourselves time and place for constant spiritual birthing and then careful nurturing in the desert or dry place where all things may best be made plain within while remaining secret from the external illusion? The external illusion challenges each entity in its journey constantly. Therefore, a portion of this holiday or holy day which you know as Christmas may well be devoted to the consideration of these movements or dynamics in the life of the growing spirit within. That which comes from you must needs first come to you. The desert is the perfect sequel to the poverty and simplicity of the manger. In all humility console yourself in secret as each new phase of being begins its development. And only when it can stand and walk within you may you then go forth in the manifestation of illusion and speak of those things which you have realized. We are with you as you continuously begin a great story of birth and death and transformation. May your learning be filled with light. We can only give you our opinion that darkness shall never overcome that light. But that opinion we do give. Arise and shine in good time and know that you are not in any sense alone. For all who seek, seek one thing. All are one thing. In the beginning was love. What is your incarnation? Love. How may you manifest it? That, my friends, is worth some work. I am Oxal. I leave you in the love and the light of the one infinite Creator. Adonai.

(Jim channeling)

I am Latwii, and I greet you, my friends, in love and light. We are privileged once again to be able to join your group. We thank you for extending this invitation to us this evening. May we ask then if there might be a question with which we might begin our humble service?

S: Yes, Latwii, I have a question. What can you tell me, if anything, of the phenomenon known as twin souls?

I am Latwii, and am aware of your query, my sister. We find that this term and others among your peoples has become somewhat overworked, shall we say. There are among those who seek the truth many concepts which fascinate the mind. The very seeking of truth opens new vistas and presents the mind with information and experience of such a revolutionary nature, shall we say, that often it is difficult for the seeker to discern those concepts which have merit from those which merely attract attention. The concept of the twin soul, soul mate, and twin flame or twin ray is a concept which has some basis in what you may call fact, but which offers little of value in the seeker's experience. Though there are entities who have from the great reaches of time and space as you know them come into the earth planes as groups and even as a type of mate, there is, in our humble opinion an overemphasis upon such a phenomenon to the point where the searching for one's, shall we say, other half becomes a replacement for the searching for truth. Therefore may we say that such phenomena do exist, yet are quite insignificant when viewed in relations to the purpose for such incarnation.

May we answer you further, my sister?

S: No, thank you, Latwii.

I am Latwii. We are most grateful to you, my sister. May we attempt another query at this time?

K: Yes. What can you say about an entity or entities in general who are almost incapable of making decisions. Even the decisions that really demand attention. What I'm asking is, is development stunted, or why do some entities have such difficulty in making decisions?

I am Latwii, and am aware of your query, my sister. As with any distortion which any entity may express, the causes are not only many, but often complex in number. For example, an entity may have the difficulty in deciding due to some blockage within the entity's energy centers having to do with clear perception of the self or other selves and the relationship between. Another entity may also experience a difficulty in making the decision because of a great desire never to infringe upon another's free will, yet see the great difficulty in achieving this high ideal and moves not, that it may not infringe. Yet another entity may suffer the difficulty of making decisions because of the ability to analyze having been, shall we say, hampered or hindered in early incarnational experience so that the information necessary to the mind for action is slow in accumulation. Another entity may feel the paralysis of non-movement of difficulty in decision making as a portion of a process of balancing actions at another time which moved with too great a speed, shall we say, and with carelessness. Therefore it is not easy to discern which situation has resulted in the inability to make the decision. We hopefully have not been unable to make a decisive statement.

May we answer you further, my sister?

K: No, thank you. You've covered a lot of territory and I thank you very much.

I am Latwii. We thank you, we think. May we have another query at this time?

Carla: I'm not sure. (That's a joke …)

We are uncertain, as to whether to laugh.

Carla: I have a question. I hardly know how to put it, but I know everybody has these experiences. I just had one where I was utterly unable to like a fellow human being. I was perfectly willing to love him, but the guy was beyond me to love …

(Side one of tape ends.)

Carla: … these characters as I'm looking at myself in the mirror. My problem here is I can't figure out what portion of myself I dislike. Because my whole reaction to this person's vibrations, even on the telephone was panic, basically, I wanted to get away. What's occurring in these unfortunate circumstances and what is there to learn?

I am Latwii, and am aware of your query, my sister. Again there are numerous points to consider. One may indeed look at such an entity and see those facets of the self which do not well reflect, shall we say. If an entity is too boisterous, is presumptuous, makes statements of arrogance, one may see that one is unable to accept such facets of the self. But it is also the case that an entity which has developed such characteristics to the extent that mastery, shall we say, of them has been achieved, an entity may develop the type of being which is indeed a vexation to a gentler spirit. As the pond in stillness lies without a ripple on its surface, the stone when thrown into the pond causes the disruption which does distort the beingness of the pond. As you look at an entity such as the one which you have described, you may see the entity as offering a very great amount of what you have termed catalyst. The amount may be in such degree that the very heart of the being which is yourself is much disturbed, as one could well expect from an overstimulation of this nature.

May we answer you further, my sister?

Carla: What is there to learn?

I am Latwii. As always, my sister, the lesson to be learned is some aspect of love and acceptance. It may be, however, that the love to be learned may have an aspect of wisdom connected to it. That is, how best to love such an entity. It may be that to love such an entity in the most helpful way to that entity would be not the simple acceptance of every portion without comment, but the gentle directing of love in a manner which would attempt some form of sharing the self as an instructive technique so that the entity might know that as you accept it, you also have responses that are somewhat disturbing that you wish to share so that the entity might know that it is being perceived in such and such a manner by yourself as you love to the best of your ability.

May we answer you further, my sister?

Carla: M was talking earlier about not throwing pearls before swine and giving back the reflection of what she received. And this is basically what I'm hearing you say. The thing that bothers me about that is that I personally would prefer not to give my opinion of a person regardless of how much the person bothers me unless the person asks me. Is that a distortion that I would be better off leaving in the closet? Is it better to go ahead and be outspoken when another person is outspoken, in other words be a reflection of whatever you're receiving? It seems to me that sometimes to give what you get is the pits because what you're getting is not wonderful, or it's not positive, is not helpful. Is there a question in there?

I am Latwii. We feel we have discerned your query, my sister. We do not mean to suggest by our previous statement that you reflect to such an entity that which you are receiving, for to do so would be to put yourself at the mercy of any entity of any nature which approached you. The great lesson of your density is the lesson of love, acceptance without condition. You spoke as to the lesson which could have been learned with this particular entity. We spoke of a refinement to the lesson of love, that being the inclusion of a portion of wisdom with that love. The way of wisdom is to speak clearly and honestly without a dedication to the outcome, only wishing to speak clearly. Therefore, it is possible to refine the lesson of love with such an entity, and we stress "refine," which suggests that you do indeed accept such an entity fully. And this refinement may take the form of speaking in a manner which is most delicate, that is, speaking to what is perceived as a stumbling block, shall we say, that the entity may not be aware of. This is not judgment. A simple discernment instead, which offers on the, shall we say, on the outstretched hand of love the morsel of wisdom which is given in love and suggests a refinement which may be helpful to the entity. This, of course, is most helpful only when asked, and in this case we note there was no such request. Therefore it may be that such refinement would not be possible. In any case, the refinement is offered only when asked, and is freely offered with no dedication to its acceptance, no, shall we say, argument of its good points; the simple expression given and whether it be received or rejected being considered unimportant.

May we answer you further, my sister?

Carla: No, thank you. Thank you very much.

I am Latwii. We thank you. Is there another query at this time?

M: Yes. Maybe this is the wrong approach to life, but I've often found people who throw tension at me. When I throw it back at them, as they throw the ball to me and I throw it back, they will comment on my tension and I will say I've just thrown the tension back that you threw at me, and sometimes I think they learn by the reflection of themselves in me. Is this wrong?

I am Latwii, and am aware of your query, my sister. Again we assume you are aware that there are no wrong actions. The action of which you speak, as all actions, will teach a certain lesson to a certain entity in a certain degree of efficiency. You may do whatever you wish and be aware that service is offered, for there is no way that one may not be of service. As you move through your incarnation you will discover various ways of increasing the efficiency of your service as you become more consciously aware of the effects of your thinking upon your experience.

May we answer you further, my sister?

M: No, I think that was very helpful. But I do have a question that's not philosophical. I have weird experiences on occasion, and this is a sample of it. My daughter and I were in the car Thursday and we were stopping someplace and I said to my daughter, "Do you smell gasoline?" She said, "No, I don't smell a thing". I said, "I smell it, it's gasoline." She said, "I don't smell a thing." So that I was positive it was gasoline, I was trying to figure out how I could smell it in the car, and then I said to myself, "Oh, I got gas an hour and a half ago, and I bet I left the gas cap off." And so, she got out of the car and looked and the gas cap was off and I went to the gas station and picked up the gas cap and went on. Now why did I smell that gasoline and she didn't? From where did I get that smell? Because she said there was no smell in the car.

I am Latwii and am aware of your query, my sister. To simply say that your senses are more acute than those of your daughter is not completely accurate. For in such an instance, not only the sense of smell may be involved, but also what might be described as the sense or awareness of things as they should be. It might be that your sense of responsibility for the well-being of your journey, your daughter, and the vehicle had been alerted by the subconscious noting of the gas cap's omission and this therefore became the primary stimulus for the remembering analogy through the olfactory senses.

May we answer you further, my sister?

M: No, I don't completely understand you still, but I think that's a good answer. Thank you.

I am Latwii. We thank you, my sister. Is there another query at this time?

K: Yes, right along the line that M has mentioned about the gas cap, I've always facetiously and yet with some sincerity said, "Well, that's just my guardian angel watching after me." And I've always said that and essentially it is, I'm assuming the subconscious mind perceiving what the conscious mind does not perceive. Is that right?

I am Latwii. In some cases, my sister, this is correct. But it must also be noted that indeed those beings which you may describe as guardians or guardian angels do have their effect and do communicate certain thoughts at the appropriate moments. It is not usually possible to discern whether the thought has come from the subconscious or from such a guardian. Both are often utilized by the higher self to relay messages from the higher self to the incarnated self which moves in the illusion.

May we answer you further, my sister?

K: Well, no that explains a lot of riddles in my life because I never worry about what's going to happen to me when I go out because I always think that guardian angel is there, so in truth, that guardian angel is there! Okay, that's fine. Thank you. Let me go back to this other idea and just see if I can clarify this a little bit. In the earlier conversation I said that I had my description of love, at least the way I perceive it at this point. Love is unconditional acceptance of another entity, making no demands on his behavior or what he does. And I find sometimes that this is very much like, well, indifference, at least I don't hurt him and he doesn't hurt me, regardless of what has been said or done. Now, is that concept of unconditional acceptance and indifference, are those concepts opposite to each other or are they about the same? That's a pretty awkward way to say it, but it's the best way I can say it right now.

I am Latwii, and am aware of your query, my sister. The effect of both of these concepts is quite similar in that the entity feeling either the indifference or the unconditional love does not have a response that could be considered in a significant distortion. In other words, the actions of the other self do not generate within the one feeling the unconditional love or the indifference an emotion which moves the entity from the center of self. Yet the entity feeling the indifference has some portion of the self which has been held in reserve, shall we say. This holding of the self in reserve is a slight distortion of the inner being which therefore requires the balance, the balance being the releasing of the self which has been held that it might be expressed. The entity expressing the unconditional love has no action within that is held, but allows the free expression of the compassion similar to that which one might feel for the newborn infant in its innocent actions. Such an infant is easily seen as worthy of unconditional love. When one can feel such, shall we call it, emotion, for any entity at any time for any reason, then that balance of unconditional love has been achieved.

May we answer you further, my sister?

K: No, I believe that answers the question. Thank you.

I am Latwii. We thank you, my sister. Is there another query at this time?

Carla: Could you say that indifference was quite a bit like unconditional denial or rejection?

I am Latwii, and am aware of your query, my sister. Such terminology suggests the addition within the entity experiencing such a condition of a somewhat negative concept. This is quite possible. To exist—we correct this instrument. It is possible for such to exist within an entity, that is, that the indifference is distorted towards rejection. It is also possible that the indifference would not have such a distortion. It would be necessary to look at each particular case as an individual situation.

May we answer you further, my sister?

Carla: No. I don't want to get into semantics. It's just, I have noticed previously sometimes that when people are really angry with you, it's basically a distorted expression of love. But when you're looking at blank indifference, you're really looking at unconditional denial of your being practically. Not that it's a negative denial, it's just that you don't exist. And it's far harder to deal lovingly with that sort of a person or to make some kind of a communication with that kind of a person than to deal with a person who is honestly upset with something that you've said or done or if there's a problem of communication because of the fact that anger, even though it seems like a negative thing, usually comes out rebounding into a very positive thing, whereas indifference doesn't have much of a snap to it.

I am Latwii. To comment upon your comment. We may suggest that it is most difficult for indifference to be pure, shall we say. It is most often the case that as you have stated, the indifference is the perimeter of rejection and must first be penetrated before the truer feeling of the heart is known. Indifference is an—we correct this instrument—indifference is a state of being which is most difficult to achieve and maintain for it is the natural inertia or character, shall we say, of one's being to respond in some fashion to those experiences and entities which surround one, thereby the use of catalyst is greatly facilitated. Whereas if indifference truly exists, then the use of catalyst is greatly hindered and in the case where true indifference is felt, the use of catalyst is zero.

May we …

Carla: Thank you.

We thank you, my sister. Is there another query at this time?

K: Yeah. I don't want to beat a dead horse, but let me see if I can clarify this maybe for all of us. Particularly for me. I've worked in lots of situations in life that could have torn you apart; you do have to try to protect the self or you get in as bad a state as the people you work with. And when I talk of unconditional acceptance, that's what I mean. They have a right to be as ornery as all get-out from my point of view. Or they have a right to do this or that which is totally opposed to the way I think it should be done. But when I'm talking about indifference, I'm talking about stepping outside of the situation and letting the situation be. If there's nothing I see I can do, then from my point of view, it's just smart to step out of and recognize the fact that you really can't help it very much. Now from that point of view, [that] is what I'm talking about when I say indifferent. I am indifferent because I don't see anything I can do to help the situation. Now in that context, it seems to me that indifference is in a sense a caring thing. Is that right?

I am Latwii. In this instance we find that the word indifference is not the correct description for the situation, for where caring exists there is not the indifference. If you have removed yourself from the situation which you do not feel you may affect, then you have in some degree built a perimeter, shall we say, around your caring, yet the caring exists. And should the situation change sufficiently, you may once again remove the perimeter and exercise the caring. Whereas if true indifference existed, there would be no caring to generate the future action.

May we answer you further, my sister?

(Inaudible)

I am Latwii. We thank you. Is there another query at this time?

M: Yes, I have one. I want to beat the dead horse a little more. To me, love is where another human being brings out the best in me, positive responses, whether they feel the same way about me or not. If I love them, then they bring out positive response in me. Or, if it's both ways, if two people love each other, they bring positive responses in each other. Is that a definition of love?

I am Latwii, and am aware of your query, my sister. One may define any emotion or term in any way as most entities, of course, do. The bringing out of the best in another may be seen as one portion of love, that being the inspirational quality, yet one may see that the action called loving may also include the ability to accept the worst in another with the same degree of enjoyment, shall we say, that the best qualities are enjoyed.

May we answer you further, my sister?

M: Yes, I'm a little confused. Do you mean that I would love a person that was extremely unpleasant, and consistently extremely unpleasant, that that would be a person that I would especially love?

I am Latwii. We have attempted to suggest that within the boundaries of love, as defined, there are indeed no boundaries. By this paradox we mean to suggest that love is exercised by one who loves toward the object of love no matter what expression the object of love has created. The child eating the bowl of soup may spill the soup and create the mess, yet receive love. The child may simply sleep and yet receive the same love. The child may injure the playmate, yet receive the same love.

May we answer you further, my sister?

M: Well, I'm not sure I exactly … I can understand loving something in a person who could do no better, such as a child. But say a person was very vicious, I would find that difficult to love them in the same sense that I would love a person who was kind and considerate. What is your opinion of that?

I am Latwii. In our humble opinion, my sister, each entity is but a child. For the child on your planet is seen as one small in experience, not aware of the total ramifications of each and every action. Yet the child grows and becomes what you people call an adult but this does not mean that the entity knows whereof it acts. The one you have called Jesus, while upon the cross, prayed to the one Creator that it should forgive those about it, for they knew not what they did. Yet were they not adults? Each upon your planet is but a child in the great search for truth and when one looks at each entity traveling that path, that journey of seeking, one can see the many ways that the ignorance is expressed. And even that entity which you may call vicious does not yet know the full import of its actions, but shall someday know them and shall make a balancing action that all shall be made whole. And it shall itself see the child within, always seeking, yet never fully knowing. Thus the child moves forward that it might know the light and grow more fully into it.

May we answer you further, my sister?

M: Yes. I can understand that you should love all other selves, but what I was meaning was that there are a few people that you come in contact with who do inspire you and who seem to bring out the best in you. And everybody can't do that. So there are a limited few people about who you can say, "I particularly love that person." Now, I don't mean that you don't love everybody, your other selves in the larger sense, but don't most people have a certain number of people that bring out the best in them?

I am Latwii. This, my sister, is correct for most entities, for there are a few, shall we say, easy questions on every test. May we answer you further?

M: No. I think you've answered me very well.

I am Latwii. We hope we have been of some small service. May we ask if there might be another question at this time?

Carla: Thanks, Latwii. I thought that your answers were especially inspirational.

K: Does the instrument have enough energy to answer another question?

I am Latwii. We believe that there is sufficient reserves for another query at this time.

K: I wanted to ask a question about the harvest. It seems that many, many people just by listening to the TV are aware that something comparable to a harvest is near. Before the harvest, do the people on the planet have to go through great catastrophes of, well, say, floods and famines and all that sort of thing, earthquakes, etc., etc.? Before the harvest do all of these, will all of these things take place?

I am Latwii, and am aware of your query, my sister. Returning to our analogy of the test. When the student has prepared itself over the long period of the course in a sufficient manner, it is not necessary as the final testing approaches to engage in the last minute, shall we say, cramming in order that the exam which approaches might be passed. Upon your planet there has been much procrastination, shall we say. The harmonizing of the vibrations of the entities who have populated your cultures in the history of your planet is a record of a difficult progression and somewhat inefficient learning of the lessons of love. Those incarnate upon your planet at this time have the opportunity of taking this final exam under conditions which most likely shall approach those which you describe due to the difficulty experienced throughout the major cycles of your planet. The difficulties shall add to the opportunity of graduation much like the student remaining awake the night before the exam for long hours going through the grueling process of covering that material which had previously been omitted and under such stress attempting then to present itself in such a manner at the time of examination that the examination is passed. Whereas if the entity had been more attentive to the requirements of the course over the longer run, the final examination would not be so traumatic.

May we answer you further, my sister?

K: No, I believe that answers it.

(Tape ends.)

Year 1983
January 2, 1983 to October 30, 1983

Sunday Meditation
January 2, 1983

(M channeling)

[I am Hatonn,] and I am now with this instrument. I greet you with the love and the light of the infinite Creator. As this instrument likes philosophy, I would like to stress the point of one person. No one person goes down alone. The people who dislike him or the people who hate him feel justified in their feeling, and they go down too. The people who love him are diminished, and even casual acquaintances, people who only see him pass and never speak to him, have a less interesting environment. Part of them go down with him. And if a man goes up he does not go up alone. People who dislike him or hate him cannot justify their opinions. His friends are inspired by him, and people who see him pass are enriched. No man is ever alone. Do not say, "Well, it was only one man," because it is never only one man. I am Hatonn. I leave this instrument.

(Carla channeling)

I am Hatonn, and I am now with this instrument, and we have for some time called, "Wait-a-while," for this instrument always says "Wait a while" when we attempt to contact this instrument. However, we find that there is a request from each of the other instruments that this instrument be used for some of your time and so we shall use this instrument [a little while]. We greet you once again in the love and in the light of the infinite Creator. We wish you blessing and glory and peace. It has often been said among your peoples, "Wishes are not worthwhile. Wishing is not substantial." And, my friends, it is this point of love to which we would speak this evening.

What a great invisible web there is that contacts all that there is, but in your density especially what a great connection there is betwixt each entity upon your planet. The one known to you as Jesus suggested that if an entity fed or visited or aided another entity, even one which was looked upon as not important, the entity was feeding or visiting or aiding the Creator. That is your unity, that is your reality. You are one, my friends, because you are all the Creator, each shining in your unique facets like the jewel that you have made of yourself, yet each a portion of the whole that is the creation. How many times have you wished, and had it became so? We suggest to you, my friends, that the faculty of hope, of faith, of wishing, of dreaming, is one of the most powerful resources of your mind, and that it alerts your entire being so that what you call your future is designed again and again by each wish, each desire, in order that you may receive that for which you wish. In your illusion the connection between wishing and having is usually invisible, for in the illusion time walks with you like an unwieldy giant, distorting true relationships and making them appear unreal. However, the faculty of hope operates in what you may call time/space where there is no time as you know it, and the connection between hope and the desire fulfilled is quite plain.

Therefore, my friends, the first thing we would suggest that you do is be cautious and careful in your wishes, your hopes, and your desires, for you do inevitably set in motion those things which will occur in order that your hopes may be fulfilled. You shall not hope in vain, but if you hope without depth, without heart, then what you receive shall be shallow and unsatisfying. In this season upon your planet that you experience at this time, shall we say, your plant life has completed its hope. For each seed that lies within the deep and dark ground awaiting the biting frost is the hard shell of a living wish for life, for growth, for service.

That is the second thing that we would suggest that you would consider in relation to wishing. When you wish, hope, desire or seek there shall in natural patterns occur a season of incubation. You have planted the seed, you must now release that seeking to the hard frost of meditation and silence. In time, upon your planet, comes the spring and behold, the seed that has fallen in good ground blooms and flourishes and graces many by the richness of its flowering. So shall your desires come to you, bloom upon bloom, ramification upon ramification, until all is hundred-fold more than you could have wished.

This is the third thing we would suggest to you, that in many cases the seed that you have planted by desire, wishing, by hope blooms into a bloom that is not recognizable, for you as an entity will have been changed by that same silence. You will already have became transformed and you will be seeking yet further. And when you find manifestations flowering about you, it may be most difficult to apprehend the personal nature of an impersonal event. And you say to yourself, can this be what I hoped for? Yes, my friends. Each thing that occurs is a flowering of what you hoped for. Each event has been incubated and has grown. Meanwhile, you yourself have grown beyond the person that you were when first you hoped.

We describe to you a difficult road, a sometimes confusing road, but it is the road of transformation and it shall, as you continue to discipline your desires, your wishes and your hopes for your future, begin to offer to you a great multitude of blessings, the flowering of many previous hopes and meditations. We ourselves hope to be of service to you. Our only purpose in speaking through instruments such as this one is that in some way we may aid you as you move through moonlit nights in your inner search, through the brightest noons in your outer search, through all conditions and all surprises. We are aware that each finds inspiration in a different manner. We can only hope that we can be of some small aid to each, for it is our way of learning and growing. As we are of service to you, so our hopes come into full power and our inspiration is a hundred-fold multiplied.

We would at this time wish to transfer to the one known as K. I am Hatonn.

(K channeling)

I am Hatonn. This instrument has been caught by surprise because she was sitting here enjoying what has been spoken already. However, as this instrument looks back on the desires of many years, this instrument is able to see the validity of the statements that have been made, and we would suggest further that as each of us goes into the new year, we might ask ourselves the question: What do we wish the end of the year to be like, or what do we wish the next several years to be, as you think of time. Because, indeed, we are planting as literally for our future, as we call it, as we know it, as literally as we plant the seed in the ground in the springtime. It is obvious as one views the world in which we live that some seeds have not brought the best results. Therefore, we will simply leave you this evening with this thought planted firmly in your mind for consideration. It has been a great pleasure to be with you, as always, and we leave you rejoicing in the love and the light of the infinite Creator. I am Hatonn.

(Jim channeling)

I am Latwii, and I greet you, my friends, in the love and the light of our infinite Creator. It is our privilege once again to be asked to join our vibrations with those of this group. We thank you for requesting our presence. We hope that our desire to be of service by attempting answers to your queries will bear the fruit which will be useful in your journey. May we therefore ask at this time for the first query.

C: Yes, Latwii, could you enlighten me as to what is the emotion of anger?

I am Latwii. To begin, may we suggest, my brother, that if one investigates that emotion called anger carefully, one will discover that it is what you might call the other side of the coin which is love. For if one attempts to love, one attempts to give freely of the self to another. Yet upon your planet this concept finds few pure expressions. The concept of love has become mixed, shall we say, with your concepts of trade and barter. Conditions have been put upon this concept so that when one gives of the self, gives of the feelings and the emotions of the heart of the being, quite often it is expected by such an one that the one receiving the love must also in some like manner return it. Thus, the love is not given freely. When this perception persists within the being of one loving—that return must be made, that return is not being made—there frequently begins the growth of that emotion which becomes the anger. This feeling of anger is a distortion of the love which has not been reciprocated. The anger grows as the entity feels it has been, shall we say, shortchanged or betrayed. Thus, if you will look to the heart of anger you will find some distortion that will lead you to the heart of love.

May we answer you further, my brother?

C: Yes. I'm asking these questions because I'm having an extremely difficult time at the present of dealing with anger, and earlier today I had a release of this emotion, and afterwards, looking backwards, I could not see myself during the release, and those around me, including my young baby, did not seem to even recognize me when I was in that state. Is there something else taking control when one's frustrations are suddenly released?

I am Latwii, and am aware of your query, my brother. Though it is possible that entities of an elemental or even a negative nature might utilize such instances to reinforce the concept of separation which anger demonstrates, it is most usually the case that just as the expression of love in its pure form has been distorted and blocked, thus causing the anger, so also has the expression of anger been blocked for a portion of what you call time. This causes within the entity so blocking the anger a buildup which might be likened unto the iceberg, where only the tip is apparent and the small trigger is all that is necessary for the remainder to come to the fore and for the entity expressing the anger that has been built up and blocked to appear as another entity. If this anger and its blockage, the love and its blockage are examined, the entity will find within this situation the great opportunity for experiencing and expressing love in its pure form. For when the anger finally comes boiling out, then the situation is such that it is most difficult to ignore further and the reconciliation can begin and this path may then lead to the heart of love.

May we answer you further, my brother?

C: Yes. I have an extremely difficult time dealing with frustrations as they occur and keep many things bottled tightly within me. It is very rare that I am able to open myself to others and release the anger before it gets to a point where I simply blow. I don't ask for specifics, but would appreciate it if you would speak to me on how one might release one's anger before it builds to a point where one blows.

I am Latwii. My brother, may we suggest that you observe the garden in the spring. As the seeds have been sown and sprout, so also sprout those seeds not intended, the weeds. And when this garden is ignored day after day, the weeds became strong in growth, and begin to overtake the seeds that were intended to be the garden. As you move through your illusion, take time each day in your meditative state to examine the catalysts which you experienced each day. Where you find anger, it is not necessary that it be expressed towards the entity in your physical illusion for the catalyst to work and teach you the lesson that you desire. You may instead experience that anger within meditation, and allow that anger to build until it does overwhelm your senses as has occurred this day. Then see within your mind the balance to the anger. For but a moment visualize the unconditional love. Then allow your inner senses to move from the overwhelming anger by their own energy towards the love. Allow this to occur until you feel love in the same proportion that you felt anger. Then see yourself as having two means for the Creator to know Itself within your being, and feel then the acceptance of yourself for yourself while expressing both anger and love.

If you would look at your life and your lessons each day in this manner in meditation, you will be accomplishing the same as the gardener who pulls the weeds each day so that the fruit of the garden may have a chance for harvest.

May we answer you further, my brother?

C: No, thank you. You've been of great help to me.

I am Latwii. We are most grateful to you, my brother, for allowing us this service. May we ask for another query at this time?

M: I have one, and it's about as unimportant as C's was profound. And it's really none of my business, but I would like to know, if you feel it's proper, if you would tell me what kind of bodies you have in the fifth dimension, and what kind you had in the fourth dimension, and do you have two or more sexes? It's really none of my business, so if you feel I shouldn't know, you don't have to answer me.

I am Latwii, and do not blush at such a query. We of Latwii inhabit the density of five. That is the density of light, the seeking of wisdom. In our particular density our progress upon the evolutionary path now allows us to become more closely aligned with that known as light, for we desire and seek the light. Therefore, we do not only know the light, but we become it, which means that in relation to the physical we may shape our vehicle according to our desires.

Therefore, during those few experiences upon your planet where the appearance of a being of light has been requested with the proper purity—and such occurrences have been recorded throughout your history—an entity of the fifth density may appear in whatever form is best understood by those so requesting the appearance. Most usually this form is as your own for obvious reasons. The entities inhabiting the density of love, the fourth dimension, have a physical vehicle which corresponds to the physical vehicle which was the second-density ancestor or parent, shall we say, [of] your own vehicle, for example, having been derived from the higher ape family. The density of six, that is, of singleness, of unity, the balance between love and wisdom, may also form itself as it chooses, and each of these densities includes the concept of polarity so that the sexual union, in forms quite different from your own sexual union, may be experienced.

Beyond the density of unity there is no longer the need to recycle the physical vehicle. Therefore there is no …

(Side one of tape ends.)

(Jim channeling)

I am Latwii, and am again with this instrument. May we ask for another query at this time?

K: Yes, Latwii, and I'm going to have trouble putting my thoughts into words, but I'm going to take a stab at it. As I indicated here a time or two, I've spent my life trying to get some sense out of the meaning of life, and in my early days I couldn't see very much sense to it. And it seems to me that since the early sixties a—literally a barrage of light or information has been given to us. That at least life makes more sense to me, and the purpose for being on this planet has become clearer.

Now, my first question is, am I alone, is this just my assessment of what has happened over fifteen years or has this happened generally to the people, say, in our country?

I am Latwii, and am aware of your query, my sister. As the, as you have called it, graduation or harvest draws nigh, the seeking of the peoples of your planet becomes more and more intense due to there being in motion the activity which this group has became aware of as the seniority of incarnation by progression. This is to say that those now incarnate on your planet are those whose previous incarnations have gleaned the lessons desired efficiently enough that they have the greatest chance to achieve the harvest with one remaining incarnation, or in some cases, two.

Therefore, as those with the greatest opportunity for harvest incarnate, the calling for the lessons of love and assistance in learning them increases. These callings are answered in many ways. One manner of answer is the incarnation of those known to this group as wanderers in waves or in groups. This began in earnest with the birthing of the concept of freedom which was born at approximately the same time in its intenser form as was this country some two hundred of your years ago. There have been various events which have been prominent in allowing further waves or groups of wanderers to incarnate. The second of what you call world wars was most important in this regard, for the release of that energy known as nuclear was of such a profound nature that a great wave of wanderers incarnated at the cessation of that conflict. These wanderers then begin to reach what your peoples call their maturity during the period you have referred to as the 1960s and this flash of light, shall we say, took many forms, yet was felt around your planet.

May we respond further?

K: Yes. Has this flash of light, so to speak, that I certainly am aware of—I'm sure that many others are also—has this occurred, say, in the third world and in Asia, or has it become more evident just in the western world, or say, in our country?

I am Latwii. My sister, we find that though your nation is quite unique in many respects, it being what has been referred to as the melting pot of your global populations, that it is not alone in experiencing the effects of this flash of light, as we have called it. The entire planet has become aware of the more intense seeking for love and light and more aware of the response to this calling, this seeking. The response and awareness has not manifested in the same manner in each region of your planet. Many of the nations which you have described as the third world nations have experienced much greater trauma. The traumas have taken the forms of wars, starvation, disease and displacement of populations. Upon your planet these are seen as great tragedies. Yet, my friends, if you shall put yourself in the place of such an entity experiencing any of these phenomena you will find great opportunity for learning the lessons of love in a very short period of what you call time.

May we answer you further, my sister?

K: No. I believe I understand what you're saying. Right now that's the only question I have.

I am Latwii. Is there another query at this time?

M: Yes, I would like to know, when a person is an alcoholic, do they choose to be that before they are born, or is it something that happens after they're born?

I am Latwii. Before the incarnation the entity, often with the help of what you may call guides or angelic presences, sets out the lessons which it desires to learn in the incarnation which approaches. In some cases it might be that a certain means of learning the lesson is set in motion. In many cases the entity will allow a variety of means to be held in reserve, shall we say. These various means of learning the lessons, which always relate to love in your density, are then activated as necessary by the deeper portions of the unconscious mind, most usually the higher self, so that the entity might learn those lessons which it desired. The means of learning which you have referred to as alcoholism may be one of many set aside or put in reserve, shall we say, and activated only when other means have not proven efficient. In our previous response we noted the great efficiency of trauma in teaching the lessons of love. For some entities the lessons must be more intense according to their own choices. For others the lessons may be learned in some areas with less of what you may call trauma.

May we answer you further, my sister?

M: Well, if they recover and give up alcoholism, is that necessarily an asset in their journey?

I am Latwii, and am aware of your query, my sister. It cannot be said with certainty that the response to, in this case, the alcoholism can be seen as efficient or less efficient. For one entity to continue in the state of the alcoholic might be the most efficient of continuing to learn the lessons of love. For another entity, to refrain from that state of the drinking and drunken being might be the most efficient way to learn the lesson of love. It cannot be said with certainty how one particular entity best learns the lessons which it has set before it. Only after the incarnation when the review has been completed may the entity see the efficiency of the learning of the lessons.

May we answer you further, my sister?

M: Well, do some people then feel that their incarnation after they have reviewed it was not successful, and some people feel it was very successful if the degree is there of success?

I am Latwii. This, in general, my sister, is correct, for each of you moves within an illusion, within a forgetting. You move within a darkness. Though your days be brightly lit, still, as you seek within your being for the truth, you seek in moonlight, for it is not clear to those who have forgotten that each is the Creator that such is the case. And as you move through your illusion you carry the small candle of your consciousness with you to dimly light your way. Only after your incarnation has been completed does the love and light of the one Creator which exists at the heart of your being shine clearly over the pages of your life so that you may then see the efficiency with which the lessons were learned, and might then see the lessons which need the learning in the next incarnation.

May we answer you further, my sister?

M: No. I think that's all I can take at this time.

I am Latwii. We hope we have not given you indigestion.

M: Thank you, Latwii.

We are most grateful to you, my sister. Is there another query at this time?

C: Yes. It concerns lessons, and goes directly back to my questions earlier. There are times when usually by basis of us going through them beforehand we can see where a lesson is being presented to another, and there are times when we tend to learn the lessons for the other instead of stepping back and letting them experience, learn for themselves. How does one know—what can one do to keep from interfering with another's lesson even though one may really want to jump in there and do it for them?

I am Latwii, and am aware of your query, my brother. May we first begin by saying that there are no mistakes within your learning. It is also to be noted that it is not possible to directly learn another's lesson for that entity. What occurs in your daily round of activities is a natural progression of interaction which allows the opportunities to be presented to each entity to learn those lessons that are desired. You may feel that you interfere with another. Yet, if you will observe the so-called interference you will see the opportunity to learn a lesson being presented.

Do you wish in this instance, may we hypothetically query, therefore to impose yourself upon another? If this is not your desire, how then do you balance the actual or supposed imposition? By removing the self. So, you see, what you might see in one instance as the interference with another's learning is simply your own learning seen from another perspective. Whatever your experiences within your illusion, the opportunity to learn the lessons you desire is always available. You cannot make mistakes. You may learn more quickly or more slowly, more efficiently or less. Yet, always do you learn the lessons you desire and always are those about you offered the identical opportunity.

May we answer you further, my brother?

C: That's a big help. It's also a load off. This is a situation that seems to occur regularly, and I know that somewhere along the line a particular guide has a hand in it which I thank you for. But there are times when you refuse to give something, whether of yourself or material, and you immediately turn around and it's taken from you in one form or another. And I've always found it's a very awakening type of occurrence. A guy I will refer to as George, I've known him for a long time, seems to not let me get too astray with him. But is that a reciprocal action, is that a common occurrence when one really sort of blocks out a lesson?

I am Latwii, and am aware of your query, my brother. In general, this is correct. As one refuses to give in certain areas, then one is, in truth, refusing to give to the self, for are not all one? To bring this point more clearly home, the entity often asks on the subconscious level to know more clearly the truth of this unity. In such cases there are those presences which you have described which aid the entity by seeing to it that a certain thing which has not been given suddenly disappears within the life of the one refusing its gift to another. This allows the entity to discover that the action of refusing to give to another is the self refusing to give to the self. For whatever action you experience in relation to another is most clearly seen as your relationship to yourself.

Therefore, as you love others, the love for the self grows. As you feel anger towards others, the anger for the self grows. This is the way of the creation, for the Creator must learn from Itself. And you are the Creator which learns from yourself, whether it be that self encased by your physical vehicle or any other self with which you come in contact.

May we answer you further, my brother?

C: No, thank you very much.

We thank you. Is there another query at this time?

K: Yes. I have one more that seems appropriate just at this point. I don't want to tire the instrument so it need not be a complicated answer if the instrument is tiring. As I indicated, in the last two or three days I've been reading the book *Eagle's Nest*, and one of the goals of the warrior, which I perceive as a disciple, is the detachment. And Buddha talked about detachment as being a goal to be desired. Would you say something about the meaning of detachment and how it applies to us?

I am Latwii, and am aware of your query, my sister. Each of you, as we have said, moves within an illusion. The veil of forgetting is drawn so that it is not possible for a clear perception of the nature of your unity with all things to be known to you. Therefore, you learn through being attached, shall we say. You learn by desiring, by sowing the seeds of wishes. Do you then draw unto yourself those events to fulfill the wishes? By observing your response to such events, your emotions may be discovered to be positive or negative, and by achieving the balance within the self of each emotional response, the entity becomes what is called balanced or regularized according to the expression of each energy center or chakra. This then allows the entity to experience what various of your religious cultures have called the non-attached state of being. We might refer to this more clearly as a finely tuned type of compassion so that whatever catalyst the entity encounters, the entity is aware that it is seeing the Creator experiencing Itself. And the entity's response is love, compassion and understanding. This is the balance which has been spoken of by the description of detachment.

May we answer you further, my sister?

K: No. I believe that's okay for the moment. I'll have to think about that. Thank you.

I am Latwii. We thank you, my sister. Is there another query at this time?

L: Yes, on this planet prior to the birth of Christ a religion on philosophy was founded by an entity named Zoroaster in Persia. This religious philosophy was fairly rapidly assimilated into Islam and no longer exists. What was the mission of the entity we call Zoroaster and what was his polarity?

I am Latwii, and am aware of your query, my brother. As each entity on your planet attempts to do, this entity attempted to serve the one Creator by expressing its perception of how the path of evolution might most efficiently be traveled. The precepts and tenets which it put forth during its incarnation were basically of the positive nature, yet as with all such religions or mystic traditions the polarity was not pure. For it is, as we have said many times, an illusion within which you move, and you seek for the truth in moonlight. And in moonlight that which is true can be dimly revealed, yet that same moonlight can also deceive. The one you refer to had some distortions towards the negative which are apparent to those aware of the concept of polarity who take the time to study these teachings.

May we answer you further, my brother?

L: Yes, I'm interested in where this entity is now. Is he incarnate on this planet or working with anyone incarnate on this planet or some world altogether different?

I am Latwii. We find that this entity has continued its path of evolution upon this sphere and resides as a third-density entity continuing to learn the ways of love.

May we answer you further, my brother?

L: So, I understand that as the entity is physically incarnate on this planet?

I am Latwii. This is correct. May we answer you further?

L: No, thank you.

I am Latwii. We thank you. Is there another query at this time?

K: Well, yes. Is his influence positive, or is it polarized now in the positive or is he still mixed?

I am Latwii. Though this entity, as most upon your planet, continues the efforts towards positive polarization, there is, of course, the mixture, for within your density the lessons are seldom learned with complete efficiency.

May we answer you further, my sister?

K: No, thank you.

I am Latwii. We thank you. Is there another query at this time?

A: Yes, Latwii. Is there any underlying reason that certain third-density entities choose prior to incarnation to experience ongoing severe trauma for lessons rather than milder degrees or a specific length of time that might be traumatic? Do you understand what I'm asking?

I am Latwii, and we believe that we perceive the heart of your query. The amount of what is called trauma can be and is in most cases chosen by each entity previous to the incarnation according to the, shall we say, number or intensity of lessons the entity desires to learn. This may be likened unto the student taking many classes or many hours of credit which weigh heavily then upon the allotted span of time. The entity could take fewer lessons and experience less trauma, yet not learn the lessons which would allow the graduation. Since what you call time grows short upon your sphere for the learning of the lessons within this great cycle, many entities therefore attempt great quantities of learning in a short period of what you call time. This brings the trauma, and the trauma offers the opportunity to learn love.

May we answer you further, my sister?

A: No, thank you. You answered very well. Thank you.

I am Latwii. We thank you, my sister. Is there another query at this time?

J: Yes. In the same way that hope and desire fulfill themselves in actuality, does fear outline the nature of the developing future? I mean, does what we fear come to pass also?

I am Latwii, and am aware of your query, my sister. We may describe fear as a negative hope, which is to say that it too shall come to pass. For the balance [of] the desire of not experiencing is the desire to experience. Where you have fear on the conscious level it is often the case that the opposite, or the desire, is experienced upon the subconscious level. In such a situation the entity with the fear shall draw unto itself that which it fears in some form so that it might balance that fear with the acceptance of what was feared. Since all is one, there is, in truth, no need to fear any thing, for all things are the Creator and all things are the self as the Creator, thus fear also is a seed which allows this fruit to be born.

May we answer you further, my sister?

J: Yes, I have another question. Could you talk about right and left brain function and activity and how—and whether it is possible to consciously balance right and left brain activity?

I am Latwii, and am aware of your query, my sister. Within most of your peoples' physical brains, there is the division between what might be seen as the active and receptive modes of perception. The right portion of most entities' brains is that portion which is logical, rational, verbal and moving in spatial fashions, able to analyze and utilize the words in a logical fashion. Within most entities' left portion of the brain is the portion which may be seen as the receptive.

We correct this instrument. Our previous description should be associated with the left brain function, the rational. To continue. The right brain, therefore, may be seen as the intuitive, somewhat illogical, that which is musical or artistic, and for an entity to attempt the balancing or equal activation of these brain functions is the process of what we have previously called the use of catalyst or the balancing. To achieve this end, it is necessary only to observe the daily activities, the various distortions, biases, preferences and tendencies which are already in motion within the life stream. Then, in meditation the entity might magnify such distortions or biases until they are overwhelming to the senses. Then by imaging for the moment the opposite, and allowing the natural progression of conscious movement to overwhelm the senses in the polar opposite, the entity experiences within the being the balancing of both tendencies and therefore brain functions as well.

We would suggest to each entity so visualizing this process that the great unconscious which is the storehouse of each entity's beingness might be seen as the analog to the left—we correct this instrument—to the right brain function of the intuitive senses. The conscious mind therefore is the analog to the left brain function.

May we answer you further, my sister?

J: I'm kind of mixed up on left and right, but I'll straighten that out later. Could you talk just a little bit about the nature of ego?

I am Latwii …

(Side two of tape ends.)

(Jim channeling)

I am Latwii, and am once again with this instrument. To answer the last query, the instrument is suffering some fatigue, and if more queries are desired after another query or two, we would suggest the transfer of this contact.

To continue our response to the concept of the ego. We find that the great use and misuse of this term renders it quite ineffectual as a useful designation of any portion of the entity's being. It is frequently seen as a portion of the self which must be removed, this perception associated with those of the Eastern religious philosophy. The ego is also seen by others, those described as the Scientologists and those who study the psyche of your peoples, as the self which acts, that is to say, the conscious being. Others see the ego as the, shall we say, show-off or arrogant portion of the self. This is a description which is common to the lay person of your culture. Therefore, the term itself has suffered such distortion that we cannot use it with efficiency in describing the activities or perceptions of your peoples.

May we answer you further, my sister?

J: Thank you, no. That is fine.

I am Latwii. We thank you. Through this instrument we may attempt one further query before transferring the contact.

Carla: Well, what would you call it, if there is an it? Ego, I mean. You just wiped it out, but there's something there. Is there an undistorted way of putting it? Could you comment on that?

I am Latwii. We thank you, my sister, for clarifying your query. We shall attempt a response by suggesting that the clearest perception of that known as the ego may be seen by observing portions of the system of energy centers which each possesses. The orange ray typifies the expression of the self in relation to the self and to another. The relationship of power of self over another is most significant here. In the yellow-ray energy center the expression of the self as a portion of a group which may express power over another group is significant in relationship to the nebulous term of "ego." In the blue-ray energy center the concept of communication with other selves by the self is significant in describing a portion of the ego's supposed function. This is not satisfactory as a means of describing that commonly referred to as the ego, yet is as close as we can come. But we feel we have fallen short by at least a country mile.

May we attempt a further response, my sister?

Carla: Only by my guessing that what you're trying to say is, there is nothing intrinsically right or wrong with the conscious portion of the self in its relationships to others, but only in the misuse of power. Would you say that that's sort of what you're aiming at?

I am Latwii. We thank you, my sister, for your query and continued clarification. We would go one step further in suggesting not only is there nothing right or wrong, as you have called it, with the conscious self or ego, but there is nothing right or wrong in any aspect of your illusion, for all is one.

May we ask if this is sufficient response to your query?

Carla: You may. Thank you very much, Latwii. That's just fine.

I am Latwii. We thank you, my sister.

Carla: Why don't you let this poor boy rest?

I am Latwii, and shall attempt that feat. If the one known as L would be agreeable, we would at this time attempt to transfer our contact. I am Latwii.

(L channeling)

I am Latwii. I am now with this instrument. We ask a moment's grace to make ourselves at home, so to speak. I am Latwii, and I greet you in the love and the light of the infinite Creator, and now that we have things a bit more shipshape, we are prepared to continue our efforts to respond to your queries. Are there any queries?

Carla: I'd like to ask first if this would be a good time to retune the group. It's been over an hour and a half since we began, and I'm wondering if we should get up and sit down and retune?

I am Latwii. In examining the fluctuating state of attunement in the group, we are inclined to agree with the recommendation as presented, although would be willing to continue in the present capacity if the reattunement process would overtax the patience of those who have developed itchy feet. We would suggest, therefore, that a brief recess of several minutes be allowed at this moment that the necessary flight to plumbing facilities be allowed as well as the opportunity to reinvigorate those areas of your physical vehicles which have had the bodily fluids compressed from their tissues for an extended period. If this is acceptable to those present, we would suggest that those not desiring to flee the room remain within its confines in the relative darkness now present.

K: I have a suggestion, Latwii. We might save time, if anybody wants. I have exhausted my poor little …

M: I have, too.

K: … poor little brain tonight. I have no more questions. And maybe we might save everybody—if there are no more questions we might verbalize that.

I am Latwii. Are there any further questions?

(No further queries.)

I am Latwii. If there is a statement to be made, we shall pause.

Carla: I think you're done.

[I am Latwii.] We think so, too.

K: We want to thank Latwii tonight. We've asked him a lot of questions. We've all got a lot to think about.

I am Latwii. My sister, as always, we are grateful for the opportunity to extend our meager efforts and learning to those brothers and sisters who desire to share what little we have to offer. And for these opportunities we are sincerely grateful. As there are no more questions and in that your queries and one instrument have been simultaneously exhausted, we shall take our leave as well. In the love and the light of the infinite Creator, my brothers and sisters …

(Tape ends.)

Thursday Meditation
January 13, 1983

(S channeling)

I am Hatonn, and am now with this instrument. We greet you, my brother and sisters, in the love and the light of the one infinite Creator. We are pleased to be called to this meeting this evening, my friends. Those within your circle have experienced our contact for quite a period of time, and have advanced well along the path of being a telepathic channel. We congratulate them heartily for the desire and the love that they have given to this service for others. The desire which is shown is indeed pleasurable for us to see. We appreciate the effort, but we feel that there may be only a little confidence lacking. Therefore, my brother and sisters, we at this time would like to share this small story with you, and as has been done in the past, go from instrument to instrument, as we feel this is the best way of upping the confidence of each instrument.

There was a time in your past, my friends, that for many, many of your years the people upon your planet were seeking, looking, striving. But my friends, they knew not of what they were looking. There seemed to be an ever-moving mirage in front of them. They would go one step, and that for which they were seeking, my friends, would seem to move three or four more in front of them. So, at one point, many of these people decided consciously to forget the mirage that never seemed to be within the grasp of actually holding in the hand. They saw more and more only what was a step in front of them, that they could pick up and hold to themselves and possess. This seemed like reality. This seemed to have some consequence within themselves, something with meaning, something they could physically see and have.

So, as time progressed, and as more and more of the peoples saw that there was an immediate pleasure in possessing things of their illusion, the mirage seemed to be forgotten.

We would like at this time to transfer this contact. I am Hatonn.

(A channeling)

I am Hatonn. And over the years as generations passed, the mirage was forgotten by many. A few spoke of it to their children, but there was uncertainty in their words, for the mirage was not something easily described with the words that could describe the food that was eaten, or the ground that was walked on. The children as they were told of the mirage would wonder of what it was, and once again footsteps started towards the mirage, and once again the mirage would take its three steps back. As the children grew older, many of them also started taking what was in reach, what could be seen and touched, and called this what was real, while a handful continued to seek for what they were not sure of, for the mirage which was in front of them, which they did not understand but wished to know.

There was no sure path ahead of them, no line which to follow, and the path was always laden with the temptations of something that could be held, touched and seen, smelled. But their desire was so strong to learn, to seek out more, that they were able to overcome the temptations, and not feel satisfied by them. Along the pathway these few individuals found that there were other similar people seeking the same mirage. A few of their elders also continued on, and they saw that a few children were also starting out on the path. There was some comfort in seeing others along the pathway, and this too almost caused them to stop seeking, to stop in the pathway with others, and to find the comfort from that as those before found comfort in the tangible objects that they owned.

And we would like to now transfer this contact. I am Hatonn.

(Jim channeling)

The journey which these people had long undertaken was one which had gained somewhat of a mysterious air among the few who still continued its path. Through there was some consolation to those pilgrims seeking the ever-changing mirage, this consolation was felt only by those few who undertook the arduous and seemingly profitless journey. By now most of the peoples had long forgotten that the possibility of such a journey existed. The illusion which had from time to time entranced the peoples had by now become quite heavy upon the shoulders of their consciousness, and their attention was weighted down with the necessity of day-to-day survival, and the accomplishing of those tasks which though as mundane and repetitive as could be imagined, yet were the focus for most in this culture.

There was from time to time the speaking that was heard from solitary voices within these peoples, which reminded the people that there was something beyond the illusion which was not mundane, nor was it boring, nor did it weigh heavily upon the existence and the attention and determination to live. The speaking often mentioned the illusive quality of the search, and did nothing to encourage the perception that the journey towards this mirage was easy. Therefore, few among the peoples listened, for already it was felt and generally accepted that life as it was was difficult enough. Why undertake yet more difficulty for that which could not be touched, could not be exhibited for others to see once it had been gained?

We shall now transfer this contact.

(Carla channeling)

I am Hatonn. And though all that is clay rebelled against considering that which was invisible, there came a time when clay mixed with the mirage, as that which is followed so long must most certainly take. And there was that being which was both clay and unearthly. The entity began to teach, and those things that he said seemed to move in and out of the world of clay. And as he said those things, he would extend a hand and a healing would occur, for part of the mirage was hope. And as he taught again, the heavens would open, and those about him would see the glory of the creation. This glory was part of the mirage. And yet again he would speak, and all that seemed broken in the beliefs of the past seemed to be made whole once again. For reconciliation is a part of the mirage. And again as he would speak, someone would spitefully scorn him and he would show love. For love above all is part and parcel of the mirage. And ultimately, when all the signs and wonders had been seen and news ran from mouth to mouth, this entity of clay and mirage was killed by those who feared him. And darkness, the darkness of clay, came to this people. And yet as they felt forsaken, so did a great light shine upon them and they saw the manifestation of the mirage personified and gone. Once again the people were left with a choice between that which could be seen to value and that which cannot be seen, but can be felt to value. However, the manifestation of the dream, having once been seen, was enough to instill within the hearts of those who sought the mirage, generation upon generation, hope, reconciliation, love and light.

We shall transfer.

(S channeling)

I am Hatonn. The mirage which you seek, my friends, is ever there. And if you would but look within the self you would find the mirage. You will find the love of one and all that is one throughout the creation.

I am Hatonn. We leave you now in love and in light. Adonai, my friends. Adonai vasu borragus.

Sunday Meditation
January 16, 1983

(M channeling)

I am Hatonn. I am now with this instrument. It may seem this instrument is talking about something that happened this evening, but she isn't. What happened this evening she thinks is funny, but the topic she is going to talk about is anger. One of your members asked about anger at your meeting, and I would like to discuss it. There are many types of angers. Sometimes it is very good. In an emergency, if you need to protect yourself, anger is very helpful. Even in an emergency when you have to do something. If you expect company and you have to get ready, then knowing the company coming at the last minute sometimes gives you the energy to accomplish what you need to accomplish. But I would like to talk a little about another type of anger. Some people build tension within them, but yet the anger is not productive. Sometimes it is the release of tension. If one is angry about insignificant things oftentimes it is really a form of letting off steam and this can be very dangerous. If you can filter this tension through another entity, you can distill some of this tension. There are other people that can be helpful—your so-called religious priests and preachers, rabbis. You even have people, counselors who help release tension. You even have marriage counselors that release tension. Some very wonderful people are not able to accomplish their desires because of this inner tension and they should make some effort to get relief.

There are many types of anger. Sometimes it is caused by sickness. Sometimes it is caused because you're tired. Sometimes it is caused because you are trying to control your other selves. There are many forms of anger and I hope some of these may be applicable to your discussion of anger.

I am Hatonn. I leave this instrument.

(C channeling)

I am Hatonn, and am now with this instrument. We greet you again in the love and light. Friends, in your day-to-day lives you each face many varying situations from moment to moment. Each is in itself a lesson, one that is designed to aid you in your journey through this illusion. Each lesson will be taken and learned from or put aside, ignored. But you cannot ignore them for long. In each entity's incarnation, those lessons ignored shall make the cycle and return, strengthened anew, tougher than before. Your peoples as they grow stronger may be able to handle the tougher lessons, but there are those who find that the tougher lessons begin to bury them.

These times, my friends, many are the individuals who swing on the pendulum of emotion. Some may withdraw deep within themselves. They may experience what you call depressions, the uselessness in their inabilities that they perceive. Some may choose to vent their frustrations and inabilities in an angry rage, taking out their perceived inabilities on others and themselves.

My friends, your emotions are indeed an extremely useful tool you have in your growth, but as they are useful, so may they harm. When either extreme of emotion is reached, that entity suffers. The entities around him or her may also suffer. They can mislead and block growth. Each in their illusion will experience the swing of the pendulum, but the pendulum need not stick on either. Acceptance of each of life's situations as lessons will aid each in finding a more useful path through the lessons of this experience. We of Hatonn wish to say again that at any time you feel the need, we will be with you when you ask [us] to aid you in your meditations in times that are good for you and those that seem too much. My friends, take each moment for what it is worth. Learn from it.

I am Hatonn, and would at this time transfer this contact.

(L channeling)

I am Hatonn. I am now with this instrument. My friends, the illusion within which you exist is a complex one. The tools which you must master to attain the development you seek are tools of unique intricacy and require an apprenticeship far beyond that of the various trade—correction—trades which many within your illusion seek to learn as a method of employment. For the tools of the physical realm, being instruments for the manipulation of that which is already created, have both form and function that remains relatively constant within your illusion. The tools with which your real lessons are experienced, however, are of a more ethereal nature in that each situation, each lesson that you encounter requires that the scholar perceive the lesson and, as a master craftsman, carefully forge and hone those tools with which one seeks to acquire attainment.

The emotions that you experience within your illusion are a small portion of the vast supply of such tools available to those who seek. They may indeed be likened to a set of chisels or punches that are uniquely appropriate each in its own manner for a specific opportunity. The emotion—anger, for example—may be likened to [a] broad cold chisel which may be used in conjunction with the hammering of one's personal will or intention to produce a seam or opening within the illusion of an other self in perceiving beyond the particular illusion which they have established at a given time. Obviously the appropriate tool for a specific task is the—correction—is determined only through meditation and careful selection. For the self who desires to employ such a tool must first acquire the mastery of the tools lest in its usage damage be the result. The mastery of one's emotions, therefore, is recommended for those who would seek the path of service to others. For the carpenter cannot accomplish his constructive tasks if he is at the beck and call of the various tools which he supposedly employs.

My friends, the analogies we use are often difficult to apply when one seeks to extend their meaning beyond that which is verbally expressed by the instruments who serve us so well because of the difficulty in translating our concepts into the symbols you refer to as speech. Yet, my friends, the translation and the illumination which may be sought as one meditates upon our feeble efforts at analogy may be found within the purity of one's own heart. For it is through love of one's other selves your selfless acts are motivated and it is through this motivation, this desire to serve, that the Creator extends His touch to His own tools, His children who desire to serve.

My friends, the nail which binds the boards together is a tool which serves. So, also is the hammer which drives the nail and the hand which swings the hammer. The chain of service extends in an unbroken line to the original creative Force. Therefore, my friends, be aware that when one acts in accordance with this creative force, one may be assured of the correctness of one's efforts toward service through the peace one experiences as a tool properly in service.

At this time we will relinquish our use of this instrument that our brothers and sisters of Laitos may perform their service of extending their vibration to those who would deepen their meditative state. I am known to you as Hatonn.

(L channeling)

I am Hatonn. I am again with this instrument. At this time, my brothers and sisters, we will be of most service by bidding you farewell that our brothers and sisters of Latwii might perform their own special act of service for those present. Adonai, my brothers and sisters. I am known to you as Hatonn.

(L channeling)

I am Latwii, and I greet you all in the love and light of the infinite Creator, and would like to express our appreciation at being invited to be of service to those present in our small way. At this time are there any questions that we might attempt to answer?

Carla: Latwii, when Nona comes through and begins a healing by the vibrations that are given, does that continue then until the situation is finished in accordance with the will of the Creator?

I am Latwii. My sister, first it is necessary to understand that the will of the Creator within a specific instance of healing versus non-healing resides largely in the will of the individual who is subjected to the healing force. If the individual desires healing and is receptive to a continuation, the vibration is encouraged and one might say that the entity, whether consciously or not, makes the Nona vibration a part of the individual entity's own vibration, in effect attempting to adopt that vibration so as to maintain the healing force. However, if the entity is resistant to changing the condition which created the physical imbalance, we are without doubt that our brothers and sisters of Nona would be reluctant to force the issue, so to speak.

May we answer you further?

Carla: No, I knew that. I was just testing you, Latwii.

I am Latwii, and, my sister, we are grateful for the opportunity to pass the test. However, we might suggest that a more rigid test be applied in that we are to some extent possessed of the answer book to the test which you apply.

May we answer you further?

Carla: No, thank you, Latwii.

Is there another question?

M: Latwii, if we have no more questions could we get Hatonn back?

I am Latwii. My sister, we would hazard the assumption that our brothers and sisters of Hatonn rarely leave the presence of those here. We are aware that our brothers and sisters of Hatonn have no pressing desire to communicate another of their ponderous lectures. However, they are always within earshot, so to speak, of those who seek their vibrations or guidance.

May we answer you further?

M: Does that mean Hatonn will come back?

Carla: Yes or no, L?

I am Latwii. My sister, we ask that you bear with us in that it is our desire to communicate accurately specific information. Our brothers and sisters of Hatonn are present at this moment. Our brothers and sisters of Hatonn, further, have nothing which they desire to communicate to this group at this particular moment. However, our brothers and sisters of Hatonn are always listening should one desire to communicate to them. If it is your desire to communicate a message to our brothers and sisters of Hatonn at this moment, we most earnestly assure you they are indeed listening.

May we answer you further?

M: I felt they wanted to speak through some of these instruments that were cut off. K, for instance. I have a feeling that Hatonn wanted to speak through K, S—different ones of them. Nobody has any questions for Latwii.

I am Latwii. We are increasingly aware there are no further questions, and will bid our friends adieu momentarily and vacate the stage, so to speak, that our brothers and sisters of Hatonn may return to offer whatever extemporaneous comments they might elect to verbalize through whichever instruments indicate a strong desire to act in service in this manner for our brothers and sisters of Hatonn. Therefore, at this time, we shall [return] whence we came.

K: I really have nothing else to add.

(Carla channeling)

I am Oxal. I greet you, my friends, in the love and in the light of the one infinite Creator, a glorious central sun of the creation and all that therefrom has sprung, an endless and infinite beauty and love. As light we are drawn to light, and we come to this group. We thank you for requesting our presence. Before we would begin, we would address two minor subjects which may be of aid to two of those now physically present. Firstly to the one known as M.

The intention of any meeting of like-minded seekers is guided and formed by the desires of those present. That you felt a presence was certain. However, my sister, as you become more proficient in your tuning and your awareness of the varying presences, it is well to question each spirit and challenge each, and after assuring yourself of the Christ consciousness within each, discover then the called name of each spirit. We use this term advisedly, for there are great differences between those spirits of inner planes and those of what may be called outer plane, the difference being the difference between an individual often of great wisdom, love, light and knowledge, and a group, often vast, of individuals so like-minded that the group speaks with one name. We would suggest that in the context of challenging and determining each entity's identity, the concept of challenging the spirit be retained in full as it is as useful when dealing with societal complexes as it is when dealing with the denizens and masters of the inner planes.

Therefore, you were indeed sensitive enough to abstract from the noise of the metaphysical universe a signal. However, it was not that of Hatonn. Also, we would suggest that not all instruments must needs speak at each meeting. The needs of the group are served by the extremely fortunate circumstance of this group wherein the ability to serve as vocal instrument is widely cultivated among its members. Each piece of information, each emotional shading of wisdom or love has its own best instrument or instruments. Therefore, the picking and the choosing of the instruments is a great …

(Side one of tape ends.)

(Carla channeling)

… as well as the one known as A. We are not an easy channel, shall we say, to successively interpret. The narrowness of the band causes the fading away of the signal if the instrument is somewhat shy of the tuning necessary.

The second note is to the one known as R, who we greet and welcome to this group this evening. Due to this particular instrument's previous training, there is some slight possibility that a trance state might be that which overtakes the instrument without the desire being present [for] *(inaudible)*. This is at all cost to be discouraged, and it is suggested that the entity consciously close some of the receptive nature gained in the training in order that all may be clean, clear and simple within so that the vibrations which are within this dwelling have only positive and life-enhancing effects upon those sensitive to the vibrations and used to disciplines which sometimes, shall we say, branch off from the discipline of this endeavor which all of the circle seeks to continue this evening.

We would speak but briefly now through this instrument as the meeting grows somewhat long. However, there is a call for information which we are extremely grateful to have the opportunity for sharing. As we heed those words which have been spoken by our brothers and sisters of Hatonn and Latwii and Laitos, and as we observe the patterns of energy within this dwelling, we are aware that when speaking of the removal of the emotional distortion so that one may be of service to another, one may not expect of oneself the direct removal of anger by placing the angry self in meditation. This may seem, as this instrument would say, as the Catch-22. An angry self needs meditation, but cannot find it. A meditative self is not angry.

Therefore, we suggest the angry self step back from the entire observation of self, not in meditation, but prior to any attempt at alteration of the situation at meeting the catalyst at hand. This instrument, in her human opinion, would concentrate upon the role of other selves in aiding one who is angry and has experienced the joy of being of seeming aid when offering the peaceful self to the angered other self. However, may we suggest to you that our opinion differs. The only alterations that will remain part of the garment of the self are those alterations made within the self for the self. And in this context, we would remind you of a phrase from your holy work known as the Bible. The phrase is, "O pray for the peace of Jerusalem. They shall prosper that love thee."

My friends, when an angry person looks at the self, what does he see? Almost inevitably because of the strength of your illusion, he sees an imperfect and mistaken self. But where in this consideration of self is the primal perception of the one original Thought? Where, my friends, is the Creator which is perfect and full of light and love? If you look at the interior of your heart as a great land full of mysterious places, cities, countrysides, caves and grottos and fantastic creatures, then you may see one portion which is completely unchangeable. All else may come and go and be permutated as you transform yourself. But your holy city, that portion of yourself that is of the Creator and has never left the Creator, resides within that great land of beingness which is yourself. Swim the sea of consciousness until you come to your own Jerusalem, my angry ones, my discouraged ones, my despairing ones, my overjoyful ones, and find in sorrow and utter joy the peace of what is called in that phrase we have quoted, "Jerusalem." This is your true and happy home. Anger cannot touch it nor sadness or despair nor mania. This is yours. This is you. And your awareness of this portion of yourself will lead you, guide you, succor you, and heal you until you can bring yourself to bear upon yourself, until you can go into meditation knowing that the one resource without which you cannot endure is yours. O pray for the peace of Jerusalem, your Jerusalem, each of you.

We would condition those instruments of whom we have spoken in order that we may briefly speak through each before leaving this most kind and gracious light source. It is a great blessing to bathe ourselves in the circle of your love. We would now transfer. I am Oxal.

(A channeling)

I am Oxal, and we greet this light of your circle once again to speak a few words through this instrument so that she might become accustomed to our vibration. Indeed, it shall be brief, and you shall hear on *(inaudible)* message, and we shall now transfer and condition the other instruments. I am Oxal.

(Carla channeling)

I am Oxal. We thank each instrument which we have conditioned. We are attempting to make the one known as S more comfortable, and also the one known as A. We are most privileged to have been able to work with each instrument, and we shall be with you at any time which you may need our particular service. We cannot leave you, for we are part of the oneness. We cannot leave this density, for we wish to be of service. Each light that shines in darkness is a great service. We encourage each to perceive the light within and without each day. We shall leave this instrument, glorying in the love and the light of the one infinite Creator. Adonai, my friends. Adonai, adonai.

(C channeling)

I am Nona, and come once again to this group for there is indeed a great calling to aid those present and those here in spirit who wish to aid others with their physical and spiritual needs. We join with you in the sending of love and light.

(C channels beautiful chanting from Nona to the end of the meditation.) ❧

Sunday Meditation
January 23, 1983

(S channeling)

[I am Hatonn.] We greet you, my brothers and sisters, in the love and light of the one infinite Creator. We would like to express our appreciation and joy in being called among you. Our small and at times seemingly meaningless messages, however, we hope may be at some point in your lives in your illusion of some help. This evening we would like to tell of a small entity who in his life would at times jump from here to there with no direction in mind. He continuously sought for whatever materialistic things his life might offer in the way of joy and happiness. In this small entity's life he acquired many items, items that for a short while might bring happiness as they would intrigue the imagination for a short period of space and time and then would be laid aside to acquire another object.

This pattern was repeated for many, many years until the small entity became larger, and then once again in the much later years became bent with age. This entity sought many, many years for things of the illusion which he could hold, but, my friends, he did not contemplate the one small fact that this illusory thing that was called happiness was at all times within his reach and would not have been a passing matter if he had but looked within, if he had but taken but a few moments of each day to look within himself to contemplate the actions of that day, to see within himself the balance of the negative and the positive. This balance, my friends, this balancing of your mind, of the emotions which riddle your life, of the catalyst with which you have chosen to dealt, of the lessons you have chosen to learn, with this balancing, with acceptance of all things within, this, my friends, is where peace is to be found, not without, but from within. From the portion that is one with the Creator and if allowed to manifest itself within your life can bring about the desired balancing.

We feel at this time the desire to transfer this contact to another instrument. I am Hatonn.

(M channeling)

I am now with this instrument. I greet you with the love and the light of the infinite Creator. In your illusion there is much teaching. Some people have so much within them they find *(inaudible)*. If they can step out of themself for a short time each day and maybe see the humor in their lives, if they can laugh at themselves either alone or with a friend, some of their tension can be relieved. Laughter is a wonderful safety valve. If you can see the humor in what you say or do or what happens to your environment, you can relieve a lot of your tension. Try to find something humorous instead. If you cannot find anything humorous, at least step out of yourself and give the tension time to dissipate. See yourself from a distance, and your problems won't be as great.

Remember, you do not have to solve all your problems; you only have to live through them. You will make it to the end, one way or another. In the end you will find that a lot of the things that caused you so much worry really were insignificant. Step out of yourself and appreciate the things about you. If you cannot laugh, at least see beauty. Appreciate the sunrise. Appreciate the sunset. Appreciate your loved ones. If you cannot laugh, if you have not advanced to the stage of laughter, start with gratitude. And if you cannot be grateful, at least step out of yourself. Put some distance between you and your problems. Life is not as serious as some people make it. Get some pleasure out of living.

I am Hatonn. I leave this instrument.

(K channeling)

I am Hatonn, and again I greet you, my friends, in the love and the light of the infinite Creator. We would like to say a few words through this instrument about how to step out of yourselves. As you are aware, there is unity in the universe, and nothing is left to chance. Even though it may appear to you that everything is in chaos, this is not true, because there is a pattern and unity in the universe. At the cellular level all is one and all is known. Try to imagine yourself under a tree, and then imagine yourself part of the tree and the tree a part of you. And then imagine that as you enjoy the beauty and the shade of the tree, the tree also enjoys your presence. This kind of imagination can run rampant as we imagine ourselves merging with everything about us. We can furthermore imagine that everything about us rejoices in the infinite Creator, because indeed all are one. In the final analysis, all is love. We only see things as separate and at cross-purposes. It might even be helpful to imagine that you love your enemy, if you have one. This might take some doing sometimes, but to pretend as a small child pretends is indeed helpful. Before you go to sleep tonight try some exercise that would help you to feel that you were part of everything about you and that all is at peace, and that all are joyful because indeed the inner self does know.

It has been a pleasure to be with the group tonight. It has been a pleasure to serve you, as always. I leave you now in the love and light of the infinite Creator. I am Hatonn.

(Carla channeling)

I am Oxal, and I greet you, my friends, in the love and in the light of the infinite Creator. May the splendor of that light be known to you each day, for surely you are of the race of light and it is your birthright to know that light and that love. We thank this group for calling us this evening. We have not spoken overmuch with your group for some time and it is a privilege which we enjoy.

Stars look down upon you as you rest in sleep, and a deep and gentle rain falls, and in the middle of that slumber, one of your telephones awakens you with its insistent sound. One asks you to remove yourself from comfort, place yourself in the rain, and drive one of your vehicles some miles to where this one is stranded. This one is your sweetheart, your beloved, the sun of your waking hours, the dream on your sleep, and you do not feel the rain and the miles cannot go by quickly enough.

This one is an acquaintance, an annoyance, and it is all that you can do to refrain from saying "No."

You stand by the well in a hot and arid land and you hold a dipper of water, precious in a dry land. The well is deep and it costs great effort to get each drop of water from deep beneath the sandy ground. One comes to you travel-stained and weary and asks for water. This one is the Messiah and you gladly give what you have earned with such hardship.

This one is a stranger, whose looks are alien and whose ways are not your own, and you hand him an empty dipper and go away.

You get into a boat to cross a river. The water flows. The other side will calm your thoughts, rest upon the affairs of your world. The one who guides your boat is Gautama Buddha. And you gaze in wonder upon the water itself, the farther shore forgotten in the miracle of the present moment.

The one who guides your boat is a man with a stubbled beard, jersey clothes, and your gaze once again turns to the far shore.

It is an interesting illusion you live in, my friends. Whom do you see? To whom do you react? What is the nature of your brother, your sister, yourself? If you look upon each surface, you shall always find the mundane. If you find love, then you rush to acknowledge it. If you find the perfection of him at the well who can give you greater water than that of this illusion, you will give all that you have in order to associate with the giver of such great wealth. This incident was written in that book which you call the Bible, the one known as Jesus saying, "I have water. I am not thirsty. I can give you water that will allow you never to thirst again."

There are those who help you in your life, those who steer your boat, and you gaze at the shore, not at the one who plies the oars. But is that one not perfection? You know the name called Buddha. But what does this name represent? A man who has found the moment. It is so. Each of you can feel the greatest amount of desire for a sweetheart, for a teacher, for one who is enlightened, and yet all, beginning with yourself, have these aspects at the core of beingness that creates each entity. Whom do you wish to delete from those who are perfect? You cannot delete even one. Not even one who freezes this night, drunken and penniless. Not even one who fattens himself upon power in its dishonest use, not even one who has stolen all that he has, not even one who cannot recognize reality—not even yourself.

The night is full of stars, and we speak as if from a great distance from beyond those stars. We weave a web of inspiration, but we are fools and we speak to the foolish. For if we were truly wise, we would not be speaking. We would be existing in unity with all. This we are not doing. We are attempting to learn wisdom. And so we are aware. Are you? It is the attempt of a fool to see perfection in the illusion. Yet it is the responsibility of the seeker to be a fool. For those who are wise in your world will their wisdom and it shall be buried with their bones. There is no one, no entity at all that is not absolutely necessary for the wholeness of the universe. Each portion of the creation is utterly desirable. The next entity who seeks money from you upon the sidewalk is Buddha, Christ, your sweetheart. How fast will you run to aid him? What drink will you gain from him that will let you never thirst again? What priceless present moment can you find with a derelict?

I am Oxal. I leave you within the illusion, knowing that you are at least looking through the bars of this prison you have chosen. You have chosen this prison, this illusion just so that you yourself may find perfection, reality, the ideal that is so obviously not there. We are with you and leave this instrument, blessing each, for to be foolish in the seeking of an ideal is divine folly. Seek carefully, and with love. In that love we leave you and in that light we cannot help but leave you. We are Oxal. Adonai, my friends. Adonai vasu borragus.

(Jim channeling)

I am Latwii, and I greet you, my friends, in the love and in the light of the infinite Creator. We are pleased that this group has chosen once again to ask for our humble service. We bring it, as always, rejoicing as we come, thankful for the opportunity of being with you and of searching with you for the truth of our existence. May we then ask if there is a query with which we might begin?

M: Are all the fourth dimension groups acquainted with one another, or are they isolated the way the third dimension is?

I am Latwii. To answer your query, we may begin by suggesting that although those of fourth density are more fully aware of the unity of their being, there is for many still some inability to perceive the, shall we say, individualized existence of others like unto themselves. Those of the density of understanding do indeed perceive …

(Side one of tape ends.)

(Jim channeling)

I am Latwii. To continue. Universe. The existence of those who dwell within and learn understanding and compassion is an existence which is far more broad than your own, for the veil which separates your conscious from your unconscious mind is being removed more and more fully within this density. Therefore, to summarize. Though it is more possible for such entities to know the fullness of the existence of their own kind, shall we say, many yet seek to complete this understanding.

May we answer you further, my sister?

M: No, thank you, Latwii.

I am Latwii. We are thankful to you, my sister. Is there another query at this time?

Carla: Is there ever a point at which knowledge of the infinite is part of an individual entity or social memory complex?

I am Latwii. As the progression through the densities of this octave continues, the knowledge of unity with all portions of the creation increases. This has been likened unto the gaining of what might be called spiritual mass. As this awareness of unity progresses into that density of seven, there is the movement into timelessness which necessarily precedes the full rejoining of each portion of an entity's awareness with the unity from which it sprang.

May we answer you further, my sister?

Carla: Yeah, there's a joke about a guy that knows everybody in the whole world. And yet that's a finite number of people, entities compared to the infinite of all of the galaxies and all of the populations. It just, you know, intellectually boggles the mind to think about knowing everybody, every entity. Maybe you can't approach it intellectually, huh?

I am Latwii. To respond to your query, may we suggest that the faculties of the mind are indeed quite boggled by such an experience. Therefore, it is of necessity that the infinity of mind give over in function to the infinity of spirit, that through this foundation source of beingness all that exists might be known as a portion of the great Self which is the one Creator. Your creation exists that this one Creator might know Itself, and as the process of evolution occurs for each entity then the Creator gains in knowledge of Itself as each portion becomes aware of more of its identity as the one Creator. The reciprocal knowing of the small self as the great Self and great Self as the small selves reaches this stage of what we have called spiritual mass increasingly so that the fullness of all creation is seen to be contained within the fullness of the self.

May we answer you further, my sister?

Carla: No, I really liked that answer. Thank you very much.

I am Latwii. We are pleased to have packed an answer in our briefcase which has pleased you. May we attempt another query at this time?

K: Yes, Latwii. As we attempt to know the higher self or the inner self, and as hunches and intuitions come, it's been my experience that if I follow them, I make the right choices. Is it true that the inner self or the higher self is capable of directing our lives in every respect if we are aware of the, well, let's just say hunches or whatever we want to call it?

I am Latwii, and am aware of your query, my sister. This is one means whereby what you have called the higher self may indeed aid in guiding the individual that is your waking self through the illusion of the lessons you have chosen. It is also possible that other portions of the self take part in this activity. Also to be included as a source of those intuitive hunches and flashes which occasionally illumine the mind is the concept of the guides or guardians which watch the progress of each within your illusion.

When you feel an intuitive feeling, you are being spoken to by a greater or deeper portion of your own being. Whether this portion be that known as your higher self, your own unconscious programming, guides or guardians, or friends of light is of little concern for the moment. What is to be noted is the impulse towards action or thought. To listen to such is indeed quite efficacious in traveling that path you have chosen, but it must be remembered that you cannot make mistakes. And to not listen to such an impulse will simply mean that you shall reach your destination eventually by another means.

You may see the balancing of the intellectual and analytical abilities of your mind with the intuitive information from your subconscious mind as that which is most helpful in accelerating your evolution of mind, body and spirit, for with the analytical abilities of your conscious mind, you are able to chart the path which you shall travel. By listening to those intuitive impulses which spring from some portion of your subconscious mind, then is your conscious mind informed as to larger parameters within which it might have its sway. Thus, the two portions of your mind operating in balance provide you with the means by which you are able to move upon your path of evolution within your illusion.

May we answer you further, my sister?

K: No, thank you. That answered it quite well. Thank you.

I am Latwii. We thank you, my sister. Is there another query at this time?

A: Yes, Latwii. I was wondering what the significance was or what the reason was for when people—when they are praying—put their hands together, as in the statues of the praying hands. Why do people do that?

I am Latwii. We find that the answer to this query for most entities is simply to do that which has been taught them, but the answer which we see you seek runs deeper than this. The foundation for each ritual which the cultures of your planet has created—we correct this instrument—have created, rests within some symbolic representation of unity, for it is unity which underlies each religion and philosophy, and unity which each religion and philosophy, to some extent, distorts. To join the hands is to join the seemingly separate portions of the self together in a symbolic action which exemplifies the unification of the being—the right and the left, the positive and the negative, that which knows with that which does not know, that which seeks with that which gives. The descriptions we have given are various means of looking at the individualized entity which seeks in prayer to know some portion of unity. To join the portions of the self known as the hands, which in your illusion seek many things, is the symbolic function which shows the entity seeks unity, seeks to make whole that which seems broken, seeks for the healing of that which seems diseased, seeks for the knowledge to fill the void of unknowing within the self.

May we answer you further, my sister?

A: No, that was most helpful. Thank you.

I am Latwii. We thank you, my sister. Is there another query at this time?

(Pause)

I am Latwii. We find this evening an early end to those queries which may be answered in our humble attempts to be of service. We thank each present for asking for our humble service once again. In your meditations, my friends, please feel always free to ask our presence there as well. We shall leave this group at this time, as always, rejoicing in the love and in the light of the one Creator. We are known to you as those of Latwii. Peace and blessings be with each. Adonai vasu borragus. ❧

Sunday Meditation
January 30, 1983

(C channeling)

I am Hatonn, and I am now with this instrument. We greet you, my friends, in the love and in the light of the one infinite Creator. We wish to speak a few words on what for you is indeed of great difficulty in your illusion, that being what you know as choice. You, as all entities, are free-willed in each thing. Each of your life situations is to you many different options of which you weigh and choose. Each entity's choice becomes that entity's responsibility. When your choice is made and the moment accepted, neither hate nor love the choice, but accept it for the moment. With each choice you are … with each choice take a step. Use your …

We are experiencing some difficulty in maintaining a good contact with this instrument. We would, as he requests, now transfer this contact to another. I am Hatonn.

(Jim channeling)

I am Hatonn, and greet you once again through this instrument in love and light. To continue. As you make your choices in this illusion, you will find that each choice brings yet more possibilities for choice. You operate within this illusion in a manner which might be called trial and error, though we would de-emphasize the error aspect, for we do not feel that any choice can be error. Yet from your experience you may discern those choices which are less efficacious than other choices, but this discernment is only possible as you continue to make choice after choice. You will find that the experiences which you gather through the making of choices will offer you hints, shall we say, that will aid you in further decision making, so that the entity which is able to analyze through the use of the mind those experiences which it has encountered is then able to take the gleanings of this analysis with it in meditation, and is able to allow new thought forms and possibilities in thinking to occur within the being.

Then this entity is able to continue a process of evolution which you may simply call growth, as you continue to expand and grow in your ability to utilize your mind, your body and your spirit complexes in an ever-expanding understanding, if we may use this term, of the nature of your illusion. Then you will find a pathway which lies before you that becomes more and more distinct. For as you choose, you become more polarized, shall we say, by the choices you have made, and this polarization then becomes likened unto a momentum within your very being. The momentum of your choices to be of service, however you have chosen, then shows to the attentive entity the path which is most efficacious within each situation that it shall face in what you shall call your future.

Do not be afraid to choose, my friends. Do not fear that which is called the failure by many of your peoples, for there is in truth no such thing as failure. There may be instances wherein your choices shall not yield the results which you had hoped they would yield when you made the choices. Yet this is only a function of your imperfect understanding of what it is that will truly benefit your evolution in mind, body and spirit. Rest within the assurance that you cannot fail as you choose and choose and continue to choose the path which you travel. You do not understand the complete overview, shall we say, of your journey, for this is not the density of understanding. You operate within a forgetting that increases the value, shall we say, of the choices that you make and the path that you travel in your total beingness.

Therefore, forget you the fear of failure. Choose and continue to choose fearlessly then, knowing that each choice has the opportunity to teach. And if you will listen with your inner being, discern with your mind, and join the two in meditation, you shall lead yourself through your own choices along that path which is the most efficacious for the growth that you so earnestly seek at this time.

We would now attempt to close through another instrument, if possible. We shall now transfer this contact. I am Hatonn.

(A channeling)

I am Hatonn, and greet you through this instrument. We would speak but briefly in closing to give the reminder that if ever our presence is desired, all you need to do is ask and we shall be with you. Seek us out in your meditation. We are with you always. We shall leave you tonight in the love and the light of the one infinite Creator. Adonai. We are known to you as Hatonn.

(Jim channeling)

I am Latwii, and greet you, my friends, in the love and the light of our one infinite Creator. What a privilege it is once again to be with you. We sincerely appreciate the opportunity which you extend by your invitation. We are always excited to speak to this group. This group has been our longtime friend, shall we say, and to join with friends is indeed an honor and a great joy. May we then ask if we might be of assistance by attempting to answer queries this evening. May we ask for the first query?

C: I'll try to get a question out of this, and try not to ramble too much, and try not to ask for anything specific. But of late I've been extremely nervous and confused and unable to make decisions. I can't seem to distinguish what is the proper avenue to take to serve others around me. When I meditate on it, it seems that a feeling that no matter what the choice, I would be serving myself more than others. Could you talk to me about such a state of confusion?

I am Latwii, and shall attempt to penetrate to the heart of your query, my brother. Within your illusion are many opportunities for learning. The greatest opportunities present themselves as what your peoples call the problem, the crisis, the trauma, for when things are going smoothly, my friend, what is being learned? Quite often, little of value. But look you then to the situation which presents the crisis. Within the self one seeks in such a situation to resolve the crisis. Yet if the crisis be of such proportions that the entity cannot put, shall we say, all the pieces together to complete the puzzle in one fell swoop, then the entity finds itself mired, shall we say, within the crisis.

To put it more properly, may we suggest that the crisis is within the entity, and the depths of the crisis begin to appear great. If you will look at any situation which might be called a crisis, any such situation has the ability to awaken the deeper portions of an entity's being so that awareness is increased. The awareness is increased usually through what may be called the pain, the suffering, the tears. The trauma of the situation which is not resolved or balanced within the thinking of the entity experiencing it begins to carve out within the entity new boundaries of perception, new potentials for experience. As the entity consciously works with the catalyst of the crisis, the opportunities for learning expand, yet are often unrecognized as the entity continues the process of working with the catalyst. Confusions often occur as the entity attempts to make decisions that shall, it hopes, end the crisis.

There are various resources and forces within the deeper mind, as well as aid from those presences which you may call angelic or guides, which provide the entity with the impulse to resolve the situation in the most efficacious manner possible according to the entity's chosen polarity. Therefore, the entity may find the, shall we say, easier solutions quite difficult to make, for the easier solutions are not always the most efficacious. The entity is provided with aid from the inner resources that allow it to make the most helpful choice according to the polarity which it has chosen. The situation of crisis, then, allows an intensive experience of choosing to continue along a certain path of polarity to the entity. The crisis is, shall we say, the cutting edge of consciousness. The entity may go in either direction, the service to self or the service to others. The more intensive the lesson, the greater the crisis, the more opportunity for learning.

Do not fear that you shall make the wrong choice, for no choice is final and each choice builds upon previous choices and will lead to yet further choices, so that the entire process may be looked upon as one which continues to provide the opportunity for increasing the polarity of the individual. As you move through this situation, attempt to view it as often as possible from what might be called a neutral situation or position. Perhaps within your meditation you may be able to remove yourself from the emotional colorations which lend to your confusion, and place your attention in a position which allows you to look down upon the situation, shall we say, and see yourself and all others within it as actors upon a stage. Look then to the dynamics of the movement and interaction. See that part which you play. Become the author of the script. Attempt to discover what potentials await your learning. What is the lesson that is being taught? How has it been learned? How might the learning be increased? Attempt to remove yourself periodically in such a manner so that you might gain an overview and a more full appreciation of the process which presents you with great opportunities for learning.

In such a discipline, then, your deeper mind and those entities which aid through it may be able to give you clearer guidance so that your choices might be more informed and effective. Attempt to remove yourself from fear and to remove fear from yourself, for this, like any emotion, only distorts that which is seen and experienced. Go forth in joy and confidence knowing that you have great opportunity to learn and to share the love and light of the one infinite Creator which seeks to be known in each moment that you experience.

May we answer you further, my brother?

C: No, thank you very much, Latwii. That gives me quite a lot to work with. Thank you.

I am Latwii. We thank you, my brother, for this opportunity to serve. May we attempt another query at this time?

A: Yes, Latwii, I have a question and it has to do with my channeling. I was wondering if you could aid me at all in why I might be having difficulties in picking up a channel. At meditations now I seem to draw a blank even though the tuning seems to be well and I've been mediating daily, but I'm a little confused on why I'm drawing a blank.

(Page 7 is missing from the original transcript.)

personal origin. The concept itself is more clearly transmitted from Confederation entity to the instrument. Each process and transformation which the instrument opens the self to will require of the instrument that it increase its desire to be of such service and increase its willingness to be the fool, shall we say. Yet as these continual exercisings—or mental pushups as we may call them—continue to be offered to the instrument, the entity will find the ability to transmit Confederation philosophy is quite enhanced and the service which it wishes to offer is likewise enhanced.

May we answer in more depth, my sister?

A: No, that will give me something to work with.

I am Latwii. We would simply comment at this time in response to both queries that it is often the plight and pleasure of the seeker to find the opportunities for increasing service and oneness to be presented in situations which provide the trauma, the doubt, the confusion, and the difficulty in perceiving clearly. This is the nature of any exploration into that which may be called the unknown. Rejoice, my friends, in your doubt, in your confusion, in your frustrations, and in your angers. For they are signposts which alert you to the fact that your seeking is increasing, and the opportunities for knowing the love and light of the one Creator are also increased.

May we attempt another query at this time?

A: I have none, but thank you for that last bit, Latwii.

C: Yes, thank you.

I am Latwii. It has been a great privilege, my friends, to be with you this evening, even for what you might call a brief moment. All such gatherings are treasured by we who are known to you as Latwii. We cannot express to you our gratitude in the appropriate terms which would be understood clearly. We feel the appreciation within those who have had queries this evening for that which we have humbly offered in service. May we express, then, to each present the same gratitude increased manyfold, for you provide us with a great service by asking for our humble service. For each, we seek to know and to serve the one Creator who resides within each portion of the one creation, and by such offerings of service have you allowed us to increase our knowledge of the One Who is present in all. We shall leave you at this time in the love and in the light of the one infinite Creator. Be at peace, my friends. Go forth in joy, for yours is the great journey into unity. I am Latwii. Adonai vasu borragus.

Sunday Meditation
February 13, 1983

(S channeling)

I am Hatonn, and am now with this instrument, and greet you, my brothers and sisters, in the love and light of the one infinite Creator. As always, with great joy we greet you. We are so pleased to be among those that are truly joyous to share time, as you perceive it, with others of like mind, of the same desire in striving. For in so doing, does it strengthen your own desires in striving. For in sharing with other selves, you are able to see within your own selves, and as this happens, my friends, we encourage you to continue.

This evening there are a few points we would like to consider, one of these being the looking within, the taking time to consider the well of strength and knowledge that comes from looking within your own self, to see the Creator that is within each and every one of you. We speak often on the subject of meditation, my friends. We realize this may at times be most boring to you, but this, as with other simple messages, can never be stressed enough. For it is through your daily meditation and through your daily prayers that you are able to accomplish that which you have set out to do in this lifetime. If there are a few moments of the day which are routinely set aside to turn the eyes inward, so to speak, then this would serve to help in a way that would perhaps better serve you than possibly reaching out to your other selves, expecting an answer from them that might possibly be an infringement upon your own free will, should they answer.

My friends, we would not at any time expect you are asking to do that which is not comfortable and can only hope to serve you, and ask that within our words you accept what is comfortable with you and discard the rest. We share our simple messages with much love for you, and even though at times it may seem as though we seem to be in the position of the parent scolding the errant child, this is not the way of our messages at all. But the thought that we send through these instruments we send with much love for your continued striving and growth.

We would at this time like to transfer this contact to another instrument. I am Hatonn.

(Carla channeling)

I am Hatonn, and I greet you through this instrument in love. We shall continue through this instrument.

What do you consider enough meditation? Indeed, what is the ultimate result desired? Firstly, let us examine the creation to discover that each entity experiences the Creator and the creation and therefore cannot help acting in a correct manner regardless of the action. Secondly, let us consider the possibility that the Creator is most efficiently experienced if the experiencer is experiencing the

Creator in such a way that he is at all times aware of the presence of the original Thought of the Creator, and further, is capable of manifesting the original Thought in each moment.

Is this possible, my friends? It is our limited understanding that indeed this is the intent of consciousness—to know itself in such a way that is finally and completely unmasked so that there are no divisions and all things become infinite in diversity, yet truly and obviously one. We would ask you to consider a story that is within the holy work which you call your Bible. The one whom you call Jesus spoke of giving, and indicated that it was difficult to give properly from abundance, but that rather the proper giving was that of the widow whose sole treasure was two coins which she gave. This, said the one known as Jesus, was the far greater giving.

My friends, do not be falsely led into consideration of monetary generosity of any sort by this parable. The parable has to do not with the giving of coins, but of the giving of a life. If your whole life equals two coins, and you give it all, it is acceptable. If your existence equals a million coins, and you give five hundred thousand, it is not acceptable. The charge that you give yourself by desiring to know the truth is that charge to give yourself to the truth when you find it—not a portion of yourself, not a tithe of yourself, but all that you have been, are or will be, and in the giving, release the self from bondage.

Imagine yourself as the coins dropping into the box. Now they have not fallen nor are they clasped in the hand. Now they are free to be infinite. And how can you do this for one second without the constant discipline of meditation or some activity which affects you personally in a centering, clearing and joyful manner? Can you possibly give yourself completely to the experience of the Creator as the Creator truly is without discipline? Can you expect to express love for one second in its original form without discipline?

You see, my friends, the search for truth is like the addiction which is in this instrument's mind as the topic of conversation before the meetings. You become addicted to the joy of being whole. This enables you to do a great deal of work, for there are no sales on truth. You will not find it cheaply. There are not bargain days and any who promises will be promising speedy happiness and speedy despair. There are no gimmicks, there are no shortcuts.

There are simply glimpses of the utmost joy, feelings of going into another world where all is as beautiful as a thought that you have just had.

To keep your faith in yourself enough alive to continue an arduous and long journey, now let us turn to meditation. If meditation is the fuel that will enable each entity to experience the truth, then seeking is the fuel that will enable you to meditate. We ask you, what is meditation? Do you think of sitting upon a mountain? Do you think of old men in white robes with long beards? That is not a full representation of the wisdom one gains in meditation and the time it takes to get it. But we ask you instead, my friends, to think of meditation as a process, as the trip up that mountain. You are in your street-soiled clothing, and it is warm day and the valley below you has the stench of too much civilization. As you climb, the smog recedes, and the warm, clean air begins to glow about you. A white butterfly dances before you. And you laugh at the sweet smelling air and the butterfly and the fine day that you have found in the high place.

After much climbing, when you are weary, you come to a perfectly smooth lake. It is so pellucid that you can see to the very, very bottom. You remove your clothing, and swim across this lovely, quietly melting lake. And as you walk up the other shore of this tarn, you find that there are new garments waiting for you to pick—garments fresh, sweet smelling as the day, comfortable and pleasant in every way. All that is without you is now cleansed and ready and you walk to the mossy, natural seat that overlooks vast distances. And you settle yourself and you allow all things to flow away, for you have been washed clean and that which is before you is new.

You do not need to ever come out of that meditation. The more you practice the experience of meditation, the more the process will be a portion of you. Then that process itself begins to give you the will to call upon the state of mind in which the kingdom of heaven and the Creator are near, or indeed are all about you. Those things which are full of the stench of complication, semantics and civilization may be seen as from that viewpoint. You may choose that viewpoint any moment. You may behave in the light of your relationship with the Creator, rather than your relationship within an illusion to the Creator, as that portion of the Creator is experiencing itself. Choose. And each time that you do, know that it is your choice and that when we speak to you of meditation, boring though that subject may seem, we wish only to give you the basic tool for renewal of the sense of the original Thought that each of you seeks with such determination.

I would transfer at this time. I am known to you as Hatonn.

(K channeling)

I am Hatonn, and would say a few words through this instrument in closing. We want to continue with the thought of addiction as one seeks truth. Or in reality the seeking of truths is the seeking of the self, the understanding of the self, and as you discover more of the beauty of the self that each of us is, it indeed is like an addiction. The more one discovers, the more one is capable of discovering. And indeed, it becomes like finding a brilliant jewel, and the more one finds, the greater the addiction. And, one might even say, the greater the addiction, the more one finds. And you will spend all of eternity discovering more of the self, because the infinite Creator resides within each self. Life takes on a totally different meaning as one truly discovers the beauty and the depth and the color that resides in each of you. One stands in awe indeed, as one begins to understand the Creator really does reside in each of us. Your life need not be powerless. As you live day by day and continue in your meditations, and as these thoughts grow within you, you will indeed be like the light set on the hill. It is indeed worth the time you have spent in seeking.

We repeat that it has been a joy to be with you. And we leave each of you now in the love and the light of the infinite Creator. I am Hatonn.

(Jim channeling)

I am Latwii, and I greet you, my friends, in love and light. It is our privilege once again to join your group in response to your request for our presence. We join you with great love for each of you and with an eagerness to serve which is, shall we say, our constant companion. May we then attempt our service at this time by fielding your first query?

M: Latwii, I have a query. What is the best way to help a person who has some form of addiction?

I am Latwii. My sister, we feel that in such a situation, the support one gives such an entity is most important. To support one who has a strong attachment to any thing, idea, person or pattern of existence is to give of the self without reserve for the purpose of letting the one to be served know that whatever its condition, with or without the addiction, the entity is acceptable to you. To give this support is to build within the entity's understanding a firm foundation upon which it might stand and move as it attempts to balance the distortions which seem out of balance. It is often the case that such entities who attempt to help one who has what you have called an addiction will attempt to help the entity free itself of that addiction through various means. This is the beginning of treading on very shaky ground, shall we say. To attempt without being specifically asked to enter into such a delicate situation is not usually recommended, but to support the entity as it makes it own efforts in that direction is most helpful in almost every situation.

May we answer further, my sister?

M: Yes. If a person is, as we were discussing before, non-functioning, what is the best approach?

I am Latwii. When an entity has suffered the bearing of such addictions to the point that it is unable to function within the normal definition of your culture, then it is often necessary to aid such an entity by providing, shall we say, the common sense support of attempting to secure the shelter, the food, the clothing, the medicine, and the companionship for such an entity that it might be nurtured to the point where once again it is able to make those decisions for itself. It is important that the door to these decisions always be left open for such an entity, yet it may be necessary in some cases that the entity be assisted through that door.

May we answer you further, my sister?

M: No, thank you. I think you've explained it very well.

I am Latwii. We are grateful to you, my sister. May we attempt another query at this time?

Carla: Well, following up on that, the alcoholic— the experience that I have had with my relative was such that when she was sober, and in that state very intelligent, she suggested that she was suicidal, and that if she drank, she was attempting to die, and that any encouragement from any member of the family would only hasten her death. Consequently …

(Side one of tape ends.)

Carla: … sturdy in their own right, and by her own suggestion, in this case, simply refusing to see her if she drank. This she felt was her only chance at becoming sober again. However, if I follow you correctly, even though it worked, spiritually it was very shaky ground. Is this correct?

(Jim channeling)

I am Latwii, and shall attempt clarification. The general suggestion which we have given, as all general suggestions, must bear the light of the specific situation. To give support to an entity who is suffering these difficulties may take many forms. Our suggestion is that one love without conditions. How this love is expressed is not set firmly or strictured rigidly. One may love and support another in specifically the manner in which the entity of which you speak desired. When an entity speaks in such a manner and asks for that type of assistance, then to love most purely, it might be the case that these desires are met. It may be many—we correct this instrument. It may be that many such entities would desire this type of assistance, and that it would be successful in aiding their recovery. Others may need some variation. If one can know what another needs by hearing those needs from the other, then one may best serve as one has been asked. If one knows not how to serve, one then must follow the heart. The love then that is given may take another form. Begin in love, refine with the wisdom which you discover either through your own discernment or through the lips of the one needing service.

May we answer you further, my sister?

Carla: No, thank you, Latwii.

I am Latwii. We thank you, my sister. Is there another query at this time?

K: Yes, Latwii. Let me just see if I understand a little bit better. The support and the love that you talk about I'm assuming would carry with it the notion that there is no judgment at all about the problem that the person is experiencing. For instance, for the most part our conversation with alcoholics oftentimes is judgmental. And so this support and this love would have to come across in such a way that the one who is addicted would know that we do not hold any judgment at all against the alcoholic. Is that true?

I am Latwii, and am aware of your query, my sister. It is our recommendation which we humbly offer that in any situation of this nature that it is most helpful to act from a position which has no judgment within it. For to judge another is to build a barrier between you and the other and then all succeeding actions must be filtered through that barrier. This tends to distort the love and the wisdom which you have to offer so that it appears to the other less than what it is. To remove the judgment is to attempt to see clearly and is that action which allows the clearer giving of assistance.

May we answer you further, my sister?

K: No, thank you, I think that clears it up.

I am Latwii. We are thankful to you. Is there another query at this time?

Carla: Just one final one on the same subject, only backwards. Can you generalize about the purpose for experiencing the addiction? There seems to be an addictive type of personality. There seems to be an addictive type of body, chemically. There seem to be some very distressing things that go on during addiction to some substance like alcohol or hard drugs or tranquilizers, yet people repeatedly seek that addiction out. Can you generalize on why?

I am Latwii. We are not fond of generalizations though they are most frequently our lot. In addressing queries such as have been asked this evening, it is necessary to speak in general terms in order that an overview can be given, yet to speak in general terms is to limit oneself greatly. For each entity is quite unique, and though each entity does fall within certain groupings and may be, therefore, in some cases, spoken of in general terms, yet one cannot look at each entity within any group and speak accurately in all instances. Therefore, we shall attempt a generalization with those qualifications understood.

Entities who experience what you call addictions to various substances such as the alcoholic beverages and the, as they are called, harder drugs, are oftentimes entities of great sensitivity and creativity. Entities within the culture in which you now exist who contain within themselves delicate sensitivities, budding creativities, and who yearn to express that which they feel they are, yet who also find such expression blunted by the general, shall we say, milieu, become sometimes frustrated, and find that their only solace is to turn inward and to ponder how to exist as a finely tuned being in what seems to be a gross and greatly overpowering world. Such an entity will often turn inward to such an extent that it becomes reclusive. Such an entity will find there are various aids to intensify this reclusive nature. The aids of the drugs and alcohol tend to turn the entity further and further in upon the self so that those sensitivities which began the entity's yearning and seeking for expression, become themselves blunted so that they no longer motivate the entity in the manner which found no expression. It is often that the turning inward and the use of the substances which alter the mind is specifically chosen that the mind might be altered, for it is the sensitive mind and the sensitive heart and the sensitive being that it seems to the entity began the pain. And yet these can be, shall we say, stilled in some degree, but then the entity assumes there will be no pain. Yet, can the spark of life which glows within any be extinguished? It is often a long journey until the entity discovers that the spark must live. And how that spark shall live is the decision which each must make.

May we answer you further, my sister?

Carla: No, thank you, that was very inspiring.

I am Latwii. We are most grateful to you, my sister. May we attempt another query at this time?

K: Yes, Latwii. I really think I know the answer to this, but I'd like to have your opinion. Do people—do some entities—well, in fact, lots of entities—before they incarnate again decide to live their lives in ignorance? Some people just seem, from my point of view, some people seem to hold on to ignorance as if it were something to be praised or enjoyed—they literally seem to hold on to their ignorance. Now do some entities choose this kind of a life before being born into this planet?

I am Latwii, and am aware of your query, my sister. Each entity before incarnating sets before itself a basic scheme or blueprint for the life which will follow as the incarnation. The lessons to be learned all stem from love within your illusion. How these lessons shall be learned is quite varied and unique to each entity. The veil which falls between the conscious and unconscious mind serves the purpose of allowing the entity to follow its path without a clear understanding of what that path is in order that the path, when followed, might carry weight within the total beingness of the entity. For an entity, then, to attempt to learn the lessons of love, it is necessary that the limitations of this knowledge of oneness with all be firmly in place. This is the challenge, to discover love within all of the experience without having more than a basic clue as to the nature of the love and the lessons awaiting the entity.

The distortion which you have described as ignorance, may also be chosen in order that the lessons of love might be learned on a very basic level. For an entity to exercise the ignoring of most of what is about it is to increase the effect of the veil and to increase the difficulty of the lesson. Yet if the lesson be learned under these circumstances, it carries great weight in the total beingness of the entity.

In short, yes, my sister, the quality of ignorance is quite a valuable tool to many who seek the lessons of love, and is freely chosen as a tool to aid that learning.

May we answer you further, my sister?

K: So, in a case like that, one does the entity a disservice by trying to enlighten, so to speak, is that right?

I am Latwii. This is not necessarily so, for each entity acts within an illusion which is populated with others such as itself, and the others serve as what might be called mirrors. It might be most helpful to such an entity to aid in its elimination, for no entity acts alone in truth. And each entity aids each other entity by interacting with that entity. To mirror the essence of another is to illumine the essence of another. And when you attempt, however you attempt, to aid another, you do indeed serve that other, for there is no way that one cannot be of service. To think in terms of service and disservice or right and wrong is to limit the perception, for in truth all actions and all inaction is service. All is service. The service may vary, yet the service exists and has its impact. There are no mistakes. Rest assured that you serve.

May we answer you further, my sister?

K: No, thank you very much.

I am Latwii. We thank you, my sister. Is there another query at this time?

(Pause)

I am Latwii. We are aware that we have exhausted the queries within this circle, yet we are aware that there is one who we perceive wishes to enter the circle, yet is hesitant. We shall therefore, take our leave of this group at this time. We rejoice in your beingness, our friends. Call upon us to join you in your meditations whenever you wish our presence. We leave you in love and light and blessings of the One. We are known to you as Latwii. Adonai vasu borragus. ❧

L/L Research

L/L Research is a subsidiary of Rock Creek Research & Development Laboratories, Inc.

P.O. Box 5195
Louisville, KY 40255-0195

www.llresearch.org

Rock Creek is a non-profit corporation dedicated to discovering and sharing information which may aid in the spiritual evolution of humankind.

ABOUT THE CONTENTS OF THIS TRANSCRIPT: This telepathic channeling has been taken from transcriptions of the weekly study and meditation meetings of the Rock Creek Research & Development Laboratories and L/L Research. It is offered in the hope that it may be useful to you. As the Confederation entities always make a point of saying, please use your discrimination and judgment in assessing this material. If something rings true to you, fine. If something does not resonate, please leave it behind, for neither we nor those of the Confederation would wish to be a stumbling block for any.

CAVEAT: This transcript is being published by L/L Research in a not yet final form. It has, however, been edited and any obvious errors have been corrected. When it is in a final form, this caveat will be removed.

© 2009 L/L Research

Sunday Meditation
February 20, 1983

(M channeling)

[I am Hatonn.] I am now with this instrument. I greet you with the love and the light of the infinite Creator. Many times people feel alone but in reality you are never alone. There are people who have gone away, and there are people who are coming who are involved in your life. They give you support of which you are not aware. You do not just have your friends in the third dimension, but you have friends in the third dimension that you do not even know because of the illusion of forgetfulness. Sometime you feel that your problems are more than you can bear, but in the total line of your soul there will be happiness and contentment to lessen your sorrows. Never feel alone. There are always many souls concerned with your welfare. If you will just remember this one sentence a lot of the loneliness of your third dimension will disappear.

I am Hatonn. I leave this instrument.

(S channeling)

I am Hatonn, and greet you, my brothers and sisters, in the love and in the light of the one infinite Creator. We thank you, as always, our friends, for allowing us to share in the very beautiful vibrations that encircle you together as one on one thought of seeking the Creator in this way. We would like this evening to share with you a few thoughts on the subject of being one with your brothers and sisters.

This, our friends, is not at all times easy to accomplish. You may look on one who is not so agreeable, and perhaps tend to think that this person is not a part of you. But yet, my friends, is each and every one you come in contact with each day of your lives a part of you and you a part of them. For within the creation there is only the separation that is brought about within the illusion. Within the Creator, my friends, there is no separation. All is one.

Each day as you are involved in your daily routine and as you meet your brothers and sisters, would you, if you knew that the one that you consider a stranger, if you knew, my friends, that he was the one known as Jesus, would you treat him perhaps as lightly as you do that stranger? For he, my friends, is as the one known as Jesus, as are you. We put out these thoughts to you, my friends, that you may stop for a moment and consider again the beauty within each and seek to see the inner beauty of each of your brothers and sisters. Do not stop at the outer covering, for with a little effort you may indeed find the beauty that you have been seeking.

We would like to transfer this contact. I am Hatonn.

(C channeling)

I am Hatonn, and am now with this instrument. As you continue to seek, you will find that you will become ever more sensitive to those around you. As you begin to go within, to see the beauty and the love that is you, you will find that you will also reach out and look at that same beauty in others. Others may not be able to see as you do, and you may well find there are times that your reaching out may tend to shut others in. Your path and your knowledge as it begins may seem lonely at times, for it does seem paradoxical, that reaching out can shut you away from others. But do not be disheartened. Continue and you will find that with your growth you can begin to reach others, be more a part of them, share with them, experience together as one. The beauty, the peace of touching others is indeed a wondrous thing. So continue to reach out and do not be disheartened if first attempts are rejected. The rewards are great. The love to be shared is great.

I am Hatonn, and would, if we may, close out this message through another instrument. I am Hatonn.

(K channeling)/

I am Hatonn. I am now with this instrument, and in closing we would like to remind you of the admonition in the book known as the Bible. In numerous places in the Bible we are told to rejoice always, even in tribulation. My friends, rejoicing diminishes what you see as problems. This may be difficult to comprehend, but if you will give it a little thought you will recognize the truth of the statement, that rejoicing does indeed diminish our problems, or what we perceive as problems. And it is always well to remember that the power within us is greater than any problem we may face. So, my friends, you can take heart under all circumstances. And remember that rejoicing is the panacea for all ills.

It has been a pleasure to be with you this evening, and, as always, we leave you in the love and the light of the infinite Creator. I am Hatonn.

(Jim channeling)

I am Latwii. I greet you, my friends, in love and light. We are most honored to be called to your group again this evening to offer our humble service, that is, the attempt to answer your queries. We remind each entity that though we enter into this service with great joy and eagerness, we are fallible messengers, and our advice, though it may seem studied and somewhat perceptive, is only meant to serve as a guide, and is but a trinket when compared to that which resides within your very being. Therefore, may we attempt now the first query?

M: I have a question. I've been reading the psychic Ruth Montgomery's new book, *Threshold to Tomorrow*, and she says that Einstein has come back and is in the body of a Swedish engineer [Bjorn] *(inaudible)*. Do you feel that this is probably true?

I am Latwii. This is, of course, a possibility which upon careful investigation upon our parts could be determined. Yet, we find that information of this nature is not our specialty, shall we say. Our specialty is the transmission of those thoughts and concepts which those present might find of use in accelerating the evolution of the mind, the body, and the spirit. Usually entities who seek in that manner shall find that information of the sort which this question contains is only of peripheral use in the evolutionary process. Entities such as the one of which you have spoken are most usually of great distortion towards service to others, and therefore it would not be at all unusual to expect such an entity, even if harvestable, to return to this plane and illusion in order that the fruits of its own efforts might be shared with others and nourishment might be given.

May we answer you further, my sister?

M: No, thank you, that's very good.

I am Latwii. We thank you, my sister. Is there another query?

K: Well, yes. Along the same line, I've heard only recently that a group of people who have been hypnotized indicate under hypnosis that lots of children are being born now for the express purpose of trying to save the planet, and there was some indication that the children were from other densities, such as perhaps the fourth or fifth density. Could you comment on that?

I am Latwii, and am aware of your query, my sister. Indeed, at this time on your planet there is the birthing of a great number of entities of various origins who have come to aid the planetary consciousness in its evolution, for indeed, your planet evolves with your peoples. Many have come as what you have called wanderers for many thousands of your years. These have been in small numbers until what you call recent times, that is, the last two centuries. During this period the number of these entities has increased greatly in order that the vibrations of your planet, which have through the three great major cycles tended to be somewhat of the heavy or gross nature [may be assisted.].

There have been also within recent times, that is, the last half century, the beginning incarnations of those which shall form a portion of the fourth-density positive population of your planet. These entities have been harvested from third-density planets from other what you call solar systems and have been given the honor of early incarnation upon your planet as harvest is begun. Their incarnations are hoped to aid this harvest as the lightness, or shall we say, the distortion towards love of their vibrations is added to the cumulative planetary vibration. These entities also enter into a forgetting, yet they bring with them skills which are not so easily forgotten, and there are many of small experience—what you call children—upon your planet at this time who demonstrate skills which are normally called by your peoples extraordinary or paranormal. These skills are the subconscious remembering of lighter vibrations which have been brought with the entity for the purpose of aiding the evolution of this planet.

The majority of incarnations at this time upon your planet, however, are of two types. The largest by far of the portions are those entities who have spent many, many incarnations upon your planet as third-density entities attempting to learn the lessons of love. Their attempts have been successful enough that they have the possibility of attaining harvest in the positive sense in the short period of time which remains before the harvest is complete upon your planet. The smaller portion of entities incarnating is that portion which also has attempted to achieve graduation, shall we say, in the negative sense, or the service-to-self sense. Thus, you will find upon your planet at this time a great polarization in consciousness occurring. That is, you will find great examples of love of others and service to others, and great examples of love of self and power over others.

May we answer you further, my sister?

K: No, that answered the question very well, thank you.

I am Latwii. We thank you, my sister. Is there another question?

K: Yes. One follow up on that question has occurred to me. You indicated that the lesser portion was the negative, and some of them are very powerful. I'm assuming some of these powerful people are in politics. Is that right?

I am Latwii. It is possible for each entity to view the culture in which it exists and to see those structures of organization which are based upon a few with what you have called power exercising that power over a great many which do the bidding of a few. You will see about you many structures in your society, not only within the arena called political, but those of your armed forces, your economic institutions, your business concerns, and so forth. The principle of negativity is that principle which intensifies the illusion of separation which is implicit within all creation. The illusion of separation is then used by those who have gained a knowledge of the negative polarity to dominate those who are not what is called elite, shall we say. Whatever characteristics are determined and determine the elite, then, are those characteristics which are used to separate the elite from the non-elite. Therefore, you may see the distortion towards negativity within many, many portions of your environment, and, indeed, within the self, for are not all entities one, and do you not contain all things?

May we answer you further, my sister?

K: No, that's very good. Thank you.

I am Latwii. We thank you once again. Is there another query at this time?

M: I have one. Within a lifetime, is there ever a person who is decidedly negative or positive who changes, and what would cause that great change within a lifetime?

I am Latwii, and am aware of your query, my sister. It is most unusual for an entity to completely change the polarity during an incarnation within the third density, for within your density the great forgetting which occurs makes progress, shall we say, difficult enough that when one polarity is discovered to be successful or helpful to the entity in its evolution, it is most usually intensified so that the efficacy is continually enhanced. There are many, many cases, however, where entities, shall we say, mix their polarities, not having the knowledge of the principle of polarization. The great majority of entities upon your planet, for example, swing in might be called the potential well of indifference, moving at times in service to others with great sincerity, moving also as the pendulum at times in service to self with great dedication. This is normal upon this particular planet at this time. For an entity to change completely the seeking from one polarity to the other and be efficient in that seeking is most unusual.

May we answer you further, my sister?

M: Well, I was thinking, say, of an alcoholic who was very destructive to himself and other people who changed—say, belonged to AA, and became quite helpful to other people. Would that be a change of polarity or not?

I am Latwii, and am aware of your query, my sister. We come to the problem here of semantics, for such an entity most usually will be one whose background is more distorted towards the previously mentioned potential well of indifference, being neither intensely positive nor intensely negative. The transformation which occurs due to the, as you mentioned, alcoholic nature being transformed to one of abstinence and service to others is a transformation which is then more purely positive and has not then usually moved from the negative sense, but has moved from the unpolarized state wherein the seeking was not of pure enough nature, either positive or negative, for the entity to move from its confusion. The entity may at the transformation of what you have spoken then choose a more purely positive seeking, and become more and more efficient in that seeking, and move itself from its confusion.

May we answer you further, my sister?

M: No, I think that explains it very well.

I am Latwii. We hope we have been of service. May we attempt another query at this time?

(Pause)

I am Latwii. We find that we have exhausted the queries, and perhaps one of your members. We hope that we have not been too ponderous this evening. We thank each present for inviting our presence. We are always honored to join this group, and we remind each present that a simple request for our presence in your meditations shall find us joined as one, more consciously than we are always joined. We shall now leave this group, rejoicing in love and light and leaving each in that same love and light. Peace to each and blessings. We are known to you as Latwii. Adonai, my friends. Adonai vasu borragus. ✜

Sunday Meditation
February 27, 1983

(Carla channeling)

I am Hatonn, and I greet you, my friends, in the love and the light of the infinite Creator. It gives us great joy to share our thoughts with you this evening, and as we touch each of you in thought we send all our blessings that your journey may be filled with light and love. We especially greet those new to this gathering and one who has not been with us for some great time as you reckon. And so you all go out seeking the adventure of learning, and so have men gone out seeking that great adventure since consciousness began. The track is irresistible and yet there are many ways by which the seeker may slow himself down. Very often the wide paths, the most traveled and the most popular are those which accommodate those entities who desire to move at a slower pace. We are aware that each in this group desires to quicken the pace and so we would talk to you this evening about courage.

It has perhaps been suggested to you that the end of your seeking will be knowledge and understanding, that you will find the answers that you seek. Indeed, we have suggested that you will find the answers that you seek. We have never intentionally suggested that you will find a key to the understanding of those answers, only that you are heard and that answers are forthcoming. The path which is narrow is a path the end of which is the realization that you do not know anything. The reason this path is narrow is that not knowing is uncomfortable, and continuing on for any length of time upon a path which promises further unknowing as the fruit of your current unknowing is simply not a very delectable path, and therefore it is not much traveled by your peoples.

But we ask you to look around you, my friends. What do you understand? Having considered what you may understand, we ask that you evaluate its importance in your spiritual quest. Are you seeking to know who you are? Very well, a noble and great quest is this, as it contains all of creation in its depth and breadth, for you and creation are one. Seek, my friends, to know who you are. But if you seek with integrity you will find that your answers do not leave you smug. You do not ever know. It takes a great deal of courage to go far along on the path that you discover the feelings and the character and the fruits of who you are and still be able to face the ultimate mystery of your identity. Those without courage will settle upon an answer, and that answer will keep them from changing, or at least changing as quickly.

Let us observe the master known as Jesus. This teacher talked about himself only in the context of his relationship to the Father, to the Creator, to the One Who is all things. He was, as you are, aware of that relationship. He was aware that he was both created and Creator. He did not know anything beyond that, and each step that he took was taken after meditation, and under the guidance of that which he did not previously know, which many have called the Holy Spirit and others have called the higher self. How much courage can you bring to your quest? Love is ever and always nearly manifested to those who quest, and that love is blinding in its power, and you know it is there, and you seek more of it. Do you have the courage to accept your conscious unknown, for surely you have spent enough hours in despair because your actions were but a shadow of what you know, as you might say. You think, "My will is strong and my heart shall be light and I shall meet all obstacles with love, that love that I know, that love that I feel, that love that I seek." And yet, these things you do not always do. You do not know. It is the seeking, continuous, balanced between seriousness and joy, fresh each day, that accelerates your rate, speed, and leads you upon an ever narrower path.

And this, my friends, is good, for it is the narrow path, the path of courage, the path of fearlessness in the face of not knowing that will grant you more and more a sense of being able to reach into the resources of your higher self, of your deeper self, of your inner self, of Christ consciousness, and manifest the true joy of faith and will. It has often been noted that justice is blind among your peoples. We would further note, so is love, so is seeking. Do not let the dimness of your mirror images ever discourage you for long. Do not let your own lack of manifestation ever discourage you for long. Do not let any error, as you may consider it, discourage you for long, for this creation is the Creator's. You live in a creation of love and in an illusion of mystery. See far enough to find the love and have the courage to release yourself from the responsibility of certain knowledge. Those who are certain about philosophy and those things of the spiritual evolution have simply placed themselves on a slower path where they will be borne upon the shoulders of their comrades, given more encouragement, offered frequent rests, and sustained by many comforts. Courage, my friends. You who have it shall inherit a great mystery of being as can no one who seeks certain knowledge. You seek the wind. It is invisible, it is infinite, and it will come and go when it will. Do you suggest that you shall know it, that you shall measure it, and put it between the pages of a book? Or do you instead seek to be it? Lift your wings, my friends, and soar in the love and the light that is yours for the seeking, yours for the taking, and yours to manifest in glory.

We leave this instrument bathed in the sweetness of meeting with comrades and again thank you that we may share our thoughts with you, humble and poor though they may be. We ask that you grasp firmly the concept that we are fallible beings such as yourselves. Therefore, take what you will of what we say. Use that which seems good to you and discard the rest without a moment's hesitation. We are here to inspire and to encourage, not to confuse. We thank you for the great service you do us by allowing us to be of some small aid. I am Hatonn and I leave you in the love and in the light of our infinite Creator. Adonai, my friends. Adonai vasu borragus.

(L channeling)

I am Latwii, and I greet you, my brothers and sisters, in the love and the light of the infinite Creator. We are speaking slowly while we are establishing a good contact with this instrument. We ask your patience that this might be accomplished, for the instrument is somewhat fatigued and out of practice.

At this time we would present ourselves in hopes of being allowed to perform whatever service we are capable of in answering the questions you may elect to offer. At this time are there any questions?

Carla: I've been wondering about the reason so many school children have been given such harsh diseases to cope with these last two or three years. The latest epidemic was very uncomfortable, and much worse than the usual measles and strep. Stomach cramps and what not. Is there some other reason other than chance catalyst that this was presented to this particular generation of kids?

I am Latwii. I am aware of your question. My sister, we would recall for you the awareness that you possess concerning the qualifications that entitle the more recent incarnations upon your planet to be allowed to incarnate. As you remember, the schedule, if you will, is based upon the likelihood of accomplishing a sufficient polarization to continue the journey, so to speak. In the case of a number of the most recent incarnates, the quantity of catalyst experienced within a relatively short period of that which you term time is necessary to allow the newly incarnate the opportunity to successfully receive the equivalent of a cram course in human experience.

May we answer you further?

Carla: You're talking about seniority by vibration?

I am Latwii. Your assumption is correct. We would emphasize, however, that the term seniority is somewhat misleading, for there are those who are of a lesser developed state whose particular circumstances or required lessons are of a nature that would lend themselves well to being accomplished in the particular milieu experienced on your planet at this time. The odds, if you will, for these entities are greatly enhanced by the particular characteristic of that which they are likely to experience, and in so doing have the opportunity to complete the stage of work which they have undertaken.

May we answer you further?

Carla: Then you're inferring that the supply of those who may be expected to make harvest is less than the supply of physical vehicles that are being born so that those who have no excellent chance of making harvest, or some, are still able to incarnate. Is that right?

To a degree that is correct, my sister. It might be examined under the light of the willingness of those non-incarnate to be of service in patiently awaiting to allow one who is less likely to be harvested an opportunity to excel, and thus achieve harvest due to the particular circumstances available within the experience range presented by the physical vehicle. For example, one whose particular requirements for growth would include an opportunity to experience great physical and emotional stress might have to wait for several eons to find such ideal circumstances as those which are currently present on your planet. And, we might add, the potential future holds a high degree of likelihood that the circumstances for intense catalyst in these areas are greatly enhanced if an entity who seeks harvest, and is approximately, yet not actually at the harvest potential, perceives an other self who would be tremendously benefited by the opportunity to incarnate at this particular moment in time, the service-oriented near-harvestable entity might be moved to delay his or her incarnation so as to extend the service of such a delay to allow the incarnation and potential harvest for the entity of lesser accomplishment who also seeks incarnation under the particular circumstances available at this time.

May we answer you further?

Carla: No, thank you. I'm impressed by the courtesy of the ones who are willing to wait another seventy-five thousand years so that somebody else can have a turn. That's a whole new light on the word courtesy.

I am Latwii. My sister, we would not be hesitant to point out that this also is taken into consideration.

Is there another question?

(Pause)

I am Latwii. As there are no further questions vocalized, we shall assume that those present have exhausted their supply of queries and we shall ourselves be of service at this point in releasing our use of this instrument to allow those present to continue in their usual fashions. In the love and the light of the infinite Creator, my brothers and sisters, we are known to you as Latwii.

Carla: In case any of the other channels are wondering whether to speak, I do feel a presence here, and I am not getting any signals, so it must be for somebody else.

C: I felt this feeling before the meditation tonight, but I'm totally unsure what it is. That's why I'm staying quiet.

Carla: Okey-doeky.

C: It's that I feel strange.

Carla: Spirit, if you are new to this group, we challenge you in the name of Christ. If you come in the name of Christ, the Christ consciousness, and the one white light you are welcome. If not, we bid you be gone now and forever. Hum. He must not have been a nice one. He went away. We are now open for prayers.

C: A quick one.

Carla: Yeah, it was a fast one, a weak little fella. You all right, C?

C: Yeah, I'm all right.

(Tape ends.)

Sunday Meditation
March 6, 1983

(S channeling)

I am Hatonn,) and I greet you, my friends, in the love and the light of the one infinite Creator. We are pleased to be with you this evening, and we are honored that you have called upon us to join you and we are, as always, overjoyed at the oneness we find when this group is joined together as we all share in our seeking. We are often concerned about your people, but we are also filled with happiness when we know that there are those upon your planet who are endeavoring to seek the Creator, each in his own way. We all seek the same light, though we follow different paths. Each of us goes his own way, though we all go toward the same place. We are individuals, yet we are one. We are alone, yet we are together. Our togetherness is often not seen as completeness togetherness. There is an illusion that we are separate, but it is only an illusion. For we are all a part of the creation; we are all the creation.

We constantly seek the same light, and we seek it whether we see ourselves as one or as individuals, for there are many upon your planet who are unaware of their oneness with the Creator. Still they seek. It may often seem that we are in the dark. We often feel alone. We often feel frightened. But if we will look for the light, it will always be available to us. If when we are in what might be called the depths of our despair, we may only seek out a point of light, that light will be shown to us. It will lead us out of the darkness, and we will know the way. But first we must seek that light. If we choose to remain in the darkness, we will remain in the darkness. It is up to each individual to strive toward the light. It is our nature to strive toward the light as the flowers upon your planet strive for the sun. It is something within their being that makes them grow toward the sun.

And so it is with you, my friends. It is within you that same striving. You will seek the light whether you are aware of your seeking or not, for it is inborn within your very soul. As you seek the light, you find that it becomes brighter, easier to find, and easier to follow. You are never alone, my friends. You always have the light. Seek this light when you are in those depths, my friends, for seeking the light is finding the light.

We will leave this instrument now and would transfer to another. I am Hatonn.

(Jim channeling)

I am Hatonn, and greet you once again, my friends, in love and light. We have been attempting to contact the ones known as M and C but find some weariness within these instruments, and therefore shall continue through this instrument. We find this evening a great concern among this group for that concept which your peoples call health. You have spoken this evening of many ways of viewing the healing process which is necessitated when that condition called health deteriorates in some fashion. We would hope to offer you yet another perspective. No more sure, shall we say, than any other, yet our own.

You and your peoples exist within an illusion within which you find a portion of yourself seemingly divided from another portion, that is to say, your conscious mind does not seem to have a ready access to that which you may call your unconscious mind. This, shall we say, darkness of knowing or veiling which separates one portion of yourself from another, in effect makes it possible for your conscious choice to be free of the great overview which the unconscious mind can provide, for the unconscious mind is your direct link to all of the creation, and were its resources fully available to you, you would have no doubt as to the nature of your being, that is, the one Creator.

The advantage of not being able to tap this resource easily is that the choices you make with your conscious mind as you travel through your illusion are choices which then carry much more weight in your total beingness. The portion of the Creator that resides within you then is given greater experience with much more intensity, variety and purity than would be possible were you to rest in the blissful state of knowing your unity with all which the unconscious mind can provide.

Therefore, as you move through your illusion, you will find your ability to accomplish the movement, the experience, the growth, the learning of the lessons of love enhanced by the choices you make. Yet, my friends, you are well aware that not all choices are as efficacious as others. There are many factors which may lead to what you call ill health, some of which are choices which eventually are discovered to be less efficient than others. It may be that the path which one has set out before an incarnation includes the necessity of making such choices, for it is well known among your peoples that the, shall we say, trial and error method teaches well.

If you will look upon each choice, not with the concept of right or wrong, good or bad, but as an experience which teaches, you will then see that even a choice which leads to what you call ill health due to a certain disharmony or imbalance in the choice can teach as much if not more in many instances than choices which do not include the need for the ill health. It is often felt by the people of your planet, especially your culture, that the, shall we say, good life includes perfect health and income which supports one's self and family in comfort, friends which gather to share in merriments, and so forth, the general being a smooth flow of experience, one after another.

Yet, my friends, does anyone live such a life? If not, why? Could it be that there is more to what you call your life than the smooth and easy flow of events? Could it be that the strength of your will to seek the light is increased when you encounter the difficulties. Could it be that each of you before your present incarnation programmed these difficulties so that when certain lessons had been learned, there would be the challenge to continue learning, for it often appears among your peoples in their current condition that when there is no reason to learn, learning occurs not. When there is the need to learn in order to resolve the difficulty, then learning occurs of necessity. You may see the condition of your health in some instances as a type of barometer which can indicate many things according to the individual. For one it may be a reflection of the lessons that are being well learned or attempted, for another it may be reflection of the harmony which is being experienced and radiated from that being. For another it may that the state of health reflects certain lessons which need the recognition in order to be attempted.

In all cases, we may suggest that healing occurs in what you may call the metaphysical realms or inner nature portions of the entity, and then are manifested in the physical vehicle as the last portion of the health recovery, and are triggered solely by the inner choice made by each entity. Many are the ways which your peoples utilize to achieve healing. Whether the way includes the visitation to your orthodox medical physicians or the visitation to what are called psychic healers or the change in diet, exercise, sleep and rest patterns, or whether the trigger is the simple choice of an entity to do or not do a certain act, the healing occurs first within the entity at the metaphysical level of what might be called the higher self. It is at this point and this level that the Creator within moves to restore balance when the lesson that necessitated imbalance has been learned, for you do not have random or accidental experience upon your plane, though much appears so. Each experience carries the potential for learning, and each experience has been designed and programmed for that purpose by each of you before and during your incarnation. The veil of which we spoke keeps this knowledge from you that the process might be completed successfully, for if you were aware of how, shall we say, the game was played, it would be but child's play to complete it.

The challenge you have before you is to seek within and through that veil, that you might glean greater and greater portions of the great plan for your evolution which you have created by your choice before this incarnation. Therefore, it is always our suggestion when asked concerning how to accomplish healing that the first step be to seek in meditation the nature of the lesson which stands before you when you experience what you call disease, whether it be of mind, body or spirit. To seek within is to look in the only direction which you shall find a clear reflection, for you have chosen the experience which you face, and it is that inner being which has chosen it. To look elsewhere is to invite a less than clear perception of what the nature of your experience is.

As you continue your inward looking, you will find that the puzzling pieces of your experiences begin to fit, one upon the other, and a continuous stream of images and inspirations then become available to you so that you might continue the process of learning [that] which the disease symbolizes, and which the disease has brought before your attention in a manner which you cannot ignore. Meditation is one means by which you can begin to choose a more balanced path of seeking, and therefore continue to make the choices which will heal the imbalances which other choices have set in motion.

We at this time would make one final attempt at closing our contact through another instrument if there is the desire upon that instrument's part to aid in this manner. We shall transfer this contact at this time. I am Hatonn.

(K channeling)

I am Hatonn. Again we greet you in the love and the light of the infinite Creator. We would close this session with you by saying a few further words about health, since the one known as Carla is absent from the group tonight, and since it is evident that all of you are concerned. My friends, on your planet and in your culture there is a belief system about health that tends toward the illness or disease that you find all about you. You have the notion that it is widespread among your peoples, that you are supposed to be sick. My friends, the body is very capable of healing itself. The cells of your body are in tune with the infinite source of creativity of the universe, but you feed into your subconscious mind concepts about illness that fill you with fear and anxiety, both of which are enemies of good health. You look to others for healing rather than looking within. There are those on your planet who have been healed during the dreaming state. This is quite possible, but if your belief system says otherwise, you will not seek the dreaming, the healing from the dreaming state.

We have given you food for thought. Each of you will have to resolve the question of health and illness for yourself, even as you have to resolve each decision that comes before you. However, we would leave you with the cheerful thought that your body is completely capable of healing itself. Therefore we suggest that you continue to seek and find the answer individually. And, as always, we leave you rejoicing in the light and the love of the infinite Creator. I am Hatonn.

(Jim channeling)

I am Latwii, and I greet you, my friends, in the love and the light of the one infinite Creator. We are most honored once again to be asked to join your group. It is always our pleasure to blend our vibrations with yours. This group has been for a great portion of what you call time now our special adventure, shall we say, for we do not speak to many upon your planet, and these opportunities to speak in this manner are precious to us. Our service this evening, as always, shall be an attempt to answer your queries. We hope you realize that our humble responses are indeed nowhere near infallible, yet we offer them with some insight and with great joy. Therefore, may we ask if we might attempt the first query at this time?

M: I have a question. I don't know whether you can help me with it but it seems like throughout my entire life, every so often I get divine spark of truth that satisfies my brain for awhile. And for about a month or so I've been looking for another spark, and I can't find one. Would you mind giving me a divine spark of truth that will keep my brain going? It feels as if it's starved. I've heard elaborations of good ideas, but I haven't gotten a really new one in about a month and this leaves me rather uncomfortable. I need something, some divine spark of truth that will feed my brain for about a month.

I am Latwii. We are unsure as to our ability to provide such a spark to one who is used to the flame of truth in many forms. It is most difficult to say what is a profound revelation to one entity as compared to another, yet we are aware of certain general truths which seem to hold sway, no matter to whom they are applied. We may humbly suggested that for the truth which you seek you might look at that feeling of being uncomfortable, for is not such a feeling as full of truth as the feeling of comfort which comes from inspiration?

May we answer you further, my sister?

M: Well, I'm not exactly sure, but I'll think about it. Thank you.

I am Latwii. We thank you, my sister. We hope that we have not made the spark too opaque. May we attempt another query?

R: Yes, Latwii, I wonder if you could tell me if the condition in one of my ears is related to my seeking in any way, or if that would be an infringement?

I am Latwii. We do not mean to be facetious, my brother, but there is no condition which you can experience which is not related to your seeking. The condition which you have spoken of is indeed most appropriately associated with your seeking, and may be evaluated by continuing your practice of meditation upon the nature of the condition, for each such condition manifests in a way which symbolizes the lessons which are being attempted, and those especially—we pause that this instrument might be comfortable. To continue. Each such symbol then, points to the lesson which most needs attention at the moment, as you would call it. If you will look at the portion of the body which has been affected and note its function, you will begin to see the connections which are being pointed at, shall we say, and from this point you may proceed further along the path which lies before you.

May we answer you further, my brother?

R: Yes. What purpose are the tones in the ears, and what are the differences between right and left?

I am Latwii. When an entity has for some time been considering a certain concept, a certain path, and has been attempting to determine how to proceed with the inner seeking, and how to reflect it in the outer expression, there will often be a communication from what you might call inner planes, guides, the higher self, and various other angelic presences that will attempt to signal the conscious mind of the entity, and provide a clue as to the path which would be most efficacious. These signals take many, many forms. Most often noticed among your peoples is the coincidence of events where within the experience of the entity in the material world there will be manifested a, as you would call it, coincidence, that points the way. Others may term this a synchronistic event, and this is but one means of such communication. The means of which you have spoken is not as usually utilized, but is …

(Side one of tape ends.)

(Jim channeling)

I am Latwii. To continue. For the entity to experience the tone in the right ear, is for the entity to recognize the appropriateness of the thought or action which preceded the tone. The left ear tone, then, signals the inappropriateness of the thought or action which preceded the tone. There is a third tone which an entity may experience, occurring at the crown chakra just above the top of the head, as you call it, which signifies neither appropriateness or inappropriateness, but signifies the balanced nature of thought or action which preceded the tone.

May we answer you further, my brother?

R: No, thank you.

I am Latwii. We thank you, my brother. Is there another query at this time?

K: Well, yes, since we're on health tonight, and I don't want to tire the instrument too much here, but in one of my meditations about three or four months ago, I was having so much pain in my lower back, and particularly when I sat down, that I requested healing in my meditation, and I seemed to get the response, "Well, heal yourself." And it seemed to be pretty dogmatic and emphatic, sort of the way I would say things sometimes. Now I have been healed. Now my question is, did I heal myself? I guess I'm wanting some reassurance, but did I heal myself or can you give me any notion of what happened?

I am Latwii, and am aware of your query, my sister. In this instance, as in all such healings, the healing indeed was of self by self. But as you know, there are various portions of yourself and the portion of yourself which has partaken in this particular healing is a portion which is much closer in unity to the one Creator than is the portion which is manifested as your conscious self. When healing is desired with enough strength, and has been accompanied by the appropriate amount of learning, then the conscious self may petition the higher self, as you call it, that that source of providing catalyst, shall we say, may also provide the balance which will be reflected in healing for the conscious self. As you meditate and as you meditated, your petition was noted. Advice was given. Advice was taken, and healing occurred. May we hasten to add that in all cases of such healing it is the Creator which moves within and which restores the balance. Yet are you not the Creator?

May we answer you further, my sister?

K: No, I believe not. It did seem like it took me a long time to learn the lesson because I sure had pain a long time, but thanks a lot, Latwii.

I am Latwii. We thank you, sister. Is there another query?

S: Yes. Latwii, can you give me any information about my friend, *(sounds like)* Morzack, if that's the correct pronunciation?

I am Latwii. We may speak only in general terms in this matter, for as each seeker travels the inner journey, there will be those friends which are drawn to the seeker according to the nature of the seeking which is manifested. As you experience your incarnation, you will find the lessons that you have laid before yourself learned in such and such a manner, and you will find that there are friends which appear from time to time to aid in this process. No entity is alone. Each entity is surrounded by many presences. Which presence will manifest at which time is determined by the needs of the seeker and the nature of the seeking. To be at peace with the communications which the seeker will experience from time to time, we would suggest that each seeker determine a certain ritual that will allow the challenge of any entity making communication so that the entity making communication may be felt at all levels of being to be of a positive nature, to be of a service-to-others nature, and all such entities greatly appreciate this challenge, for it is an indication that the one whom they wish to serve is more aware of the nature of such service and more able to benefit by it.

Therefore, as you continue your journey of seeking, know that you are not alone, that there shall be those who will make themselves known to you in one way or another according to your needs.

May we answer you further, my sister?

S: No, thank you, Latwii.

I am Latwii. We thank you. Is there another query at this time?

M: Well, I would like a little information, Latwii. I'm not particularly sensitive to any form of pain, and I don't believe in sickness. Now is that just … Does that affect the fact, the reason I don't have any pain, that I don't believe in sickness? And if I have a slight pain, I tell my mind not to feel it, and it doesn't feel it. Is that done by me or is it done by, say, a previous incarnation that I decided to be this way? Why is it, everybody else seems to have so many pains and … I know I'm not particularly sensitive to pain because when the dentist drills my teeth he never puts any Novocain or anything on it because I don't feel it. Is that something I've done or something that was planned?

I am Latwii, and am aware of your query, my sister. All choices [are those] you have made, many before this incarnation, and [many] indeed as a result of previous incarnations, for each incarnation may be looked upon as a class or course in which certain lessons are desired according to their efficiency, shall we say, in learning. The next course or incarnation is determined to be of such and such a nature so that new lessons may be learned or previous lessons may be refined. It may be that, as in your case, there is a certain need for the, as your peoples call it, maintenance of health upon a rather constant level so that lessons may be focused upon which do not require the use of the ill health, as your peoples have called it. Many upon your planet feel that people are quite similar in their experience and each may be likened to another in its experience of the various stimuli which your illusion offers, for example, pain. Yet, if careful study were made of each entity, there would be a great diversity discovered. Your case may sound quite unusual to many, yet it is but another example of the great diversity of the one Creator throughout all creation.

May we answer further, my sister?

M: Well, maybe. In other words, did I choose before I was born not to feel pain and have bad health, or did I … is my attitude here in this life causing me not to have bad health? Was it before this life or during this life? Is it my attitude now? I don't believe in sickness. Is that a factor or not?

I am Latwii. Your attitude, may we say, was quite carefully chosen before your incarnation.

May we answer you further?

M: No, thank you. I believe that does answer it.

I am Latwii. We thank you, my sister. Is there another query at this time?

S: Latwii, I have a quick one. I assume that my challenging ritual is effective. Can you confirm this for me?

I am Latwii. We may suggest that your ritual has been effective, for it is born of your heart and the desire to seek the truth.

May we answer you further, my sister?

S: No, thank you very much.

I am Latwii and we thank you, my sister. Is there another question at this time?

(Pause)

I am Latwii. We see that we have passed from the silver-tongued speech to the golden silence. We thank each in this group for allowing us to speak this evening. We remind you that our words are but guideposts, hopefully pointing the way to an inner seeking which will provide you with the true treasures of your being. Take what words we speak as lightly as the wind that blows in your spring season, and move gently along the path in peace. We leave this group at this time, rejoicing with you in light and love, in peace and in power. We thank you, my friends. We are known to you as Latwii. Adonai vasu borragus.

L/L Research

L/L Research is a subsidiary of Rock Creek Research & Development Laboratories, Inc.

P.O. Box 5195
Louisville, KY 40255-0195

www.llresearch.org

Rock Creek is a non-profit corporation dedicated to discovering and sharing information which may aid in the spiritual evolution of humankind.

ABOUT THE CONTENTS OF THIS TRANSCRIPT: This telepathic channeling has been taken from transcriptions of the weekly study and meditation meetings of the Rock Creek Research & Development Laboratories and L/L Research. It is offered in the hope that it may be useful to you. As the Confederation entities always make a point of saying, please use your discrimination and judgment in assessing this material. If something rings true to you, fine. If something does not resonate, please leave it behind, for neither we nor those of the Confederation would wish to be a stumbling block for any.

CAVEAT: This transcript is being published by L/L Research in a not yet final form. It has, however, been edited and any obvious errors have been corrected. When it is in a final form, this caveat will be removed.

© 2009 L/L Research

Sunday Meditation
March 13, 1983

(Unknown channeling)

[I am Hatonn.] It is a great pleasure to speak to you this evening through this instrument, and we would, at this time, speak to you in parable.

When a child, young in years, wearies of walking, he has in your culture the opportunity of asking for a tricycle. Originally, this tricycle was a very tall wheeled machine known as a velocipede. Upon it, the adventurous young person would dare life and limb, for the front wheel was very, very tall, and the two rear wheels very small, and the element of skill and concentration and art was great. But now, those who desire that no risk be taken have offered to your culture not only the tricycle made of metal, off of which a child could conceivably fall and bruise himself, but also the soft plastic safety of the big wheeled tricycle that cannot fall over. Upon it the child cannot come to harm. Of course, the child cannot then risk himself or dare an adventure, except in imagination, but this satisfies those who keep watch over him and are concerned for his safety.

When a child reaches a certain age, if it is of an adventurous spirit, [it has the opportunity] to request a bicycle. The element of risk returns. The child can dare the many tricks and performances common to those who cry out, "Look, Ma, no hands!" and swerve around corners at breakneck speed. They are not going anywhere, these older adventurers, they are risking themselves. Eventually, the child becomes man or woman and uses whatever means of transport is available, towards some end. He clambers into a car or upon the bicycle or motorcycle because it is necessary to move from one point to another, and perhaps the adult no longer dares the risks for the simple adventure of it. For perhaps now the adult sees purposes that unfold as the life unfolds before each one.

Now, my friends, as adults, the risks, the journeys, and the daring are interior. And yet, still there are those who could condemn you to the spiritual equivalent of the big, soft, plastic, three-wheeled environment. All your risk in your journey would be in your imagination. It has not been the choice of this creation and of the Creator to offer to each co-creator with safety. Not the three-wheeled, low-slung vehicle, spiritually or otherwise. You are free to risk, to dream and to dare. You are also free to go nowhere, to go only to those places which have meaning within an illusion which is bounded by geography, physics and the demands of your physical body. Those who find little joy in their experience are often those who have, of their own free will, chosen to limit the degree of risk in their seeking.

Let us turn in our thinking to a parable given by another. In this parable there were two sons. One son took his inheritance and spent it foolishly and sinfully, according to the notions of that day. The other son remained safely with the family, taking no risks and making no obvious mistakes. Yet, when the prodigal son had been reduced to the lowliest job possible within that culture he fell upon his knees, and he realized that he had left a loving father and sinned against him, and he determined to ask of that father for the lowliest job in the household. He had risked and he had lost everything, and yet when he came to his father's house, the father instead said, "My son who was dead is now alive. Rejoice! Prepare a feast and bring all of our friends to celebrate the return of one who has been gone, one who has been lost."

The other son, peddling carefully through life upon three low-slung wheels, adhering to his father's orders, felt not love but jealousy, for he had missed his journey, he had taken no risks and he did not know his identity nor appreciate his son-ship to the father, and said, "My father, you never gave me a party. I've always done everything you told me to." What could the father say? He looked at one son, who was foolish but brave, who'd come back loving and penitent, and he looked at the other son who measured every bit of service, and he could only say, "All that I have is yours. It has always been so, but cannot I give a party when your brother, who was dead, has come alive again?"

Each of you look into your heart and search out that which you measure, that which is low to the ground because you do not wish to risk a fall. Examine it carefully, my friends, because it may be an opportunity for you to enhance your journey. You seek to know the Creator, and you know that the nature of this seeking will be of a kind of return for you. Know that you have come from the Creator, and it is to that consciousness that you return. Therefore, must you not journey away in order to come back? Can you ever return if you do not set out? Whether it is a small thing, or a large, do that which is true to you, even if it is a mistake in actions. When it is due to fear that you will lose control over others or yourself, if often the intemperate and unwise choice, action brings about a catalyst that provides you with many mistakes, much learning, new understanding, and an ever abundant return to feast with the Creator in the kingdom where bread is of the spirit.

I would, at this time, transfer this contact. I am Hatonn.

(Unknown channeling)

I am Hatonn, and I am with this instrument. We would like once again to greet you in love and in light and would only say a few words in closing. We would like to express our joy in being allowed to share our message with you, the message of the Creator, the simple one of acceptance and love. We would like at this time to transfer, if the one known as A would allow us to do so, for we feel that the contact is beneficial for her at this time. I am Hatonn.

(A channeling)

I am Hatonn, and I greet you through this instrument, once again, in the love and in the light of the one infinite Creator. We are pleased with the chance to have our thoughts spoken through this instrument, and we are glad to see her climb back upon the horse. We have enjoyed sharing our thoughts with you and hope that, in some ways, it can shed a new light for you, for in learning in this illusion, there are many ways to see a lesson, and the brighter the light, the easier it is to see the lesson.

We shall leave you now, as we came, in the love and in the light of the one infinite Creator. Adonai. We are known to you as Hatonn.

(Jim channeling)

I am Latwii, and greet you, my friends, in the love and in the light of our infinite Creator. We are pleased, once again, to be called to your group. We rejoice with each of you at the honor of joining vibrations. Without further adieu, let us offer our service of attempting to answer your queries. May we begin with the first query?

A: Latwii, I am hoping you can help us with our Friday night meetings, and first of all ask how we are doing on achieving purity in our contact, for it is something we strive for as channelers.

I am Latwii, and am aware of your query, my sister. We feel that the discussion which preceded this meeting is quite sufficient to allow the realigning, shall we say, of the policy to admit those who have some knowledge of the nature of the meeting gained by reading those books which have been prepared for such a purpose. We feel that those who are what you may call the core of this group, are well aware of the necessity for tuning carefully, and do indeed tune as carefully as possible when the tuning time draws near. Yet, when entities have lesser desire and knowledge for this type of experience enter your circle, then the circle suffers some de-tuning. We feel that to expose these entities to the material available as a prerequisite to joining the circle shows respect to the tuning of the circle. The old and new entities, and, indeed, in the new entities, is a portion of the initial building of that respect which shall aid the tuning and the purity of the messages received.

May we answer you further, my sister?

A: Um, I know this will really touch a lot on our free will decisions, but where was there a great deal of distortion in your message and in Hatonn's messages in the past meetings, or is that too much on the free will?

I am Latwii. To give a complete answer to this query would indeed take from you the ability to discern that which is discernible to you. You have within your inner awareness and your intellectual capacities as well the ability to, shall we say, gain a feel for what transpires and for the nature of the messages as they are delivered. Look then to your own resources for the tools to make this discernment more readily available, my sister, and may we answer you further?

A: No, thank you.

I am Latwii. We are grateful to you, my sister, and thank you for your care and desire. May we attempt another query at this time?

Carla: I'm a little puzzled. When we have an intensive meditation and a new channel asks about the quality of channeling, the answer is usually fairly specific. What is the difference between that question and the one that I raised?

I am Latwii. In the case of the new instrument, there is genuine doubt as to the purity of the contact. In the case just queried upon, there is not such a pure doubt and the service to be most helpful is to reinforce that which is known, not by verification in a yes or no manner, but [by] coaxing that which is known forward [within the instrument's mind.]

May we answer you further, my sister?

Carla: So, if A truly was in the dark, and really had no clue, then she would have been able to find out about the channeled source, is that correct?

I am Latwii. This is largely correct, my sister.

May we answer you further?

Carla: No, no, I am just reminded of something Ra said once about how interesting it is that people ask so many questions that they already know the answers to. I guess we want confirmation. Thank you.

I am Latwii. We are very appreciative, my sister, to you, as well. May we attempt another query at this time.

Carla: I guess you want me to save the questions about things that have happened to me and the channel and Don for Ra, right?

I am Latwii. Our desires, my sister, are to serve in whatever manner is possible. We therefore ask if there is a way in which we might be of service?

Carla: Yes, there is, if it isn't an infringement on free will, because I really don't think I know the answer, and I would like to—all three of us—would like to have a Ra session soon. Two of the three of us are under the weather but feel that we can do it. Is that estimate of the situation accurate or would we be too low on energy, and therefore be taking too much of a risk?

I am Latwii, and shall attempt response to this query, though the instrument has some doubts as to our ability to clearly transmit that which is available. We shall begin, with the instrument's kind permission as he attempts to stand aside. We feel that your group has the requisite energy and harmony necessary for the conducting of a session with those of Ra. Though your group does have the deficit in certain areas at this time, well known to each of you, there is the ability to function in the metaphysical sense, which is the overriding factor in such sessions.

May we answer you further, my sister?

Carla: Since Jim is the power part of the triangle, is there some danger that the kidney problem might go on longer because he is expending physical energy and visualizing white light?

I am Latwii, and I am aware of your query, my sister. We find that this entity shall be able to function as necessary without the further damage to those organs of the renal structure for it is not a portion of the healing process that will be called upon in the activity of which you have spoken.

May we answer you further, my sister?

Carla: Just one thing, it's the only other thing that I could think of that wouldn't infringe, for sure, for sure. Is there anything that can be done to aid either Jim or me in building ourselves back up, each in our own way, and becoming healed of the things that have been wrong with us so that we might be able to be more, regular in our sessions than just having maintenance sessions and having trouble again?

I am Latwii, and to answer this query in the most helpful manner, we feel that we shall move from that which you may call the mechanical to that which we hope is the heart of your query, for there are those who are far more able than we to speak upon the mechanics and though there are also those who are far more able than we to speak upon the heart, we shall attempt this speaking. As you prepare yourselves to travel through your illusion, whatever the destination or purpose at the moment, to be most prepared to partake fully and to be of the greatest service at each moment one may look to the heart of love, and to see that love reflected in each moment is to know that one is prepared for all things.

As you look about you, and as you move with those about you, and as you dance with your creation, find the harmony of the moment. Find the means by which the love within may be shared with those about you. The dance of your illusion is most important, for it is an illusion that seems to lack love. The magic of the moment is to find that love, for it is in each moment. It is within your being. To dance with those in love and harmony is to be prepared to know the one Creator, and to serve each of its portions to your greatest ability.

May we answer you further, my sister?

Carla: No.

I am Latwii. We thank you, my sister, and may we attempt another query at this time?

Carla: If no one else has one, I'd like to ask one more unrelated. I can't remember whether I saw it in the news or heard it in the paper or whether it was just—but there was a woman with muscular dystrophy or multiple sclerosis who felt that she had the right to die because the nature of her life was not such that she could be of service to anyone else, basically. There has been a movie made on the same subject. A man being a sculptor who could no longer sculpt. He wanted to have the right to be taken off the machines that were keeping him alive. What are the metaphysical implications of determining, while still conscious, to end an incarnation, no matter how benign the circumstances sound? One does have the tendency to wonder whether or not it is a suicidal thought, and if it is a suicidal thought, whether that might not simply be prolonging the lesson rather than the other way around. What are your thoughts on that, Hobson?

I am Latwii, and am most happy to respond, dear. We shall begin by removing the concept of the suicide, as your peoples call it, for we find it overlaid with emotional content that distorts. We shall, indeed, re-correct this instrument, we shall de- …

(Side one of tape ends.)

(Jim channeling)

I am Latwii, and we shall continue with the concept of desire or perhaps dedication. When an entity finds itself in an incarnation lacking in that desire and dedication to learn those lessons which it has chosen to learn, and lacking in such an extent that it in some way contributes to the ending of its incarnation in what might be called a premature manner, then it shall find as it reviews the incarnation so ended that there was indeed the lack of desire, and it shall then find within itself the desire to complete that which was left incomplete. Therefore, such an entity may find that the lack of desire in one incarnation shall be balanced by a rededication to those lessons not learned and that situation not well used, and shall, once again, enter an incarnation in which the situation and the lessons and the desire dance together to find that there is the learning of love.

And may we answer you further, my sister?

Carla: Yes, just to finish up. The only variation on that theme, of course, is when there is a flat brain wave but the body is still being kept alive by allopathic means, you know, a heart machine, a lung machine, and all that stuff. At that point, pulling the plug seems to me to have no karmic, no anything—force—it's just simply the acceptance of what has already happened. Would you like to confirm that, or could you comment on it?

I am Latwii and am aware of your query, my sister. Indeed, in most cases, this may seem to be so, yet, it cannot be stated unequivicably—we correct this instrument—unequivocally, that such is always so, for, as you know, there are no mistakes, and a random catalyst is less and less apparent to those entities now incarnated upon your planet. This is to say that the advent of those machines which you call the life-support systems may have use to some entities. It may be that some final, last portion of a lesson can be learned while utilizing such a machinery.

Carla: No kidding!

It may also be the case that there are no further lessons, therefore, the machinery is unnecessary. We cannot state which case applies without knowing these specifics. Each entity can look to the inner knowing for that information.

May we answer you further, my sister?

Carla: Well, can one really? I mean, there's a poor dumb relative with a "living will" in her hand saying this is the "living will" stating her husband's desire is to be unplugged, if he ever gets in this situation. How does that person know how to perform the best service?

I am Latwii. We repeat that there are no mistakes. You may do as you will in each case. There are always ramifications and results from action. That is the nature of action. When you review your incarnation you will undoubtedly find those situations which you had hoped might produce results other than were produced. This will give you the means by which you may refine the learning which you intended. It is not necessary, shall we say, that you measure up to a certain grade in each situation. Do not be overconcerned with the details of each situation that you encounter. Look instead to the overall basics that are developed and balanced, especially those concerning love, forgiveness, acceptance, understanding and compassion. If you begin with such considerations, you begin at the heart of your lesson, and it is the heart of that lesson that you seek in each tiny experience.

May we answer you further, my sister?

Carla: I would hardly consider the decision that would bring about the death of someone—clinical death—a tiny experience. I think I get the drift. Thank you very much.

I am Latwii. We thank you, my sister, and, indeed, we do not mean to call that which you call death a tiny experience, but we are speaking to the general tendency to look upon each experience as large.

May we attempt another query at this time?

(Pages 14 and 15 are missing from the original transcript)

tion that we are of the Creator, we, therefore, are of yourselves.

May we answer you further?

Carla: No, thank you.

We thank you, my sister. Is there another question?

Carla: Yes, just one other question, Latwii. These people who are living in these illusions different from ours from our point of view, who worked with them many years, they are irresponsible and someone has to care for them. They have to be literally taken care of as though they were helpless, and oftentimes they are very disruptive to everybody around them, in fact. And my question is, do these entities, when they are crazy, to use our word—it's as good as any that I know—do they serve as a catalyst for those around them or do they give them an opportunity to serve the Creator?

I am Latwii. My sister, we would, if allowed, extend your question and respond by observing that those around oneself always have the potential of being both catalyst and the opportunity to be of service. There is no self who is not capable of being of service at any opportunity to another self.

May we answer you further?

Carla: No, thank you.

We thank you, my sister. Is there another question?

(Pause)

I am Latwii. As there are no further questions, we will take our leave with the observation that this has been a ducedly good time. In the love and the light of the infinite Creator, my friends, we are known to you as Latwii.

(Carla channeling)

I am Nona. We greet you in the love and the light of our infinite Creator. We come at the request of one who is not present and one who is present. We are most grateful to offer our healing of vibrations through this instrument, in love and light and light.

(Singing)

(Transcript ends.)

Sunday Meditation
March 20, 1983

(Carla channeling)

I am Hatonn, and I greet you, my friends, in the love and in the light of our infinite Creator. It is our privilege to blend our thinking that together we may sing in harmony and rejoice in creation. We greet you in the love and in the light of our infinite Creator. We show this instrument a picture of a door, a steel door with a steel handle. The walls about the door are blank and there is no designation for this place. This is a gateway. Yet impressed upon the heart of those who face this door is a phrase taken from one of your holy works: "The first shall be last and the last shall be first." You who stand before this door are not only capable but are also actively and continuously monitoring your supposed spiritual readiness to move through this door. And as you see those things in your existence which may seem to you to be of a simple nature, of a trouble-free nature, you may think to yourself, "I shall not spend my time thinking and analyzing upon these portions of my life experience, for then, perchance, I should miss the thinking and the contemplation that must be done for these other portions of my life which are not simple and easy."

There is no one barometer which says that an experience is spiritually neutral, has been handled well, or in need of examination. However, we shall surely tell you this. Each of you has many, many portions of life which are greatly, in your own estimation, in need of work. And in your own estimation, perhaps you feel the time that you have for meditation and contemplation should be spent in these areas. It is as though your life, or as this instrument's lateness to church, you are ten minutes late to an ever-running appointment with your life. You are forever behind; you are forever attempting to catch up. That which is of the spirit is not neat nor is it tidy, and unless you are a prophet, you will not find order as you seek the love and light of the Creator. In prophecy is order. In love there is divine confusion, and we come to you as messengers of love.

We ask you, my friends, to look most carefully at the halcyon, tranquil and peaceful moments that make up your daily lives. There is as much work to be fruitfully done in this examination as in the constant repetition of your penitence at being ten minutes late for your appointment with life. Do you think love wears a wrist watch, my friends? Do you think that you could miss a portion of a service, a part of a ritual designed to offer you your birthright? No, my friends, that is not possible. You made a journey to a far distant land and took upon yourself a heavy chemical body. And as if this body were a ship, you embarked upon a marvelous odyssey, and you sailed and you sang and you observed the stars, took your bearings and headed your course as you wished it to go. And so you do now.

You cannot be late, nor can you miss that which is within you. It is an illusion that you are experiencing, that of missing, that of needing to be penitent. To recognize an error in calculation is sensible, and this will come from balancing your various emotional feelings in meditation. But to find what is behind the curtains of those good times that are not seasoned with the salt of love is also a fine thing to balance in meditation. Have you loved as the Creator loves you? Have you cherished the joy of those about you? Have you nurtured those who do not yet know their own divine identity? Take your ship and let the wheel hum beneath your hand. Let the rigging sing with the sounds of the crystalline winds of creation. There is no need to accept those things which are unhappy without balance. There is surely the same need to examine good fortune. Until your experience sings with joy, there is more to do.

Now, my friends, we speak in most general terms and have not attempted to speak to the subjects of each entity with himself or of entities within families. These are separate subjects, and the questions that come to mind as one examines these far more personal questions of the great ship, the illusion, have to do with the intensity and the rapidity of reaction of the experiences that occur. It is far easier to work spiritually with an acquaintance than with a mate, and yet the deepest work is done with mates and friends who are held in an oath of perfect honesty and perfect love, so that there are no lies, good or unfortunate, no flattery, and no dodging. This is much more difficult, my friends.

At this point we would like to transfer this contact. I am known to you as Hatonn.

(Carla channeling)

I am Hatonn. I am again with this instrument. We find that each channel requests that we finish as we have begun through this instrument, and we shall most happily do so. We greet you once again in love and light. When you arrive at yourself, my friends, you find the most personal work of all and the one requiring the most perfect honesty. It is difficult to be responsible for your thoughts and yet, if they are unhappy, within your being shall you be balancing them. And if they be contented, within your being shall you gaze beyond those curtains of contentment to find life and joy and sometimes that which is discontentment which has been ignored, as if some leftover guest at a party had forgotten to go home.

You are in some ways, my friends, many people, and you stand before a door. We have described this door to you as being of steel, for though in some messages the door betwixt conscious and unconscious in the roots of mind has been called "veil," we call it "steel." Let us not deceive you as to the difficulty of what you attempt to do. On your side of this blank and featureless door you work with yourself consciously and prayerfully. If you have the will and the faith to reach in your dreams and open the door, you may see that those things about yourself, your families and your entire life that seemed so full of contentment, had many hidden guests. You will see that your difficulties produced much gold. One glimpse beyond the lintels of that doorway is an enormous aid.

May we ever more strongly suggest a continuing effort in meditation. And as you balance, balance all, judge nothing and view without rancor, bitterness or bias all that occurs. Remember that you are a creature of love. A great power created sun and galaxy and universe and consciousness and you. Center yourself upon that point and go forth with your mind filled with love and your heart full of light that you may do those things which are truly prepared for you and may rejoice in doing them that you may be whom it is you wish to be, that you may smile and dream and laugh. For is it not your birthright to encompass all creation? And is not that creation unspeakably beautiful?

We leave you now, my friends, in the love and the light of the infinite Creator. We are known to you as Hatonn. Sail forth, O sailors of life and know that the winds are with you, and there are those who shall always answer your call. Adonai, my friends. Adonai vasu.

(Jim channeling)

I am Latwii, and I greet you, my friends, in the love and in the light of the infinite Creator. We are pleased to be asked to join your group, and, as always, we come in joy. Your numbers this evening are few, but we are most appreciative of the great feeling of harmony which you offer in the blending of our vibrations. We thank you, my friends. May we ask if we may serve you at this time by attempting to answer any queries?

Questioner: Yes, Latwii, could you tell me the nature of sexual energy? I'm interested in knowing more about what it is and how it's used, etc., etc.—anything you can tell me about it.

I am Latwii, and we shall attempt a response to this query which does some justice to your great desire, though we feel we shall be somewhat limited by the breadth of this topic. Each entity has an energy of mind, of body, and of spirit which is that known as a vital energy. The combination of these energies enlivens the entity that it might continue learning in the vehicle which you call the body. In your illusion this is the yellow-ray chemical body. The energy of the physical vehicle is an energy which is usually described as a sexual energy. This energy is available to each entity in one of two natures or modes: that of the female, which awaits the reaching of the male, which reaches.

These two expressions of the one infinite Creator are a portion of each entity, be they male or female, yet each entity, as a male or female, will express one in predominance over the other, and has this energy to give in an exchange with a sexually polarized other self. The amount of energy which is available to each to transfer in what you call sexual intercourse is a function of a number of factors, one being the entity's ability to express and manifest its sexually polarized nature in thought and beingness, another being the amount or nature of the balance of the entity's mind, body and spirit complexes which is reflected in the unblocking and activation of the successive energy centers.

When two entities of sexually polarized nature join in what you call sexual intercourse, these two major factors then determine the amount of energy which is transferred. As you have discussed before your meditation began, the male offers the physical refreshment of the female and the female offers the inspiration of mental and mental/emotional energy to the male. By this dynamic interchange of energy, there is the potentiating, each of the other, in a mutually enlivening fashion so that the experience which each shares with the other is enriched and enhanced in the ability to further utilize the catalyst of the illusion and learn those lessons programmed before the incarnation. Such an energy exchange may be seen as a sort of a celestrial—we correct this instrument—celestial lubrication. We are happy that our pun was enjoyed.

May we answer you further, my sister—we correct this instrument—my brother?

Questioner: I understand you can't see the beard in the dark. No, thank you.

I am Latwii. We thank you, and shall keep our eyes peeled for that beard. May we attempt another query?

Carla: Well, just keeping abreast of the situation, I noticed that you said in the energy transfer—and I don't believe we've ever gotten any information from Ra either on this—there is physical going to the female and mental and mental/emotional to the male. At some point, when one wants to begin studying the sacramental nature of sexual energy transfer, spiritual energy transfer has to begin. Do both male and female have that to share in transfer of sexual/spiritual energy?

I am Latwii. Indeed, my sister, each entity, whether male or female, has the energy of the spirit which may be shared. This is the work of the adept working within the indigo or gateway center. As this center is activated, the experience of joy and the sacramental nature of each moment then becomes available to each sharing this experience. Many among your people have given this experience many names. That which is known as the cosmic consciousness experience will suffice for the moment. As each enters those conscious realms which are cosmic, the deepest portion of the mind is touched. This in turn, contacts the shuttle known as the spirit complex. Then as the spirit shuttle travels the great circle of One there is the contact with intelligent infinity which each then feels as an experience of the one infinite Creator.

May we answer you further, my sister?

Carla: So the keys to working at or—I hate to say work when we are talking about something that enjoyable—working at making that experience more available and working at making it more wholly sacramental would have to do with the work you did with yourself before you came to the sexual intercourse? Or would it have more to do with—in other words, I didn't quite understand whether you were talking about, when you contacted the shuttle, whether you had prepared yourself before the experience or as part of the experience? By yourself or with your mate?

I am Latwii, and am aware of your query, my sister. Each must prepare the self. The preparation of the self may be looked upon as the removing of blockages or distortions from those energy centers which precede the indigo-ray energy center. This preparation of the self, however, is aided and accelerated when done with a mate of a sexually polarized and oppositely polarized nature. This is a portion of the great experiment which our Logos has harvested a learning, shall we say, and has found to be most efficient in the evolution of the mind, body and spirit. When this work has been accomplished to the sufficient level, then each entity may join together and seek the experience which we have described. The process of sexual intercourse, then, becomes as what you may describe as the fruits of the labor, and each may then drink of the nectar.

May we answer you further, my sister?

Carla: Yes. Two questions. First, the way you use the terms having to do with mates. It seems to me that you're intimating without ever actually saying it, because you haven't been asked, that the mating is an all-important process, in other words, without the very strong polarity in love and trust, a true mated relationship, this level of work is simply impossible. Is that correct?

I am Latwii. We would not use the term "impossible," but would suggest the term, "difficult." We elaborate by suggesting that for two entities to reach the green-ray energy center …

(Side one of tape ends.)

(Jim channeling)

I am Latwii. We continue. There must be a considerable investment of what you call time made by each entity, that true caring and knowledge of the other self may be gained and even greater investment of what you call time is necessary to reach the level of honest and clear communication exemplified by the blue-ray energy center. It is most difficult for entities to activate these energy centers without having spent the time that is available to those you call mates or companions. Therefore, there is the bias towards the mated relationship on the part of our Logos, yet only a bias, for the free will of each entity is paramount, and each will discover by his own experience that method of evolution which is most efficient.

May we answer you further, my sister?

Carla: Well, I catch your meaning on that one, but the only other question I had is something that I'm a bit puzzled by. I know a fellow, one of the people I pray for every week. He's right now calling himself S1, lives in Atlanta. One of the many odd things that he's done in his life is embark on a magical system of opening up what he considered the sacramental nature of sex, and he did it by choosing at random a prostitute—the man's married—and paying her for beginning sexual intercourse, stopping it just at the point before climax, leaving it at that point for some time, and then, I suppose, putting on his rain hat and going home. And doing this for some period of time, after which he would allow himself full experience once. The experience, according to S1, was quite sacramental in nature. I have been puzzled by the nature of this experience, and haven't known what that particular experience was. Could you comment on it?

I am Latwii, and am aware of your query, my sister. We may only suggest that each entity has an unique path which it shall travel. Though the journey will eventually end at a point which is unity, each shall find that point by traveling a seemingly separate path. When we speak of such topics as sexual energy transfer, we speak in an area which is large and diverse. We are limited by the necessity of speaking in general terms in order that a general understanding might be achieved. The methods used by the entity of which you speak are most unique and specific to this particular entity. That such divergent methods may be efficacious does not argue against the general nature of the mated relationship being most efficacious for the seeking of the adept.

May we answer you further, my sister?

Carla: No, I think that's probably a pretty good evaluation of Tantric Yoga. That was some variation on Tantric Yoga that S1 was practicing. No, I have no more questions, thank you.

I am Latwii. We thank you, my sister. Is there another question at this time?

S2: Yes, Latwii. Along the same lines, when this experience happens at a rather early age, could you give me any information about that when two people haven't really had that much time invested in the relationship, is it more or less an accident or an awakening, or what can you tell me about that?

I am Latwii, and am aware of your query, my sister. Again, to speak in general terms is most difficult when a specific situation is thought of. It is often the case that entities remember in subconscious fashion incarnations shared before the present incarnation and express this remembering in certain areas of the current incarnation. That area which you call the sexual sharing is an area which [is] greatly subject to such remembering. The efficacy of such sharing remembered from previous incarnations then can be experienced in the present incarnation by, shall we say, beginning where the previous incarnation left off. That this is possible is due greatly to the fact that your sexual nature is not so much a function of your intellectual or thinking process as it is a function of your greater being, that being which exists before, during and after this incarnation.

May we answer you further, my sister?

S2: No, thank you, Latwii.

I am Latwii. We thank you, my sister. Is there another query at this time?

(Pause)

I am Latwii. We are most pleased to have been able to share yet another type of energy transfer with you this evening. It is always our privilege to join your group. We remind each present that we are with you at your request at all times. We leave this group at this time, as you call it, rejoicing in the love and in the light of the one infinite Creator. We are known to you as those of Latwii. Adonai, my friends. Adonai vasu borragus.

L/L Research

L/L Research is a subsidiary of Rock Creek Research & Development Laboratories, Inc.

P.O. Box 5195
Louisville, KY 40255-0195

www.llresearch.org

Rock Creek is a non-profit corporation dedicated to discovering and sharing information which may aid in the spiritual evolution of humankind.

ABOUT THE CONTENTS OF THIS TRANSCRIPT: This telepathic channeling has been taken from transcriptions of the weekly study and meditation meetings of the Rock Creek Research & Development Laboratories and L/L Research. It is offered in the hope that it may be useful to you. As the Confederation entities always make a point of saying, please use your discrimination and judgment in assessing this material. If something rings true to you, fine. If something does not resonate, please leave it behind, for neither we nor those of the Confederation would wish to be a stumbling block for any.

© 2009 L/L Research

The Law of One, Book V, Session 102, Fragment 52
March 22, 1983

Jim: And now, in Session 102, it was once again Carla's turn to experience another psychic greeting which intensified a momentary lapse from harmony on her part. She was unable to accept a portion of my perception of our shared relationship for the period of about an hour or two, but that was long enough, due to her intense emotions during that time, for a potent working to be accomplished by our friend of negative polarity. Fortunately, most people will not have to worry about such instant and dramatic intensifications of disharmonious moments since few people or groups attract the attention of fifth-density, negative entities. But the general principle is that one who is standing close to light experiences an honor which must be balanced by the responsibility of reflecting that light as harmoniously as possible, and this principle holds for all seekers. Failure to live up to that responsibility simply brings one another more intensive opportunity to do so until it is done, or until one steps away from the light.

In the third paragraph of Ra's second response we find the key concept or attitude for dealing with any such psychic greetings, or any difficulties in general, that one may face in the life patterns. Further into the session Ra gives the basic criteria for the unblocking of the yellow-ray energy center, the one with which Carla was working in this situation. Surgery was avoided, and the spasming condition of Carla's abdominal region was brought under control over a period of about two years. A potent working, that one!

Carla: Ah, humanity! Jim's and my discord was about that age-old dynamic between men and women: monogamy. Who was it that wrote the little ditty: "Hogamus, higgimus, men are polygamous; Higgimus, hogamus, dames are monogamous"? Ogden Nash? Dorothy Parker? At any rate, this is true, or tends to be. Jim asked for an open relationship several times in our early days together. Being most honestly more a friend than a BOY-friend, being linked to me primarily by our work together rather than any romantic interest, he naturally responded to the many lovely women who came his way. In this same circumstance, it never occurred to me to seek a further relationship. I was totally satisfied to have Don as my companion and mate, and had long since left off blaming him for wanting to be celibate, and also was perfectly happy with Jim's and my friendship and intimate life together. How we do stir up confusion with our desires! Yet to desire is most proper. I think much of learning in life is involved with the right use of will and desire.

One of the major healings of my life occurred with the removal of about half my descending colon in 1992. This cleared out much old and dead matter, and enabled me to do corresponding work within myself at the metaphysical level. There was much to release, and I felt wonderful to be able to do that. The psyche and the soma, soul and body, are inextricably intertwined and pain to one will be reflected in the other. However, when the body alone is harmed, the mind is much freer to re-vision the trauma than when it is the mind and emotions which are injured. If such damage is not addressed and respected, it can move ever deeper into the body's health, unbalancing and undermining it.

After that surgery, with its attendant metaphysical work, I had released all I could of the whole tragedy of Don's death and my life, so diminished without his company. And so I became finally able to move on into new life. I was sent home with a new diet, following closely Ra's suggestions. Every look into my GI system showed ulcers, and given my 30-year use of cortisone, this is not remarkable. The diet was called "low sediment," and on it were the well-cooked meats, veggies and fruits, sugars and fats that Ra had recommended, but not on it were the usual health foods—whole grains, nuts, berries, uncooked fruits and vegetables. I think one could almost characterize it as the UN-health diet! Yet it has worked, thank the Lord, for five years so far, and I am most grateful. I think I share with many people who have chronic disease that feeling of living on the razor's edge. I have to be careful, as mistakes are costly. I do miss salads especially, but have no argument with the destiny that has allowed me these years of life I almost did not have.

One note about "Bob": he was an amazing help in one area: my feelings of suicidal nature. After Don's death, and especially after I found out what Don had been thinking, I felt totally guilty for not being able to see his fears and allay them. I felt as though it was all my fault. The penalty, I felt strongly, should be death. I was quite unwilling to take my own life. Knowing how it had affected me when Don died, I knew I could never do that to those I love. Which left me hanging between life and death. Through the years from 1984 to 1992, the forces of death circled ever closer until finally I could look death in the eye, and find the faith to affirm life and love and healing. The part prayer had in this was substantial to say the least. And Bob's prayers were especially powerful to save. He told me of these suicidal vibrations long before I could do much besides drown in sorrow, and helped me through those pangs of self-knowledge and self-judgment which were so unbalanced. And he was joined by so many others. I had the sensation of being upheld in love, safe and sound, during the whole of the 1991-92 experience which involved four trips to the hospital, critically ill and quite foundered, my GI tract closed tight.

We have lost touch with Bob, in case you would wish us to give his name and direction. He let us know he had retired from active healing, and wished to spend his time now in deep prayer on the planetary level. Our thanks and blessings, wherever you are, dear Bob.

It was not easy to find Arthur Schoen. Ra had pronounced his last name "Shane," but there was not an M.D. of any type by that name. Finally we hit upon the German spelling—although if the name had been pronounced correctly, it would be "shourn," more or less. But this IS America, so of course the name was Americanized. We actually did go see this man, but left before he could treat me, as he and Donald did not see eye to eye. This is no surprise, for Don wanted him to read Ra's diagnosis, and the doctor did not really feel comfortable consulting with a discarnate entity.

Ra's suggestion to "link hands and walk towards the sun" is good counsel indeed. Had we been able to dwell in praise and thanksgiving, much would have been altered. But things were as they were. From this remove of time, I see and give praise and thanks for every moment we had together. Whatever it has cost, it was and is worth it all.

Session 102, March 22, 1983

Ra: I am Ra. I greet you in the love and in the light of the one infinite Creator. We communicate now.

Questioner: Would you first please give me the condition of the instrument?

Ra: I am Ra. The physical energy deficit of this entity is the most substantial across which we have come. The mental and mental/emotional distortions are near to balance and the vital energy of the instrument, as a whole, is distorted towards health or strength/weakness due to the will of the instrument.

Questioner: Will Ra please tell us what caused the pain and cramping in the instrument's stomach, and what could be done to heal it?

Ra: In order to observe the cause of physical distortions towards illness one must look to the energy center which is blocked. In this situation, the blockage being yellow-ray, the experience has had the characteristics of that region of the chemical body. The so-called lacuna in the wind-written armor of light and love was closed and not only repaired but much improved. However, the distortions energized during this momentary lapse from free energy flow are serious and shall be continuing for, in all possibility/probability vortices, some of your space/time, for a predisposition to spasticity in the transverse colon has been energized. There is also pre-existing weakness in pancreatic functions, especially that link with the hypothalamus. There is also the pre-existing damage to portions of the liver. These lacks or distortions manifest in that portion of the system directly proceeding from the jejunum. Further, there is some irritation closer to the duodenum which causes the instrument to fail in assimilating foodstuffs. This is an allopathically-caused irritation.

The diet is of central import. We can go no further in observing the system of the entity as a full discussion of those distortions towards various weakness/strengths which contribute to the present difficulty begin with the lips and end with the anus. We may note that the instrument has remained centered upon the Creator at a percentage exceeding ninety. This is the key. Continue in thanksgiving and gratitude for all things.

There are stronger anti-spasmodic drugs which the one not known to this instrument, but known as Arthur, may aid by the offering. The recommendation to do this, being as it is that which does not retain or remove life and does further remove from the instrument its opportunities for study in this situation, needs must be withheld. We are not in a position to recommend treatment at this space/time beyond the watching of the types of foodstuffs ingested.

Questioner: Thank you. I'm not sure that I understood everything that you said. The last name of this Arthur, and where he is located? Can you give me that information?

Ra: I am Ra. We can.

Questioner: Will you please do that?

Ra: I am Ra. The entity, sound vibration Arthur, has a surname Schoen, and is of your locality.

Questioner: What foods should the instrument eliminate in her diet in order to alleviate these painful attacks?

Ra: The information gained from the one known as Bob is that which is to be recommended. Further, all foodstuffs are to be cooked so that those things which are ingested be soft and easily macerated. There is a complex addiction, due to long-standing eating habits, to your sugars. It is to be recommended that, therefore, this sugar be given in its more concentrated form in your time of late afternoon, as you term it, with the ingestion of the sugared libation approximately one to two of your hours after the evening meal. It is further suggested that since this instrument has been using sugars for carbohydrates that a small amount of carbohydrates, low in sugar, be ingested approximately one to two of your hours before the sleeping period.

Questioner: As I understand what you say, the instrument is to have no sugar until late in the afternoon. Is that correct?

Ra: I am Ra. No.

Questioner: I didn't fully understand what you meant about when she should have the sugar. Could you clear that up, please?

Ra: I am Ra. The concentrated sugar; that is, the dessert, the ice cream, the cookie, should be ingested at that time. Small amounts of the fructose, maple, or raw honey may be ingested periodically for, as we have said, the chemistry of this yellow-ray body is such that the sugar is being used by blood enzymes as would carbohydrates in a less distorted yellow-ray, physical vehicle.

Questioner: I'm sorry that I am so slow at picking up precisely what we are getting at here. I want to be sure that we get this right, so I'll probably ask a few more stupid questions. Was the spasm that caused the extreme pain a spasm of the ileum?

Ra: I am Ra. Partially. The transverse colon also spasmed, as did the ducts to the liver in its lower portion. There were also muscle spasms from the bronchial coverings down through the pelvis and from shoulder blades to hips. These sympathetic spasms are a symptom of the exhaustion of the entity's physical vehicle.

Questioner: Then the opening for these spasms was originally made by the yellow-ray blockage but are triggered by the foodstuff which has to do with the ingestion of sugar. Am I correct?

Ra: I am Ra. You are partially correct.

Questioner: Then what else causes the spasms?

Ra: I am Ra. We speak of two types of cause. The first or proximate cause was a meal with too much oil and too large a burden of undercooked vegetable material. The sugar of the dessert and the few sips of your coffee mixture also were not helpful. The second cause—and this shall be stated clearly—is the energizing of any pre-existing condition in order to keep this group from functioning by means of removing the instrument from the ranks of those able to work with those of Ra.

Questioner: Now, there are two areas that the instrument can look to for curing this problem. I understand that the yellow-ray blockage problem has been completely repaired, shall I say. If this is not correct, could you make suggestions on that, please?

Ra: I am Ra. Each entity must, in order to completely unblock yellow ray, love all which are in relationship to it, with hope only of the other selves' joy, peace, and comfort.

Questioner: The second thing that the instrument must do to affect this cure is to be careful of diet which includes all that Ra has just stated and that which Bob recommends from his readings. There seem to be so many different things that can cause this spasm. I was wondering if there were a general approach to food. Could Ra recommend those foods that the instrument could eat that would have no chance of causing a spasm. Could Ra do that?

Ra: I am Ra. No.

Questioner: Is that because of the first distortion?

Ra: I am Ra. No.

Questioner: Why cannot Ra do that?

Ra: I am Ra. There are no foods which this instrument can take with total confidence that no spasm shall occur. The spasming portions of the vehicle have become sensitized through great distortions towards that which you call pain.

Questioner: Is there a group of foods that is most likely to not cause the spasming or any foods that Ra could name that would be highly likely not to cause spasms?

Ra: I am Ra. Yes.

Questioner: Could Ra please state which foods are highly probable to not cause the spasming?

Ra: I am Ra. The liquids not containing carbonation, the well-cooked vegetable which is most light and soft, the well-cooked grains, the non-fatted meat such as the fish. You may note that some recommended foodstuffs overlap allergies and sensitivities due to the juvenile rheumatoid arthritic distortions. Further, although sugar such as is in your sweetened desserts represents a potential, we may suggest that it be included at this period for aforementioned reasons.

Questioner: Would Ra please estimate the length of time in our time periods for the probability of this problem, if we follow these curative measures, for this problem to continue with extreme severity?

Ra: I am Ra. One of your moon's revolutions has a good possibility/probability vortex of seeing either the worsening of the spastic condition so that surgery becomes indicated or the bettering of the situation so that the diet continues be watched but the spasms be removed. The housing of the working is within the infection within the duodenum, the stomach, the jejunum, the ileum, the transverse colon, and portions of the liver. This shall be somewhat difficult to remove and constitutes perhaps the most efficient working to date. We may suggest, again, that the one known as Bob may be of aid. The one known as Stuart could, if it wished, discover the infection which is only marginally detectable but may prefer not to do so. In this case it would be well to request physical aid from an allopathic specialist such as that which has been mentioned.

Questioner: Do you mean by that Arthur Schoen?

Ra: I am Ra. That is correct.

Questioner: You mentioned the possibility of surgery. What would be the surgery to be done, specifically?

Ra: I am Ra. The body cannot long bear the extreme acidity which is the environment of such spasms and will develop the holes or ulcerations which then do appear upon the allopathic testings and suggest to the chirurgeon that which is to be excised.

Questioner: In other words, would this be the removal of a duodenic ulcer that would be performed?

Ra: I am Ra. If the ulceration occurs, it shall be past the jejunum, and most likely include the ileum and upper portions of the transverse colon.

May we ask for one more query of normal length as this entity, though filled with enough transferred energy, has the most fragile framework through which we may channel this and our energies.

Questioner: Obviously we would like not to get to the point of surgery. The only other alternative that comes to mind other than the diet and the instrument's mental work is healing through a healer, and I would like Ra's recommendation with respect to a non-allopathic type healer and any recommendations that Ra could make for either Jim or myself to act in that capacity or anyone else that Ra could recommend so that we wouldn't have to go through a surgical operation if it seems to become necessary. If we could begin working on one of these other approaches right away, I think it would be highly recommended. Would Ra comment on that, please?

Ra: I am Ra. We salute the opening of compassion circuitry in the questioner but note that that which is being experienced by this group is being experienced within an healing atmosphere. The healing hands of each have limited use when the distortion has so many metaphysical layers and mixtures. Therefore, look not to a healing but to the joy of companionship, for each is strong and has its feet set upon the way. The moon casts its shadows. What shall you see? Link hands and walk towards the sun. In this instance this is the greatest healing. For the physical vehicle we can suggest far less than you had hoped.

Questioner: Is there anything that we can do to improve the contact or make the instrument more comfortable?

Ra: I am Ra. All is well. Find love and thanksgiving together, and each shall support each. The alignments are conscientious.

We are known to you as Ra. We leave you in the love and in the light of the one infinite Creator. Go forth, then, merry and glad in His power and peace. Adonai.

L/L Research

L/L Research is a subsidiary of Rock Creek Research & Development Laboratories, Inc.

P.O. Box 5195
Louisville, KY 40255-0195

www.llresearch.org

Rock Creek is a non-profit corporation dedicated to discovering and sharing information which may aid in the spiritual evolution of humankind.

ABOUT THE CONTENTS OF THIS TRANSCRIPT: This telepathic channeling has been taken from transcriptions of the weekly study and meditation meetings of the Rock Creek Research & Development Laboratories and L/L Research. It is offered in the hope that it may be useful to you. As the Confederation entities always make a point of saying, please use your discrimination and judgment in assessing this material. If something rings true to you, fine. If something does not resonate, please leave it behind, for neither we nor those of the Confederation would wish to be a stumbling block for any.

CAVEAT: This transcript is being published by L/L Research in a not yet final form. It has, however, been edited and any obvious errors have been corrected. When it is in a final form, this caveat will be removed.

© 2009 L/L Research

Sunday Meditation
March 27, 1983

(Carla channeling)

I am Oxal, and I greet you in the love and in the light of the one infinite Creator. We graciously thank you for your gracious invitation and cannot express to you the enjoyment …

(Sound of a telephone ringing and then a recorded message.)

(Carla channeling)

I am Oxal. We apologize for the delay. We were to wait and speak to you after our brothers and sisters of Hatonn and had sought the one known as C and the one known as L, but had found each wishing to wait before offering the service. Therefore, we shall speak in some brief manner, and then allow those of Hatonn to speak to your group through other instruments than this one.

The teacher known to you as Jesus said to his disciple, "You shall deny me." And Simon, known as Peter, said, "I shall never deny you." And yet, under certain circumstances this disciple did deny his teacher. Look you now into the recesses of your own minds and find the teacher within you and find the teaching within you. Shall you deny that teaching today? Let us examine this concept further. How does one deny what one has learned? Is it by a word, a gesture, some portion of your life that is less than you would wish it? These things may be examined to good accountability and yet the fruit of deeper teaching is a person, and when you deny your teaching, you are other than your teaching would have you be. When you strip your daily living of the outer masks, that which shall affirm or deny lies in what you are. And when you deny what you have become, then you are as the one known as Peter, saying, "No, I do not know the one known as Jesus. You must be thinking of someone else."

This entity—son—was of such a quality, such a fine and good nature and kind that his leadership was known to the teacher, and his subsequent leadership has birthed both the good and the ill of that which you now know as Christianity. This was not a weak or cowardly man, and yet he denied that he knew. My friends, how easy it is not to know. How easy it is not to be. How very difficult from time to time it becomes to be who your teachings have lead you to become. There was no rancor in the teacher's voice when he told his disciple, "You shall deny me." There was only knowledge of the difficulty of responsibility, and this is what we speak to you of this evening, my friends.

Each of you is responsible for what you have learned, for what you believe you may have learned, and for what you are considering. We do not suggest to you that there is a sure knowledge, nor one that is even available to those wiser than ourselves, for our teachers do not claim to know all that may be known in what you would call any intellectual manner. It is the heart of things to which we wish to strike when we suggest that you are responsible to be yourself. We suggest further that you will find that difficult, and we suggest further that there is no unfortunate part in this apparent dichotomy, for that which you find difficult is that from which you learn.

Therefore, your very difficulty in expressing what you have learned teaches you. There is a purpose to your mistakes, as you would call them; there is a reason for your confusion. You did not arrive upon this sphere intending to withdraw from this plane in the same condition and estate in which you came. You intended to know the Creator in more and more glory, and in more and more accountability. You intended a great safari, and your game is the nature of love. That is your prey. The caliber of your weapon is the measure of how carefully you examine the difficulties that you are having in being yourself. Never judge yourself on seeming outer behavior. Continually attempt to learn.

"Peter, Peter," we say to you, "You shall deny love a million times and in each denial you will come to know me better." And all the strangers that say to you, "Are you not the one who knows love?" that cause you to deny are aiding you. Do not forget to thank them in memory, for such are the ways of the learning of love, that the paths of the creatures who learn it are twisted, and many who appear to be fair, prove difficult. And those who are most difficult are most mightily fair, for they have given you another denial and another step.

Shall you find love, then? My friends, you have no choice. You cannot reckon with your own nature. Shall you find it quickly? In that, my friends, you have a great choice.

I bow humbly before you and thank you. If any word of mine has offended you, remove it from your mind. It gives us great, great pleasure to be of any service to this group. And we thank those who have called us. We have come in the beatific love and the infinite light of the one Creator. Adonai vasu.

Carla: Would you all each continue to meditate and tune while I ask if all is all right. Are you all right, C?

C: I'm okay.

Carla: Do you need to hold on to somebody?

C: It's just that I've had some trouble lately and I'm just not ready to channel.

Carla: I just wanted to make sure that you weren't going into trance.

C: I'm feeling [warmth,] but I'm okay.

Carla: S, are you all right?

S: Uh-huh.

Carla: Do you want to tune a little again?

C: That would be helpful.

(The group sings quietly, "Row, Row, Row Your Boat.")

(Someone is heard entering.)

Carla: Come on in.

H: Go right ahead.

Carla: No, there's a chair right here, right by the TV. Hatonn is waiting on you, I guess.

Questioner: Hi, H.

Carla: Well, I guess we better tune again.

H: Sorry to interrupt.

Carla: Hatonn's been waiting on you. I'm glad you came. How do you want to tune, H?

(Inaudible)

Carla: Well, let's try …

(All sing, "Row, Row, Row Your Boat," through again.)

(H channeling)

I am Hatonn. Greetings to each of you in the love and in the light of our infinite Creator. As is always, we are glad to visit with you and to once again speak through this instrument. As you are aware, we of the Confederation are here about your planet desiring to serve man in whatever small way that we can, and it is groups such as this one that enable us to carry on our work most efficiently at this time. And we of the Confederation thank you for the opportunity to meet with you and to speak with you and to share our knowledge, our experience, and most of all our love with you and all of your brothers upon this planet.

Each of you within this room is what you might call a channel of our energy and our love, for all of you are instruments of the Creator. There has not been born one upon your planet that in truth is not a servant and a channel of the Creator's love. Every man has a role, as does every woman, to fulfill within their given lifespan. Most do not become aware of the role that they play until they have completed it. Few are given the knowledge and the directives that give them knowledge of what to do and whom to serve.

If you seek within your life the fulfillment that can only come through service to your Creator and your fellow man, then open yourself to the guidance that can be provided to you directly from the Creator in your silent meditations. We have always stressed to your group that meetings such as this one are beneficial, for the group energy, the group spirit and the group love is well for you to experience. It is enlightening and it is fulfilling, but it is not complete. It is for you as an individual to give time to the Creator in your meditations, for He has given this life and this time to you. Most of the people upon your planet at this time wander about, living their daily lives with no awareness of what they see or where they go. Those of you within this room have begun a journey that we wish all of your people would begin, for the time of awakening, the time of tribulation is at hand. We have always spoken of it to be approaching, but the time has come that it is now at hand.

Look about your world. Witness the turmoil. Witness the separatism, faith against faith, country against country. You can see that your planet is growing apart from one another and it is only through the efforts of groups such as yours and the individual efforts of each and every person involved that can enable this planet to grow together as one and take its proper place within the universe and in service to the Creator and hand in hand with we, your brothers of the Confederation. We wish not to alarm your peoples; we wish to enlighten them. We do not desire to see discouraging words spread amongst your people. By this we mean that it is not your duty to tell of the dangers or of the difficult times that lie ahead to your friends or your acquaintances. You need but love them with your spirit, share with them your light. The unspoken word is most often the most effective when it is given with your love.

With this, I shall pass to another instrument. I am Hatonn.

(Carla channeling)

I am Hatonn, and I greet you once again through this instrument. We had intended to speak, if permission were given, through the one known as L. However, this instrument is somewhat uncomfortable, and we find that it is not, shall we say, a good opportunity to speak through this instrument. We would, therefore, close through the instrument known as K. I am Hatonn.

(K channeling)

I greet you, my friends, again in the love and the light of the infinite Creator. We have just indicated through the previous instrument about the tribulation and the difficult times that lie ahead. But, my friends, levity and joy are most infectious and you can do more for your loved ones, your friends, and even for the planet in its difficult times by remembering that all, indeed, is one, and that what appears to be catastrophe is a way of cleansing, is a manner of cleansing your planet. So we would greet each one of you again with levity and joy and harmony and peace and all those qualities that lift the spirit of your peoples.

And, indeed, you do have reason to rejoice. We observed in the beginning of your session a certain dourness, shall we say, that need not exist among you. So we close this session, encouraging each of you to let the light shine with joy and peace and power that is available to each of you. Listen to the inner self as the hints come from time to time of who you are and what you are. You will find that indeed those about you will receive a blessing. And now we leave you in the light and in the love of the infinite Creator with rejoicing and thanksgiving for having been with you. I am Hatonn.

(Side one of tape ends.)

(Jim channeling)

I am Latwii, and greet you, my friends, in the love and in the light of our infinite Creator. We are honored to be called to your group, and to once again to be able to offer our simple service of attempting to answer your queries. We feel there are many present this evening with such queries. May we begin with the first.

C: Latwii, of late I've been experiencing great difficulty. I'm unable to meditate. I've been experiencing some physical difficulties, emotional and mental as well. I've gotten to the point where, as tonight, I'm so unsure of the contacts, I seem to be … it's just not comfortable anymore. I was wondering if the problems I'm experiencing are due to the denial of blessings, and if so, any creative suggestions you might have.

I am Latwii, and am aware of your query, my brother. We may speak only in general terms, for when a student such as yourself faces the difficult lesson, it is most helpful for that student to find the path by means of its own efforts, that the path may be known in each portion, and walked with sure feet. But we may make a general observation. That is, as you find yourself confronting the confusions, the frustrations, the angers, the doubts, the dissension with those whom you feel love at the base of your being, know that in each opportunity lies love. Know that the difficulty of the testing to find the love develops the strength to find it.

As you are in the midst of those lessons you have programmed to learn, you will often feel quite helpless and despairing. At these moments it is helpful to remember that your life is whole and perfect as it is, that you experience at that moment the illusion of difficulty for the very purpose of finding the wholeness, the balance, and the love within your being, and the being of each entity around your. Be not discouraged when the lesson is difficult, but find the heart of love at the heart of your being through the faith and the will to continue. The Creator has given you each experience as a treasure, and through each experience do you then grow closer in oneness to that Creator.

May we answer you further, my brother?

C: I am aware of that helpless feeling of which you speak. What disturbs me is that at this time, not the feeling of being helpless, but the feeling that I'm harming those around me. It's because I felt that I was doing harm that I've been away from these meditations these few weeks. Is—well … What does more harm at this time, my staying away from all participation?

I am Latwii. My brother, the source of the difficulty for any entity is the limitation of the viewpoint. If you will look upon your experience and the experience of each entity about you as the experience of the one Creator, with no separation between you, you will see that there is nothing but service, and in truth there is no harm, there is no polarity, no right or wrong, for you are one.

May we answer you further, my brother?

C: Not at this time, thank you.

I am Latwii. We are most grateful to you, my brother. Is there another query at this time?

L: Yes, Latwii. I came down with an illness about a week ago, and I'm still suffering some of the effects from it. Can you give me any indication of why these conditions are still hanging on?

I am Latwii, and again, my brother, we may speak in general terms. When the physical vehicle experiences the illness, as you call it, one may look to the symbolic function of that illness to determine the configuration of mind which has not well used the catalyst programmed for learning certain lessons. You are a crystal being. You have the centers of energy described by the rainbow. As you look to each, and to the difficulties which your physical vehicle expresses, you may make the correlations which shall show you in symbolic form the catalyst which provides further opportunity for learning certain lessons.

May we answer you further, my brother?

L: Yes. Also, earlier this week I was involved in what seemed to be a pretty pointless auto accident. Is there anything you can tell me about any significance for its having occurred? Any information you can give me? I assume that it occurred for a reason, but as yet I haven't been able to uncover any significant reason for it having happened at all.

I am Latwii, and am aware of your query, my brother. We may suggest that there are some instances in which random catalyst strikes. Yet, even random catalyst has the value in teaching love in some fashion. Therefore, one may look to each experience and attempt to find the lesson therein. For us to accomplish this for you is not our proper role, for this is your learning, which we would not take from you.

May we answer you further, my brother?

L: No, thank you.

I am Latwii. We thank you, my brother. Is there another query at this time?

K: Yes, Latwii. I was reading, just this week, in the book, *Unknown Reality*, and I'm going to paraphrase the statement, I think I can get it pretty close, that sickness and suffering are simply the misguided use of creative energies. These energies are neutral. They can be sickness and suffering or they can be health. So sickness and health are simply opposite sides of the coin. And it has been said that suffering is good for the soul, but this statement says that suffering is not good for the soul unless the soul learns not to suffer. So, would you comment on that pretty powerful statement? Or at least to me it's pretty powerful!

I am Latwii, and am aware of your query, my sister. We may suggest that the viewpoint spoken is helpful and is, in our humble opinion, in large correct. Yet we would also add another side or two to the coin. To describe sickness or ill health as the use of energy in a misguided manner may also be stated as the use of catalyst to learn lessons programmed by what you call the higher self. One may use the catalyst of the everyday life well or poorly. One may use such a catalyst so poorly that the physical vehicle becomes encumbered with the symbolic energy center blockage in a painful and crippling manner. This is, shall we say, to apply the board to the center of the forehead of attention. Is this misguided? Or is this simply the means by which the entity shall learn. We choose not to judge with terms of "misguidance" or "incorrect" or "wrong," but simply observe the action of catalyst upon an entity.

May we answer you further, my sister?

K: Well, from what I read, and from what I gather you say, I sense a discrepancy. What I'm assuming, the purpose of the catalyst is to learn to be well or whole. Is that a fair assumption? To learn some kind of a lesson, shall we say?

I am Latwii, and am aware of your query, my sister. We do not feel a discrepancy exists but that the differing means of viewing and describing growth exists. We would agree again with your statement that to discover your wholeness and perfection is a great portion of your learning, for indeed you are whole and perfect, for you are one with all. Yet it is also the choice of each entity before incarnation in learning that lesson of wholeness to program certain lessons that will teach love of all as one, and these lessons may require the application of the board, shall we say, from time to time when the attention seems to falter and the catalyst is not well used.

May we answer you further, my sister?

K: No, I believe that answers it. Thank you.

Carla: I'd like to pursue it a little further. May I assume that no matter what the person is like, whether the person is sick or well, whatever, the person's purpose remains constant, and that is to learn in this lifetime. I assume that's correct?

I am Latwii. My sister, again we find agreement with the greater portion of your statement. Yet, from time to time catalyst is so well used that additional lessons become possible so that the basic purpose, to gain experience and to polarize in the sense that you have come to know as service to others or self, may be seen to remain as underlying themes of the incarnational patterns.

May we answer you further, my sister?

Carla: Well, I think you just skipped about two questions and got to the end. Where I was headed, for those who didn't hear those other two questions, was—my reasoning was that perhaps when people were well they were using catalyst with the same amount of sensitivity, and feeling the slings and arrows of outrageous fortune and all that, with as much sensitivity as a person who was getting these slings and arrows in the form of an illness or suffering.

However, in a person who had gotten to this point, it simply did not produce suffering, it produced an observation of the problems, and a learning without the addition of suffering. In other words, suffering isn't necessary; suffering occurs because of, just as K said in the beginning, when the catalyst comes in you choose to find that it hurts instead of finding that it does not hurt. We basically have the choice, and some people have found that they do and therefore they learn—this was what I was assuming—without having the suffering involved. And these people are well, but they are still learning, that was where I was headed, and that's just what you said. So, that's not a question. I just wanted to confirm that was the direction that your answer took.

I am Latwii, and we find that we were indeed on similar paths. We may comment in short by suggesting that we deal with two concepts when we speak of using catalyst well or poorly. These are the concepts of the development of will and faith. As an entity constantly chooses to be of service to others or to be of service to self, to radiate light and love or to absorb light and love, the entity will develop the strength of will and faith that will make the traveling of its path ever [more] sure and ever more filled with the nature of that path. For the entity who chooses service to others, the constant choosing or polarizing in this direction begins to shine as a light above such an one, that the path be lighted and grow protected. The strength of will to make that choice, and the faith to know the choice as power are the factors which guide such an entity.

May we answer further, my sister?

Carla: No, Latwii. I thank you.

I am Latwii. We are most grateful to you, my sister. Is there another query at this time?

M: Yes, I have one on the same subject. I grew up in a family where it wasn't fashionable to be sick, and the irony of the whole thing was, nobody was ever sick, nobody took an aspirin. And is it possible to have an attitude of good health that really is a factor in not getting sick?

I am Latwii, and am aware of your query, my sister. It is indeed possible such a choice has been made before the incarnation, and has become a portion or part of the great puzzle that shall be assembled by the entity during the incarnation.

May we answer you further, my sister?

M: No, thank you, that was fine.

I am Latwii. We thank you. Is there another query at this time?

C: Latwii, I would like to ask a question about the colors and chakras. I'm aware of the color scheme that Ra has given forth, but there are other sources of information that have given other color schemes, not so different, but some of the chakra colors are different, and also that there are other sub-chakras in the ankles, knees, wrists, elbows, shoulders, and could you comment on this please?

I am Latwii, and am aware of you query, my brother. To begin with the last portion first. There are indeed a great many sub—as you call them—chakras within the physical vehicles, and within the other lighter bodies of the mind/body/spirit complex. These are for the advanced student who has mastered the basic function and purpose of each of the seven major energy centers within the physical body and has begun some work upon the penetration of the eighth, which is located above the crown chakra.

The colors of each chakra or energy center are far less important than the function of each center. Those colors given by the social memory complex known to this group as Ra proceed from lower, or groin, to higher, or crown, in the rainbow fashion of red through violet. The functions, as we mentioned, are of most import. That is, for the red to serve as the foundation for all that proceeds in the experience of an entity, that being in a primary function the sexual reproduction, and is a center which is not usually worked upon in a conscious fashion, for it is the beginning, and it is as it is. The orange being then the further refinement of the prana, as you may call it, that enters through the red into the personal expression of being, whether it be the expression of power over others in what you have come to know as the service-to-self sense or in the beginning expression of love and acceptance of others and self. The yellow continues the refinement of the in-streaming prana of the one Creator so that the entity begins to expand this expression of love into groups with which it identifies. The green being that great opening into compassion, understanding, forgiveness and acceptance. The blue further refining this energy into the clear and free communication of self with each other self. The indigo refining further the prana of the one Creator in a way which combines that of which we spoke earlier, the development of will and faith.

This is the birth of the adept, the entity who is consciously aware that it seeks unity with the one Creator. At this center activities of what might be called a paranormal nature are possible. The working of what is loosely known as magic is here first begun, that is, the conscious use of the unconscious mind. With the violet ray we again complete the circuit, and find a center which is not consciously altered by incarnational experience, in that it is the register or the mark of the entity, revealing the balance of mind, body and spirit. When the entity has sufficiently cleared each of the energy centers within the physical vehicle, then it is possible for the entity to reach from indigo ray through violet to the eighth energy level, and contact those portions of the one infinite Creator known as intelligent energy and intelligent infinity, the latter producing the experience of unspeakable joy as the entity knows the full presence of the one infinite Creator.

May we answer you further, my brother?

C: Thank you. I would like to ask another question concerning fourth density that we're all moving into. I would like to know more about body functions in the fourth density. Could you comment on that?

I am Latwii, and am aware of your query, my brother. The body which shall be inhabited by those of the fourth-density positive remaining upon this sphere is a body which is much more densely filled with light and the force of life which we have spoken of as the prana or love/light of the one infinite Creator. Many among your planet, in studying those things of mystery and of an occult nature, describe this body as the astral body. It is the green-ray energy center equivalent to the body you now inhabit as the yellow-ray energy center body. It is a body which responds much more fluidly and instantaneously to the will and faith developed in the indigo-ray energy center so that those actions or artifacts which are desired are much more easily constructed through the indigo-ray energy center's contact with intelligent energy. This allows for the further development of the, what might be called, discipline of the personality which allows an entity much greater freedom in travel, in contacting telepathically all those about it, whose thoughts are seen to be quite transparent, and to do all things which serve as catalyst and as means for processing catalyst. The body is therefore much more malleable and subject to that which has created it, that is, the mind of the mind/body/spirit complex.

May we answer you further, my brother?

C: When you say "travel," does that mean teleportation?

I am Latwii. My brother, in some cases, most usually in the later progression through this particular density of love numbering four, this is true. The ability to travel by what you have called teleportation, or what we would call the discipline of the personality, is an ability which is developed more and more by the entity which seeks to accelerate the process of its own evolution. There are many, many entities within the fourth density who are unable to travel in this manner, and must use those types of mechanical devices for travel that you now use, though such devices are also quite far advanced, yet they are mechanical and not yet of mind.

May we answer you further, my brother?

C: Thank you. I'm most grateful.

M: I'd like to extend that a little further. If I saw a fourth-density being, would I feel that they are similar to us or would I feel that they are quite different?

I am Latwii, and am aware of your query, my sister. Most fourth-density beings would seem quite different in appearance if you should see them, and we mention that seeing such an entity is possible only by such an entity's desire to be seen, for each entity has evolved from a second-density physical vehicle, and has evolved through the third density utilizing that vehicle, and continues the utilization of the basic form of that second-density vehicle through the fourth density, and only with the fifth density graduation is able to change the form by the power of the mind.

May we answer you further, my sister?

M: No, thank you. That answers my question.

I am Latwii. We thank you. Is there another query at this time?

Carla: Ask the condition of the instrument. Is the instrument fatigued or is he okay for continuing?

I am Latwii. We find a sufficient reserve of energy available for another few queries. Yet we would suggest the drinking of the water.

(Pause)

Carla: You want me to drink it? Sorry, Latwii, didn't see the hand coming.

L: Good thing he didn't have to go to the john.

(Giggles from group.)

(Jim channeling)

I am Latwii, and am once again with this instrument. We appreciate your levity, my friends, and we thank the one known as Carla for the drink and the laugh. May we ask now if there might be another query?

A: Yes, Latwii. I had two, but Carla took care of one of them. The other was pretty short. As you were giving your answer about fourth density, a story came to mind. I was just wondering if it was a rather simple analogy, and that was of Jonathan Livingston Seagull and his life of change, and is there a similarity?

I am Latwii, and am aware of your query, my sister. Indeed, we find there is great similarity between the story of which you speak and the concept of which we were speaking. The concept is that of transformation. At each juncture in an entity's life there comes the opportunity to be that which the entity was unaware that it was before the juncture, that …

(Side two of tape ends.)

(Jim channeling)

I am Latwii, and once again speak through this instrument. That the entity is more able to fully express the nature of the one infinite Creator within its own being, that this is done in steps, is most important. For within your illusion, you experience a great seeming illusion, that of inhabiting a physical vehicle with certain characteristics and abilities and seemingly without others. And to express the full nature of the one Creator in a moment is the work of many incarnations and many stages that prepare the entity's various vehicles and energy centers for the increased flow of prana or love/light of the one Creator through its being.

May we answer you further, my sister?

A: No, thank you, Latwii.

I am Latwii, and we thank you. Is there another query at this time?

K: Yes, one other question along that line. Were some of our forefathers wanderers from the fourth density. Well, let's say—let's take Emerson, for instance. Was he from the fourth density?

I am Latwii, and am aware of your query, my sister. Though we find that this entity, the one known as Emerson, was of a nature which you have come to know as a wanderer, that the density was not that of love, but was that of wisdom.

May we answer you further, my sister?

K: Are you saying then that Emerson was from the fifth density?

I am Latwii. This is correct.

K: Then I am assuming Franklin and Jefferson and several of the men who wrote the Constitution were from the fifth density also. Is that right?

I am Latwii, and am aware of your query, my sister. Many of those which you now know as the so-called founding fathers of this culture were indeed wanderers who had incarnated in what you may call a great wave of incarnations that they might offer together the concept of freedom and the freedom of choice to entities upon your planet. Most wanderers who return to planets such as your own come from those densities of five, that of wisdom, and six, that of unity. Few come from the density of love, the fourth density, for there is required for any such wandering entity a great deal of the strength of will and what you might call foolhardiness. That takes much experience and use of catalyst to develop. Usually the entities of the density numbering four are not so well prepared for such a rigorous experience, for each such entity partakes of the process of forgetting which all upon your plane partake, in that the lessons learned in this, the choice-making density, might carry more weight within the total beingness of the entity.

May we answer you further, my sister?

K: No, that helps a lot, Latwii. For having been a student of American history, that helps me to understand where these fellows got all their smarts. Thanks a lot. I always wondered where they got all their smarts.

I am Latwii. We thank you, my sister. Is there another query at this time?

M: Yes, I have one. This may sound presumptuous, but several weeks ago I was talking to this dog, and the dog told me that some humans could come back as a pet animal if all they needed was love and a lack of responsibility for, say, seven or twelve years. Was this dog correct?

(Chuckling from group.)

I am Latwii, and am aware of your query, my sister. We recognize the great humor in speaking to one such as that of which you have spoken, yet we remind each that you speak at all times to the one Creator, and there is wisdom all about you. It is, to the best of our knowledge, not a usual practice, shall we say, for an entity to choose to place the mind/body/spirit complex in a less advanced physical vehicle, and to further limit the potential for the expansion of the viewpoint, but it is possible for a portion of a mind/body/spirit complex to inhabit by magical means second density and first density creatures and artifacts.

May we answer you further, my sister?

M: No, thank you, but I guess then there was some merit to what the dog said?

I am Latwii. There is some merit, my sister, in all words and concepts, wherever they originate, and there is some misdirection in each as well, for the nature of the word is to limit that which is limitless.

May we answer you further, my sister?

M: No, thank you.

I am Latwii. Is there another query at this time?

Carla: I have known rogues who were much loved, and who did not have any responsibility, and who were quite human. Could this be what the dog meant?

I am Latwii. To a rogue, another rogue is easy to spot. May we answer you further, my sister?

Carla: Yes. That's what I thought that was probably what the dog meant, but I was also thinking about the seeming heartbreak of kids that are born with fewer marbles than the package normally contained and are indeed much loved and indeed do not have responsibility. And many times the parents will express an enormous amount of joy at continuing care of a little one, even though that child will always be no more than a two-year-old. Is this another instance perhaps, of what the dog is speaking of on a more serious line?

I am Latwii, and am aware of your query, my sister. It is indeed possible that an entity may choose to learn the lessons of love by limiting the mental or physical energy complexes, and that it will enter into agreements with those about it during the incarnation to not only aid its own learning of love, but to aid their own as well as they provide that service which is necessary for the, shall we say, making up for the limitations.

May we answer you further, my sister?

Carla: Just one more question and I'll quit. Nona just left. Did she leave because the group is getting too tired to listen to the healing sounds? Is the healing that she left still with us? Or was there some other reason?

I am Latwii. The Nona influence has departed for the moment but shall return upon request.

May we answer you further, my sister?

Carla: No, thank you, Latwii. Thank you, you've done yeoman's service tonight.

I am Latwii, and we find there is sufficient energy for a final query at this time.

C: Latwii, could you comment about the information that's coming through in a set of books called *A Course in Miracles*?

I am Latwii, and am aware of your query, my brother. We find in this instance that we must speak again in terms that are general. For us to determine for another the path to take is not, in our humble estimation, proper. We may suggest then that the student of its own evolution look to any source of information with the broadest possible viewpoint, taking information that seems of value, leaving that which seems of less, and using that which is gleaned as feels appropriate.

For one student at one time there is a need. For that student at another time, the need is different. For each student at all times the needs are unique. One source may be helpful to some at one time, and not at another. Each processes catalyst using unique circuitry, thus all need not be the same to be equal in will and faith.

May we answer you further, my brother?

C: Thank you, no. That was fine.

I am Latwii. It has been a very great honor to speak to this group, and to greet new friends and old alike. We thank each present for inviting our presence. It is a privilege which we treasure. We remind each that we are but your humble and fallible brothers and sisters of those of Latwii. Take what we have offered that has value to you. Leave that which has none. We send you each our love and our light and our joy. In that love and light and joy, we leave you now. In the name of the one infinite Creator, we bid you adonai.

(Carla channeling)

I am Nona. I am with this instrument. We greet you in the love and in the light of the infinite Creator. We were sorry to distress this instrument, but we wished to bide with the instrument known as C. For as many in this group are in need of healing and have requested for each other that the energies be with you, we wished to offer that which we have not done before, that is that to sing in harmony. We would start with the one known as C and continue with this instrument. We thank you in love and light. I am Nona.

(Carla channels chanting from Nona in lovely two-part harmony.) ❧

L/L Research

Sunday Meditation
April 3, 1983

(S1 channeling)

I am Hatonn, and I am with this instrument. I greet you this evening, my friends, in the love and in the light of the one infinite Creator. We are, as always, pleased to be with you this evening. We hope you are all experiencing the great togetherness that comes with this day of blessing. We feel an overabundance of love emanating from your planet on this holy day. We are overjoyed to see such love and such togetherness when many people among your planet are joined together in love and brotherhood, and though this happens most often on what you call a holiday, it is nonetheless important. We seek to find the love and the light as it grows in brightness and we see that on days such as this the love and the light coming from your planet increases on days when many of you are joined together in your seeking and in your thanksgiving.

The creation is of love and of light and is increased by the love and light which joins us to you, for the love and the light is one, as we are all love and light. We often speak to you of love and light, and we hope that you are aware of the significance of these words, for love and light is all. Love and light is without; it is within; it is everlasting; it is eternal; it surrounds you; it is within you. You each have the ability to take the light that is within you and send it outwards to others, for if each entity sent its love and light to others, what a brilliant light it would be. It would be all-encompassing. It would be as if you were all aware in one moment that you were all a part of this love and this light. And while many are aware, many stumble and many do not feel or see the light that shines within them and upon them.

So we would hope that you would always send your love and your light to those with whom you come in contact, for each entity is energized by this light, whether they are aware of it or not. Each entity is touched when they are touched by another, for to send your light to another is to share your love with them. They may not see this as anything more than kindness, cheerfulness or good will, but they indeed see it. It is an honor and a privilege to be able to aid an entity with the love and the light within your heart. Each entity has within them a light. The light is ever expanding, ever growing, ever reaching outward. It has the ability to help others, it has the ability to heal others, it has the ability to comfort others, and though you may think your love, your compassion, or any kindness you may expend on another entity often goes without reward, let me assure that it never goes unnoticed. There is always a result when you send your love and your light to others, for you are sending your love/light to creation. The Creator sends love and light to each of you, and in return [you] send love and light to the Creator. It is always and totally encompassing. It is unity, it is all.

It is indeed with a great deal of honor that we are able to speak to you through this instrument, for we have wanted to spend some time with this instrument this evening. We thank you all for your invitation and we would wish to transfer this contact to another instrument at this time. I am Hatonn.

(Carla channeling)

I am Hatonn, and having consulted with the one known as S2, we find that it is better for us to speak through this instrument in order that the one known as S2 may be comforted and rested as she has been of great service already in your recent past. We greet you once again in the love and the light of our infinite Creator and we shall continue speaking of light—light, limitless, ever abundant, ever echoing and reechoing in its vibrations. We speak to you of one known as Jesus whose presence is called to this planet more in your diurnal period than at any time, as you call it, except for that season which you call Christmas. We speak to you of the light, for you are all light. We speak to you of a man who did not allow his light to be placed beneath a basket. We speak to you of a dark world, for such is the nature of illusion. Each of you comes into the world as a light, but the world is in darkness, and knows you not and receives you not, and yet you shine in the darkness and though the world does not know you, you set upon your journey, your eyes twin lamps of love, beaming as watch towers, as light houses, as warning signs to those who see or wish to see.

That teacher known to you as Jesus was on a journey. Scarred and broken, he died. But that did not stop him for long. He went in his new body upon the road again into Galilee as it is written in your holy works. He did not leave the road for long, for he wished his light to shine, no matter how dark the world which seems to be about us all. And he met those upon the road and he broke bread with them and spoke to them and shone and glistened and then was, as each of you shall one day be, gone into other illusions, into other partial darknesses, for you shall attempt to refine and refine and refine once again your understanding of your own nature, for that is your nature, my friends—light.

When love created material, the material it created was light. Light is creation, and all that is within creation is light. That is why light has the power to comfort, to bind, to unbind, to heal, to do all things. Light is the very stuff of which the universe, the galaxies, the constellations, the creation itself is formed, and the energy of love which free will causes to move, moves within that light and through that light into all those which are of the light. And my friends, there are none which are not of the light.

We would say to you two things. Be aware of light. The illusion will cause you to be aware of darkness, and darkness does not know light, it cannot see light, and shall not discover light. But you are light. Choose, my friends, to enter into meditation, to come close to your nature, to find your own light and to allow it to shine forth as you stand upon the watch tower of a dark world. The light will see many things. Let no darkness come between you and love.

We suggest to you one more thing before we leave this instrument and that is that you are on a journey. You are on a great gamble, and you must risk yourself or you shall not proceed upon your journey. The light that you seek and that you are will aid you in your risk, but a risk it is, my friends, to choose. We risk and you risk. But, my friends, the game is divine. And losses are far more temporary than the inevitable lightsome outcome. Therefore, be of good cheer and encourage each other, lending praise and joy to your common endeavors, letting your light flow endlessly, purely and powerfully. All the world sings of light at this time of your year. The springtime blossoms turn to the light and rejoice. The very grasses of the meadows turn and move and rustle at the glad wind of the Creator that brings the sun ever nearer and keeps it in the sky ever longer. So are the seasons of your life. So are the resurrections of your journey. And so is the nature of your journey.

Know always, my friends, in the deepest night, on the shortest day, there is that light within you. Doubt it not, but find it and risk all to find it again more clearly, more lucidly, more plentifully, more abundantly, and then open yourselves and shine.

We leave your radiant group, rejoicing and making merry at the lengthening days and the beautiful light within this group and within your planet. We leave you in the love and the light of the Creator that is in all and is all. I am known to you as one of Hatonn. Adonai, my friends. Adonai vasu.

(S1 channeling)

I am Latwii. I am Latwii. I am pleased to greet you, my friends, in the love and in the light of the infinite

Creator. We hope we did not surprise you by speaking so soon, but this instrument requires a great deal of conditioning before she will allow us to speak so we have been preparing her for quite some time. We are honored that you have called us here this evening, and we are also honored that this instrument has wished to speak our words. She is always hoping that we will contact her. She seems to be rather fond of us. We also are fond of her. We hope to be able to be of some service to you this evening, and humbly ask that you would consider those words which have been spoken tonight by our brothers and sisters of Hatonn, for we also feel the warmth and the love and the light emanating from your planet today. It gives us great joy, and we are always happy when we are able to experience such a loving vibration from all of you.

We are hoping to be able to speak through this instrument more often, for it is indeed an honor to be able to speak our words through any instrument that calls upon us. We are often seen—we correct this instrument—we often seem to be a source of joy among this group, if we may be so bold as to brag a little bit. We hope to be of service to you in the answering of questions that you might have, so we would leave this instrument and allow another [to complete] this portion of our transmissions. We leave you temporarily in the love and in the light of the one infinite Creator. We are known to you as Latwii.

(Jim channeling)

I am Latwii, and greet you once again in love and light. We now begin our task of attempting to answer your queries. May we ask then, for the first query?

R: Yes, Latwii. My question concerns the work environment, and the feeling I've had recently of it being a very, not necessarily depolarizing, but just not conducive to any kind of growth, in fact it seems to be the opposite, and I don't really know what my question is, but it's become a problem. My meditations have become erratic, and I'm going through some kind of a strange period of time. I wonder if you could offer any words of wisdom or advice, maybe? I need the job.

I am Latwii, and am aware of your query, my brother. We look at the situation which you describe. We see one who seeks truth. We see the lessons which lie before you. We see the opportunities to learn that which you wish to learn. We see also that from time to time, as in the life of any, shall we say, serious seeker, there will be those times when the training aids which you call your reality will be less efficiently used. For the entity upon the journey there are times when rest is of aid, and there are times when the journey is speeded, and less rest is needed. Be aware that each situation in which you find yourself has the potential of teaching of you just that which you wish to learn.

What do you wish then, my friend? The environment in which you find yourself will be that which meets your wishes and your desires, though you may not know that this occurs as it occurs. For much is hidden from the conscious mind. Be not over-discouraged when the mysteries seem to far outnumber that which is gleaned with any clarity. That you inhabit an illusion is obvious to your conscious mind as you continue your seeking. That the illusion shall remove itself and make clear that which guides your incarnation is not so obvious. Yet, this is the process in which you partake at the present. You look about you and you see the difficulty. With yet another eye you may see the opportunity. With yet another eye you may see the lesson learned.

If for a moment or two each day you might exercise, shall we say, an objective indifference, you may develop other eyes to see. By this we mean to say, look upon yourself and your environment as though you were seeing another being. Describe that which you see in objective terms so that instead of saying, "I feel a difficulty because …" you may say, "I see an entity experiencing such and such …" This may aid the perception of the general run of the pattern of energy which tends to confuse and overload your circuits, shall we say, from time to time.

May we answer you further, my brother?

R: No, thank you.

I am Latwii. We thank you, my brother. Is there another query at this time?

S1: Yes, Latwii. I have a question that's somewhat of a personal nature so I realize you may have to answer in general. I believe this last week I have discovered a main lesson that I am here to learn, and I was wondering, since this hit me in the head like a board, and I'm quite curtain of it, if you would be able to confirm it for me?

I am Latwii, and am aware of your query, my sister. We find that you have indeed gotten your attention, and have noticed that which you have placed before your incarnation. The journey which each travels is long and has many turns. At some turn there will finally come a realization of yet another factor or characteristic of the journey, so that increasingly so the pilgrim comes to know the self, the journey, and the lessons.

May we answer you further, my sister?

S1: Not on that subject, but I do have another question. I'm trying to think how to phrase this. Give me a moment, and I'll try to put it into words and get back to you in a little bit, okay?

I am Latwii. We are honored to await your query or attempt the next at this time.

Carla: Well, just to fill in the gap, I guess my question's like R's, just a matter of perspective, but ever since I got this tummy ache which won't go away, I've wondered if there's anything more that I can do than I'm doing. As far as I know I don't have any energy blockages. An examination of conscience doesn't reveal anything. I've attempted to follow the things within the illusion like what to eat, and things like that. What more can I do at this point to not just end my stomachache, but end the concern for me that people around me feel?

I am Latwii, and am aware of your query, my sister. We find that you have various portions to this particular distortion, as has been mentioned by those calling themselves Ra. The nature of your difficulty has many levels of the metaphysical nature. We find that the close adherence to diet is that which in the short run shall provide the greatest measure of relief, in that no further irritation of the sensitive intestine tissues will be initiated. We find the work done upon the energy center blockage most helpful with few, shall we say, corners to soften. Yet the container is solid. We can only suggest the continued rejoicing and giving of …

(Side one of tape ends.)

(Jim channeling)

I am Latwii. To continue, my friends. My sister, as we were saying, to walk with the one Creator, to rejoice at the opportunity to be and to serve, is most helpful and central in this instance. For there are so many levels of the metaphysical nature to this distortion that one must return immediately to the heart and to the Law, the only Law, and that is the Law of One. As you are one, so you see the Creator. As the Creator sees, It sees Itself in many forms and in many situations, each of which allow It to know yet more of Itself. The experience which you now face is that of the Creator. As you find yourself in the center of yourself you will find yourself able to use this experience as the Creator uses it. Rejoice in your beingness. Praise the Creator. Know that though you inhabit an illusion within an illusion, you are one with all. You are the Creator, and all is well.

May we answer you further, my sister?

Carla: Yes, thank you. But I would ask for another. If I were to ask you for a mantra, for one phrase to focus on in order to work with as many levels as possible in the metaphysical, what phrase would you think of?

I am Latwii, and we might suggest the simple repeating of simple phrases which touch the heart of being, such as "I am love," "I am light," "I am one," "I am whole," "I am perfect," "I am the one Creator." You may decide to focus upon one or more at any time, whether in meditation or singing as you go about your daily activities. You may find another phrase from that distortion which you find helpful in the worship which might be more meaningful. Any phrase which focuses upon the central nature of your being, that is as a being of love, light and unity, as a being which is the one Creator, is most helpful.

May we answer you further, my sister?

Carla: Gee, Latwii, you mean there's no tummy ache mantra in your dogma? I guess I can make do. I'm just teasing you. Thank you.

I am Latwii. We thank you, my sister. We hope our mantras do not give you indigestion. May we attempt another query at this time?

Carla: One little follow-up, and this is simply confirmation. Is this fainting bit just energizing, sort of wholesale, as long as I'm this weak we might as well go for broke, that kind of thing? And not seeing and all that?

I am Latwii. My sister, we find that you have discovered the basic nature of the recent greetings which have given you yet further opportunities to serve the one Creator in the positive polarity.

May we answer you further?

Carla: No, thank you. Thank you very much.

I am Latwii. We are most grateful to you, my sister. Is there another query at this time?

S1: Yes, Latwii. I believe I have formulated my question into words. This entity that I have called upon and has contacted me during my meditations, I have been receiving telepathic communication from this entity. I wanted to know if you can give me any advice as to the advisability of this. Is there any potential danger in accepting this communication? It's become a great comfort to me.

I am Latwii, and am aware of your query, my sister. We find that the entity which has been in close contact with you is one which has been called by the nature of your inner search, and which attempts to aid you at this time in the way which is most efficacious and understandable to your current perception. That telepathic contact has been made is a function of, shall we say, your training and ability developed within this circle of seekers, and has been utilized, for it is a language, shall we say, that you understand. When such contact is allowed, it is advisable that it be preceded by the tuning which you have utilized and faithfully utilize on a continuous basis. The desire which you express in your seeking for the highest and best, shall we say, information available to you is central, for it is your desire which determines that which you receive. Strive then to maintain if possible a purity in your seeking that the information which you receive will be of equal purity.

May we answer you further, my sister?

S1: Yes. Can you tell me if this entity is mainly here to aid me or would it be, if this entity were to come to me in groups such as this, would you advise channeling the entity or is the entity more or less of my own calling for basically my own information?

I am Latwii, and am aware of your query, my sister. We find in attempting to answer this query that the, shall we say, boundaries of being, of both your being and the entity's being, are not so clearly drawn that they may be described with complete accuracy. By this we mean to say this entity has responded to your call. You are not consciously aware of the total nature of that call. The call also may with time evolve and become transformed so that it also changes. The nature of the service to be provided by this entity therefore, would correspondingly change. Therefore, it is partially beyond our ability to perceive what you call your future, partially our desire not to infringe upon your free will, and partially due to the changing nature of the situation or its potential for change that causes us to be unable to give a clear and specific response to this query. We may suggest that at the present moment the situation appears to be one which is for your benefit in the majority.

May we attempt to answer further, my sister?

S1: Is what you're saying, that this entity may be available for channeling at another time but for the time being I should more or less keep this entity to myself?

I am Latwii, and might respond most efficaciously by suggesting that this was a significant portion of our response. Yet, might we suggest further work with this entity so that perhaps with the passage of what you call time, and the gaining of experience, the answer to this query might be made known to you by this entity and by your own choice.

May we answer you further, my sister?

S1: No, Latwii, that's exactly what I was after. Thank you.

I am Latwii. We apologize for taking so long to complete our beat around the bush. May we attempt another query at this time?

Carla: Well, Latwii, if everybody's finished, I would like to know something before you leave. At the very beginning of this meeting I had a contact, and challenged it because it was new, and it went away. Immediately, instantly, poof. Well, that's unusual for a negative entity. I mean, that is, I've never experienced that with a negative entity. There is usually a moment of resistance, and then the leaving. And when I analyzed the name that I'd been given, it's a name that means "No one" in Latin. That was as close as I could come was, "Ne Mo," "Nemo," which I believe is strictly Latin, meaning "no one." Latwii, was that you checking to make sure that I was—was that your idea of a joke by any chance, Latwii?

I am Latwii. And we find in this situation that your instrument was greeted by one which is of what you might call the inner planes, and somewhat of a lesser vibration. This entity was simply hoping that it might have an opportunity to speak through an instrument which was experienced and able to convey its simple thoughts. The entity may be seen to be of an unpolarized nature at present, looking for opportunities to polarize.

May we answer you further, my sister?

Carla: Would this be somebody's Uncle George that doesn't know he's dead yet or something? That kind of unpolarized being?

I am Latwii, and may respond by suggesting that this entity is more familiar with its current state of being, and has chosen to wander about the inner realms with occasional attempts made at contact with entities such as are gathered this evening, that it might speak and partake in some manner with the process of polarization which it is aware it also partakes in. This entity would be more served than would the group, in our humble opinion, yet each may choose its own path.

May we answer you further, my sister?

Carla: Yes. I surely would never channel an unpolarized entity. However, we always as a group wish to aid the planet as a whole. Would we then be aiding this entity by sending it love and light as a kind of healing to its nonpolarized state?

I am Latwii. My sister, it is always a service to send the love and light of the one Creator to any portion of that one Creator.

May we answer you further?

Carla: Nope. We'll do it. Thank you.

I am Latwii. May we attempt another query at this time?

S1: Yes, Latwii, just out of curiosity, are you aware of this entity known to me as Morzack?

I am Latwii. As we investigate the entity of which you speak we are familiar with your perception of its blending of vibrations with your own, and familiar with the manner in which the contact has been made. We must, in order to acquire this information, look into those portions of your being which you have given permission to look. Though you give conscious permission for the general perception of this entity and your experience with it, we find there is a trust or a boundary beyond which we may not move. Therefore, this is our limit of what we might share with you at this time.

May we answer you further, my sister?

S1: I don't quite understand what you mean by the boundary. Is the boundary within me in my subconscious?

I am Latwii. This is correct, my sister, for it is the unconscious mind of each entity which allows the experiences that will teach those lessons desired to reach each entity. Though your conscious mind perceives some portion of each experience, much is yet veiled to it. The entity of which you speak has been called to you not only by what seems to be your conscious choice, and indeed is such in port, but also by that which is your unconscious mind responding to those programs, shall we say, placed before the incarnation. There are portions of these programs which remain within the unconscious mind, and are not perceived consciously, and which yet hold the ability to affect your future. Thus, we may not peer into them closely enough to describe them to you without infringement. Thus, we do not.

May we answer you further, my sister?

S1: No, thank you, Latwii.

I am Latwii. We thank you, my sister. Is there another query at this time?

(Pause)

I am Latwii, and as we find that we have exhausted the queries and the instrument at approximately the same time we find this happy coincidence an opportunity to thank each present for the continued invitation to those of Latwii to join you, to rejoice with you, to seek with you, and to speak with you. We are humble messengers of the vibration of light. We remind each that our words or any words are but guideposts pointing directions which may or may not be traveled. Take then those words which have meaning. Think upon them, meditate upon them, use them as you will. Leave those which have no meaning, and we rejoice with you in your choice. We shall now take our leave of this group, again thanking each for the honor you bestow upon [us] with your invitation to blend our vibrations with yours. In love and in light, in unity and in the power and the peace of the one Creator, we leave you. We are known to you as Latwii. Adonai, my friends. Adonai vasu borragus.

(Carla channeling)

I am Nona, and I greet you in love and light. We come but briefly among you, and for a most happy request. There are several in this group who request thanksgiving. That in itself is a healing and we are most happy to oblige. The thanksgiving of *(inaudible)*, the thanksgiving of truth perceived, the thanksgiving of sorrow known to be of the most helpful nature. We cannot tell you our gratitude, and hope that we do not pierce your eardrums, for your request to us for joy is great. We are of Nona, and leave you after the vibrations in love and in light.

(Carla channels chanting from Nona.)

Sunday Meditation
April 10, 1983

(C channeling)

I am Hatonn, and I am now with this instrument. We greet you, as always, in the love and the light of the one infinite Creator. It has been some time since we have been able to speak through this channel, and we will speak but briefly through this channel, for he wishes to break back into the channeling process slowly as he has been some time in doubt. To doubt, to ask questions is but one way to learn.

We are having difficulty at present and would pause for a moment to better attune ourself to this instrument. I am Hatonn. We would at this instrument's request transfer this contact, for he feels he needs more time before he can fully operate again as a vocal channel. We will now transfer.

(L channeling)

I am Hatonn. I am now with this instrument. We are grateful for the willingness of the instrument known as C to re-offer himself for service in acting as our instrument that we might communicate with our otherselves. We are aware of the difficulties that he is experiencing, both in the facility of channeling, and the awareness of the moral significance of the action. We again are grateful for his service.

At this time, my friends, we would like to share with you a small story concerning a creature which lives beneath the watery surface of that which you call the sea. The creature is that which you term a mollusk or a clam-like shelled entity. Its awareness of itself and its universe is quite limited, for primarily its interests are limited to the acts of eating, excreting, and occasionally reproducing. The consciousness resultant from this situation, as you may well imagine, is quite limited as the entity we described is not only uninformed of the world upon which you exist, for example, but also quite uninterested. However, we shall cease describing and return to our story.

The entity was created in physical form and sought to continue its life in what must appear to those present as a very bland, eventless existence, for in truth, the lack of event was that which was sought. However, this entity had the apparent misfortune to choose to incarnate near the site of that which you term a generating facility on land which resulted in sudden releases of very hot water into the clam's environment. As this resulted in great discomfort, the entity was faced not only with the choice between remaining and possibly stewing or using its rudimentary equipment to gradually, over a period of years, remove itself from the environment. However, the entity was first forced, for such are the ways of lessons, into perceiving that an environment or universe existed beyond the limitations to which it had become accustomed, and firmly, yet dimly, regarded as the limits of the universe, for the increasingly warm temperatures could hardly be ignored.

The entity of which we speak, reflexively, slowly, began to move, to attempt to push itself slowly away from the uncomfortable environment. Many of its brothers and sisters also undertook identical journeys at the same time while others elected to remain behind, clam-like in their unwillingness to perceive or even acknowledge that other forces existed besides themselves. Years passed, the journey undertaken was at last completed, and in the manner of such creatures, the clam of whom we spoke eventually relinquished its hold on its incarnation in this fashion.

My friends, this may seem to be an uneventful tale, yet we ask you to examine your own progress on your journey. For is it not true that too often one must find the temperature of one's environment exceedingly uncomfortable before one seeks change of one sort or another, and in seeking that change find that the change must entail a change of oneself. So a journey is begun. One stretches muscles, so to speak, that one was only dimly aware of and more often than not strives only to leave behind that uncomfortable state which one once occupied in search of that which is unidentified, totally unfamiliar, yet toward which one is drawn as if following an instinctive beacon within the soul. And alongside each who follows the path, quite often unrecognized in the day-to-day struggle to climb one more rung, to circumvent one more difficulty, are brothers and sisters, quite similar, each struggling to surmount its own problem, each on a very similar path, journeys that though quite separate are yet quite common.

My friends, the creature of whom we spoke was fashioned in a manner which protects through a lack of awareness of that which surrounds. Yet, my friends, at this point the comparison fails, for each of you has been blessed with the ability to perceive the commonness, the sharing of the journey which you have undertaken jointly with those who surround you. My friends, strive to recognize within one another, within the stranger who at a corner crosses a street in time with yourself, that your journeys and yourselves are one, that his or her beacon rings forth within the soul with the same note as that within your own. It is often possible in your world to ignore the fact that your journeys are common. But, my friends, you differ from the other creatures we have described in your ability to communicate with one another. You are able to choose not only to seek or ignore your seeking, but also to aid or ignore the need for aid.

We realize the complexity of the puzzle before you, for we are aware that you consciously seek to avoid inflicting your will or your ways upon others. Yet, my friends, there is no failure, no offense in bringing forth your light in presenting yourself openly that those who seek your help may find it. We know that each of you further has felt the doubt within the soul, the suspicion of unworthiness, the self-doubt of the value of one's assistance. We are aware that at times those of you who seek to be of assistance by serving in the capacity of an instrument are quite rightly consumed with doubt both of your worthiness to perform the task you have undertaken and your ability to accurately represent that which is placed within your mind. My friends, we can only comfort you in these situations of doubt with a reminder of that which was said on your planet so many years ago, that if you wish to learn, that the door will open if you will but knock, that if you wish sincerely for an opportunity to serve your brothers and sisters, you have but to ask and that opportunity will be provided.

The one who spoke these words, my friends, went on to add that he who asks his father for sustenance will not be given a snake to hold in his outstretched hands. My friends, we ask you to be aware that the Creator has provided for His own, for all of His children. We ourselves are simply your loving other selves. Yet the tool that is provided by the Creator for our communication with you is a gift from that source. We offer, therefore, for your evaluation the question: When one asks for sustenance, what will be provided? My friends, be confident in your acts of love. Accept the blessing of the opportunity to be of service and go strongly forward with your desire to do so. Be not afraid and do not feel the necessity to provide yourself with assurances and safeguards, with necessities to validate your service to yourself, but rather, in the words of the source we described, go forth with but your staff and your scrip[4] and serve.

At this time we will relinquish our use of this instrument that our brothers and sisters of Latwii might perform their service of answering questions.

---

[4] scrip: pilgrim's knapsack.

In the love and light of the infinite Creator, I am known to you as Hatonn.

(L channeling)

I am Latwii, and we greet you in the love and light of the infinite Creator. We are aware that this instrument has been used somewhat extensively by our brothers and sisters of Hatonn quite recently. However, we are most anxious to refamiliarize the instrument with our vibration, and to exercise the instrument as we are less frequently able to accomplish this task lately and desire to give the old whiz-bang a tune-up. At this time, are there any questions?

K: Yeah, I have one, Latwii. You always say at the end of the session that if we just make a request that you will be with us or you'll hear it. Okay, I made a request this week, not for me, but for my daughter. And I don't know whether you answered the request or … I said, if you weren't in the business of healing or getting her through this three days, because she had a terrible cold, that would you stand around and see if you could find another entity to help. Well, anyway, it worked out beautifully, and I was just interested to know if you really did work out the circumstances or what happened.

I am Latwii. My sister, we were quite grateful to receive your contact and request. However, we must confess that we, to a large extent, passed the buck, so to speak, to our brothers and sisters that you know of as Nona, and that the entity to whom your service was directed was experiencing an amount of discomfort and stress. In reference to the details of the situation, however, we must explain that it is not our line of work to alter the circumstances that one has selected for their personal growth, but rather to encourage them in attaining that growth, which service we did attempt to provide.

Is there another question?

K: No, that's very good. I figured that's the way you would do it, but anyway I was just curious to know if you heard the request. Thank you.

We thank you, my sister, and we are quite pleased that [you] recognized our touch, so to speak.

Is there another question?

M: Yes, Latwii. When a person has an imbalance in their physical being or in their life, how can they tell if it's karma or if it's an incorrect attitude on their part?

I am Latwii. My sister, the most truthful and obvious answer is to seek within one's own soul for the answer. We are quite aware that the simplicity of such an action seems to make it difficult to perform, yet in all honesty, that is the most accurate and effective manner.

May we answer you further?

M: No, thank you.

We thank you, my sister. Is there another question?

K: Yes, one other question, Latwii, and we've touched on this before, but I've had some unusual dreams recently, and my question is, do we make our dreams or are we given dreams sometimes in order to help us when we ask for help?

I am Latwii and, my sister, without frivolity we must acknowledge that the answers to your questions are yes and yes. We would take the liberty of adding further detail in this manner. The mind of which you are aware is quite capable of generating dreams for entertainment or for one's education. Using this particular instrument, one can therefore acquire dreams which provide situations for growth, for in truth is not the world within which you exist merely an additional dream? The desire for learning, for attainment, is the incentive that allows you to bring into your life that which provides catalyst, be it in the somnolent or waking state. We would further remind you, my sister, that each entity is a portion of a larger entity and that—and that which is needed will be provided.

May we answer you further?

K: That last statement, let me see if I understood that correctly. That each entity is a part of a larger entity, is that what you said?

I am Latwii. My sister, consider the smallest finger upon your hand. It is a finger in its own right. It is a portion of you yourself, which in turn is a portion of the consciousness of your planet, which in turn is a portion of the Logos within which you function, which in turn is a portion of the Creator Itself. Just as your physical vehicle provides the sustenance, the needs for the growth of each cell within your finger, so also does that of which you are a portion provide the spiritual nourishment required for your growth …

(Side one of tape ends.)

(L channeling)

Is there another question?

(Pause)

As there are no more questions, we shall relinquish our use of this instrument and gratefully thank each of you for giving us the opportunity to perform our small service. In the love and the light of the infinite Creator, we are known to you as Latwii.

(Carla channeling)

I am Oxal, and I greet you, my friends, in the love and the light of our infinite Creator. It is a great privilege for us to blend our life streams with yours, and we thank this instrument for catching the signal which we offered to it, for it is an unexpected contact. However, there has been a call and we would speak briefly. We would speak to you, my friends, of binding and unbinding, for there are those questions upon your minds which may perhaps be perceived more clearly after some meditation upon the nature of your being. Firstly, let us establish the subjectivity of being. Consider two women. One marries, and one day the honeymoon is over and she says, "Oh, it is my fault, I have somehow destroyed the perfection of my life as I planned it." The second woman in the identical circumstance, nodding her head in recognition of circumstance, will still say, "Thank you for the good times, for they are a gift and they teach me what it is to live fully. And thank you too for the challenge, for it teaches me to pay attention."

The first woman then becomes ill, and she says, "I have failed to take care of myself. I have had a hard life; I am afraid that my body is not what it used to be." The second woman in the identical circumstance, smiling ruefully at the circumstance, says, "Thank you for the health that I have had, and the health that is to come, for they have been gifts, and shall be so again. And teach us how to live more fully. But thank you, too, for this challenge, for through it I shall learn better how to pay attention."

Thus, my friends, we intend to demonstrate that the circumstances of your life, though they be as they are, are subjective in meaning. That meaning is only decided by you. Therefore, all is decided by you. We reach this point in our reasoning in order that we may gently but strongly urge you to consider meditation upon the responsibility for your own thinking. It has been written in one of your holy works that that which you bind shall be bound, and that which you unbind shall be let loose. Are you then a ruler of a universe? Yes, you are, for you are co-Creator, one with all that there is, a dazzling and perfect portion of the one light. And as you see things, so they are. And what you see is final until you change what you see.

In some cases, my children, you see not only yourself but others, and you bind others to you and you unbind them from you. And yet, they too are shafts of the same sunlight, perfect and one. Shall you then judge to bind and to unbind for another? Do not all entities do this? And is it not always to some degree an error in thinking? For are you not all one being with no judgment between parts, but only a desire to serve? No matter what you have done to another, you have done far worse in judgment of yourself, at one time or another, if you shall pardon the misuse of this term. Therefore, use your meditation to release the coils of subjectivity from about yourself and your other selves, for you in your meditation have room for only one thing and that is love. That is what you came here to this orb in space to spend your portion of consciousness at this opportunity learning. Shall you not then grasp the opportunity? As you become more distorted and more subjective, you move further from the love you seek so wisely to know. Seek, then, and leave subjectivity behind on a regular basis that you may be one with all eternity, that you may shine with the stars and glow as does your sun with the good and fertile brightness of life.

We leave you in joy, and we lift each of you in our arms to bless you and send you upon your way. May you be merry and full of that life of which love is the very essence. I am Oxal. I thank you for calling us to your group this evening and for listening to our impoverished thoughts. Please accept them as imperfect and discard any concept that causes any difficulty. For truth, as you seek it, must be seen by you, not for you. Therefore, discard anything that you perceive as less than truth and use what remains. I leave you in the love and in the light of the One. Adonai vasu borragus. ✤

Sunday Meditation
April 17, 1983

(Carla channeling)

I am Hatonn, and I greet you, my friends, in the love and in the light of our infinite Creator. We thank you for the great blessing that you give to us by allowing us to speak with you through this instrument. We thank you for your attention, and the gift of open ears and open hearts. We thank you for wishing to know the truth. Knowing the truth is an inestimably ruthless process of continually altering the viewpoint and widening your faculties of love—we correct this instrument—of observation. What is your source? That is a question central to your quest for truth, for that from which you come binds that which you are. If you can imagine a moment incredibly far distant in time, as you call it, when you took all of creation into your hand and flung it from you, then you can imagine the impulse which guides your destiny. You are as a whole person abiding still in the Creator, but a splinter of your consciousness was flung for each, and that splinter of consciousness has become you as you now sit in meditation. The journey has been a long one. You have seen creations and planes and densities and lives and through all of them you have been under the influence of that force of yourself which flings you outward, and at the same time calls you home.

As you sit in meditation, parts of that journey flash before you, colors and visions and the sensation of speed, and any experiences you have had to come to this moment of peace. This is the precious moment of all creation. This instant is the excellent instant, far excelling past or future, for here your heart lies and your consciousness rests and you can receive and give forth the breath of creation, love and light. In and out you are filled with nothing but light, nothing but love. How interesting that you arranged this illusion so that it would be impossible for you to go through your incarnation in this state without renouncing nature, the nature of your body, your mind, and your emotions. Do you trust yourself? If you do, then you must know that you had good reason to hide from yourself the perfection of this moment. There were some points that you wanted to learn better than you knew them before. There were some parts of the spectrum of your light and your love that you wished to emphasize and explore.

As you move forth from meditation, attempt to keep in mind that you did not make a mistake of any kind in choosing the circumstances and the seeming accidents of your life. You chose well, each of you. You gave yourself food and you gave yourself an appetite. You gave yourself mental food, the food of the intellect and the mind, the food of analyzing, synthesizing, attempting to know and understand. You gave yourself emotional food, desires for love, experiences of love, experiences of apparent lack of those emotions you need. You wanted to catch your own attention and fix it. You wanted to make a point or perhaps several points for yourself and to yourself.

It is not just the physical body that needs food. Spiritually speaking, you consume far greater amounts of experience and digest far more experience than ever you do earthly food. For it is the food of the mind, the heart, and the spirit that you have indeed stopped here, a splinter of light, a split second in a long journey on this orb you call Earth to experience. And what of your future? You are an eternal and everlasting part of the One. And although in the One there is properly no past, present or future, in the subjective terms of this illusion which you now experience and which we share with you, time is passing, and there is a future before you. It is a future in which you call that splinter of yourself back to yourself as the lessons are understood, as the points are made, and as you experience yourself in yourself and with others, more and more you shall be drawn closer once again to the source whence you were flung with such a greedy and extravagant hand before the beginning of time.

Breathe in, then, the joy of this moment, and sense the relaxation, the resting and the peace that you share with those who dwell in meditation as do you. There are some not with you. And yet, because they are in the same condition of experience, you are together in joy, together in peace. Your time will pass, and some may read these words and will then sit in meditation and still you shall be able to join that blessed company of all those who seek and sit in the listening silence of your joyful quest.

We share your joy, and thank each of you for the great privilege of blending our joy with your own. Let your hearts be light as a fluttering gauze curtain at a window in the sunny breeze. For the wind is rich with blessings and there is music amongst the trees. I am known to you as Hatonn. I leave you in the love, in the light, in the joy of the infinite One. Adonai vasu borragus.

(Jim channeling)

I am Latwii, and I greet you, my friends, in the love and in the light of the infinite Creator. It is our privilege once again to be asked to join our vibrations with yours. We thank you for the opportunity to serve you by attempting to answer your queries. We remind each that our humble responses are merely opinion, perhaps somewhat different than yours, perhaps with a somewhat wider perspective, yet it is but our opinion. Please accept that which has value and leave that which has none. May we then begin with the first query?

Carla: I have a question. I got a telephone call this week from a friend who asked me how to remain faithful to all the ideals of love and light and service to others that we work on in this group when the situation looks hopeless, and there doesn't seem to be any point in carrying on. I felt that my answer was inadequate, and so I would ask if you could perhaps comment on this question?

I am Latwii, and am aware of your query, my sister. Indeed, when the situations which we have termed "catalyst" present themselves to the seeker, the seeker may look upon such catalyst with a polarity viewpoint, that is to say, one may look upon the situation and see people and events not in keeping with the desires of the seeker, and the seeker may wish to change those people and events and maintain faithfulness to the ideals of service to others. This is a great dilemma, for in truth, if one wishes to be pure in what you have called the positive polarity, there can be no wish to change another person or event, for each must be accepted as each is, for each is whole and perfect. Each is the one Creator. This is a great lesson, which takes much of what you call time to learn. Therefore, as a portion of remaining faithful to those positive ideals which each in this group upholds, then it might be recommended that the viewpoint include the possibility that no person or situation be asked to be other than it is, that each indeed be accepted, loved, forgiven, that the same be done with the self, and that then the self is taken by the seeker as the primary tool for upholding the ideals of service to others, and the self is transformed by acceptance of self and others so that love is given no matter what. In such a way does the positive polarity become purified and refined, that the beacon of love and light within the heart of self might shine more brightly.

May we answer you further, my sister?

Carla: No, it was a beautiful answer. I think it's probably the hardest single lesson that we foolish humans have to learn. But it's a useful answer. Thank you.

I am Latwii. We thank you, my sister. Is there another query at this time?

M: I have one, Latwii. What causes people to have periods in their life when they have absolutely no desire to go forward or backward? In other words, just basically, is it a lack of energy or is there a reason why they go through this stage?

I am Latwii, and am aware of your query, my sister. Look for the answer to this query to the seasons and cycles that you observe upon your planet. After the fall, the harvest, there is a time of rest, then followed by a regeneration of that which was harvested. So it is within each entity. As the lessons of your incarnation are learned, you will find within your being various cycles of seeking. There will be times as luxuriant in the seeking of lessons as your summer is in the spawning of life forms. There will be times when the difficulties rage as does the thunderstorm, the wind, the hail, the rain. And yet each portion of the cycle of seeking adds a part that becomes that which you seek.

As you observe those times within yourself of peace and rest, enjoy that portion of the cycle, for, indeed, all things change, and you shall find new lessons presenting themselves within the fertile and peaceful ground of your being.

May we answer you further, my sister?

M: No, I think that was very helpful. Thank you.

I am Latwii. We thank you. Is there another query at this time?

M: I have another if no one else has one. What causes some people to have a nervous breakdown or become disoriented in the same set of circumstances where another person may not be affected at all?

I am Latwii, and am aware of your query, my sister. For the answer to this query, may we suggest the concept of the limitation of the viewpoint. For an entity to exist within your illusion there is the seeming inborn necessity to gather about the center of the being a grouping of beliefs, those concepts which are relied upon to provide support as the entity journeys through the incarnation. As each entity journeys, each gathers about the self a variant set of these beliefs. We may suggest your restaurant, for example, a few from column A, a few from column B, and so forth. Some viewpoints contain a wider perspective, shall we say, and when added to others, yet further increase the perspective of the seeker.

This is another way of suggesting that that which is seen and accepted as a belief then is an ally which aids in perception and in utilizing the catalyst which comes before the attention. The fewer and more narrow the concept, the less efficient is it in this process. Some entities, therefore, are more limited by their own belief system in what they are able to accept and use efficiently as catalyst. Therefore, catalyst of a given nature, of, shall we say, intensity which require the ability to accept a wider viewpoint would cause greater stress upon one with less ability to accept the wider viewpoint.

May we answer you further, my sister?

M: Yes, I'm still not quite sure—take people who are unfortunate enough to hear voices and to be paranoid and to really have miserable lives. What's the basis of this problem?

I am Latwii, and am aware of your query, my sister. Such an entity may have a variety of reasons for its behavior and response to those inner voices which from time to time become available to each entity upon your planet. An entity, to take one example, may have the belief system imbedded from youth that any such voice heard within is of the devil or is what may be termed evil or satanic, and when such a voice is heard, the entity may respond as though this belief were true, whether or not such a voice was of a negative source. Repeated experience with such a voice might cause the entity to feel itself possessed, to feel unworthy, to feel as though it was going what you have termed insane. This need not be true, yet can be so if believed. This is but one small specific example. There are a myriad of potential examples with each having different ramifications.

May we answer you further, my sister?

M: No, thank you, that was very helpful.

We are pleased to have been of some small aid. Is there another query at this time?

K: I have a question. When you're trying to understand another person's point of view, and trying not to change them, and in the process you try to see their point of view so much that you don't believe in your point of view, and you almost become crippled in your ability to act on what you think is right, are there some helpful suggestions to have more belief in what you're thinking and feeling?

I am Latwii, and am aware of your query, my sister. To begin, may we suggest that if you look upon each point of view that you could possibly imagine within your illusion, you shall see an infinity of possibility. You are each. That you do not yet recognize that is a portion of your learning. If you feel a discomfort as you pass through various beliefs, as you change your mind from time to time, as you evolve in your own understanding, consider the possibility that each individual point of view has its balance. That is to say, each lesson is paired with its opposite, for example, patience and impatience, anger and love, acceptance and rejection. This list may be continued infinitely. As you see a certain bias developing in your belief, attempt to learn also its opposite so that your learning be balanced, and develop also the ability to accept yourself, for including each point of view within your being, that the one Creator might know Itself further …

(Side one of tape ends.)

I am Latwii. To continue. In such a fashion, then, you shall move in a balanced manner and construct the architecture of your being with a stable foundation without bias in any direction which would risk the stability of your being.

May we answer you further, my sister?

K: Thank you, Latwii.

I am Latwii. We thank you, my sister. Is there another query at this time?

M: If I have a pain anywhere, I can tell that part of my body not to feel pain, and it won't feel it. And I wish there was some way I could help other people to have that same talent because so many people are in pain in various parts of their body, and I don't know whether there is something innate within me, but I don't know why I can tell a part of my body—like a tooth for instance, if it's acting up a little—I can tell it not to, and it won't. Is there anything that I could do to help other people so they wouldn't be in so much suffering, or why can I do it and I can't explain it to anyone else?

I am Latwii, and am aware of your query, my sister. It is always the case that the entity entering the incarnation brings certain abilities, as would the carpenter its tools to the job it wishes to complete. Some are not well understood. Many remain latent throughout most of the incarnation, their use discovered at what you would call a later date. The tool or talent of which you speak is one which you shall find an increasing understanding attached to as you explore your own use of it. It is often most difficult to impart the use of such a slightly understood talent to another. Therefore, may we suggest the meditation upon this ability, not just its mechanical use, but the value which you obtain from it.

May we answer you further, my sister?

M: Well, just quickly. Is it a form of self-hypnosis?

I am Latwii, and am aware of your query, my sister. To describe this talent in these terms is somewhat accurate, yet somewhat misleading as well, for the focusing of the attention is necessary for both hypnosis and the use of this tool, and each requires the increasing use of the unconscious mind. Yet, you are not quite, shall we say, hypnotized or in a trance as you accomplish this talent. The ability to concentrate, which is one of the benefits of meditation, is central to this particular talent, and there must be, shall we say, a certain opening made within the veil which separates your conscious and unconscious mind. This opening is a portion of this talent brought with you and may be enhanced by the application of concentration.

May we answer you further, my sister?

M: Is there any chance that I could explain this talent to people that are in great pain or is it just a personal talent?

I am Latwii, and am aware of your query, my sister. You could indeed attempt such explanation, yet would find a variety of responses from those to whom such explanation was given, for each entity varies in the ability to use that which you could explain. You would be, as we mentioned before, further hampered by the lack of your own understanding of the deeper significance of this phenomenon. Therefore, we continue to recommend the meditation upon this significance.

May we answer you further?

M: No, thank you. That's very helpful.

I am Latwii. Thank you, as well. Is there another query at this time?

(Pause)

I am Latwii. We feel that we have exhausted the queries for the evening, and again extend our deepest appreciation to each entity present for allowing us to blend our vibrations with yours this evening. To join you in your seeking for truth is a joy which we eagerly anticipate at each moment in the timeless span of our existence. We remind each present that a simple request for our presence in your private meditation is all that is necessary for us to join you there and once again blend our vibrations with yours. We shall at this time leave this group, yet in truth, always are we one. We are known to you as those of Latwii. Adonai vasu borragus. ♣

Sunday Meditation
April 25, 1983

(M channeling)

I am Hatonn, and I am now with this instrument. I greet you with the love and the light of the infinite Creator. I would like to say why this instrument is not channeling. Her soul is hibernating. It is going through a period of healing, and cannot give information at this time. I am Hatonn. I leave this contact.

(Carla channeling)

I am Hatonn, and I greet you, my friends, in the love and in the light of our infinite Creator. It is a great privilege to speak with you and we thank the one known as M for allowing us to exercise her newly acquired skill to a small extent. It is helpful when one is in a period where one is not offering oneself as instrument to allow the practice in order that the tuning and the recognition may remain fresh in the mind.

We find among those upon your planet a constantly amazing degree of slumber which is the equivalent of completely blocking the channeling of any inward view. This is unfortunate, for the outer gifts among your peoples are largely those of difficulty and strife. The nature of your illusion is such that the apparently logical reaction to a majority of the events in any existence is a negative emotion or a negative action. Few among your peoples actually desire to be negative or gain any true satisfaction from negativity.

But there is a great majority of those who slumber [and] know not how to wake. The unblocking, the [awakening] of the vessel which you experience as your physical vehicle in most cases must be a conscious thing. Without a desire to become an instrument for that which is invisible and inner, the entity most usually remains clogged with the reactions which the illusion draws from the entity.

We do not advise the taking of the metaphysical temperature, for judgment is impossible from your point of view, which is limited. No matter what you think about yourself, it is very likely somewhat incorrect or at very best biased. However, there are signs that you have begun to unclog your own vessel, that you have begun to function as an instrument. These signs are simple ones and include cheerfulness, calm, kindness, love, generosity and compassion. Most of all, above all, a joy which is the natural reaction of the self to its surroundings, which communicates to others in a radiant manner as a the signpost of the instrument which is functioning properly.

We do not use the word "instrument" in a narrow sense, meaning a local channel such as this one, for in this context each entity upon the planetary sphere may be seen to be an instrument capable of the most magnificent contributions towards the metaphysical light which your planet needs so very much at this time, as you would call it. There is no one, probably, among your peoples who can honestly vow that he or she is cheerful, kind or loving one hundred percent of the time. Your illusion was not intended to allow you to build up that kind of record. Your illusion was intended to make it a definite challenge to spend even half the time that you are awake giving instead of taking, loving instead of withholding, reaching out instead of removing.

Therefore, my friends, concentrate upon simple goals, upon attaining some fair portion closer and closer to fifty percent of your thoughts and actions which are kind or intended to be loving or intended to [be] joyful. You do this in the face of a world in which the illusion exposes you to many unfortunate and irreconcilable disappointments. If all things are well with you, then it is a friend of a loved one who is struggling. You gaze at one with who has come face to face with the traumas of broken marriage or advanced and debilitating old age or the loss of a mate or a child or some other heartbreak, and there is nothing that you can say that will make the one who grieves comforted because the illusion causes many conditions to appear utterly disconsolate. But if you go back to meditation, if you return to that portion of yourself which is silent and holy, you find gifts there heaped upon one another which answer the illusion but which you cannot explain.

Now, this is unfortunate, seemingly. You find gifts within you, and yet you cannot explain them. How, then, can you help others? You find your joy, you find love, you find the source of unity within you that binds all things as one. You find that comfort which faces death, disappointment and heartbreak, and says that every tear shall be dry. "This I know," and you cannot communicate it. What then shall you do? My friends, you shall be instruments. You shall desire first in meditation for yourself to know the free-flowing beauty of love, the infinite and merciful kindness of creative compassion, the utterly simple faith that beneath all appearances lies a consciousness that is one with you and with the universe which precludes judgment. These things shall you find, and you shall not cease in your seeking until you have found these gifts, for they are your birthright. Do not be satisfied with less. Open that door of silence and ask, for the asking is irresistible, and then in the fullness of the answer let the flow begin and become you as much and as often as you are capable of functioning in this manner.

It is who you are that is the true instrumentality of your being. Your actions may seem wise or misapplied. Your intentions may be scrutinized many different ways. But your being is unmistakable. It is your metaphysical signature. Your consciousness does your work in the world for you, and those words and actions which you undertake merely underscore others' perceptions of who you are. There is no action or word that you can do or utter that will mean an iota if you have not consciousness. And if you have consciousness, the most clumsy word or action will suffice to allow others to experience the love and the light that flows radiantly through you.

We would at this time emphasize that in your analyzing of your own behavior and your balancing of the various distortions, you pay special attention to your function as a listener. Many are the well-meaning instruments who feel moved to serve and who then err on the side of doing and talking. If you are talking, you cannot listen. If you are doing, often you cannot hear. And in serving others, the function of listening is central. Entities are seldom what you expect. Things that appear simple at first glance may be found to be coming from a bias in that person whom you wish to help which you must listen carefully to [to] comprehend. And only with this level of knowledge achieved can the word or the action be appropriate.

Nevertheless, it is by far your central activity to be who you are. We ask that you seek diligently to find this, to articulate this, and to experience yourself as this consciousness that is you. Each of you is unique and utterly perfect. Each of you is a crystal in the sun ray. And there is a rhythm to the turning of that crystal in order that the shafts of beautiful light may flow through you in the clearest and most lovely manner, that you may indeed radiate to those about you, and indeed to yourself, for you are the great feeder of your own self. There is a great portion of your physical life which is almost starved unless that inner self that seeks turns to the self, accepts it, forgives it, loves it and grants it the power to be truly whole. As you come out of meditation, acknowledge who you are and grant yourself that power, for it is only as a portion of the one infinite Creator that you could possibly have that thought, and that is just what you are.

We leave you, my friends, riding upon the waves of light that arise in this group. We are always with you if you should desire us to aid you in achieving a deeper state of meditation. Merely mentally request our presence and we shall be with you. I am Hatonn. I leave you in the love and in the light, the joy and the power of the one infinite Creator. Adonai. Adonai vasu.

(Jim channeling)

I am Latwii, and I greet you, my friends, in the love and in the light of our infinite Creator. We are pleased that you have asked us to join your group again this evening. It is our privilege to do so. We always look forward to blending our vibrations with those of this group that we may attempt our simple service of attempting to answer your queries. We then shall ask for the first query.

M: I have a question, Latwii. K is going through a difficult divorce right now, and there's material things to be divided, and the children's time. Could you give her a few helpful hints that would help her sail through this time?

I am Latwii, and am aware of this query, and the need for the aid. We shall attempt a response in this manner: by first suggesting that the situations such as this one in which the seeker will find itself from time to time, that is, the typical situation, the potential problem where disharmony is apparent, is a situation in which the exceptions one has are of primary importance in the perception and the resolution of the seeming difficulty. This is to say that as you encounter such difficulties, it is recommended for the greatest harmony possible that a great attempt be made—through force of will, if necessary—to see each entity as the Creator and [to] accept each as each expresses some facet of the Creator, for you have not gathered together for the time which you have shared by chance. You have come together for that time as Creator speaking to Creator that certain lessons might be shared, that certain experiences might be enhanced, that the Creator might know Itself more fully, that you might know the Creator more fully, that you might know yourself as the Creator.

Therefore, if you can take what we might call the larger view, and see each entity as the Creator and love and accept each entity as such, the self included, then you build a strong harmony where perhaps seeming disharmony once existed. You will then build the remainder of the situation and its resolution upon a firm foundation, that is, love and acceptance, blessings and joy. It is most often the case that the strength of the seeming difficult catalyst will act upon the mind of those involved, and most usually produce lesser feelings, shall we say, those of resentment, of anger, of disappointment, of confusion, of jealousy, and so forth. Each of these emotions may be worked with by the seeker and may be transformed into love. The process is aided by the conscious ability of the seeker to take the larger viewpoint of which we spoke. Such a viewpoint is as the alchemical process in which the pseudo-scientists of old attempted to change the lead to gold. The viewpoint which sees the Creator indwelling all about and within the self is the viewpoint which changes each difficult emotion and situation into an opportunity to know, to love, and to express the one Creator.

May we answer you further, my sister?

M: Well, I thought that was a good answer. I'm not in the situation so I don't know if K would like to elaborate on any phase of it. You would have to ask her.

K: No. I knew I needed to come tonight. Thank you.

I am Latwii. We are most grateful to each of you, our sisters. May we attempt another query at this time?

M: Well, I have a rather insignificant one. I found out in many situations when logic doesn't work, I try illogic, and it works beautifully. And I would like you to explain that to me. I'll give you a simple example. I have a lawnmower, and this friend of mine put it out facing the garage and we tried and tried until we wore ourselves out, and it wouldn't start and I said, "I can't understand it, it always starts for me on the second time, but I turn it the other direction." So I turned the lawnmower around with the house, which of course was illogical, which direction it was [facing], turned it around towards the house, and it started the second time. Now the position of the lawnmower surely shouldn't have made any difference, but it did. Now, how do you account for that illogic? It's happened in a number of situations lately.

I am Latwii, and am aware of your query, my sister. The general concept is that the intuition shall feed the intellect. For the intuition is connected to that portion of the mind that is unconscious, and is quite infinite in the resources which it contains. It contains the food for thought, shall we say. The intellect then takes this food and arranges this food and arranges it in what you may call a logical fashion, logical perhaps only for a certain entity, yet uses it as a food and expresses certain directions, tendencies and actions according to the arrangement. If the intellect is not fed, then it must operate on, shall we say, an empty stomach. As you are aware, this often hinders the efficiency of any entity's operation.

Therefore it is most helpful to blend the use of that known as intuition or more distortedly, illogic, with the use of that which is intellectual, or more distortedly, logical. To speak specifically to the situation which you have described, there may have been in this situation certain needs, shall we say, of the entity known as the lawnmower to be spoken to or addressed …

(Side one of tape ends.)

(Jim channeling)

I am Latwii. We greet you again, and shall continue. This entity may have needed to have been addressed in a fashion which included a certain attention or compassion for its being. By the process of reversing its direction it was being shown such affection and attention, and may have responded more to such affection than to the direction of its pointing.

May we answer you further, my sister?

M: No, I think you've answered it very well. I like that lawnmower and it likes me and I think that might have been a factor. I think you've answered it perfectly.

I am Latwii. We are grateful to have been of service. May we attempt another query at this time?

K: I have a question. I feel so fortunate to be here, and I feel like I'm taking from the group. I'm getting things that are really helping me, and I'm wondering what I can do besides learning to meditate better, what I can do to contribute to the group. I feel like I'm taking.

I am Latwii, and am aware of your query, my sister. My sister, we are most familiar with the feeling which you express, for we ourselves have felt that feeling often in connection with this group, for we are humble messengers and feel the greatest privilege at being asked to provide our simple service. We can only suggest to you that which we suggest to ourselves, that is that your part is merely to be whoever you are, for you are the Creator experiencing Itself and your experience, though different from each other entity within the group is just as valuable. To be, without concern as to how you are to be, is most helpful, for that which you are and which you shall express will then have a clear path into expression without having to traverse the various concerns and fears that one must be or do in a certain fashion in order to be helpful. Your very being is of infinite worth.

May we answer you further, my sister?

K: Thank you.

I am Latwii. We thank you, my sister. May we attempt another query at this time?

Carla: I'm curious about something. Last summer when I sang to the vegetables, some of them overgrew. Can you send too much love and light to second density so that they grow faster than is good for them?

(The telephone rings and the answering machine message is heard.)

I am Latwii, and am aware of your query, my sister. We paused while your recording device performed its duty of love and service.

To answer your query, we are unaware of the possibility of sending too much love or light to any entity of any density. That such entities of your second-density vegetable life form may utilize such love and light for abundant and extravagant growth is quite understandable and possible. Such entities in receiving this abundance of nourishing love will then produce in a manner which may or may not equal the expectations normally held for such forms of life. Yet, whatever the yield, it will be one infused with love, and that which you have given shall return to you multiplied, and shall dwell then with you and shall rejoice in the service which you have enabled it to provide.

May we answer you further, my sister?

Carla: Well, would it help the plants if I told them what I was hoping for before I sang? Would that help them know how to grow?

I am Latwii, and am aware of your query, my sister. Such speaking to these entities will be of aid in opening their receptivity, shall we say, both to the general infusion of love, and to the manner in which you request that love be used. Such entities when so spoken to are most often greatly delighted to be so spoken to, and will comply with your wishes to the fullest of their extent to do so.

May we answer you further, my sister?

Carla: No, thank you. I've got that one okay, but that phone machine reminds me of a question that I've been wanting to ask. What in the world do I do to these electromagnetic machines that screws them up so badly? And should I just never touch them? Or is it I? That's what I'd really like to know? Can you tell me that? I feel that it has to be me because it happens so often, but I guess I ought to establish that first.

I am Latwii, and am aware of your query, my sister. Your record is unblemished, my sister, in the dealing with such machines. It includes a long list of electromagnetic malfunctions which have been produced by the unusual electromagnetic configuration which is a portion of your, what might generally be described as, aura field. This unusual configuration has been programmed and utilized by your choice before this incarnation and during, in order that you might partake in the work which you now undertake. The, shall we say, discombobulating of various mechanical devices of the electromagnetic nature by this unusual configuration in your electromagnetic field is an effect which takes various forms in various types of your equipment.

The machine of which you now speak has various portions within its inner working which have been affected, and are not able to fully complete their assigned tasks because of the, shall we say, shorting to some degree of the circuitry which is programmed to function in a certain manner, but which must satisfy itself with an alternative functioning due to the infringement of your ever-so-gentle touch. We would suggest, as have our brothers and sisters of the social memory complex known to you as Ra, that if the normal functioning of such machinery is desired, that such machinery not know your touch.

May we answer you further, my sister?

Carla: No, thank you.

I am Latwii. We thank you, my sister.

Carla: I do have one more question coming, though. Is there any positive use to this "ever-so-gentle touch" that screws up machines?

I am Latwii, and am aware of your query, my sister. The touch of which we have spoken has many valuable uses upon other types of entities, those which are of need in the, what you have called, spiritual balancing. For this touch has the capacity, shall we say, used in the metaphysical sense to balance those spiritual energies which have for one reason or another found imbalance, and this you have accomplished in what you call your past.

May we answer you further, my sister?

Carla: No, thank you, Latwii.

M: I have a question on the same subject. If she has to touch a machine, could she have a conversation with the machine, and tell it that she has to touch it, and would it block the sensations that she has? Would it be helpful or would the machine care?

Carla: Yeah. Would that work?

I am Latwii, and am aware of this query, my sisters. The intention would be appreciated by the machine entity, and would be some consolation to the machine as it then proceeded with the inevitable malfunction.

(Laughter)

May we answer you further?

Carla: No, thank you.

I am Latwii, and we join in the humor. May we attempt another query at this time?

(Pause)

I am Latwii, and we perceive that we have exhausted the queries for the evening. Again, may we express our great gratitude at being asked to perform this simple service. We remind each of our fallibility, and that what we have expressed, though the best and highest of our opinion, is yet but our opinion. Take that of value. Leave that of none, and go forth both within your illusion and within yourself full of the knowledge that within your being, within the hearts of your being lies the answer to all your queries. Use our words as signposts to go further and deeper within the heart of your own being. We are with you there, and travel always at your side. We are known to you as those of Latwii, and we leave you now in the love and in the light of our one infinite Creator. Adonai, my friends. Adonai vasu borragus. ❧

L/L Research

Sunday Meditation
May 1, 1983

(C channeling)

I am Hatonn, and am now with this instrument. We greet you in the love and the light of the one infinite Creator. My friends, the peoples use three small words, the words, "I love you." These words are bandied about. They have been spoken many times without thought, but the meaning they hold. The words mean nothing without the knowledge of what they can mean. As the populations of this planet increase, and as you find there is less and less room for each individual, the knowledge of the meaning of the words will help you communicate with your fellow …

We would pause for a minute. I am Hatonn. We are still experiencing some difficulty in our contact with this instrument. We will attempt to adjust.

I am Hatonn. Our contact is strengthened, though tentative, as this instrument is still seeking to renew his channeling abilities that he had come to doubt. We would, if we may, begin again.

We wish to speak on communication between the entities on your planet. You and all those on your planet often find it hard to transmit feelings to one another. People become bogged down by language and by being unable to touch their inner selves to convey those things they feel. Many words, including the word love, have been subject to distortion, for it is often used superficially and empty of meaning. Love, as you are becoming aware of, need not be spoken to be conveyed. The light [that] is in you, once you have become aware, reaches out and touches those around you. You give of yourself to the other without words. A simple touch, when done as freely as you can offer it, conveys much more than the words of your language.

As you continue your journey attune yourselves to the love within you, within others. Become not bogged down by the rhetoric, but communicate yourself by using yourself. The light within you shines if you let it. A touch may convey it.

I am Hatonn. We would now transfer this contact to another instrument. I am Hatonn.

(Carla channeling)

I am Hatonn, and I greet you once again through this instrument in the love and the light of our infinite Creator. We shall continue upon this subject through this instrument.

Shall we examine the assumptions which each seeker makes concerning the quality of his or her communication with other beings. Perhaps the primary assumption, my friends, is that you must have ambition to seek and to grasp that which it is you wish to know, and therefore that which you wish to communicate. You wish to take upon yourself the essence and the meaning of love. Although it is written in your holy work the Bible, "Seek and ye shall find, ask and you shall be answered, knock and it shall he opened," there is a point at which the seeking with the conscious self as ambitious seeker ceases to make metaphysical sense, and indeed becomes counterproductive to the serious student.

Therefore, you seem to be upon the horns of a dilemma. You must seek in order to be a seeker. You must have ambition, you must grasp and reach ever further than you *(inaudible)*. And yet in order to fully be a seeker there is that point at which such grasping and seeking is a negative or unhelpful method of being, and of transmitting your being through communication to others. The cause of this is the very nature of taking. Examine the nature of those who take. It may all be done in the most noble spirit. But do you wish for yourself that you may become somehow glorious as the Creator is glorious? Do you seek in your relationship to be someone to whom that other person may look with respect? Do you seek somehow the glory of that great wisdom which is love?

In all that you do in your occupations, in your preoccupations and your hobbies, do you seek somehow to make an impression, to take and build, to grasp a reputation or an opinion from yourself or from others? Do you even have a fantasy that you might one day experience the glory that is your birthright? We would be surprised, my friends, if there were any who could answer, "Nay." For it is the nature of those who labor diligently to attach importance to the tasks and to wish for results. But the first rule of communication is that there is no taking but only giving.

Therefore, in the process of communication, you must give all that you have away. Is your difficulty that of a relationship? Then you must give that relationship completely away. You must lose everything so that you have no stakes in the outcome of the relationship. There are no impressions to be made. There is no grasping for meaning. You are simply there to listen and to give, with no possible loss. You may apply this to any of the areas of your illusion. Any reputation that you have, any pride, any thoughts that you wish to be of more service but the structure of your environment first must change, need to be left behind. For you who have anything at stake have too much to lose to communicate love.

Is there any thing, any possession of mind or body that you fear to lose? In your mind let it go. Release it and bid it farewell. You will be bidding farewell constantly, for this process of amalgamating to the self those things which seem useful is continuous to the student, and in the process of communication, each thing must be given up, for only in the full light of compassion which has no stake and nothing to lose can you truly hear the voice of another being who speaks.

You may do many things, my friends, in your attempt to experience the oneness of all creation, and each thing that you do is fine and wonderful and worthy. But the glory is not within the attempts, but within the realization which comes to those who have given up all things. That all is the Creator. You may give away everything, and for the first time experience true plenty. In fact, until you give away all things, you will not experience plenty. You will not communicate love without significant distortion. Each entity has a unique way of expressing itself. For you to communicate with one other entity, you must come into a vibratory agreement with that entity's deeper self. Not with that entity's words, but with the entity's self. If you have anything at all at stake, you will not be free to communicate with even one entity.

If you are able through meditation to keep the realization fresh that your beingness does not depend upon any thing, but is and has been and will be as it is, then you can begin to experience those gifts given to what that same holy book has called the poor in heart. We realize that this may be confusing to those who are attempting with a full heart and sincere purpose to seek the one infinite Creator, for there is a great deal of intention and purpose needed to set one's feet upon the path and to keep one's feet moving, to pick oneself up when one falls, to open oneself to the comfort of meditation when one does not even feel worthy of such a state of being. But each of you is already full of purpose, full of desire and seriously seeking. Therefore, the balance is necessary. You seek for yourself, and then you give what you have sought back to the infinite Creator. You can lose nothing. You can gain nothing. You are always on this journey. You are always on the brink of an utterly indescribable joy.

Therefore, my friends, let your hearts be light, and your voices merry and never feel that you have reached the last resort as you communicate. Simply remember that whatever it is that you are holding in your hands or in your heart or in your mind can be safely given away. That is how one loves by action. You are blessed with infinity. Whatever you give away is yours again in infinite supply. We ask that you come out of meditation with a thought for the joy of giving. Imagine how surprised a burglar would be if he came to your house and you said, "My friend, my brother, take all that I have. Take my shoes. I have more." Such an attitude can convey more to one who needs to speak with you than all the fine speeches in the world. Whoever is performing has a mask beneath which lies the eyes of the Creator. Communicate with that Creator and cease not to meditate in order that your contact with infinite love may always be free-flowing so that you may touch it and it may touch others.

We would like to take this opportunity to thank the one known as S1 and the one known as S2 for serving as vocal channels. We appreciate the desire to listen, and therefore will take our leave through this instrument, allowing them a rest. We would leave you with this thought. It has sometimes been said by those who come to this group and find their questions answered helpfully that perhaps this person or that [person] is or is not worthy. Just such a case occurred the previous meeting at this domicile. We therefore wish to say to the one known as K what we say to each of you so that you will see that it is truly intended by us. We are extremely grateful for the opportunity to share our thoughts with those among your peoples who are seeking the truth. If you all were not within this domicile, and if you were not in possession of questions that needed the answers, we could not serve. And if we did not serve, then we would have ceased being useful to the group. Therefore, there is no one who desires to hear our thoughts who is not paramount in our blessings, our affection, and our thanks, for only in serving you are we served. This is our method of learning about the Creator. We learn from you and we are infinitely grateful for the opportunity you provide. As always, we caution you to toss away those things which do not make sense, and to keep that which is helpful, for we speak with the same inadequate tongue as any being. However, we have the great fortune of speaking to the Creator, and we salute each of you. We too are the same Creator.

We leave you upon the winds of time and change. We leave you in your illusion, that marvelous prison which you have selected in order that you may learn how to escape. We leave you in the love and the light of the infinite Creator. I am Hatonn. Adonai vasu borragus.

(Jim channeling)

I am Latwii, and I greet you, my friends, in the love and in the light of our infinite Creator. We are pleased once again to be asked to join your group, and to provide our humble service of attempting to answer your queries, those treasures of sharing which you have brought with you this evening. May we ask then for the first query?

R: Latwii, I'm confused somewhat on the mechanism of the sexual energy transfer. I'm wondering, I know that the male and female both must experience orgasm, and my question is, I hope I don't embarrass anyone, but my question is, does the male orgasm have to take place within the female for the energy transfer to take place? I'm not sure I understand the complete workings of the mechanism of that …

(Side one of tape ends.)

(Jim channeling)

I am Latwii, and am with this instrument once again. To continue that which we had barely begun. It is not necessary, my brother, that the orgasm be achieved for the sexual energy transfer to be accomplished, especially among the entities who are well polarized and mated, shall we say. The energy transfer in such situations is a constantly ongoing phenomenon which is greatly enhanced by the conscious sexual sharing of love, compassion, understanding and forgiveness. There are those disciplines among various cultures and orders of the peoples of your planet that have pursued the sexual energy transfer without using the culmination known as orgasm. The practitioners of that known as Tantric Yoga, for example, utilize such methodology. For those who wish to utilize that culmination, shall we say, known as the orgasm, it is indeed most helpful if the orgasm of the male occur within the female sexual organ region, as we note is the normal methodology of most of your peoples. This is mostly a, shall we say, symbolic region, though not just symbolic, yet that the orgasm occur here is most helpful for this is the base chakra or energy center and is activated by the physical sensations which have been shared by the two entities engaging in the transfer of energy. From this point then, the energy centers are activated in order, and when there are no significant blockages at the next energy center, then the energy which has been transferred proceeds through that center until it meets the point of resistance at which point the transfer is culminated. At each energy center there is a certain vibrational nature to the transfer which enhances the vital energies of both entities.

May we answer you further, my brother?

R: No, Latwii, thank you.

I am Latwii, and we are most grateful to you, my brother. Is there another query at this time?

Carla: I m not sure because I'm not a very good student, but it seems to me that the Ra material suggested that energy transfer could take place—if only one of the two partners had an orgasm, that it would be shared. Is that true?

I am Latwii, and am aware of your query, my sister. This is correct, and is a further ramification of this type of energy transfer which we had not yet covered.

May we answer you further?

Carla: I'd just like a confirmation of something that I was talking about with a friend earlier this week. Each of us had had experiences where in sexual orgasm it seemed that there was a linkage not just with a mate but with the universe. But it didn't happen but maybe two or three times in a lifetime so far. Could you confirm that you can't tell me how you do that?

I am Latwii, and am aware of your query, my sister. We find ourselves in this particular response limited greatly by that which we may share as our form of energy transfer at this time, for the type of experience which you have described is that of the indigo-ray energy transfer which is most rare upon your planet. This is the work of the adept. To describe that methodology for any entity seeking adepthood is to travel that for the entity, and this we view as an infringement. An entity in sharing with another in the sexual energy transfer may from time to time strike the heart of its seeking, shall we say, just as the novice who aims the arrow at the target shall from time to time strike the center or the bull's-eye. The methodology for repeating this procedure in a manner which is sure is a methodology which must be discovered by the practitioner in order for it to be effective, for each shall find his or her unique methodology, though each shall travel a similar path.

May we answer you further, my sister?

Carla: Okay, so it was your basic beginner's luck? All right. Just one more question. Is the path traceable, the same, by each mated pair that is vibrating all the way up through indigo or is it unique to each mated pair?

I am Latwii, and am aware of your query, my mister. Without meaning to confuse, may we suggest that both possibilities are correct. To explicate, may we suggest that the lessons to be learned are represented by each energy center, the green being the sharing of unconditional love with the other self, the blue being the acceptance in a free and open manner of the other self, and the giving to and receiving from the other self of clear communication, and the indigo being the work of the adept that seeks to change conscious perception by utilizing the unconscious mind. Each energy center and type of lesson must be mastered by all who seek adepthood, yet the method of mastery is unique to each entity, and to each pair of entities it is doubly unique. This is because each entity has preincarnative programming which allows the pursuing of these lessons in a manner which is a culmination of many previous incarnations. Each [is] also traveling the path of the seeker, yet traveling the path in quite an individual fashion so that various lessons are learned in various manners of learning in various climes with a multitude of those joining in the seeking throughout the many incarnations.

May we answer you further, my sister?

Carla: Just let me boil down what you said and see if I got it. What you're saying is the requirements are constant but the methods of meeting the requirements are as various as the people. Is that what you said?

I am Latwii, and, my sister, we appreciate your ability to distill that which we spend many words upon.

May we answer you further?

Carla: No. I'll let somebody else have a go.

(Pause)

Carla: Well, as long as nobody else has a question, I have another question. I was confused a little bit by the message tonight, I didn't understand it. I guess I'll have to read it. As we've studied, it seems that the function of will is very important. And it seemed that what Hatonn was trying to express was almost a negation of will. I guess it's only natural that there should be a lot of paradoxes, but that one about turning your back, sort of, on your seeking in order to communicate confused me and I wondered, especially since we keep being reminded about the function of the will, what is the function of the will in communication? Do you will to lose that which you have gained? What … I'll just stop there and you can say anything that comes to mind. I was confused.

I am Latwii, and am aware of your confusion, my sister. We hope that we may aid in this matter, for as the seeker continues the journey there is the need for the constant refinement of the means of seeking. Our brothers and sisters of Hatonn attempted to provide this means of refining for your consideration. You are each aware that the effort of the seeker is great when the seeking becomes conscious. The seeker looks all about the self for answers to the basic questions of who it is, of what is life and how shall this life be lived. There are many groups upon your planet who provide various answers to these queries. Many seekers travel to many groups, and as the shopper at a sale, tries on many clothes and many possible means of looking at the universe about the self, and at the self within the universe. Many techniques are used to still the mind, to center the attention, to provide healthy thoughts and food for mind and body, to repeat various phrases, to sing various songs, to dance various dances. Each seeker then gains a repertoire of means by which the evolution of mind, body and spirit might be pursued, and each seeker then uses these means in such pursuits. The road is traveled, the turns are found, the sun and the moon alternate in shining upon the journey, the winds of change blow across the face which continues to push forward. Eventually the seeker must look within the self for the final inspiration that motivates the seeker to take one more step, and yet one more step.

The message which our brothers and sisters of Hatonn attempted to deliver concerned this point at which the seeker begins to refine the seeking so that the dedication to an outcome in any situation is released. For though the will is built at first by such dedication it is as the crutch that eventually must be laid down in order that the seeker may walk with its own strength. To give up the stake in any outcome of an event is not for the beginner. One must take the first step first. To give up the stake and the dedication is another way of suggesting that the seeker be that which it seeks, that the seeker be that which it has been for all time and before time unrolled its scroll of beingness. The seeker then is exhorted to be that which it seeks—the one infinite Creator. For, in truth, the seeker is the one infinite Creator and though it may use many crutches to come to that point of realization, eventually to be the Creator the seeker no longer seeks with any crutch but is that which it is. And this is a refinement of the will which is directed then in another fashion with a much lighter touch, shall we say, yet in paradoxical fashion a touch which has great power.

May we answer you further, my sister?

Carla: You knock me out, Latwii. I'll have to read that, but thank you.

I am Latwii. We thank you, my sister, and hope that we have not bruised you with our punch. Is there another query at this time?

S: Yes, Latwii. Can you offer any advice or make a comment on our informal meditation meetings at home?

I am Latwii, and am aware of your query, my sister. We find great joy and purpose within these gatherings which of late have graced your domicile. We can only suggest the continuing adherence to those principles which you have set before you, most importantly being the tuning. We find a great dedication in this respect, and commend each of you for your efforts, and thank you for your great service.

May we answer you further, my sister?

S: No, Latwii. But we thank you also for showing up.

I am Latwii, and it is our privilege and pleasure to join you, always. Is there another query at this time?

(Pause)

I am Latwii. We find that we have exhausted the queries for this evening, and would therefore take our leave of this group at this time. We leave you, as always, with the joy which is known by those who feel the love and the light of the one Creator emanating from a group such as this one, and from each portion of the creation that sings in harmony with those who seek the truth. We thank each of you for your devotion to this seeking, and remind you that we are with you at your request always in joy, in peace, in love and in light. We are known to you as those of Latwii. We leave you now in that love and light, in the power, and in the peace of the one Creator. I am Latwii. Adonai vasu borragus.

L/L Research

L/L Research is a subsidiary of Rock Creek Research & Development Laboratories, Inc.

P.O. Box 5195
Louisville, KY 40255-0195

www.llresearch.org

Rock Creek is a non-profit corporation dedicated to discovering and sharing information which may aid in the spiritual evolution of humankind.

ABOUT THE CONTENTS OF THIS TRANSCRIPT: This telepathic channeling has been taken from transcriptions of the weekly study and meditation meetings of the Rock Creek Research & Development Laboratories and L/L Research. It is offered in the hope that it may be useful to you. As the Confederation entities always make a point of saying, please use your discrimination and judgment in assessing this material. If something rings true to you, fine. If something does not resonate, please leave it behind, for neither we nor those of the Confederation would wish to be a stumbling block for any.

CAVEAT: This transcript is being published by L/L Research in a not yet final form. It has, however, been edited and any obvious errors have been corrected. When it is in a final form, this caveat will be removed.

© 2009 L/L Research

Sunday Meditation
May 8, 1983

(C channeling)

I am Hatonn, and I am now with this instrument. We greet you, as always, in the love and the light of the one infinite Creator. We come tonight in this time of rebirth of your planet when nature renews itself as another life cycle begins. As we have spoken to you before, each of you goes through a process of growth. At times the growth will be slightened or set back, as all the plants on your planet, when after a period of warmth and rain are faced with renewed cold, but the desire to continue growth is something that is within all of us and all may continue. As each setback occurs it may be learned from and overcome, for once the foot has been set upon the path, the need to continue increases. Each lesson and experience leads to an enlightening and a continuation.

My friends, remember always that as you travel, there are those who will help and give what aid be needed. Travel forward with the senses open, with the heart open, to encompass that which you may meet. Be not afraid to give of yourself. Be not afraid to ask for help. You have many kindred spirits journeying with you. We of Hatonn are always willing to do what we may to aid. You need but ask and we shall join with you.

We would now like to transfer this contact to another. I am Hatonn.

(S1 channeling)

I am Hatonn, and greet you once again through this instrument, my friends. We would only stay shortly with this instrument so that the one known as S2 could also have the opportunity to practice this area of his service, if he would just relax.

My friends, this day upon your planet has been indeed a most beautiful one. There are those who see only what they wish to see, and in the clouds and the coolness they see a grayness. And with the sun their spirits revive, and they once again rejoice. Are you like this, my friends? There are times when it is difficult to see the sun behind the clouds but it is there. The beauty always remains no matter how dark the sky overhead may seem. If you look closely enough, you may be able to see more beauty than you firstly expected. The book may have a plain cover, but the inside carries much, much more. We urge that you be not content with seeing only the outer actions of your brothers and sisters, seeing what you may at first perceive as gray skies. Look within, my friends, within your brothers and your sisters, within yourselves. See the light, the love, the beauty of the creation that is within. Be not content with only the vestiges of a fine veneer. The inner core is so beautiful when perceived and accepted.

I am Hatonn, and would now transfer this contact.

(S2 channeling)

I am Hatonn, and I am now with this instrument. We would continue thus by saying that looking for the core, and finding the inner goodness, and not seeing only the outer, which can be plain. A lot can be missed, a learning experience that could not be learned. But by perceiving what is hidden, what can be implied and learning what's there, a most wondrous beauty can be found. For all are the Creator, and all has their part, and being a part of the Creator, thus can all be perceived.

We would at this time like to transfer this contact. I am Hatonn.

(Carla channeling)

I am Hatonn, and again I greet you in the love and the light of our infinite Creator. We shall conclude through this instrument with thanks to each who has been of service at this gathering. There is a premise which each within this group shares which calls us to you and calls you together. That premise is that you as an entity are unfinished. If you were finished, the metaphors we use of journeys, seeking and learning, would be inapplicable because a finished thing does not need to journey. It is static and rests as in a museum, a completed project, a piece of art. This is not your concept of yourself. Rather, you resist the teaching of your culture which says that that at some point you are finished, you are grown. You say, "No, I am not. There is more than I am perceiving to the world about me, and I wish to have the tools of a more accurate perception in order that I may work upon myself."

This is why you are here. One may phrase this in many ways, but this is why you are here. You are not satisfied to gaze at the veneer, at the surface, at the appearance, at the constant coincidences, surprises and events of daily life. You do truly wish to penetrate more and more the eggshell, the cocoon, to reach out, young though you may be, burst out of the shell, out of the cocoon and gaze upon a new world.

We would ask you a question this evening. If you do so truly and earnestly wish to learn more, and do so truthfully feel that you are not finished, why is it, my friends, that so often you form judgments that seem to be carved in stone and resist change? Do you think that everything is worthy of your attention in the illusion except for those things which you have already decided are so? It is an interesting question, and one we urge you to ponder whenever you find yourself prey to a sudden attack of surety. When you are absolutely and positively certain that things are as they must be in an area of your life, it is then time to ponder the unfinished nature of your great infinite and eternal personality.

What do you want to keep when you shed this cocoon, when you crack this shell? The emotions you accept and allow to become biases will be those things which you keep. Therefore, examine your biases or judgments, your reactions, your opinions and seek in them the seeds of new growth. We do not say this is a simple matter, although it is. We are aware of the effort which it takes for one who is within an illusion to bring light to bear upon a cherished misconception. Nevertheless, my friends, if you do not find love within each and every bias, pull that bias apart and find out how the wood shall be grained beneath the veneer, how the butterfly shall travel when it is free of that particular cocoon.

Before we leave this instrument, we and our brothers of Laitos would wish to spend some few moments with the one known as K, familiarizing this entity with the feeling of our contact. We also wish to spend those same moments with the one known as R. If you would be so kind as to allow us to pause at this time. I am Hatonn.

(Pause)

(Carla channeling)

I am Hatonn. We thank each. Our blessing is with you, and as the last rays of your planet's sun light the room in which you sit, so we travel from you. Our thoughts are always with you and you may request our presence at any time. Look always for the light, and when you see it now, remember the light within you, and then you shall be free of darkness and you shall bloom as do your flowers. I am of Hatonn. I leave you in that great inner light which is only faintly mocked and fondly remembered by your sun. I leave you in the infinite love of the infinite One. Adonai. Adonai.

(Jim channeling)

I am Latwii, and greet you, my friends, in love and light. We are privileged, as always, to be asked to join your group this evening. We thank you once again for your joyful invitation which we gladly accept. We of Latwii are here to attempt to answer those queries which have meaning for you for which you have concern. May we then begin our humble service by asking for the first query?

S2: I was wondering. Is there a reason for having a rash and what do you recommend would be a good cure for such of the kind that I have right now?

I am Latwii, and am aware of your query, my brother. The first portion of your query is the more easily answered, for, indeed, my brother, there is a reason for each situation or condition in which your physical vehicle finds itself in a distortion of what you may call disease. The basic reason for any such distortion towards disease is that an opportunity to learn which has been less than efficiently used by the mind and by the thinking processes of the entity has then been given to the physical vehicle in a symbolic form that the entity might more easily notice the opportunity which was first missed.

Therefore, for the cure, shall we say, to any such malfunction of the physical vehicle, it is most helpful to look to the symbolic form which the malfunction represents. This may require that the entity suffering such malfunction engage in a substantial portion of contemplation and analysis of what the symbolic meaning might be. This action then might be helpfully followed by meditation upon the fruits of such contemplation, allowing the crystal thoughts to sink to the heart of the being accompanied by the desire to know the truth and the desire to evolve in mind, body and spirit. This desire shall fertilize and water the crystal seeds of your thoughts, so that there might be what you would call an intuitional inspiration rising from the deep portions of the self into the conscious mind, and allow the opportunity which was first missed to be utilized, and therefore allow a healing to occur within the being.

May we answer you further, my brother?

S2: Do you have any suggestions—well, first off, I'm probably asking a question you can't answer, but I'm going to ask it anyway. Do you have any suggestions as to what it is that I'm not—I assume there's a lesson or catalyst I'm not utilizing correctly. Do you have a suggestion as to what areas I should concentrate on?

I am Latwii, and am aware of your query, my brother. We may speak in general terms only in this matter, for as you are aware, the process of struggling with the so-called problem allows a spiritual strength to be nourished within the seeker. This density which you inhabit has one primary lesson. That is the lesson of loving, forgiving and acceptance or that which may be called compassion. When there is less than love, less than acceptance, less than forgiveness in any area of an entity's life, then there is the opportunity to grow, shall we say, that very lack which is experienced. For the lack of such provides a vacuum which attracts to that lack in the entity experiencing the lack that which is missing. Love, acceptance, forgiveness, tolerance and the ability for what you might call the light touch are those aspects of unconditional love to which one may look in general in order to see where there might be the lack in the life as it is experienced by the entity.

May we answer you further, my brother?

S2: No, that's fine. That really is a lot of help to me. Thank you.

I am Latwii, and we are most grateful to you, my brother, for allowing us to serve. Is there another query at this time?

K: I have a question, Latwii. I'm having a terrible time with procrastination. I know that often in the past when I'm putting off something, when I first jump in then things come easily, and I'm spending a lot of time sleeping so I won't have to do things. And I really wish to get out of that rut, and I don't seem to be able to do it. Do you have any suggestions?

I am Latwii, and am aware of your query, my sister. We again may speak in general terms and suggest that the meditation upon the difficult situation, and the growing desire to rectify it is most efficacious, for within the heart and the deepest portions of the self of each entity lies the knowledge of what lessons are being sought, and what lessons have been programmed before the time of this life began …

(Side one of tape ends.)

(Jim channeling)

I am Latwii, and shall continue through this instrument. As you meditate, and again fertilize your meditation with your desire to know the truth, you shall open deeper portions of yourself, those portions which serve as resources to the conscious mind. The intuitional inspirations then shall travel through the same openings, and become apparent to your conscious mind. You may find then in this manner that there are a number of possible solutions or possibilities that shall be presented to you as a result of such mediation. The intuitional inspirations may offer the more specific type of suggestions as to what lessons are being made available to you through the situations which you see and describe as the procrastination in a more general manner. You may also discover that the desire which you take with you in meditation to seek the truth also returns to you enhanced, and becomes, shall we say, a motivational force or factor which allows you then to utilize the specific inspirational hunches which rise from the deeper portions of your being.

May we answer you further, my sister?

K: *(Inaudible)*.

I am Latwii. We thank you, my sister. Is there another query at this time?

R: Latwii, I'd like your advice on surviving in what I consider to be a very negative atmosphere with very negative requirements for survival, and how to maintain … It's hard to put into words. How to maintain an unguarded, I guess, attitude or an unguarded—reject an unguarded attitude in this environment. It's hard to … For quite some time now I've been able to maintain what I consider to be a positive attitude in a negative surrounding, and just recently, very recently, I, in a way of speaking, picked up the knife and cut a throat to guarantee my own security, and it's bothering me. And I want to know, is it possible to survive in negative places without being negative, and if so, how?

I am Latwii, and am aware of your query, my brother. Though the survival of the positive polarity becomes more difficult when surrounded by the increasing negative influences, we may reaffirm that indeed it is possible and even probable that such survival may be enjoyed by those who seek the light and love of the one Creator in the positive sense. Remember first, my brother, that you inhabit an illusion. What seems to be one thing may be another. What seems to be the negative polarity surrounding an entity may also be the opportunity for finding the positive aspect of the same catalyst.

To remember that you inhabit an illusion is most helpful, for if from time to time you forget and believe with you thinking that what surrounds you is real, then you are more likely to respond in an illusory manner, shall we say, playing by the rules of the game which is not real. This of course intensifies the catalyst for the entity so entrapped until the entity, by the trauma of its own experience, is brought to the realization that there is much more to what is true, good and beautiful than what it had previously imagined.

May we now move to another aspect of the catalyst which seems negative. All of your creation, all of any creation, is based upon an illusion, the illusion of separation. It would seem to one observing creation that certain things, in fact all things exist apart from each other. Yet, are not all one? Therefore, as you face the catalyst of your daily round of experience, remember that each portion of the creation, though an illusion, also contains the love of the one Creator. Your mission, shall we say, if you should choose to accept it, is to find that love. This is the work of the adept, for it requires that which has the magical or metaphysical power of transformation. As you look at what seems to be negative, look for the Creator. The Creator is there. Look for love. Love is there. If then you can find that love, that light, the one Creator within the situation and within yourself, then you, as Creator, may speak to that situation which also is the Creator. And it may be transformed by your recognition of it as the Creator.

My friend, this is not an easy path, nor was it meant to be. The burden of your journey weighs heavy, yet the strength that you gain grows daily. You shall seem the fool to many. And so shall you be. For the fool knows that it inhabits an illusion and seeks to become one with that which many would run from. This is the way of the fool, running in the opposite direction towards the difficulty, for no difficulty is seen.

[May we answer you further, my brother?]

R: No, Latwii, thank you. I only wish I could take you to work with me sometime. Thank you.

I am Latwii, and, my brother, we are with you there as well. May we answer another query at this time?

S2: Latwii, I was wondering. You said that my—what my primary lesson in this existence is, and the reason why I had a disease, was because I had not responded to some catalyst as effectively as I should have. Could it be that, or is it possible that I could be receiving catalyst for, let's say, an extension of the sort of basic requirement, if you understand what I mean?

I am Latwii, and am aware of your query, my brother. We spoke in general terms in our previous response to your query, and indicated that love was the primary lesson to be learned. It is quite true that each entity shall refine the means by which this lesson is learned, and shall refine these means in many, many ways so that unto each entity falls unique configurations of catalyst programmed, may we add, by the entity itself that it might learn certain lessons.

You see, you are the professor which constructs the tests and the queries. Then you forget who you are and join this illusion, and begin the class of love and become the student taking the test which it seems it has never seen before. Yet, as you continue upon your journey, you shall discover that you become more and more familiar with the questions and the testing, and you shall discover more and more the unique nature of each catalyst, each question, each test.

May we answer you further, my brother?

S2: No. Thank you very much, though.

I am Latwii, and we thank you, my brother. Is there another query at this time?

Carla: If I could suggest, perhaps we should close because of C's discomfort.

I am Latwii, and we are most happy to serve in this manner as well. We wish for the one known as C the comfort of the cessation of the coughing difficulty. We thank each present for inviting our presence. We are with you always. In the present situation you are simply more aware of our presence than at other times. Ask for our presence in your meditations if that would serve you, and we shall be most honored to respond and join you there. At this time we shall take our leave of this group. Yet, as we seem to leave, we are with you in love and in light and in unity. Peace and blessings be with each. We are known to you as those of Latwii. Adonai, my friends. Adonai vasu borragus.

Sunday Meditation
May 15, 1983

(Unknown channeling)

[I am Hatonn.] I greet you, my brothers and sisters, in the love and light of our one infinite Creator. It is a great joy to us to join you this evening for so large the gathering of your peoples in the seeking for which you have come together, is a wonderful sight for us, to blend our vibrations with yours, to become one and to share in your oneness.

My friends, this evening we would share a few thoughts on the subject of becoming one with your brothers and sisters, with your other selves. There comes a time in each life when one will experience doubts in their seeking. One might wonder at the path that has been chosen, when one struggles with the concept of seeing a brother or a sister who is not quite as one would expect and still within the self would realize that though there are conflicts, there is still the oneness, the sameness, the reflection of the self in the entity that is causing the conflict.

My friends, this opportunity which has been made available at a certain point in many lives is indeed a great step, one which with love, with the sharing of the heart, the mind, and the spirit will perhaps cause some of the doubts to be allayed. The path you have chosen, my friends, as you well know, may have many bends, many [bows], but the blessings which are bestowed are so beautiful. The lessons you have chosen in the pre-incarnative state to undergo are those that have the capability of becoming one within yourself, bringing the lesson home, so to speak. As the harvest becomes closer, my friends, these lessons of love and of sharing yourselves by learning the experience of becoming one with those that you perceive as being troublesome to your spirit, are great lessons and are wise to be thankful for.

At this time we would like to transfer this contact. I am Hatonn.

(Unknown channeling)

I thank you for the light.

[**Carla:**] Let's all picture a bright light completely encircling and holding this group.

(Unknown channeling)

I am Hatonn. I greet you now through this instrument once more in the love and in the light of our infinite Creator. We shall continue now through this instrument.

Let us compare perception of other selves by consciousness as a type of mirror. The type of mirror which the illusion surrounding you provides for your use is the type which is used in your carnivals. Far from receiving an adequate reflection each mirror is purposefully warped in order that an imperfect and distorted image is seen by the one who goes to the carnival. Some mirrors seem to reflect a jolly and harmonious image and cause one to laugh, other mirrors seem to reflect to us a looming and menacing shape. And so you go through the illusion day by day, perceiving and categorizing the images from the mirrors as good, as evil, as friend and stranger, as harmonious and inharmonious, and you do not realize that you are in a carnival, and that, my friends is the only reason that the carnival mirrors are in place. The more emphasis that is placed upon the distortions, by the carnival goer, the more distorted the images will become, the more complex, the more interesting. Each carnival goer chooses the nature of his entertainment, by choosing to see the image he prefers to see while watching for it, by finding it, by naming it, and calling it his own.

At some point in the carnival, either by good fortune, by inspiration, or by the cold use of intellectual gifts it may become apparent to the carnival goer that there is an exit from the house of mirrors. And so the carnival goer which has decided to seek the exit leaves the hall of mirrors. Behold, he has entered another hall of mirrors! Those you discard are discarded, those you do not recognize remain the portion of the reflecting surface of your consciousness, and so begins a new carnival, and at the new level of awareness that the seeker has found and cherishes and nurtures by meditation, the carnival goes on, the flags wave, the merry-go-round plays its merry tune and still you see a distorted image of each other self, less distorted than before in many cases, until one day by good luck or inspiration, or the cold use of intellect, the carnival goer again finds the exit.

There are many, many mirrors, many rooms full of them and many exits, for your seeking and your learning is a process we cannot offer to you, the instantaneous realization that will last. We can promise to you that such moments will come to you, the mirrors will be blown away in the wind, and you see clearly, as if through glass with no lead to keep an image reflected, but you look at yourself in everyone you see, and you are indeed one with all that there is, and you say again and again, there too am I, and this realization is wonderful and joyous, but we cannot promise to you that you may keep [it], for you are within the illusion which you inhabit, in order to work with mirrors.

For a great portion of your incarnation you will be dealing with a carnival. It may be possible in a life-long friendship of mate or bosom friend that all the mirrors be vanquished and that you may see yourself face-to-face and rejoice that you have known the Creator. It is more likely that you shall only be able to do this intermittently, but to know what you are after is the key to seeking. As long as you seek you shall find. This promise written in you holy works is no part of any lie, we can only ask that you take care in what you seek, for you shall find it.

We ask that if at any time you become discouraged, you stop at the first available moment and look into the one mirror that you carry with you, that will give you a true image. We ask that you look into the silence, for there is a center and a hope, a joy and a love in the midst of that silence that can create a new kingdom for you and for your planet. Let your desire be turned to that which you have a proper need to attend to, your own consciousness.

My friends when you lift up your consciousness into the great mirror of light you offer a gift to yourself, to all those around you, and to your planet, the nature of which is indescribable. You can leave the carnival, there is a way out, and while you are gone and have raised yourself up into a focus to find in this illusion, you may descend once again and join the carnival and ride the horses on the merry-go-round and eat the cotton-candy and laugh, and choose to find in the hall of mirrors good and kindly images. How do you choose to see yourself? It is your illusion, it is your choice. We do not deny any of those things which are negative, seen against the positive standard of a happy, smiling, vibrant illusion; we do not deny hate or death or jealousy, pain or anguish or loss, we only say to you that they are a part of that which is an illusion and that at the heart of each of these things is a transformation which is so positive that joy leaps from every tear that you may shed in the learning of these lessons.

Therefore, whatever face you see, it is your choice, put your name to it and do not let world opinion of any type or degree sway you, for you can be a messenger of light. You may give that message to anyone whose path intersects yours simply by seeing that other self as the Creator. We ask that you begin always by attempting to gain a true reflection of yourself, for it is only when the carnival goer is lifted from the hall of mirrors that the mirrors become part of a manageable, reasonable and loving consciousness. This day, has the carnival become a bit hectic? Do you wish more for yourself? Very well then, my friends, begin that process by utterly forgiving yourself. By loving yourself most dearly and by lifting yourself through meditation to the light, what consolation there is in that light, what healing there is in that love.

We are aware that there are questions in this group, and therefore we would pause only to offer our vibration to those who find that it deepens their meditative state. If you would be patient we shall pause briefly to share our blessing on each of you. I am Hatonn.

(Pause)

I am Hatonn. I leave you, my friends, through this instrument, but never in the unspoken sense. We are always pleased to be with you, if you so desire. We ask that you be most discriminating as you listen to us, as we are imperfect and fallible, much like yourselves. Use what thoughts we have that are of help to you, discard the rest. Our own selves, our greater selves, we greet you and bid you farewell. We are those of Hatonn. We leave you in the ineffable love and the infinite light of the one Creator. Adonai. Adonai.

(Pause)

I am Latwii, and I greet you, my friends, in the love and in the light of our infinite Creator. It is with great joy that we join your group this evening. Again it is our privilege to be asked to provide our humble service of attempting to answer those queries which may be of value to you in your seeking. May we then ask for the first query.

Questioner: Latwii, in another meditation, I channeled the one Onoma, and as I channeled vocally I began to feel my hands leading to move in gesture, and I had not experienced anything like this before. Could you make any comment about what was happening?

I am Latwii, and I'm aware of your query, my brother. As various instruments partake in the process of vocalized channeling there is frequently an abundance of the energies being transmitted that requires some outlet so that there is not an overloading of the normal means of transmission. In your particular case this outlet was the use of the manual appendages to serve as a diversion for the excess of energy that the ones known as Onoma were providing that evening. Your particular sensitivity on that evening allowed what might be viewed as a mismatch in the energy to be transmitted compared to the receptivity or normal level of receptivity of your particular instrument, therefore the one known as Onoma found the use of your, as you call them, hands, to be most efficacious in relieving your instrument of the excess of energy.

May we answer you further, my brother?

Questioner: No, thank you very much.

We thank you, my brother. Is there another query at this time?

Questioner: Yes, Latwii, are there more clairvoyants and psychics and healers now or at this point in time than there were, say, oh, twenty years ago?

I am Latwii, and I'm aware of your query, my sister. You may notice an increase in not only the absolute number of such entities, but also in the percentage as a proportion of your planet's total population.

May we answer you further, my sister?

Questioner: So the answer is yes. The answer is yes to my question? Is that right?

I am Latwii. This is correct.

Questioner: Thank you.

We thank you, my sister. Is there another query at this time?

Questioner: Is this due to third-density, fourth-density kids being born to wanderers or both?

I am Latwii. There are, my sister, not only these factors to be considered, but more as well. Not only have those known as wanderers incarnated with latent abilities awaiting activation in service to this planet and not only have the children of the harvest of other third-density planets begun early incarnations on this planet which shall be, as you know, a positive fourth-density planet …

(Side one of tape ends.)

(Unknown channeling)

I am Latwii, we shall continue. There are also those native to this third-density planet who have by what you may call seniority of vibration incarnated with hopes of achieving what you may call the harvest, or the graduation into the next density of being. These entities have through many incarnations upon this planet developed certain abilities that now are able to be used in greater ease and facility than at any previous time, as you call it. You may also consider the increase in the vibratory level of the catalyst which each entity faces in the daily round of activities. This increased level or intensity of opportunities for growth allows many entities to be able to utilize the catalyst in a fashion which develops those abilities which may be called psychic or of a paranormal nature.

May we answer you further, my sister?

Questioner: No, thank you.

I am Latwii, we thank you. Is there another query at this time?

Questioner: Yes, just one more question along the same line. I was talking with a clairvoyant yesterday and she said that I had a healing aura about me, and I had not really heard of such a thing before and, well, would you comment on that, about a healing aura about anybody?

I am Latwii, and I'm aware your query, my sister. To one who is sensitive to the energies which surround each entity the perception of those energies may vary according to the, shall we see—we correct this instrument—shall we say, to the depth of sensitivity of the clairvoyant, as you call it, entity. One may see the ease of the melding of the mind, the body, and the spirit reflected in the aura and interpret this balance of the being as a healing aura, for indeed such an entity, having balanced the self to a certain degree is able to generate the feelings of peace, serenity and joy, which are most soothing and quite healing in their manifestations.

Another entity of the clairvoyant nature may look at the same auric energies and note that indeed within the field of energies lie the specific abilities of this entity to serve as what your peoples call the healer, having incarnated with these abilities either in potentiation awaiting the activation or in partial activation.

Therefore, it is both necessary to look at the one who is perceiving the auric energies and its ability to so perceive, and to look at the one being perceived to determine if there are those specific abilities defined as the healing abilities contained within the auric field or if there is a more general configuration of mind, body and spirit which in some also provide the faculty of healing.

May we answer you further, my sister?

Questioner: No, that's fine. Thank you.

I am Latwii, and I thank you, my sister, and greet you after your absence.

Questioner: Thank you also. We missed you.

Is there another query at this time?

Questioner: I have one. This morning my message was to forget what I feel are earthly moral responsibilities or obligations and to let myself go on my path freely, not to tie myself down to one area. Can you expand on that?

I am Latwii, and I'm aware of your query, my sister. We may speak in a general sense about the nature of such a message, but cannot be specific for when the self at its deeper levels begins the communication with what you might call the conscious waking self, there is the direction from the inner being which is being reflected as clearly as the conscious self can perceive such reflection and the necessity in such cases is that the conscious self seek more and more to perceive more and more clearly those messages which arise from within.

The concept of allowing the self to move along the path of evolution in a free and open manner is a concept which has meaning to an entity which works with the blue-ray energy center of the throat. Such a configuration of energy is then experienced by the seeker in a manner which promotes the clear communication of the self with the self and with other selves, accepting the self and other selves and freely expressing the self to all which surround the self. In this manner the giving of freedom and acceptance to others springs from the giving of freedom and acceptance to the self for you are also a mirror and reflect that which is your being to those about you.

Therefore, as you seek to move freely along your path of evolution, you shall also give that freedom to others and shall inspire such freedom to those who come in contact with you. It is therefore helpful to consider the deeper ramifications and implications of such a message as you meditate upon it, that you might continually refine that journey which lies before you, and which you have long traveled, making refinement upon refinement. And as you continue upon this journey you shall find those messages arising from within your deeper self to be more and more frequent, more and more clearly perceived.

May we answer you further, my sister?

Questioner: No, thank you, Latwii.

We thank you, my sister. Is there another query at this time?

Questioner: This is a hard question to get into words, but I'll try. A friend and I this last week, or week and a half, have been experiencing a sense of pressure and tension, almost a sense of reverberation from the planet, as if the planet itself is in some kind of special pressure or tension. Just a number of symptoms and we wonder if there is a particular reason or cause? Can you comment on that?

I am Latwii, and I'm aware of your query, my sister. The planet, the entity upon which you walk is also partaking in the process of evolution, for all portions of the creation are one and move with the Creator as It becomes aware of Itself. As you know, the cycle which is now ending upon this planet is very close at hand and its transformation has not been what you might call smooth for many upon this planet have had difficulty in realizing the love that exists in each moment, each situation and each entity. Therefore, the seeming inharmonious expression or perception in the mirror has been experienced by many upon this planet's surface for a great portion of what you call time so that these vibrations of disharmony have entered into the planet itself and as the planet begins its transit into that density of love, there is the momentary mismatch of vibratory frequencies. This mismatch becomes apparent to those who are sensitive in many ways, but we can assure each that the mismatch or stress suffered is but momentary and in its way, also offers greater opportunity for each entity upon the planet and for the planet itself to find that love in the moment which has not been found previously, for love is at the heart of all creation and no moment is without it's own infinite share of that love. Therefore, when such distressing feelings are felt, rejoice that the planet is giving birth to itself and each entity upon it, and that the birth is attended by love.

May we answer you further, my sister?

Questioner: No, thank you. That's what I expected.

We thank you, my sister. Is there another query at this time?

Questioner: Yes, let me go just a little bit further. These vibrations that are more intense now, that you mentioned a moment ago, are they beginning now to sift down to, well, say, the average person who has been going about life totally unaware of what's happening?

I am Latwii, and I'm aware of your query, my sister. This is correct with the qualification that for many upon your planet who do not yet feel with the sensitive inner being, that the vibrations' intensities are reflected in a more gross or general manner. That is, many will be found to speak of what is called "the good old days," when times were more peaceful and there was time to reflect and a feeling of ease was more apparent. You will see the return to such days in mind, in entertainment, in clothing, and in the various ways that your peoples express their inner being and feeling. Therefore, such intensity of vibrations are—we correct this instrument—such intensity of vibrations is noticed by each entity upon your planet, yet noticed in a infinite variety of ways.

May we answer you further, my sister?

Questioner: No, that makes sense. Thank you very much.

We thank you once again. Is there another query at this time?

Questioner: Just a little follow-up question on that one. [When] I first was asking the question, I was thinking that this was like a labor pain, but I didn't want to say that, but then you said those words. When human beings give birth the labor pains usually increase in frequency and intensity. Is that going to be the pattern for the planet?

I am Latwii, and I'm aware of your query, my sister. Though the future is not known, we can look upon the direction in which your planet and its various populations are moving and can suggest that such shall be most likely the case, for the planet has for a great portion of what you call time known its populations by their hostile expressions of power over others and these vibrations have created an inertial residue which seeks to be balanced in the short period of time which remains in order for the balance to be achieved. It is most likely that it shall be allowed its full run, shall we say, and the intensity of catalyst shall continue to increase so that the use of catalyst in the remaining time might be most efficient. You might consider the great learning which comes with the situation which you call traumatic. In but a brief span of time, great transformations can occur when the entities involved in the situation are, shall we say, made aware of the need to call upon the great and deeply held inner reserves with which each entity enters each incarnation, but which each entity is but faintly aware exists within.

May we answer you further, my sister?

Questioner: Thank you, no, that's fine.

Questioner: Latwii, to what extent can one person send positive vibrations to another person?

I am Latwii, and I'm aware of your query, my sister. Depending upon the entity's clearing and balancing of the energy centers, the degree of ability is variable and ranges from most ineffective to infinitely effective.

May we answer you further, my sister?

Questioner: No, thank you.

I am Latwii, and we thank you, my sister. Is there another query at this time?

Questioner: How's the instrument holding up?

We find the instrument somewhat weary, but able to continue for another short span of your time. May we ask if there is another query?

Questioner: Well, as long as you've got a query left. I ran across a very unusual situation recently. I met a friend's wife who had a most unusual thing happen to her twice. She became pregnant, in a heartbeat it was discovered, and she went quite a ways with the pregnancy, four or five months, so that she was big, and then the pregnancy disappeared. You would think it were a hysterical pregnancy except for the fact that the husband's a doctor and he heard the heartbeat of the child. What type of entity needs this form of nurture and where are these children going? Let me add that I do not doubt this woman's word or the ability of her husband to use a stethoscope.

I am Latwii, and I'm aware of your query, my sister. In the situation of which you speak, you may see evidence of the entity which needs but a short span of time within your third-density illusion in order to accomplish the task which it has set before it. It is most common among your people's perception of the way of the incarnation that the incarnation shall begin with a, as is called, normal pregnancy, birth, childhood, adolescence and some portion of the adult years experienced before the passing from the illusion is accomplished. Yet, if one could look with unfettered eye at the experiences which are truly occurring within your illusion, one would see a great array and variety of means of being and learning those lessons which this density has to offer.

The experience of which you have spoken is not as uncommon as one might believe, many are the entities at this time in your planet's evolution which seek but specific and short-term experiences within your illusion. The lessons which are then learned are of great value for most usually such lessons are of the nature of completion, that is, the graduation is at hand and but one course credit remains.

May we answer you further, my sister?

Questioner: Just one thing. These children were not stillborn; there is no physical evidence they were ever there. Where did they go?

I am Latwii, and I'm aware of your query, my sister. These entities move into this illusion as each has moved into this illusion, and leave this illusion in the same manner, though the entities living, as you call it, within this illusion have not become totally aware of their presence.

May we answer you further, my sister?

Questioner: Do you think there's any chance at all I could understand what you're saying? Or do you think that it's probably beyond me?

I am Latwii, and we shall attempt clarity. The concept is so simple that we apologize for assuming that the questioner was familiar with it …

Questioner: Never assume!

We suggest that all exits, shall we say, from this illusion are exits in which the third-density yellow-ray physical vehicle, whatever its degree of manifestation, is left, so that the etheric or indigo-ray body may be entered, the incarnation reviewed, the lessons discerned, and the further needs for incarnation determined. Therefore, the exit is from the yellow-ray body to the indigo-ray body in each case, whether the incarnation has been, what you call, long in years or hardly apparent at all.

May we answer you further, my sister?

Questioner: So what you're saying then is that in the case of this unusual woman, she is capable of absorbing the physical material used to house the child which had such a short incarnation, so that it did not have to be spontaneously aborted and gotten rid of all at once, but simply absorbed into the body of the mother. Is that what you're saying?

I am Latwii, and I'm aware of your query, my sister. This is partially correct. The entity exiting the physical vehicle also provides some degree of assistance in the absorption of that vehicle which it exits. There are in other cases entities which may be seen as what you may call the guides or angelic presences which also provide such aid as does the entity's higher self or oversoul, as you may call it. Each situation is unique and each situation will be provided the aid which is appropriate, that aid having been pre-incarnatively chosen by each entity involved.

May we answer you further, my sister?

Questioner: Well, is this great service that R is performing the key to her inexplicable weight gain?

I am Latwii, and I'm aware of your query, my sister. We find in this instance some bar upon the distance we may travel attempting to reveal the nature of this situation.

Questioner: That's OK, I had a hunch about it anyway. Just checking, thank you.

I am Latwii. May we ask if there is another query at this time?

Questioner: This feels like a personal question, but I'd like to try it anyway. Latwii, are you presently embodied in a space/time location?

I am Latwii, and I'm aware of your query, my sister. The nature of our existence at this, what you would call, time is such that we inhabit the analog of a space/time physical vehicle within the density of light. Therefore, the vehicle which we inhabit, though it is an analogue of the vehicle which you inhabit, would not be able to be perceived by the great majority of your peoples in any way because of the, shall we say, density of light contained within it, which to your physical senses is quite without substance or perceptibility. When we communicate through instruments such as this instrument, we transmit in a time/space or thought form, so that our space/time physical vehicle generates a form of thought that may penetrate the interlocking densities and planes within each density to reach the instrument which opens itself to our thought form.

Therefore, to answer your query, our normal, shall we say, existence is within a space/time physical vehicle of light, but when we communicate with groups such as this one, we partake in the analog to your meditative state and transmit our thoughts in a thought form vehicle.

May we answer you further, my sister?

Questioner: No. No, thank you.

I am Latwii, we thank you, my sister. May we ask for one final query at this time?

Questioner: Thank you, Latwii. Where is it best to bring a new way of medicine to this society?

I am Latwii, and I'm aware of your query, my sister. We find that there is no place which does not call for the type of healing of which you speak, for the sorrow and suffering and ignorance of the truth of unity within each is great upon your planet at this time. There are many who seek wholeness and do not know that already they are whole; there are many who seek love and acceptance and do not know they are love, they are loved; there are many who exist within the illusion and believe that the illusion as they perceive it is all that there is and they call in their subconscious mind for an exit to the illusion. However, it can be found and yet they are unaware that to look within the self is the exit into unity.

Therefore, as one seeks to be that known as the healer, in whatever form that healing may take, we may suggest that you cannot miss the mark, for all about you are those who call for that healing that you have to give and may we humbly suggest to each that the greatest healing is that love which is at the heart of your being and may be shared at each moment of your existence with each entity you meet. There is no greater magic nor healing than the love, the forgiveness, and the compassion for those who walk along the path of evolution with you.

Therefore, give as you can, be as you are, and those gifts which are yours shall shine as beacons in the night and shall be noticed by all who call and the healing shall occur, for such is the way of the one infinite Creator, that all cycles shall be completed, all the pieces of the creation shall be reassembled into one, and all who seek love shall find it all about them.

At this time, we feel it appropriate to take our leave of this instrument, for we find that this instrument is somewhat weary. We thank each present for calling for our humble service and we remind each that we are but your brothers and sisters in light, fallible and imperfect. Take that we have offered which is of value to you, leave that which is not. It is our privilege to be with you whenever you call, in your private meditations or in your group meditations such as this evening. We leave you now in love and light, in the power and in the peace of the one infinite Creator. We are known to you as those of Latwii. ✻

L/L Research

L/L Research is a subsidiary of Rock Creek Research & Development Laboratories, Inc.

P.O. Box 5195
Louisville, KY 40255-0195

www.llresearch.org

Rock Creek is a non-profit corporation dedicated to discovering and sharing information which may aid in the spiritual evolution of humankind.

ABOUT THE CONTENTS OF THIS TRANSCRIPT: This telepathic channeling has been taken from transcriptions of the weekly study and meditation meetings of the Rock Creek Research & Development Laboratories and L/L Research. It is offered in the hope that it may be useful to you. As the Confederation entities always make a point of saying, please use your discrimination and judgment in assessing this material. If something rings true to you, fine. If something does not resonate, please leave it behind, for neither we nor those of the Confederation would wish to be a stumbling block for any.

CAVEAT: This transcript is being published by L/L Research in a not yet final form. It has, however, been edited and any obvious errors have been corrected. When it is in a final form, this caveat will be removed.

© 2009 L/L Research

Sunday Meditation
May 22, 1983

(S channeling)

I am Hatonn, and we greet you this evening, my friends, in the love and in the light of the one infinite Creator. We are pleased that you have invited us to your group this evening. As always, we are happy to be able to share in the love and in the light that emanates from this group. We are, as always, pleased to know that there are groups such as yours that join together and together help each other to find the way to the light, and are able to help each other as each seeks to find the truth that is all, that is one. For though you look at each other as a—we correct this instrument—though you look at each other as separate entities, from where we are as we look down upon your planet, we see not this individualism. We see a group of entities that are blended together as one, for thy light shines continuous. It does not look to us as an evening sky filled with separate twinkling stars; it appears to us as a soft warm glow that reaches from one end of your planet to the other. It is whole, it is continuous, and we are happy to be able to share that warm glow with you as we come to help you in our small way. We are always happy to spend time with you and look forward to your invitations.

We would transfer this contact at this time. I am Hatonn.

(K channeling)

I am Hatonn. We would like to exercise this instrument for a few moments tonight. Again, it is a joy to be with you. In her imagination during the tuning tonight this instrument saw herself floating joyfully and almost carelessly among the stars. She found it a very delightful experience, and, my friends, you can visit the stars any time you wish. It will be very helpful to the frayed nerves, healing to the mind and the body. It even provides growth for the soul. As one takes a long look at life, it is unnecessary to be so totally involved in the day-to-day happenings, and yet it is the nature of the peoples who walk your planet. Again we repeat, it need not be so.

We appreciate the opportunity of exercising this instrument, and will now leave this instrument. I am Hatonn.

(Carla channeling)

I am Hatonn, and I greet you now through this instrument once again in the love and the light of our infinite Creator. We are aware that as you are interested in how we see you, in order that you may see yourselves more clearly, so you wish to know how we see ourselves because you think that an understanding of that which is to come in your future development as portions of the one consciousness will aid you in your present development. There are reasons why information about what you call the fourth density which we inhabit is of limited use and the most cogent reason is the stricture of language itself.

Your language was designed to express your illusion. The language of our illusion is conceptual and has no grammar. There are few of your planet's languages where this is remotely applicable. For the most part, we do not speak but use the mechanism of thought transfer which we use to convey images to this instrument. In this case, we are sending a very strong signal and the instrument has an adequate receiver. In the case of two fourth-density entities, the harmonics of tuning are such that a subtlety which we cannot express in any terms but those of capacitance and inductance is achieved. There is a oneness in our communication which belies the separateness of our physical vehicles to the extent that it is our subjective reality to be one. There is no possibility of disguising, distorting or hiding our concepts, one from another or one from himself.

Although in your illusion it seems almost impossible to comprehend, when this situation prevails, true anger, misunderstanding or resentment is quite impossible. It does not take imagination to wear another man's shoes, as this entity would say; we do wear each other's shoes all of our experiential time together. Nor is there a parting when the physical bodies move along divergent courses. There is still a great deal of variety amongst a fourth-density population such as those of Hatonn. Therefore, we choose those with whom we live our lives, as you would put it. As the entire population learns through incarnational experience to refine energy transfers of green and blue ray, as this instrument would express it, we finally become one. We no longer have sharply differentiated groups. We have begun to learn the lessons of wisdom, that is, to be single-minded and glad of heart. At that point we may be said to be a functioning social memory complex, though one in its comparative infancy according to our own teachers.

You will notice that although we are aware that you are curious as to how we live, we have not discussed mating, families, politics, business or other facets of what you now experience as necessary portions of the illusion. These portions of your illusion pertain to the unblocking of those energy centers which keep you from learning the lessons of love. On a personal or individual level you block your learning when you become overly possessive, concerned, anxious, jealous of another. Among your peoples, that which you call love often has the expectation of this very blockage called possession. We suggest to you that in your exploration of the true meaning of this terribly overused word, you attempt to discover how to love completely. By this, we mean how to set a beloved one free; free to fall down, free to make errors, free to choose another, free to come or to go, free in trust, in sacredness, and in honor.

Should you do this with your mate and your friend, those whom you love shall be blessed, and you shall find what it is to love. There is much of a blocked nature amongst your peoples in the areas of the individual interacting way of the group. The position for which one is paid, the team for which one fights, whether it be game or war, the ceaseless blockage of the other self as one who may be taken advantage of, manipulated or used. These blockages are those which are yours who work upon the lessons connected with removing the obstacles to seeking love. In the personal relationship you learn to love one other self. Through that learning it becomes clear that you are loving yourself.

In the interaction with groups you gain an even larger prospect. Your vantage point has grown, you have identified yourself with one group, and you must now see the other groups as yourself. The entity who gazes upon a seeming enemy and sees the Creator has granted freedom to the part of creation upon which he gazes. Indeed, love and freedom walk hand in hand. You may ask yourself many times how you can possibly, for even a brief period of time, love to the extent that the illusion is penetrated, and all other selves become one with you and one with the Creator. But we assure you that it is within the grasp of each seeker acting imperfectly, foolishly, haphazardly, and oftentimes at odds with himself to still manifest that which he seeks, for to the seeker is given a great gift. To the seeker is given the power that is the power of the seeking itself. And though you be weary or foolish or hopeless or confused or alone, yet you have the seeking within you and it becomes your birthright. It becomes your inheritance and it will manifest within your experience one way or another to the extent that you continue to seek.

We do most heartily encourage you in that great process of evolution. We are on the same path. We have worked with the blockages which now concern you. We work now with the refining of love into wisdom. We have a great deal to learn. We have an infinite amount of time, space and illusion in which to learn. We wish you the joy of your journey and reach our hands out to you as fellow travelers. We are known to you as Hatonn. We leave you in the love and the light of the infinite Creator. Adonai, my friends. Adonai vasu borragus.

(Jim channeling)

I am Latwii, and I greet you, my friends, in love and light. We are privileged once again to be asked to join your group. We feel a great honor each time that we are able to blend our vibrations with yours, the mutual seeking of truth. Our humble service is one which we offer in great joy, for as we are able to be of service to you we are serving the one Creator. May we then begin by asking for the first query?

S: Yes, Latwii. Last night at our meeting we had some problems where you had to leave us somewhat unexpectedly. You stated that I was having some problem with my physical vehicle, and all that I noticed was that my eye was watering, and I had become confused over forgetting part of a question that had been asked, and I tried to not worry about it and just relax and try to pick up what you were sending me, but I was somewhat distracted. And also R was concerned that maybe he had inadvertently asked a question that was maybe too specific in nature, and therefore we were a little confused as to the reason for you closing the meeting, so to speak. Can you make any comment on this?

I am Latwii, and am aware of your query, my sister. To begin, as we were using your instrument during the meeting which you have spoken of, we were aware that the portion of your own being which we utilize in each transmission had become somewhat unsteady due to your concern over the portion of the query which had not penetrated through to our perception. This produced within your conscious experience but a slight amount of distortion, for you were attempting to retain the contact in a steady and stable manner using the relaxation that you have spoken of. The deeper ramifications of this difficulty which you experienced were of a profound enough nature at that time that we felt it appropriate to end the contact so that there would not be the unbalancing of your deeper mind complex which had been attempting, as you call it, even more precisely by calling upon deeper levels of not only relaxation but meditation, and meditation approaching the trance state.

Your great desire to channel even more precisely was in this case not as helpful as it might be in most other cases. The intensity of interest which your new group has generated has been matched by your own desire to precisely reflect those concepts given to you by those of the Confederation, and in this instance where you were not able to, shall we say, live up to your own standards, then your response on the conscious level to relax was intensified upon the subconscious level so that the imminence of trance caused us to seek the end to the meeting since the proper protection for that type of contact was not available.

May we answer you further, my sister?

S: Yes. If this should occur again, can you give me any advice as to what to do? Did I try to relax too much or should I … What can you tell me about how to protect myself and what to do if it should occur again?

I am Latwii, and am aware of your query, my sister. In the event that such a situation should repeat itself, we can only suggest that your attempt at relaxation carry with it the boundary beyond which you do not seek to pass, that is, consciously seek, then, the relaxation that will allow the concepts to flow smoothly through your instrument, but also consciously see, if you will, in your mind the boundary betwixt the deeper states of relaxation and meditation and trance. Then you will have imaged within your being the field within which you may safely roam.

May we answer you further, my sister?

S: No, thank you, Latwii. You've been very helpful.

I am Latwii, and we thank you, my sister. Is there another query at this time?

Carla: Well, I'm curious about the whole subject of trance because I don't understand how it works myself. But before I ask that question which you can just tell me that you can't answer if you want to, I was just wondering if it would help S if there were another channel in the group or if part of the strain is in basically working without a net, that there is no one else who channels in the group?

I am Latwii, and am aware of your query, my sister. It is the decision of the one known as S to proceed as she has proceeded, that is, to be of service to those who have interest in this type of experience. This is a more, shall we say, daring type of service when there is not present another instrument which can serve as the, shall we say, backup or as you have described it, the net. This type of service allows a quicker type of progression in the service of vocal channeling, for …

(Side one of tape ends.)

(Jim channeling)

I am Latwii, and shall continue through this instrument. It is well known to the one proceeding in the singular fashion that it shall bear the entire weight of the service of vocal channeling. Thus the progress and opportunity for progress is greater. Also of a greater nature is the opportunity for the difficulty which will remain the mystery until queries can be asked of another instrument. This is not usually a great difficulty, but can provide the frustration and puzzlement as has been witnessed by the group which met upon the evening past.

May we answer you further, my sister?

Carla: Yes, if you think that it's in my interest. I'm curious about what you said about trance because I've always wondered from the very first Ra contact just exactly what happens to me. Because as far as—when I go into trance—because as far as my own recollection is concerned, I am only going to sleep. But if it is a protection for me not to know, then I would prefer the protection.

I am Latwii, and am aware of your query, my sister, and can respond in a general fashion since there is some necessity for the complete understanding to remain the mystery for the present. The seeking which you have pursued throughout this incarnation has been of an intense nature, and has not included the preparations for what is called the trance state by any form of working or ritual or any training of a specific nature. The purity of your seeking and the intensity of your seeking has, shall we say, filtered to the deeper portions of your mind and allowed those portions to respond in a manner which has as its product the service which you offer in the trance state. This, of course, has been determined in a general fashion by your own decision and the agreements with others before this incarnation began.

May we answer you further, my sister?

Carla: Apparently not, thank you.

I am Latwii, and we thank you, my sister. Is there another query at this time?

K: Yes, Latwii, I've got a whole bunch of stuff in my mind that I'd like to have an answer to, but let me see if I could ask a simple question. Since I went to Chicago, and was in that symposium for two days with some very, shall we say, unusual people—at least I thought they were—my mind seems to have been bombarded almost with—this is where I'm at a loss for words—things of the mystical nature as we think of mystical, I guess is the best way to say it. Is this the result of my going to the symposium or is there just—is almost everyone who has any ability to perceive bombarded with these unusual experiences?

I am Latwii, and am aware of your query, my sister. Among your peoples there is the saying, "When it rains, it pours." You may look upon the experience which has recently passed and those which have followed it as the products of the, shall we say, opening of a door within your mind which has allowed certain opportunities to be noticed. Such opportunities are always available to any seeker. It is necessary to make way for the opportunities to be noticed. You may see your recent experiences as the result of your own choice at a deeper level of your being to make way for new experiences, that you may discover more and more the mystery of your own being, the nature of the illusion which you inhabit, and the means by which you may progress through this illusion. Therefore, you have created the opening for opportunities to be noticed and you have noticed them.

May we answer you further, my sister?

K: No, that answers it very well. Now, right along the same line let me ask another question. When I reviewed this book, this little autobiography of Dean Kraft, *The Portrait of a Psychic Healer*, I did it with trepidation because of the, well, I don't know whether it's proper to use a closed mind, but I really questioned whether I should review this book for these women. But I got a response that really surprised me. Now, my question is this. Were those women seeking or—I'm assuming they were seeking that information, and I was the one who had the fear. They were really seeking, themselves. Is that right?

I am Latwii, and am aware of your query, my sister. You are correct when you assume that these entities were seeking that which you had to offer, else there would not have been the opportunity or the offering to join with the seeking. Your own hesitancy, and, shall we say, fear of presenting this particular information may be looked at as likened to the whetstone which sharpens the knife so that it may serve as an useful tool. The fear served to hone your ability to present this material in a manner which cut away that sharing which would be less than optimal, and left that which would be helpful to these entities.

May we answer you further, my sister?

K: Well. How about that! Then that explains—maybe that's the explanation for this. We ordinarily have about an hour for the book review, and three of the women were delayed about thirty minutes, which left me thirty minutes, and I had planned for an hour's review, and so I sat there and wondered what in the world I would do—how I would refine it to thirty minutes. Was that all planned? Or at least did it serve a purpose for me to have to refine that to thirty minutes?

I am Latwii, and we may respond in the affirmative, my sister. That indeed there are such plans which make themselves known only after they have been carried out.

May we answer you further, my sister?

K: Well, no, that answers that bit because I sure did get squirmy when I wondered what I was going to do. No—thank you very much.

I am Latwii, and we are most grateful to you as well, my sister. Is there another query at this time?

M: Well, I would like a little help, Latwii. I'm going to have to give a talk on Paul, and I was wondering if you could give me some insight?

I am Latwii, and am aware of your query, my sister. We find in this instance that the information which we may share is again of the general nature, for to speak specifically of that which you would use in a future, as you would call it, time is to guide your actions to a point which we view as an infringement, for even the smallest type of information which is then used in a, shall we say, verbatim nature is not that which we wish to offer.

We can, though, speak upon this manner of sharing your being with other selves by suggesting that when you speak to those who seek from you any type of guidance, inspiration or simple information, that you share in a manner which reflects your true self and inner being, and, that is to say, when speaking upon any subject, it is most helpful to share that which you truly feel about the subject, to share, if possible, in a way which reflects the nature of your being. For in any type of speaking or sharing with others, this is in effect what you do. To attempt to do this upon the conscious level of your being is to refine that sharing as much as is possible for you to do. It is not only the information which you share which is sought from those with whom you share, but it is also upon the deeper levels of their own being and seeking that the call is given forth to know that being who shares with them. Therefore, to give of yourself in a manner which clearly reflects your nature is most helpful and will serve to illustrate and make a more richly enjoyed experience for all those with whom you share.

May we answer you further, my sister?

M: No, thank you.

I am Latwii, and we thank you, my sister. Is there another query at this time?

S: Yes, Latwii. I was talking earlier about a dream I had this week that didn't seem to fit the mold of being one to awaken me to blockages. It seemed important to me at the time. I wondered if you can comment on this. Are there dreams that really don't mean anything, that just come into your mind for some reason? Or is this something I need to ponder further?

I am Latwii, and am aware of your query, my sister. In the field of the dreams we find that there is a great range and variety available to the seeker according to the calling of the seeker at the moment. The dream of which you speak is not a dream of what you may call a random nature, though such dreams do exist, and though random are useful in themselves, but this dream was, as you have surmised, unusual in nature. Though we cannot give the specific nature of this dream, due again to our concern for your own free will, we can suggest that meditation upon the deeper ramifications might be useful. That you have remembered this particular dream is significant, for it is not, as you have noted, your nature to remember the dreams of the night.

May we answer you further, my sister?

S: Would you correct me if I'm wrong? What I'm assuming then is that I have possibly incorrectly discerned the meaning of this dream, and need to look at the dream more symbolically, and kind of look deeper into it. Is that what you're saying?

I am Latwii, and this is in general our suggestion, though we would emphasize the aspect of looking deeper for those portions of the symbolism which have yet to be noticed.

May we answer you further, my sister?

S: No, you've been very helpful. Thank you, Latwii.

I am Latwii, and we thank you, my sister. Is there another query at this time?

K: Yes, Latwii, let me ask another question along this line of dreams. I have just recently read the book, *Memoirs and*—oh, I forgot the exact title—*of Carl Jung*. It's almost like an autobiography in the sense it is an autobiography of his life and his dreams were so vivid, and they guided his life and his therapy. Were these dreams given to him for the benefit of mankind or were they just a revelation of himself. Was it self-discovery?

I am Latwii, and am aware of your query, my sister. We find in this instance that both assumptions which you have made are correct. It is possible for any entity which seeks to utilize the dreaming faculty to utilize this faculty with the same vividness of experience which the one known as Jung was able to utilize. As the seeker becomes aware that work in the evolution of mind, body and spirit may be accomplished while sleeping, shall we say, and is made aware that the messages obtained from this dreaming activity are useful in the activating and balancing of energy centers, then the process becomes, shall we say, self-generating, and more information becomes available to the conscious mind from the unconscious mind as the two begin to function with a sympathetic resonance, shall we say. The continued seeking by the conscious self creates an opening in what you have called the veil which separates the conscious from the unconscious mind, and through this opening, then, the symbols and images and messages from the unconscious are made available to the seeker in the form of dreams, and also in the form of what you may call the intuition or flashes of intuition and inspiration which occasionally lighten and brighten the conscious experience.

This entity also had determined before its incarnation to be of service in the general manner in which it finally was of service, that is, to provide its other selves with an avenue to the unconscious mind that those great resources which are a portion of each entity might be made more available to each seeker, and therefore the path to the one Creator might be widened just a bit more through this entity's efforts.

May we answer you further, my sister?

K: Yes, that was very good. I have thought for a long time that Carl Jung was a sort of forerunner, shall we say, of the raising of the consciousness that we're even experiencing now. Is that a fair assumption?

I am Latwii, and am aware of your query, my sister. As the planetary and racial consciousness factors continue to, shall we say, proceed in evolution, the needs and requirements of humanity in general also are transformed so that with each age there is a certain vibrational seeking which is expressed by humanity as a whole. Thus, during the incarnation of the one known as Jung, there were the needs which not only he but each who incarnated attempted to meet as the other self portion of the incarnation was pursued. Thus, as each entity incarnates, the time, shall we say, or the milieu in which the incarnation shall occur is considered with two major components in the forefront, that is, how the entity may progress in its own evolution, and how it may be of service to others if that be its path during the incarnation.

So, to summarize our somewhat lengthy response, may we suggest that you are correct in your assumption, and it is the great seeking at this time which has resulted in the greater awareness being expressed by humanity, and the greater need for continuing this progression of awareness.

May we answer you further, my sister?

K: No, that's very good. Just one final question about Jung. I read that after he read the *Tibetan Book of the Dead*, that he always kept it on his desk. And that seemed, being a Westerner or an Occidental, that always seems strange to me. Could you comment on that? Why would Jung, if he did keep the *Tibetan Book of the Dead* on his desk, why? What good did it do him?

I am Latwii, and am aware of your query, my sister. The one known as Jung was concerned that those who passed through the gates of what is called the death of the physical vehicle might be aided in ways which his culture was not able to provide aid. Therefore, when those of his immediate circle were gathered about to discuss the concerns of their own seeking, often the conversation would turn toward the great mystery which followed the process of death. This entity sought to aid such other selves in a manner which he felt was of service, and of the greatest service possible. Therefore, he kept many references to that transition called death at close hand so that he might share the best of the research which he had found with those who had gathered to do likewise. This book, then, was one of many which had been placed close at hand for his ready reference.

May we answer you further; my sister?

K: No, that was very good, Latwii, and I thank you very much.

I am Latwii, and we are most grateful to you, my sister. Is there another query at this time?

(Pause)

I am Latwii, and we find that we have exhausted the queries for the evening, and we are most grateful for the opportunity of sharing our humble perceptions with you, and we remind each that we are but humble seekers of truth and are quite fallible. Therefore, take that which has meaning to you, and leave that which has none. We are always with you, my friends, and again remind each that it would be our great honor to join you in your meditations should you but request our presence. At this time, then, we shall take our leave of this group, but in truth we shall always be with you. We are those of Latwii, and we leave you now in love and light. Rejoice in the power, the peace and the joy and the mystery of the one infinite Creator. Adonai vasu borragus.

Sunday Meditation
May 29, 1983

(S channeling)

I am Hatonn, and we greet you, my dear friends, in the love and in the light of the one infinite Creator. We are happy, as always, to join your group this evening in the unity which abides in this dwelling, for when people upon your planet are joined together in unity in the love and in the light of the Creator, there is a warm glow that emits from such a dwelling and it is pleasing to us, for this lets us know that we are indeed sharing the path with many of your peoples. We all seek to know the truth, to know the answers, for we all are sometimes confused, and we often wander aimlessly, but when we join together in unity we are more [able] to see the light that is ahead of each, for the love and the light surrounds all and we are all joined by this love and this light.

We wished only to exercise this instrument for a few moments, and she has, as always, been most cooperative and receptive to our contact. We thank her for this. We would allow this instrument to spend some portion of your time listening as this is what she wishes to do this evening. We would therefore transfer this contact at this time. I am Hatonn.

(Carla channeling)

I am Hatonn, and I greet you, friends, once again in the love and the light of our infinite Creator. This instrument has no idea of what we wish to say through her this evening, and one of the things which we would like to say is that this willingness to speak without concern for the product of the speech is necessary for those who wish to serve by being vocal channels. There are many, many ways to serve, and this is but one of them. However, in each way that you serve, one of the keys is the same sort of relaxation into a faith in the process of a kindly universe at work within your life. Just as this instrument speaks without knowing the next sentence, yet because she has tuned and prayed, she opens herself with the intent to do this service. So, in your chosen service to another, the greatest efficacy may be found in relaxing into the flowing of a kind of communication from your heart and the deeper portions of your mind to your actions. In such a way you become inspired, and, indeed, you become inspiring. That is, you may inspire others by your lack of fear and concern, and by your wholehearted desire to serve, as well as by the radiance which is peculiar to those who have learned the value of faith governed by a carefully tuned desire.

Faith is much like the traveler who is weary. The traveler may move ahead in a blind faith that the end of the daylight shall bring shelter and the traveler will indeed find somewhere upon which he may rest his head. There is another traveler who is equally weary who governs his faith in the kindness of the universe by as clear a perception as possible of the nature of the country in which he roams. It is far easier for the faithful weary traveler to exercise faith in the midst of one of your townships than in the midst of a wilderness. However, blind faith has its lessons also and sometimes when there is no way to judge the future so as to be a more intelligent user of faith, we recommend the attitude which allows our traveler upon his journey weary doing that which it is he must do whether or not he is in a wilderness. If a traveler departs from faith, he departs from that which is the governor of his journey.

In your idiom, let us say the traveler is a man who sells items during the week and arrives at his home upon your so-called weekend. Where does faith enter this very mundane situation? The traveler is not merely selling items. He is presenting himself to each entity whom he meets. He is faithfully assuming the basic nature of goodness that lies in sympathetic resonance between himself and those to whom he sells, those to whom he comes at the end of the day and asks for shelter. Thus, you may see in the most mundane of situations that faith; that faith which is basically a simple bias towards the opinion that all within the universe is one thing, that we are all part of that one thing, and that we all may understand each other at some level as part of one thing.

Sometimes the weary traveler will lay his head upon a pillow of sod and sleep beneath the stars because sometimes faith does not produce that which one hopes or expects. It is then that faith is truly blind and truly necessary. It is in the face of apparent unkindness from the universe, from those about you, from those close to you that you may rely most heavily upon the blindness of love.

Let us look at the foundations of faith. All that we speak of has to do with one original Thought, that Thought which created all that there is. Your basic material for seeking is yourself. If you see the surface of yourself, if you concentrate upon your imperfections and your impurities, you may find much about which you might be unhappy in yourself. You might lose faith in the basic strength and unity of your character. So you must meditate and look within until you find that great fulcrum upon which your universe will turn that is your own identity. Who are you? You are one who seeks, and you are what you seek. We ask that you seek within yourself continuously, daily, during many moments of each day if possible until you are as often as possible with contact with the one original Thought within yourself. And you shall have faith, faith of that which is invisible, faith in that which is infinite, but faith in that which you have examined yourself.

From this resource springs the faith with which [you] greet the world, the love which you show to the world, and the joy which you dare to manifest in a world that is all too dark with sorrow and despair. The lesson of faith is written in life-forms all about you. But it is difficult for those who casually move through an unthinking existence to be aware of this truth. Within your yearly cycle, all that seems to hold promise in tree and flower and bush withers and dies. The sun wanders far from you. The grass is gone, brown and dry, and ice cold strikes the very earth. Yet trees and shrubs and perennial flowers are not cursed with intellect nor do they have its advantages. They never doubt that the seeds they hoard will bloom again, that the life that is within will be perfected and manifested in due time. And, yes, it happens. The trees come into leaf, the flowers give their lovely scent to the air, and you stand once again upon luxuriantly green and vibrant grasses drinking in the confirmed faith and hope and joy of tree and flower.

My friends, you will be knocked completely away from joy, from faith, and from hope not once but many times. It is through this process of apparent loss, disharmony and difficulty that you learn how to love, to seek, and to be. Rejoice, then, at your own folly, at your difficulty with others, with everything that seems to be a stumbling block. Thank it, be grateful to it, and then turn to the sweet smelling meadow of meditation. Feel the gentle breezes of an infinite creation waft across your inner self, hearing the sound of bird, the kindliness of love, the overpowering joy of the One infinite One. You are not alone. You are one with all that is. Spend your tears as if they were precious coins, and save the greater energy for faith, hope, compassion, love and joy. It is these coins that will repay you again and again no matter how many times your faith must turn blind, no matter how many wildernesses pillow your weary head.

If the instrument known as K is willing at this time, we should like to close through her as we would like to exercise her. We leave this instrument. I am Hatonn.

Sunday Meditation, May 29, 1983

(K channeling)

I am Hatonn. Again we express the joy of being with you, and it is a joy to find you on your journey afraid. This instrument has been forced many times to fall back on nothing but faith. And once you learn, my friends, that there is an inner self and an inner faith that will support you in your difficulties and confusion, then life does take on a new meaning and you do indeed become a light to those about you. You may recall that the one known as Jesus talked about a very tiny bit of faith being important, and the more one exercises faith, the more one has. And in fact the more one exercises love and faith and hope, the more one has.

The beauty and the quietness of the evening together is always a blessing to us as well as you. Therefore, we leave you this evening in the love and the light of the infinite Creator, and rejoice with you as you go about your journey of faith. I am Hatonn.

(Jim channeling)

I am Latwii, and I greet you, my friends, in the love and in the light of the one infinite Creator. It is our privilege once again to be asked and to be able to join your group in your quest for truth. We are aware that there are many queries awaiting the asking, and it is our joyful honor and humble privilege to attempt answers to these queries which may be of some aid in your spiritual journey. We remind each present that our words are intended not as final answers, but as those signposts which point possible directions for your consideration. We would then ask each to weigh our words with the proper amount of concern and discernment so that your journey might indeed be decided by your own decisions.

May we at this time ask for the first query?

S: Yes, Latwii. I'm so happy to be able to talk to you. After last Sunday night's meeting, Carla and I were debating, trying to figure out where I had missed the target with my dream analysis, and with her help it seemed that I was taking night classes, so to speak. I wanted to know first of all if you can tell me if I now have the correct analysis of the dream, and if this is correct, in reading through Book IV I came across an answer where Ra stated that a great amount of polarity [work] could be done doing this work at night, and I was wondering if that is what's going on—if there's anything I can do to improve my ability to continue in this manner?

I am Latwii, and am aware of your query, my sister. As we scan that analysis which you have determined, we discover that there is a great portion which is correct, yet we would add that each entity has many teachers which appear within what you call the dreaming state and according to the call of the one who dreams the response shall be according to the teacher which is most suited to respond.

To address the second portion of your query. The efficient use of catalyst, which is another means of describing the polarization process, may be increased when the dream is recalled in the conscious state and is scrutinized for the message which lies just beyond the symbolism which adorns most dreams. To train the self to remember such dreams and messages is a task which few attempt upon your planet, yet is one which is mastered with experience.

To use, then, in the conscious state the message of the dream in the same manner one would use from any consciously experienced situation is that process which shall aid in the polarization of the entity.

May we speak further upon this subject, my sister?

S: Yes. I'm bit confused, then. I seem to have interpreted it incorrectly. What I assumed it meant was that the work done during sleep was effective in polarizing. Is that incorrect?

I am Latwii and am aware of your query, my sister. The work which is done during the dream has little effect upon the conscious self, the self which moves through your illusion. Unless the message of the dream is recalled by that conscious self and is worked with by that conscious self, though there is work done during the dream, the work may be viewed as the potential for polarization which resides within a deeper portion of the mind complex. To bring this potential for work to the conscious mind is that process which shall aid the conscious mind in its polarization. Most entities forget the message of the dream, and indeed the dreaming process itself. Therefore, for most upon your planet the potential for polarization lies untapped within the deeper portions of the unconscious mind. There are other processes which may be completed during dreams, such as the healing of various imbalances within an entity's deeper mind, but the polarization process must be tapped and made available to the conscious mind for the process to be efficient.

May we answer you further, my sister?

S: No, thank you, Latwii. I think I finally understand.

I am Latwii, and we thank you, my sister. Is there another query at this time?

K: Yes, let me ask one more question about the dream. In order for my spiritual self to benefit from the dream or in order for me to become more balanced from the dream, I not only have to remember it, but I have to be able to have some understanding of it and make a decision regarding the dream? I didn't say that quite the way I want to. In remembering the dream, as I try to understand it, and if I think I have some understanding of this dream, then I must make a decision about it and my life now will reflect that decision that I made about the dream. Is that correct?

I am Latwii, and am aware of your query, my sister. To clarify this point is our intent. We shall refer to a law of your physics which states that for each action there is an equal and opposite reaction. In your daily life you experience the …

(Side one of tape ends.)

(Jim channeling)

I am Latwii, and greet you again in love and light. We shall continue.

The message of your dream refers to the same experiences which you face in your daily life. The message of the dream points to certain expenditures of energy, certain actions, certain behaviors, certain distortions or imbalances which you are manifesting as a means of learning their equal and opposite, that your total journey shall be balanced in your thinking and in your actions. Therefore, to benefit most efficiently from the message of the dream, it is most helpful for the entity not only to see what the message is, but to realize that that message describes but half the learning. For if you see impatience, then also must you view patience for the learning to be seen as a whole. If you view anger, then also must you view love. If you view rejection, then also must you view acceptance, and in your meditative state be able to see both as means for the Creator to further know Itself through your being and the various distortions which you hold within your being.

When you are able to examine your life and see those expenditures of energy in a balanced fashion, and are able to accept yourself for each distortion, and able to see each as a means of the Creator knowing Itself, and of knowing yourself, and of you knowing the Creator, then you shall find that balance within your being that allows the pure white love/light of the one Creator which is your source of being, and which enters your being as a crystal. Then you shall allow that white light to remain white as it passes through the jewel of your being.

As you notice distortions in your daily life, and have them pointed out to you through your dreams, you see in effect how the white light is refracted and broken into colors as it passes through your being. That it should remain white is the goal, in one way of speaking, as you learn the lessons of love and acceptance of all.

May we answer you further, my sister?

K: No, thank you very much. One other question. I was in a meeting. I saw a meeting advertised in the paper about one, about someone speaking on healing energies, and since I had read this book and been to the conference, I was interested, so I just went, since it was announced publicly. And the woman who spoke made a comment that I didn't understand because it was a meeting of my first time, and I didn't know anybody there, I wasn't about to ask anybody a question. But she made the comment during the course of the evening that several in the group were surrounded by a white light, so nothing could hurt them, and so they could feel nothing. And that really stumped me. I didn't understand it at all. Would you comment on that? In the first place, I don't know how she saw the white light, if she did, and I did not understand the meaning. Could you comment on it? If not, I'll certainly understand.

I am Latwii, and am aware of your query, my sister. We may comment and shall attempt to clarify if possible this entity's statement. We remind you, my sister, that each entity such as the one which you describe will view such occurrences with the distortions which are native to that entity's being. We may suggest that the viewing of such white light surrounding other selves may be the result of many and various causes. For example, this group at the end of its meeting sends the healing love and light to those known in need of such. If one able to view what may be called the auric energies were to look at the entities receiving such healing energies, this entity would see a white light surrounding the recipient. For a certain period of time, then, the recipient would be surrounded by what would be perceived as a protective shield of love and light.

Another possible cause of such white light surrounding an entity might be that the entity itself has in some fashion invoked such protective white light from perhaps those you may call guides or guardians or other angelic presences. Perhaps prayer has been used to seek the aid of such presences, and the prayers have been answered. It is also possible that an entity might before the incarnation, due to previous incarnational experiences, surround the self with a certain degree of this love/light that a certain degree of protection might be afforded the entity so that other lessons may be learned, previous lessons having been learned without protection. There are other possible causes of such surrounding of light for an entity, but we hope that these few will give you an idea of the variety of causes which may be responsible for an entity being surrounded for a portion of what you call time by love/light.

May we answer you further, my sister?

K: So this light really can serve as a protective barrier against harm of any kind. Is that right?

I am Latwii, and am aware of your query, my sister. This is basically correct, though the concept would be more precisely stated if it were named in the positive sense. For example, the white light allows the presence of the positive or service-to-others nature of beings and experiences to coexist with it. The harmful or negative are not precisely shunned or shielded, for they do not seek coexistence in such a situation.

May we answer you, my sister?

K: No, that's very good. Now, she also said one other thing. She said because of the very rapid pace at which we are moving into the Age of Aquarius that mental telepathy is increasing rapidly. For instance, she said if we pick up thoughts at the rate of, say, three at this point in time, perhaps in a year it would be increased to eight or ten, just by comparison, and she gave examples of having picked up other's thoughts, and analyzed it, and found out they were not hers. She had picked them up. Would you comment on that?

I am Latwii, and am aware of your query, my sister. It is our perception that the vibration of change of the atomic structure of your illusion has indeed made the transition to what is called variously the New Age, the Age of Aquarius, or the density of love. Due to this transfiguration of the nature of your illusion, the what are normally called paranormal experiences are much more common upon your planet at this time, for it is the density of love and understanding in which you now reside, and it is the nature of this density to express itself through entities such as those upon your planet in a manner which utilizes the power of the mind to create, to communicate, and to become one with its environment.

May we answer you further, my sister?

K: No, that's fine, thank you.

I am Latwii, and we thank you, my sister. Is there another [query] at this time?

S: Yes, Latwii. Along these same lines of protection. I was sitting on the couch a couple of weeks back, and C came in to me and said, "The fire scared me," and she seemed like she was a little bit frightened, but she has a real vivid imagination and I didn't pay that much attention to her. She wasn't crying or anything. And I was walking through the dining room and I looked down and saw that she had taken a pair of tweezers and plugged them into the light socket, one half of each tweezer in the two light sockets so that there was a full connection. The light socket was black and there evidently had been a fire there. And when I saw it, it horrified me, you know, I couldn't imagine her not being dead, or at least, you know, burnt or very stunned. And I said, "C, is this what you were talking about?" And she said, "Yeah." She said, "The fire came right out of there." And I said, "Well, did you put that in there?" And she said, "Yes," and I said, "Well, didn't you even get a shock or didn't you get burnt?" and she said, "No," that she hadn't felt anything, but she had left it alone because the fire came out, and the fire had frightened her. And I was wondering if maybe she had some sort of protection at that particular moment?

I am Latwii, and am aware of your query, my sister. This entity of which you speak, as well as many upon your planet, has the access to those guides and guardians which ceaselessly watch the entity entrusted to their care that they might be of service where possible, might guide where appropriate, and might speak in various ways in those instances in which the ear of the entity has opened. The child of which you speak at the moment in which the, as you call them, tweezers were placed in the electrical outlet was protected by its own desire to be of service, calling to its guides, as you call it, and there was the minute yet effective barrier placed between the implements called the tweezers and the entity's fingers that the circuit was not able to be completed.

Many upon your planet and, indeed, most within this dwelling at this time can remember instances in which the experience was most frightening, and, as you would call it, dangerous and life threatening, yet the entity somehow survived. The miss by the inch, the moment's delay, the unexplainable incident—there are many ways that the guides and guardians may choose to implement the protection when the entity in their care has foolishly strayed for the moment and has asked in the subconscious mind that aid be given. In this way each of you may recall such protection.

May we answer you further, my sister?

S: No, thank you, Latwii.

I am Latwii, and we thank you, my sister. Is there another query at this time?

Carla: I've always wondered whether the protection which I think of in terms of scripture a lot, "For He shall give His angel's charge over thee to keep thee in all thy ways," might apply especially to children. And I wonder why that is if that is so. Is there some special quality about children that invites angelic protection or is it simply the innocence and helplessness of the young soul that seems to protect the child? Or is it an illusion?

I am Latwii, and am aware of your query, my sister. The passage to which you refer is indeed true for all those children upon your planet. The children, though, may be seen in a wider perspective as any entity which lacks the conscious sophistication necessary to provide its own protection. Thus, many, many are the children upon your planet under this protective shield. There are many ways in which an entity may pass from your illusion, and the premature passing is an event which reduces the ability of the entity to learn those lessons necessary for the graduation, shall we say. Therefore, those entities who are at the heart pure in desire to learn and to serve are those which constantly call for the protection of those in whose care they have been given that they might learn those lessons which they have agreed to undertake before this incarnation. That the lessons shall proceed is the point of importance. That such entities are protected as they travel this journey is, shall we say, an aside and may be noted for its function.

May we answer further, my sister?

Carla: Noted, but not striven for? In other words, not a part of. I have heard people say, "Every morning when I get up I surround myself with white light so that I will be protected during the day." That isn't nearly so desirable, you're saying, as the attempt to seek purely because that attempt carries with it its own protection, is that what you're saying?

I am Latwii, and am aware of your query, my sister. You are quite correct in your analysis of our statement. To consciously attempt to protect the self in a daily ritual which focuses only upon that protection without knowing what precisely the events shall be is to focus on an aspect of the creation which is that of assuming separation and seeming difficulties instead of focusing upon the unity of all and seeking purely to know that unity as the experiences are gathered and the entity finds itself learning more and more of that unity through these experiences. The protection which is with those who seek in the positive sense is there and in special, shall we say, instances may be called upon that it might be more apparent. To call upon such protection constantly without the specific intent is, shall we say, to turn the focus slightly from the pure desire to seek the truth.

May we answer you further, my sister?

Carla: I hope we're not wearing you out. That intrigues [me] by the thought that when we say the Lord's prayer, we say, "Lead us not into temptation, but deliver us from evil," which does seem to be focusing upon a protection without regard to precisely what it is we're expecting. Of course, at that point we are petitioning Christ consciousness or our higher self or whatever we perceive as the Creator to aid us. Comments?

(Pause)

I am Latwii, and am aware of your query, my sister. Please forgive our pause. We were unsure whether your query was complete. We can comment by noting that the intent as this group begins its meditation for the using of the Lord's prayer is the tuning which we have strongly suggested. Therefore, we see the appropriate use in this instance.

May we answer you further, my sister?

Carla: I'll leave it for now. Thank you.

I am Latwii, and we thank you, my sister, though we feel you have further queries residing within your mind.

Carla: You're right, but I'm concerned about the weariness of the instrument, who I know has had a long day.

I am Latwii, and we thank you, my sister, for your concern. We find the energy available for another query or perhaps two.

May we then ask at this time if there would be another query?

K: Yes. Right along the same line, I read someplace in the last year or so that we should in our meditation or our prayer, because of the perilous times through which we will be going, and are going in lots of places, that we should surround our loved ones in our meditations when we do our meditating or when we're doing our praying, we should surround our loved ones with love and light for protection, and even the automobiles they drive and everything they own, that we could protect our loved ones and their possession by surrounding them with love and light. Now I have to confess that sounds a little far-fetched to me, but I thought if it had validity I might try it. Would you comment on that?

I am Latwii, and am aware of your query, my sister. To surround those near and dear with the protective love/light of the one Creator is indeed a means of providing protection and healing energies to such entities. We have attempted this evening to make a slight distinction in the use of this protective energy, that is, that it be used with a specific intent in mind, that some service might be rendered because of its use. We have attempted to discern a slight difference in attitude that accompanies the, shall we say, overuse of this protective process from the specific use which attempts to verify and reaffirm the unity of all creation. To use such a protective device, shall we say, without regard to any specific purpose is to make a slight distinction in the attitude or in the configuration of mind which then perceives danger and division within the one creation. That there are difficulties for each entity cannot be doubted. Yet are these difficulties [not] also a portion of the one Creator and of the self, and are they not experienced so that lessons might be learned from their experience having to do with love, light and unity, the acceptance of all, the forgiveness of all, and the understanding of all as love, as the one Creator?

Therefore, all protection is within the realm of unity. To use it in a specific situation in order that the learning or the experience or the service of the one Creator might be accelerated because of that specific experience is less a distortion of that unity than is the constant and unspecific use of protection which begins to see the universe as a dangerous and divided place in some respects.

May we answer you further, my sister?

K: No, I think I understand that. Thank you very much.

I am Latwii, and we thank you, my sister. Is there a final query for the evening?

S: Well, Latwii, just briefly. I have a lot of people that I'm concerned about so I send a lot of love and light out to these people, some of which I don't even know, but I just send it because I know there are people that are hungry or are in pain or are unhappy. I don't necessarily send it as a protective device, but just so they'll have some love and light there. In this instance would the same thing be accomplished if I were just to send the planet in general this love and light or would that be too general? Do I need to be more specific?

I am Latwii, and am aware of your query, my sister. Now we move into yet another area in which service may be rendered from what you may call the distance. In this respect, the sending of love and light to be used by the entity in need is an action which is most helpful to the entity which faces the difficulty. In this regard the distortion from unity is much, much less than the previous cases which we have attempted to clarify, for as you send the love and light to another, it is the recipient's decision, shall we say, as to how this love and light shall be used. The deeper portions of the mind are those portions most closely aligned with all that you know as the creation, and these portions of the mind may call upon any portion of the one creation for assistance.

When the recipient of your love and light decides deep within its being to call for some type of assistance, then there is that which you have sent that is most easily called upon, for it is sent within the recipient's apparent illusion, and those deeper resources and portions of the deep mind then can use your gift as well as other gifts, shall we say, of the one Creator that await the calling and await the desire for unity to be expressed within the recipient's being in a more refined manner which may be seen as the healing.

May we answer you further, my sister?

S: No, thank you, Latwii.

I am Latwii, and we are most grateful to you, my sister. We find at this time, as you would call it, that we have used this instrument up to the point which we feel is appropriate. The weariness begins to overtake this instrument, and the focus is not quite precise with the attention. Therefore, we would thank this group for allowing us to speak our humble words and for allowing us to attempt to answer those queries which have meaning to each. We remind each that we are but your humble brothers and sisters, quite fallible, and most hopeful of serving even in our fallibility. We remind each also that a simple request for our presence in your meditations is all that is necessary for us to join you there. We are always with you. We would leave this group at this time, rejoicing with each in the love and in the light of the one infinite Creator. We are known to you as those of Latwii. Adonai, my friends. Adonai vasu borragus. ❧

L/L Research

L/L Research is a subsidiary of Rock Creek Research & Development Laboratories, Inc.

P.O. Box 5195
Louisville, KY 40255-0195

www.llresearch.org

Rock Creek is a non-profit corporation dedicated to discovering and sharing information which may aid in the spiritual evolution of humankind.

ABOUT THE CONTENTS OF THIS TRANSCRIPT: This telepathic channeling has been taken from transcriptions of the weekly study and meditation meetings of the Rock Creek Research & Development Laboratories and L/L Research. It is offered in the hope that it may be useful to you. As the Confederation entities always make a point of saying, please use your discrimination and judgment in assessing this material. If something rings true to you, fine. If something does not resonate, please leave it behind, for neither we nor those of the Confederation would wish to be a stumbling block for any.

CAVEAT: This transcript is being published by L/L Research in a not yet final form. It has, however, been edited and any obvious errors have been corrected. When it is in a final form, this caveat will be removed.

© 2009 L/L Research

Sunday Mediation
June 5, 1983

(S channeling)

[I am Hatonn,] and I greet you, my brothers and sisters, in the love and the light of our one infinite Creator. How joyfully we join you this evening, my friends. We have experienced also the joy of your coming together in your time in this place to perhaps find comfort, joy in the being one with other selves who are also aware of the struggles along the path of love and light. We thank you, my friends, for allowing us this opportunity to be with you. We of the Confederation of Planets in Service to the One Infinite Creator have always enjoyed the opportunity of serving, and in this manner of telepathic communication through the free will use of an instrument would like to think that our small messages may indeed be of some service.

My friends, have you looked about you today? Have you reveled in the beauty of your planet, in the voices of the birds, the greenness of the trees and the grasses, in the beauty of the sky, the dark rich soil which allows the second-density entities to prosper? My friends, it is indeed easy to get caught up in the trappings of your illusion, to overlook the small wondrous ways of the creation, to look about and see the abounding love that is so apparent from the Creator. My friends, take a moment. Enjoy the love, the oneness, the beauty of the creation. Indeed, all is one. And, my friends, even though it may be difficult to realize, you also can be no other than beautiful because you too are a portion of that creation. You too are one with your other selves. Do you see beauty in another self? How can you deny that beauty in yourselves, my friends, for you and he are one. Do not be so harsh upon yourselves, my friends. If you but take a moment to see the love in another and the beauty of another, take also that moment, my friends, to see the beauty of the Creator within.

I am Hatonn. At this time we would transfer this contact.

(Carla channeling)

I am Hatonn, and I greet you once again through this instrument in the love and the light of the infinite Creator. We shall continue through this instrument but thank you once again for the ineffable pleasure that your request for this rambling of ours gives to us as we attempt to serve you, the thoughts which you may hold or toss away as you find value in them.

You are aware, my friends, that you live in an illusion. You see the illusion made foolish and blurred many times in an incarnation. You see the string that holds up the conjurer's hat. You see the hidden dove in the pocket. From time to time you are given glimpses of a finer and more carefully tuned reality, or as we prefer to call it, illusion, for there is nothing but illusion out of which to make your consciousness that of the Creator. It is simply a choice of which illusion you wish to choose.

One choice which affects subsequent choices quite centrally is the choice of what to desire. When people become aware that they live in an illusion it is often a logical response to desire to experience that which is not illusion. It is an illogical response, and one which you will not learn listening to our words, to assume that in the receiving of this desire you will find a constant and unremitting happiness, peace of mind, or tranquility. We promise you no such foolishness. If you wish peace of mind, we urge you to go back to sleep. However, we are aware that each of you has already irrevocably chosen to wake up, to know the illusion for what it is, and to choose the experiences that you will have. Of course you wish to experience tranquility, peace of mind, and happiness. And so you shall. But when these things are goals in themselves, you reduce the speed with which you will be able to further untangle your illusion to a near standstill.

The one who is on the way will experience some discomfort, for there is always the discomfort of travel. You do not have everything that you had in your domicile. You have not packed for every possibility. You are caught short and stranded and made uncomfortable because you put yourself at risk against the unknown. In seeking the truth, the truth is always beyond the next bend. The truth escapes at precisely the speed you travel so that it is always in front, and you have always learned more than you knew before if you take responsibility for what you have already learned.

Now let us return to our comments about the moment. The decision that you may make which will profoundly affect the many choices that you make is the decision to seek love—not any kind of love, not any description of love—to seek love. To seek love is to seek one of the primal distortions from the infinite Creator. To seek love is to seek the great intelligence that fills the energetic consciousness of the universe with purpose. To seek love is to seek that which is omnipotent, omnipresent and closer to you than anything that you will ever experience or seek to experience. The experience of finding that love is rare. Even so, that love is so close and so near and so transparent and so powerful that it will pick up your life and move it at an ever-increasing acceleration towards truth. The reason for this is that people expect love to mean something, a physical thing, a mental experience, an emotional onslaught, a sweet peace, the great "Aha!" of philosophy. Whatever people expect, it is not what love is, because love is in this moment, and has been in every moment that you have experienced this day.

As we speak to you, the moments tumble by, numberless, limitless, thousands and thousands of moments. Can you reach out and grasp even the tiniest moment filled with love? Ah, you can feel that about which we speak because you are becoming tuned to love, you are resonating with love, you are being filled with love at this moment, and you become thereby a powerful person. But it is now another moment. And when you are not sitting in meditation, you are often in the situation of manifesting the love that is in the moment. Now you know why we urge meditation. Now you can feel the love of the moment, be taken by the rush of the wind of love, be stormed and overcome and be in the moment. And there are those who are in that moment for a short period of your time, and there are those who find that moment and do not leave it for hours or weeks or years as you measure time. But you choose to come out of meditation and go about your daily life. Now you see how the choice of what you decide affects so many other choices in your life's experience.

If you desire happiness or peace or tranquility there are many moments that must be discarded. If you desire to know love which is the Thought, the one Word or first Thought, the Logos of the infinite Creator, then you will be uncomfortable and accountable at the same time. You will be attempting to find the love in a moment that does not intrinsically appeal to you. And this will occur time and again because you will be learning. We do not say to you that it gets easier; we say to you that it becomes more exciting, that the possibilities for service to others grow greater, that there are certain advantages to declaring yourself clearly in a universe which is crowded with intelligence, for there are many kindly and loving intelligences which will tabernacle with you as you glory in the unity of the love of the one Creation in its infinity.

We would close through the one known as K. I am Hatonn.

(K channeling)

I am Hatonn. We would close this evening by saying that the joy we feel and the joy you feel by coming together in meditation is in itself enough. The peace that all of us experience together, we as well as you, is healing, and we are all uplifted through the experience. As each of us go our separate ways you may feel separate, and yet we are not separate. We are always with you. We leave you now in the light and the love of the infinite Creator and give thanks again for having had the opportunity to be with you. I am Hatonn.

(Jim channeling)

I am Latwii, and am with this instrument, and we greet you, my friends, in the love and in the light of the one infinite Creator. We are most privileged to be with this group once again, and we rejoice in the opportunity to serve in our humble way those present this evening. May we begin our service then by asking for the first query?

K: Yes, Latwii, I seem always to be the first one to start, but if that's the way it is, then here goes. I have a friend who—we've been talking about dreams today, and she says that she has a recurring dream. And she's had it for years. And she's always lost in this dream. Sometimes she can't find her way home, she doesn't know what street her home's on, in fact, she's just lost. And could you make any comment on a recurring dream like that?

I am Latwii, and am aware of your query, my sister. The recurring type dream is most usually that message from the unconscious portion of the mind or deeper self which attempts to give to the conscious mind a basic message or theme for the incarnation. This is a recurring phenomena for it is a foundation stone of the seeking process for the entity experiencing the recurring dream. It is similar to the child which has attempted to learn a simple childhood game, shall we say, and finds some portion of the game beyond its ability to master, and therefore in later experiences, as the years pass, discovers that this portion reappears, and again provides the opportunity for the mastering. The entity continues the experiences and finds that until there is the mastery of the lesson, the lesson continues to appear.

May we answer you further, my sister?

K: No, I thought that was probably about what the dream meant. Now then, would you comment on the dream I had last which was very much like a vision within a dream concerning my mother-in-law?

I am Latwii, and am aware of your query, my sister. We find in this instance that the experience of which you speak has indeed a most profound and vivid nature when seen in harmony with your own learning. We cannot, as you are aware, make the mystery plain, for to do so would be to take from you that opportunity which strengthens your own being as you participate in the untangling of the symbols. We can suggest the viewing of each portion of the dream as being found upon a scale, with one end being symbolic and the other being what you might call actual or real, though these terms are not satisfactory. As you look at a dream and its contents, ask what each portion stands for within your own being and experience. That you have lost something in the dream and it later appears in the possession of another who offers it to you is most important. What is it that has been lost? Why does it appear in another's possession and why that other? And why would that other offer it to you? Questions such as these are helpful in untangling the meaning behind any dream, and even may be extended to the awake state, as you would call it, and the experiences which this state of consciousness contains. For each experience in your life stands not only upon its own but has ties or offers pathways to deeper understandings for the seeker of truth.

May we answer you further, my sister?

K: No, that's fine, thank you. One other question. What was the meaning of the golden light that surrounded us?

I am Latwii, and am aware of your query, my sister. The light which you have perceived within this dreaming experience is a light which you view as the all-sustaining beingness of the one Creator which surrounds, informs and enables, and, indeed, ennobles each entity and experience.

May we answer you further, my sister?

K: No, that's fine, thank you.

I am Latwii, and we thank you, my sister. Is there another question at this time?

M: Well, this is a little bit personal, but do you have—have you ever had a reincarnation on Earth, or have you ever been acquainted with any people in our Earth history, either the Bible or our own history?

I am Latwii, and am aware of your question, my sister. We of Latwii, as is the case with each Confederation member, have had those among our, what you have learned to call, social memory complex, who have offered themselves and their services in the capacity of what you have come to call the wanderer. That such entities have gone from our beingness to your beingness from times of old is a truth which we rejoice in the experience of, for by the offering of such service, thus do we glorify and praise the one Creator. Thus also do we grow in understanding of our own beingness and the beingness of your peoples which when we are able to fully comprehend these natures we shall find that they are indeed one. We have not experienced incarnations in what you would call the third density in any other fashion, for our own third-density planet of origin lies in another, what you would call, solar system.

May we answer you further, my sister?

M: That was very helpful, but do you have any—even though you may not have had a third density experience here, do you know anything more about the people in our history—the knowledge we have on them is so limited—Ghandi or Jesus, any of the people? Would you have an expanded knowledge that would be helpful to us about them?

I am Latwii, and am aware of your query, my sister. Though such knowledge is accessible to our seeking, and is available because of certain experiences that we have shared with the peoples of your planet in the capacities of which we have just spoken, we find that such information lies outside of our chosen field of service, that is, we are more of the philosopher's bent than the historian's recordings of the peoples and places of the drama which your planet now completes. That we wish to offer information which is helpful to those who seek the truth is a fact which also mitigates against the over-concentration upon information of an historical nature, for it is not usually helpful in the evolution in the mind/body/spirit complex for that entity to devote attention in great degree to the lives of others when the life of the entity itself begs for close examination.

May we answer you further, my sister?

M: No, thank you, that was very helpful.

I am Latwii, and we are most grateful to you, my sister. May we ask if there is another query at this time?

Carla: As long as we're on dreams, I would like to ask about a couple. Firstly, I dreamt that Jim's parents were looking back over a life in which they had won a house in a raffle when they were in high school. And they used to go over and sit in the empty rooms when they fifteen and sixteen and gaze at them while finding a toy in their crackerjack box. They were explaining to me at the age which they are in this lifetime, which is about sixty, that they had in fact fulfilled all the dreams they had had as children for this house that they had won. They had finished the garage, and they had finished the family room, and so forth. I'm wondering if you could confirm that I was attempting to tell myself something about the relative value of the prize in the crackerjack box and this particular dwelling in which this meeting is taking place and its possible purchase, to me?

I am Latwii, and am aware of your query, my sister. Again we find that the general comment is the extent of our ability to serve in this instance, for as you have surmised there is the connection between the symbol of the crackerjack prize and the dwellings which have become important, shall we say, to those entities …

(Side one of tape ends.)

(Jim channeling)

I am Latwii, and am with this instrument once again. We shall continue. The entities which joined you in this dreaming experience, as you are aware, have placed great value in that dwelling which they, indeed, had long sought and finally found. There is the symbolic relationship which needs the examination from your own perspective between the dwelling which was found by these entities, the dwelling which you now attempt to purchase, and the relationship to the prize, shall we say.

This is not an unusual situation, for each entity as it seeks in whatever way it seeks will find that there are various goals set before it. Each goal exists not only for itself, as we have mentioned, but stands as a symbol for yet a deeper seeking. The attitude of the seeker in the attempt to attain the goal is most important. The entities within this dreaming experience were portrayed as the high school aged lovers who long sought the house. The trinket within the box of candied corns was the corresponding symbol for this particular seeking. Yet there lie beyond the symbol deeper meanings, as we have mentioned, for each goal which is sought. The attitude of the seeker determines the depth of the penetration and the access to these deeper meanings, for the one who seeks more and more purely to be of service to others, to find the love and joy in each moment, and who sees the unity of all creation sees a different world, a different goal, and a different message from those entities who are not as aware of the nature, shall we say, of the reality which they inhabit.

May we answer you further, my sister?

Carla: Not on that particular subject, no. That was great. Thank you. I have another question just out of curiosity. I hope I'm not wasting your time. Also last night I dreamed something interesting to me, and that was it was like a history novel—I dream a lot of adventures that I'm always protagonist in—and in this particular adventure, I had a farm in space/time and periodically I had to scan it in time/space because there was such a thing as—in the dream it was called "time squatters." And what these were were outlaws of one kind or another who were able in this particular universe to pay for the technology to be moved to that same piece of land but at a time at which it was not inhabited, back in the past or in the future, and there were some dangers because these outlaws did dangerous things to the land, and anything that was past could affect the future, so the time squatters were a danger. Is there a universe in which there are time squatters?

I am Latwii, and am aware of your query, my sister. We do not mean to be facetious, but shall state that each in this dwelling is such an entity, for if you will look at the continuum which you call time, you will note in the overview which may be gained from moving the attention to time/space that, indeed, times past, present, and what you call future are one time, as you call it. You perceive this one time as a linear type of experience in which there is a time which has been completed, a time which is occurring and a time which shall occur at a later, as you call it, time. Yet the river of time is one river. The space which you now occupy has itself been occupied by others at other times, shall be occupied by yet others at future, as you call them, times, and yet all these times are one, and in the great scheme of things, as you call it, all the entities and all the times, and all the places are one thing, one process, one experience, one evolution.

Yes, my sister, you have in your dreaming experience individualized and made more real, in a specific experience of your own, this simple fact of all existence. That it might be used in such a specific fashion as was the case in your dream is also a possibility within certain realms of being.

May we answer you further, my sister?

Carla: No, thank you.

We thank you, my sister. Is there another question at this time?

Questioner: I have a question, Latwii. You are of a philosophical bent, and you have a sense of humor, and you experience joy, and our calling. Do you experience sorrow, and if so, about what kinds of things?

I am Latwii, and am aware of your query, my sister. We of Latwii experience sorrow as an experience of other selves which do not yet know the nature of their own being, and experience that which they experience much as the entity who has the blindfold upon the eyes and wanders in the seemingly dark and dangerous jungle, and finds that there are areas of difficult passage. We of Latwii attempt to be service to such entities first by hearing the call, then by blending our being in time/space with the entities who call that we might become one with such entities and feel that which they feel in order that our service might be, shall we say, tailor-made to be of the most aid without infringement upon the free will of such entities. We of Latwii, therefore, do not feel that which you call the sorrowful feeling as a portion of our own being or experience, for we have moved from the blindfold stage, shall we say, and have removed that obstacle to sight and have been blessed with the sight of the one infinite Creator and the one infinite Creation which is our own being, and is our experience on what you might call a perpetual basis. We, however, do feel a type of yearning for further completion of our evolution, and this yearning or feeling of incompletion then urges our progress or evolution.

May we answer you further, my sister?

Questioner: No, thank you.

I am Latwii, and we are grateful to you, my sister, for this service. Is there another query at this time?

K: Yes, just one more question, Latwii, from me. My daughter has had a superior class this year and she had a great deal of apprehension about it. She thought the parents of these superior children would give her a hard time, and, the typical mother that I am, I began to visualize light around P and each of the children. I would visualize the classroom filled with light and these smaller lights moving around in the classroom. And then I would visualize these smaller lights, which were the children, going home and being a blessing to their families. Now I did that in my meditations much of the year, and P has gotten along just great this year, and so have the children. But this is why I'm asking the question. Friday was the last day for the children, and several of the parents came to school and brought gifts, and P came home from school and said, "Mother, we had a hug fest today," she said, "you never saw so much hugging in all your life." She said, "Parents hugged me, and I hugged them, and the children hugged me, and I hugged them, and we spent a whole lot of the day hugging." And, you know, it was such a good feeling after she had started off with so much apprehension. And my question is this after that long explanation, did my visualization have anything to do with what happened?

I am Latwii, and am aware of your query, my sister. We find in this instance that it is quite evident that your efforts were partially responsible for the fruits of your daughter's efforts. There is the relationship which is the parental relationship shared in this instance that enables the sending of light to be more efficient than were the sending completed by another outside of this particular relationship, for the situation of the teacher and students and parents is, shall we say, one of an harmonic resonance with that which you share with your daughter. Therefore, your abilities were enhanced, shall we say, and the sendings of light were therefore configured in such a specific manner as to be more useful.

We are pleased to say that any entity which is in a relationship of a close nature with another is therefore able to be of a more specific aid to that entity. We say that we are pleased to make that observation for we know that each in this circle this evening stands in relationship to another entity that is in need of such aid, and we are aware that those present wish to be of service in this manner, and might take some solace or comfort in knowing that the service which is intended shall be enabled by the ties which already exist, for knowledge aids the service as the light is configured in such and such a fashion.

May we answer you further, my sister?

K: No, that's very good, Latwii. Thank you very much.

I am Latwii, and we thank you, my sister. Is there another query at this time?

(Pause)

I am Latwii, and we find that we have exhausted the queries once again. We are pleased that we have been able to utilize this instrument this evening for the performance of this humble service. The feeling of the group in the conservation of this instrument's energies has been helpful in making those responses which we have made of the, shall we say, highest quality. We thank each entity present for seeking our service, and for allowing our service. We shall be with each whenever requested, and rejoice at the blending of our vibrations with yours. We shall now leave this group, rejoicing with each in the love and in the light of the one infinite Creator. We are known to you as those of Latwii. We leave you now, my friends, in joy and in peace. Adonai vasu borragus. ☙

L/L Research is a subsidiary of Rock Creek Research & Development Laboratories, Inc.

P.O. Box 5195
Louisville, KY 40255-0195

www.llresearch.org

Rock Creek is a non-profit corporation dedicated to discovering and sharing information which may aid in the spiritual evolution of humankind.

ABOUT THE CONTENTS OF THIS TRANSCRIPT: This telepathic channeling has been taken from transcriptions of the weekly study and meditation meetings of the Rock Creek Research & Development Laboratories and L/L Research. It is offered in the hope that it may be useful to you. As the Confederation entities always make a point of saying, please use your discrimination and judgment in assessing this material. If something rings true to you, fine. If something does not resonate, please leave it behind, for neither we nor those of the Confederation would wish to be a stumbling block for any.

© 2009 L/L Research

The Law of One, Book IV, Session 103
June 10, 1983

Ra: I am Ra. I greet you in the love and in the light of the one infinite Creator. We communicate now.

Questioner: Could you first please give me the condition of the instrument?

Ra: I am Ra. The physical distortions of the instrument remain serious. Further, the vital energies of this mind/body/spirit complex are much diminished, although acceptable for the needs of this working. This is to be noted as the lowest or most distorted vital reading of this all-important energy. The mental and mental/emotional distortions are as last seen.

We find the will of the instrument, having been unwisely used, to have encouraged the distortions of vital energy. It is well that the instrument ponder this.

Questioner: What is the situation with respect to the physical problems with the digestive portions of the body that the instrument had previously?

Ra: The yellow-ray—We must correct ourselves. I am Ra. Please expel breath across this instrument's chest area.

(This was done as directed.)

Ra: I am Ra. The channel is now satisfactory. We find the yellow-ray, chemical body of the instrument to be exhausted, but to be attempting the improvement by action such as exercise and diet. We may state that the infection has not completely left the body complex, although it is far less virulent.

Questioner: What is the present situation with respect to our fifth-density, service-to-self oriented companion?

Ra: I am Ra. This entity has, for some period of your space/time, been at rest. However, it has been alerted to the workings taking place and is soon to be your companion once again.

Questioner: Can Ra recommend anything that the instrument can do, or that we can do, to improve any of the energies of the instrument?

Ra: I am Ra. This is previously covered material. We have outlined the path the instrument may take in thought.

Questioner: I didn't mean to cover previously covered material. I was hoping to add to this anything that we could do to specifically focus on at this time, the best possible thing that we or the instrument could do to improve these energies, the salient activity.

Ra: I am Ra. Before responding we ask your vigilance during pain flares as the channel is acceptable but is being distorted periodically by the severe physical distortions of the yellow-ray, chemical body of the instrument.

Those salient items for the support group are praise and thanksgiving in harmony. These the group has accomplished with such a degree of acceptability that we cavil not at the harmony of the group.

As to the instrument, the journey from worth in action to worth in *esse* is arduous. The entity has denied itself in order to be free of that which it calls addiction[5]. This sort of martyrdom, and here we speak of the small but symbolically great sacrifice of the clothing, causes the entity to frame a selfhood in poorness which feeds unworthiness unless the poverty is seen to be true richness. In other words, good works for the wrong reasons cause confusion and distortion. We encourage the instrument to value itself and to see that its true requirements are valued by the self. We suggest contemplation of true richness of being.

Questioner: Is there anything else that either we or the instrument could do that would specifically work on the vital energy of the instrument to increase it?

Ra: I am Ra. We have come up against the full stop of free will.

Questioner: In that case I have a few questions on Card Number Seven in order to finish off our first run-through of the archetypes of the mind. There is a T with two right angles above it on the chest of the entity on Card Seven. We have guessed that the lower T has to do with the possibility of choosing either path in the transformation and the upper two angles represent the great way of the left and the right-hand paths in the mental transformation that makes the change from space/time into time/space, you might say. This is difficult to express. Is anything correct in this?

Ra: I am Ra. Yes.

Questioner: Would Ra comment on that?

Ra: I am Ra. The use of the tau[6] and the architect's square is indeed intended to suggest the proximity of the space/time of the Great Way's environment to time/space. We find this observation most perceptive.

The entire mood, shall we say, of the Great Way is indeed dependent upon its notable difference from the Significator. The Significator is the significant self, to a great extent but not entirely influenced by the lowering of the veil.

The Great Way of the Mind, the Body, or the Spirit draws the environment which has been the new architecture caused by the veiling process and, thusly, dipped in the great, limitless current of time/space.

Questioner: I am guessing that the wheels of this chariot indicate the ability of the mind to be able to move in time/space. Is this correct?

Ra: I am Ra. We cannot say that the observation is totally incorrect, for there is as much work in time/space as the individual who evokes this complex of concepts has assimilated.

However, it would be more appropriate to draw the attention to the fact that although the chariot is wheeled, it is not harnessed to that which draws it by a physical or visible harness. What then, O Student, links and harnesses the chariot's power of movement to the chariot?

Questioner: I'll have to think about that. I'll come back to that.

We were thinking of replacing the sword in the right hand with the magical sphere and putting a downward-pointing scepter in the left hand, similar to Card Five, the Significator, as symbols more appropriate for this card. Would Ra comment on that, please?

Ra: I am Ra. This is quite acceptable, especially if the sphere may be imaged as spherical and effulgent.

Questioner: The bent left leg of the sphinxes indicates a transformation that occurs on the left that doesn't occur on the right, possibly an inability in that position to move. Does this have any merit?

Ra: I am Ra. The observation has merit in that it may serve as the obverse of the connotation intended. The position is intended to show two items, one of which is the dual possibilities of the time-full characters there drawn.

The resting is possible in time, as is the progress. If a mixture is attempted, the upright, moving leg will be greatly hampered by the leg that is bent. The other meaning has to do with the same right angle, with its architectural squareness, as the device upon the breast of the actor.

Time/space is close in this concept complex, brought close due to the veiling process and its

---

[5] Carla made a New Year's resolution to give up buying clothes for herself for one year.

[6] tau: in heraldry, a type of cross called a "tau cross."

efficaciousness in producing actors who wish to use the resources of the mind in order to evolve.

Questioner: I am assuming that the skirt is skewed to the left for the same reason that it is in Card Number Four, indicating the distance service-to-self polarized entities keep from others, and I am also assuming that the face is turned to the left for the same reason that it is in Card Number Five, because of the nature of catalyst. Is this roughly correct?

Ra: I am Ra. Please expel breath over the breast of the instrument from right to left.

(This was done as directed.)

I am Ra. That is well.

Your previous supposition is indeed roughly correct. We might also note that we, in forming the original images for your peoples, were using the cultural commonplaces of artistic expression of those in Egypt. The face is drawn to the side most often, as are the feet turned. We made use of this and, thus, wish to soften the significance of the side-long look. In no case thus far in these deliberations, however, has any misinterpretation or unsuitable interpretation been drawn.

Questioner: Our appropriate time limit for this working, I believe, is rapidly approaching, so I would like to ask what was the problem in this session when twice in this session we had to expel breath over the instrument's chest?

Ra: I am Ra. This instrument is unaware of the method used to contact Ra. However, its desire was particularly strong, at the outset of this working, for this working to transpire. Thus it inadvertently was somewhat premature in its leaving of the yellow-ray, physical body.

In this state the object was dropped upon the instrument which you call the tie-pin microphone. The unexpected contact caused injury of the chest muscles and we would advise some care depending from this working to avoid stress so that this injury may heal. There is a metaphysical component to this injury and, therefore, we wished to be quite sure that all portions of the environment were cleansed. Since this place of working has not its usual level of protection we used your breath to so cleanse the environment, which was at risk.

Questioner: Is the reason for this lack of protection the fact that it has been a considerable time since we have worked in here?

Ra: I am Ra. No.

Questioner: What is the reason?

Ra: I am Ra. The lack of regular repetition of the so-called Banishing Ritual is the lack of which we spoke.

Questioner: From this I assume that it would be most appropriate to perform the Banishing Ritual daily in this room. Is this correct?

Ra: I am Ra. That is acceptable.

Questioner: I don't want to overtire the instrument. We're running close to time here. I will just ask if there is anything that we can do to improve the contact or to make the instrument more comfortable, and anything else that Ra could state at this time that would aid us?

Ra: I am Ra. We find the alignments quite fastidiously observed. You are conscientious. Continue in support, one for the other, and find the praise and thanksgiving that harmony produces. Rest your cares and be merry.

I am Ra. I leave you, glorying in the love and in the light of the one infinite Creator. Go forth, therefore, rejoicing in the power and in the peace of the one infinite Creator. Adonai.

The Law of One, Book V, Session 103, Fragment 53
June 10, 1983

Jim: The information in Session 103 concerns the continued spasming condition of Carla's abdominal region. Large amounts of pain accompanied the spasming and caused her to be less and less able to function in any manner of service at all. Thus she felt useless, and her natural joy became reduced and was the focus for this series of questions. Further, Carla had decided to stop buying clothes for a year because she felt that she had devoted too much time and attention to a transient part of her life, and wished to break that habit, and this decision added to her loss of joy.

Carla: By June of 1983, Don and Luther, our lessor and the owner of the house in which we had lived for all of the Ra sessions, were locked in a Mexican stand-off. Because Luther raised the asking price an arbitrary $5,000.00 in the middle of negotiations, and because Don was absolute in his refusal to buy the house without Luther's adhering to his original price, all bets were off. At this point, I was just trying to get Don's deposit out of escrow. Luther would not release it after we agreed not to buy the house. He felt it should be his, regardless. Luther was not a great help. Eventually, I was to agree, long after Don's death, to give him over half the escrow amount. It really didn't seem to matter what was fair. There was more confusion because our lawyer for the purchase of the house did not do his paperwork. I did not want to go to court, feeling that Don would not have done so. Nothing would resolve; everything felt like we were moving in molasses. This was the sort of baffling energy that seemed to have overtaken us. Nothing seemed to work well, me included. Don was feeling poorly, too, though in a vague and generalized way rather than anything acute. Jim alone was regaining health every day.

I was concerned about Don without knowing why, really. At this stage of his mental illness, it was very subtle. He simply felt very low, and was very prone to think and plan for the worst case scenario. While he, all his life, was always rigorously careful and cautious in his dealings, a change of address was in order, and his normal response was not this slow. We had to move. But month by month, looking constantly both here and in Atlanta, we could find nothing that Don was pleased with. I would target this point as the time period within which I was becoming aware that something was really wrong. As was always our pattern, I responded to the feelings of concern by asking for help and communicating. Don responded to the same with an increase of reserve. He could be firm about only one thing: that nothing we were looking at was the right place.

In this atmosphere, we were all uneasy, unsettled. I tend to get busy when I get worried. I was busy. All the records were in order. I went on my walks and did my time in the whirlpool and tried to remain hopeful. I felt constantly a bit irritated with Don, because I could never figure out why he rejected every single house we found in the listings or saw from the street. He seemed to be dragging his feet for no reason. Don was never one to share in his motives for doing things. He just said no, much as Nancy Reagan suggested later. It wasn't a solution for either environment. This is the first place I can think back and say, HERE I was feeling both of us losing ground, Don and myself.

I was heavily dependent upon him. I had been raised a most independent person, and I had to learn to let go of everything except what Don needed from me. And Don had needed all my choices to be made around him. He wanted me to be at home and right there, a person he could count on to be loving and willing to do whatever he decided. He never really consulted me, and it sounds very chauvinistic, but he did not mean this personally. He simply consulted no one. He never had. And his view on women was so bad that I could only look better! I quickly formed the opinion that when I stopped getting interference for an idea, that idea was the right one. It took me at least the first six years of our relationship to figure out that no matter what, I should never take a job that took me away from him, even as far as my desk. He even stopped me from working on our projects, many times, when he was at home. "When I am off, you are off," he would say. So I had pretty much given over my decisions to him. It is to be noted that I was aware of the unhealthy tinge of this relationship. However it was and remains my opinion that this was the absolute best Don could do in the way of having a relationship. And that was good enough for me. Where Don was concerned, I was ready to do whatever he needed. Period.

And at this point, with my health compromised and aiming for more sessions, I was not "allowed" to do much except follow my regimen and try to keep my weight above 80. I was whole-heartedly into this model for living, for what mattered most to me from the first was to see Donald really happy, as only the contact with Ra made him. So our every effort was towards that goal: just to have one more session.

However, what had always before gone hand in hand with my dependency was his willingness to steer our course, indeed, his insistence upon that. I was glad to give this leadership over to him, and to do what he said. He was far wiser than I was or ever could be. When he stopped giving orders, and indeed seemed not to know what to do, I was quite lost. My mode was to find out what he wanted and do it. But with the question of moving, we entered an arena where I could not succeed. No house, no apartment, was acceptable. I do not find it at all odd that I had "lost my joy." I was totally bewildered. My sense of reality had been compromised.

The comments about clothing address a facet of my personality of which I am not proud, but do own: I absolutely love to wear a new dress or pair of socks or whatever else might catch my fancy. My childhood had been very low on pretty clothing, as our family finances were tight. My mother and I, when I was grown and her career as a psychologist had begun, had a standing date on Saturday for lunch and shopping which we kept faithfully until her death in 1991. I would find wonderful things with her, as she was a champion shopper, looking through great masses of sales racks with the patience of an archeologist, sifting for good labels and just the right bargain. To this day, when I can, I love to go bargain-hunting, and just thrill to be able to wear something new.

I kept my promise to myself, and did not buy clothes for myself for a whole year. However, I cheated, in that I bought things for Momma, and she bought things for me. I kept the letter of the promise anyway!

Session 103, June 10, 1983

Questioner: The instrument asks the question why she lost her joy in the recent past? Could Ra comment on that?

Ra: I am Ra. The instrument made a free will decision not to address the physical catalyst causing great pain by means of the allopathically prescribed chemical compound which the instrument was sure would be efficacious due to its reliance upon the suggestions of Ra. Thus the catalyst was given in a more complete form. The outer service to others became nearly impossible, causing the entity to experience once again the choice of the martyr; that is, to put value in a fatal action and die or to put value on consciousness of the creation of the one Creator and, thereby, live. The instrument, through will, chose the latter path. However, the mind and mental/emotional distortions did not give the support to this decision necessary to maintain the state of unity which this entity nominally experiences and has experienced since its incarnation's beginnings.

Since this catalyst has been accepted, the work begun to remove distortions blocking indigo ray might well be continued apace.

Questioner: Could Ra recommend work appropriate for removing indigo-ray blockage?

Ra: I am Ra. We cannot recommend for the general situation for in each case the distortional vortex is unique. In this particular nexus, the more appropriate working is in the mental and mental/emotional powers of analysis and observation. When the strongest and least distorted complex is set in support, then the less strong portions of the complex shall be strengthened. This entity has long worked with this catalyst. However, this is the first occasion wherein the drugs to dull the pain that sharpens the catalyst have been refused.

Questioner: Can Ra recommend anything that the instrument can do or that we can do to improve any of the energies of the instrument?

Ra: I am Ra. This is previously covered material. We have outlined the path the instrument may take in thought.

Questioner: I didn't mean to cover previously covered material. I was hoping to add to this anything that we could do to specifically focus on at this time, the best possible thing that we or the instrument could do to improve these energies, the salient activity.

Ra: I am Ra. Before responding we ask your vigilance during pain flares as the channel is acceptable but is being distorted periodically by the severe physical distortions of the yellow-ray chemical body of the instrument.

Those salient items for the support group are praise and thanksgiving in harmony. These the group has accomplished with such a degree of acceptability that we cavil not at the harmony of the group. As to the instrument, the journey from worth in action to worth in esse is arduous. The entity has denied itself in order to be free of that which it calls addiction. This sort of martyrdom, and here we speak of the small but symbolically great sacrifice of the clothing, causes the entity to frame a selfhood in poorness which feeds unworthiness unless the poverty is seen to be true richness. In other words, good works for the wrong reasons cause confusion and distortion. We encourage the instrument to value itself and to see that its true requirements are valued by the self. We suggest contemplation of true richness of being.

L/L Research

L/L Research is a subsidiary of Rock Creek Research & Development Laboratories, Inc.

P.O. Box 5195
Louisville, KY 40255-0195

www.llresearch.org

Rock Creek is a non-profit corporation dedicated to discovering and sharing information which may aid in the spiritual evolution of humankind.

ABOUT THE CONTENTS OF THIS TRANSCRIPT: This telepathic channeling has been taken from transcriptions of the weekly study and meditation meetings of the Rock Creek Research & Development Laboratories and L/L Research. It is offered in the hope that it may be useful to you. As the Confederation entities always make a point of saying, please use your discrimination and judgment in assessing this material. If something rings true to you, fine. If something does not resonate, please leave it behind, for neither we nor those of the Confederation would wish to be a stumbling block for any.

CAVEAT: This transcript is being published by L/L Research in a not yet final form. It has, however, been edited and any obvious errors have been corrected. When it is in a final form, this caveat will be removed.

© 2009 L/L Research

Sunday Meditation
June 12, 1983

(K channeling)

[I am Hatonn, and I] greet you, my friends, in the love and light of the infinite Creator. We would like to exercise this instrument briefly by saying that your coming together in meditation serves much the same purpose to each one of you as the fertilizer does for the plants, or in this case, as the one known as M uses fertilizer on her roses. And as you have been discussing and as you already know, they're beautiful, and without the fertilizer and the care they would not have the beauty they do. Sometimes you may feel that your meditations are not so important, and yet I can assure you, my friends, they are. Your week is different when you come together and feel the sense of unity and quietness that goes with meditation. As we have said many times, it is our joy and pleasure to be with you. We are delighted to have friends with us who have not been here before. We greet them in the love and the light of the infinite Creator. We wish to thank this instrument for permitting us to use her, and now we transfer contact. I am Hatonn.

(Carla channeling)

I am Hatonn, and again I greet you in the love and the light of the infinite Creator. We shall continue through this instrument. It is written in one of your holy works that a small amount of leaven leavens the whole, and that without that small amount of leaven, all is without virtue. You may think of your meditation time as yeast time, for without the inspiration which you may garner from silence the activities of the day may seem quite profitless and uninteresting to you. How many times in this past week have you wished only to arrive at the end of your diurnal period and lose yourself in sleep? Each time that you have thought that thought you have indeed lost yourself, for you and all that you are are a creature of this moment. It is meditation that impregnates your life with immediacy. It is contemplation that livens your feelings with joy. If you are lucky enough to have a point of view which includes inspiration and joy, we applaud you and urge you ever onward in your quest to refine those virtues, to become ever more a creature of the moment, a creature who knows that this moment is full of love.

If you are having difficulty experiencing joy and peacefulness, if moments are lost to you, we ask that you try the leaven of meditation. When we ask those among your peoples to meditate, we know that there is a great deal with which each seeker must contend before meditation is even possible. We know of the seeming mountain of chores, of the illusion that you do not have time. However, meditation stretches your time, gives you more than you had, delivers more than it takes. In your terms, it is a cost productive enterprise. It is far better to find yourself a location and a time for daily meditation and to move to that time and place even if it is only for a few moments each day. However, if this cannot be arranged, any time and any place will do. The primary element of meditation is your desire to seek truth and your decision to seek that truth in silence. Those who seek and do not believe there is an end to the seeking may nevertheless experience those things which meditation will bring about. However, it is admittedly easier if those who seek have some faith in the efficiency of the technique and in the content of silence.

We speak of a Creator, but we do not ask that you believe in a Creator. We ask that you be seeking a Creator because what you shall seek you shall find. We ask that you give as much care to the purity of your seeking as possible because the principle of reflection is ever present in those who seek. If you can consider yourself divesting yourself of your world-stained garments and dressing yourself in metaphysical cleanliness, settling down in a most fragrant and beautiful meadow, and simply listening, you will discover that you have indeed heard the silence. You will discover, perhaps not at once, perhaps cumulatively. But that which you give to this effort you shall reap many times back again.

As you sit in meditation, little by little those things of this world may fall away, all the inharmonious portions of your experience are put aside, and out of the silence comes that portion of yourself which is your greatest self, that portion which is almighty, infinite and everlasting. That portion of yourself is the Creator. Some have called this Creator, and we find this a good name, although among your peoples that word is often misused. Most of all that Creator can pour its infinite supply of strength, love, compassion and patience into those portions of your life which constitute your daily round of activities to the precise extent that you desire and allow this to occur. It is a not a great commitment in time to meditate, but it is a great commitment in a timeless sense, for once you have begun you shall change, and your life will be leavened and become different than you ever expected that it would be.

I am Hatonn, and would now transfer to another instrument.

(M channeling)

I am Hatonn. I am now with this instrument. I greet you with the love and the light of the infinite Creator. I would like to continue on the subject of meditation. It is a very beautiful and positive thing. Some people have seen waves in motion when they meditate. Some people see floating clouds in the skies. Some people see green trees. It is a positive thing. It is very difficult for trouble to intrude if one is truly meditating. It affects each person differently. To a Christian his soul can soar to the very gates of heaven and all eternity is within its grasp. There is a beautiful quiet silence in meditation. It does not leave the person when you are finished. There is a serenity that you carry through the rest of the day, and people around them can absorb some of this serenity. Another expression in your holy book is, "Be still, and know that I am God." Too many people are so busy and so involved that they find it difficult to quiet down and have a personal contact with the Creator. Meditation is very helpful to give you an understanding of yourself in your infinity.

I am Hatonn. I leave this instrument.

(Carla channeling)

I am Hatonn. We had intended to close through S, and found that this instrument was desirous of listening. We find that the one known as C is also desirous of receiving the meager amounts of poor information that we have to give. We thank both of these instruments for many times of service, and would be most happy to close through this instrument.

We know that it is often said among your peoples, so often that it sounds useless to say, "Who are you?" But this, my friends, is the central question of your incarnation. We are members of the Confederation of Planets in the Service of the Creator. It is our imperfect but considered opinion that you are the Creator. It is our opinion that you are dealing with an illusion which tells you in many, many ways that you are not the Creator, and that those around you are not the Creator, and that if the Creator exists, the Creator must be a fool or a madman. We say to this, "Amen." This is indeed the intention of the illusion. It was not formed carelessly. It was designed to be somewhat discouraging because each discouragement, given reflection, is an enhanced opportunity to learn.

Who are you? How much do you want to know about yourself? What ethic do you wish to carve out of that knowledge as you deal with others? How strong do you wish to become? How powerful, how loving? What kind of environment do you wish to feel about you? How would you desire your world to be? We suggest meditation. Contemplate, reflect and then, my friends, listen. For there is within you a voice that is totally silent and that will be the greatest influence your life will ever have if you wish it. You may learn of love very quickly by meditation or you may learn of it very slowly. You cannot help but learn about love, for that is the true nature that lies behind your dreams, your illusions, and your disappointments. Love is your companion and it is closer than your voice or your breath. Feel within you at this instant that love that enlivens you and lifts that life you live into merriness and joy. Feel that all about you have the same identity and the same potential experience. Then wander into the illusion once again armed with a little yeast. You'll need it. Life is sometimes very unloving.

As always, we caution each of you to take what we have to offer, use what seems good, and discard the rest without backwards glance. We are quite capable of error, and are only your brothers and sisters, a step or two ahead, an eternity on the same journey. Thank you for the music of your hearts. We are known to you as Hatonn. We leave you in the love and the light of the infinite Creator. Adonai vasu borragus.

(S channeling)

I am Latwii, and we are happy to greet you this evening, my dear friends, in the love and in the light of the one infinite Creator. We hope that we have not startled you, but we have been with this instrument for some time, and she was anxious to speak our words so that she might alleviate the pain in her neck which we have caused. We are, as always, pleased that you have invited us here this evening, and we are honored that you find some use in our appearance at these gatherings. We hope that we shall be able to be of some assistance to you this evening, and we would transfer this contact so that we might set about the business of answering those queries which are present this evening. We leave you for a brief moment in the love and in the light of the one infinite Creator. We are known to you as Latwii.

(Jim channeling)

I am Latwii, and greet you once again in love and light. May we then begin by asking if there is a query which we might attempt to respond to?

M: Latwii, I have something that's been bothering me. That little girl that disappeared. Is it just that she was in the wrong place at the wrong time, or was it predestined, that horrible thing that must have happened to her?

I am Latwii, and am aware of your query, my sister. As we look at this entity and its experience, indeed, as we look at your planet and peoples as a whole, we see the Creator in many portions striving to learn those lessons which each portion has determined is most helpful in the evolution of the mind, body and spirit at a certain time. That you inhabit an illusion that does not show a clear reflection of the unity of all creation is important, for the actions taken within this seeming darkness and forgetting therefore carry much more weight within the total beingness of each entity within the illusion. Each of you suffer those difficulties of varying degree throughout your incarnation, and these are opportunities, perhaps more severe tests in many cases, for each of you to learn the unity, the love and the light, and the joy in each moment of your illusion.

Thus, the entity of which you speak has partaken in the same process of evolution, and within the illusion it may appear that, indeed, a tragedy has occurred. Yet from our humble point of view, we see the Creator knowing Itself more and more fully with the aid of other portions of that same Creator. There are no mistakes. The illusion which you inhabit may seem difficult to understand. But there is an order and purpose to each event, and each event is an opportunity for the Creator to be known more fully.

May we answer you further, my sister.

M: No, that was very helpful. Because although I didn't know the little girl, I felt a personal sense of loss since I heard about it, but now I feel there is a method in the madness. Thank you.

I am Latwii, and we thank you, my sister.

C: Yes, Latwii. First I want to say thanks to you and our brothers and sisters of the Confederation for the aid you've been in the upheavals of the last month, not only in my household but at Pooh Corner. And I would like to ask that during all the things that have been going on I've experienced many different emotions. I've felt like I've found myself, and I've also felt like I've totally lost myself. But I find that decisions at this time are extremely difficult to make. I can't seem to find what is right for me because I feel so many different things which I feel responsibility to. I feel a need for more of a sense of security. Is this idea of security both physical and emotional? I'm having an extremely hard time understanding what this is, and why I can't seem to let go with D at this time, having decided that for the children it would be best for us to relocate and start again. The security question is really doing a number on my head. And I wish if you would speak to me briefly on what this thing that I refer to as security is, and how one can grow, not necessarily beyond it, but to be able to deal with it more readily?

I am Latwii, and am aware of your query, my brother. We do not mean to discourage you by suggesting that the concept which you call security is an illusion. To seek that which does not exist is to chase the dream which evaporates upon the waking. Your illusion is constructed in such a way that that which you call security is often seen as a desirable goal, and for those who seek such, there are most important lessons to be learned, for as we have previously stated, there are no mistakes, there is only learning.

Within your illusion it would seem that if one could only pull together certain ingredients, the financial stability, the family and friends with secure and rewarding relationships, the recognition of peers, the path of traveling into the future which seems steady, then one could be secure. Yet, as the child upon the beach building the castle of sand, as one element is gathered for but a moment, another seems to slip away, as the waters of the illusion and the catalyst erodes what seemed to be secure. And, my friend, this is not an accident. As your attention becomes focused on those difficult situations, it becomes honed as the blade of a knife and becomes able to focus upon deeper and deeper aspects of the illusion and of the self and of the journey through the illusion by the self. The catalyst works as a file upon the blade, sharpening that attention that it might see deeper and deeper and cut further and further through the illusion to the center of the being of the self. That the true nature …

(Side one of tape ends.)

(Jim channeling)

I am Hatonn—we correct this instrument. I am Latwii, and am pleased to speak through this instrument once again. This instrument forgot to complete the process of the challenge of the contact as is its procedure, and was momentarily, shall we say, in improper tuning.

To continue with our response, and we ask forgiveness for its length but hope that its importance might justify its length, the blade of the attention then reveals layer upon layer of the truer nature of the being. And each lesson, then, is seen to contain two portions in polar reflection, that is, to know love, one may experience much anger; to know clarity there may be much confusion; to know patience, there may be much impatience. Therefore, when you are experiencing any of the polar emotions, look then in your meditations to the opposite which seeks to be known.

We cannot give you direct advice, as you know. Therefore we feel it is most helpful to suggest meditation for those times which are difficult. The limitation of the viewpoint is that which causes the distortion of the viewpoint to be experienced. If you can expand that point of viewing so that the unity of all creation is more available to your seeing, then you shall see with new eyes and those answers which have eluded you in your past shall appear to the new sight.

May we answer you further, my brother?

C: Just here in the last month the lessons have been to me, they've seemed really, really intense. I remember in a regression that I'm following attempting to learn lessons my father and his father before had attempted within this illusion. Over the years I've seen what has happened to my parents because of these particular lessons, and I don't want this to reoccur with me. The lesson this time has been about all I believe I can stand, and several times it's gotten down to the point where I've felt like just getting away by myself for awhile to try to get myself collected. I find myself really torn because I feel there's a blockage within me, and that due to this blockage I'm unable to fully open myself to D, to fully accept her love. I do feel that there have been other times when I was able to get beyond this blockage, but I found the blockage redeveloping the other day. I know you can't deal with problems of the specific person, but anything you tell me about blockages that people may feel would be of great help at this time.

I am Latwii, and am aware of your query, my brother. The experience of which you speak is that experience of what may be called the yellow-ray energy center located at the solar plexus region. It is the nature of this center to allow the expression of the entity of its beingness to those with whom it is in close relationship. The nature of the fully unblocked yellow-ray energy center allows the entity to express complete acceptance of all those within its reach of relationship so that the wishes of the entity for these others is that they be happy, and do that which has meaning for them.

The fully unblocked yellow-ray energy center, then, expresses the love of the entity in an unconditional fashion for each of those with whom the entity experiences a close relationship. When there is any kind of condition set upon the giving or receiving of love to or from another entity, then there is the blockage of that center which the entity experiences as the catalyst or the difficult situation which may express itself in confusion, frustration, anger, fear, and if it is not worked with in the minimal manner by the mind complex, then is given to the body complex as a form of what you may call disease formed in a symbolic fashion so that it might be noticed in its new configuration, whereas its previous mental configuration passed without the proper notice.

When you feel any type of difficulty in loving another such as the one which you have mentioned, look at the experience which you discovered the difficulty within. By using the powers of analysis and contemplating the nature of the difficulty, you may form the seeds of what you may call a solution that you may take with you into meditation attempting to experience once again in meditation the difficulty until it is overwhelming to your senses. In this process of balancing, then when the overwhelming experience is felt, for but a moment see in the eye of your mind its opposite, in this case, the acceptance. Then let that image go. Allow a process of natural discovery to occur so that your senses and seeing in the mind's eye moves from the overwhelming difficulty, and the entity and the difficulty begin to take on new characteristics so that as this process continues, its end result is the equal experience of an overwhelming nature, but of the polar opposite experience, that is, the complete acceptance in this specific situation.

If you can accept yourself as the Creator for having both of these means for the Creator to know Itself contained within your being, then you will have begun, and we stress begun, the process of balancing the blockages or distortions to the yellow-ray energy center. This process may be continued for each situation in which you find the difficulty in completely accepting another within your relationship range of experience. This is not an easy process. The lessons of your illusion at this time contain intense catalyst. These are great opportunities for learning that love and unity and joy and forgiveness and understanding exist infinitely in each moment, in each experience, in each entity. To learn that, you begin with the opposite experience. As the pendulum of your being moves to the extreme of both ends of its arc and as you become aware of its movement you shall be able to center that pendulum until it rests quiet and still as the one Creator rests within your being.

May we answer you further, my brother?

C: You've been very helpful. I would like to ask about something that occurred two weeks ago.

Carla: Hold off, C, let me ask the group something. I'm picking up a real fluctuation in the energy, and we either need to retune or we need to draw to a close. Want to vote on that? Would you mind retuning briefly or is everybody tired?

C: Since it's *(inaudible)* it might be better to go ahead and draw to a close.

Carla: Anybody else?

S: I'm willing to go on.

Questioner: I am too.

Carla: Okay, let's retune.

(Group sings, "Row, Row, Row Your Boat," three times in a round.)

Carla: Okay, that's good. Carry on, old chap.

(Jim channeling)

I am Latwii, and am once again with this instrument and this group. We thank the diligence of the one known as Carla and each member of this group remembering that the tuning is most important for the quality of the content and the information which is transmitted. We thank each for the patience which each is able to offer to our sometimes lengthy responses. May we then ask if there is another query to which we may respond?

C: I'd like to ask one more, then I'll be done. As I was saying before, on one particularly stressful evening, I started receiving conditioning that I recognized as Nona, and as I was receiving it, I also began feeling that someone had been hurt, and I expressed this to D that I was picking this up but I couldn't hit on anybody specific. As I was telling D, an ambulance came across the hill with siren going, and as it passed us I felt an energy release and was quite drained for a period of time after that. Here of late I've developed, it seems, an ability or have been sensitized empathically. I want to know, is this the case and in the situation of which I spoke, was I of any assistance to whoever it may have been in the ambulance at the time? If you can?

I am Latwii, and am aware of your query, my brother. As you seek upon your journey, you shall find various experiences and abilities within your grasp. You supposition is correct that your ability now is expanding into the area of the healing realms, and indeed your aid was greatly appreciated by the entity to which it was sent.

May we answer you further, my brother?

C: No, you've been very helpful tonight. Thank you.

I am Latwii. We are most grateful to you, my brother, for allowing us to perform our humble service. Is there another question at this time?

M: Latwii, I just wonder if so much of the younger generation is afraid of failure and as a result, even if they're succeeding, the specter of failure just is there and—in C's case if he failed as a—if he lost his job, if he failed as a husband, if he failed as a father, life would go on, and he would find a new meaning. Is it that people cannot accept failure? We all fail and if you can't be comfortable with failure, I don't understand how you can be comfortable with success. Because that is the other side of the coin. And is C [being] afraid of failure in some field the reason he's uncomfortable? The world's not going to fall apart if he fails at everything. He still is a delightful human being. And is the younger generation afraid of failure or why are they so tense?

I am Latwii, and am aware of your query, my sister. We shall not attempt to describe the one known as C in any terms such as being afraid of failure, but shall simply state that for those within your illusion at this time the catalyst is most intense, and is quite likely to cause many entities to retreat for the moment until the grasp of the situation can be gained, for it is felt by most upon your planet now that the times are most difficult in ways which are seeming to threaten that which has been secure in what you know of as the past. Therefore, the mass consciousness, shall we say, of your peoples is that which does find some fear at that which seems to be failure.

As you have correctly surmised, there is a greater viewpoint or larger viewpoint which might be taken, that, indeed, the experience and the life shall continue, and it shall be enriched but there must for many be the fear of failing before the entity is able to continue the life experience, for there are many experiences upon the journey of the seeker, and the so-called failure is but one. Many of these experiences have the, shall we say, designation as "bad" or "to be avoided" pinned upon them, and therefore take more time to assimilate, yet each shall eventually learn each lesson, and love shall be found, and the purpose of each incarnation shall be realized.

May we answer you further, my sister?

M: No, thank you.

I am Latwii, and we thank you. Is there another query at this time?

S: Yes, Latwii. Before I ask my question, I'd like to ask if the energy level of the instrument is okay?

I am Latwii, and we thank you for this concern. We find that this instrument is growing somewhat, shall we say, fatigued, but there is the energy available for two or three more queries of the usual length, shall we say.

S: I had an experience this week that I would like you to comment on. I assume that you know what I'm talking about, so I will just briefly state that I suddenly found myself in a state similar to sleep and also similar to unconsciousness. My body was shaking quite a bit, and I was aware of this shaking. When I came to or woke up, whatever the case may be, my sunburn and my pain were for several minutes totally gone. I was wondering if there was anything beyond a physical nature—if you could tell me what had occurred?

I am Latwii, and am aware of your query, my sister. We may speak in general terms with some specificity, yet may not penetrate the total gist, shall we say, of this experience, for some yet remains for your own discovery. The process of the seeker in seeking the truth sets in motion many opportunities for the seeker to experience that which is sought. That portion of yourself which you have come to call the higher self often sends a symbolic message to the conscious seeking self so that by the process of contemplation and meditation the conscious seeking self might penetrate further into its own being, and find more of that which it seeks within itself. As you seek to know in order to serve, that seeking shall manifest in many and various ways. To desire the healing of ignorance or of any diseased portion of mind, body or spirit is a desire which shall be realized in various steps. Your experience was of this nature and you may in your meditations ponder the possibility that there is more to this experience which is available to you at this time.

May we answer you further, my sister?

S: I'm afraid you always leave me with a puzzle. I would like to ask you briefly another question about dreaming. If one has a dream that one wants to figure out and use, is it necessary to look behind all the symbolism that goes on, and all the people that you come in contact with, or is it sufficient to, say, realize one particular feeling such as unworthiness that carried throughout the dream, and if that was the main message that you got out of this dream, is it correct that this is probably what you have set for yourself to balance?

I am Latwii, and am aware of your query, my sister. We would suggest utilizing both methods which you have mentioned. For the general, shall we say, understanding of the dream it is helpful to be aware of those underlying currents or major themes that one feels. To hone the understanding, if we may use this misnomer, of that theme, it is most helpful to attempt to assign some sort of grasp of meaning to each portion of the dream which you are able to remember, for each portion reflects some aspect of the major theme.

May we answer you further, my sister?

S: No, thank you, Latwii. You've been very helpful.

I am Latwii, and we are grateful to you, my sister. Is there another query at this time?

M: Yes. K is going to England, and do you have any words of wisdom that would make her trip more enjoyable and more knowledgeable?

I am Latwii, and am aware of your query, my sister. Yes. *Bon voyage!*

K: *(Laughing)* Well, thank you, Latwii.

I am Latwii and we thank you, my sisters. Is there a final query at this time?

R: Latwii, how can I improve my health, and the health of others around me?

I am Latwii, and am aware of your query, my brother. This is a most central and large subject for each entity which seeks the truer nature of its own being and the illusion in which it moves. In general we may suggest that this desire might be enhanced by continuing to seek the love and the light of the one Creator within each moment that you experience, within the face of each entity which you encounter, within each portion of your own being. Look about you and consciously, moment by moment, attempt to find, to see, and to radiate the love and the light that exists in each moment. If you can, within your own being, continue to fan that flame of seeking and to share it without reservation with each entity whom you meet. You shall be at once doing two things: enhancing your own seeking and lighting the way ever more clearly on your own journey and with that same flame of seeking you shall be lighting the way for others. For as one finds more of the love and light of the one Creator within its own being and shares that love and light with others, the entities about one will find an inspiration which shall be most beneficial.

To seek this unity, this love, and this light is a process which enhances what your peoples call the health of the being. We would use the term balance but shall not quibble with terms at this point. To be in health or in balance is to walk the journey in will and faith, to have the will to seek and share and to have the faith to know there is that which might be found and shared. To develop these characteristics, the will to seek and the faith to know that there is that which can be found, is most helpful to any entity who wishes to be in a state of balance or health and to share that with others.

May we answer you further, my brother?

R: No, thank you.

I am Latwii, and we thank you, my brother. We would at this time suggest the ending of the queries, for this instrument is somewhat fatigued, and we are not able to transmit the clear message when there is the overriding feeling of fatigue. We thank each entity present for allowing our humble service. We are filled with joy at your seeking and your harmony and we rejoice with you in the love and in the light of the one Creator. We are with each upon your request in meditation to offer our conditioning vibration. We again thank this group for seeking our humble and poor advice as responses to your queries. Whatever words we offer are but the merest of trinkets when compared with the great treasure of your own being which each of you seeks, and which each of you must surely find. We shall leave you now in the love and the light of the one infinite Creator. We are known to you as those of Latwii. Adonai, my friends. Vasu borragus.

(Carla channeling)

(Carla channels a lovely song without words from Nona.)

I am Nona. We have shared with you in the healing love and light of the infinite Creator. You are with those who desire the healing vibration. We will be with each who mentally calls upon us. We thank you for the privilege of being able to serve *(inaudible)* this instrument in love and light. I am Nona. Adonai.

Sunday Meditation
June 19, 1983

(Carla channeling)

[I am Hatonn,] and I greet you in the love and the light of our infinite Creator. May we welcome those who have joined this group this evening. Our hearts *(inaudible)* and we rejoice that we may once again speak with you through this instrument to share the blessing of communication and comradeship. You are aware, of course, that we are with you if you so desire, that we are aware that on the other hand it [is] very helpful to hear our thoughts and to feel the force of them as you would a conversation with a friend, rather than an inner voice.

We gaze now at the topic which we would choose to speak with you about this evening, and we find ourselves discarding many. We would speak to you of the one original Thought of the infinite Creator, that great and powerful Thought of love which is the foundation of the creation, and indeed is the creation. But we find that you have been working with this concept for some time. Our thoughts move then to the topic of light, the manifestation of love, and we would give you information upon how to become a more radiant being, how to manifest love in your life in the service of others. But we find that you have taken this up, each one of you, and have embraced it and have pursued service to others. We then bethink ourselves of meditation, for it is most important that all outer work [be] founded, strengthened, undergirded and covered with the armor of the contact within in silence which meditation offers. And we could abjure you to be more faithful in your meditations. And yet we find that indeed each is pursuing a path in which meditation plays some part, and in which the individual is already attempting to make use of meditation.

We have not run out our chain of conversation with you. We gaze at the possibility of speaking with you about the unity of all creation, and we find once again that each of you works with this concept. Indeed, we find that we must speak with you about the nature of creation as you find it at this particular point in your experience.

Many times the metaphor of the way, the path or the road has been used to describe the journey of a metaphysical seeker. It is far too often assumed that this path, in addition to being narrow, stony, difficult and winding, is the same path as that of your neighbor. Therefore, we would examine the idea of your journey. Indeed, the central metaphor that links your illusion with reality is the journey. You have launched yourself into a journey. And in common with all of your peoples you are journeying. You do not journey down a common path except insofar as all of creation is fundamentally one, for you are unique. The lessons that you have before you are unique. The gifts that you are given to take with you are unique. And companions who you chose are uniquely your own. The name of every road is love but there are no markers.

We ask you to move in imagination from the metaphor of a journey upon land where in the dust you may see at least the footprints of those who have gone before you, to the journey upon the sea. Sit in your wooden boat and listen to the timbers creak and guard well your weather, for this is your boat, this is your path, this is your journey. The ocean is trackless, merciless, and secretive. What you have to guide you are things that seem very far away, as far away as the stars. You have your ideals, your desires, your seeking. From those you must estimate what sea lane you shall travel. Your journey is a moonlit one, a perpetual shadow land which only by the greatest of purity of effort can you brighten into a brighter light. When you strike land, you do not know what the treasure is. You must explore. You do not know if this is the island of your treasure. You do not even know precisely what the treasure may appear to be.

And so you sit and listen to the timbers creak and hope for a good wind and you hone your desire as sharp as a new-minted knife that you might sniff the freshening breezes of seeking and cast yourself once again into your journey. This is the inner work. This will continue. Your refinements done in moonlight have virtue because you are acting within such heavy illusion. When you have prepared yourself, and listened, and smelled, and seen through meditation and the sharpening of the desire to seek the truth, you will find yourself at the end of this incarnation gazing back over your sea voyage with joy indeed. For great progress is made in difficulty, and little in times of ease and repletion. So get used to the feel of the hawser ropes as you cast off. Adjust yourselves to the smell and the sound of devotion. There it is that you wish to go. Far from comfort, far from safety, entirely at risk, seeking the one Treasure.

We would not let this image pass without speaking of that which balances all of the hardships of the sailor's travels. For when good souls meet together, do they not always throw a party? Suddenly, many times in your incarnation, you shall come across festivities and you shall feel free and make merry and rejoice, and this is a gift given only to those who seek. You might simply glance in another's eye and know that you are seeking in deep water together. It does not take much to make a party when two souls recognize one another. Much of what you experience in positivity and joy at a meeting such as this one has to do with the seemingly unlikely possibility that those in deep water and completely alone could suddenly happen onto a party. And yet, where you are gathered, the great light shines, joy is felt, love is shared. Each is strengthened, and does indeed make merry and so grace the one infinite Creator with the lightsome laughter and the lifted *(inaudible)*.

My friends, no matter what the situation in the illusion, we urge you to do two things. Seek the Creator with a whole heart and a desire to know in order to serve and wait for a party; wait for joy. It has been written in your holy work called the Bible, "Weeping may spend the night, but joy will come in the morning." The metaphysical sea is awash with salt tears but there is no lack of joy. Therefore, comfort yourself, and above all continue your voyage with as much dedication as you may find within you. Precisely this much, no more and no less. Daily meditation has as one of its most important aspects the regulating of your seeking. For you, as all entities who are conscious, go through seasons, and you are not always the same in your strength, in your faith and in your will. In your meditation, therefore, fill yourself with that love which is unlimited. But allow that same intelligence to inform the voyage. If your will lacks, allow the sails to go slack, and do the work that is required to restore them to will, hope and faith. Do not abandon your boat. We strongly suggest you remain on board that great platform of yourself.

(Tape ends.)

L/L Research

L/L Research is a subsidiary of Rock Creek Research & Development Laboratories, Inc.

P.O. Box 5195
Louisville, KY 40255-0195

www.llresearch.org

Rock Creek is a non-profit corporation dedicated to discovering and sharing information which may aid in the spiritual evolution of humankind.

ABOUT THE CONTENTS OF THIS TRANSCRIPT: This telepathic channeling has been taken from transcriptions of the weekly study and meditation meetings of the Rock Creek Research & Development Laboratories and L/L Research. It is offered in the hope that it may be useful to you. As the Confederation entities always make a point of saying, please use your discrimination and judgment in assessing this material. If something rings true to you, fine. If something does not resonate, please leave it behind, for neither we nor those of the Confederation would wish to be a stumbling block for any.

CAVEAT: This transcript is being published by L/L Research in a not yet final form. It has, however, been edited and any obvious errors have been corrected. When it is in a final form, this caveat will be removed.

© 2009 L/L Research

Sunday Meditation
June 26, 1983

(C channeling)

I am Hatonn, and I am now with this instrument. We greet you, my friends, in the love and in the light of the one infinite Creator. My friends, as you strive to serve, as you journey on, the journey may well be trying for you. You may find yourself becoming weary. In these times it is sometimes helpful for you to take a time and reflect upon those things that you have done as part of your journey. It is often easy to lose sight of the whole as you aim yourself down your chosen path, for as one singles out a specific means to serve, other opportunities may well be passed by. When you become aware that you take your chosen goal so seriously that it is all that you may see, take time, meditate, and reflect upon it, for in your illusion—and that is what you exist within—your opportunities are many, the lessons are indeed varied. My friends, be patient as you travel but be not afraid to attempt to see the whole. Your life has many facets. Each is important.

I am Hatonn. We would, if we may, now transfer this contact to another instrument. I am Hatonn.

(Carla channeling)

I am Hatonn, and I greet you through this instrument in the love and the light of the infinite Creator. We shall continue through this instrument. It has been given you to discriminate in your free will among those experiences, thoughts and interpretations which come your way in the course of your daily lives. Your power of discrimination is at the heart of your being, and not to use it is to reject a tool the use of which accelerates your progress as a seeker of that which is true. The culture in which you dwell would have you believe that there is one ethic or mode of conduct, one way of interpreting situations which satisfies all circumstances. This is most emphatically not so, in our meager understanding.

At one time you may have a decision to make, an idea may be calling you, and as you look behind you see many loose ends, many things that you have left undone, a family that you wish to greet and assure comfort, of friends whom you wish to bid good-bye. And it is of no purpose to go ahead with your new idea until you have made a lasting and bountiful peace with all that you leave behind. At another time an idea may call you, and you look back and see precisely the same situation. And yet in that instance, to turn back for a moment is to lose the idea, and you must rush forward, leaving that which is behind behind, and devoting yourself to the present moment.

This example is simplistic and most decisions are far less dramatic, but there is that much difference between one situation in your seeking and another. The two situations may be outwardly identical, but you as a seeker, as a person, and as a human servant of your own higher self are two completely different responders to circumstance. How can one know when to act and when to wait? As we have said, there are so many things to capture your attention, and all are deserving. What, then, shall you accomplish today? How shall you serve the Creator today?

You are aware, my friends, that unless you are in touch with that portion of yourself which is silent and which waits for your inward seeking, you will forever be in darkness. It is seldom that a true decision dealing with spiritual matters can be made logically. You must have recourse to the contemplation of that silence which speaks within you. One who works without this meditation is like a carpenter who builds a house armed only with the roughest tools. No surface can ever be finished nor corner can be squared. The pitch of the roof can never be even when there is no level. Such is the poverty of the intellect when it works without the aid of the meditative self. It is understandable that you become discouraged at times, weary and ready to release all of your burdens. But you who know that this is an illusion may take it under advisement that it is not comprehensible to us that you would leave so many of your tools behind as you go about making your decisions.

You have been given many gifts; as many as the beauties of your wildlife, your trees, your shrubs, your sun, and your breezes. And just so are the virtues of your inward self. If you were for just a few seconds in total contact with that self, your limitations, the confusions, and your weariness would cease to exist. You would see light, and you would see unity, for you are all that is, and all that is you. Moreover, the husks that we gaze upon and deal with as we meet each other in the illusion of the incarnational experience are not those bodies that we see when we grasp the nature of our inner selves. If you could imagine a light so bright that it completely fills and overflows the habitation in which you dwell, and if you could imagine every being upon all of your planet and in all of creation dwelling in such a light, then you would begin to become aware of the original nature of the creation.

What an illusion you experience, and to a certain extent how much of an illusion do we experience, my friends! How much is the light dimmed, how greatly all the outlines disappear. And yet it may not be so. Move into the light and feel yourself cleansed, refreshed and awakened to that light which is whole and without blemish. It may seem that that light and the light that is in you cannot be brought into this illusion, cannot be brought to bear upon your decisions. But meditation is the tool whereby you open a corridor between that husk and shell you experience that grows weary and discouraged, and the original creation that you are. It is possible to experience and retain the characteristics of the original Thought of the Creator. It is possible to deal with other selves in the light of that oneness which they share in the original Thought of the one infinite Creator. It is not probable that you shall each day be able to find and to retain that light and that love. It is recommended that the attempt be made ever new each day.

I am Hatonn. I see that we have lulled one of our members to a peaceful doze. It is time for us to take our leave. We bless each, and say to each of you again, you shall be discouraged, of course, but take each day as a chance to find and retain the original Thought of the Creator. Know that the illusion is an illusion, and that you must be foolish enough to cease from acting only from logic, for illusions are not logical, and the lessons that you came here to learn will be learned very slowly if you are burdened with intellect to the point that it rules out the seeking of the truth, which is often very illogical. No two days, no two situations are the same, nor are you the same. Do not be fooled by the illusion. Do not be fooled by the seeming constancy of your own personality. You progress; you must keep up with yourself.

And so we say to you, seek the original Thought, that, though never changing, informs you of your progress, and shines a level light on your world. We leave you in that light and in the love of the infinite Creator. We are known to you as the brothers and sisters of Hatonn. Adonai. Adonai.

(Jim channeling)

I am Latwii, and we greet you, my friends, in the love and in the light of our infinite Creator. It is our privilege once again to speak to your group. We thank you for blending your vibrations in the seeking of our humble words, and we remind each that our words are indeed humble, and are as but as potential signposts upon your journey. May we then ask for the first query this evening?

Carla: I have a question for R concerning his wife, C. For quite some time she has experienced black dots in front of her eyes, rather like black ash falling and lately it's gotten quite a bit worse, always black. R and C have thought that it may have something to do with some heavy drugs that she took when she had a very bad injury to her leg, and they wondered if you could make some comment about the black dot situation?

I am Latwii, and am aware of your query, my sister. In this instance, we find that it is possible to speak in somewhat more than general terms, though we may not and cannot penetrate the heart of this situation, for such penetration is of necessity the honor and duty of the seeker. But we may suggest that though this appearance has its origin in what you may term an accidental situation, in another sense one may be assured that there are no accidents. The trauma of the accident, as it is called, and the treatment which followed had origins within this entity's higher self, as you have come to know it. Therefore, though it might be seen that the medication which was administered had its effect, the medication itself was as the catalyst, and presented this entity with the experience and opportunity for growth which the higher self deemed proper.

It is, as in all such physical manifestation of catalyst, recommended that the entity look upon the nature of the phenomenon and its physical expression as symbolic of a deeper lesson, that those spots which float past in the ephemeral vision be analyzed for their deeper meaning and then meditated upon so that the deeper portions of the mind which contain additional clues may release these insights into the inner vision of the entity in meditation.

We cannot prescribe treatment beyond this suggestion, for it is not our place nor is it the proper use of such an instrument as we now use to attempt to give such specific advice. We remind that entity that it travels its journey in perfection and wholeness, and each such event which it shall encounter is also perfect, and the perception of this perfection of journey, of self, and events by the entity is the most important beginning that can be made, for it is within the basic attitude of an entity that any healing may occur, and the attitude shall then attract the further opportunity for the learning and the healing.

May we answer you further, my sister?

Carla: Yes. When I read the question in the letter, I thought immediately of something that I've noticed in myself, and I don't know how many other people have, but I assume many have, and that is that any time I look at a fairly blank space where you can actually see some space, like looking out of a car window or something, I always see what seems to be a dancing pattern of little dots. They're very small. I never knew what they were, and thought they were some mechanical function of the eye or possibly the beginning of vision through the mechanical eye of what prana looks like. And I'm wondering whether something like what has happened to C could just be a distortion of this normal perception? Let me ask this question in two parts. First of all, is what I'm describing that I'm seeing a normal perception?

I am Latwii, and am aware of your query, my sister. That which you have described to those who are of a certain nature of being is what you may call normal. All entities upon the close examination of their physical vision will discover some small alterations in that vision in that movement of a certain kind and patterns of that movement will be noticed. It is our humble opinion that the entity for which you query has experienced another type of phenomenon which has some relationship to that of which you now query, but which is also of a nature unique to this type of lesson and this particular entity.

May we answer you further, my sister?

Carla: No, I think you've successfully pulled the wool over all our eyes. Thank you very much.

I am Latwii, and though we do not wish to be sheepish in our responses, we find that there are certain areas of our responses that we must touch upon with a certain amount of gentleness, that our words may then be used as means for further seeking rather than as the ending point for such seeking.

May we attempt another query at this time?

S: Yes, Latwii. I have a question which I will state in personal terms, and hope that you may comment in general. I'm wondering why I'm so personally tired all the time. I get a good night's sleep, I take lots of vitamins, and I'm good for about three and a half hours in the morning and whatever doesn't get done by then, doesn't get done. I've seen a doctor who has prescribed antidepressants for me, which on looking them up a little bit, I've found out they're anti-anxiety. Although I do often feel anxious, I don't often feel consciously depressed. And I was wondering if maybe there is more to this lack of energy than perhaps my doctor is aware of. I do have an idea, but I would just like any light that you can shed on this.

I am Latwii, and am aware of your query, my sister. As in our previous response, we again may state that each physical experience …

(Side one of tape ends.)

(Jim channeling)

I am Latwii, and am again with this instrument. To continue our response, my sister. The nature of your physical vehicle has the purpose of reflecting to you the contents of your mind, for it is the evolution of your mind which is most important within this illusion. Therefore, one may look upon the phenomena which passed through the physical vehicle as messages in need of more attention that have first begun as configurations of the mind. You may look upon the experience of weariness, then, not necessarily as that which shall be cured, but perhaps as that which shall be utilized. You may wish to ask yourself what purpose may weariness serve? What opportunities are opened in the experience of physical weariness that would not be available should the weariness be absent, and the energetic movement be its replacement?

There are, as we have stated before, no accidents or mistakes. Whether you utilize the current physical catalyst well or poorly, quickly or slowly, is your choice. You have come to learn and to serve. When it is appropriate, your higher self offers catalyst to aid in this process. You may look at all which occurs within you and within your grasp as a speaking to you that has the purpose of aiding your evolution.

May we answer you further, my sister?

S: Yes. If, then, my weariness has been programmed by my higher self for me to utilize, it seems to me that it's telling me that I need to physically slow down a bit. If I use prescriptions to overcome this weariness, am I defeating what I have programmed for me, and will it then come out in some other way, or could the overcoming of this weariness allow me to better serve?

I am Latwii, and am aware of your query, my sister. You cannot, in our humble opinion, defeat the catalyst which you have joined in the programming for your current incarnation. You can deny it for the moment, and delay it for a period of time, and perhaps treat to the point of removal of some of its physical symptoms, yet you shall at some point experience another message perhaps more symbolic, perhaps more difficult to penetrate, yet always are the opportunities forthcoming that you might utilize this illusion in your evolution. It is, shall we say, likened unto a training aid for you and for each within the boundaries and definitions of your culture and this illusion. Certain acceptable means of acting and being are given, yet no situation has any definition other than aiding and being able to accelerate your evolution. How this is accomplished, and the speed with which it is accomplished, and the efficiency with which it is accomplished is your choice.

May we answer you further, my sister?

S: No, Latwii, thank you. As always, you've been most helpful.

I am Latwii, and we are most grateful for your service as well, my sister. May we attempt another query at this time?

Carla: Well, her query triggers something that's been troubling me. When I had a good deal of intestinal trouble I got a reading from Ra on it which was very detailed. And one of the things that Ra recommended was that if I wished I could go to a certain person, a doctor, whom I did not know at the time but found in the phone book, and get a prescription for an anti-spasmodic drug. Ra then said something about either using the drug or dealing with the catalyst without the use of the drug, and since I wasn't absolutely flat on my back as I would be with arthritis if I didn't use drugs, I decided to try using the catalyst without the use of the drug, and I've continued doing it to this time.

The thing that I've noticed about this catalyst is that it goes on for a long, long time. It doesn't simply end. It doesn't resolve itself quickly. It seems to have all kinds of ramifications in manifestation, and also in my understanding of the causes of it. I haven't really gotten a handle on it yet. What really bothers me is that since it's taking me a long time, and since I'm uncomfortable a good deal of the time because I've accepted the catalyst instead of taking the drugs that would remove the discomfort, those around me and especially the two people closest to me are constantly having to deal with my catalyst because I'm unable to do this or I'm feeling a little poorly to do that or something. There's a spillover into other people's lives, and it almost seems, like, unfair to others to work out your catalyst because it turns out being everybody's catalyst that lives in the household.

It seems to me that I'm almost being a stumbling block because of my decision to go ahead and work through this catalyst without the use of drugs. Could you shed any light on the confusion?

I am Latwii, and am aware of your query, my sister. It is only within the illusion that the experience of time holds sway. That which appears to you, my sister, as taking an inordinate amount of that which you call time may from another point of viewing be a glorious opportunity to advance not only your own evolutionary process but to provide the opportunity for those close to you to do as well. Each of your peoples dwells within this illusion in order to learn and to serve. The purpose for the incarnation is not to experience little in the way of learning, for most upon your planet are capable of great service and great learning.

As you experience what seems to be your very own catalyst, you must remember that all beings are one, and those who are near need also from you to experience those portions of yourself which aid their evolution and allow them to learn and to serve. It may seem that some catalyst detracts from the comfort of another, and this may be so, but are you here to experience comfort? We realize that that commodity is in somewhat short supply when spoken of in reference to your physical vehicle. Yet one may look upon the most, as you would call it, heavy of physical burdens, replete with great discomfort, and see a great opportunity presented for finding the love which exists in infinite quantity in each moment.

You are aware that you have not chosen an easy path. You are aware as well, my sister, that the opportunity to serve is great with this group. With the honor and duty of such great service, there is also the necessity of working with great catalyst, for it is the work with such catalyst that refines and hones an entity's ability to serve and to learn. You and each within this group and upon this planet have not been given more than you can bear. This is the law: to those who can bear much, then shall much be given. To those whose shoulders are not quite as strong, then shall the appropriate burdens be given, for it is only in the bearing of the burden that the spiritual legs are strengthened and the journey quickened.

May we answer you further, my sister?

Carla: No, thank you. It does sound like it would be fun to be skip around without a rucksack, but I accept it as it is a part of the journey.

I am Latwii, and we appreciate your seeking and your acceptance, and we hope that our words, humble though they be may, in some way assist in this endeavor. May we attempt another query at this time?

S: Yes, Latwii. Are you saying that if I listen to my higher self, and slow down a little bit, that those members of my family will actually be able to find their own socks?

I am Latwii, and am aware of your query, my sister. We would not make such a *(inaudible)* …

(Group laughter.)

… assumption. There are some situations which do not seem probable. Yet, my sister, in good humor, may we also suggest that such may not be the point of the incarnation.

May we attempt to answer you further, my sister?

S: *(Inaudible).*

I am Latwii, and we thank you, my sister. Is there another query at this time?

K: I have a question, Latwii. When I go home to New York every summer there's a woman who reads my tea leaves, and she's been so on the money about things that are going on. I'm drawn to her like a moth to a flame, and she's not really given me any advice, but if she were to do that, I'm curious, is there any way you can tell what orientation a person is, whether it's service to self or to other, or do you go with your gut feeling or do you have anything to say on that?

I am Latwii, and am aware of your query, my sister. We can only suggest for this entity and your evaluation of its service that which we suggest to each in the evaluation of our service, or any source of information which you may find interesting and perhaps helpful in your journey of seeking. That is to look with your conscious mind at all such services, all such information, and match it with that which you have found helpful in what you call your past. Determine if there is some kernel of truth available. Meditate upon that which you have contemplated. Ask within your own being for inspiration. You are not without inner resources, my sister. These may be utilized in the evaluation of each experience within your illusion. Indeed, it is most necessary, as our brothers and sisters of Hatonn have stated this evening, that the proper amount of meditation be used to refine and seat that which has been consciously contemplated and experienced. You have the tools available, and do know how they may be used.

May we answer you further, my sister?

K: No, thank you.

I am Latwii, and we thank you, my sister. Is there another query at this time?

(Pause)

I am Latwii, and it appears that we have exhausted the queries for the evening. We hope that our words will be of some aid to those whose seeking has drawn them this evening from our being. We remind each that should any word offend or displease, it may immediately be discarded. We look upon those within this group this evening and see many portions of the one Creator existing within an heavy chemical illusion moving from one experience and lesson to another with desire that is of great proportion. Yet, my friends, we would remind each that your illusion shall not give way to desire. It is not so constructed. It is constructed that you will continually find what you have called the difficult situation, the confusions, despair, frustration, loneliness, anger and so forth. Your great desire shall allow you to utilize these opportunities to find the love which you came to find and which, indeed, is available in each situation.

This is the purpose of the illusion, to provide the darkness in which to find light, to provide the burdens, the carrying of which develops strength, to provide the difficulties in seeing the Creator in all things, that you may indeed see that Creator in all things. Take heart, my friends. Have courage and know that your desire shall see you through. It is as it must be for the great process of evolution to occur. You work now within an illusion which provides the greatest of opportunities for learning each lesson that you desire. Rejoice with those who seek and walk with you. Be at peace at the center of your being, though all around you there seems to be only chaos and confusion. We are with you, my friends, as are the legions of light which seek to aid you in ways quite difficult to understand, but ever present and available. We are those of Latwii, and we leave you now in the great and glorious light of the one Creator, bathed in His love. Adonai, my friends. Adonai vasu. ☙

L/L Research

L/L Research is a subsidiary of Rock Creek Research & Development Laboratories, Inc.

P.O. Box 5195
Louisville, KY 40255-0195

www.llresearch.org

Rock Creek is a non-profit corporation dedicated to discovering and sharing information which may aid in the spiritual evolution of humankind.

ABOUT THE CONTENTS OF THIS TRANSCRIPT: This telepathic channeling has been taken from transcriptions of the weekly study and meditation meetings of the Rock Creek Research & Development Laboratories and L/L Research. It is offered in the hope that it may be useful to you. As the Confederation entities always make a point of saying, please use your discrimination and judgment in assessing this material. If something rings true to you, fine. If something does not resonate, please leave it behind, for neither we nor those of the Confederation would wish to be a stumbling block for any.

CAVEAT: This transcript is being published by L/L Research in a not yet final form. It has, however, been edited and any obvious errors have been corrected. When it is in a final form, this caveat will be removed.

© 2009 L/L RESEARCH

Sunday Meditation
July 3, 1983

(Carla channeling)

[I am] Latwii, and I greet you in the love and in the light of the infinite Creator. We thank you for calling us this evening. It is a great privilege to be able to speak through this instrument. We are not often able to do so. We would like to offer a brief message to you and then we shall bow out so that our brothers and sisters may also speak.

Once upon a time there was a planet full of people much like yourselves, and all of these people brushed their teeth every day without fail. One day a toothpaste company came around and revolutionized the world. It invented a new compound which made your teeth sparkle called dioxyethexene, and all the people flocked to buy this wonderful toothpaste with dioxyethexene. What the toothpaste company did not realize, and what the people did not realize either, was that if, when you were brushing your teeth with this toothpaste, you would speak one unfortunate word, if there were more than two oxygen molecules standing around, your jaws would become stiff, and you could no longer speak.

The first to go were the truck drivers right in the middle of the first sentence they spoke after brushing their teeth. Suddenly, there were many, many silent trucks driving down the road and the CB channels became empty. The next to go were all the housewives who said "I hate these …" They had been intending to speak of washing dishes; they never got the words out. Soon their husbands joined them in speechlessness, as they uttered many unfortunate words on their way to their work.

Before the first day was over, well over ninety-five percent of the world had become silent. Human speech was seldom heard. Even great judges had become speechless when they said, "I hereby judge you …" That, my friends, was the last word they would say. Preachers as a whole lasted into the second day, but they too unfortunately had developed the habit of saying rude things about other churches, and sooner or later on the second day they too became speechless, and could no longer preach from their pulpits of love and glory. All the war machines ground to a halt, for there was no one to give the orders.

And finally, for just a few moments, there was on this very small planet only one person left who could speak. The best, the kindest, the dearest person of all, he kept looking around him and could find no one to speak with. And finally he said, "I'm the only one who can still speak. If that isn't the da …"

We ask you, my friends, how long would you speak if dioxyethexene were in your toothpaste? How careful are you? Do you know that all vibration is real and that each word is a vibration? We ask you to consider your vibrations that they may flow from you in love and touch those about you in radiance. Where there is a smile, a laugh, an understanding, or even in some circumstance that knowledge that truth has been spoken but fairly, there you may see communication used aright. Where there is frustration, sadness, anger or judgment, there you may see the negative power that you have. It is yours to use if you wish. But do you truly wish it?

I am Latwii. We shall leave this instrument, and return through another channel. It has been a great privilege to use this instrument. We had just figured out how to use this instrument without blowing out all her circuits, and she stopped being able to answer questions. And we are so pleased to be able to use her knowledge, and to be able to use her sense of humor. May your evening bless you. We leave you in the love and the light of the one infinite Creator. I am Latwii.

(C channeling)

I am Hatonn, and I am now with this instrument. We greet you in the love and the light of the one infinite Creator. We join you tonight not to be our usual morose selves, for it would not be appropriate after the delightful tale of our brothers and sisters of Latwii. My friends, we rejoice in the love and the light that emanates through the small but united group which though small at this time reaches far. It is joined by those close to and a part of this group. The unity you have found, love and fellowship, is not broken by the distance, is not broken by your time. Love shines and reaches far. We of Hatonn have indeed been privileged to be of what small service we have been and may be with this group. Your times together physically may be short but the spirits remain connected. The love that each gives unto the other is helped in ways you may never know. Rejoice in your love, rejoice in your fellowship. We are known to you as Hatonn. Adonai, my friends.

(Jim channeling)

I am Latwii, and we greet you again, my friends, in the love and the light of the infinite Creator. We must make some small adjustments in order to speak through this instrument, for our speaking through the one known as Carla is much more, shall we say, finely tuned, and this instrument has somewhat the consistency of lead, and must therefore require an additional jolt, shall we say. We feel that we have good contact at this time, and it is once again our privilege to attempt to answer those queries which those present have to offer to the group. May we therefore ask for the first query?

C: When I first began attending these meditations, there was a period when I was experiencing physical difficulties, and I don't believe you were doing the questions and answers then, but the one doing it scanned my physical and spiritual being and was able to make some helpful comments. I was wondering if you could do that—make some general comments about some blockages that I'm experiencing?

I am Latwii, and am aware of your query, my brother. We may, without infringement, make only the general comment. These general comments may then be meditated upon and utilized for the specific actions of your own choosing. The thinking of identity may be seen as the most important ingredient in the maintaining of what you call physical health, for in most cases your physical vehicle is functioning as a system of feeding back to your attention those areas which in your thinking have been neglected or blocked in some way. Therefore, when you see in your thinking or in your behavior—and here we stress the thinking over the behavior—certain patterns, you may correlate these patterns with energy centers, and if there be difficulty in the pattern of thought which has not been noticed sufficiently enough by the mind then you may see it reproduced within the body complex.

The red-ray energy center, as it has come to be called in this group, is a center which is not often worked directly upon, for it is the beginning, the foundation, the, shall we say, given for your physical vehicle.

The orange-ray energy center concerns the expression of the self in relationship to the self. It is the physical expression of what you might call power, if it be of the positive or negative variety. Difficulties in this center will be noted in the physical vehicle as the inability of certain means of expression, usually of the lower gross motor muscles of the legs, feet and in some cases the hands and arms, for these appendages are those portions of your physical vehicle which allow the power-filled nature of your being in relationship to yourself to be expressed in your immediate surroundings.

Difficulty in the yellow-ray energy center may be seen as a reflection of the entity's inability to fully accept those within its immediate range of relationship, and an inability to let these entities be that which they are. Conditions which are set upon these entities in order that they might receive the affection of the entity are those blockages of this energy center which express themselves in the region of the abdominal cavity, for the solar plexus energy center is most prominent in its effects in this region.

The blockage of the green-ray energy center is somewhat common upon your planet, for it is the lesson of this vibration which most have attempted for a great period of what you call time to learn, that is, the unconditional love and acceptance of all beings, whether in relationship with the entity or not. The difficulty in this energy center has little specific correlation to the physical vehicle at this time, for, as we mentioned, it is that lesson which is set before the peoples of your planet, and is in general not yet grasped.

The blue ray of clear and free communication and inspiration is seldom activated in your populations, and is therefore infrequent in its effect upon the physical vehicle of most of your entities. But in those who have made some progress in its activation there may be seen the difficulty in some area of the speaking when this speaking is blocked.

To speak of the indigo-ray energy center is to speak of that which is most rare in your peoples at this time, and its effect upon the physical vehicle therefore is even less noted.

When an entity sees any physical difficulty in its physical complex, it might most helpfully and efficiently look at the effect of the difficulty upon the entity's life. For it is this symbolic blockage which has been transferred from the mind complex to the body and noting the difficulty and its means of inhibiting the entity's expression is most helpful then in determining its source and in pointing the energy center which has been blocked.

May we answer you further, my brother?

C: You say the green-ray energy center has been or has begun to be activated. Once that has occurred, is it possible for it to be deactivated?

I am Latwii, and I am aware of your query, my brother. This is not only possible, but is quite frequent in occurrence. Any energy center which has been activated may from time to time be blocked in part as the lessons of that center are continually refined.

May we answer you further, my brother?

C: Maybe in a minute I'll think of a few.

I am Latwii. We are happy to allow your consideration of our humble words. May we answer another query at this time?

R: Yes, Latwii. S asked me to ask you if there any information you could [give] her on Morzack, and also what their specialty is with the Confederation?

I am Latwii, and am aware of your query, my brother. We find in this instance that it would be most helpful for the one known as S to inquire from this entity itself that information. We can, again due to certain limitations, speak in general terms. Each entity such as the one of whom you speak, that known as S, has a variety of entities on which to call for inner assistance in the evolutionary process. As we spoke earlier this evening, each thought and word and action which emanates from your being is a vibration which *in toto* reflects the frequency or strength of your calling. As each entity refines the calling, this through the learning of certain lessons, and the drawing towards the self of other lessons, then other, shall we say, teachers about us or presences are attracted to this entity, and make their services available in whatever form the entity is able to understand. Since most in this group are most familiar with what is called the telepathic contact, members of this group may then expect some type of telepathic contact from time to time from those entities which are answering the call for service, for all of creation listens and serves.

The entity which the one known as S has come to know is such an entity, that is, one wishing to be of service to the one known as S, and may be worked with in the meditative state in whatever manner the one known as S desires. We cannot make the choice for the one known as S as to the best means of working with the one known as Morzack but can suggest that she use her own intuitive abilities to seek also this information. It may be found through the, shall we say, trial and error method or it may be found immediately if the receptivity is of the proper nature. In either case there is the assistance available, and it shall find its own course with the aid of the desire of the one known as S.

May we answer you further, my brother?

R: No, Latwii, thanks.

I am Latwii, and we thank you and the one known as S as well. May we attempt another query at this time?

C: This is not a question, this is just to thank you for your answers, for your story tonight. It had great meaning for me.

I am Latwii, and we are very happy, my brother, that our little story and humble words have found meaning for you. Each will find a different meaning and each will determine its use. Is there another query at this time?

(Pause)

I am Latwii, and we are somewhat surprised that we have exhausted the queries so early in the evening, yet we are pleased if we have been able to provide some semblance of response to those queries which were asked. We thank you, my friends, for your patience with us, for your continued seeking of our poor and foolish words. It is our privilege and great joy to speak with your group. We hope that we have been of some small aid. We are with you in your meditations at your request. We leave you now, my friends, [in the glory,] the love and light of the one Creator. Blessings on your journey in unity with the One. I am Latwii. Adonai vasu borragus.

(Carla channeling)

I am Oxal. We greet you in the love and the light of the infinite Creator, and are most privileged to be with your group. This instrument was searching for Morzack, however, this instrument is tuned more to our frequency by nature than to that of Morzack, which is a social memory complex quite close to our own vibratory frequency. Therefore, we were called as stand-ins and are most happy to serve as second best, as it were.

We speak to you of something which this instrument has within her mind at this time; that is, the patriotic holiday. We ask you to consider what a patriot is. A patriot is one who willingly arms extremely large numbers of killers and sets them upon other patriots in order to acquire portions of the creation. There are no patriots in second density. It takes the advanced consciousness of third density to organize slaughter. Examine your relationship with the group which is the nation to which you are patriot. The phrase that we find running through this instrument's mind is, "We do not wish to be anything but peaceful, but if they fight us, what are we to do?" You see, my friends, your energy centers are not crystallized. You have not been refined. You are barely able to activate that which you have learned to call the yellow ray of solar plexus. You have barely begun to master the complexities of group action. To invest group action with that which you have learned to call green ray, all-compassionate love, is to remove the "they" from the equation of "us and they." Then there is no one to fight, no one to lose, and no reason to be patriotic.

We find to our amusement that this entity attempted but did not succeed in learning the national boundaries of the planetary land masses of your planet. We find that she attempted to learn the pink ones, the yellow ones, the green ones and the blue ones. If you will carefully examine that portion of the creation upon which you may stand after removing …

(Side one of tape ends.)

(Jim channeling)

There are no colors to differentiate one nation from another, no boundaries, no true reasons for defense. We ask you to consider how much of your birthright you wish to claim in this incarnation. You will have to lose the sentimental overtones, the heart-swell of national song and sentiment if you are to claim the lesson of love. The kingdom of love lies beyond you. It is within you that you have not yet mastered it, and like a horse that cannot be ridden, that gallops wild and free while you are a slave and oh, would you like to get upon its back and ride free as the wind, full of love, full of light, with the wind of creation upon your eyes and all the cares of little minds and petty lives calmed away. If love is wild, then you must tame it and claim it and make it yours by loving life above all those things that block you from it. Hear that gypsy that is compassion gallop within you. What shall you do to ride away upon that marvelous love? Ride away and change all with which you come in contact. What is freedom? Freedom is service in love. Perfect love is not patriotism, in our humble opinion.

I am Oxal. We again thank you for allowing us to come and speak with you. We leave you in search of our birthright. We leave you in sunlight and in perfect love. We leave you in the Creation, for where else is there? We leave you [in] unity, and so we do not leave you at all. Adonai, my friends. Adonai. Adonai. ✣

L/L Research

L/L Research is a subsidiary of Rock Creek Research & Development Laboratories, Inc.

P.O. Box 5195
Louisville, KY 40255-0195

www.llresearch.org

Rock Creek is a non-profit corporation dedicated to discovering and sharing information which may aid in the spiritual evolution of humankind.

ABOUT THE CONTENTS OF THIS TRANSCRIPT: This telepathic channeling has been taken from transcriptions of the weekly study and meditation meetings of the Rock Creek Research & Development Laboratories and L/L Research. It is offered in the hope that it may be useful to you. As the Confederation entities always make a point of saying, please use your discrimination and judgment in assessing this material. If something rings true to you, fine. If something does not resonate, please leave it behind, for neither we nor those of the Confederation would wish to be a stumbling block for any.

© 2009 L/L RESEARCH

THE LAW OF ONE, BOOK V, SESSION 104, FRAGMENT 54
JULY 27, 1983

Jim: Ra made a point in Session 104 that seems to us to be one of the central principles which govern our evolution through the third density. It was in reference to the amount of exercise which would be most appropriate for Carla when her body was near normal and when it was weakened by one distortion or another. Ra suggested that it should be exercised more when weakened by distortion because "It is the way of distortion that in order to balance a distortion one must accentuate it."

In the next response Ra refers to the use of gifts with which one has entered the incarnation as a kind of "Use it, or lose it" proposition.

When Book One of *The Law Of One* was being published by The Donning Company under the title of *The Ra Material*, we were asked to write an introduction. In one portion of that introduction Carla was writing about the concept of reincarnation. When we got the galley proofs back from The Donning Company we noticed that a sentence which we had not written had somehow appeared in what we had written. It was truly "subjectively interesting."

Ra's eloquent closing was in response to a series of queries concerning our oldest cat, Gandalf, who then was going blind and losing weight, apparently in preparation for death. We have considered leaving this material out, once again, because it has little general application, but we have left it in because Ra's desire not to infringe upon our free will is notable and well illustrated here.

Carla: When people try to improve their living habits, they always go for diet and exercise as being the first things to change. I think these changes have a mental and emotional benefit as well as a physical one, in that it feels as good for the mind as the body to be doing something when there is a concern. The concern for me, by all three of us, seemed never-ending. I don't watch soap operas; they move too slowly for me to keep an interest. But certainly at this point we were living in one. I was steadily losing weight, even eating more than I ever had. So the focus was on diet and exercise. I think we all felt better because we were trying to work on the problems actively. It did, however, seem to take up so much time! Much of the days seemed spent on maintenance. We all were stressed by the situation.

I always have loved my childhood summers spent dancing at the Noyes Rhythm Foundation's camp in Portland, Connecticut. It exists still today, and is a wonderful place altogether, one I cannot recommend highly enough, for you can live in a tent, dance on a sprung wood floor to classical piano music in an open pavilion with greenswards and forest about in an absolutely unspoiled environment. The teachers still follow Florence Fleming Noyes' original method of instruction, which posits that all things have their own rhythm, so one may dance a starfish or a star, a bear or a horse or a blade of grass. It teaches that all things are alive, and that they are all one consciousness. It is very like the Isadora Duncan style of dancing, but with a much elevated philosophy driving the technique. You can be a beginner and still have a wonderful time. I certainly did, and I measured the exercises I was doing at that time with the yardstick of the dance. The walking came up short! But I was faithful and kept up with the routine. Jim usually was kind enough to walk with me, which motivated me greatly.

I see here, for the first time, really, that Ra was echoing Don's request of me, which always was to take more time just to sit. I am an avid reader, and have always loved to toss myself headlong into a romance or science fiction or fantasy novel. To this day it is not unusual for me to read a book a day. Ah, if only the books were "good literature"! but NO! I love to read just for fun, and winkle away to adventure-land. As time has passed, I have more and more found the time to rest in silence, but still tend to read too much.

The stomach problems were to plague me for some years; indeed, still. But things were greatly aided in 1988, when my doctor finally figured out that my gall bladder was infected. Ever since 1982, they had been reading the picture of my gall bladder as showing some sludge—not an operable problem. However, in actuality it was simply infected, and not working at all. Until the sick organ was removed, I was to suffer greatly. And four years later, in 1992, I had the second cleansing operation, when half my colon was removed. These days, I still deal with discomfort throughout the GI tract, but it is not beyond management, and most days I can do well and just put such aches and pains out of my mind. When the sessions were going on in 1983, however, I was in sorry shape. The stress of knowing things weren't right with Don was undoubtedly a factor here.

One can note the way Ra moved fluidly between the psyche and the soma in working with illness. They linked the severity of the pain to work in consciousness, which I was pursuing as intensively as I could, but to slow avail. When one has felt unworthy for a long time, one is slow to learn self-respect of the deep and lasting kind. I was embarking on a life-lesson which was all about learning to be wise and live. Don was also embarking upon a journey, a much darker one. He was learning how to love completely and die.

Meanwhile our beloved cat, Gandalf, was getting old and creaky. How he loved us! He wanted only to be on us, or beside us, always. His devotion never let up, even when, in Georgia some months later, we had to lift him to the food and sand-box, as he could no longer walk. He would move heaven and earth just to be with us, and I got in the habit of carrying him with me so he would not have to walk on his sore paws.

It may seem like Donald spent a lot of time on this kitty, but you have to remember how much like a child such a special pet is. We had no children; being celibate, he wasn't likely to sire a family. But we did have Gandalf and Fairchild. They meant a great deal to us, as our cats still do to Jim and me.

Notice how the tuning started drifting as Don persisted in trying to get specific information from Ra. It is abuse of a well-tuned channel to ask for specific information, I think. And notice how Ra's suggestions for bettering a situation always begin with rejoicing in, giving thanks for and praising the situation, whatever it is. To Ra's way of thinking, when the attitude with which you met the moment was praise and thanksgiving, you'd be best prepared to meet it well. Simple advice, hard to follow, but worth it.

Session 104, July 27, 1983

Ra: I am Ra. We greet you in the love and in the light of the one infinite Creator. We communicate now.

Questioner: Could you first please give me the condition of the instrument?

Ra: I am Ra. The readings are somewhat less distorted towards physical bankruptcy and vital energy loss than at the previous asking. There is still considerable bias in these readings.

Questioner: The instrument would like to know what is the optimum amount of aerobics, walking, and whirlpool exercises for the best condition at this time?

Ra: I am Ra. We shall answer in two ways. Firstly, to speak to the general case which pertains to this instrument in varying degree. Each form of exercise is well accomplished approximately three to four times per your week. The amount of exercise, all quantified as one sum, is approximately one hour per diurnal period.

We now answer in a second way, distorted in this response to the duple conditions of yellow-ray, physical difficulty and mind complex distortion. The swirling waters then must needs be viewed as being appropriate four to five of your times per week. The walking and the exercising as much as is desired by the entity. The total of all these should in no case exceed ninety minutes per diurnal period.

The yellow-ray, physical body has been experiencing that which is called lupoid changes in much tissue of muscle and some of the organs as well. The exercise regains the wasting physical muscular strength. In some ways the walking is the more appropriate exercise due to the proximity of the entity to second-density creatures, particularly your trees. However, the habitation you enjoy does not offer such opportunity and instead offers the proximity to creations of mind/body/spirit complexes. This does not feed the mental/emotional needs of this entity although it produces the same physical result. The exercise fulfills more of the mental/emotional need due to the entity's fondness for rhythmic expressions of the body such as those found in athletic endeavors derivative of the artifact system which is known among your peoples as the dance.

We suggest the support group encourage any exercise except that which exceeds the time limit which is already far beyond the physical limitations of this body complex. It is the way of distortion that in order to balance a distortion one must accentuate it. Thusly, the over-wearing of the body may, if correctly motivated, produce a lack of deficit at which juncture the lesser exercise limitations should be put into practice.

Questioner: The instrument has determined that the unwise use of her will is its use without the joy and faith components and constitutes martyrdom. Would Ra comment on that, please?

Ra: I am Ra. We are pleased that the entity has pondered that which has been given. We would comment as follows. It is salubrious for the instrument to have knowledge which is less distorted towards martyrdom and which is rich in promise. The entity which is strong to think shall either be strong to act or that which it has shall be removed. Thus manifestation of knowledge is an area to be examined by the instrument.

We would further note that balancing which, in this entity's case, is best accomplished in analysis and manifestation seated with the contemplation of silence may be strengthened by manifested silence and lack of routine activity. We may go no further than this recommendation of regularized leisure, and desire that the entity discover the fundamental truths of these distortions as it will.

Questioner: Is there anything further that we can do to help the instrument's stomach and back spasming problem?

Ra: I am Ra. The greatest aid is already being given to the fullest. The encouragement of the instrument to refrain from the oil-fried nature of foodstuffs in its intake is helpful. Cheerful harmony is helpful. The spasms must subside as a function of the entity's indigo-ray work and, to some extent, the recommendations made in response to a previous query. The definitive refraining from over-stepping the already swollen boundaries of physical limitation is recommended. The infection remains and the symptoms are now far less medicable, the entity having chosen the catalyst.

Questioner: Can you tell us what is wrong with our cat's, Gandalf's, eyes?

Ra: I am Ra. The one known as Gandalf nears the end of its incarnation. Its eyesight dims and the aqueous membrane becomes tough. This is not a comfortable circumstance, but is one which causes the entity no true discomfort.

Questioner: Is there anything that we can do to alleviate this situation?

Ra: I am Ra. There is a course of therapy which would aid the situation. However, we do not recommend it as the condition is more benign than the treatment.

Questioner: I don't understand. Could you explain what you meant?

Ra: I am Ra. A doctor of the allopathic tradition would give you the drops for the eyes. The cat would find the experience of being confined while the drops were given more distorted than the discomfort it now feels but is able to largely ignore.

Questioner: Can the cat see at all?

Ra: I am Ra. Yes.

Questioner: Does it seem that the cat will lose all of its vision in the very near future, or is the cat very near death?

Ra: I am Ra. The one known as Gandalf will not lose eyesight or life on most possibility/probability vortices for three of your seasons, approximately.

Questioner: I feel very bad about the condition of the cat and really would like to help it. Can Ra suggest anything that we can do to help out Gandalf?

Ra: I am Ra. Yes.

Questioner: What would that be?

Ra: I am Ra. Firstly, we would suggest that possibility/probability vortices include those in which the entity known as Gandalf has a lengthier incarnation. Secondly, we would suggest that this entity goes to a graduation if it desires. Otherwise, it may choose to reincarnate to be with those companions it has loved. Thirdly, the entity known to you as Betty has the means of making the entity more distorted towards comfort/discomfort.

Questioner: Could you tell me who you mean by Betty? I'm not sure that I know who you mean by Betty. And what Betty would do?

Ra: I am Ra. The one known as Carla has this information.

Questioner: I'm concerned about the possibility of moving. If we did move it would make it very difficult for Gandalf to find his way around a new place if he can't see. Does he see enough to be able to find his way around a new environment?

Ra: I am Ra. The vision is less than adequate but is nearly accommodated by a keen sense of smell and of hearing. The companions and the furnishings being familiar, a new milieu would be reasonably expected to be satisfactorily acceptable within a short period of your space/time.

Questioner: Could we administer the drops that you spoke of that would help his eyesight so that he wouldn't be confined? Is there any way that we could do that?

Ra: I am Ra. It is unlikely.

Questioner: There's nothing that we can do? Is there any other possibility of using any techniques to help his eyesight?

Ra: I am Ra. No.

Questioner: Is this loss of eyesight … What is the metaphysical reason for the loss of eyesight? What brought it about?

Ra: I am Ra. In this case the metaphysical component is tiny. This is the condign catalyst of old age.

Questioner: Would the drops that you spoke of that would aid the eyesight … How much would they aid the eyesight if they were administered?

Ra: I am Ra. Over a period of applications the eyesight would improve somewhat, perhaps 20, perhaps 30%. The eye region would feel less tight. Balanced against this is rapidly increasing stiffness of motion so that the holding in a still position is necessarily quite uncomfortable.

Questioner: Then Ra thinks that the benefit derived from these drops would not be worth the cat's discomfort. This would probably … Is there any way that the cat could be given anesthetic and the drops put into the eyes so that the cat was not aware of them?

Ra: I am Ra. The harm done by putting the allopathic anesthetic into the body complex of this harvestable entity far overshadows the stillness accruing therefrom which would allow administration of medicaments.

Questioner: I'm sorry to belabor this subject so much, but I was really hoping to come up with something to help Gandalf. I assume then that Ra has suggested that we leave things as they are. How many applications of drops would be necessary to get some help for the eyes, roughly?

Ra: Approximately 40 to 60.

Questioner: Each day, or something like that?

Ra: I am Ra. Please expel breath over this instrument's breast.

(This was done as directed.)

Questioner: Is that satisfactory?

Ra: I am Ra. Yes.

Questioner: I had asked if the drops should be administered once per diurnal period. Is that correct?

Ra: I am Ra. This depends upon the allopathic physician from whom you receive them.

Questioner: What is the name of the drops?

Ra: I am Ra. We have a difficulty. Therefore, we shall refrain from answering this query.

Questioner: I am sorry to belabor this point. I am very concerned about the cat, and I understand that Ra recommends that we do not use the drops and we won't. I just wanted to know what it was that we weren't doing that would help the eyesight and I apologize for belaboring this point. I'll close just by asking Ra if there is any further recommendation that he could make with respect to this cat?

Ra: I am Ra. Rejoice in its companionship.

Questioner: When we got our introduction back from our publisher on the book which originally was called *The Law Of One*, in the introduction Carla had been speaking on reincarnation and there was this sentence added, "For although originally part of Jesus' teachings they were censored from all subsequent editions by the Empress." Would Ra please comment on the source of that being placed in our introduction?

Ra: I am Ra. This follows the way of subjectively interesting happenings, conditions, circumstances, or coincidences.

We would suggest one more full query at this time.

Questioner: Prior to the veiling process there was, I am assuming, no archetypical plan for the evolutionary process. It was totally left up to the free will of the mind/body/spirits to evolve in any way that they desired. Is this correct?

Ra: I am Ra. No.

I am Ra. We leave you in appreciation of the circumstances of the great illusion in which you now choose to play the pipe and timbrel and move in rhythm. We are also players upon a stage. The stage changes. The acts ring down. The lights come up once again. And throughout the grand illusion and the following and the following there is the undergirding majesty of the one infinite Creator. All is well. Nothing is lost. Go forth rejoicing in the love and the light, the peace and the power of the one infinite Creator. I am Ra. Adonai.

Sunday Meditation
July 31, 1983

(S channeling)

I am Hatonn, and greet you, my brothers and sisters, in the love and the light of the one infinite Creator. We thank you, my friends, for letting us be part of your gathering, to share your vibrations of love which so strongly fill this place this evening. My friends, it has indeed been a beautiful day. It has been a time of rejoicing, for there are indeed multitudes of your people who now seek peace, and desire to see that peace surround[ing] your planet bring more and more into a oneness with the Creator. This expression of the love of the Creator has grown, and we sincerely hope will continue to grow, for as your planet continually nears the harvest, this expression verbally and by thought will more and more increase your planet's vibratory level. My friends, we are so pleased and so happy to see this. It fills us with joy to see the oneness of your people expanding, for throughout the world there are groups such as yours who sit in meditation attempting to share this love further and further. There can be no greater service than this. As each strives to serve the Creator, each will indeed grow in that love.

We would like to transfer this contact at this time. I am Hatonn.

(Carla channeling)

I am Hatonn. I am now with this instrument and greet you once again in the love and the light of the infinite Creator. We shall continue.

We are aware that all may not seem to be full of peace and joy and love among your peoples. Indeed, the quality most desired from third density is its opacity. It is not intended that you be able to see through the illusion readily. We find in this instrument's mind the image of young men who play "King of the Mountain," and a game which this instrument calls "Chicken," and who run after anything in a skirt. We ask that you look at your countries, your national culture units. Those especially which concern you as you dwell within the reaches of your United States are that country and that which you call Russia. And as you look, you find these countries behaving as young men, each one daring the other, and playing chicken, and chasing any country in a skirt, so to speak. This is immature behavior developed by societal units which have not reached the age of wisdom and which wield power.

We are aware that this part of the illusion seems to declare a grave and malign influence that would deny not only love in its surface and shallow sense and all the good expressions that from it flow, such as peace and joy, but that which is at the root of love, that being the original Thought of the Creator. Yet that original Thought feeds the illusion with its acceptance of biased consciousness while remaining without that illusion. That which love is possesses the qualities which formulate your language's improbable attempt to describe singularity—that is light, power and compassion.

That which will occur among your peoples, and which is known among many as the harvest is not a function of an incarnational experience wherein certain factors seem to be ineuphonius. That harvest is a function of many unique portions of the Creator who [have] been conscious and who have been learning for many thousands of your years. The free will of each of those portions of consciousness shall draw a picture that is to come, and it shall draw it in a state of being that is outside your immediate, your illusion. It is as if we were to say that all that you see, measure, feel and touch has no value. This is not so, but it surely must seem as if this is what we are saying.

Can governments rise and fall? Can peoples think and err and sleep, and yet the harvest occur? Seemingly, this cannot be. And yet that which you and that which many are who shall be harvested in time/space in your, what you call, future shall be due to the rhythm and pulse of a portion of love which is intelligent and which has specifically and carefully detailed the circumstances which will surround this opportunity. Thus we say to you, there is far more peace, there are many more groups such as this one. We are overjoyed at the progress being made. There will be a harvest. That there will be any harvested at all is our joy.

We ask you to consider all the works of your hands, minds and your hearts, all the things which you may have built up for yourselves, all your appetites and your means of satisfying them, and we ask you to consider which of those things feeds that portion of yourself which is aligned most closely with the one original Thought, with love. The world about may do what it will. It cannot touch the work that you do mining, as it were, for a gold within yourselves. In meditation, in silence within lies information for those who wish information, inspiration for those who wish that, hope, *(inaudible)*, faith. All these are derivative of love, and feed back into love, and the key to your own progress towards your own harvest is first in your dedication to learning what the truth may be within you, and secondly to your decision to allow that love to radiate to those about you, not by what you do but by what you are.

We would very much like to use other channels within this group as we have not had a chance to exercise any of them for a period of your time. Therefore, we shall offer one thought and then move on to another channel. That one thought is all-important. We ask that you consider our words as you would consider the words of a friend or a neighbor. We have existed in consciousness coherently for some of what you would call time longer than you, and perhaps there are some viewpoints worth sharing. We hope so. That is why we are here. We hope that one or two may find our words useful. We have an equally strong hope that no one accepts our words or any words as infallible. The truth lies within you, and all must be brought before that great and mighty court. We would at this time transfer this contact. We thank this instrument. I am Hatonn.

(C channeling)

I am Hatonn, and am now with this instrument. There was some initial difficulty establishing contact with this instrument and [as] we have not been together for some time, we wish to speak but briefly through this instrument. We wish to ask you to remember that while you meditate within this group that [there are] those who, though not physically present, are with you at this time adding their energies to yours, for this group stretches far and has touched many. We have indeed been privileged to have been allowed the chance to speak to and through so many through your years. It has indeed been an opportunity for us to continue our growth as we attempt to serve as we may.

I am Hatonn, and would at this time like to transfer this contact to another instrument. I am Hatonn.

(K channeling)

I am Hatonn. We would close this evening by saying a very few words through this instrument. My friends, as you wish for peace, you can extend peace by being peaceful, and you bring joy by being joyful. And you extend love by loving. And one learns to be peaceful and joyful and loving by exercising the will, by choosing to be peaceful. We also have the ability to increase hate upon the planet by exercising hate. It's this simple, my friends. So when you pray for peace on your planet, we would ask that you remember there is one way for you to bring about that peace. So we leave this challenge with you, and may we repeat it has been a joy to be with you. We have missed your presence in meditation. And we leave you in the love and the light of the one infinite Creator. I am Hatonn.

(Jim channeling)

I am Latwii, and I greet you, my friends, in the love and in the light of our infinite Creator. It is our privilege once again to be called to your group in order that we might attempt to answer those queries which are with you. May we repeat the words of our brothers and sisters of Hatonn, and suggest that our words be viewed as those of a friend, for we are in no way infallible but wish only to serve as we are asked. May we then ask if we might begin with the first query?

M: I have a question I'd like for you to give me a little information [on]. We've had two epidemics, one of herpes and the other of AIDS, and I was wondering if it could be brought on—not that I would have anything against homosexuality, because I guess they're born that way—if they had a contact or two, but one man in the paper that had AIDS said that that he had had thirty-five contacts during a week. And that does almost seem ridiculous. And have these diseases been brought on as a warning?

I am Latwii, and am aware of your query, my sister. Though we may look at any such disease in general terms and give a description which may be satisfactory concerning its nature and purpose, we must preface this general description with the suggestion that each entity which experiences such a, as you call it, disease, has an unique configuration or lesson to learn within the general pattern. With that disclaimer we may suggest that the widespread profusion, shall we say, of these types of diseases of the sexual nature and function have, for those entities experiencing them, the general purpose of creating a bias towards the mated relationship, for it is the time of what you have called the harvest, yet few there are capable of being so harvested.

The catalyst, therefore, which aids in this evolution is by the choice of all on the subconscious level increased. One most efficient way for evolution to occur is through the mirroring process which the mated relationship provides the entity seeking adepthood as the purifying communication and honest observation describes in ever clearer terms the nature of the lessons to be learned. Each entity then is offered a greater and greater opportunity to accelerate the evolutionary process in the short time that remains upon your planet. When this opportunity is not fully utilized, there then comes the reminder. When certain entities have not utilized the opportunities which they chose before the incarnation to utilize, then they, in their subconscious beings, provide themselves with the symbolic reminder of that opportunity's need to be noticed.

Therefore, you will find upon your planet today, and especially this country within which you reside, the increasing experience of physical dysfunction related to the sexual energy transfers when made indiscriminately.

May we answer you further, my sister?

M: I wasn't exactly sure whether you felt that these diseases were brought on by not using good judgment or whether they were supposed to be helpful to the people.

I am Latwii, and shall attempt clarification. These diseases are reminders of an helpful nature potentially which serve to, shall we say, focus the attention of the entity who has not used catalyst for experience well in the thinking processes. Therefore, the catalyst is then given to the body where it might be noticed where it was ignored by the mind. This is to aid the evolutionary process.

May we answer you further?

M: No, I think that was very helpful.

I am Latwii, and we thank you, my sister, for your query. Is there another query at this time?

Carla: I just have a small one. Ra said that the foundation ray, the red-ray energy center, is almost never blocked because it's the foundation. Are these diseases largely due to orange-ray blockage, in terms of energy centers?

I am Latwii, and am aware of your query, my sister. The blockage is again unique for each entity, yet there are certain general characteristics which may be described. Some experience the combination of orange and blue-ray blockage, these centers focusing respectively upon the relationship of self with an other self and the clear communication with that other self. Others will include the green-ray energy center, and the need to unblock the compassion for acceptance circuitry. …

(Side one of tape ends.)

(Jim channeling)

I am Latwii, and am once again with this instrument. To continue. The orange-ray energy center is that which is often combined in such diseases with the green-ray energy center as the entity needs to open the circuitry which leads to compassion, and is utilizing, or wishes to utilize, one other self in that effort. There may also be instances in which the yellow-ray energy center is blocked in conjunction with any of the aforementioned centers as it deals with the acceptance of all other selves with which the entity has common exchange, shall we say.

May we answer you further, my sister?

Carla: Just to clarify. So you're saying that the orange-ray blockage which is basically fear of possession, fear of being possessed, or desire to be possessed, or desire to possess, is usually overlaid by also a lack of clear communication or also a lack of compassion, that it shows up in the genital area which seems like if it were orange and blue it would show up in a different part of the body. I was confused by that. Is that correct, what I'm saying? Is that a clarification of what you said, fear of possession, etc., overlaid by lack of compassion, or inability to speak clearly, or no desire to speak clearly?

I am Latwii, and am aware of your query, my sister. Your restatement of our observation is reasonably accurate. There is for each entity a simple series of attitudes in relation to love which need the learning within this illusion. Each energy center has its part to play in the refinement of this learning. The diseases spoken of this evening offer themselves as catalyst when certain avenues of opportunity have been ignored. Therefore, one may look at each energy center and the balance of each with each and find an unique configuration for each entity, though your description is in broad terms reasonably accurate.

May we answer you further, my sister?

Carla: I'm just curious about one thing. The description which you've given of the things that are blocked and the disease that occurs seems to be a disease that occurs to positively-oriented people. The negative polarity would be using sexuality in a completely different way? Is that correct?

I am Latwii, and am aware of your query, my sister. This statement would be correct for those of the negative path who are consciously following that path with a great degree of purity. Many upon that path are unaware of the required purity, and therefore experience similar manifestations of this disease as do those upon the positive path.

May we answer you further, my sister?

Carla: No, thank you.

I am Latwii, and we thank you, my sister. Is there another query at this time?

K: Yes, Latwii, a totally different thought. I want to make a statement about a dream I had, and then get an opinion. Recently I was dreaming, it was sort of haphazard dreaming and didn't have very much content after I woke up it seemed, but in the midst of this dreaming, I was aware of the plant in my living room having lost a leaf or two. When I went to bed the leaves had not fallen, but in the midst of this dreaming I become aware that the leaves have fallen off of the plant, but it isn't clear in the dream that they are my plants, I'm just aware that some leaves have fallen off of somebody's plants. And then I go on with this sort of haphazard dreaming. When I woke up it was as if I walked directly to one of my potted plants in my bedroom, and lo and behold, there were two leaves that had fallen from that plant, and it looked just like the leaves I had seen while I was asleep. Now this is my question. Was my subconscious mind aware of what happened or is this sort of an indication of the unity of all things? Would you make a comment about that?

I am Latwii, and am aware of your query, my sister. We may comment by agreeing with both suppositions; that, indeed, the sub- or unconscious mind has knowledge of all that which it is one with, which of course is all things. We may further suggest that there are occasionally instances of such a communication from the subconscious mind to the conscious mind for the purpose of reminding the entity that it has great resources at its disposal.

May we answer you further, my sister?

K: Yes, I'd like to push that just one little bit further. Then, that being the case, then it's possible that my subconscious mind or the unconscious mind could pick up something, well, say, something that happened across the other side of the world as far as that goes. It would be possible, I think this is what I'm trying to say, then it would be possible for the subconscious mind to pick up something anywhere? Is that right?

I am Latwii, and am aware of your query, my sister. It is indeed possible for such to occur, and indeed this is not as unusual a situation as one may think, for often such insights, shall we say, occur to an entity yet in a form which is not easily recognizable. So the conscious mind then is constantly privy to a multitude of signals, most of which are filtered out by the focus of the attention. Therefore, to most precisely become aware of another portion of the self seemingly hidden from the conscious mind requires a fastidiousness in the focus of attention which you may liken to your tuning process that is used before each of these meditations.

May we answer you further, my sister?

K: No, thank you very much, but I have another question. It's on a different subject. I read a book recently about the Masters of Shasta supposedly who have met people from time to time in the astral body. And supposedly this mountain has been a very important place to those who are capable, shall we say, or desirous of spiritual experience. Would you comment on that, the Masters of Mount Shasta?

I am Latwii, and am aware of your query, my sister. It is often the case that certain areas or portions of a planetary are so situated that the web of, shall we say, love/light or prana which surrounds your planet may find an easy entrance point. The location of which you speak, and many others as well, is such a point. To be considered as well in this particular situation is the additional fact that many of your peoples who seek the one Creator, having become aware of this point, then also invest this point with the power and purity of their cumulative seeking, thereby enhancing the possibility of such contacts you have described briefly.

Therefore, we have two equally important factors which permit the, shall we say, experience that is not ordinary upon your planet, that is, the physical location at an energy nexus or vortex and the investment of that place by the seeking of, shall we say, the pilgrims.

May we answer you further, my sister?

K: So, you're saying that even the seeker increased the power or the, yes, that even the seeker increased the power on Mt. Shasta, it was not only a point where the contact could be made, but the seekers themselves enhanced the power. Is that what you're saying?

I am Latwii, and am aware of your query, my sister. This is correct. May we answer you further?

K: No, thank you. That's very good, thank you.

I am Latwii. We thank you. Is there another query at this time?

K: Yes. On that very thing. We've read so much about the gurus of the Himalayan mountains, and especially in Tibet. And I'm assuming that the mountains were—because of their height and all—were a good place to make spiritual contact, but I'm assuming the seekers have increased the power in the Himalayan mountains so that it is a very spiritual place. Is that true, also?

I am Latwii, and am aware of your query, my sister. This is correct. The thought that a place is of a certain nature need not be initially correct in order for the place to become of that nature when such thoughts continue to manifest in such and such a manner. To summarize, remember that each thought is a thing which exists in what you may call time/space, and may be brought into your coordinate system, shall we say, by the continued thinking of that thought.

May we answer you further, my sister?

K: Then some of these gurus really have lived to be more than four or five hundred years old because of the power that has been generated in these mountains? Is that true?

I am Latwii, and am aware of your query, my sister. Only indirectly, my sister, is this statement true. The power of such an area aids the evolutionary progress of the seeker, yet it is the faith and will of the seeker that is the most important ingredient in, shall we say, achieving the goal. When the love and the light of the one Creator has been contacted, shall we say, by the adept, and when the adept consciously becomes aware of its unity with all creation, then such phenomena as the living for what seems to be an extraordinary length of years becomes a side effect of that contact with unity by the adept in such a place.

May we answer you further, my sister?

K: No, that's very good. That makes sense. Thank you very much.

I am Latwii. We thank you, my sister. Is there another query at this time?

K: Does the instrument have enough energy to answer one more question?

I am Latwii, and am aware of this query, my sister. We find this instrument is able to be utilized for another query or two. Is there another query at this time?

K: I'd like for somebody else to ask a question if they like. If not, I have one more question. I was in the bookstore the other day and I read a part of a book by Ruth Montgomery. The title of the book is *The Threshold of Tomorrow*. And she's talking about the numerous walk-ins on the planet today, and she's even bold enough to mention the names. In her first book, *Strangers Among Us*, she withheld the information, but in this book she's very bold to mention the names of people we know who are walk-ins, and they are here for the express purpose of helping the planet through the crises. Would you comment on that?

I am Latwii, and am aware of your query, my sister. We can only make general response for it is not our desire to speak to the specific validity, shall we say, of any living entity's efforts, for we do not wish to be the judge, that is, for those who read such information. The phenomena of what has been described as the walk-in entity is a phenomenon which is occurring upon your planet but is, shall we say, much rarer in its manifestations than is imagined by many who write upon and consider such possibilities. It is a situation which is most rare, for the third-density being which agrees to leave this illusion and allow its physical vehicle to be inhabited by another density's entity is one which willingly forgoes the opportunities of continuing its incarnation and does progress in some manner, yet will find its progression for the, shall we say, short run, greatly ended. There are a few who would push to partake in such an exchange for that reason unless there was a greater service which could be provided by so partaking.

May we answer you further, my sister?

K: No, thank you.

I am Latwii, and we find that the energies are dwindling within this instrument, and therefore we shall take our leave of this instrument and this group. We leave you, my friends, rejoicing in the unity which we share. Remember that we are with you in your meditations at your request and rejoice in being able to blend our vibrations with yours. We are known to you as those of Latwii, and we leave you now in the love and the light of the one infinite Creator. Adonai, my friends. Adonai vasu borragus.

(Carla channeling)

I am Nona. We greet you in love and light. We are having difficulty maintaining contact with this instrument. We have been called to send healing vibrations to the one known as M. We request of those who call that the call be repeated that ye may establish contact with this instrument. We shall pause.

(Pause)

We thank you and after we finish with our sounds, we shall leave you in love and light.

(Carla channels a vocal melody from Nona.)

Sunday Meditation
August 8, 1983

(Unknown channeling)

I greet you, my friends, in the love and in the light of our infinite Creator. To be with you is an exquisite pleasure and we thank you for requesting our presence. The opportunity to share our thoughts with you is the greatest opportunity for which we could ask.

We should like to offer philosophical thoughts and *(inaudible)* and we shall move from one channel to another with some frequency and therefore we suggest that if you have *(inaudible)* and challenged us mentally that you may dispense with the beginning and ending greetings until the end of this session.

Once upon a time there was a wooded *(inaudible)*, a beautiful leafy glade and within that small forest lived many creatures that you would call spirits of nature; others have called them fairies and elves. To them *(inaudible)* smallest *(inaudible)* was as a towering tree and the red clover was enough to make *(inaudible)*. We shall transfer.

(Unknown channeling)

(Rest of tape is inaudible.)

Sunday Meditation
August 14, 1983

(Carla channeling)

[I am Hatonn,] and I greet you in the love and light of our infinite Creator. We have been blending with your group for some time, and we thank you for the great privilege of being able to speak through this instrument, and to share our humble thoughts with you. We would speak with you this lovely evening about that which you may call discipline. Many and many are the sources and the messages which you may read or hear which are of an inspirational nature which express to you the perfection, the unity of the present moment. And many are the blissful moments that you may gain from taking in such beautiful and consoling thoughts. So far from being sarcastic are we that we would suggest that you make a practice of availing yourself of this idealism, this beauty, this vision of perfection, and unity on a daily basis, not only through meditation but insofar as you find it helpful through inspirational works.

However, if you do seek truly, you will find that inspiration carries with it a mandate for action, and it is that action which takes a discipline of the inner self. Such disciplines are not much understood in your culture. The discipline of the mind, the character, the personality, is hardly recognized unless it bears substantial and obvious fruit in the social life, and is therefore not much valued by that cultural web in which you find yourself experiencing the illusion at this time. However, without the discipline to take responsibility for what knowledge you have gained, you will find yourself on a treadmill, and you will in the end be disillusioned, if you will excuse the pun, and you will consider that all the inspirational writings and speeches that you have heard are foolish and that there is no use in them.

When we speak to you of love and light and peace, we do not expect to do anything more than to inspire you to begin or to intensify your own efforts at seeking, that probing the unknown which holds within it the treasure which you call the truth. And as you seek you will find on your own a subjectively interwoven series of apparent truths. If you do not claim them as you discover them, they will escape you, and you will have to discover them again and again and again. If you claim that which you know and begin the unending attempt to manifest within your being that which you have learned, then you shall proceed, and the penetration of the illusion which hides from you the true nature of love will be accelerated accordingly.

My friends, it is so easy to think that the feast, the love, and the unity that you experience in moments of inspiration will be a natural fruit of your attempting to manifest these qualities through your being. However, this is far from the truth. When you choose to seek the truth, you embark upon a very personal journey, and one which will differ from person to person because of the unique nature of each being. Therefore, the first fruit of seeking may well be dissension, and the peace that you find will only be found at the end of a process of communication that may be very painful. When you seek the truth, you are acting as a creation inspired by an ideal. You move according to the winds of your own particular needs and energies, and those closest to you, if they are also seeking, shall also be in motion.

Perhaps you may look with dismay upon this first fruit of seeking, and yet we say to you it is entirely necessary within third density to use the illusion in order to open communication to the level of spiritual verbalizations. If you have a disagreement, count yourself blessed, for you may then use your manifested seeking to turn towards another self openly and fearlessly. Without seeking and grasping the principles of the discipline of the self, it is almost impossible to communicate clearly and with a minimum of bias. The chance to do so is precious indeed, and because success is so hard won it is worth a great deal. We come among you only as brothers and sisters and do not wish to add to your burdens, but we do challenge you to retain that fine sense of the ideal, that great seeking for the one original Thought, while gazing with a clear and careful eye upon each situation that seems to be quite out of keeping with all the effort and all the love you have given to that situation.

Do not let your heart falter because there are great difficulties, minor disagreements, or poor feelings. Know that your third density is doing what you planned for it to do, and now is your chance to use it wisely. When you were a child, did your parent see fit to discipline you? How much more wise is your higher self which offers you disciplines. You are not weak to be patient or poor in heart to strive for cheerfulness. You are not failing your brother or your sister when you step back from a confrontation that would leave a brother on one side and a sister upon another, and strive to reestablish by clear communication through dissension the final understanding that you are one being. If you have compassion, then you must seek discipline.

We shall at this time show some discipline by refraining from exercising the other instruments within this domicile, for they have come to listen and to be refreshed. Take refreshment from all that you can. Drink deep in the glory and the beauty that is around you, but do not feel betrayed by apparent disharmony. Isn't it just like you, each of you, seekers all, to plan for yourself some hard times, some rough knocks, so that you might more clearly express your grasp of the truth and your penetration of all apparent separation.

We give this instrument a vision it does not understand. This instrument sees the hammer descending upon the anvil and the rock breaking. We attempt to say to this instrument that that which is not tempered will break. Go through the fire of experience willingly, my friends, and be tempered a bit at a time, that with experience you may bend and learn and become stronger, and serve more and more that great ideal that you so cherish. On the surface the spiritual path seems poetic and dramatic and will attract many who will become weak-hearted. Know, my friends, the spiritual path is for those who are tough and wish to become tougher. Perfect compassion involves an unbelievable personal discipline, for how in this great illusion can you naturally believe that all others are one with you?

We of Hatonn are one with you. This we know. We offer our vibration to you during meditation. You need but mentally request it. We thank each of you for the opportunity of joining a circle of light that expands until the universe rings, for in joining as a group, you join light with light and the resulting energy is monumental, and that which you would not believe. But we say to you, you aid the planet and you aid us as we learn in our service to the One. We commend, as always, meditation on a daily basis, and so leave. We are those of Hatonn. Adonai vasu. We leave you in the love and the light of the One Who is All.

(Jim channeling)

I am Latwii, and I greet you, my friends, in the love and in the light of our infinite Creator. It is our special pleasure and privilege to greet each of you this evening. We thank you, as always, for requesting our presence. We come as humble messengers of love and light, and of the unity of the creation of the one Creator. We hope that our service of attempting to answer your queries will provide you with some small amount of aid and food for thought. We remind each that our words are but our opinions, most fallible, yet offered with a great desire to be of service. May we then ask for the first query?

Carla: Dr. B has an electrical machine, and she's unwilling to use it on me until she gets a reading. Can I ask you about it or do I need to ask Ra?

I am Latwii, and am aware of your query and desire, my sister. The machine of which you speak is of potential aid if used with the proper mental attitude. This attitude is most necessary for it is the, shall we say, force or enabler which you will use to form the channel through which the healing energies will be able to move. More than this we cannot say without infringement. The attitude is of your construction of necessity in order for it be most efficacious.

May we answer you further, my sister?

Carla: Is there any setting on the machine which would be harmful or should I ask Ra? This is information she specifically asked for.

I am Latwii, and am aware of your query, my sister. There are certain settings, as you call them, which may prove less than helpful. There is a certain intuitive grasp which is necessary for the one known as B that can be used to determined these settings. We cannot speak as to the specific setting, for it is not within the nature of this type of contact to be able to transmit information of such specificity.

Carla: Okay, then all I have to ask Ra is just a very specific question about settings. Good. One more little question. After the one thing she did on me, I experienced a good deal of pain in the general area of my kidneys which was outside the general area of back spasms which I've had an unrelated problem with. I suspected quite strongly that what had happened was I had released into my body too many toxins and I had failed to drink enough water. Could you confirm that?

I am Latwii, and am aware of your query, my sister. We may say that this assumption has a large degree of correctness. There is also the shaping, shall we say, of the proper mental attitude of which we spoke previously which would aid in the use of this instrument. This again we recommend as a topic for your pondering and meditation.

May we answer you further, my sister?

Carla: No, thank you. I appreciate your going right up against the Law of Free Will with the information [I wanted].

I am Latwii. We thank you, my sister, for your seeking and your understanding. Is there another query at this time?

A1: Yes, Latwii. I've got a situation which has been occurring for the past three or four weeks. And, well, I'll be explaining it to you, but I'd like to have some reasons of why it might be happening, if you can help. What it is, is during the Friday night meditations after the tuning, I can hear the first words of, "I am Hatonn," and then a few seconds later I hear, "I am Hatonn, and we now leave you," then I hear, "I am Latwii, and we greet you," and then I hear, "I am Latwii and we leave you." And the whole meditation appears to take about five minutes. And once we have sent love and light, I have this problem of using—from the elbow down—my arms. It takes about ten minutes to regenerate the hands. The first week I kind of let it go by, and the second week I thought I might just be exhausted and sleeping through it, but with this many occurrences I'm beginning to question whether or not something else might be going on. And I've it given it thought, and I can't come up with anything, so I'm asking now. Can you help?

I am Latwii, and am aware of your query, my sister. We may be of some small aid in this area by suggesting that each who joins a circle of seeking such as this circle will take from the information given that which has meaning to the entity. Each will hear in some fashion that is most helpful to that entity's journey of seeking the truth, no matter what is spoken and generally available. In your particular case, the turn of your mind and seeking of recent time, as you call it, desires that nourishment which is of a most unique and personal nature. Therefore, it is the case that you seem not to hear the words, yet upon a deeper level receive the sustenance, and are not consciously aware of the information verbally transmitted. This is your pattern of seeking at this time. The process entails a somewhat deeper level of meditation which may have as an aftereffect the numbing or the making inoperable of certain portions of the physical vehicle.

May we answer you further, my sister?

A1: One more thing. I don't think I am, but I just want to make sure that I'm not causing any negative action within the group, or also, you know, a reverse effect of hindering anyone else's growth by not being fully conscious during the meditation.

I am Latwii, and am aware of your query, my sister. To aid a group such as this one in the shared seeking, it is most fundamentally necessary for each entity to seek as purely as possible. The method of seeking is of lesser importance. Therefore, if each comes to the circle of seeking with a desire which is as pure as possible, and comes [with] a mind that is as open as possible, and a heart which accepts each other self, then the fundamental requirements for aiding in the shared seeking are met. It is, of course, helpful to remain in a non-trance state in such a circle, for the proper protection for that special type of seeking is not provided in such a circle.

May we answer you further, my sister?

A1: Latwii, thank you, you've helped a lot. Now I don't have any more questions.

I am Latwii. We thank you, my sister, for your service. Is there another question at this time?

Carla: I'd like to check up on A1. I was wondering if the problem with the lower arms could be mechanical. I've got some of the same problems that she does with the arthritis, and I've found that propping up my elbows has helped my comfort after the sessions quite a bit. Do you think that it is this same syndrome of arthritis in the joints and lessened circulation and nerve function that may be the aftereffects of being in one position for too long?

I am Latwii, and am aware of your query, my sister. These are helpful suggestions, and we may concur in our estimation of their correctness. The joints which have the poor circulation and which must withstand motionless periods for some time are more susceptible to the numbing effect and difficulty in use after the motionless period is ended. The one known as A1 may experiment with different …

(Side one of tape ends.)

Carla: *(Inaudible).*

(Jim channeling)

I am Latwii, and am with this instrument once again. Our puns are often unnoticed, and we appreciate the notice. We will now resume with the asking for the next query.

Questioner: What can we do to help A2 during this crisis that she's in now?

I am Latwii, and am aware of your query, my sister. As those entities about you move through their incarnations, there will be those times in which it seems as though great difficulties threaten their being and the continuance of the incarnation in a stable fashion. To be of the greatest aid to any entity which is undergoing that which is seen as difficult or traumatic, it is first most helpful to look in what might be described as the overview, that is, to see the entity being presented with an opportunity for greatly accelerated growth. It may not be understood in the smallest degree just how the growth will occur, yet in a universe of unity, there is nothing but opportunity for the realization and expression of that unity by each entity.

Therefore, if you can, begin your efforts with this view and you will note a greater ease in the attempt to aid an other self which seeks assistance. Then if you can, radiate or communicate to this other self your vision of the perfection of the opportunity, and the assurance that all not only will be well, but all is at this moment well. Then you and the other self stand upon the bedrock of truth as well as it can be understood in this illusion which seems so difficult and threatening from time to time.

If then you can refine further your efforts of service by seeking in your own meditative state that which might be most helpful to the entity, and share this assistance with love and acceptance of the entity, the situation, and without a dedication to any particular outcome, then you will have given a gift which is most helpful in that it is given freely, with love and with concern.

May we answer you further, my sister?

Questioner: No, you've been very helpful.

I am Latwii. We thank you, my sister. Is there another query at this time?

(Pause)

I am Latwii, and though we feel there are still several queries forming themselves, we feel that it is the appropriate time to take our leave of this group, and perhaps have the honor of attempting these queries when they are more firmly formed. We thank each in this group for seeking our humble service. We are with each in meditation upon request and are most honored to be able to blend our vibrations at any time our presence is requested. We leave you now, my friends, in the all-encompassing love, and the clear shining light of the one infinite Creator which resides in each portion of your being and within all creation. We rejoice with you in the truth of our unity. Our blessings and peace be with you. We are known to you as those of Latwii. Adonai, my friends. Adonai vasu borragus.

(Carla channeling)

I am Nona. We greet you in love and in light, and for several requests we offer the sounds through this instrument of a healing nature.

(Carla channels a beautiful vocal melody without words from Nona.) ❧

Sunday Meditation
August 21, 1983

(Carla channeling)

[I am Latwii,] and I greet you in the love and in the light of the one infinite Creator. We are most pleased to have been called to speak through this instrument without the answering of questions for the moment and hope that we may serve you. We greet and bless each and surround each with love, for surely this circle is beautiful in its clarity of seeking and the light that emanates from that seeking, and that identity which you have forged as a group which gives you a life beyond yourself which is that of the light source which is of great planetary aid.

We cannot ever express too much the importance of the dedication of each to the mutual seeking of truth, the discriminating gaze upon all materials which may aid the seeker and the sincere desire to be kindly affectioned one to another. For as you love one another, so shall you be illuminated, so shall your group be illuminated, and so shall your sphere be illuminated. The nature of seeking develops within the seeker that which is far beyond the individual and the personal in its nature. You may indeed find portions of your being becoming impersonal in that you gaze at the particular and personal circumstances which engage your attention within the illusion you enjoy, and draw from that illusory experience impersonal and general conclusions which may seem to the casual observer to have little to do with the circumstances.

We find the great majority of your people still waiting for an awakening. We are not concerned with those who do not wish to awaken. We have not come here to serve by persuasion but only by request. We do not wish to persuade the sleeper to awaken, the sluggish to become adroit, the negative to become positive. We wish only to lay before you a vision, a view, an ideal, if you would, which is our experience of the creation and the Creator at this time which makes for us the life that we choose to lead, and the illusion that we choose to experience. This we share with you in the awareness that as others have done for us when we were as you, so now may we serve as those who speak of those concepts which you may wish to consider which form the construction of the philosophy and practical ethic by which we have our being choose our actions. And so we continue, my friends.

We give you a view of joyful and merry universe resounding with the hearty and never ending laughter of the Creator that loves to experience Itself and to learn about Itself from Itself, a Creator that is doing just that through us and through each of you. Therefore, we bring to you a framework in which you may see your illusion as a unified experience in which those things you term good, those things you term bad, and those things which you term neutral are all blessed by one light. That light is the light of the Creator creating, experiencing and learning about Itself. When you open your eyes, you are opening the eyes of the Creator. No less judgment can you make about yourself, for consciousness is one and you are conscious. You are also unique due to your experiences which by the role of the free will many times over has made you the being that is of the Creator, of the version which is you.

As you look out of your eyes, the eyes that you meet are those of the Creator. It is sometimes difficult to penetrate the illusion that the eyes into which you look are those of the malcontent, the murderer, the rapist, the evil man, the anyone who does not meet with the standards you have set up for yourselves in order to make an order of the illusion. However, all of these people are the Creator, and not a splinter of the Creator, for that is the manifestation, but the Creator in wholeness, for that is the root of the conscious mind. Therefore, you cannot say, "This is a splinter, this is a portion, this is a spark of the Creator, and the light has been greatly distorted in this part of the creation," without causing a distortion in your understanding. You must see that each is the Creator, totally and wholly and without hindrance of any kind. The remainder is a manifested illusion.

We began by speaking with you of the light which you generate as a group. This is an appropriate concept to consider in each relationship which you enjoy. If you have the faith in another being that each of you manifests in each other at this moment, you will then be able to vibrate in harmony with each entity, even as the entity seems to be straying from the light which you prize and which you jealously guard.

We ask that you perform two processes when you engage in relationship with another being. Firstly, you must realize that you are the Creator. The center of your being is whole, and you do not need any thing, neither emotion nor material nor any other manifestation from another, for you are perfect as you are. The release which this will give to you in your somewhat less than ideal condition will be substantial, for if you do not need anything, then you are free to listen, and to discover what you may do to be of service to another, and to work in harmony with another as you are now working in harmony in order that this instrument may be used as a channel, and have the energy to transmit this message.

To continue this first process through to the logical conclusion will cost you a bit of time, perhaps no more than a second or two, and preferably, in order to cause the momentary centering process to be minimal, a daily period of meditation in order that the center is always on view.

The second process is the free and willing giving of the attention to the Creator which is manifested to you. This is where your reactions will sometimes seem to be unresponsive to a situation. You may seem detached or happy when sadness was expected, as you listen and gather the harvest of harmony with another and celebrate that unity by seeing in a greater perspective the ebb and flow of an entity's life as it moves in perfect freedom. Regardless of whether you are understood or misunderstood, the valuable light generated by seeing the Creator and coming into harmony with the Creator in your dealings with others is still the same. The only way in which that light can be multiplied is if the one whom you listened to gives the same honor to you in return. Ah, then the light is tremendous.

In no case can your light be taken from you, for you have within you all of creation, all the light, all the world. You are unity. To say you are a part of the Creator is confused. To say you are the Creator is confused. You see, my friends, language is a poor thing, and we are poor at using it as you well know, but the joy that is a portion of the release felt by the vision of the Creator lovingly at work in dealing with self is immeasurable.

We offer these thoughts to you that you may consider and take that which is good, leaving, of course, those things which we have said badly or wrongly in your estimation. You must know we have only opinion to offer. We could speak in grand terms and pretty language and perhaps even through this instrument using this method tend to set up a method of convincing you that we were sure and invincible in our truth and our prophecy. But why would we wish to do that, my friends? We have not worked through the densities that we have accomplished in order to influence people. We have come to our present experience because, in part, others gave us things to consider, visions to see, ideals to dream when we were in situations that did not seem ideal or seemed unbalanced, tame, boring and quiet.

You see, my friends, those who have a settled existence wish to be gypsies, and those who are troubled wish to be peaceful. That is the balancing self, and each shall experience the other extreme again and again until the desires are seen for what they are, that is, a portion of the great balance of experience that is available for those upon the positive path, as it has often been called. We wish you the joy of that positive path, and assure [you with] our thought that as you wish to be light beings, so you are. It is not a *(inaudible)* for most to keep the vision the self as Creator, and other self as Creator dancing forever within the mind, but you may grow closer and closer to that ideal and of the seeking, for the truth of our statements will inevitably bring you closer and closer to this very realization, for in the end, this realization is all that there is: we are one; we are the Creator; we are love manifested as light.

This instrument was not expecting this contact, and we have had a good time using this instrument, and staying very serious, and giving you all kinds of good advice, and hopefully [you will] remember not to care anything about our opinion but only your own opinion. We thank you for allowing us to share our thoughts with you outside of the question and answer format, but there was a calling for this information such as it is.

We would like to exercise those channels which may wish to avail themselves of this opportunity before we attempt to answer any queries. Therefore, we would at this time with a sweeping bow, as this instrument would say, leave this instrument in order that we may exercise others. I am Latwii.

(S channeling)

I am Latwii, and we greet you, my dear friends, once again in the love and the light of the one infinite Creator. As usual, we have had to nearly knock over this instrument, and we apologize for the delay but this [was] her request, and we are happy to oblige. We are, as we have stated, so happy to join you and share in the love and love and light that is present here this evening. It is our sincere hope that we have brought a small amount of light and love into the love and light that is in much abundance here this evening. We are honored that you have invited us here this evening, and, as always, we are grateful for the opportunity to share those moments that we find so enjoyable in this group. We shall leave this instrument and attempt to make ourselves known to another. We leave you momentarily. I am Latwii.

(Carla channeling)

I am Latwii, and am again with this instrument. We find that the three creators we have not spoken through this evening are requesting that a little more experience be given them before the grand Latwii debut occur and we concur. We are grateful that we have had the chance to work with each and are pleased with the contact that we were able to initiate. We must admit we are not the easiest contact for some to tune into as we are a narrow band compared to, for instance, Hatonn or Laitos, those which each is familiar with in the usual course of meditation.

We therefore wish to assure that the next time that you see your friend lying beneath the felled tree, even though the friend thinks that you are lazy when you say how lucky you are to get all that catalyst, you must bear up and retain your own opinions of the nature of the creation. However, we suggest that you not be quite that extreme or you may not be able to share your perceptions with anyone except trained psychological personnel.

In merriness and joy we leave you in order that we may answer a question or two through the instrument known as Jim. You know that we leave you in love and in light, for what choice do we have, my friends? If we left you in apples and sausages, it would still be love and light. All else is an illusion, a beautiful rhythmic tapestry of color and rhythm to which you put the pattern. May your patterns be beautiful. We are those of Latwii. We give you adonai as lecturers, and yield to the question and answer format. I am Latwii.

(Jim channeling)

I am Latwii, and I greet you, my friends, once again in love and light or apples and sausages. We are pleased to once again find ourselves in our customary role of attempting to answer those queries which are important to you this evening. May we then begin with the first query?

K: Well, as usual, it seems my role to start the questions, and by the way, apples and sausages fit together. I was very interested in what Latwii said about seeing everyone as a part of the Creator, and intellectually I think I can buy that. I certainly can see the Creator in the rose and the tree, etc., etc. But I'm going through a real hard time right now. My husband has always been lazy in mind and in body, and I had not been aware of how lazy until his retirement. And I'm just having a hard time with time in seeing the Creator in him right this minute. And if you've got any pointers for me—now I know you're not going to solve my problem for me, but if you've got any hints as how I can see the Creator in what I perceive as laziness, would you comment on that?

I am Latwii, and am aware of your query, my sister, and shall indeed attempt a comment. As we look upon your planet and the peoples that inhabit it, we see many variations of perception and behavior. We see the illusion which bars clear-seeing from each eye, and we see somewhat the purpose for the bar. For each entity to look deeply at each other entity is necessary in order that a truer nature of being be discovered. The experience which results from the true seeking, the arduous seeking, is experience of great value, for it is hard won, and much difficulty has been overcome. As you look at this entity of which you speak, and see that which you describe as the laziness, you see that which is not a prominent portion of your own being as you now manifest your beingness. You see that which has little, shall we say, good press amongst your peoples and certainly that which is seldom attributed …

(Side one of tape ends.)

(Jim channeling)

I am Latwii, and am once again with this instrument. To continue, my sister. That aspect which you call laziness is indeed a manifestation of the one Creator, for there is a great portion of the one infinite Creator which is not manifest, which has not moved into the creation, which seeks not action, accomplishes no work, and simply exists [in] the fullness of its being. In your illusion, when such beingness is exhibited it is seldom understood even by those which exhibit its nature. In truth, my sister, there is little understanding for any manifestation of beingness or of action within your illusion. Understanding, indeed, is quite seldom found in your illusion, for as we previously spoke, there is a great bar upon the clear seeing. This is necessary that the experiences which you learn within this illusion might be hard-won, and being hard-won might then carry more weight within the total beingness which is your birthright and which is the one Creator.

Therefore, as you look at the entity of which you spoke, you see not a portion of the Creator. You see the one Creator manifesting a portion of Itself which plays a part in the great lessons of balance which are so important within your illusion. You do not see so you may see. You do not understand so you may understand.

May we answer you further, my sister?

K: No. I understand it academically or intellectually, and will work on it emotionally. Thanks a lot, Latwii.

M: Latwii. I would like to discuss this a little further because I would be a person who if you wanted to be judgmental would be called lazy. But really you should say they lack energy. And the truth of the matter, anybody would rather move than sit, if they had energy. So, instead of having sympathy for a lack of energy in a person, isn't lazy a judgmental term?

I am Latwii, and am aware of your query, my sister. It may not only be said to be a, as you said, term of judgment, but might also be somewhat inaccurate. It might be the case that the entity does not suffer from a lack of energy, but has chosen for some reason not to express the energy and has chosen not to move into activity for the nature of its lessons require that type of inactivity that might be viewed by some as laziness, and the lessons available in such an environment might include the entity accepting the judgment of others as being lazy and learning to love and accept those who seem not to love and accept the entity.

May we answer you further, my sister?

M: No, I think you've clarified it for me.

Carla: I'd like to ask a question. I'm still pondering a little bit because in the Ra material we've learned over and over again that when you see something in another person, it is the person acting as a mirror for you, and the longer you've been with that person, the clearer the mirror. Now, I see no way in which I can possibly view K as lazy or lacking energy or any other way you want to describe. My guess is that hers is a perfectly accurate term, meaning that there is energy available, but the guy who chooses not to use it, he's still asleep, right? I understand that this is a lesson, but how is this acting as a mirror for her? How is her nature mirrored by such a diametric opposite?

I am Latwii, and am aware of your query, my sister. The great Law of Free Will prohibits a specific explication upon this point, for, indeed, it is true that each entity is a mirror for each other, and points the way to the lessons which need the learning and the balance. For an entity to look upon another and see that which does not seem acceptable is a part of the process of learning to accept either in the self or in an other self that which seems unacceptable. It may be that the entity unable to accept certain behavior has that behavior within the self and needs therefore to accept it both in the self and in an other self. To others who know both entities, it may seem that only one exhibits the behavior which is not acceptable. Many are the distortions in perception, especially within those entities which seek the balance. It may also be that the entity which cannot accept a certain behavior is merely refining the acceptance of another entity, and is using a certain behavior to trigger full acceptance.

May we answer you further, my sister?

Carla: No, thank you. That was fine—good.

I am Latwii. We thank you, my sister. We are always pleased to be of some service, however small. Is there another query at this time?

S: Yes, Latwii. I realize it's getting late so feel free to make your answer brief. I have a very complex question which I have been sitting here all night trying to formulate into words. So I will just ask you to please sift through them, and do what you can do. What I'm looking for is insight. I'm experiencing difficulty with discipline. I have trouble meditating on a daily basis. I meditate easily and enjoyably when I'm with a group, but it's very difficult for me to discipline myself to go in the bedroom by myself, you know, at a given time on a daily basis and meditate. That's half of the question or problem. The other deals along the same lines, discipline or will power. In this instance I'm talking about things like smoking, overeating, lack of exercise, drinking too much. I know these are catalysts, and I need to meditate to work these things out. But if you can give me any information or insight into any, well, like I said, sift through the words, and is there anything you can tell me at all?

I am Latwii, and am aware of your query, my sister. We have completed our sifting, and view that which we may. Now we believe we may begin. The topic of discipline is one which deserves a great deal of attention, and we feel we shall not do it justice in our response but shall make an attempt, for the discipline of the personality is the great work of all densities. It begins within that illusion which you now inhabit. To focus the attention of the mind is to control, to use a poor term, a great power, a creative force of infinite potential. That this force begins in what seems as chaos in undifferentiated focus is fitting, for its eventual goal is to be single-pointed, and to lead the seeker on that path which has been called straight and narrow.

But before such can occur, much exploration must precede that fine focusing. It is necessary for each seeker to shine the light of consciousness in all directions in order that the one Creator which each seeker is might know what resources surround it, what potentials wait, what choices can be made. This is a time within your illusion of the gathering of motivation, shall we say, of the development of the will and the faith to exercise that will as choices in the seeking continue to be made, and as these choices become more and more finely focused and tuned to that straight and narrow path. You will do what you do and choose as you choose for as long as is necessary for your will to finally move in a certain direction. You shall not move until the time is right, until you have gathered about your being the desire to move in a certain direction. To move before that time is to move unwisely, for you have not yet gathered the desire to propel the movement and to maintain the motion.

When you feel the need to move and when the need is true, you shall move, you shall choose. For you direct your movement from portions of your being not totally conscious. You shall do that which is appropriate, for there is nothing else you can do. In an universe of unity, you see, there is no mistake and each action or inaction seeks the true balance, and each has a purpose. To know that purpose is not always possible, but to seek that purpose within your illusion is always possible. Therefore, my sister, do not be overly concerned for what you call your lack of discipline, for it is not truly a lack, but a skill which is constantly being gained, and when it is finally manifest in a way which seems to your discrimination to truly be discipline, then the skill will have been refined to such a point through long effort that it will be the fruit of your labor. Yet the fruit is not the only measure of that labor or that skill.

May we answer you further, my sister?

S: No. I knew there was a method to my madness, I was just having trouble grasping onto it. Thank you, you've been exquisitely helpful.

I am Latwii, and we are pleased, my sister, to have been of service. Is there another query at this time?

M: If no one has one, I would like you to tell me whether this is old age or some pattern I have. When I was young I could focus ninety-five percent of my brain on anything in a large or small circle that I chose to focus on so that I would have photographic memory recorded in my brain. And now I'm doing good to focus fifty percent on anything, probably twenty-five percent, and I really don't care. Now what is that change? Is it old age or is it a different attitude?

I am Latwii, and am aware of your query, my sister. The pendulum, shall we say, has begun its movement in yet another direction within your conscious being, and that which was now seeks its balance, for there is value in what is called the perfect or photographic memory, and there is value in a diffusion of attention which allows the mind to be fed from another source, that is, the unconscious mind. Therefore the process which you now experience is a balancing process which attempts to feed your conscious mind in a way which it previously was not fed, therefore enlarging your perception in a way which is not consciously known.

May we answer you further, my sister?

M: No, I understand then that my attitude is different, not necessarily old age. Is that right?

I am Latwii, and would in general agree with your summary, but would add that that portion of the incarnation called old age is also an attitude in many respects.

May we answer you further?

M: No, thank you. That was very helpful.

I am Latwii, and we thank you, my sister. Is there another query at this time?

K: Yes, right along that same line, Latwii, and I'm not sure whether I can put this into words, well, I'm sort of like S now, pondering for words. My daughter made a statement to me today. Well, we got into a big philosophical conversation, and I made a statement that we as westerners, and particularly as Americans until the Vietnam war, did not stop long enough to say, "Who am I, and what am I here for, and where am I going," that we were just so busy. And she said, "Well, mother, you were busy all the time." And I said, "Yes, that's true, but now my busyness has very little importance, it seems. I'm just using up energy that's there, and needs to be used, and what I do has no great importance. There is something inside me that's much deeper that's going on. And that's what I'm really aware of and working on."

Now I know that's said badly, and probably makes absolutely no sense to anybody else. But is that the evolutionary process that goes on in all of us?

I am Latwii, and am aware of your query, my sister. The process of which you speak is a process which is in some form or another a generalized process of your peoples. The process is to begin with that which seems significant, and to enlarge the point of view so that greater significances are seen, and that which once was important is placed within a larger framework. The process may be described as the process of acceptance. Each entity is as the one who plays the game you call cards, poker for example. The hands are dealt. Each card seems significant. The hands are played. Each hand seems significant. The game then seems significant, and each card formerly played loses some significance. Another hand is dealt, another hand and another. Game after game after game is played. Some victories and some losses are recorded. The entity becomes, shall we say, an old hand at playing this game. The significance of each game grows less. Wisdom accrues and the entity looks with wizened eye at each card, each hand, each game, and the significance grows less. The entity becomes aware that more exists than one card, one hand, one game, and the entity's view enlarges until eventually and hopefully the entity is able to accept all cards dealt, all cards played by self and other self, and is able to look beyond the game and see a greater significance.

May we answer you further, my sister?

K: No, that's very good, Latwii. Thank you very much.

Carla: Well, let me follow up on that because it seems to me that what you inferred, well, that what K inferred was that when she worked as a psychologist, her work was important, and that now that she's not working as a psychologist, and is not of obvious service to other people, that her work is not important, and what you inferred in answer was that her work with patients and her work now is all the same, it's a hand of cards. The outer work … you're minimizing the actual importance, in other words, it's difficult to lead an important life, is what you're saying. The real importance is in getting the overall picture. Is that correct? Is that a correct inference from what you said?

I am Latwii, and am aware of your query, my sister. This is basically correct. It will seem to the beginning poker player that an ace is more important than a deuce. It will seem that two or three of either are more important than one of either. Yet it is not the specific card or specific work that an entity does which is importance. It is the acceptance of that card and that work, and the learning of that lesson which is important. The nature of the process is the important thing, shall we say, and not the means by which the nature is accomplished.

May we answer you further, my sister?

Carla: No.

M: Well, if you're not exhausted, I have one more question about cards, now that you brought it up. Over a period of fifty years of playing cards, I have noticed that the good cards in playing bridge run either north-south or east-west, and they'll run that way for a long time. Now, what is the phenomenon that makes the cards run good and north-south or east-west for a long period of time? They eventually may change, but if I have a choice of sitting, I'll sit where the cards are running good, and I tend to win that way. Now what is that phenomenon?

I am Latwii, and am aware of your query, my sister. Within all games, shall we say, within all patterns of your illusion there are movements of the energies which are not often understood by the players within the games. This is so because each of us within any illusion exists within an ordered universe, a universe of unity. The energies which express in any pattern or illusion, therefore, are a function of the nature of the game, shall we say. To give an analogy, one may look at a body which you call an ocean. The game which is played by the wind, the sun, and the earth with the water has a pattern. The waves crest, the currents flow, because those elements which play the game of ocean form thus and so. In a smaller scale, a game which you may

describe as a form of cards has no less the force of such energies within its plane. Those entities which partake in the game are much like the sun, the wind, the earth, and the water. There are certain attractions, certain expelling or repulsions. There are added unto these energies the conscious and unconscious desires and force of will which affect the flow, shall we say, as they are shuffled, dealt, played, shuffled, dealt and played. The energies in motion are not visible to most eyes, yet act as surely as do sun, wind, water and earth.

May we answer you further, my sister?

M: No, that's very helpful, thank you.

I am Latwii, and thank you, my sister. We find energy available for one more query of average length, shall we say, for this instrument has nearly played its hand.

Carla: Okay, I'm curious about something that happened to me, has happened to me before, happened to me today. I was in church, and shortly after the beginning of the service I lost track of time and consciousness, and when I became aware of my surroundings again, several minutes had passed, two or three, I'm not sure. I had this time almost no memory of the content of what had occurred while I was gone. I awoke with a tremendous feeling of praise, praise, joy, joy, almost just a rhythmic, it was almost indescribable, but that was the basic feeling, "Praise the Lord." And I felt closer to Christ than I—I knew that was my closest moment to Christ in some few days or weeks. My pardon to all those in the group who are not Christian. Don't let me give you a hard time, but I am so. I'm very curious whether it's safe, metaphysically safe, physically safe for me to wink out like that and come back, and if it's not safe, what I can do to protect myself from losing consciousness, and if it is safe, what I can do to remember the content long enough to be able to write about it, because I know people that read my Christian writing would be very interested in the experience, provided I could remember it.

I am Latwii and am aware of your query, my sister. We feel that we shall only be able to scratch the surface of this subject, but shall attempt response. May we first suggest that to bring back the fruits or pearls of the experience may not be the goal or even a portion of the experience. When this is appropriate it will occur of its own course or movement. The experience has as its general nature a movement from the conscious to the unconscious mind for the purpose of experiencing a deeper portion of your own being in relation to the one which is called by your peoples Jesus, and which serves as a model for your own being. This movement is triggered by the rituals which are a portion of what you call your church worship, and by a conscious and unconscious desire upon your part to be fed in the magical sense by these rituals. That you are unaware of the nature of this happening coincides with your lack of knowledge concerning the means by which you function as instrument in the contact with those of Ra.

We may suggest some form of protection be used in such a situation, which would mean that in your future worship in group church environment that you give some form of praise and thanksgiving as you build the shield of light about your being. We cannot speak in more specific terms in this particular response, for we are aware that there are some portions of this experience which are most valuable for discovery upon your own effort and cannot make those discoveries for you.

May we answer you further, my sister?

Carla: No. I'm just grateful you didn't tell me that I had to hold the hand of the person next to me because she's a soprano and she wouldn't understand. You know, you're really very helpful to everybody. Thank you very much for your services.

I am Latwii, and am most grateful to be able to be of whatever service is possible, and thank each in this group for the service which each provides us by allowing us to speak and by weighing our words with careful discrimination.

K: I thank you also, Latwii, and I'm going to work on that business of laziness and I think I'll unravel some of it. Thank you very much.

I am Latwii, and am filled with the joy of the thanksgiving which this group generates at present. We must at this time take our leave of this group, for we have somewhat fatigued this instrument, and shall be with each upon the request in your meditations. We leave you, my friends, in the love and in the light of the one infinite Creator. We leave you in your own love and light, for it is in great abundance, and in truth we do not leave you, for we are one. We are known to you as Latwii. Adonai, my friends. Adonai vasu borragus. ✤

Sunday Meditation
August 28, 1983

(C channeling)

I am Hatonn, and am now with this instrument. We greet you, as always, in the love and light of the one infinite Creator. My friends, for you and your people it seems that you spend a great deal of your time with [your] back turned, pretending to separate yourselves from the others around you, listening but with deaf ear to needs of others. So many stay tuned out to the very planet on which they live. Like a huge television, channels are changed. If you can slow down for moments at a time and look around and see your brother and your sister, reach out with yourself for even the briefest moment, feel love within them and within yourself, you may take another step, you would see those others as part of the one which each seeks. My friends, as beings seeking to grow and be one, [the] love in you that is you grows only when you allow it to be shared. Take time. Be part of your world, turn towards your fellows, share.

I am Hatonn, and would, if we may, transfer this contact to another instrument. I am Hatonn.

(Carla channeling)

I am Hatonn, and I greet you now through this instrument. Again we are grateful and bow to the winds of desire which have called us to speak with you this evening. That which we say can only act as catalyst for you, my friends, and we diligently warn you against assuming that we know the truth. We are fallible beings. We are, however, beings with a point of view which you are calling for at this time, a point of view that goes beyond the limitations which seem to be so densely set about each of you, limitations of the many demands and requirements of your physical bodies, the maintenance of them in this particular culture which you enjoy, and the great mazes and hedges which have grown in your own minds which, in addition to enabling you to function in this illusion, cause you to be unable to penetrate in many cases that very illusion that causes you to suffer.

And so we would ask you to follow us in mind as we bring you to another place. For when we speak of time, we must first bring you away from time, so we would bring you through all imaginable densities and experiences, planets, suns and galaxies until you have found the wide open, vast and limitless zero that is at the core of timelessness and of your own being, and see within that timelessness all, an unmoving, timeless, infinite, black all. You are the Creator and you are all. There is no time, there is no experience, and you reach within yourself in infinity to make the shattering decision to create, to watch, and to learn. And gathering yourself, you fling that infinite allness into infinite directions, and you create the one Thought, the one Energy which molds the darkness. Suns appear, brilliant, lucid, infinitely caring and full of the Creator, full of the one original Thought. And they in turn gather themselves and fling those energies and recklessly hurl the round reaches of their magnetism. And suns spawn planets and spin in families, and the families spin to become galactic families.

There is now light and darkness and each of the suns decides and chooses more and more what shall be the nature of this creation. How shall love be expressed and experienced? Oh, what infinite amounts of thought and care have gone into what so many have called random chance. And you, small portion of a sun which is a small portion of the Logos, how many experiences have you passed through to choose this one, how many colors, how many wonders, how many miracles, how many joys and sorrows and infinities have you passed to choose this experience? You are not here by error or chance. You chose this as being of great beauty and tremendous correctness. This confusing, dismaying, unsettling illusion is of your particular choice. How you cherished it before you came! How careful you were, and how satisfied you were before you began this expression of the Creator within the illusion of your Earth [walk].

And now you are in time. Now the die is cast and you have appeared. You have taken your choice. It is yours to enjoy. Many and many are the ways it is possible not to enjoy that experience that you now have, for the illusion is harsh and relentless and is designed to fool you completely. It is the great confidence game designed to convince you that you are a creature measured by birth and death, that those things that the culture defines at this time to be desirable are your desires, that those values that are held in fashion at this time shall be yours, and that all that you experience as difficult must be quickly blocked out and erased so that you may [be] distracted from such unhappiness, and find that happiness that is your birthright.

So often, to find happiness without leaving the illusion is to choose either solitude or the imprinting of your desires over the incarnations of those about you. You have forgotten much. You have forgotten the joy that you felt at being able to work with those with whom you have chosen to work. Why have you forgotten this, my friends? We will tell you, it is simple. You are caught in time. It is well to back away and realize that you have designed an often uncomfortable and frequently unhappy existence in order that you may rejoice, and we mean, my friends, rejoice with all your heart at discomfort and pain. It is the same discomfort and pain that you feel when you put your muscles to a new task, a task that has never before been completed or even tried. The pain is good, and when you achieve that which you could not beforehand do, how pleased you are at the progress you have consciously decided to make.

This is the nature of your incarnation. You are in your own way an athlete, each of you. The most helpful training is meditation, but the painful exercises are usually those involving those about you because that is when you finish practicing and you begin the race. That is when you offer yourself as manifestation. You might say, "Look, I have new spiritual muscles I have exercised, now I shall pit myself against my own record and shall attempt to use those muscles even better or for the first time," and you manifest that which was not before within you, that which is not of time. For can love be of time, my friends? Time erodes beauty, and love is so often of beauty. But have you noticed that love so often endures? That is the riddle, my friends. That which is true love is not of beauty but of essence. And in so many ways you begin to cherish the essence of each other, and you watch yourself be uncomfortable and in pain because you simply are not like any other creator. You are co-Creator, and you are unique, and there is not another like you, and you will not be comfortable because you will not find a twin. You will not find one who agrees with all, who does all, who is all, amenable forever. And had you the fortune to find such a twin you would become dissatisfied because perfection is boring. You were not placed by your own wisdom in this density to be bored.

Yes, my friends, spend time. Spend it as if it were the most precious kind of legal tender. Spend it as if it were money on which there were at least three zeroes. Every minute of your time that you consciously spend and give because you are manifesting the Creator is worth far more than that which man has made out of man's mind can ever be worth. And when you are dry, and you are confused as this instrument is this evening, and you are uncomfortable and in pain, when you are bared, go back and exercise in meditation by opening the door that leads outside of time, outside of races, streets, avenues, towns, names, places, situations, leads out of all particulars into the great source of love.

We wish each athlete a good season, and a personal best that you may ever strive to improve. We wish that you may love one another, and know one another as the Creator. More and other than that we cannot wish, for there is, to our knowledge, no other thing that is true. We leave this instrument in the love and the light of the infinite Creator. We are most grateful that you have called us and so very hopeful that we have been able to find the words that may aid you in your thinking at this time. We are always available by mental request. We are those of Hatonn. Adonai, my friends.

(Jim channeling)

I am Latwii, and I greet you, my friends, in the love and the light of the infinite Creator. It is our special privilege to join you this evening. We are always filled with joy at the opportunity to blend our vibrations with yours, and to attempt to be of some small service by answering those queries which you have brought with you. May we begin then with the first query?

C: Yes. During this last week I've been getting up extremely early. And one morning I was up early enough, I had a few minutes, and I sort of laid back down to close my eyes to rest for a few extra seconds, and when I did, it seems that I left my body, for I was suddenly looking upon a scene that was very brilliantly colored, and was not like the fuzziness that's sometimes in dreams, but was exact in shapes, and it didn't seem to be any place on this planet. And I wasn't at this time trying at all to get out of my body. I believe I was out of body because when it occurred, shortly after it occurred, B woke up, and when he did it just suddenly ended, and I was left feeling very weak and dizzy. I would, if you can tell me, like to know if, indeed, I did leave my body, and if so why did it occur when I was making no attempt to do so?

I am Latwii, and am aware of your query, my brother. The event of which you speak is a vivid example of those occurrences which occur from time to time within the life experience of the one who seeks the truth of the nature of its being, much like the dream which also is not consciously sought, as you would describe. So such experience will occasionally become available to an entity at a time which may seem somewhat unusual in the perception of that entity. Yet, my brother, if you will examine the nature of such occurrences even within your own experience, you will discover that it takes but an instant for great portions of, shall we say, a truer reality to be made known to the entity who seeks such.

The experience of which you speak is one which contains elements of what you have described as an out-of-body experience, yet there are many such experiences that fall under this general heading. The salient feature of such an experience is not necessarily whether it occurred, either in or out of this or that body, yet is the vividness of the experience, and its impact upon your perception. Such experiences have many purposes, as many as there are entities who have such experiences. In general we may suggest that this experience occurred at a time which you were ripe for it to occur in that you were seeking the nature in a deeper sense of your own being and of the illusion which you inhabit. When an entity experiences certain difficulties within an illusion, it is often helpful for that entity to touch home base, shall we say, and be re-energized by the truer nature of that reality, and that energizing might strengthen those channels from the conscious to the unconscious mind and allow further experience.

May we answer you further, my brother?

C: Any experience that I've had of this nature seems to occur in the same place within the house in which I live. Even the same positioning in the spot. Is there some energy built up in the spot which aids these occurrences?

I am Latwii, and am aware of your query, my brother. This is indeed so, my brother, and is so for each experience and each place in which it occurs for each entity at all times. To clarify, let us suggest that your mind, your body, and less perceptibly but even more profoundly, your spirit are palettes with colors which you paint according to your perception of any experience. This then allows, through the repeated nature of experiences for each entity, to design, shall we say, certain rituals of experience and perception that allow further such experiences and perceptions. For example, in the place in which this meditation is now occurring many such meditations have occurred, and each entity present as well as others not now present have colored this place with those vibratory colors from the palette of mind, body and spirit that allow for this experience to be repeated with greater and greater ease. If you experience an emotion, thought or enabling force in any place in a repeated manner, then that place is, shall we say, tuned by the repetitions of previous experiences, and allows further experiences along similar lines.

May we answer you further, my brother?

C: Yes, you may. As it occurs, it happened at the meditation last week. I've gotten into the habit of coming in and taking a certain spot for the meditation. Last week I know I was tired but I could not achieve a comfortable state in that spot. Something other than weariness seemed to be with me and kept me in extreme discomfort …

(Side one of tape ends.)

(Jim channeling)

I am Latwii, and am aware of your query, my brother. And now we speak of those anomalies which accompany the general description which we gave in our previous response. There are often those instances in which an entity will add a new ingredient to the ritualized situation which will allow yet another result, shall we say, to occur. When, for example, an entity has concerns of a certain nature rambling about in the mind, shall we say, which may also find expression in the resonance of the body to the concerns of the mind, then the entity, as in your case, brings a new ingredient into the ritual or recipe and the cake, shall we say, to continue our analogy, therefore has a different texture, flavor and configuration. The concerns which were with you on the evening of which you speak are those which would have been with you whatever seat you would have taken, yet were somewhat ameliorated by the familiar surrounding and completing of the larger portion of the ritual of joining the group in a certain position with a certain desire and frame of mind. Yet the new ingredient was enough different that your comfort was reduced noticeably.

May we answer you further, my brother?

C: It seems that now I have lost all desire to resume occupancy of that position, and am currently feeling extremely strong energy at this moment in this spot. Can you comment on what is occurring at this time?

I am Latwii, and am aware of your query, my brother. We may suggest that when the rider is thrown from the horse, the rider may blame the horse or may consider another grip upon the rein or the saddle or the frame of mind. And when another grip has been found, the rider may enjoy success upon the horse from which it was thrown, and may also enjoy a similar success upon yet another horse, for it is the rider which determines the success and not the horse.

May we answer you further, my brother?

C: No, thank you very much.

I am Latwii, and we thank you, my brother. Is there another query at this time?

Carla: I promise I'll only ask one, and it's probably a stupid one, but it has been rattling round in my mind for a couple of days. Jim and I were talking about the mated relationship, and all the red-ray activity, and I said that I thought I was probably too rigid in my thinking of other mated relationships. When I really thought about how active my own libido is, and how often I am sexually aroused by total strangers, and I never think about it, because I've found through dating and through mated relationships that I am more comfortable with one man than several, so it never really occurred to me to question. But Jim's response was, "Well, whatever all that red-ray stuff is about, I want to have catalyst, and to progress in my evolution, and I'm greedy, and so I choose the mated relationship consciously because I know that that is the most efficient way available to progress."

And I guess I really want more of a comment than an answer to a question. I just wonder what the possibility might be that we may have the wrong slant on it. For instance, I have been praying for an acquaintance who had a mate have an affair with another woman, and she grieved terribly, and was ready to leave the couple because of it. I don't know anything about this person except that it is a friend of a friend of mine, so I just had been praying, sort of, in the dark but I know her pain was very keen. There isn't a reason for the pain, if you analyze it, and there certainly isn't a reason to quit the relationship, and yet this kind of thing goes on all the time, and people seem to want to force each other sometimes into mated relationships, and I feel definitely that that's wrong. I don't know. Could you comment on the whole thing, the red ray thing? Surely everyone has the same constant bombardment that I do. I surely can't be more highly sexed than the rest of the world.

I am Latwii, and am aware of your query, my sister. We love your stupid questions, my sister, and take great joy in attempting some form of response which may be of service. To begin, the red-ray, as this group has come to call it, energy center is that which serves an entity by providing a very simple service. The service is similar to the service which the magnet is provided with the iron filing. It is necessary for entities within your illusion to feel an attraction for one another within certain groupings, shall we say. The male and female grouping is most helpful for the reproduction of the species, and for beginning of that relationship which shall potentially for the length of the incarnation, and through the excellence of honesty, and in the mirroring effect of honesty provide both entities with continuous opportunities for polarizing [in] the sense of service to others, in most cases, and shall allow the opportunities for love to be learned.

It has been found through many, many experiments within various third-density illusions that the journey to adepthood is best accomplished by those entities of the mated relationship, for in such a relationship the universe in wholeness is made available to each as each refines the red-ray energy which began the relationship. The key ingredient in this journey is the honesty of the sharing of self with other self, for it is necessary in your illusion that perception be as clear as possible in order for catalyst to be utilized as efficiently as possible. You live within an illusion in which perception is most difficult upon a level of clarity which speeds your evolution. It is therefore necessary that the highest degree of clarity be sought and be utilized by each entity. If the relationships were, for example, of a serial nature it would be much more difficult for the trust to build the foundation of honesty, for it takes what you call time for that trust to develop.

The experiences that each entity shares with each other in this relationship develop that trust foundation with the tool of clear perception and honesty. Then each experience which the couple shares may be refined and utilized by higher and higher, shall we say, energy centers, culminating in the birth of the adept, the one who is able through conscious effort to penetrate the illusion, and to see and be the unity of all things. This is a difficult journey, a journey which requires great dedication, and a single-pointedness of mind and purpose. It is that type of discipline which the mated relationship strengthens as the difficulties are seen as catalyst and are refined and worked with until they become the gems of experience, and further add to the stable foundation upon which the two journey together.

May we answer you further, my sister?

Carla: Only to pursue the last part of the question, and that just had to with jealousy and my realization that it's almost impossible to avoid it. For instance, I am sexually mated to the instrument that you're using. If I wished to give him a present by finding him a red ray sexual partner that was younger and prettier and different, and if he wished to give me a present and found me a younger and prettier man, whatever would appeal to me, I'm not trying to be specific, in neither case I think would either one of us, as clear and honest as we always have been with each other, get off without experiencing jealously, nor probably would the other person even take the other person up on the offer because of the feeling of, what would you say to that new person in your life afterwards; what would be the point? And yet, it's really a candy store out there. It's really just fun and pleasant. For some reason it isn't actually that way. I guess that's really what I'm after is—it really looks, at least in this culture, to be just like a little candy store with all kinds of pretty girls for the men, and pretty men for the girls, but take any candy out of the jar, and it gets sticky, it gets difficult, and the only non-difficult relationship really does seem to be the one with trust as you've been describing. And that seems to be full of joy as well as difficult. Is the reason for the candy store thing, is that strictly cultural or is it intended so that we'll have a choice?

I am Latwii, and am aware of your query, my sister. All experience is available for the entity's choosing, that in each choice some progress might be made in the evolution of mind, body or spirit. There are, in the case which you have mentioned, many possibilities for basic choices to be, shall we say, to be distorted towards certain biases. For example, in a culture in which the red-ray sexual activity is both repressed and displayed, shall we say, for sale, there may be a confusion within the minds of many entities who have not consciously recognized the purpose which the red-ray sexual activity plays within the life experience. Therefore, many entities within your culture seek to enjoy a certain flavor, shall we say, of the experience, yet avoid certain [other] flavors of the experience. Many may focus upon the basic attraction nature, and seek no further. Others may progress some distance further upon that path, and find the difficulty which offers catalyst yet not desire to utilize that catalyst, [choosing] instead the sweeter experience of finding another candy to taste.

In a culture which has not promoted, shall we say, a unified view of the red-ray sexual experience, one may expect to see a great variation in the culture's population as the population enters the candy store and attempts to choose what candy it might taste, and what then it shall do with the other candies. Shall the candy be refined, and be transmuted into a nourishment for mind, body and spirit or shall it, shall we say, provide the cavity for the teeth, which then is a catalyst of quite another nature, yet with lessons quite profound to the entity who has not yet discovered the purpose of the red-ray sexual activity or the mated relationship or the nature of its own being.

May we answer you further, my sister?

Carla: No. I never did [get] it straight about whether one could ever completely rid oneself of jealousy. But I think I'll save it for another day, for I think that everyone is getting tired. Thank you very much.

I am Latwii, and we thank you, my sister. Is there another query at this time?

(Pause)

I am Latwii, and we observe a lull in the query process which promises some length. Therefore, we would take our leave of this group and this instrument, rejoicing in the opportunity to be with each in this group, and thanking each for seeking our vibration. We are with you upon your request at any time which you request our presence. We are known to you as those of Latwii, and leave you now in the love and light of our infinite Creator. Adonai, my friends. Adonai vasu borragus.

Sunday Meditation
September 3, 1983

(Carla channeling)

I am Hatonn, and I greet you in the love and in the light of our infinite Creator. We thank you and bless you that you have called us to be with you this evening. The honor is great and our words are poor but we hope that we may be of some small service to you as you are of great service to us in allowing us to share your meditation and the stream of your living, for in this sharing we learn a great deal from you, and the service you render us thereby cannot be described.

This evening we would like to tell you a story. There was once a young man. He was faced with the burden of adulthood. All things lay before him, and he did not know what he should choose. But of one thing he was sure, and that is that he wished to get that out of his life which he would feel was enough, for all his life he had heard his parents say, "We would like to do this or to have that but we do not have enough time or we do not have enough money." The young man was quite determined that he would accomplish the possession of enough.

We shall transfer this contact. I am Hatonn.

(R channeling?)

I am Hatonn. I am now with this instrument. We shall continue. The young man of which we speak desired things which were greatly different than those which his parents failed to achieve, for as he looked and searched for fulfillment in his life, he found that it would be enough to do that which he truly felt was his purpose in incarnating into this present life. For the young man spent many years viewing his parents and their difficulties, viewing his own hardships and realizing that the world was but an illusion, and that there is only one thing to be achieved and that is the spiritual growth of each and every individual in whatever way that they feel is comfortable and adequate and for their purpose.

Each of us walk a different path, yet all paths eventually shall lead to the same point, the point of union with the creation and its Creator, and if you do nothing in your life other than fulfill your own spiritual hunger, then you have done enough. For in doing so, you shall be assured that that which is to manifest around you in your world will be in harmony with the direction that you seek. Though many times you will experience difficult situations, within each test there is a lesson to be learned, and with each learning you pass farther and farther, and through this passing you gain the knowledge and fulfillment for which you have incarnated.

Man upon Earth now faces a dilemma which shall indeed test his spirit, and those that are weak shall have difficulties but those that are strong shall have the greatest, for they are prepared to burden the hardships of their fellow man as well as their own in reaching out their hands to assist those whom they are able to help. We urge that you seek within yourself the fulfillment of life and of spirit. It is imperative that you take time to yourself to offer prayer to your Creator, to meditate, and to attempt to reunite your consciousness with that of the Creator, and to attune yourself to the energies that are beginning to flow more and more freely within your environment, for if you are sensitive you will gain great strength from the influx of positive energies from what you would call the next dimension or area within your universe.

Earth passes quickly into this space. Those who harmonize with the greater energies shall in one way or another graduate with this Earth sphere, and those who do not shall experience a form of death through which they may incarnate once again into their present dilemma to attempt to seek the answers which they have not found within their experience. Many of your peoples still seek material life, still place all the importance upon the gain of material objects. This is not necessarily wrong, but it indeed should be a secondary goal. Life is short as you know it, but it continues forever, for beyond this experience shall be another and another, and in each life there is only one, one thing that you need, and that is to continue your spiritual direction, for it is enough. It shall provide you with all that is needed.

I shall now transfer this communication to another instrument. I am Hatonn.

(Carla channeling)

I am Hatonn. Having found that the remaining instruments wish to listen, we shall return to this instrument and complete. In the prayer which you prayed prior to this meditation you made a request of an invisible presence or force, "Give us today enough to eat." This prayer was taught to a small band of students by a good teacher, and it encompasses an accurate view of the relative importance of having enough. The seeking within the illusion for enough, if it goes beyond that which is easily measured, will go awry and will cause great frustration. There will not be enough sooner or later, one way or another.

Within your illusion, depending upon how you have chosen to learn the lessons of love, you will find what you consider to be shortages of power, money, influence or love. In fact, all of these shortages are some distortion of love and may be viewed as opportunities to discover the true nature of love. If you do not have enough money, you may find that your discomfort distracts you from seeking. But if you exercise another point of view, you may find that your lack of abundance has produced a simplicity that frees you to love. If you lack power you may feel victimized, but you may also take this opportunity to practice the realization that that entity or group of entities which victimizes you is in fact part of you, and together with you is the Creator, and is therefore infinitely lovable.

Any distressing situation, any shortage, can be the opportunity you intended for yourself in order that you might balance within yourself some aspect of the nature of a unifying and powerful love. If you have the faith to examine situations, especially recurring situations or conditions which seem to say to you, "I do not have enough," you may well find therein the key to your reason for personal study during this incarnational experience. You will not have discovered what it is you may do for those about you, but before you serve others, it is well to feel that you have a plentiful and bountiful selfhood, that you are standing upon solid ground within your own being, and that you are not faced with internal weaknesses which will make it impossible or improbable for you to be of service to others.

The inner work, the work upon the self, is not selfish. For it [is] only the whole self that can serve the Creator it sees in others. What you see is a reflection of what you are. If you have not found enough, then you will continually view outer shortages. If within yourself you have discovered the wholeness of your being and the adequacy, indeed, the perfection of your consciousness, you will then find that same consciousness buried however deeply in the illusions about you. You may think to yourself that you cannot possibly find a whole and complete being within yourself. It is certain that your culture does not encourage you to feel whole. However, through meditation and the discipline of analysis of your thoughts and your actions you can find the keys that open the door to wholeness.

This wholeness is another word for love, for love is that which is not broken or battered or in any way imperfect. Love indeed is creative and multiplies that wherein it dwells. Sometimes you may feel as if your situation were that of a certain crowd spoken of in your holy work called the Bible, gathered upon many hills, many thousands of people, and you have a few loaves of bread and a couple of fish. And you feel completely inadequate to nourish that which is about you, those who need you. You feel that you do not have the food, the nourishment, the love that is necessary. But this is the point. Such is the power of love as it flows through you from the infinite source which has created all that there is that that which you have will be enough. You are enough and you have enough.

And so our young man could grow old and die and never find enough unless the attention had been turned to the inner silence that beckons all who seek, an inner silence so filled with joy that those who have felt it recognize others by that one smile that says to the world, "Yes, I have felt it too, I have known infinite bounty, I have felt the sunshine of a universe scattered carelessly, abundantly and wastefully upon my upturned spirit. I have asked; I have received." Those who have received radiate that which they have received, and give it again a hundredfold.

And so my friends, please do not think ill of your poverty, whether it be of power or of money or of the right words or of enough love or of the ability to deal with a situation correctly today. For a little while you have left eternity, and you are living in time. You brought infinity with you; you brought the infinite love that created you and is you with you. Claim it. It is your birthright. Whatever has gone wrong this day, whatever will go wrong tomorrow, be serene still in the confidence that that small effort that you can make, that tiny bit of love that you can bring through, that widow's mite of what is needed, will multiply for you, and you will live abundantly.

You know that there is much help if you wish to claim and call upon that help. You are not and never have been alone in your experience. There are those who you would call angels who are with you at all times but especially upon request. There is your own self, of which you are only a part in this incarnation, sometimes called your higher self, which comes as you call it. There is the fullness, infinite and invisible power of love if you but call within yourself. There is the light of truth if you but ask.

We hope to inspire you to seek the truth. Any thought which we may share with you could be spoken incorrectly or could be misunderstood by us, for we are not perfect, but are merely your brothers and sisters. We wish mainly to encourage you to continue seeking love, to continue then seeking to manifest that love in your very dark world, for such love burns like a light and lightens the fragile earth which binds you to this illusion. We rejoice with you that you have this opportunity to seek and to strive and to choose what you will do. We can see all the choices and much of truth. Our choices are made for us. We have been through our choice. We now serve and attempt to refine that choice. You are moving more quickly in your spiritual evolution than you ever have or ever will again, for yours is that glorious moment a mere lifetime long when you have the opportunity to choose forever to love.

We are those of Hatonn, and as you love, so do we. We greet you and bid you farewell in the love and in the light of our infinite Creator. Adonai vasu borragus.

(Jim channeling)

I am Latwii, and I greet you, my friends, in the love and in the light of our infinite Creator. We are especially privileged to be able to join your group once again this evening. We thank you, as always, for it is a great honor to offer our humble service to you, that is to attempt to answer your queries. We remind each that we too are fallible beings, having as resources somewhat more experience, shall we say, than do you, but having our own catalyst to work with as well in order that our experience might be refined. May we begin this evening with the first query?

Carla: Well, if people are shy of starting out, I'd like to ask a dumb question. Is it a sexually determined characteristic to enjoy wearing pretty clothing or is it just culturally determined in this culture that women are vainer than men?

I am Latwii, and am aware of your query, my sister. Within your culture, and indeed within most cultures upon your planet, it is a portion of the biological female's characteristics to await the reaching of the biological male, for that which reaches is a male principle. That which awaits the reaching is a female principle. The female entity, in order to attract the reaching of the male, dons some sort of apparel that serves as a symbol of its attractiveness, shall we say. This apparel varies from culture to culture but serves a similar purpose in that it focuses the attention of the male upon the female in order that the species might be joined and reproduced.

May we answer you further, my sister?

Carla: There have been some times in history when the men were at least as interested in fashion. I'm thinking especially of the reign of Queen Elizabeth II, and the restoration years in English history, and the Greeks and the Romans which had sort of "exquisites," I guess you'd call them. Was that just waves of biological males with a lot of female memories going through incarnation at that time?

I am Latwii, and am aware of your query, my sister. This may contribute to such a phenomenon but it is also the case that [the] similar form may serve another purpose. For the male to reach and demonstrate the male principle it is often helpful for the male to establish its stamp or mark or identity, shall we say, for all to see, then that male entity or grouping of such is firmly established in its beingness of the eyes of those about it, and may reach with surety of self towards the female as a group and in individual expression.

We remind you that it is also the case that each biological male contains female principles, and each biological female contains male principles, so that the expression of each is often of a mixed nature, yet the characteristics of each remain most firmly established male principle to male entity and female principle to female entity.

May we answer you further, my sister?

Carla: This must be very boring to everyone else. Just one more question. I'm trying to understand something about myself. I have absolutely no desire to attract a new male and I feel fairly solid about my situation as it is, and I still enjoy dressing up just because I enjoy dressing up, not for anybody except for myself. Is that a female principle? it does not seem to be sexually oriented, perhaps it's just derivative …

(Side one of tape ends.)

Carla: … as a matter of fact, I think that women these days are more attractive in jeans, you know, than skirts.

(Jim channeling)

I am Latwii, and am once again with this instrument, and am aware of your query, my sister. We may speak in general upon this topic, for it is an area in which you now work in your spiritual evolution. The donning of certain apparel of what you may describe of an attractive nature may also serve any individual, be it male or female, as a means of verifying the nature and value of the self. The environment which surrounds an entity will mirror to that entity in its perception what it feels about itself. The entity will construct an environment which reflects its opinion or its desired opinion of its nature and its worth.

May we answer you further, my sister?

Carla: No, thank you.

I am Latwii, and we thank you, my sister. Is there another query at this time?

S: Yes, Latwii. I had an experience a few months back or a few weeks, I'm not sure how long ago it was, and I explained it to R, and he told me that he had had this same experience as a child. And I was wondering if you could make any comment on it. I was drying my hair and looking in the mirror and all of a sudden it struck me that that wasn't me, and it was really strange. It was like the image was looking back at me, and it looked so peculiar that I actually moved my head back and forth to see if it would move. And I was wondering if you could comment on this occurrence?

I am Latwii, and am aware of your query, my sister. The, shall we say, veil which shrouds the conscious—we correct this instrument—which shrouds the unconscious mind from the conscious mind is from time to time penetrated or pierced by an entity. In the instance of which you speak, this type of penetration occurred, and there was, shall we say, the bubbling up through the veil the memory of and picture of a previous incarnation. This is not as [an] unusual event as one may think, for from time to time the configuration of seeking and of belief system of an entity will be of such a nature that such remembrances occur in just the fashion you have described, though many more occur within what you call the dreaming state or within the daydreaming state, as it is called.

May we answer you further, my sister?

S: Well, I'm a little confused. As far as remembering a previous life, the face that I saw in the mirror was the face that I have now. Was what I was experiencing that that was not really me now? That's how it seemed to me.

I am Latwii, and believe we have the gist of your query. Please ask further if we have misperceived. The unfamiliar portion of that face which you saw in the mirror is the portion which had been drawn to your conscious mind, and came through the veil from your unconscious mind as a memory of what you would call a previous incarnation.

May we answer you further, my sister?

S: No, I understand. I would like to ask—an occurrence like this or an occurrence where I blacked out and had the thing with my sunburn—these and a lot of strange dreams. Are these happening more frequently now—is this a result of my continuous seeking, and can I expect to experience these things more frequently as I learn more?

I am Latwii, and am aware of your query, my sister. We feel that your observation is correct.

May we answer you further?

S: No, thank you, Latwii.

I am Latwii, and we thank you, my sister. Is there another query at this time?

Carla: Well, if everybody's through, I just have one last one that I was kind of curious about, an aspect of S's experience having to do with blanks. It seems as though a lot of psychics use glass or crystal, and things happen with reflection, that there's a power somehow that is focused for the individual using it either consciously or unconsciously. Could you comment on that?

I am Latwii, and am aware of your query, my sister. The use of such crystal is a use which intensifies the entity using it, specifically the entity's energy of what you would call seeking. The entity which desires to know more of the nature of its being and of the creation through which it moves attracts in some fashion the answers which it seeks, for those answers are a portion of that being since all beings are the one creation. The crystal, the mirror, the surface of the still pond, may all serve to intensify this seeking and to allow the entity so seeking to experience, shall we say, a clearer perception of that which it seeks.

May we answer you further, my sister?

Carla: Well, let me put that another way. It seems that you have a space/time illusory manifestation, a crystal, glass, a reflective surface, and it is having a time/space or completely different part of the what we would call closer to reality—it is having a time/space effect. It's a space/time thing having a time/space effect, or it is an illusory thing having a real effect? Is it that reflective things are some sort of a bridge between the two worlds, the two universes?

I am Latwii, and am aware of your query, my sister. Your supposition is, in general, correct. There are certain substances, most notably the crystals—of which the great pyramid is one well known example—which focus the instreaming love and light or prana of the one Creator in a fashion which allows an entity who seeks purely to experience an answer to seeking, shall we say. This is indeed a joining of that which is not visible with that which is visible or that which is metaphysical with that which is physical. Your illusion is filled with both and both may be joined in the perception of the seeker in order that that which it seeks may be made known to it in such and such a fashion by the combination of the two principles.

The, shall we say, two-dimensional surfaces such as the glass or surface of the pond in its effect have a somewhat different focusing ability, and act more to reflect to the seeker those images which reside within its own conscious and unconscious mind. This again joins that which is not visible with that which is visible and forms an image which conveys to the seeker a portion of that which it seeks.

May we answer you further, my sister?

Carla: No, I think that's very interesting. The next time I find myself upset about something, I think I'll go look in the mirror. Thank you.

I am Latwii. We thank you, my sister, and would remind you that each entity and experience is a mirror.

Is there another query at this time?

(Pause)

I am Latwii, and we have discovered that the queries seem at an end for the evening, and we would once again thank each present for inviting our presence. We rejoice at each opportunity to share our humble thoughts with you. We are with you in your meditations at a simple request. We are known to you as those of Latwii. We leave you now, my friends, in the love and in the light of the one infinite Creator. Adonai vasu borragus. ☥

Sunday Meditation
September 18, 1983

(S channeling)

[I am Hatonn,] and greet you, my brothers and sisters, in the love and in the light of the infinite Creator. We would ask your patience this evening, my friends, for it has been a long while since we have had the privilege of speaking through this instrument, and need a few moments to tune in to her vibrations, so to speak, and to make her more comfortable with ours once again.

We are, as always, my friends, extremely pleased to be called among your gathering. There are those groups among your peoples who are more and more seeking the humble message we have to share, and in any gathering, whether large or small, the opportunity to share our most humble words is appreciated. We have been long seeking those who in their willingness to serve others would allow us to impart what amount of wisdom we have, and the service you impart is great, for in sharing with one, my friends, do you not share with all your brothers and sisters? In some infinitesimal way there will always be a link between you and each of your brothers and sisters. This link, my friends, is not always consciously felt but is still there. One act of service does not only touch one, it touches all; it touches your planet. In each wholehearted loving service you impart, you indeed further your planet onward into the fourth density. There are times when this realization is forgotten or misplaced but the service still goes onward, goes forward, is projected into an ever-enlarging sphere as does a pebble thrown into a pond creates ever larger circles.

We would at this time transfer this contact. I am Hatonn.

(Carla channeling)

I am Hatonn, and am now with this instrument. I greet you once again in the love and the light of our infinite Creator. A great linkage exists between you and all that exists, and you are taking part in what you may call the drama of each existence that has ever been, is now occurring, or will ever be. This is a difficult truth to evaluate, and we would guess it is even more difficult to evaluate its importance. There is a longing in each of you for a dramatic happenstance, a change within the consciousness which will say to you, "I am still making progress; I have made progress at all."

However, this drama which we discuss with you is divided into two great acts. One portion of it is a drama of those asleep. The sleepwalkers randomly bump into each other, and into the furniture of the stage, they fall into the spotlights, crash into the orchestra pit, and cause the audience some amusement. There is a moment in each actor's life some time after he has determined that he is within a drama when the actor decides to write the play. He will choose his character and he will write his own lines.

This is the division, the great before and after which yawns away into eternity back to the beginning of your creation, and towards its end, once you have the opportunity to make what may be a dramatic choice. For many of you it may well not even be dramatic then, for you will have already made the choice in a previous incarnation, and this entire incarnation will be that action which rediscovers the choice and then sets about refining that choice. Therefore, you will not see the drama that others about you luxuriate in.

Let us look within your holy work. This instrument has thought much about the parable of the sheep that was lost. There were one hundred sheep. Ninety-nine sheep know where they were. They had chose to come home. In an undramatic way they munched and thought and moved around within a restricted space. But one sheep had wandered off. The entire attention of the shepherd went out to the sheep that was lost. Tossing the fate of the ninety-nine to the winds, he went after the single lost sheep. And so it is that when one which has never before chosen decides to choose, the creation resounds with joy. Another has made the choice. Back at the sheepfold where most of you are, the rejoicing is done. You are now one of those who will rejoice when the lost sheep are found. But the changes in your own thinking will occur, little by little by little. You will learn how to use the tools of mind, body and spirit by a process of refining that is agelessly slow and painstakingly careful, and many times will see your gains as losses and your losses as gains, and will spend much time involved in incorrect biases about yourself.

Much of this can be averted by reminding yourself constantly that you must not expect drama in your spiritual existence. The joy of experiencing love will come to you if you seek it, but it will also leave you. You will manifest great understanding and radiate the love and light that you have spent so many hours seeking in silence, and then other times you will not. Were you able to penetrate the illusion from one end to the other, it would be doubtful that you would have chosen this illusion, for it would not be doing the service it is intended to do. It would not be causing you to learn to refine upon your choice.

You may look back and think about that sheep, that foolish, seemingly unimportant sheep that got all the attention, and you may wish that you might even get lost so that you may rejoice to be found. But we say to you, you have better things to do. Try to think of yourself as royalty. What would occur had you been born a prince or a princess destined one day to rule and lead a people? Your life would be much restricted compared to others. You would behave in a more regular fashion. You would bow to many responsibilities. You would sometimes question the honor of royalty, and even though in some ways your position might seem to others to be admirable, you yourself might wish for freedom, freedom to do what you will.

And so you are, my friends, each of you. You have accepted a crown. The crown sits upon your head and it weighs you down. You are already rescued. You have already chosen to love. There is no chasm to bridge, there is no great drama. Honor and responsibility are yours and your advances, though they seem small, are greater, though they are more hard-won. Never kid yourself that the choice was the hard part, for in most cases the choice is made in a burst of the joy that the first understanding of love and light gives off. The refining of that love and that light, the manifestation of service to the one infinite Creator, is a task that is full of joy but could not be more demanding or more continuously puzzling.

And here you are, my friends, with your part in the drama. You are still upon the stage, you have stopped falling into the orchestra. You are many times writing your own lines and perhaps part of you has even made it into the audience where you observe yourself and give yourself reviews. You would be hard upon yourself, harder than others, but you find comradeship along the way, and always and ever that stage, so firm beneath your feet, so solid beneath the illusion. That stage, my friends, is a kingdom that you have never left and that you will never leave. You dwell within the kingdom of love, you dwell with the Creator always. Lift up your heads and feel your crown grow lighter as the great sunlight of the Creator strengthens your will and undergirds your faith.

We would like to close through the instrument known as C, and would now transfer this contact. I am Hatonn.

(C channeling)

I am Hatonn, and am now with this instrument. The steps that each take in this illusion may seem for you to apply [too heavy] but with the continuation along your chosen path comes patience. The one path found as patience finds a peace and a knowledge, but things move slowly, but they move, they grow. Not that we may see, but they do. You may at times have pause to look over your shoulder and realize that without your conscious knowledge you have moved. You have passed a point which you will never pass again. My friends, find your patience, open your eyes and continue. Each will know his own pace. Each one's pace is his, and you will find that you will move.

I am Hatonn. It is indeed a privilege to be allowed to speak our humble words to you. Each of you will take them as each needs. We hope that we may be of service to you. We are always at your call. I am Hatonn. We leave you now in the peace and the love of the one infinite Creator. Adonai, my friends.

(Jim channeling)

I am Latwii, and I greet you, my friends, in the love and in the light of our infinite Creator. We are again privileged to be able to join your group in the seeking of truth. We thank you for the service of asking for our presence and for your patience in assessing our humble service at this time. We would then ask if we may begin with the first query?

S: I have a question, Latwii. A few weeks ago Hatonn talked on reaching a point in the seeking when you no longer seek. This has been coming back in the past couple of weeks and is in my thoughts constantly. Could you just expound on the subject a little bit?

I am Latwii, and we shall be most happy to attempt clarification of this point, which may at first seem quite contradictory and confusing to those who have long sought the nature of truth, shall we say. The seeker is one who is conscious of the process of evolution. Though each person learns as the one Creator, many do so in a manner which you may consider unconscious. To use our brothers and sisters of Hatonn's analogy, there is the stumbling into the spotlight, the falling into the orchestra pit, and eventually the entity begins to write the script, which is another way of saying begins to seek in a conscious manner the keys which shall unlock door after door within the inner self, and reveal those treasures of being that await such seeking.

At some point in this process there is another transformation which occurs. This is the transformation in which the seeker not only knows intellectually with the conscious mind that it and all it observes are the one Creator, but experiences more and more the being of the one Creator within its own being. The one Creator is found within and the entity is found everywhere within the one Creator. As this process becomes more apparent and becomes that which is experienced more and more within the incarnation, the seeker discovers that it is that which it seeks.

This is more than semantics, my friends. To seek is to suggest that the one who seeks spends the efforts looking for that which it is not, yet wishes to become. To know that the self is that which is sought, is the one Creator, is to de-emphasize the seeking and to be that which was previously sought. In this transformation the entity looks upon a new creation. The entity looks upon itself as it surveys that which it is and which formerly would have been seen as that in which it existed. In this transformation there is a greater responsibility assumed by the one which formerly focused its efforts upon seeking. Now this entity, our former sturdy seeker, is that which it sought, and shoulders the responsibility of being all that is. This is not an event which is lightly undertaken, and is most properly placed within that realm of what you may consider the advanced nature of being.

May we answer you further, my sister?

S: No, thank you, Latwii.

I am Latwii, and we are most grateful to you, my sister. May we attempt another query?

(Side one of tape ends.)

(Jim channeling)

I am Latwii, and we rejoice with those sounds which surround your evening, and we rejoice that we have been able to join with you this evening. Though we have not expended great effort, each effort is treasured, and we thank you for your service which you provide by requesting our humble presence. As you seek and as you are, we are one with you. We travel that same path. We are your brothers and sisters, and together we are the one Creator. We are with you at your request in your meditations, in your thoughts, and in those moments when companionship is desired. We take our leave now of this group, though in truth we remain with you. We are those of Latwii, and leave you now in love and light. Adonai vasu borragus. ✢

Sunday Meditation
October 2, 1983

(K channeling)

I am Hatonn, and I am now with this instrument. I greet you, my friends, in the love and the light of the one infinite Creator. We wish to take this opportunity to exercise this instrument briefly because it has been a long time since we have had the opportunity. Many changes have occurred in the group since we had the opportunity of exercising this instrument, and we would like to say the changes have been toward growth. We rejoice greatly in the opportunity that we have of being with you tonight, and since this instrument is a bit rusty, we shall wait or transfer to someone else. I leave you in the love and light of the infinite Creator and transfer the contact.

(T channeling)

I am Hatonn. I am now with this instrument. It is a pleasure to speak to your group and to be invited to join with you. We of the Confederation have sat with your group numerous times throughout the past. We have had the opportunity to speak to [you] through numerous channels such as these present tonight, yet it is always a very welcome experience for us, for this is our main source of communication with the peoples upon your planet at the present time. We are in your skies and we have been seen often, yet this is an irrelevant factor, for what we offer is not our presence but our knowledge and our experience. We are not an infinite source of information. We, too, journey through our life experience for the purpose of learning and we have found through our experiences we have come to a point in time, as you would call it, where we must share with others that which we have learned in order to continue our own progression, for service of a spiritual nature shall always be—correction—service of a spiritual nature shall always take shape in this manner. That which you receive you shall share in order to receive more. It is as in a circle, all things must go around and around, or shall we say, even a spiral, increasing in its magnitude yet flowing in a pattern which continually swirls from one to the other and unites all.

We of the Confederation share with you our love and our experience and this is all. There may be a time in the future of your planet where we shall be able to work with you hand in hand. But for now, our service to you is these simple words, and your service to us is inviting us to share with you that which we have to speak. We of the Confederation love deeply this opportunity to work with you, and we thank you for your presence, we thank you for your patience. It gives us great pleasure to have people upon your planet who are willing to accept our words and speak them without fear, for as those present who have had the opportunity to channel can attest to, there is a great deal of ridicule that accompanies such as this. In the days past this group was exposed to a greater number of people, and in that time it was very difficult, for the energy was so great for the channels and the people attending the meetings to keep from sharing what they had learned with all those that they met. It is wise to keep to yourself that which you receive until you understand how to properly utilize the gift of knowledge that we share with you. The greatest way to serve your fellow man is through your actions, not your words.

I shall transfer this communication. I am Hatonn.

(Carla channeling)

I am Hatonn, and speak now through this instrument. I greet you once more in the love and the light of the one infinite Creator. May we take this opportunity to express our appreciation for this group's willingness to hear our greeting, for it is not of ourselves that we speak. We speak of love and light. We are messengers of a Creator that is infinite, and expresses Itself through that which cannot be imagined but which is known to all in one distortion or another as love, this love that is so tremendous and so vivifying that it has enlivened the universe and created it from light.

Why are you all one, my friends? Why do we insist upon proclaiming your unity? You are all one thing; you are light, a manifestation of one original Thought. That Thought is love. This cannot be understood, but we are so grateful to be able to proclaim the love and the light, the infinite Creator. There cannot be too many times or too many ways to speak of that which is when all that is illusion is subtracted and all that is distorted has become light.

We shall continue now with that which we were discussing. It is impossible, perhaps, for you to know the magnitude of the work that you create by your offering of your being seated in this circle with like-minded people. You make an offering that would indeed stagger you by its magnitude. For you, as you multiply your wills together and send your desire towards the stars asking for truth and seeking a light, you are such a source of planetary healing that we are aware as you might be aware of lights as you came into an airport and gazed at the city about you. Perhaps it would be a small airport and the sources of light would be few. Perhaps it would be large city and you would see many, many lights.

As we gaze upon your planetary energy web, what we see are the lights that have been lit at this time. This particular time, being the Sabbath for many of the people which inhabit this portion of your sphere, has many lights. Many of those lights are strongly colored, tending towards the less pure seeking, being very brilliant but therefore being murky in coloration due to the lack of seeking for the truth and the certainty that the truth has been found and can be contained, that the Creator has been caged and explained. Fewer, but brighter, are groups such as yours who meet to offer in silence consciousness and dedication to seeking in the faith that truth is a possibility, a marvelous, reached for possibility. This quality of seeking lights up your sky and radiates, for you wish to know how you may serve that truth.

We say to you, know that you are, as you seek, the precious ones of the Creator. You choose yourselves much as in your holy works you read of the chosen people. This chosen nature is quite valid, however, you choose yourselves. You choose to become responsible for seeking, for manifesting, for giving, and for seeking again. You choose a voyage. In your culture that which is rare and precious is placed, as treasure always is, in a secret trove where no one may steal or corrupt that which is precious. So we ask you to consider the hushed, silent portion of your consciousness that is involved more or less in seeking. It is not the function of the seeker to show the treasure of that seeking to all, but rather to allow any fruits that may have come from the seeking to manifest in a natural way.

Therefore, we never suggest that you proselytize or attempt to sway opinion, for, indeed, you are only exposing that within you which is most precious, and which you need to nurture, protect and value. But as you value and nurture these desires to seek, as you meditate and seek the silence within, as the power of the original Thought brings love into your life, you will find that you are manifesting to others qualities which will aid those about you. You may allow this to occur and indeed encourage it, for this is a natural fruit of seeking. However, the seeking itself, that inner journey, we encourage you to protect as if it were a baby, for it is a baby that you carry within yourself. Nurture it with meditation and you encourage it to grow in wisdom, and you discipline it by the regularity with which you examine it with thoughts and your being.

And in the end, in secret, you find a fierce joy, a delight that you share with an invisible and infinite source. This joy is the heart of the presence of the original Thought that will through a long and varied journey express to you many opportunities through which you may see the face of the Creator in yourself, in circumstances, and in your co-creators, those about you. The more of that joy that you experience inwardly, the more resilient shall be the radiance of your being.

Now, we gaze upon you, thank and bless you; a place of light made of people, one of hundreds which seek the Confederation for inspiration this evening. How light your planet seems as you gather together and join in an infinite proclamation of consciousness, for what is consciousness? That which you are before you think is the Creator. The original Thought is not a thought as you understand thought, for your mentations are pale indeed. It is a power; you call it love. Treasure yourselves aright, value that which you are doing, and know that as you go forth you shall stumble and fall many times by your own estimation, and many other times you shall consider that you have done well. We suggest that you not keep score. Many is the time that you shall score incorrectly. Only continue to seek and above all to nurture that inward thrust towards truth. We can only encourage, not truly teach. You are your own teachers, for all that you wish is within you.

We bathe in the light of this group, and thank you that you have been so gracious as to have allowed us to speak our humble words. How little we have to offer you compared to what you have to offer us. You hearten us, for it is not difficult for us to seek; our illusion is far less dense. For you, my friends, the challenges are so many. How we encourage you. We shall be with you at any time that you may wish us. We leave you now in that love and light of the infinite Creator of which we have spoken. We leave you in joy, and in truth we do not leave you at all for we are singularly one with you. We are those of Hatonn. Adonai, my friends, adonai.

(Jim channeling)

I am Latwii, and I greet you, my friends, in the love and in the light of our infinite Creator. We are most privileged to be able to join with your group this evening, and we thank each present for seeking our vibration. As always, it is an honor to attempt to answer those queries which each brings for the inspiration of the seeking. May we then begin and ask for the first query?

Carla: I have a question. I had a brief vision late last night or early this morning, just as I was drifting off to sleep. And I thought that the person that I envisioned, that I saw, was the archangel Michael. He put his sword away, and he was rubbing his hands together, and he said, "I love it when a plan comes together." That's all I saw. I found out today that it's the feast of the archangel Michael and all the angels, and I wondered if people who were sensitive like I am to various influences have experiences like that due to the amount of prayer from churches like the Catholic church that concentrate on saints a lot more than the Protestant ones do, or if it was just an odd experience?

I am Latwii, and am aware of your query, my sister. We might say that each supposition which you have made is in some degree a portion of the explanation for this particular vision. We may comment by suggesting that your particular bias in the direction of the observation of certain days for certain saints, as you call them, plays a large role in this situation. Also your nature of being sensitive to impression is greatly responsible for the general nature of the vision's appearance. Also to be considered is the information registered in your subconscious mind from a previous conversation of a similar nature which was incorporated in a somewhat humorous manner in this vision. Thus, from many sources within your own being are drawn the resources which composed this particular vision. For the vision's meaning we may suggest contemplation and meditation.

May we answer you further, my sister?

Carla: Yes. The bias which I follow is that each of us has a Comforter, another word for the Holy Spirit, and the action of this force, whatever it is called, I don't think you have to be Christian to have an awareness of the force itself, it sustains you one way or another. Could you comment on my guess that whereas I tend to get very articulate messages from this force, nevertheless the mechanism basically works for everybody, it's just that in some people's lives the working of this force, or this source of information, this comfort, might be dreams, might be coincidence, or many other ways in which the Comforter or the Holy Spirit or whatever you could call it, the higher self, might work. But it's one, no matter what your bias, the force itself that occurs is one very substantial force which is the true one. Would you comment on that or is that clear enough?

I am Latwii, and am aware of your query, my sister. We believe that we have the gist clear enough to be able to respond in this matter. Indeed, there is a force which protects and guides each entity as it seeks its source, for all entities are part of this one force. You are additionally correct in your supposition that there is what many on your planet have called a Comforter which lends assistance in a more specific manner than the all-encompassing force of the one Creator.

An entity serving as a comforter responds to the seeker's special call at those instances within the incarnation which may be described as sacred, shall we say. In such moments the seeker's intense desire for the revelation of truth in the incarnation is such that the comforter is that which is called and that which responds by the feeding of a certain kind of spiritual food, a certain manna, as you would call it, which enters first the unconscious realms of the mind complex, and then, shall we say, rises so that in some way the entity perceives this assistance. The entity perceives in whatever manner the entity is able to perceive according to the system of beliefs which it has constructed during its incarnation. Thus, each entity perceives in a slightly variant and unique fashion.

There are also other presences which lend assistance to the seeker. These are frequently referred to as guides of one nature or another. Each seeker has at least three such guides: one of a positive or radiant or male nature; one of the magnetic, receptive or female nature; and one which you would describe as androgynous, being of a more balanced nature. Each seeker may also from time to time be assisted by other angelic, shall we say, presences and beings according to the needs, the desires and the seeking of the seeker. Each such assistance is perceived in whatever manner has meaning to the seeker.

May we answer you further, my sister?

Carla: Well, it's fascinating, but I think I should let other people have a chance to ask questions. So for now I'll let it rest. Thank you.

I am Latwii, and we thank you, my sister. Is there another query at this time?

(Side one of tape ends.)

(Jim channeling)

I am Latwii, and am once again with this instrument. We must apologize, my sister, for we must ask for the repetition of the query, for this instrument was not fully functioning during this reversing of this tape recorder device.

Questioner: What is Matira's relationship to me, and what can you tell me about her?

I am Latwii, and am aware of your query, my sister. In this instance we may speak in general terms only, for to give the specific information requested would be to infringe upon the free will of the seeker. The entity of which you speak is one which has a relationship to you similar to those beings of which we have just spoken, though it is not one of the specifically mentioned types of relationship. This entity seeks to be of service by providing the type of assistance which it feels most appropriate to your particular needs as they arise in your own process of seeking. We look upon this relationship as one which is most beneficial for the continued growth of the point of viewing, for the entity's service in general is that which expands the point of view.

May we answer you further, my sister?

Questioner: Well, when and if this little group should disband, can we contact Hatonn or someone else through Matira?

I am Latwii, and am aware of your query, my sister. The Confederation of Planets is available in the vocalized channeling format to any group which seeks in a pure manner, which is to say, the philosophy of the Confederation concerns the evolution of entities upon your planet, and we are what you would call philosophers who have a desire to share our opinions and learning with the understanding that they are opinions and quite fallible. We cannot prove our existence, our message, your past, your present, or your future journey in any way. Our service is most ephemeral, and is meant as an inspiration along the way. Any group which uses the tuning devices that have been shared within this group, and has the desire to seek as purely as possible, and which is familiar with the vocal channeling contact may seek and receive information from the Confederation of Planets in the Service of the Infinite Creator, for that is our purpose at this time, to share that which we have come to know as our truth with those upon your planet which seek that sharing.

May we answer you further, my sister?

Questioner: No, thank you very much.

I am Latwii, and we thank you, my sister. Is there another query at this time?

Carla: No, could you run that by me one more time, real fast, because I don't quite … Her question was could she contact Hatonn through Matira, and you just said Hatonn enjoyed speaking vocally. Would that mean that Hatonn wished to speak only through vocal channels? In other words, straight to a person and not through a guide on the inner plane. Is that what you intended to say, and just didn't come right out and say? I didn't hear it, if you said it.

I am Latwii, and am aware of your query, my sister. Our response was intended in the general sense. That is, that communications of a inspirational or philosophical nature could be received by any group through any type of instrument if that group sought with the requisite purity and desire and tuning mechanisms that have been utilized within this particular group.

May we answer you further, my sister?

Carla: I'm still trying to figure out if you said that Hatonn could be contacted through Matira or whether you said … I guess what you're really trying to do is take the emphasis off what the name of contact is and put the emphasis on the nature of the message. Am I right? Take the emphasis off the messenger, and put the emphasis on the content of the message?

I am Latwii, and am aware of your query, my sister. This is in part correct, for we wish always to emphasize the nature of the message, for the nature of the message is very simple. We are all one and we all seek that unity. Whether that seeking finds manifestation in a contact such as this contact, a contact through a guide or through personal inspiration through those books and resources which the seeker peruses or through any other means is not important The message of unity, the seeking of love and light in that unity, is the important—we correct this instrument—is the type of contact and experience which is that which we wish to emphasize. The means of the messages being transmitted is less important.

May we answer you further, my sister?

Carla: No, that's very helpful. Thank you.

I am Latwii. We thank you, my sister. Is there another query at this time?

K: Yes, sort of along this same line. This has happened to me for a long time, I guess it happens to everybody, but some thought will come to me seemingly out of nowhere, I don't know where it comes from. I haven't read it or I haven't heard it to my knowledge, but very shortly, maybe within a week or two, I will hear this on the radio or I'll pick up a book and find the same thought in it. Now my question is, is there an atmosphere of these thoughts, and are all of us picking up these thoughts at about the same time? Where do these thoughts come from?

I am Latwii, and am aware of your query, my sister. It is most difficult to describe in your words the source, shall we say, in specific terms, of such thoughts. One means of such description might include the concept of pools of thought which surround or are available to each entity at all times. From time to time, as you would call it, the entity dips into one pool, and then another, and may dip into many simultaneously. These pools are available throughout all of what you call time, and are indeed timeless so that what might appear at one of your times to be separate from another of your times might in the nature of your being be one time or experience.

Thus, when you first thought the original concept, and then seemingly later experienced its further ramifications, you were dipping into one particular pool of thought in one experience during two of what you call time periods. These pools of thought are drawn to you by your desires, by your seeking, just as the iron filings are drawn to the magnet. That which is called for is received. This is, shall we say, a law: that which you desire will be drawn unto you. As you continue your journey of seeking, you will discover that there are streams or pools of thought which serve as resources for your further contemplation. These are what you have frequently called sources of food for thought. These pools rise within your subconscious mind and become available to you through many types of experiences. The intuitive insight, the dream, whether in sleeping or daydreaming, the mental contemplation, the meditation, all are means of perceiving such pools of thought.

May we answer you further, my sister?

K: No, that's what I thought, but it helps to have you expound on it. That was very good, thank you. Now, I'd like to ask a question about some dreams I've had, and wondered if they were sort of archetypes. This past summer I've been trying to discipline myself to remember my dreams, whereas before I'd been a little careless, shall we say. I've been off and on—now I'm on. But I've dreamed numerous times about a bird or a baby that's about to be born. One dream, I was holding an egg in my hand, and whatever it was, a chicken or duck or whatever it was, literally broke open the egg, and I could see the yellow wing, holding it in hand and it was a very exciting thing, to have that egg hatch right in my hand. And of course I wake up before the thing comes out. I just get to see that yellow wing, but it's about birth and all about me. It seems I'm trying to get ready for this new birth that's about to come about, and things are not quite ready, and I'm just working myself to death to try to get everything just right for this baby that's about to be born. It's not my baby, it's just a baby that's about to be born. Now what can you say? Is that an archetypical dream or is this just my silly dreams?

I am Latwii, and am aware of your query, my sister. We look upon this experience as one which, indeed, reaches those roots of mind which you have come to know as archetypical. Each entity which seeks the truth of its being and of the creation in a conscious manner will frequently experience such dreaming as you have described. Those experiences of a new birth may be looked upon as representative of the archetypes of transformation, for each moment provides infinite opportunity for the seeker to transform some portion of its being by finding the love, the light, the unity within the moment, no matter how that moment might camouflage such truth with seeming discord and distress.

As the seeker continues these minor transformations there are, shall we say, various octaves or levels of transformation which then become available, much as a threshold which requires a certain degree of strength to surpass, and when that strength is gathered then a great change in perception and being is apparent. The viewing of the birth of the egg, that which is encased, and which is freeing itself from the encasement, is quite frequently of a personal nature so that the seeker experiencing the dream is seeing a symbol of its own birth or the birth of some portion of its being and thinking. In other cases, the entity is perceiving the tides of being of its race or kind and is, shall we say, tuning into a greater process of transformation of which it is a smaller part. In most instances both such situations pertain, for as one entity is transformed, all in some degree are transformed, and as all are transformed, each is transformed, for in truth, all are one.

May we answer you further, my sister?

K: No, that was very good. Another dream that has—I've become a great believer in dreams even though I used to make fun of my grandmother for believing in dreams. I've been converted. Another dream I'm assuming is along the same nature, I'm assuming is an archetype. This has occurred again and again throughout my lifetime, periodically. Somebody is about to be buried, and here we're all about to bury this person and this person just begins to move around in the casket, and, you know, here we are with a live corpse on our hands. I used to wake up literally scared to death with that dream. That dream doesn't frighten me anymore, but I dreamed that just recently. Now, I'm assuming that's an archetype also. Is that true?

I am Latwii, and am aware of your query, my sister. We may preface our response by suggesting that the conscious seeker would have great difficulty in finding any dream which did not tap some archetypical portion of its deeper mind. To respond now more specifically to your query, we might suggest that this particular type of dream is most useful to that conscious seeker which many upon your planet have called the adept, for in times most ancient upon your planet, there were those initiates who sought to increase their seeking by going through that experience which may be likened to the burying of the self while alive, and the experience of the death of perception to the physical world and the resurrection of the perception to [a] greater or divine plan for [an] entity within its incarnation.

Many upon your planet at this time seek such experiences within what you have called sensory deprivation chambers. The experience of self with self at such a time is most profound, and at some point each seeker must make what you would call the peace or sense of grasp or wholeness with the concept you call death, for the seeker to know that the death is a great transformation but not the end of its beingness, at some point within each seeker's journey. The dreaming experience which you have described is a portion of that learning and may be considered most valuable when it is carried to its completion within the dreaming state, for this experience will allow the seeker to expand its point of view concerning that experience called death.

May we answer you further, my sister?

K: No, that's very good. Thank you very much, Latwii.

I am Latwii, and we thank you, my sister. Is there another query at this time?

T: Yes, I'd like to go back to the thoughts on the thought pools that you mentioned earlier, and are these thought pools entity, non-entity or liaison entity or none of the above?

I am Latwii, and am aware of your query, my brother. We hope that we do not confuse by suggesting that all of the above are correct, and in addition there are as many forms to such pools of thought as can be imagined by entities, for each entity, as we have noted, will draw unto it those thoughts which it desires, and will form them in such and such a manner. If a great number of entities form certain thoughts in a similar manner such as with what you have called the service of worship within various of your churches, then certain thoughts may take the form of angels, of archangels, of rituals, of processions, and so forth. These forms of thought, then, may be called upon by such entities, and there may be a sustenance or a nourishment gained from the calling.

May we answer you further, my brother?

T: No, thank you. That is excellent.

I am Latwii, and we thank you for your service, my brother. Is there another query at this time?

Carla: Just while we're talking about pools of thought, I was thinking about tidepools. You divorced these pools of thought from the notion of time, and suggested that we really are living a simultaneous existence, we are living in an eternal present. We simply don't see it that way because of the illusion. But I was wondering if there were tides that pulled at those pools of thought so that as K first asked, many people might feel the surge of the tide and therefore feel the—have a tendency to seek for that thought or to reach into that thought at the same apparent time, the tides being impersonal events. Could you comment?

I am Latwii, and am aware of your query, my sister. This is, as you have surmised, a very large subject, and there is little likelihood that any supposition would be totally incorrect cor—we correct this instrument—concerning its nature. There are, as you have supposed, certain tides of energy or vibrations of light and love which surge in rhythm and become available to the planet as a whole, so that each upon the surface of your planet, if seeking that type of vibration, may become aware of it in a conscious fashion while unaware of it if not seeking it, yet and nevertheless [be] moved by it in some degree.

There are those vibratory levels of energy influx which are constantly being made available to your planet and its peoples and are being made available in a fashion which slowly increases in the strength or frequency. Thus, tides of thought or energy do periodically surround your planet. These great oceans, shall we say, of thought energy are of a general nature as in comparison with those we were previously speaking of which were more of the individual group or racial origin.

May we answer you further, my sister?

Carla: No, that was fascinating. Thank you. I would like to know if you would please check the instrument to find out if he is too fatigued to go on.

I am Latwii, and we appreciate your conscientiousness in this regard. We find the instrument is available for two or three more queries and would welcome them at this time.

Carla: Would a quick retuning be in order?

I am Latwii, and we suggest the continuing as has occurred, with no present need for retuning. Is there another query at this time?

Questioner: Yes. We seek to do more than we are able to accomplish at this time. We like to know how we gain more energy to do more.

I am Latwii, and am aware of your query, my sister. You may observe that experience of fatigue and consider that as you are seeking to do more, as you call it, you are continually expanding your capacity to do more in the service of the one Creator. As you continually expand this capacity, you will notice that there is the residual effect of fatigue. As you continually expand your capacity, you may experience what you call continual fatigue, for this is a constant process and this process is not always consciously apparent to your perception. Thus you may feel you have not moved in your ability to do more service, yet if you could take the larger view, that view, looking upon the incarnation from beyond the incarnation, you would see great progress.

Indeed, it is not a portion of this illusion to give a clear perception of one's progress. The seeking within this illusion is done within what one might call a great darkness and forgetting, even to the clearest seeking eye. As you desire to seek and serve and to enlarge your capacity to do both, thus shall you do both, for as the filing is drawn to the magnet, thus is that which you desire drawn to your desires and your being.

May we answer you further, my sister?

Questioner: No, thank you very much.

I am Latwii, and we thank you, my sister. Is there another query at this time?

K: Just one more, Latwii, right along this same line. I guess all of us would like to go out and feel that we are really serving, but that doesn't seem to be the way things work out all the time. But during my meditation or as things work out during the day, I feel the urge as I send caring, healing, peaceful thoughts to family and friends, or just around the planet. Is this serving the Creator or [is] this a type of service, even though this person does not know that I am sending healing thought? Is this a type of service?

I am Latwii, and am aware of your query, my sister. Indeed, my sister, there is no action which is not service. Most actions by your peoples are of a service nature that is unconscious. Most present this evening seek to serve in a conscious manner, and to serve as efficiently as possible. Many do so in just the manner you have spoken, for, indeed, all creation is one being, and as you send a thought of healing, of love, of light, of support, of comfort, of caring to any other being upon your planet, all receive such and are able to partake of it if so desired. For in those realms which are the foundation of your illusion, in the metaphysical realms, a thought is indeed a thing which is seen, which is felt, which is used. It is such a foundation which supports your present material illusion, and not your material illusion which supports the metaphysical realms.

May we answer you further, my sister?

K: No, that makes sense. Thanks a lot.

I am Latwii, and we thank you, my sister.

(Pause)

I am Latwii, and we find that we have exhausted the queries and this instrument at approximately the same time. We are grateful to each for seeking our humble service. We remind each present that our words are but fallible opinion. Take those which have meaning and use them as you will. Leave those which have no meaning. We are most honored and overjoyed at each opportunity to speak to this group. We are with each upon request in your meditations, and would be honored to join our vibrations with yours then. We shall leave you now in the love and in the light of the one infinite Creator. We are known to you as those of Latwii. Adonai, my friends. Adonai vasu borragus. ✣

Sunday Meditation
October 16, 1983

(S channeling)

I am Hatonn, and greet you, my brothers and sisters, in the love and the light of the one infinite Creator. As always, my friends, it is indeed a great joy for us to share with you, and we are greatly pleased to be with you this evening, for in this time of change we are honored that you would still wish us to be with you, and the service each of you would perform is dear to our hearts. We are overjoyed that you would still allow us the service of attempting to help in what small way we may in your search for the original Thought, in your seeking of the many paths to the Creator. The path of that search may be an arduous one, and yet, my friends, do not forget the moments such as this that make of that path a joyous one. In your oneness with your brothers and sisters you see the Creator.

There are many times each of you may feel set apart from many of your brothers and sisters upon your planet's surface. But this is not so. Each must follow his heart to the Creator and each must learn to allow his brother or his sister that choice, that freedom to follow his own way, for each path does indeed eventually lead to one point, and no matter how one gets there, the end will be the same. Just as each of you have chosen, maybe for a short while, to be a part of this group in its seeking, there are many other groups who seek in their own way. These are no less right than your way. Each must find in his heart the place that will touch him as each of you have been touched. Remember, my friends, there is no right and no wrong, only experience in the creation.

We would at this time transfer this contact. I am Hatonn.

(C channeling)

I am Hatonn, and am now with this instrument. My friends, you are embarking on a journey, a quest for continuance of the path you have chosen these past years. You face what to some seems the loss of the heart, the force that brought and held you together. My friends, each and every one is vital, each is part of the whole, and that which has been learned is yours no matter if those things you have become accustomed to change, each has the knowledge each has gained. Each, if they so choose, may continue to share in these intimate groups their love. We and our other brothers and sisters of the Confederation will always be at your call if so desired by you, to be with you at times like these when vocal channeling is desired, are with you at any time you call us. We have been honored for so long to be able to speak to this group through your years. Though many have come and gone from it, it is still very much our honor to continue.

My friends, each of you here has made great strides, and each here has much further to go. Often it will seem that you struggle to reach the top of the mountain only to find a higher mountain beyond. My friends, as one mountain is climbed, so may another. Each of you has become aware of the love and the light that surrounds you, that is you. Each has been able to find the warmth within that allows you to be one with your fellows, to share their joys, their sorrows.

We must pause for a moment. I am Hatonn. The instrument is experiencing some difficulty due to the beverage he had previously consumed, but we feel now that we may continue.

My friends, call us when you need, call when you want to share. We wish to be of service in what way we can. I am Hatonn. We would now take our leave. We leave you in the love and the light of the one infinite Creator. Adonai, my friends.

(Jim channeling)

I am Latwii, and I greet you, my friends, in the love and in the light of our infinite Creator. It is a great honor to join you this evening. We blend with you now our love and our light in the mutual seeking of truth. It is again our privilege to provide our humble service of attempting to answer your queries. We rejoice in that service, and ask now if there might be a query with which we might begin?

S: Yes, Latwii, I have a couple of questions, one being the subject that was being discussed before the meeting started concerning the aspect of Jesus Christ as the Savior, according to the Bible, the only way to get to God. Would you comment on this?

I am Latwii, and am aware of your query, my sister, and it would be our joy and privilege to comment on this concept which has been much discussed and misunderstood by many peoples since the one known as Jehoshua walked on your planet. This entity was born a man as each upon your planet is born, and through many years of pure and sincere seeking was able to blend his vibrations with those of the one Creator which are available to each entity, but which are [in] some fashion distorted so that experience may be gained.

The one known as Jehoshua or Jesus was able in his life pattern to remove the distortions to such an extent that he was able to experience that type of consciousness which may be called Christed, christened, pure. This enabled him to speak with authority when he said, "I and my Father am one. No one comes unto the Father unless he comes by me." These are the words which are often misunderstood, for many upon your planet feel their meaning is simply that one must just believe in the one known as Jesus the Christ and that known as salvation will be his.

This is what might be likened unto the child's perception of truth. It cannot be said to be untrue, but it cannot be said to be the complete truth, for within those words lie much which is still covered to the simpler perception. The simple believing in an entity, no matter what the entity's purity, is not sufficient to gain for the one so believing that known as salvation, salvation itself being much misunderstood. Our humble definition of such a term might be that grade necessary for what you call the harvest, a polarity of service which is sufficient to enable the entity to be graduated, for this entity now understands in a conscious manner, or perhaps yet still in an unconscious manner, the need to serve and to evolve in mind, body and spirit. And it is this evolution, this process of seeking and the fruit yielded therefrom, that is, the service to others, which enables an entity to gain that broadly described as salvation.

If one shall come unto the Father, the one infinite Creator, by the path followed by the one known as Jesus of Nazareth, then such an entity shall in the life pattern demonstrate the desire to seek the truth and the service to others that is of such a nature that the so-called salvation is imminent, the graduation draws nigh and the harvest shall be completed. It is not by mere belief in another entity—though faith, indeed, in the seeking of the truth is necessary—that an entity shall come unto the Father. The one Creator, the Father, resides within each entity. Each must go within the self in the life pattern and find the deepest truth available therein; and when that truth is found, manifest that truth in the experience of each day. Then the salvation shall be available by the efforts of the seeker following the same path the [one] known as Jesus of Nazareth followed.

May we answer you further, my sister?

S: No, thank you, Latwii, not on that subject. I do have another question that I hope you might be able to put a little insight into. It seems that during the week I have all different kinds of questions, and then on Sunday nights they all disappear. Either that, or the questions cannot be put into words. Why is that? Can you comment on that?

I am Latwii, and am aware of your query, my sister. We may comment by suggesting that for the sincere seeker it is often the case that the well-framed question will provide the answer in a process of conscious and unconscious contemplation and meditation which occurs within the seeker's being. That is to say, that when you perceive a query arising within your mind, it is a natural process for the self to continue with the query in many forms so that the same basic question is re-formed many times within the mind of the seeker. As the question is thus re-formed, or mulled over, as you would say, there arises within the seeker potential answers, shall we say. The purity with which the question is asked, with which the truth is sought, is a force which reaches down into what you would call the subconscious mind and attracts those pieces of information which have what you might call an electromagnetic configuration that is similar to the query, and thus is drawn to that query.

Often such answers are recognized in the conscious mind, and it is known that the query has for the moment been answered. Often such answers will remain in the unconscious mind, yet radiate a certain sort of surety so that the entity no longer seeks with such determination an answer which it somehow feels has been achieved.

May we attempt further response, my sister?

S: No, thank you, Latwii, that's very sufficient. Thank you.

I am Latwii, and we thank you, my sister. May we attempt another query at this time?

(Pause)

I am Latwii, and we feel that the queries for the evening, though small in number, have covered those areas of concern. It is always our joy to speak with your group, whether for a long or for a short period as you would measure time. My friends, that which you call time is an illusion and when we join in the seeking of truth that seeking is timeless and is brilliant and vivid on the walls of creation as the rainbow across the sky after the rains have fallen. We are with you at your request, and are most happy to be able to join with you at any time in your private meditations or in your group meditations such as this evening.

We join with our brothers and sisters of Hatonn in wishing you well as you undertake a new portion of your seeking as a group. We assure you that we shall be with you and shall lend our assistance whenever possible whenever requested. We join in your great seeking and we rejoice in your great seeking. We leave you now in the love and the light of our infinite Creator. We are those of Latwii. Adonai, my friends. Adonai vasu borragus.

(C channeling)

I am Nona, and I am now with this instrument. We would, if we may, join with you as you send healing to those in need.

(C channels a vocalized melody, very quietly and with gentle intensity, from Nona.)

The Law of One, Book V, Session 105, Fragment 55
October 19, 1983

Jim: After a good deal of searching we finally did find a house north of Atlanta to which we were about to move in November of 1983. We decided to query Ra about the metaphysical cleansing needs of this new dwelling before moving there, and that was the purpose of this session. As Jim was giving Carla her pre-session massage he noted reddened welts, symmetrical in nature, on both sides of her back. They were similar to the welting which had covered her body when her kidneys failed at age thirteen from glomerulo nephritis. Apparently, if Carla had chosen to meet difficulties in completing our lease agreement with our landlord by allowing a feeling of separation from him to occur or had allowed this same feeling of separation to grow for Don as he hemmed and hawed about what house to choose in Atlanta, that allowing of separation of self from other-self could have been energized by our negative friend until her self was separated from her physical vehicle, and her incarnation would have been at its end. She had to deal with our landlord, who had numerous requirements for our leaving that he felt justified in making, and with Don's mental condition, which was beginning to show further signs of the long-term stress to mind and body that commuting and worrying about his job had brought about. Strikes and bankruptcy were continually threatening Eastern Airlines and, though he knew it would be easier to get to work from his base in Atlanta, he had great difficulty in even looking at houses in Atlanta, much less choosing one, because of his life-long love of Louisville and the comfort and beauty of our home as we had known it together. But our home was up for sale, and we had to move somewhere.

My first trip with the twenty-four foot U-haul truck saw me lost in the mountains of northern Georgia. Many curves and turns later I found our new home in the countryside around Lake Lanier. It was midnight when I saw the house for the first time—Don and Carla had picked it out—and I immediately began searching in the darkness for each window and doorway to perform the ritual of cleansing with salt and blessed water. It was an inauspicious beginning to an unusual experience there.

A small beginning is made near the end of this session to query again on the archetypical mind, and Ra's comment at the end of this session is a key part of the mystery of Don's illness and his death.

Carla: By the time Don accepted the house we moved into, he was in a settled state of disorientation, something unknown before this time. I, too, was quite at low ebb. Dimly grasping that I needed to be exquisitely correct in all ethical dealings, and willing to go to almost any lengths to remain in the light, I did manage to keep the anger and vast irritation I felt with our landlord out of my actual dealings with him. We packed up the kitties and Don flew us down to Atlanta. Friends drove our cars down, another friend drove the second rental van, and we piled into a huge and glamorous—and decidedly non-winterized—lakefront house in Cumming, Georgia. As if warning us that this trip was going to be dicey, Jim's first attempt to take the van to Georgia found him fetched up, barely sixty miles from Louisville, with a broken truck. We disregarded this event, and pressed on.

The whole five months that we were there was like a sit-com, overlaid with bizarre situations. Cumming was the county seat of Forsythe County, a place notorious for its prejudice against any race but Caucasian. On a Saturday, one could drive through the little town and see Ku Klux Clan members in regalia, except for their head-masks and hats, handing out brochures at the stop lights. Grandmothers, children, all ages and both sexes wore these sad little costumes and waved racial hatred around as though it were cotton candy. I had planned to join the Robert Shaw Chorale, but when I sang my piece, there was a misunderstanding, and the judges thought I had sung a wrong note. So I did not get accepted, something I had not even thought of. I had been singing all my life, and I was a competent chorus member. But I was out. Instead, needing to sing, I found a little group in the Cumming area, and plodded along while I was there with Irish folk songs and the like, fun to sing but not the marvelous prayer experience I had always found classical sacred choral singing to offer. I planned to sing, on Sundays, at the cathedral there, St. Philip's, and had made every arrangement to do so. But they would not let me start singing until after Christmas, a practice the church had been forced to adopt after people tried to drop in for Christmas and not sing the rest of the year. Meanwhile, I found a mission church five minutes from our house which had no choir whatever. So I stayed in tiny All Saints' mission, and sang the old Anglican hymns during Eucharist. Every expectation was baffled. Nothing worked out as envisioned.

The worst of it was that Don had more, not less, to do in order to arrive at work. He had to run the whole gamut of paralyzing traffic from far north of Atlanta to south of it, where the airport was. And the weather seemed fated to make things harder. It was extremely cold in Georgia that winter, and when icing conditions were there, as was the case several times, there was absolutely no way to drive anywhere. I can remember Don having to stay in a motel he managed to slide into the parking lot of, unable to reach either home or work. Christmas Eve found me singing two services at All Saints' while Jim and Don bailed water from burst pipes. By the time the New Year came, the wet carpets had begun to become moldy, and both Don and I were allergic to mold and mildew. As luxurious as the house was for fun on the lake in summer, it was nothing short of a disaster as far as winter living went. I got ulcers on my toes because they were so cold—the floor was never warmer than fifty degrees, ever.

Since all this was wrong with the house, we immediately began looking again for another house, both in Atlanta and back in Louisville. We never had one settled day in Georgia and, pretty as the state was, I cannot say I would wish to be there again. Until Don found the house we now live in, in March, we were in a constant restless perch, having no real order to things. Our belongings remained boxed, our feelings fragile. I was the one who dealt with the new landlord, which was not a picnic. Don was very insistent that we move immediately for the whole time there, so even though we did stay in that one place for five months, the landlord and I had to talk at least weekly so that he could be apprised of our latest plans—none of which worked out. Finally, in March, he asked us to leave, so that his family could use the house themselves that summer. It was at that juncture that Don flew to Louisville by himself over a weekend, found this lovely and venerable old bungalow in which we still live, and agreed to buy it.

Buying a house was something Don had always felt was unwise for himself to do. And as soon as he had done it, he began to regret it. For Jim and me, this was most difficult to bear, as we had unwisely let ourselves hope that we would come to this little exurb and really settle in and just live as we had before. But Don remained convinced that we must move, again, while always turning down any possible place we found to look at. When I found a house twenty thousand dollars cheaper, with a duplex design which would give Don and me a full home plus an apartment for Jim, and Don turned that down too, I realized that something was really wrong. Things were in a fine pickle.

In this atmosphere, it was faintly off-balance even to try to pursue the work and questioning about the archetypical mind which we had begun, but persist we did, cleansing the new working room daily and hoping for the day when we could have another session with those of Ra. I remember feelings of great hope and faith welling up within me as this period spent itself, and wonderings about what in the world was happening with Don. None of us knew anything to do except *persevere, and follow Ra's suggestion to meet all with praise and thanks. Or try!*

Session 105, October 19, 1983

Ra: I am Ra. I greet you, my friends, in the love and in the light of the one infinite Creator. We communicate now.

Questioner: Could you first please give me the condition of the instrument?

Ra: I am Ra. The vital energies of this instrument are in a much more biased state than the previous asking, with the faculties of will and faith having regained their prominent place in this entity's existence and balance. The physical deficit continues.

Questioner: I am sorry that we have to ask so many maintenance questions. We seem to be in a confused condition now with respect to our abilities to continue in the direction that we wish to with respect to the archetypical mind.

I would like to ask what caused the symmetrical welts on the instrument's back, and is there anything further that we can do to heal the instrument and her condition, including these welts?

Ra: I am Ra. The welting is a symptom of that which has been a prolonged psychic greeting. The opportunity for this entity to experience massive allergic reaction from streptococcal and staphylococcal viruses has been offered in hopes that this entity would wish to leave the incarnation. The previous occurrence of this state of the mind complex which occurred upon, in your time-numbering system, the ninth month, the twelfth day, of your present planetary solar revolution caught your fifth-density companion unprepared. The entity is now prepared.

There have been two instances wherein this entity could have started the reaction since the first opportunity was missed. Firstly, the opportunity to separate self from other-self in connection with the choosing of an house. Secondly, the possible vision of self separated from other-self in regard to the dissolving of mundane bonds concerning the leaving of this dwelling. Both opportunities were met by this entity with a refusal to separate self from other-self with further work also upon the indigo-ray level concerning the avoidance of martyrdom while maintaining unity in love.

Thusly, this instrument has had its immunal defenses breached and its lymphatic system involved in the invasion of these viri. You may see some merit in a purging of the instrument's yellow-ray, chemical body in order to more quickly aid the weakened body complex in its attempt to remove these substances. Techniques include therapeutic enemas or colonics, the sauna once or twice in a day, and the use of vigorous rubbing of the integument for the period of approximately seven of your diurnal periods.

We speak not of diet, not because it might not aid, but because this entity ingests small quantities of any substance and is already avoiding certain substances, notably fresh milk and oil.

Questioner: Is there any particular place that the integument should be vigorously rubbed?

Ra: I am Ra. No.

Questioner: Could you please tell me what caused Jim's kidney problem to return, and what can be done to heal it?

Ra: I am Ra. The entity, Jim, determined that it would cleanse itself and thus would spend time/space and space/time in pursuit and contemplation of perfection. The dedication to this working was intensified until the mind/body/spirit complex rang in harmony with this intention. The entity did not grasp the literal way in which metaphysical intentions are translated by the body complex of one working in utter unity of purpose. The entity began the period of prayer, fasting, penitence, and rejoicing. The body complex, which was not yet fully recovered from the nephrotic syndrome, began to systematically cleanse each organ, sending all the detritus that was not perfect through kidneys which were not given enough liquid to dilute the toxins being released. The toxins stayed with the body complex and reactivated a purely physical illness. There is no metaphysical portion in this relapse.

The healing is taking place in manifestation of an affirmation of body complex health which, barring untoward circumstance, shall be completely efficacious.

Questioner: Is any consideration of the appropriateness of the house at Lake Lanier which we intend to move to or special preparation other than that planned advisable?

Ra: I am Ra. We believe you have queried obliquely. Please requery.

Questioner: We plan to cleanse the property at the Lake Lanier location using the techniques prescribed by Ra having to do with using the salt for 36 hours, etc. I would like to know if this is sufficient or if there is any salient problem with respect to moving to that house that Ra could advise upon at this time please.

Ra: I am Ra. The cleansing of the dwelling of which you speak need be only three nights and two days. This dwelling is benign. The techniques are acceptable. We find three areas in which use of garlic as previously described would be beneficial. Firstly, the bunk bed room, below the top sleeping pallet. Secondly, the exterior of the dwelling facing the road and centering about the small rocks approximately two-thirds of the length of the dwelling from the driveway side.

Thirdly, there is the matter of the boathouse. We suggest weekly cleansings of that area with garlic, the cut onions and the walking of a light-filled perimeter. The garlic and onion, renewed weekly, should remain permanently hung, suspended from string or wire between workings.

Questioner: Just so that I don't make a mistake in interpreting your directions with respect to the second area outside the house, could you give me a distance and magnetic compass heading from the exact center of the dwelling to that position?

Ra: I am Ra. We may only be approximate but would suggest a distance of 37 feet, a magnetic heading of 84 to 92 degrees.

Questioner: I know that it is unimportant for our purposes and from the philosophical point of view I don't want to do anything to upset the Law of Confusion, so don't feel that it is necessary to answer this, but I was wondering what condition created the necessity for such continual cleansing of the boathouse?

Ra: I am Ra. The intent is to create a perimeter within which the apiary denizens will not find it necessary to sting and indeed will not find it promising to inhabit.

Questioner: Are you speaking of bees or wasps or creatures of that type?

Ra: I am Ra. That is so.

Questioner: Are Jim's plans and ritual for the deconsecrating of this dwelling sufficient, or should something be added or changed?

Ra: I am Ra. No change is necessary. The points necessary to be included in consecration or deconsecration of the place are covered. We may suggest that each second-density, woody plant which you have invested during your tenancy within this dwelling be thanked and blessed.

Questioner: Is there any other suggestion that Ra could make with respect to any part of this move that is planned, and will it—will we have any problems at all in contacting Ra in the new dwelling, and if so, will Ra tell us about those and what we could do to alleviate any problems in contacting Ra in the new dwelling?

Ra: I am Ra. We weigh this answer carefully, for it comes close to abrogation of free will, but find the proximity acceptable due to this instrument's determination to be of service to the one infinite Creator regardless of personal circumstances.

Any physical aid upon the part of the instrument in the packing and unpacking will activate those allergic reactions lying dormant for the most part at this time. This entity is allergic to those items which are unavoidable in transitions within your third-density illusion that is, dust, mildew, etc. The one known as Bob will be of aid in this regard. The scribe should take care also to imbibe a doubled quantity of liquids in order that any allergically caused toxins may be flushed from the body complex.

There is no difficulty in resuming contact through this tuned instrument with the social memory complex, Ra, in the chosen dwelling, or, indeed, in any place whatsoever once physical and metaphysical cleansing has been accomplished.

Questioner: I have come to the conclusion that the meaning of the hawk that we had about a year ago when we started to move the first time had to do with the non-benign nature of the house, in the metaphysical sense, which I had picked. If it would not interfere with the Law of Confusion I think that it would be philosophically interesting to know if I am correct with respect to that.

Ra: I am Ra. What bird comes to affirm for Ra? What bird would be chosen to warn? We ask the questioner to ponder these queries.

Questioner: We have been, you might say, experimentally determining a lot of things about the body, the next portion of the tarot, and have been experiencing some of the feedback effects, you might say, between the mind and the body. From everything that we have done so far with respect to these effects the great value of the third-density, yellow-ray body at this time is as a device that feeds back catalyst to create the polarization, I would say. I would ask Ra, if initially when they were designed for third-density experience the mind/body/spirits— not the mind/body/spirit complexes—had as the major use of the yellow-ray body, the feeding back of catalyst and if not, what was the purpose of the yellow-ray body?

Ra: I am Ra. The description which began your query is suitable for the function of the mind/body/spirit or the mind/body/spirit complex. The position in creation of physical manifestation changed not one whit when the veil of forgetting was dropped.

Questioner: Then the yellow-ray body, from the very beginning, was designed as what Ra has called an athanor for the mind, a device to accelerate the evolution of the mind. Is this correct?

Ra: I am Ra. It is perhaps more accurate to note that the yellow-ray, physical vehicle is a necessity without which the mind/body/spirit complex cannot pursue evolution at any pace.

Questioner: Then you are saying that the evolution of that portion of the individual that is not yellow-ray is not possible without the clothing at intervals in the yellow-ray body. Is this correct?

Ra: I am Ra. No.

Questioner: Would you clear up my thinking on that? I didn't quite understand your statement.

Ra: I am Ra. Each mind/body/spirit or mind/body/spirit complex has an existence simultaneous with that of creation. It is not dependent upon any physical vehicle. However, in order to evolve, change, learn, and manifest the Creator the physical vehicles appropriate to each density are necessary. Your query implied that physical vehicles accelerated growth. The more accurate description is that they permit growth.

Questioner: As an example I would like to take the distortion of a disease or bodily malfunction prior to the veil and compare it to that after the veil. Let us assume that the conditions that Jim experienced with respect to his kidney malfunction had been an experience that occurred prior to the veil. Would this experience have occurred prior to the veil? Would it have been different? And if so, how?

Ra: I am Ra. The anger of separation is impossible without the veil. The lack of awareness of the body's need for liquid is unlikely without the veil. The decision to contemplate perfection in discipline is quite improbable without the veil.

Questioner: I would like to examine a sample, shall we say, bodily distortion prior to the veil and how it would affect the mind. Could Ra give an example of that, please?

Ra: I am Ra. This general area has been covered. We shall recapitulate here.

The patterns of illness, diseases, and death are a benignant demesne[7] within the plan of incarnational experience. As such, some healing would occur by decision of mind/body/spirits, and incarnations were experienced with the normal ending of illness to death, accepted as such since without the veil it is clear that the mind/body/spirit continues. Thusly, the experiences, both good and bad, or joyful and sad, of the mind/body/spirit before veiling would be pale, without vibrancy or the keen edge of interest that such brings in the post-veiling mind/body/spirit complex.

Questioner: At the end of an incarnation, before veiling, did the entity appear physically to have aged like entities at the end of their incarnation in our present illusion? Did the Significator look like that?

Ra: I am Ra. The Significator of Mind, Body, or Spirit is a portion of the archetypical mind and looks as each envisions such to appear. The body of mind/body/spirits before veiling showed all the signs of aging which acquaint you now with the process leading to the removal from third-density incarnation of the mind/body/spirit complex. It is well to recall that the difference betwixt mind/body/spirits and mind/body/spirit complexes

---

[7] demesne: In feudal law, lands held in one's own power; A manor house and the adjoining lands in the immediate use and occupation of the owner of the estate; The grounds belonging to any residence, or any landed estate; Any region over which sovereignty is exercised; domain. [< AF *demeyne*, OF *demeine*, *demaine*. Doublet of DOMAIN.]

is a forgetting within the deeper mind. Physical appearances and surface and instinctual activities are much the same.

Questioner: Then I was wondering what was the root reason for the change in appearance that we see as the aging process? I am trying to uncover the basic philosophical premise here, but I may be shooting in the dark and not questioning on it correctly. I am trying to get at the reason behind the design in this change in appearance when it seems to me that it would be just as possible for the mind/body/spirit or mind/body/spirit complex to look the same throughout an incarnation. Could Ra explain the reason for this change?

Ra: I am Ra. When the discipline of the personality has led the mind/body/spirit complex into the fifth and especially the sixth level of study it is no longer necessary to build destruction of the physical vehicle into its design, for the spirit complex is so experienced as a shuttle that it is aware when the appropriate degree of intensity of learning and increment of lesson have been achieved. Within third-density, not to build into the physical vehicle its ending would be counterproductive to the mind/body/spirit complexes therein residing, for within the illusion it seems more lovely to be within the illusion than to drop the garment which has carried the mind/body/ spirit complex and move on.

Questioner: I see, then, that it is, shall we say, when an individual reaches a very old age it becomes apparent to him in third density that he is worn out. Therefore, be is not attached to this vehicle as firmly as he would be with a good-looking, well-functioning one.

After the veil, the body is definitely an athanor for the mind. Prior to the veiling did the body serve as an athanor for the mind at all?

Ra: I am Ra. Yes.

You may ask one more full query.

Questioner: I believe that I should ask if there is anything that we can do to make the instrument more comfortable or to improve the contact since in the last session I was not able to get that question in?

Ra: I am Ra. We find the weariness of the group well-balanced by its harmony. That weariness shall continue in any future circumstance during your incarnations. Therefore look you to your love and thanksgiving for each other and join always in fellowship, correcting each broken strand of that affection with patience, comfort, and quietness. We find all meticulously observed in the alignments and give you these words only as reminder. All that can be done for the instrument seems done with an whole heart, and the instrument itself is working in the indigo ray with perseverance.

We have previously mentioned some temporary measures for the instrument. If these are adopted, additional liquids shall be imbibed by the instrument and by the questioner, whose bond with the instrument is such that each difficulty for one is the same in sympathy for the other.

I am Ra. I leave you rejoicing merrily in the love and the light, the power and the peace of the one infinite Creator. Adonai.

Sunday Meditation
October 23, 1983

(S channeling)

I am Hatonn, and greet you, my brothers and sisters, in the love and light of the one infinite Creator. We, as always, thank you for allowing us to join with you in your camaraderie, your singing and your sharing of the love amongst one another. It pleases us greatly, my friends, to become one with you in your seeking of the Creator. We have often in the past spoken of your seeking. My brothers, my sisters, we, at the risk of becoming extremely boring on this subject, would like once again to stress the wideness of your paths. There are those who in their seeking reach out for an object to hold to, relinquishing all else that they may come in contact, hoping to bring into perspective an illusion, my friends, that is extremely difficult to be brought into a perspective. The spiritual path that is sought is one of many turnings and should not, my friends, be limited.

This instrument is experiencing some difficulty, and we would at this time like to transfer the contact, perhaps later returning to this instrument. I am Hatonn.

(Carla channeling)

I am Hatonn, and greet you once again through this instrument in the light. We continue, once again thanking each for the privilege of being allowed to share our thoughts with you. The one thing from which all else has been removed in spiritual writings has often been referred to or compared with a precious gem, a pearl of great price, or a jewel. The crystalline quality of that which you seek is, indeed, one with the gem, but the nature of that crystalline goal which you have set for yourselves and for which you have given all is mutable, moveable and infinitely changeable, far more [than] the qualities of water, which may be steam or rain or ice or sewage.

The one certainty in your variable path is that it will change, because what you have chosen as the pearl of great price is something called the truth or love, or as we would perhaps most accurately describe it, the one original Thought or Logos that is the manifested Creator. It does you little good to seek the unmanifested Creator because you are the unmanifested Creator and if you realize that, you have manifested that which is unmanifest. Therefore, what you are seeking is the first manifestation, and you are using this great tool in order to progress.

However, the quality of truth is such that as you approach its boundary, it will recede from you, constantly giving you more to look for, to understand, to use, to experience, and to finally again use up, so that you once again reach the boundary point where you feel you have discovered at least some part of the nature of love. Each discovery of love should be celebrated as the wonderful event which it truly is. We are not discouraging you from shouting with gladness when you make a breakthrough, when the difficult place becomes easier, when the nature of life becomes clearer—by all means, raise your hands, your hearts, and your voices, and give praise because the Creator has just learned more about Itself.

But then, as if you had climbed some mist-covered peak and finally emerged from the cloud line to see a wonderful vista, you finish clapping your hands, you gather your gear and you lower yourself once again into the low ground of common third-density human experience, for that which you seek does not exist simply as a moment in which you have seen truth. It exists eternally upon the next mountain that you wish to climb and within you in the lowest of places.

We are not saying that you deserve to be of a certain nature, that you are worthy, that you have earned the nature of manifested love. You have done nothing to earn this—it is your birthright. It is within you; most have forgotten it. Therefore, a great portion of your seeking and the touchstone of your ascent upon every mountain of truth is recognition, for each truth will be recognized rather than learned. You know already all of truth, for you are truth; you embody the Creator; you manifest the very nature of love, and you change constantly.

We would at this time transfer this contact to another instrument. I am Hatonn.

(S channeling)

I am Hatonn, and greet you once again in love and light. These changes, my friends, are always with you, will always be with you. There will be times in your existence in the third density when the changes will seem to be happening so quickly. You stutter, you blink, and it seems as though you cannot take them all [in] at once. When an entity does to refine his seeking, the recognition of these phases, the growth of the Creator [within], will be more readily accepted. Be joyful, my friends. Each of you are bright with the light and love of the Creator. It shows more brightly, and warms us as we join with you. Those brothers and sisters you meet each day are also warmed, even those who may not as yet recognize that in their physical existence, still my friends, recognize in their hearts. Each has much to share. Do not be afraid, my brothers and sisters, that your light will not seem to make any difference—for it does. Be happy, my friends. Rejoice as each path widens and grows, as each of you reach out to more experiencing of the creation and more growth. We rejoice with you, my friends, it is a great blessing, one which will reach many. The path grows broader as each of days progresses. Think, my friends, how very joyful.

We would leave you now rejoicing in that love and light of the Creator. Adonai, my friends, vasu borragus. I am Hatonn.

(Jim channeling)

I am Latwii, and I greet you, my friends, in the love and in the light of our infinite Creator. We are overjoyed once again to be able to be with your group and to offer our service in an attempt to answer those queries which are upon your minds and which point the way in your seeking at this point. May we begin with the first query?

Carla: *(Inaudible)* I may as well take a shot while thinking about him. I have a personal situation in which there is a person who very much desires to cause separation between him and me. It is the first time in my life that I have had an active and long-standing relationship with someone who wants to be an enemy. I have never made an enemy of this man. At this point this man wishes to take a sum of money from my associate for no reason except his own greed. I would prefer to calmly, rationally and without anger continue going about retrieving the money involved until that job is done.

It has occurred to me partly by suggestion, but partly by my own thinking, that it is in many ways a dangerous situation for a person attempting work such as we do to have a physical negative pull on one, and might well be worth the entire five thousand "samolians" simply to remove the negative pull. It is difficult for me to weight this set of circumstances. I have my grief; I think I have conquered my desire to be right and my desire of revenge. Could you comment?

I am Latwii, and am aware of your query, my sister. We feel confident that should your thinking continue as it has that you will indeed discover a larger and larger portion of the picture in which you find yourself a painted portion. But it is our joy to make comment as well. In this case as in all cases, we see the one Creator in various portion or distortion. This entity of which you speak is the one Creator with a unique point of view in order that it might learn certain lessons, well or poorly. The same might be said of you. The situation which binds you together is that catalyst which offers both of you an opportunity to learn the basic lesson of love in some way, well or perfect, consciously or unconsciously.

It is necessary within your third-density illusion that such lessons be learned with a forgetting, for if either of you remembered completely and wholeheartedly with total clarity your true nature as the one Creator, then you would not have the same opportunity to learn love. The intensity would not be present, the variety would be reduced, the purity would not be present. Thus, it is necessary to find oneself embroiled in difficulties. To truly learn love it is necessary to find oneself embroiled in difficulties, and then to untangle the difficulties so that when each is followed to its source, the source is seen as the one Creator residing in all things.

(The telephone rings.)

We shall pause.

(Pause)

(Jim channeling)

I am Latwii, and we shall continue, my friends. Indeed, both of you in this situation have received a call, each from the other, and each hears what each is prepared to hear. The message may not be clear, some parts may not be delivered. Yet each will have a point of view and may hold that point of view quite firmly, and shall act upon it and shall have the opportunity to expand upon it and to that entity which is able to expand the point of view to the greatest degree falls the greatest degree of responsibility for sharing the treasures of the expanded point of view.

Those treasures, my sister, as you know, are always a greater acceptance and love of the one Creator. You may consider such a situation as a great opportunity and a great responsibility, for each act of service to the one Creator bears a price. If there are great fruits to be reaped, a great harvest, shall we say, available to the expanded point of view, then there is also the responsibility to manifest that love in the greatest possible degree. We do not say there is danger in such a situation, but there is great responsibility.

May we attempt further response, my sister?

Carla: No, thank you.

I am Latwii, and we thank you, my sister, as always. Is there another query at this time?

Carla: I don't think there are any more questions. Would you like to give a dissertation on any subject whatsoever? Except money market certificates.

I am Latwii, and we are honored to participate in whatever manner we may with this group. Each within this group is most dear to our hearts and our memory. We could speak at length upon any particular subject. As you know, we are often fond of doing just that. The concept of a money market certificate is quite intriguing to us at this particular moment, for upon your planet it is an interesting phenomena that wealth is measured in such a way. We find it an appropriate means in some ways of representing the third-density illusion which seems most practical and externalized. Most will not consider that a thing is real unless it can be seen, felt and made to work. That wealth and that which is of value would be similarly treated is, indeed, a product of your illusion, for what is wealth and how often is that question asked? Each in this group measures wealth in a unique fashion, yet, those with this group might measure it somewhat more similarly than might many others upon your planet, for the very question of wealth and its nature leads to the deeper questions concerning the meaning of life and how it shall be lived, what preceded it and what shall follow it.

When these questions are asked, wealth often takes on another appearance, and for those who seek the, as it has been called, the pearl of great price, the nature of the one original Thought which resides within each being, wealth indeed appears quite limitless, incapable of being confined within [any] kind of certificate, yet available to all for the seeking, a seeking without greed.

To seek without greed that which is of value so that one might be wealthy is a quite paradoxical seeking for one upon your planet to make. Usually, to seek wealth is to seek it for the self, to amass it that it might work for the one seeking it. Yet, to seek the pearl of great price if it is to be sought most efficiently is a seeking which requires that one continually give away the wealth to others who ask for whatever one may give, for these others are none other but the one Creator, are none other but the self. And the one who seeks the one Creator begins to know the desire to serve the one Creator with every fiber of its being, every thought of the mind, every drop of devotional love of the heart, and will give whatever it has to that one Creator, and this shall return to the seeker, for who is the seeker but the one who asks as well and the one Creator who dwells in all.

Yes, my friends, your money market certificates rise and fall in their value as the supply and demand continually shifts as the waves upon the sea, and that of true wealth lies deep and still at the bottom of the ocean of your being and at the bottom of the ocean within each, and though on the surface of your illusion you move with the winds of change, deep within your being you are unchanging, you are the One.

Thus, when E. F. Hutton speaks, take note as you will, but remember where the balance of wisdom lies and where the key of love is placed.

We thank you, my friends, for the great honor and opportunity of speaking with you upon this most interesting of teachings. And we shall leave you now, only in a manner of speaking, for we are with you always. We are those of Latwii. Adonai, my friends. Adonai vasu borragus.

Sunday Meditation
October 30, 1983

(This was the last meeting of the regular Sunday night meditation group before Don, Jim and Carla moved away from Louisville.)

(C channeling)

I am Hatonn, and I am now with this instrument, and we greet you with the love and the light of the infinite Creator. We would like to take this opportunity to exercise this instrument for a few minutes. Many of you have mixed emotions about the departure of the ones known as Carla and Jim. You have learned to depend upon them, but, my friends, you need [not] fear change. It is all about you all the time and you face it daily, and change offers the opportunity for growth always. One can take advantages of the opportunities or one can carelessly let them go by. It has always been a joy to join this group, and as you know, we are always ready to join your group at any time.

Many of you have been enjoying the beauty of the trees and the weather. My friends, nature always offers you the opportunity for growth. Its stillness, its silence, its grandeur, its beauty, offers magnificent opportunities for praise, and praise, my friends, is growth. Gratitude is growth, and it is difficult to watch the change of the seasons without recognizing the infinite Creator, and as the one known as Carla has indicated, change and growth has taken place in this group in the last year or so. You are more tolerant people and more understanding as a result of your meditations. The setbacks that occur from time to time, or what you call setbacks, are not really setbacks but they are opportunities for reevaluating and learning from the so-called setbacks. Never be discouraged, my friends, because the power and the peace and the joy of the universe always surround you. Indeed, one is never alone.

We are grateful to this instrument, for having had the opportunity to speak through her, and we leave you in the love and the light of the infinite Creator and offer the opportunity for someone else to channel.

(M channeling)

I am Hatonn. I am now with this instrument. On your planet all life is accompanied by change. The cells in your body are replaced. You change from day to day, from the day you are born til the day you die. Each day you are different. Nature changes. Never wish for things to stay the same. The only way they can stay the same is if you let in, you embrace change, find it exciting, grow with it, enjoy it. See the various phases of nature. Do not wish for things to stay the same, for you are asking for yesterday. Today and tomorrow belongs *(inaudible)*. Think of change as life.

I am Hatonn. I leave this instrument.

(Carla channeling)

I am Hatonn, and I greet you once again through this instrument in love and light. We ask you to picture the stark and barren beauty of a ravine in the winter. Even the snow cannot cling to its steep sides now. There are striations of brown and white with the gallant stark skeletons of trees clinging to the hillsides. We ask you to picture a meadow. It is the first soft breath of June, the lazy drone of bumblebees, the silent flicker of butterflies, the sweet smell of the meadow and a gentle wind driving soft clouds through a blue sky. We ask you to consider the pitted craters of moons which you have never seen, of asteroids that have only come to you in imagination and pictures, naked against the zero of absolute space.

We ask you to see, to pull back until you can see, to enlarge your perspective until it becomes clear to you that all three vistas are the one infinite Creator. They are different expressions, but they are created out of precisely the same building blocks, that is, they are made of light, and they have been created because of a great force and principle, one great original Thought. That thought is love.

Do you find yourself grasping in a difficult situation, listening to useless advice and wondering where inspiration and true affection have fled? Gaze upon the ravine, gaze beneath the gnarled tree trunks to the roots which stretch quietly, quietly, gathering in winter the force which will propel new growth, new love, new beauty, new service to the infinite Creator. In the summer every being shall breathe; it shall remove from your atmosphere that which you do not need and give to you oxygen; it shall be of service in the most practical way, and further, it shall be of service by its very beauty.

Do you find yourself in a pleasant time standing with the wind drifting past your cheek, listening to the lazy drum of insects? We speak to you of an illusion. Insects sting, flowers have thorns, and you shall die. Things are never remotely contracted and compacted into the shape that they seem to hold before your eyes. That which is pleasant gapes with the prevision of ashes and earth. That which seems to be already dead holds within it the transformation of birth. And in the absolute zero of what you call outer space, in the mercilessly pitted craters of foreign moons, lies the beating heart of that which has never been separated from the original Thought of the one infinite Creator. Each particle of the universe is part of the Creator. Some portions of the universe have become individualized; a great deal of it has remained love. The resounding echo of the creation is love … love … love …

We have spoken this evening through this instrument among other things in an effort to offer to you our thanks for this instrument's availing herself to us. We say farewell through this voice, for you know that each instrument has its own tone, its own melody, and each melody is sweet. Each speaking of ours is basically the same. The changes are due to the needs of those in the circle and the personality, the experiences and the vocabulary of the channel. Thus, each of you has something you need to offer if you wish to pursue the path of being a vocal channel. Whether this be your desire or whether you wish to learn the truth, the one basic tool for education is meditation. In meditation, you move beyond constancy and beyond change, beyond sea and land and planet, beyond stars and galaxies and any idea of limitation. You move within yourself. In meditation you become a listener and you listen within for a cosmos that is completely within yourself. We encourage each to follow the dictates of that seeking for truth. But before you move, meditate. You know your own path. But in most cases, you must spend some of your time in remembering it.

We would close through another instrument. I am Hatonn.

(M channeling)

I am Hatonn. I am now with this instrument. I greet you with the love and the light of the infinite Creator. Extending some of the ideas which I have discussed, but showing them in a different way, I would like to tell you how to appreciate the scene. Most people start with the total scene. But if it is the beach, start with a grain of sand; see the beauty in that grain. And all of eternity is in the grain and all of eternity is outside of the grain. Then extend your eyes to the footprints in the sand going somewhere, going nowhere. Then watch the lapping of the water obliterate the footprints. Then see the people coming from the beach houses.

The variation of the people makes the scenery beautiful. The beach houses themselves are interesting. If you start with a grain of sand, the whole scene will be seen through eyes that can see little or much. If you had started with the total scene you would not realize it but you would really be confused because there was too much. The same is true of love. It starts with the gentle gaze, a mother looking at her child, two people liking what they see. Extend love to the touching of hands, to a true dedication that is unsaid but nevertheless meaningful. Carry this love out to the very end, and you will see the true meaning of love. But if you just try to start at the end you will never get all the variations of the theme. Start out simple and then take in things that are complicated, but you will never lose your way because everything is in a grain of sand and a gentle gaze.

I am Hatonn. I leave this instrument.

(S channeling)

I am Hatonn, and greet you once more in love and light. We would stay only a few more minutes with your group at this time and would speak a few more words. Our friends, we wish to thank you for allowing us this opportunity to share your love, to be with you. We wish to thank you also, my friends, for allowing us the opportunity to serve the one infinite Creator, to grow in the creation, to experience yet one more facet of the Creator. How much more love can be given than this, my friends, to allow one to serve and to serve at the same time? We thank each instrument for their service, their willingness to serve the infinite Creator. We ask each to look within, to see the love in each, to share that love is so beautiful, my friends, and we thank you, for the love within this group is beautiful, and has gained strength over the years. The service has been great and has touched many. The light grows ever stronger and fills us with much joy and happiness. Our brothers and sisters, we would leave you now in the love and light of the one infinite Creator. I am known to you as Hatonn. Adonai, my friends. Peace be with you.

(Jim channeling)

I am Latwii, and I greet you, my friends, in the love and in the light of our infinite Creator. As always, it is a great joy to be able to speak with your group. We rejoice at the opportunity to attempt to answer those queries which you have brought with you this evening. May we begin, then, with the first query?

Carla: What's the nature of the energy stored in meditation?

I am Latwii, and am aware of your query, my sister. We find here a most interesting query, for this energy of which you speak is an energy which has not yet yielded to the measure of any instrument upon your planet, yet many, many of your peoples are quite aware of its presence.

The nature of this energy is similar to that force which you call gravity, if one would look at that force as the inward seeking of each portion of creation for that which resides within each portion. The seeking which each entity brings to the meditative state is likened unto an energy, is likened unto that which we have called gravity. When an entity in meditation seeks in some fashion to know truth, to know the one Creator, to know the self, to seek a solution to a difficult situation, seeks illumination, this seeking, then, creates the force or the energy which becomes apparent to the entity in some fashion which is understandable to that entity. Some may feel this energy as a lightening of the head, as a tingling of the body, as flashing colors before the inner eye, as a floating within free space, or as any other sensation that finds a path from the unconscious into the conscious being. The energy, then, is released from the deeper portions of the unconscious mind by means of the entity's conscious seeking. This seeking opens a passage way or a channel through which that energy passes.

May we answer you further, my sister?

Carla: No, I'll have to read that. Thank you.

I am Latwii, and we thank you, my sister. Is there another query?

K: Then, I am assuming that this energy is multiplied many times in a group such as ours. Is that right?

I am Latwii, and am aware of your query, my sister. This it quite correct, for in a group such as this one which has been most careful to tune each entity so that the group may seek in a unified fashion, then the energy becomes greatly multiplied so that each portion of energy which each entity contributes is felt in a cumulative fashion by each entity within the group.

May we answer you further, my sister?

K: No, thank you.

I am Latwii. We thank you, my sister. Is there another query at this time?

K: Yes, it's certainly not a very important question as I see it, but I'm curious. A couple of weeks ago I read Ruth Montgomery's book, *Threshold to Tomorrow*, and I'm just curious to know if that book is being read widely?

I am Latwii, and am aware of your query, my sister. We are not usually asked to give book reviews, and this is somewhat outside of our boundaries, shall we say, of ability. But we may make a comment upon such collections of work, and that is to say that each entity which is, shall we say, in a resonant type of harmony due to the seeking of that entity will be able to read those sources of information which are available to it. That is to say, such books will receive the recognition that they attract and each entity shall attract those books and sources which are most helpful to it at each point in its seeking.

May we attempt further response, my sister?

K: So it's sort of like the adage, "When the student is ready, the master appears." Is that sort of what you're saying?

I am Latwii, and am aware of your query, my sister. This is correct, my sister. The student is constantly readying itself for an endless procession of lessons and teachers and, indeed, students of its own.

May we reply further, my sister?

K: Well, no. The thing that caused me to ask that question is Jason Winters—whose story is told in the book—says he healed himself by drinking this herbal tea which was made up of three herbs. And I read in the paper yesterday or the day before that some of the cancer clinics now are experimenting with herbs from China to heal cancer, and I was just curious about whether the story of Jason Winters caused this to come about. You needn't bother to answer that question, Latwii. It's just one of my ramblings. It just seemed maybe it was just too much to be coincidental. Could you comment on that?

I am Latwii …

(Side one of tape ends.)

(Jim channeling)

I am Latwii, and am once again with this instrument. We shall comment by suggesting that many entities suffering from that disease which you may describe as the cancer are healed in various manners. Each may then claim that the particular means of healing is the secret to the disease and its cure. And yet, many may discover that one particular method does not work and another does. In truth, it may be the case that all such discoveries for this cure have in common an unknown factor, and it is this unknown factor that has produced the cure.

If you will examine many of these techniques of curing that called cancer you will discover a general tendency or attitude that is contained within most of these techniques. That attitude has many of the attributes of that which you may call forgiveness or acceptance. When an entity is able to express the love of the Creator which it receives daily to each entity whom it meets, and is able to feel that same love within its own being for itself as well, then it is often the case that the entity sees the creation about it, and, indeed, itself through new eyes. The eyes of love, acceptance and forgiveness are the eyes which heal. That known as cancer as has been discussed by those known as Ra, which is a disease which is the result of an inability to forgive, is a disease which grows from the angers which have not found their balance in love.

May we attempt further response, my sister?

K: No, thank you. That's fine, Latwii.

I am Latwii, and we thank you, my sister. Is there another query at this time?

M: Latwii, I had an interesting experience that started about two months ago. One morning these syllables which I did not know were even a word kept going through my mind all morning, and no matter what I was doing this particular set of syllables would go through my mind. And I could not understand. As far as I was concerned I didn't even know whether it was an English word. And so I tried to look it up in the dictionary, but I'm not a very good speller and I couldn't find it. So then I called a friend of mine, who is good, and she tried to look it up and she couldn't find it either. The word was "reciprocity." And to my knowledge I'd never heard this word in my life.

And she said, "I think it's a legal term, call the reference room at the library." So I called them, and they said it meant "reciprocate." Well, I couldn't understand why that word would go through my mind all morning, because, I understood the meaning of reciprocate. And lo and behold, last week I went to the library and found—I was going to give a talk for my Sunday school class—about a forty-five minute talk—and I found this amazing book called *The Invisible World*, by Pat Robertson, and one whole chapter was called "The Law of Reciprocity." And I really felt I was drawn, and that gave so much meaning to my Sunday school lesson, this chapter on the Law of Reciprocity. Could you explain why that happened?

I am Latwii, and am aware of your query, my sister. We are happy to attempt such explanation, but are unsure if we shall be able to completely elaborate upon this experience, for it is an experience which continues within your being, and we tread carefully when the potential for infringing upon free will is present.

To begin. It is only within your illusion that time seems sequential. In fact, all those lessons you seek, and all your experiences that you shall gather within your incarnation, exist simultaneously. As you continue your process of seeking you will from time to time draw from those portions of your experience which you may call the future. These portions will enrich that which you call the present. In most instances the seeker is not consciously aware of the process of, shall we say borrowing, from the future to enhance the present. In some cases the seeker will become aware of some unusual phenomenon which has seemingly intruded into the present moment.

In your case, this particular intrusion took the form of the repetitive hearing of the word and syllables of this word within your mind. That you should later in your reference then be drawn to a book and then a lesson which would utilize this word is a natural outgrowth of this particular phenomenon. That you should become aware of its initiation, shall we say, into your consciousness in such a fashion as that which was your case is the portion which is somewhat unusual in your normal frame of reference.

You will from time to time, when your seeking is particularly intense, open those passageways into what may be called your deeper or unconscious mind which has access to that which you call the future. In such instances phenomena of this nature are more likely to occur than when your seeking has not been amplified by a greater desire.

May we respond further, my sister?

K: No, thank you. That was very helpful.

I am Latwii, and we thank you, my sister. Is there another query at this time?

(Pause)

I am Latwii, and as it appears that we have exhausted the queries for this evening, we shall take our leave of this group. We once again wish to thank each within this circle of seeking for requesting our presence. It is the greatest of honors to join with you in the seeking of the one Creator which resides within each portion of the creation. We of Latwii feel it a great privilege to be able to speak with those who seek the truth, yet we would remind each that we are but your brothers and sisters, also pilgrims upon that same path of seeking. We are delighted to share our opinions with you, but would remind each that they are mere opinions, quite fallible, and are intended only as sign posts and suggestions. The truth which you seek is already with you. Your seeking within your own being will produce those true treasures. Our words are but inspiration to encourage your own seeking. We are those of Latwii and we leave you now in the love and in the light of the infinite Creator. Adonai vasu borragus. ☙

Year 1984
March 15, 1984 to June 3, 1984

L/L Research

L/L Research is a subsidiary of Rock Creek Research & Development Laboratories, Inc.

P.O. Box 5195
Louisville, KY 40255-0195

www.llresearch.org

Rock Creek is a non-profit corporation dedicated to discovering and sharing information which may aid in the spiritual evolution of humankind.

ABOUT THE CONTENTS OF THIS TRANSCRIPT: This telepathic channeling has been taken from transcriptions of the weekly study and meditation meetings of the Rock Creek Research & Development Laboratories and L/L Research. It is offered in the hope that it may be useful to you. As the Confederation entities always make a point of saying, please use your discrimination and judgment in assessing this material. If something rings true to you, fine. If something does not resonate, please leave it behind, for neither we nor those of the Confederation would wish to be a stumbling block for any.

© 2009 L/L RESEARCH

THE LAW OF ONE, BOOK V, SESSION 106, FRAGMENT 56
MARCH 15, 1984

Jim: We lived in the house on Lake Lanier for five months—from November of 1983 until April of 1984—before deciding that that experiment had been a failure. We were only able to have one session with Ra during that time because Don's physical condition was worsening, and his worry was increasing his mental distortions as well. Most of the time Carla's physical condition was also below the level necessary to safely attempt contact with Ra. In January of 1984, Don's condition became so bad that he was forced to call in sick for the first time in his nineteen years with Eastern Airlines. He would only fly a few more trips before his death that November.

However, as we were about to move back to Louisville, Don was able to gin himself up to be in good enough condition for a Ra session so we could ask about the metaphysical cleansing needs of our new home as well as ask about Don's and Carla's difficulties. Ra's reference to Carla's "inappropriate use of compassion" concerns her response to Don's continued worrying about his job, his health, and the continuance of our work. One afternoon while, Don was sharing his worries, Carla simply told him that she would take over those worries for him, and he could do what she usually did: relax, have a good time, and be carefree. Don innocently agreed. The bond of unity between Don and Carla was apparently of such a nature that this simple agreement resulted in a deleterious transfer of energy between them. This occurred at a time when both were apparently undergoing an internal process of transformation that is usually called initiation.

We can assume that our friend of negative fifth density found targets of opportunities within these combined experiences of initiation and the negative energy transfer and was able to increase their intensity. The mystery-filled nature of the cumulative situation becomes more evident here as we do not know why Carla survived and Don didn't. We can only remind ourselves of Ra's parting words after this last session when Ra suggested "the nature of all manifestation to be illusory and functional only in so far as the entity turns from shape and shadow to the One."

Carla: At the time of this session, I had gone through every kind of alarm and concern you could possibly imagine. Don had stopped eating, more or less. He was acting extremely unlike himself, and while I had not yet realized he was psychotic and not entirely in our usual reality, I was disturbed and scared by these changes. Don's entire pattern of previous behavior with him had trained me to respond to his wishes. Don picked our meal times, our movie dates, he liked and received total control over my life. Call me dependent and you'd be right. However, it was the only way Don could bear the intimacy of a live-in relationship. I could object and be heard; I could suggest and sometimes get lucky, but on the whole, Don was an old-fashioned man who liked me to be at home, period. I awaited his fancy. Meanwhile, I read, or did quiet desk work.

Suddenly, he was always asking me what I had to do next, and then driving me, a chore which hurt his piles and which he usually left to Jim (I was at that point no longer driving, it hurt too much.) He simply sat while I went to church, to exercise class, to the folk song rehearsals. Even though Jim was swamped with things to do for L/L business, for the landlord, who had him dig a root cellar out of red-orange clay, and for the house, Don began to try hard to stay in and eat at home every night, also a radical departure from his usual wont. Jim was off-balance—I think that's as far as his humor was affected. He was puzzled. But I was in full nervous collapse.

I feel that B.C. and I really did merge into one mind, one person, in that "inappropriate" transfer between us triggered by my suggestion to switch roles, and his agreement. Between us, we had a simple dynamic: he was wise and I was loving. Actually, we shared much ground, but our deeper natures were quite polarized between wisdom and love. In that transfer, Don received the extreme sensitivity with which I receive all sense impression, and the fully expressing and open nature of my heart. And I received in full strength the stark terror that lived behind Don's calm and oh-so-blue eyes, tempered by his firm and very solid grasp on the big picture.

I have come to feel that in the time from this session, which was done two weeks before we left Atlanta thankfully to return to the blessed hills of Kentucky, until B.C.'s death in November of that year, Don was able to complete an entire incarnational course of how to open his heart. I cannot express how much agony and suffering he sustained in this time. The concrete walls that were so very strong, and had protected him always, fell away as if they were never there, and he felt everything. And how he loved! He could not watch television, even the sitcoms, because there was too much suffering. He, the lifelong observer by actual oath, cried at the Mary Tyler Moore Show. And when he was in the same room with me, he tried, over and over, to explain to me just how bad the situation was. This one thought was uppermost in his mind, always. The sheer horror of what he was feeling wiped him fairly clean of most other emotion, and he was unable to remain collected for long around me.

Meanwhile, I was utterly and damnably unaware of Don's fears that I preferred Jim. When Don began snatching me to him and kissing me, not knowing his strength, he hurt me, cracked a rib, split the skin of my lips against my teeth, left bruises, even, when he was in hospital in May, put me into the hospital with him, with sciatic nerve pain which I'd gotten having to stay in an uncomfortable chair for several hours. (To Don, this was the only chair that was not bugged.) I became frightened of Don. I began waking up in the morning to find Don sitting beside me, waiting patiently for me to awaken. When he had said "Good morning," he simply began telling me how bad everything was. No matter how I attempted to get him to relax, take it easy, do what the professionals had said about exercise and medication, and trust in time to heal—all of which I tried to retail to him, with absolutely no success, he was utterly sure nothing could get better, ever. For him, reality really began to slip away, to the point where I was afraid to ride with him. My nerves broke under this most difficult strain. I was completely downcast, for I could not find Don, and all I could think was that I didn't have him to go to—I had to keep together by myself on behalf of me AND L/L Research, because Don was no longer with us. He seemed a different person altogether. The color of his eyes even changed from deep, brilliant sky-blue to navy. I'd been doing his paperwork for a long time. I knew that Don had slightly more than two years of built-up sick time with the airlines, and had interacted with everyone who had to be notified of his illness. Everyone, to a man, wanted nothing more than that Don take all that time, if that's what it took, to get it together again. The crises in his head were not real to me, or to Jim. Only he had the awful sense of impending economic doom. Don made a comfortable salary. His expenses for all three of us and the kitties cost him about half his check, usually, each month. But Don lost all hope, and truly that being that he became was living in hell.

And how can I look at that and say that it is all part of a perfect pattern? Only by having been given the grace to see it, finally, after many years of gazing at the riveting scenes in memory, probing them and working with them over the days, months and years since Don died. Fifteen years have passed, and that gives a much clearer perspective. In accepting at last the importance of the open and giving heart to balance wisdom, Don completed the personal lesson he intended to learn. Opening his heart killed his body, but truly he was rejoicing not a day after he was gone from the physical illusion, for he appeared to me several times joyful and laughing and telling me all was well. And I, my nerves permanently less than they were before the Ra contact and Don's death, have embarked upon that balancing of the compassion I have been given and earned in this next lesson, which began the day Don died.

When I woke the morning after Don's suicide, I expected my hair to be completely white. There was no outer change. But I began a completely new life at this point. Until November of 1990, I spent my time in self-judgment almost entirely. I had found out about Don's suspicions of me, and felt that he had enlarged these fears until he'd killed himself over them. It was my fault, not because I was guilty of any sort of infidelity, but because I should have guessed what he was thinking and reassured him. But this never occurred to me, in my foolish pride. I just assumed that he would KNOW that I, that paragon of virtue, would never break an agreement. I really have a continuing problem with pride, because I do try to be exact in my ethics. I got completely blindsided with Don's illness.

It was further confusing that every doctor, social worker, and friend suggested the same thing—that Jim and I needed to let him alone, not to try to bribe him to do things, because he was going to have to make the decision to get well himself, and we would only lengthen the process if we fussed. Looking back, how I wish I had had the vision to say "NUTS" to that and just stay with him no matter what. And yet, as I tried my best to do just that, vowing to stay if it killed me, my body simply went dumb on me, and I woke up one morning pretty out of touch with reality. From March onward, my beloved Don was in full and fast decline, and I was walking through a complete nervous breakdown.

The allergies which had Don so worried about the Hobbs Park house were on his mind because of the lake house's unhappy brush with being flooded by burst pipes that frigid Christmas Eve. The damp had penetrated deep into the thick wall-to-wall carpeting in the hallway, and rendered about half the house unlivable for me and Don. When we arrived here, we found a dry basement, or rather a basement with a sump pump and no unusual drainage problems. The humidity was fine, and the place was, indeed, a very angelic-feeling place, one which Jim and I have come to love deeply. It was Don's last work in the world, to pick out this place. As always, he did a fantastic job. It has been a privilege to be able to abide here, where my Donald was alive, where he suffered and died, and where he loved me so well. Jim and I have turned to this lovely little bungalow and its modest yard, and have made more and more of it into gardens. We are still working for Don! That gives us both great comfort. Whatever we do, it is only the continuation of that which he so wonderfully began with his sharp mind and wide and thoughtful nature.

It has been a dark-hued experience for me, complete with literally years of suicidal feelings and self-condemnation. Yet through this catalyst, I have learned to love myself, really to love and care for my self without trying to justify or defend. And this is not so much an advance in loving as it is an advance in wisdom—for one learns to love the mistakes only through wisdom. While I shall definitely never come vaguely close to being as wise as Don, I can feel the gifts he left with me. My intelligence has a persistence and clarity I feel are his gifts to me. And I see it as my remaining personal lesson to follow the pattern of devotion and love through every day and hour of the rest of this earthly life. I live now for both of us, as he died for both of us. And I feel the peace that comes with cooperation with one's destiny.

Session 106, March 15, 1984

Ra: I am Ra. I greet you in the love and in the light of the one infinite Creator. We communicate now.

Questioner: Could you first please give me the condition of the instrument?

Ra: I am Ra. The parameters of this instrument are marginal, both physically and mental/emotionally. The vital energy of this entity is biased towards strength/weakness.

Questioner: What would the instrument do to make the marginal condition much better?

Ra: I am Ra. The instrument is proceeding through a portion of the incarnational experience during which the potential for mortal distortion of the left renal system is great. Less important, but adding to the marginality of distortion towards viability, are severe allergic reactions and the energizing of this and other distortions towards weakness/strength. The mental/emotional complex is engaged in what may best be termed inappropriate compassion.

Questioner: Would Ra recommend the steps which we might take to alleviate or reverse the conditions of which you just spoke?

Ra: I am Ra. We can do this. The renal distortions are subject to affirmations. The entity, at present, beginning what may be called initiation, is releasing toxins and, therefore, larger amounts of liquids to aid in the dilution of these toxins is helpful. The allergies are already being largely controlled by affirmation and the near-constant aid of the healer known as Bob. Further aid may be achieved by the relocation of dwelling and future vigilance against humidity exceeding the healthful amount in the atmosphere breathed.

The mental/emotional distortions are somewhat less easily lessened. However, the questioner and instrument together shall find it possible to do such a working.

Questioner: How serious or critical is this renal problem? Is drinking liquids the only thing she can do for that, or is there something else?

Ra: I am Ra. Note the interrelationship of mind and body complexes. This is one example of such interweaving of the design of catalyst and experience. The period of renal delicacy is serious, but only potentially. Should the instrument desire to leave this incarnational experience the natural and non-energized opportunity to do so has been in-built just as the period during which the same entity did, in fact, leave the incarnational experience and then return by choice was inlaid.

However, the desire to leave and be no more a portion of this particular experiential nexus can and has been energized. This is a point for the instrument to ponder and an appropriate point for the support group to be watchful in regards to care for the instrument. So are mind and body plaited up as the tresses of hair of a maiden.

The nature of this entity is gay and sociable so that it is fed by those things we have mentioned previously: the varieties of experience with other-selves and other locations and events being helpful, as well as the experience of worship and the singing, especially of sacred music. This entity chose to enter a worshipful situation with a martyr's role when first in this geographical location. Therefore, the feeding by worship has taken place only partially. Similarly the musical activities, though enjoyable and, therefore of a feeding nature, have not included the aspect of praise to the Creator.

The instrument is in a state of relative hunger for those spiritual homes which it gave up when it felt a call to martyrdom and turned from the planned worship at the location you call the Cathedral of St. Philip. This too shall be healed gradually due to the proposed alteration in location of this group.

Questioner: Then as I understand it, the best thing for us to do is to advise the instrument to drink more liquid. I think water would be best. We will, of course, move. We could move her out of here immediately—tomorrow say—if necessary. Would this be considerably better than waiting two to three weeks for the allergies and everything else?

Ra: I am Ra. Such decisions are a matter for free-will choice. Be aware of the strength of the group harmony.

Questioner: Is there anything, with respect to the present spiritual or metaphysical condition or physical condition of this Hobbs Park Road house that Ra could tell us about that would be deleterious to the instrument's health?

Ra: I am Ra. We may speak to this subject only to note that there are mechanical electrical devices which control humidity. The basement level is one location, the nature of which is much like that which you have experienced at the basement level of your previous domicile. Less humid conditions would remove the opportunity for the growth of those spores to which the instrument has sensitivity. The upper portions of the domicile are almost, in every case, at acceptable levels of humidity.

Questioner: How about the metaphysical quality of the house? Could Ra appraise that please?

Ra: I am Ra. This location is greatly distorted. We find an acceptable description of this location's quality to elude us without recourse to hackneyed words. Forgive our limitations of expression. The domicile and its rear aspect, especially, is blessed and angelic presences have been invoked for some of your time past.

Questioner: I'm not sure that I understand what Ra means by that. I'm not sure if the place is metaphysically extremely good or extremely negative. Could Ra clear that up, please?

Ra: I am Ra. We intended to stress the metaphysical excellence of the proposed location. The emblements of such preparation may well be appreciated by this group.

Questioner: Would the cleansing by salt and water be necessary for this location then? Or would it be recommended?

Ra: I am Ra. There is the recommended metaphysical cleansing as in any relocation. No matter how fine the instrument, the tuning still is recommended between each concert or working.

Questioner: If the instrument stays out of the basement, do you think that the humidity and the physical conditions will be good for the instrument then? Is that correct?

Ra: I am Ra. No.

Questioner: We must do something about the humidity in the whole house then to make it good for the instrument. Is that correct?

Ra: I am Ra. Yes.

Questioner: I want to come back to a couple of points here, but I want to get in a question about myself. It seems to be critical at this point. Could Ra tell me what is physically wrong with me, what's causing it, and what I could do to alleviate it?

Ra: I am Ra. The questioner is one also in the midst of further initiation. During this space/time the possibility for mental/emotional distortion approaching that which causes the entity to become dysfunctional is marked. Further, the yellow-ray, chemical vehicle of the questioner is aging and has more difficulty in the absorption of needed minerals such as iron and other substances such as papain, potassium, and calcium.

At the same time the body of yellow-ray begins to have more difficulty eliminating trace elements such as aluminum. The energizing effect has occurred in the colon of the questioner and the distortions in that area are increasingly substantial. Lastly, there is a small area of infection in the mouth of the questioner which needs attention.

Questioner: Could Ra recommend what I should do to improve my state of health?

Ra: I am Ra. We tread most close to the Law of Confusion in this instance but feel the appropriateness of speaking due to potentially fatal results for the instrument. We pause to give the questioner and the scribe a few moments of space/time to aid us by stepping away from those distortions which cause us to invoke the Law of Confusion. This would be helpful.

(A few moments pause.)

I am Ra. We appreciate your attempts. Even confusion on your behalves is helpful The questioner has, in the recent past, allowed a complete transfer of mental/emotional pain from the questioner to the instrument. The key to this deleterious working was when the instrument said words to the effect of the meaning that it would be the questioner and be the strong one. The questioner could be as the instrument, small and foolish. The questioner, in full ignorance of the firm intent of the instrument and not grasping the possibility of any such energy transfer, agreed.

These two entities have been as one for a timeless period and have manifested this in your space/time. Thusly, the deleterious working occurred. By agreement in care and caution it may be undone. We urge the attention to thanksgiving and harmony on the part of the questioner. We may affirm the previous recommendation in general of the skills and the purity of intention of the one known as Bob, and may note the sympathetic illness which has occurred due to the instrument's sensitivities.

Lastly, we may note that to the one known as Peter several aspects of the distortions experienced by the questioner, the instrument, and the scribe may be quite apparent and rather simply traduced to lesser distortions.

Questioner: What is Peter's last name? I am not familiar with who he is.

Ra: I am Ra. The name by which this entity chooses to be known is Inman.

Questioner: Does Ra think that surgery in my case would be of any help?

Ra: I am Ra. We assume you speak of the colonic indisposition and its potential aid by your chirurgeons. Is this correct?

Questioner: Yes.

Ra: Again, I am Ra. Please blow across the face and heart of the instrument.

(This was done as directed.)

Ra: I am Ra. We shall continue. The atmosphere has been meticulously prepared. However, there are those elements which cause difficulty to the instrument, the neurasthenia of the right side of the face being added to other arthritically energized pain flares.

Such an operation would be of aid in the event that the entity chose this physical cleansing as an event which collaborated with changes in the mental, mental/emotional, and physical orientations of the entity. Without the latter choice, the distortion would recur.

Questioner: Now, going back to summarizing what we can do for the instrument is through praise and thanksgiving. Is that all that we can do other than advising her to drink a considerable amount of liquid and moving her into a better atmosphere. Am I correct on that?

Ra: I am Ra. We examine the statement and find two items missing, one important relative to the other. The chief addition is the grasping of the entity's nature. The less important is, for little it may seem to be, perhaps helpful; that is, the entity absorbs much medication and finds it useful to feed itself when these substances are ingested. The substitution of substances such as fruit juice for the cookie is recommended, and, further, the ingestion of substances containing sucrose which are not liquid is not recommended within four of your hours before the sleeping period.

Questioner: With my experience with the dehumidifiers I think that it will probably be impossible to lower the humidity in that house much. We can try that, and probably if we do move in there, we will have to move out very shortly.

Is there anything else that needs to be done to complete the healing of Jim's kidney problem?

Ra: I am Ra. If it be realized that the condition shall linger in potential for some months after the surcease of all medication, then care will be taken and all will continue well.

We may note that, for the purposes you intend, the location, Hobbs Park Road, whether humid or arid, is uncharacteristically well-suited. The aggravated present distortions of the instrument having abated due to lack of acute catalyst, the condition of the location about which the assumption was made is extremely beneficial.

Questioner: Then you are saying that the effect of the humidity—we will try to get it as low as possible—is a relatively minor consideration when all of the other factors of the Hobbs Park Road address are taken into consideration? Is this correct?

Ra: I am Ra. Yes.

Questioner: I am quite concerned about the instrument's health at this point. I must ask if there is anything I have failed to consider with respect to the health of the instrument? Is there anything at all that we can do for her to improve her condition other than that which has already been recommended?

Ra: I am Ra. All is most whole-heartedly oriented for support here. Perceive the group as here, a location in time/space. Within this true home, keep the light touch. Laugh together, and find joy in and with each other. All else is most fully accomplished or planned for accomplishment.

Questioner: Is it as efficacious to cleanse the house with salt and water after we move in as it is before we move in?

Ra: I am Ra. In this case it is not an urgent metaphysical concern as timing would be in a less benign and happy atmosphere. One notes the relative simplicity of accomplishing such prior to occupancy. This is unimportant except as regards the catalyst with which you wish to deal.

Questioner: Can you tell me what the instrument's difficulty was with her last whirlpool?

Ra: I am Ra. The instrument took on the mental/emotional nature and distortion complex of the questioner as we have previously noted. The instrument has been taking whirling waters at temperatures which are too hot and at rates of vibration which, when compounded by the heat of the swirling waters, bring about the state of light shock as you would call the distortion. The mind complex has inadequate oxygen in this distorted state and is weakened.

In this state the instrument, having the questioner's distortion without the questioner's strength of the distortion one might liken to the wearing of armor, began to enter into an acute psychotic episode. When the state of shock was past the symptoms disappeared. The potential remains as the empathic identity has not been relinquished, and both the questioner and the instrument live as entities in a portion of the mental/emotional complex of the instrument.

May we ask for one more full query at this working and remind the instrument that it is appropriate to reserve some small portion of energy before a working?

Questioner: I would just ask if there is anything that we can do to make the instrument more comfortable or to help her and to improve the contact, and what would be the soonest that Ra would recommend the next contact? I would certainly appreciate the return of the golden hawk. It gave me great comfort.

Ra: I am Ra. You have complete freedom to schedule workings.

We suggest the nature of all manifestation to be illusory and functional only in so far as the entity turns from shape and shadow to the One.

I am Ra. We leave you, my friends, in the love and in the glorious light of the one infinite Creator. Go forth, then, rejoicing in the power and in the peace of the one infinite Creator. Adonai.

Epilogue

Jim: After we moved back to Louisville the mental/emotional dysfunction which Ra spoke of concerning Don occurred. Don was noted all his life for being very cool and extremely wise, emotionally unmoved by events which caused others to fall apart. His observations and advice always proved to be correct. Now, as this dysfunction worsened, Don saw himself intensely affected by even the smallest stimuli. His worrying deepened to depression and he sought healing counsel from every available source, yet nothing worked, and he resigned himself to a death which he saw quickly approaching.

After seven months of this mental, emotional, and physical deterioration he became unable to sleep or to eat solid foods. By November he had lost one-third of his body weight and was experiencing intense pain. He refused further hospitalization which we saw as the last hope for his survival. The thought of having him put into the hospital against his will was abhorrent to us, but we decided to do it and to hope for a miracle, knowing of no other possible way to save Don's life at that point.

When the police came to serve the warrant a five and one-half hour standoff resulted. Don was convinced his death was imminent, and he did not want to die in a mental hospital. When tear gas was used to bring Don out of the house, he walked out of the back door and shot himself once through the brain. He died instantly.

After his death Carla saw him three times in waking visions, and he assured us that all was well and that all had occurred appropriately—even if it made no sense at all to us.

So we give praise and thanksgiving for Don's life, for his death, and for our work together.

Though this book is a more personal portion of that work, we hope that you can see that the principles underlying our experiences are the same ones which underlie yours. Though expressions may vary widely, the purpose is the same: that the many portions of the One may know themselves and the One as One. Or, as Ra put it:

"We leave you in appreciation of the circumstance of the great illusion in which you now choose to play the pipe and timbrel and move in rhythm. We are also players upon a stage. The stage changes. The acts ring down. The lights come up once again. And throughout the grand illusion and the following and the following there is the undergirding majesty of the one infinite Creator. All is well. Nothing is lost. Go forth rejoicing in the love and the light, the peace and the power of the one infinite Creator. I am Ra. Adonai." (From Session 104.)

Carla: Jim and I have wished to open this personal material for those who feel they might find it useful, because we see in our experiences a good example of the kind of stress that working in the light will produce. The more full of enlightenment the channeling received, the more enlightened the patterns of living and talking need to be. In the case of Don, Jim and me, all of our outer behavior was correct, and it was not to be held against Don that he didn't become a talker when he got sick. He had never taken another's advice, and he did not want mine or Jim's then any more than usual. And so the tendency Don had of being paranoid bloomed until he was sure I was no longer his love. For him the world without me was unacceptable.

Looking deeper at the timing here, it is crucial that it be seen that I was at this point weighing in at around 84 pounds, at 5'4". Each session was extremely hard, and yet I never flagged in my desire to continue. I was perfectly willing to die in the process of gaining these sessions' contents. Don was very worried that I would indeed die, and fussed over me continually. There was some mechanism within him which persisted in trying to figure out how to substitute himself for me in taking the brunt of the contact. He spoke about it from time to time, and I always discouraged that line of thinking. But he did just that, in the end. His death ended the contact with those of Ra, and we have never been tempted to take it up again, as we are following Ra's own advice not to do that except with the three of us.

I want to express to each reader the profound feeling of peace that has come to me in the healing of my present incarnation. There will always be that part of me that wishes I could have either been able to save Don or to die with him. I think that is one valid way I could have gone. Then he and I would be a vastly romantic, and quite dead, part of L/L history. But this is not the lesson that was mine. Mine was the lesson concerning wisdom. Ra put it to me quite bluntly when he asked what my time was for going to Jerusalem. He was asking me whether I wanted to martyr myself. This was in the context of questions Don asked concerning the possibility of more frequent sessions. My response to that was to go on my first vacation in eleven years. Don and I had adventures, NOT vacations!

Don's lesson when our energies and mental distortions were exchanged and merged by our talk in Georgia was concerning the complete opening of his heart. By remaining an observer, he had not yet succeeded in unblocking that great heart of his. In his illness, he truly thought that he was dying that I might be well and live peacefully. There is no more utter devotion and sacrifice than the giving of one's life. It does not matter, in this context, that he was dead wrong. He never lost me, far from it. He lost himself. In his moment of death he was completely open of heart, and uncaring of the pain of living or of leaving. Of course I have many and conflicting emotions about this. But always I am absolute in my faith that Don's ending was as noble as his life as a whole. To me, he is beyond words. I just adore that soul.

My lesson was the opposite: that of adding wisdom to completely open love. My heart chakra is usually quite unblocked, but my sense of limits has long been shaky. The mind-meld we shared at that time left me with a choice of dying for Don's sake or living for his work, for L/L Research, and all we had done and been together. I did exactly what I had to do to stay in this world. It was touch and go for me for a long time, long after Don's death I was working the energy of death through my own mind, body and spirit. Through the years I plumbed the depths of despair, anger (how dare he doubt me!) grief and sorrow. I faced my own physical death and knew that the crux had come, and the joy of living was still strong within me. This was during the difficult days around Christmas of 1991. I have never been in that much extremity before, not even when my kidneys failed. But my love felt never stronger. I felt as though all was being burned away, and I welcomed that. In the heat of that pain I felt cleansing and completion. From that time, it was as if a whole new strength had poured into my frail body. As I have achieved a rise from wheelchair and hospital bed, I have felt more and more joy-filled and at the same time transparent. This is a new life I am experiencing, in a new and much replenished body. Indeed, at the age of 54, I feel a grounding and balance that are solid and healthy. I am glad to be here, and feel that have entered into the working out of the second pattern that my divided life offers. I bless Don's and my sad tale. And I bless all that has occurred. We loved; we were human. It seems as though we often erred. We did not, for we truly loved. And though I shall always feel orphaned by his absence from my side, I embrace the wonderful things that are now mine to treasure. Jim and I are fueled constantly by the blessing of being able to carry on Don's work.

Any group that stays together and works harmoniously while being of service to the light will begin to attract psychic greeting of the sorts we experienced. In this crucible, every fault and vanity, however small, is a weapon against the self. Ethical perception needs to remain very alert and cogent of issues and values being tossed around. This is a matter of life and death. L/L Research is a special and wonderful place, and not unlike many other light-houses other wanderers and seekers have lit. Many, many others are awakening now and wishing to become ever more able to be channels for light. And it is a wondrous ministry, to be there as a metaphysical or spiritual home for wanderers and outsiders everywhere. We hope this helps you and your group to stay in full communication, to refuse to offer each other less than joy and faith no matter what! And never, NEVER to make a deal with the loyal opposition!

We at L/L Research continue to keep our doors open for regular meetings, and many visitors come through our doors, through the snail mail and e-mail, and as our books continue to be spread around, those who are aware of Ra's ideas are all over the globe. Our web site is www.llresearch.org, and our snail-mail address is L/L Research, P. O. Box 5195, Louisville, Kentucky 40255-5195. We answer each piece of mail, and are *always glad to hear from readers old and new. Our hearts are eternally grateful for each other, for Don, for those of Ra and the contact they shared with us. Blessings to all who read this book.*

L/L Research
Carla L. Rueckert
Jim McCarty

Louisville, Kentucky
December 20, 1997 ❧

Sunday Meditation
April 15, 1984

(Carla channeling)

[I am Hatonn.] I greet you in the love and the light of the infinite Creator. It is a great pleasure to speak through this instrument once again and to be with each of you. This instrument was reluctant to begin, however each other instrument was more reluctant than she, desiring in common to hear our words through this instrument. Therefore, although this instrument is somewhat fatigued, we find the instrument most receptive and we are grateful for the opportunity to share our thoughts with you for you are our beloved friends, and there is no greater pleasure than in your companionship. From you we have learned so much. We thank you and bless you and offer, as always, to be with each of you, for the Confederation wishes to be of service even as we find ourselves served in the doing of this humble service.

We find in the instrument's mind a phrase which passed her ears this day. It is from your holy works and concerns the teacher you know as Jesus. It was said of him in this writing, "He can save others; himself he cannot save." This is a greatly misunderstood portion of the writing which surrounds a greatly distorted telling of this teacher's life and work. We shall explore it with you with your permission.

When you consider what this particular teacher did for others, whether you wish to consider the story as myth or as history, you will find that he indeed saved; the dead man became alive, the blind man saw, the troubled woman was healed of heartsickness and learned to love. The essence of a life of service is that there is about the person who lives such a life that which heals. It may be physical healing, emotional healing, it may be healing upon levels which are difficult for most of your peoples to recognize. But nevertheless, on a planetary level, healing. Healing of inner or auric spheres, healing of earth energy—there are as many kinds of healing as there are those who offer their lives in service to others.

When the most rigorously unselfish person begins to heal, that person comes up against one of the great paradoxes of life of service to others, and that is this, my friends: beyond a certain point, giving to others robs the self. Therefore a life of perfect service to others removes the self. That is what occurred to the teacher known to you as Jesus. This teacher literally could not save himself, for perfect compassion had expressed itself in his incarnation. And in perfect compassion lies the decision to lay down the life for others. Each of you is at this time living a life of imperfect compassion by the standards set by the one known as Jesus. No matter how beatific and angelic your thoughts, how pure your motives, there is an instinctual sense of the preservation of the self. We wish you to accept this as a balanced and unquestionably necessary frame of mind as you pursue your path of service. If you give all, if you lay down your life continuously, you become literally too fine to withstand this illusion, and therefore you offer yourself as sacrifice for many …

(Sound of cats snarling.)

(Carla channeling)

Pardon our delay, but the instrument was laughing. We wish to assure you that in no way do we suggest the kind of enlightened self-interest, as this instrument would call it, that causes one to become separate and apart from others, judgmental, or in any way a stumbling block. Indeed, one can come very close to complete service to others and still remain within this illusion. But if all others are the Creator, are not you the Creator also, and is not the heart of your work your own worth? Therefore, we ask each of you not to lose that center of joy, happiness, peace, the gifts of the spirit of light which are given to you in meditation and are your birthright.

Let us dwell now upon this joy, for we would wish that you would feel more fully that which you wish to give. We wish to take you with us into etherean heights in which colors dazzle and light sings with joy. Your spirits are as beautiful as gems, and they are all worthy to be lifted up into the light, the all-pervading, limitless light that makes all one. Where can you go that light is not when you are in meditation and you have asked to see that which is? Nowhere, my friends, is there a lack of any kind. Nowhere is there darkness or shadow. Let your hearts rest upon the gentle current of the ocean of love. Let your weariness fade away as you bask in the one original Thought. Yes, you must come back, and yes, your memory will be imperfect, and your expression will not accurately reflect the totality of your understanding. The illusion is too often too heavy for you to be able to remember. And so you must go back and yet again back, and if you cannot remember, again. Persist and the word is a knowledge that has no words, a joy that has no bounds, and an expression that is limitless.

We know that each of you recognizes this state of mind and has been in it. We know that each of you wishes to serve to the utmost. And so we wish this evening to ask that you balance the grasping of the worth of the self and its life in love as against the giving of that life in love to others. An unbalanced giving is martyrdom, an unbalanced worth of the self severely limits your potential for progress upon the positive path that each of you seeks to travel. Grasp you then the balancing pole. Fix firmly in your mind the sense of the illusion through which you may laugh and cry and still know the illusion. Then, looking neither forward or backward, step out and lift your own heart.

That which is your service will be known to you day by day. What is your service this day? What has been your manifestation? It is worthwhile to spend some time in the asking of these two questions at the ending of each of your days. But whatever the answer, however far you may have been unbalanced between self worth and giving, the morning will bring more light, more love, and a new opportunity to find that perfect balance that you may give and give and give again, dancing, balanced on your center of love so that all comes through you, and a bit remains with you, just enough for today. There is no hoarding of the self possible, indeed, if you hoard your worth and your giving you shall diminish yourself. If you give all and keep no yeast to leaven new dough, tomorrow shall be difficult.

We celebrate the return to this group of two members and cannot express our happiness. We celebrate also the reuniting in meditation at this time of the one known as M as he is now sitting in meditation. Though geographically apart, there is unity and strength in your bonds. Let us ride together, my friends, in the ship we have fashioned of speech and dreams and love. Let us comfort each other in love, let us rejoice in the unity of our identity. We are the one infinite Creator. All that you see about you—shape, delineation of all kinds, all that meets your eye is the Creator. What is your service today? There is a whole creation, the possibilities have no end, and your beauty is perfection. We leave you with the promise of our return whenever you would wish it. We leave you in the love and in the light of the infinite Creator. I am Hatonn. Adonai. Adonai.

(Jim channeling)

I am Latwii, and greet you, my friends, in the love and in the light of our infinite Creator. We are filled with great joy to once again be able to address this group. This instrument is becoming familiarized with the process of conditioning once again and finds it somewhat amusing, that his jaws should be moving without conscious intent of digesting food. The food we present is of another nature, and we join this group in the seeking for that food, the seeking of the One in laughter and in joy. As always, it is our joy to attempt to answer those queries which you have brought with you. If each would search the pockets and see if the list has been remembered, we shall begin with the first query.

Carla: I forgot my list. Could you address the subject of harvestable second-density animals, and the possibility of their living to third density, and how many of them do, and how many of them come back to be with their owners?

I am Latwii, and am aware of your query, my sister. May we say it is good to hear your voice once again in the spoken form, though may we also say we have heard you from the inner speaking as well. To address your query, we shall suggest that the creatures upon your planet who enjoy existence with you and are called by you the second density, have progressed through a cycle of what you would call time that is in comparison to your own cycle most immense. Your cycle is but an inch compared to the miles these creatures have traveled. To gain the consciousness of self is an arduous process, for all we come from the One, yet in the beginning stages of that coming and becoming, the gaining of individualization is a very slow process.

Therefore, when such an entity becomes what you would call harvestable, the prospect of one that you would call a pet returning to those you call masters is a prospect which seems but a small effort to make in the repayment of the gaining of harvestability. Such an entity may feel that the doors which have been opened by the master shall await, and it shall remain and through added devotion serve the master once again in a manner which increases the harvestability, and shall as an incidental effect increase its placement within the next density when it chooses to go through that door. Many such second-density creatures travel through that door as soon as it is open, for one of the great characteristics of the second-density creature is that of curiosity, and open doors are seldom ignored.

May we answer you further, my sister?

Carla: If a second-density entity that was harvestable had been a cat, and if it chose to return to the master once more before going through that door, would it necessarily choose to be a cat?

I am Latwii, and am aware of your query, my sister. The form which is chosen is usually the form which is desired by the master. This desire is formed by habit. It is not usual for a master who loves birds, shall we say, to suddenly switch that allegiance and desire a crocodile.

May we answer you further, my sister?

Carla: No, that's a great relief. I'll check the cats out and leave the crocodiles and kangaroos and whatnot to others. Thank you very much.

I am Latwii, and we thank you, my sister. Is there another query at this time?

S: Yes, Latwii. I have a several month backlog. Unfortunately, I didn't bring my list either. I guess as it should be, a lot of these questions were eventually answered by myself. What I was wanting to ask you about this evening is perceiving an eye looking back at one during meditation or sometimes casually and quickly just as one closes one's eyes to relax for a moment, or, you know, have a cup of tea before the kids get home. And I've experienced this twice, seeing two separate eyes, one looking similar to mine, and one looking totally different, and not having a totally human characteristic that we have here. Can you make any comment on this at all?

I am Latwii, and am aware of your query, my sister. There are, of course, many possible explanations. We do not rule out astral beeping tones …

(Laughter)

… but shall suggest that is not the case. The subconscious mind of each entity which seeks the truth contains many forms and symbols which have meaning to the entity which the entity may not be familiar with consciously. Yet, when the form or symbol presents itself in a moment which is unexpected, there arise within the entity many connotations, inspirations and suggestions in holographic form, shall we say, that present yet one more piece to the puzzle, the puzzle of what is truth and who, in truth, am I, the seeker. As you seek these forms and others, and experience various phenomena, you will most often be puzzled. The message will not be clear at once, and, indeed, may never be clear to your incarnation, yet each time the conscious mind shall be enticed by that which is mysterious.

This is the nature of the seeking. Always there are guides, signposts, surprises and that which is in general mysterious, in order that the seeker might travel further and in some sense gain an insight into the nature of its own being and the creation through which it moves.

May we answer you further, my sister?

S: No, I think I'll need to digest that a little bit, thank you. And I'd also like to thank you for your patience, and it's very nice to hear you.

I am Latwii, and we thank you as well, my sister. It is a joy to hear your voice and to feel your presence and join with your being. Is there another query at this time?

Carla: Would you care to comment on the association either between the eye within the pyramid on the dollar bill and what S experienced or the eyes on the chair when the thing that the figure is sitting on in the Tarot card—I can't remember whether it's the Priestess … no, I can't remember which one it is. It's either number three or number four I think …

(Side one of tape ends.)

(Jim channeling)

I am Latwii, and am once more with this instrument. What a motley crew we have this evening. Forgetting lists, turning the tape recorder around, and forgetting the number of the card. We shall attempt response to your query amidst such difficulties …

(Laughter)

… These symbols of which we spoke in the previous response may have a personal or general connotations. As a race of beings, your people have had and shared common experiences. The eye which peers upon the pyramid, and is found upon your dollar bill, as you call it, is symbolic of that which is also called by many the third eye, that eye which resides at the brow chakra and represents the seeing of another reality. You exist within an illusion, an illusion which seems separate, one portion from another; the night and the day, the male and the female, the right and the left, the good and the bad, and so forth. With two eyes of polarity do you see but dimly within your illusion. With the so-called third eye, which is single in its sight, does one seek to see the unity of all creation. This eye is found and has been recorded within many disciplines, from those cards called Tarot, and various lodges such as Masonic, and even appears in distorted form upon your currency. This same eye has a general meaning to your peoples and may also have specific meanings to each entity.

May we answer you further, my sister?

Carla: That's what I call a general answer. Thank you.

I am Latwii, and we thank you once again, my sister. Is there another query at this time?

Carla: Well, I don't want to hog, but I did have another question. A friend of mine asked me recently about the possibility that the desire of one person in a mated couple was enough to make appropriate the actions of both. In this case it was having to do with the decision to possibly have a child. My feeling at the time was that mutual agreement in all things, whether having a child or any other portion of the relationship needed to be the basis of the action. That was my opinion. Since then I've thought about it, and wondered about the placement of intuition. In a mated couple it's always true that one is more intuitive than the other, and in a service-to-others couple, it's very possible that the most intuitive person would feel that something is correct, and it would serve both well to agree to it even if both did not fully understand. So I wanted to ask whether one person's heartfelt belief that something was so was enough for two to agree and make it so?

I am Latwii, and am aware of your query, my sister. This is a most interesting query, for it appears quite complex, and indeed may be such unless one is able to distill the heart of love from each complexity and therein find the simplicity of love which is to serve. We may suggest that as foundation to our reply it be stated that there are no mistakes, a phrase which has found frequent utterance in this dwelling, yet let us reaffirm its truth. As you move through this illusion, you cannot err, for each movement serves and each movement teaches. The question then which the seeker must ask is, "How do I wish to serve, and what do I wish to learn?"

Of course, the answers to these queries have, in part, been programmed before the incarnation. Yet throughout the incarnation free will may alter any answer. It may be that the great desire of one for a particular action is reason enough for the action to be taken, especially if the other wishes to serve in its own way by granting that request. It may also be that difficulties shall arise when the one which lacked the great desire to begin with, but found a desire to serve later, finds some regret in the future. Yet, is this not also an opportunity to once again find love and to serve and to learn?

You see we cannot give you an answer which is clear-cut, for each has lessons and services that are unique, and when joined with another are doubly unique, and there are no mistakes. The questions we suggest the seeker then ask are as we have stated. What lessons are desired? And what services are desired? Let the decisions emanate from those answers resting upon the foundation of knowledge that there are no mistakes possible, and that love is always available.

May we answer you further, my sister?

Carla: No, darn it. I understand that you can't have a clear-cut answer, that each situation is unique. I gather that's why there is no clear-cut answer. Is that correct?

I am Latwii. My sister, not only is that correct, but each situation is also always changing. May we answer you further?

Carla: No, thank you.

I am Latwii, and we thank you, my sister, for being allowed to confuse you further and for getting away with it and appearing wise in the doing. May we attempt another query?

S: Yes, Latwii, since I'm the friend, I was wondering if the decision were made not to attempt to have a child, because I feel that there is one out there, I feel that, you know, there's just one hanging around me all the time, and if I decide to not have a child, what will happen to that individual? I mean, I'm kinda worried about him just hanging around me the rest of my life. You know, will he go on and see if he can find another mother—you know, what will happen to him?

I am Latwii, and am aware of your query, my sister.

Carla: She didn't let you get away with it.

Ah, but we have another chance. The unemployment lines for the unborn are quite long. Ah, but we assure you, my sister, that should you decide not to provide entry within this illusion for that entity which you feel awaits, that this entity shall find a suitable entry within another loving couple. For this is the way of entry within your illusion. Most prospective parents, as you would call them, are not aware of the young being seeking entry before entry has been made. As you approach the end of your cycle of being within this third density, and as entities such as yourself become more aware of how the illusion operates, more and more shall find the awareness of such beings surrounding them, and shall be able to establish a communication in the way of sensing emotions and transferring emotion, and shall ease the entry process in so doing. This feeling that you have is the beginning of that process, which may or may not continue according to mutual decision.

May we answer you further, my sister?

S: I wonder why it doesn't hang around R, or is he just ignoring it? Or does the kid feel it has better luck with me?

I am Latwii, and am aware of your query, my sister. The feeling that you have concerning the entity that is, as you say, hanging around, is a feeling which is most perceivable by the, shall we say, female of your species, for it is the receptivity of that polarity which draws unto it such beings. It would take a greater effort on the part of the male polarity to perceive such an entity. The male would indeed have to reach for that perception, and desire it as well.

May we answer you further, my sister?

S: No, Latwii, I think you summed that up pretty much, and really want to thank you because I really needed this information to help me with my decision. Thank you.

I am Latwii, and we thank you, my sister. Is there another query at this time?

Carla: Well, just to finish up that train of thought. What you're saying suggests to me that unlike lots of previous centuries and lots of old information, the children that are attempting to incarnate now have balanced karma, in other words, they can go to another mother or father because they do not have any more karma. They only wish to either do planetary work or to start fourth-density work, in other words, we're dealing with a much different kind of child these days, and the balanced karma—at least it would seem in your answer—would almost have to be balanced karma in order for the child to simply go and seek another opportunity instead of, say, hanging around and waiting for C1 or C2 to be old enough to be married so that they could still get into the same family. Is that enough of a question or should I start over?

I am Latwii, and am aware of that which you have called a question, and assure you that it is enough. We deal here with terms which have nebulous meanings, those terms being "balanced karma." This term suggests a lack of certain distortion or perhaps even a lack of karma which would then free the choices. We feel we tread on shaky definitive ground when using these terms, and would suggest that the concept which you wish to convey might more lucidly be conveyed by stating that such entities as now wish to enter your illusion do not have a balanced karma, but have a shared karma with a great number of your peoples so that many choices present themselves. Should one not be appropriate, then others, perhaps, can be utilized instead. For you see, at the end of your cycle of being within this third density, there is the possibility of experience presented to those who have polarized to a sufficient degree to become harvestable within what is a very short period of what you call time. The polarization necessary to be harvestable carries with it many, many shared experiences so that many now upon your planet have many shared or similar experiences, [and] therefore may provide more of the same, each to the other.

May we answer you further, my sister?

Carla: No, thank you.

I am Latwii, and we thank you for your query and apologize for the seeming complexity of the response.

Carla: I'll read it.

Is there another query at this time?

(Pause)

I am Latwii, and we find that we have exhausted the queries for the evening, and though it is not usual for an early ending, perhaps it is the long space of time between our speaking to this group that makes this evening seem so short. We thank each of you for asking that we join you, and present our humble service to you. We rejoice with you in your seeking. We humbly praise the one Creator with you, and we remind you that we are with you upon request, and would delight in joining your meditations at any time, as you call it. As always, we now shall take our leave of this group in word only, for we are always one with you. We are those of Latwii, and we leave you in love and light as we join you in love and light. Adonai, my friends. Adonai vasu borragus. ✣

L/L Research

Sunday Meditation
April 22, 1984, Easter

(H channeling)

[I am Hatonn.] I greet you, my friends, in the love and in the light of our one infinite Creator. It is a very great privilege to be with this group this evening. It is a very great privilege to speak through this instrument who has for so long not allowed our contact through him. It is not that he did not wish to speak our words, it is simply that he felt it inappropriate.

(Pause)

I am Hatonn. I shall now continue. As I was saying, each of you decides at each movement through free will what you will do, what you will think, how you will act. Each of you may decide at any instant to become channels, for us to remain silent. We approve wholeheartedly of either action. This instrument has for several of your years remained silent. At this time we are using him in specific way. It is not exactly the same way that the other instruments in this room are used, but it is appropriate for him at this time. So please bear with us while we speak through this instrument and recondition him to receive our thoughts.

We of Hatonn are of the density of love, and this is our message. Our message to your people is a message of love. It is a very simple message. It is a message we have repeated millions and millions of times, uncounted millions of times, my friends, to the peoples of your planet. It is a message of love for other beings. Actually, my friends, this is all that is necessary to be communicated to your peoples at this time. There are many other things that we have told you, and many other things that we will tell you. However, if this single message could be fully understood and fully applied during each instant of your experience in your present illusion, all else would be unnecessary, for you would then realize personally everything else that we have had to give you, every other concept, for we come to you to help you understand the nature of the creation in which you dwell, the creation of which you are an integral, single, unified part.

If you look about you during your daily activities, and see any part of the creation, experience any part of the creation, embrace any part of the creation, and feel for that seemingly separate part the feeling of love, you have, shall we say, made the grade. What, my friends, is this feeling of love? What is it that you experience when you feel this? It may seem a bit different for each of you, and yet it is one thing, and ultimately is only one feeling, one experience, one knowledge. It is a feeling of total unity, total compassion, total oneness with the seeming other self, the seeming other entity, whether that entity be an insect, a rodent, an owl or an individual; whether it be the most ugly, unacceptable entity that you have ever experienced or the most beautiful and attractive. If that same total feeling of unity and love fills your being on contacting either end of the spectrum of what you might call desirable, then, my friends, you have found the Creator's love.

This is the message that we bring to you. It is not complex, it is not intellectual; it is a feeling, a knowing, an all-embracing experience. It is a total unity with everything that there is. It expands your consciousness from the seeming isolation of your being to total acceptance and merging with all other consciousness and all other beings. We hope we have been of some small service in once more bringing you the single basic concept. It is the foundation of the universe. It is the Creation and it is the Creator and it is you.

We have been privileged to speak to you this evening through this instrument, and at this time we leave this instrument. Adonai.

(Jim channeling)

I am Latwii, and I greet you, my friends, in the love and in the light of our infinite Creator. It is with great joy that we join your group this evening. We thank each of you for inviting our presence.

It is our privilege and pleasure to attempt to offer our service by means of attempting answers to your queries. We would then, without further delay, ask if there is a query with which we might begin?

Carla: Could you give some general information about the transfer of personalities, and its metaphysical nature and purpose?

I am Latwii, and, my sister, we feel that we have the basic gist of your query but would ask if you are referring to that phenomena which you have shared with another in this group?

Carla: Yes.

I am Latwii, and we shall attempt a response as best we can. This instrument is somewhat doubtful that adequate response is possible through its channel but with its kind permission we shall attempt such.

The transfer of which you speak is one which is quite unusual among your peoples. For it to occur there must be a certain unity between the transferees, shall we say. There must be a harmony of being which permits an exchange to occur without loss, shall we say. Many of your people experience that which is called possession, and in this experience there is a certain loss to the personality which is being possessed and such would be the case if entities of the, shall we say, normal configuration were to attempt such a transfer as that which you have experienced. Yet with the unity which you have in common with the one known as Don, the transfer was easily effected, for it was offered with firm intention.

It is not often understood among your peoples that the primary ingredient to all your evolution is intention. That which you will occurs because you will it. If you are unsure of what have willed, observe that which has occurred. The transfer of characteristics of your personality and the reception of the characteristics of another personality, then, in this instance resulted in dual personalities residing within both entities. This was not a complete transfer, however. For such to occur, there would be much more preparation, and the skills of the adept would be consciously applied. The transfer occurred not due to such skills of the adept, but because of firm intent and of the harmony which existed and does exist between the two entities. The partial transfer was a transfer of those characteristics which were most immediately available, those, shall we say, on the surface of the personality, those which were pronounced and therefore most easily transferred, and not requiring in your case the skills of the adept.

For the one known as Don the portions transferred were of the nature of concern, anxiety, fear, worry. These, shall we say, characteristics had been surfacing for some time within this entity and had been finding avenues of expression in various directions. The portions which you yourself transferred were those of great sensitivity, great compassion, without bounds or control, so that much now seems out of control and most sensitive to the one known as Don.

May we answer you further, my sister?

Carla: Yes. After the incident took place … I have two questions, this is one. After the incident took place I had an acute episode wherein I experienced all the characteristics you mentioned, and a few more. However, the effects did not last, or if they lasted they were integrated into myself, and I have not felt less than whole since very shortly after that time. It is my perception of the one known as Don that his primary nature is that of a wise person. I do not feel perceptively wiser. However, I do feel integrated. On the other hand, some of the deeper characteristics of mine seem to be transferred to Don, and rather than an acute episode and then integration, seems to have the nature of a chronic or cycling character, and it does not become integrated or become comfortable.

And I guess my first question is why should he have to suffer and I am not, and secondly why should he not receive the extremely tough nature with extremely strong will which I offered to him when I to said him, "I'll be the strong one and you can just take a rest for awhile." Why was he not able to receive the toughness that is at my heart? That's sort of an A and B. Why is he suffering so much more than I, and why didn't he get the rest of me, the part that he needs or even the part that he needs of himself which is equally tough?

I am Latwii, and am aware of your query, my sister. We feel that the two portions of your query may be combined, for they are indeed one. The cause of what you have called the suffering is due to, shall we say, lack of transfer of that portion which you have spoken of as the toughness. The one known as Don has indeed that great quality of wisdom which is itself composed of what you would call a tough fiber, and in your actions you have without becoming aware of it expressed this quality, and have it to some degree yet. It is not an easy query to respond to, that is, why there is suffering in this case, for there are many portions to this situation, some of which we may not touch upon, for they lie within the rim of what you may call free will infringement.

We would remind each entity that this experience is a great opportunity, yet with the opportunity comes the risk; such is so at all times. The one known as Don has many portions to his personality, as does each entity, and there are many portions which are in motion in regard to his being at this time. Some of those are known and some are suspected; others remain mysterious. As that quality known as fear attempts to be expressed in any personality, the attempt is usually for the purpose of achieving a finer balance. This is the purpose of all distortion, that greater experience and balance might be offered and achieved. Each distortion has a purpose that may be expanded to many levels of perception in the life experience. The great wisdom of the one known as Don has been a valuable ally throughout the incarnation. To search carefully so that each step taken is placed with care is a wise thing to do. When one begins to doubt the results of the search, to doubt in some degree the ability of the self to step forward, then the wisdom becomes somewhat distorted, and there is the tendency towards that which you may call fear. This tendency then presents the opportunity to renew the faith in the stepping forward. When this quality of wisdom being distorted and presenting further opportunity for strengthening is affected by other forces, shall we say, then the situation becomes somewhat complex.

At each point in an entity's growth there is the opportunity to express the fullness of being that is each entity's birthright. At certain points there shall be tests. There shall be that which is called the initiation. Each initiation proceeds in a totally unique fashion in ways which are quite beyond the ability of most entities to comprehend, and are beyond our ability to express at the present time due to the desire we feel not to infringe upon free will. The actions of those entities of negative polarity which monitor this group also add their particular distortion to the situation. The toughness which you have to offer is not in this case transferred, for it was not, shall we say, upon the surface of your being, and was needed for you to be the strong one, shall we say. *(A telephone rings.)* We shall pause.

(Pause)

(Jim channeling)

I am Latwii, and am once again with this instrument. We appreciate the notes of joy, and shall complete our response at this time. To summarize that which we have taken so long to speak, and apologize for, we may say that the transfer was not of a total personality, and not of the characteristics which might be desired to be transferred should the process be understood consciously. Therefore, each received that which was available and upon the surface of the personality. The complexity of the transfer is to be appreciated when viewed from the perspective of the one known as Don, for this entity is experiencing other phenomena as well as the transfer which is playing a large role in distorting his current perceptions.

May we answer you further, my sister?

Carla: Yes. I would like to say that that was not a long answer considering what you told me. It was very concise and I thank you. It strikes me that this has been a kind of a key incident in my life. You meet people, and you've seen them before, and you realize that you have made preincarnative agreements with them to be companions or friends or whatever, and I suspect that this was a preincarnative possibility, a planned possibility, simply because I had no conscious idea that there was anything like this possible. It *(inaudible)* question is, if you can tell me that, is this correct? And the other part of the question is, is there a way to finish the job so that the compassion without the toughness can be changed to the balance that I have achieved to this point, which I would be glad to transfer?

I am Latwii, and am aware of your query, my sister. We find that such preincarnative choices have indeed been made, yet with each preincarnative choice there is the great variety of means of expression. Some abilities and faculties are left to the, shall we say, unconscious mind to serve as rudders or general guides so that the personality is powered by forces unseen or so it seems. Other characteristics and abilities are presented with conscious expression possibilities so that during the incarnation entities may, shall we say, realize the fruits of the preincarnative choices upon a conscious level. During your lives together you have expressed in an unconscious fashion and on numerous occasions this ability to transfer portions of yourself. You have with each other been able to lend portions of yourself to the other, yet this lending ability has not been as conscious a choice as the recent transfer of which we have been speaking. The reintegration of personalities is that which you have been attempting now for some time to achieve.

We find that there is a limit here to our ability to speak upon this subject, yet find the suggestions of the one known as B to be most helpful in this instance. Again we remind each entity that it is the intention which is most important in this case as in all others in which there is the conscious attempt to progress in mind, body and spirit. The sitting in silence together with the focus upon the true nature of being, the true nature of each entity's being, and the true characteristics of each entity's personality is that which is most helpful.

May we answer you further my sister?

Carla: No, I think that's been an extremely helpful answer. I have only one more question to tax your patience with, and that is, when we decided to do this, it just seems to me that a lot of friends or mates would have decided to attempt to balance by transfer in order to be of more service to other people, in order to be more balanced entities, and you say this is very unusual. Why is it very unusual, because it obviously has a lot of good qualities if you can tough it out? For service to others, I mean, it has a lot of potential for service to others.

I am Latwii, and am aware of your query, my sister. That which we find unusual in this instance is the degree of transfer. As you have mentioned, there are many upon your planet who seek to serve a mate, a family member, or a friend by transferring some portion of the self to that entity that that entity might in some way benefit, yet it is quite unusual to find two entities who have the qualities, shall we say, necessary to effect a transfer in the manner which has occurred between you and the one known as Don. There must be, as we mentioned, a firm intention, powered, shall we say, by a strong will. There must be a harmony of being between the two which is of a high degree. There must be a sensitivity upon each entity's part which allows the feel, shall we say, between those portions of the self being transferred and those portions of the other self being received. And there must be a certain conscious quality of understanding which, even though small, is necessary in order for the transfer to occur.

We speak of these characteristics which are necessary for such transfer in terms which we feel are most able to be comprehended, yet we remind you, my sister, that we speak of a phenomenon which is quite beyond the description of words, and in truth we feel we do not do justice to its qualities by our words.

May we therefore attempt further response?

Carla: No, thank you.

I am Latwii, and we are most grateful to you, my sister.

(Side one of tape ends.)

(Jim channeling)

I am Latwii, and am with this instrument once again. Is there another query that we might attempt at this time?

(Pause)

I am Latwii. Well, my friends, we had our operators standing by but we have not received another query. We hope that we have not been too laborious in our previous responses and caused each with a query to fear that that would be the fate. We shall ask one final time if there might be another query to which we might attempt a brief response?

Carla: Okay. Make a brief response to this. When I was in church this morning, it being Easter Sunday, I was relatively unmoved by the service although I was praying with my normal zeal and enthusiasm, it being my distortion to worship in that way, and suddenly I was not in the church. This has happened to me before. The portion of the service that was occurring at that time was the reading of what is called the Gospel which is part of a holy work called the Bible. And the reading was that Mary Magdalene went to the tomb on Easter morning where her teacher was and she found the stone rolled away from the mouth of it, and her teacher was gone, and she felt that his body had been stolen by somebody, and she cried. And that's where I was, and I was wearing the clothes that she was wearing, and I was crying. And I wasn't gone for very long. I came back and they were finishing up that reading. And I discovered tears on my cheeks. I don't cry, don't have any tears of my own. And I wondered if you could say something in general about the nature of that kind of experience? Briefly, of course. Concisely. And at no great length.

I am Latwii. Yes.

(Laughter)

Carla: Would you please?

I am Latwii, and now to our more characteristic response. The quality of which you speak is one which is uniquely expressed in your being and that is your empathic ability. The one known as Jesus has great appeal to your distortions, and on occasions which honor this teacher such as this particular day, your devotion to his teachings and the praise of his work and life is that quality which is the motivator, shall we say, of the focus of your empathic ability. You experience that which is read and become the entity spoken of. In some degree this quality is available to each who worships, yet the intensity of the experience is dependent upon the devotion to the one known as Jesus, and the sensitivity of the one who worships. Since you have both qualities in great degree, it is possible for you from time to time to experience that of which you have spoken.

May we answer you further, my sister?

Carla: No, thank you.

I am Latwii, and we thank you, my sister. Now that we have proven that we can speak briefly, is there another query at this time?

(Pause)

I am Latwii. We are aware of several potential queries that have not yet found their time of ripeness. Perhaps at a later meeting we shall have the honor of attempting answer to them. We would remind each entity that our words are but words, and are but our opinions. Take them for what they might be worth to you. Leave those which have no value. All words are but guides and all guides can take an entity but so far. The journey you travel is truly your own and the strength to continue it will come from your own efforts. We are greatly honored to be a part of that journey, and, in truth, we travel as One to the One through the One. We thank each in this group for inviting our presence, and we remind each that we are but a request away. We shall take our leave of this group at this time, and leave you, as always, in the love and in the light of the one infinite Creator. We are known to you as those of Latwii. Adonai, my friends. Adonai vasu borragus. ☘

Sunday Meditation
April 29, 1984

(Unknown channeling)

I am Hatonn and I am now with this instrument. We greet you my friends, in the love and the light of the one Creator. My friends, were you touched today by the rain? Did you feel gladness? Did you feel elation? Did you sit back and feel the life, the love? Did [you have] the thought of new life coming forth? Were you hurried? Did your thoughts lead you to a darkness? Each of those conditions exists. Which you see depends each you may …

We pause. It has been some time since this instrument has channeled, and we must readjust for contact, for he was beginning to slip away somewhat. We would pause briefly at this time to readjust.

(Pause)

I am Hatonn, and we are once again with this instrument. We will again try to speak through him, but will cease if he feels uncomfortable again and start through another.

My friends, each thing you perceive in the world around you are symbols which may be seen from many different sides, as with the rain which fell. It brings to some sorrow, for they see it is something to convince them, to perceive it as a barrier. It seems they cannot climb. It shuts them in with their thoughts with which they must deal. Others see the rains as a great joy. They feel the life-giving waters upon themselves and are refreshed. They open themselves to thoughts and experience both feelings that are very real. Both are lessons with which we must deal. When the rains come into lives, feel them. Let the rain touch you as you would the sun.

I am Hatonn, and we would now, at this instrument's request, transfer this contact. I am Hatonn.

(Carla channeling)

I am Hatonn, and I am now with this instrument We greet you once again in the love and the light of the infinite Creator. And again may we thank each of you for wishing to share meditation and contemplation with us. It is our great joy to be able to be of any service we may be of to you.

The transparency of your experience is dependent upon your willingness to use the tools which are yours as a birthright but which take discipline and energy to use. To one who is completely unaware of any need to pierce the illusion, the world is an opaque thing. The sky is sunny or stormy. Friends are good or false, and circumstances vary. It is the work of those who seek truth, upon arriving at each portion of what you may call truth, to apply it towards the lightening of the opacity of your experience. Each of you has often had a significant and memorable dream, and has upon awakening repeated it and told of it to others, and searched within the dream for the meaning that may be applied to better grasping what the subconscious self was attempting to communicate through this medium to the conscious mind.

Once you have planted your feet upon the path which a seeker walks, in a very specific sense you are not of this world. There is no need for you to be of this world, and the degree to which you take this world to be opaque is your choice, for you know that this world is an illusion. It is possible and indeed profitable to view portions of your experience in a waking state precisely as you do an interesting dream and attempt to determine what it was that your subconscious mind was attempting to tell your conscious mind, for, indeed, just as much as any dream, that experience which you have during your day is a quite accurate representation of what your deeper self wishes for you to engage your attention upon.

Further, it is likely that you as your great Self, hope that in this incarnational experience you not only find transparency in the illusion and begin to read the daily experience, but also you begin to act in accordance with your understanding. Please understand, the fruits of the work of the seeker are secondary to the original intention of grasping the truth, however, one who seeks and begins to find the truth then finds that unless that which is learned is now manifested, further learning will be slow, and the lessons will seem to repeat themselves. The process is from opacity of experience to transparency of experience, and with your feet planted firmly in the Kingdom of Heaven, moving back into the world of illusion with eyes which see, ears that hear, hearts that understand, hands that can reach without reserve in service to others.

Your own training is designed so that you may first be your own stumbling block, then remove yourself as a stumbling block and replace that self with a greater self that is filled from a source which is beyond this illusion which you call third density. To fix your feet firmly so that you may do these things so that you may be of help, so that you may truly listen, truly see, truly hear, it is necessary not only to meditate but also to do any other exercises that you find necessary in order to keep a sense of your center, your source, and your peace.

If you find that in meditation you are peaceful but after meditation you are not, you must seek then to discover what it is within you which cries out to be helped. You must work within your own self. Treat yourself as the precious Creator which you are. If there is difficulty, work on it, accept it within yourself. Deal with it to the best of your ability and release it into that great light which is the form of all that has substance.

There are times, of course, when there are breakthroughs, and you find that you have jumped several levels of perceptions very quickly. When this is the case, it is most usual that the lesson will not be a permanent incarnational experience but will fade to be replaced once again by the difficulties. Creation was designed [in] what this instrument would call true Murphy's Law fashion. It is designed to go wrong, to break down, to seem inadequate and to cause you to be uncomfortable. This density is designed to cause you to become aware of that about which you previously were unaware. It is not designed for the complacent or the smug or the full of spiritual belly.

Whenever you get too comfortable, be aware that your deep self is undoubtedly fattening you in order that your next experience will be one that you can find the challenge in, discover the heart of, and take with joy into all of your being. Indeed, my friends, of sun and rain, whether it be the weather or your emotional climate or any other circumstance of this polarized world, are illusions to be greeted, each with thanksgiving, indeed, with joy.

We do not mean at all to suggest that there is no such thing as a overriding sense of peace, that those who have peace have fixed their mind upon that which lasts beyond the seasons, that which does not die, that which does not become corrupt. Those who have peace have what some would call faith. Faith is not a tool which one brings to bear upon difficulties when the going becomes treacherous. Faith is a necessity. It is in faith that you move into a transparent light-filled illusion which you may at your leisure ponder and study, dream upon dream and day upon day, creating your life instead of reacting to it.

We would like to close through another instrument. We are aware that the one known as K has some reservations, and will return to the one known as

Carla if the one known as K feels the contact is not yet at an acceptable level. I am Hatonn.

(K channeling)

I am Hatonn. Again we greet you in the love and the light of the infinite One. Many changes have taken place in your lives since your last encounter. Let me assure you that you have grown in wisdom and in spirit during this period since you were last together, and may we also assure you that even in the midst of difficulties, there is always joy. Even though at times it appears to be well hidden of the clouds, even with the rain brings beautiful spring flowers. The rain and the sorrow in your own lives brings the same beautiful flowers. We look forward to being each time we have the opportunity, so we bid you adieu tonight and leave you in the love and the light of the one infinite Creator. I am Hatonn.

(Jim channeling?)

I am Latwii, and I greet you, my friends, in the love and in the light of our infinite Creator. It is our great joy to once again greet this group and to attempt to offer our service by answering those queries which you have brought with you. We are most pleased to welcome those who have long been absent, in your measure of time, from this group, for they are those which have given us great joy in the many queries which they have presented us. May we begin with the first query?

Questioner: Yes, Latwii. I am the President-Elect of the Women's Club of St. Matthews, and I would not have accepted this position under any circumstances had I not thought that I had some kind of a mission, and I don't like to use that word mission, but nevertheless, in the lack of a better one. There is so much illness, and so much stress among the members, and I really would like to be of help but I have a sense of fear and intrepidation that I may go too fast and offend rather than help. Would you comment on my frustration?

I am Latwii, and am aware of your query, my sister. We do not mean to sound simplistic when we say that you will be as you will be, and those within whom you find yourself in comradeship shall be as they shall be, and together you shall find those deeper levels of meaning which you have come to find. It may not be that you shall find these levels of meaning and fulfill such purposes in ways which you plan, for your plans are of your conscious mind more or less, and it is through such indirect avenues that the deeper mind and greater Self moves with what you might call the current of your being.

That you fear or feel anxiety for your ability to be of assistance as it is needed is a hopeful sign, for again it is through such an avenue that you may well find yourself, shall we say, that your efforts shall be the best that you have to offer. Know that you cannot make a mistake, that each offering which you share shall be of service, though the service may not be known in full by all at once. Yet, the service will exist, and shall be found. The quality of service, as the quality of any artistic endeavor, will be available on many levels. Those levels which are deeper shall take greater time, shall we say, for the seeds sown there take a special caring, yet they do sprout.

May we answer you further, my sister?

Questioner: No, I guess not right now.

I am Latwii. May we attempt another query?

Questioner: Latwii, I too have myself with a group who I would not have thought myself getting involved in, yet we have come together with a common goal, but I feel an uncomfortableness around some of the others within the group, I think partly due to my not being able to fully accept them and their ways of operating. I feel that although we have set a goal, that the differences—things that are different between us—are making us see that as two different things.

I want to stay with this project, and at the same time, I need to be able to … I am rambling on and not forming a question. It is just an uncomfortable feeling right now. I think that our group has gotten into two separate bunches, seeing the goal two different ways, and I am afraid maybe it is going to kill the whole thing. And I wonder if you might speak on how I can better open myself to the others so that I can better understand them, and maybe them better understand where I come from. If you can [put] enough of that together to make any comment back to me.

I am Latwii, and am aware of your query, my brother, and we shall certainly do our best to make a response which will hopefully be of some service. May we begin by suggesting that the experience which you now share with this group of entities is much like any experience which any entities might share together. Those of many persuasions and sets of mind come together for a stated purpose, and as you mentioned, goals are set. Yet, my friends, how many of you would be surprised to discover that perhaps the greater purpose of joining together is not to accomplish the goals that are set?

Yes, of course, it would be helpful, occasionally, if certain goals could be met for service to others, for that is, of course, the purpose. Yet, look at the mechanism by which that purpose is achieved in your daily lives. You find various attitudes concerning how to meet the goals. You find that the self has a certain point of view and can accept that which falls within certain boundaries, yet are you not here to remove boundaries? Are you not here to accept all that exists as the one Creator?

So, as you go about your work with these other selves, you will constantly find the opportunity to expand those boundaries which hold your perception and ability to accept within certain limits. If no goals commonly set were ever achieved, there would yet be the constant opportunity to accept, to love, to forgive, and to communicate clearly with those other selves with whom you find yourself journeying to the one Creator.

It is as though you are each a pilgrim and together you are a band of pilgrims, and long have you journeyed on this road, the road to the one Creator. Yet, you are the Creator, and each moment you experience the experience of the Creator. But you have forgotten this in this life, and in order to intensify your experience as the one Creator, you are as children, make up certain games, join certain groups, to, shall we say, pass the time as you journey. You are so successful in passing the time that often you forget that you journey.

Remember, my brother, you are a pilgrim. Seek your deepest goal. See the Creator within those with whom you journey. Your viewpoints will widen. Each experience of difficulty will widen that viewpoint.

(Pause)

I am Latwii, and am with this instrument once again. And you shall love that which was not previously lovable.

May we attempt further response, my friend?

Questioner: Yes, one of the problems I have been having is evidenced by the previous attempt to form a question. It is that my mind and my mouth no longer function together. I seem to have lost sight of my deepest goals. I seem to miss the here, there, wherever. I cannot, many times, make a simple comment to someone because in between the time it is thought and the time it comes out, I forget words, mutter them, stutter with them. It is just as though, wherever I am, I am not there. I am not able to fully put my energy into things, although I have been involved in many things. I have been trying. There is some empty spots. And sometimes it feels weird that I can hardly say hello to someone without either muttering it or saying half the words and forgetting the rest. It's just—I don't know if you would call it confusion or just *(inaudible)*. Could you comment?

I am Latwii, and am aware of your query, my brother. As the pilgrim journeys, there are many conditions which the pilgrim must adjust the self to. The road is not always smooth. Storms arise, and there are agreements and disagreements with fellow pilgrims. There is the consulting of the map and the occasional doubt as to the landmarks. There is the rain, the sun, and the dust, the insects. There is much which makes the journey a great challenge. There are those times in each pilgrim's life during which there will be confusion and a concentration upon the essence of one's being which seems less than clear. Less than it was, shall we say.

Such occasions arise as opportunities, shall we say, for the finer tuning of the quickest of the pilgrim. There is an analogy which we may make. From time to time, that instrument which you may call the radio will find its wave of reception wavering due to influences in your atmosphere. Perhaps a bit of attention to the tuning is all that is necessary to restore a clearer reception. This is the same process which any pilgrim undertakes upon the journey at any point during which the experience of the journey seems less than what is perceived as possible. This attuning may take a long or short period of what you may call time, for time is irrelevant. It is the essence of the tuning that is of import.

Know that whatever experience we encounter, be it confusion, lack of attentiveness, forgetting of words, difficulty in communication or distorted perceptions, that there are no mistakes which are possible for you to make, for each experience contains the heart of the Creation and of the Creator. And each experience, therefore, has all you seek available for your seeking.

May we answer you further, my brother?

Questioner: Not at this time. I feel there will be one later.

I am Latwii. Is there another query at this time?

Questioner: Just a passing query which you may not be able to answer. What was the purpose of the vigorous, clockwise, involuntary rotation of my head that took place during a fairly long part of the meeting?

I am Latwii, and am aware of the phenomenon of which you speak. We can speak without infringement by suggesting that such a movement is usually accomplished by a deeper portion of the self which is aware that there is momentary imbalance in the spinal structure which may be corrected by such a movement. This movement is for the purpose of allowing a more free flow of those energies which traverse the energy centers of the spinal column.

May we answer you further, my sister?

Questioner: No, thank you.

I am Latwii, and we thank you and thank you again for patience for the previous method of response. This instrument was not certain whether a response of any sense could be made to that query, and therefore requested greater conditioning. May we attempt another query at this time?

Questioner: Oh yes, Latwii. So many people seem to get so disturbed so very easily, and I have great sympathy for them but I don't exactly understand why. Because I have lived my entire life on an edge of a cliff, never really caring whether I went over or not. And I don't seem to go over, and I seem to have good health which I don't care whether I live. Why is there that difference between people?

I am Latwii, and am aware of your query, my sister. We do not need to be simplistic in our response but may suggest that the difference that exists between entities exists that the one Creator may know variety. Each entity has a specific vibration or frequency, shall we say, various abilities in-built before the incarnation in order that certain services might be performed and certain lessons might be learned. Each learns in an unique fashion, and if all entities were as impervious as you to that catalyst which finds them there would be a homogeneity of learning which each might be, shall we say, boring to each entity, and not provide the one Creator with variety and intensity of experience which is possible with the unique configuration of seekers.

May we answer you further, my sister?

Questioner: Well, maybe a little bit. Some of these people I know that have died have had a great desire to live, and they have died. And other people who couldn't care if they lived or not, seem to continue. It doesn't exactly make sense to me.

I am Latwii, and we will assume that you ask why, and shall respond by suggesting that the incarnation is the point at which free will and what you might [call] predetermination meet. Each entity has the complete free will to follow whatever path it chooses to follow. Yet, each entity is also programmed by its own choice by preincarnational predispositions, shall we say, so that there are those currents of energy which the entity moves upon, but anytime the entity may change the course, change the means of travel, and, indeed, change the travel completely.

May we answer you further, my sister?

Questioner: No. That's very helpful. Thank you.

I am Latwii, and we thank you, my sister. Is there another query at this time?

Questioner: Yes, you answered my question partly to my satisfaction—understanding, I think is a better way to put it, Latwii, but as I was listening to C it seems to me that he is taking himself too seriously, and I concluded that is what I have been doing also. I know I have a tendency to take myself too serious. Would you comment on the fact of what I just said, that maybe C and I are both taking ourselves too seriously?

I am Latwii, and am aware of your query, my sister. We shall not make any judgment as to whether or not one or another may take the self seriously, but shall suggest that there is a balance in attitude which may be struck between the taking of the self and the experiences of the self in a manner which you may call serious, and in viewing the self and the experience of the self in a lighter and more jovial manner: the serious attitude which ensures the entity that it shall continue focusing upon those lessons and services which it feels are its mission or purpose for the incarnation; the lighter or jovial touch [which] is most helpful for the entity to not only to endure those times which are filled with what you might call difficulty, but [which is] most helpful as the entity attempts to widen the viewpoint and see that experience and self it is familiar with on a larger scale, that which you may describe loosely as the cosmic or grand scale.

To look at any situation and see that situation in a manner which limits the situation to describable characteristics allows the entity to work with those characteristics as specific catalyst for the self. To see any situation in a manner which allows the entity to see the one Creator and to see the self as the Creator provides the entity with, shall we say, spiritual charge or energizing effect that enables the entity to continue on its journey of seeking, balanced between the intense focus and desire to know and to serve and the knowledge that the entity is the Creator and need only be without worry as to what it shall be, for it is all that there is.

May we attempt further response, my sister?

Questioner: No, that's fine, thank you.

I am Latwii, and we thank you, my sister. Is there another query at this time?

Questioner: Latwii, do you think people worry too much? *(Inaudible)* guilty?

I am Latwii, and feel that we may respond most helpfully by suggesting that people worry just enough, and are just guilty enough, so that worry is seen as unnecessary and guilt is no more felt than necessary.

May we attempt a further response, my sister?

Questioner: No, but I always wondered why I never felt guilty, and I guess I am letting other people do it. Even when I guess I ought to I don't. Feeling that I am not self-made, I just don't take responsibility for my life. And if I do everything wrong, it really doesn't bother me. Is that my destiny?

I am Latwii, and am aware of your query, my sister. We would describe it as perhaps your point of view which you have chosen for specific purposes, purposes which are unique to you yet in common with all who seek the one Creator, each in its own way.

May we attempt further response, my sister?

Questioner: No, you made me realize I don't have to feel guilty because I don't feel guilty.

I am Latwii, and am grateful to have been of some small service, my sister. Is there another query at this time?

(Pause)

I am Latwii, and we find that we have apparently exhausted the queries for the evening. We are most grateful to each of you for inviting our presence, and we hope that you will remember that words are but opinions. We offer them as our service to you, and we thank you for each opportunity in which we may do so. We shall be with you in your meditations upon request. We shall leave this group at this time, rejoicing with each in the love and in the light of the one infinite Creator. We are those of Latwii. Adonai, my friends. Adonai vasu borragus. ✤

Sunday Meditation
May 13, 1984

(Carla channeling)

[I am Hatonn,] and I greet you in the love and the light of the infinite Creator. We thank each for inviting us to join in your meditation. We are aware that there was some ambivalence at the beginning of this meditation as to the preferred tuning being possible for a good contact, and we would like to take that opportunity to say that all that is necessary for a good contact is an open mind and an inquiring heart, that we are comfortable speaking to any level of understanding, and that we do not feel the need to give advanced information, but rather we feel the need to give service.

We do not deny that some information may be considered advanced and some concepts refined compared to the basic message which we of the Confederation of Planets in the Service of the Infinite Creator offer. Yet, the heart of each message is the same, and that is that the one original Thought, when sought with a full heart, yields the spiritual path which will be most helpful to the sincere seeker.

We begin by stating this in order to assuage fears that exist in this circle that one is more advanced than another or one's state of meditation may not be acceptable. All seeking modes are acceptable, and, indeed, closed minds are also very acceptable to us. However, we cannot by the Law of Free Will communicate through channels effectively when such an entity is present in the circle. In this instance we find that it is well to go over some very basic material. We will begin by speaking of lettuce.

There was once a farmer who planted a bountiful harvest of lettuce. When spring rains came and nourished the ground he rejoiced, and each weed was carefully removed. When the beautiful sun warmed and encouraged his young lettuce, he gloried in every leaf. Each new day brought new joy to the grower of this beautiful crop, for there were new furls and petals to this beautiful plant each and every day. This farmer had only [one] problem and that was that he was reluctant to take the lettuce from the earth and claim it as his bounty. Oh, every once in a while he would pluck a precious head of lettuce from its bed and would have a wonderful salad for his family. But for the most part the lettuce remained in the ground. And one day the farmer discovered that the frost had come and destroyed that which had grown, leaving him with nothing of lettuce except the brown remains of his beloved crop.

All things about you, my friends, live and have essence just as any crop. They respond to love. Whether we speak of crops, animals, children, people or stones, this is true. The thanksgiving and prayer and praise of our hearts moving into the surrounding vibrational vortex affects that all that therein is and incubates all that will be, and then that which we have incubated and that which we have nurtured comes to maturity. It is with an equally full heart that we plant and that we harvest. If you enjoy planting but not harvesting, then half of the learning available to you in this illusion is not being used. Indeed, were this another group with other personalities, the analogy might be the opposite, for in many cases there are those souls who would seek to harvest that which they have not nurtured, that for which they have not cried, laughed, planned and longed.

But in this circle, my friends, are planters. You have planted much that is full of joy. You are aware of the love of that original Thought, and you are able to avail yourselves of it in meditation and you are attempting to do this daily. It follows, then, that there will be a harvest each and every day, that there will be love that has been nurtured, cared for, cried for and that you may harvest that love this day, this moment.

You may ask, "What sort of crop is love? I would never let lettuce lie in the ground, but I do not understand what you mean." If that is the case, my friends, turn your eyes towards yesterday and see if you find that which was not harvested and which has become as something which is dead and available no more. Turn back then to today, this present moment, and open your senses to the possibilities. You have given them to yourself; you have nurtured each and every possibility, each day is harvest day. There is no lack or limitation of the original Thought. Therefore, reach out your hands, whether mentally or physically, and accept with praise and thanksgiving and joy the harvest that is yours this day, and let your hearts be happy, for there is a principle which we have found is as steady a rudder for your density as is possibility, and that principle is love.

There is no farthest and remotest point, no depth or height, no distance whatsoever that you may go by foot or in your mind that is not governed by the laws of love, and that law is that you are free in love. You are lovely, you are beloved, and you are loving, all in perfect freedom. This is your rudder, by this you steer. And where shall you steer, my friends, what shall you plant today that you may have a crop tomorrow or, to move backwards to our previous metaphor, what course shall you plot, what vector shall you take from this present moment? Love is not limited, but rather expansive. You may choose freely of those things that are of service and then you may plant by word, by deed, but most of all by intention. Each day spend some time touching with the center of your being in meditation and sometimes surrounding that planting, and sometimes surrounding that attempting to become aware of the harvest of light.

We would at this time transfer this contact to another instrument. I am Hatonn.

(Carla channeling)

I am Hatonn, and am again with this instrument. We thank each of those who attempted to avail themselves to our contact but there is what this instrument would call a great amount of intemperance, therefore we shall end through this instrument, which is a strong one. My friends, you know who we are, for we are the Creator. Have you identified yourselves? Oh, harvesters, go forth into your fields, for the crops are high, the bountiful plenty awaits and there are so few who are aware. Therefore, harvesters, go forth with open eyes and sensitive hearts and see the bounty of the Creator. Feel the love and find in each moment the great architecture of the one original Thought that sings throughout all that is light and all that is love and all that is. We leave you in the All that is in love and in light. We are in the service of the one infinite Creator, and for your benefit we call ourselves Hatonn. Adonai. Adonai.

(Jim channeling)

I am Latwii, and I greet you, my friends, in the love and in the light of our infinite Creator. We are most honored to once again join this group by your gracious invitation. We would at this time ask if there might be a query that we might attempt an answer to, as is our usual way of serving this group?

Carla: A friend of mine is very depressed and having a lot of trouble functioning right now. Would you comment on the condition and help me to understand better what it is he's going through?

I am Latwii, and am aware of your query, my sister. The entity of which you speak is one which has long moved along that path known to the seeker. That path seldom remains the same in all characteristics. The offerings of that path are of one basic nature, that is, to provide the food for the evolution of the being. This food is, however, provided in many ways. Among your peoples it is sometimes recognized that each situation has the opportunity for a transformation of some kind, a transformation of thinking, for as you think, so are you for that portion of time in which you inhabit what you call an Earthly incarnation.

The entity of which you speak now sits at what might be called a feasting table, yet few call it such, for there are few seekers in your illusion who have penetrated the heart of being and who have eyes to see, ears to hear, and hearts to understand. The illusion you inhabit is quite heavy. The sight is difficult. *(There is a loud whistling sound.)* We shall pause.

(Pause)

I am Latwii, and am once again with this instrument. The table at which this entity sits is one which is heavy laden with exotic foods, exotic to most seekers, for they are not usually tasted. The difficulties which seem present are the difficulties of assimilating this food. When the seeker is unsure of that into which it has placed its teeth, then perhaps the chewing shall be somewhat slow. And if some foods do not taste quite right, it must be decided whether it is the food or the tasting ability which for the moment seems lacking.

We may suggest that there is one great food which shall aid each seeker upon the path, no matter what table has been set. That food, as you know, is love—that state of being and accepting which love generates is that state which shall aid each seeker to digest whatever food is placed before it, for are not all foods portions of the one Creator?

May we answer you further, my sister?

Carla: No. I think that helps me understand what Hatonn was saying.

I am Latwii, and we thank you, my sister. Is there another query at this time?

S: Yes, Latwii. I would like you to comment on something. I've been wondering lately about what most people call prayer, and using this prayer for someone who is in need, and that part makes sense to me. What I'm wondering about is people who are either praying for something for themselves or something that they see is a need or a want, maybe not entirely selfishly, for themselves or their families. And the part I'm wondering about is, while we are here we are supposed to receive everything that we need, and if we are praying for something that we have previously decided that we don't need before we got here, then it makes sense to me that that prayer will not be answered. But, since we get everything that we need, if it is decided that this is a need, won't we get it without praying? So, my real question is, what is—how does that work? It doesn't make sense to me.

I am Latwii, and am aware of your query, my sister. We shall attempt a response by suggesting that, indeed, each entity has, shall we say, programmed the basic journey that shall be traveled, has examined the general terrain over which the journey shall take place, has indeed agreed with companions to journey together, and has set before itself a certain series of lessons and services which it wishes to learn and to offer. These are general guidelines, my friend, and if it be realized that the free will of each entity during the incarnation is equal to the programming before the incarnation, then it may be discovered that there is what one might call a dynamic tension or balance that exists between that which has been determined before the incarnation and the free will that is exercised during the incarnation.

The free will, of course, also is covered by the programming, yet the programming may also be altered by the free will. Thus, an entity at any time within the incarnation may be moved by two seemingly separate forces, the programming and the free will. The actions of the entity will be the product of the, shall we say, mating of the free will and preincarnative programming. To attempt to discover how much a part each plays in forming the actions, the thoughts, and the disposition of the entity is difficult, for both forces, shall we say, are plaited up together as one might see a rope to be, yet each plays its part.

An entity may at any time use certain ritualized techniques to express both the programming and the free will. The techniques may include that which you have described as the prayer or may include what have been called positive affirmations, and may include, for those who are seekers of the rituals to a finer degree, that called the ritualized magical performance, shall we say. In each instance the seeker is calling upon the one Creator in some form to aid the service or the lesson. As this call is made, those preincarnatedly programmed abilities and propensities lend their portion as do the incarnational free will choices. Thus, the product of the ritual is that which includes both forces. The free will may, shall we say, finely tune the general parameters of the preincarnatedly programmed path or attitude.

May we answer you further, my sister?

S: Well, yes. I've had someone tell me, said they were sending out thought-forms of wanting to acquire something, and they acquired this thing but somewhat at a cost because they either had not been specific enough or maybe didn't realize what else was going to have to occur for this to come about. Now, at this point this seems kind of hard for me to believe. So what I was wondering, in this instance, do your intentions or your polarity protect you at all against something maybe you haven't thought or hadn't realized as a repercussion of that which you're trying to attain?

I am Latwii, and am aware of your query, my sister. In this particular instance it may be generally agreed that one's polarity is a great protection when the surprises, shall we say, that accompany seeking within your illusion occur to the seeker. To be more specific, we might suggest that when the polarity of that entity is specifically expressed in the form of what you would call praise and thanksgiving, the finding of joy in the moment and the radiating of the one infinite Creator's love and light to all are means of this protection and are refinements, or shall we say, products of the polarity, and the seeker then may be seen to have an armor of light surrounding its being as it proceeds with its choices to learn and to serve.

May we answer you further, my sister?

S: No, you've been very helpful, and now I can understand praying. That makes sense. Thank you.

I am Latwii, and we thank you, my sister. Is there another query at this time?

(Pause)

I am Latwii, and we discover that we have once again exhausted the queries which have been brought this evening. We thank each for the service provided to us by asking for our presence with your group this evening, for in attempting to be of service to you do we learn more of our own journey of seeking. We shall continue with this service if it be your pleasure in what you call your future …

(Tape ends.)

Sunday Meditation
May 20, 1984

(Carla channeling)

[I am Hatonn, and] I greet you in the love and in the light of our infinite Creator. We come in the name of love, and we come with its blessing which has been bestowed upon us—not by merit, for we are but foolish travelers—[but] by the happenstance of birthright, a happenstance that we share with all of creation. We are having to speak somewhat slowly through this instrument as this instrument is fatigued. However, this instrument is glad to be used and so we gratefully make use of her.

There was once a young man, an ambitious young man of great attractiveness and many desires. Very early in the young man's adult life he fell in love with the enchanting smile of the woman who became his wife. He pursued her relentlessly, for she was indeed an elfin and enchanting creature, and once having enchained her, [he] tucked her into appropriate accommodations and largely forgot about her nature, for his desires were for power and money and success, and he used every portion of his mind and will to work towards those goals.

He disliked college because it took so long to get the paper that he needed for what he wished to do. Furiously, he would rage at his wife, "It is such a waste of time!" His wife would smile her enchanting smile and go about her domestic duties.

There then came a time when this young man, having achieved his education, went to work for the most calculatedly prestigious law firm in the great city which he called his home. He did not spare any effort. He worked early and he worked late. But the cases that he was given for several years were unimportant and he would rage at his wife, "This is a waste of time!" and she would smile that totally enchanting smile and shrug her shoulders and be gone about her work, tending her garden, visiting the sick.

And while he worked in the law, he planted his roots politically, for he wished to be a mover and a shaker, a statesman; he knew he could be the best. He worked at many odd jobs and began to hold small offices as a politician, and with his first election came the constant campaigning that was to consume much of the rest of this entity's life. And as he was saying the same speech for the forty-third time, repeating the words that were only mumbled nonsense, his mind dulled from repetition, all ideals gone, something inside him would rage internally, "This is a waste of time." And sometimes he would turn just to look at his wife, and the elfin grin that he was waiting for would come, the lines a bit more deep-set, the hair beginning to turn gray, her charming smile intact.

The man did indeed become a great statesman, or so people said, for this entity late in life turned and looked at all he had done and was appalled to discover that in his own estimation that which he had accomplished was nothing at all. And he said to his wife, "My darling, you have been with me for so many years. Why did you never tell me that the goals I sought were a waste of time?" Age had not dulled her impish smile. "My dear," she said, "In my opinion you have done many wonderful things. You have been telling yourself all your life that your activities were a waste of time. Look at me," she said, "I have never earned a penny. I have not served my country. I have not made great laws or understood international positions, made and broken treaties. You have done things. I've just been along for the ride and I've enjoyed it." And she smiled.

The statesman, so old in years now and so young in wisdom, gazed at his wife and saw her for the first time. "You have never wasted your time," he said, "because every time you smile, all that is about you is lit with love." She smiled at him. "And so it is with you," she said. "So it is with you."

Occasionally, as those who are seeking look carefully into their worldly day by day existences, they may find within themselves not the smile, but the folly. We urge you to balance your perceptions of yourselves. The characters, that which we have told you, are not real. They are easy, simple, archetypical figures, understood within your culture because of the marked difference between that which nurtures and that which is aggressive. Perhaps you are too full of your own folly, and make of it a terrible shame. But remember that when you smile, you illuminate creation through the boundless power and love of the infinite Creator.

Regardless of who you are, regardless of your circumstances and regardless of what folly you may indeed have accomplished, it is sometimes helpful to focus and concentrate upon a present moment, especially in times when folly seems to be uppermost in your mind, either the folly itself or your judgment of yourself. This illusion was not created so that you would act without folly, without error, without bias. You are expected to be biased, you are expected to err with regard to balance. These are the tools with which you learn. Sometimes it takes a great deal more than a short meditation for a seeker to rediscover his own smile, his own joy, his own inner light. Nevertheless, look in your closets, search the upper shelves. You stored it somewhere. Get it out, dust it off, put it on.

It is perhaps the greatest gift of consciousness that those who are conscious of themselves may choose not only to experience catalyst but to create attitudes. If your heart is breaking, if you have completely exhausted yourself, if you are unsatisfied, if you fall short of your own measure and have not found what you seek, if the world before you seems to be so dark an illusion that you cannot see, yet you may choose to smile and to laugh and to find your joy precisely in that which breaks your heart, that which saps your strength, that which you seek but do not yet find.

Human frailty, as this instrument would put it, is an often hilarious condition. Find your joy. In the midst of acknowledging the time you have wasted and the things you have left undone and the things you have done incorrectly, an exercise of utmost importance, my friends, is the finding of your smile, for as you smile, you are healed, and as you heal you become able with more and more vigor, more and more joy to go forth in life committing whatever folly or error brings each closer to the learning of the lessons of love.

The tidiness of your universe is on paper. In actuality, it is a very untidy metaphysical world. All is in complete balance but all is illusory. The only balance is within you. There it no circumstance that will be without folly, that will be without error, that you will face without misgivings, unless you home in on your own enchanting smile, a symbol of the one original Thought. Within joy and laughter all that is untidy becomes unimportant. All things become simple because they are unified with acceptance and peace. Find and keep your smile, my friends, as we endeavor to do. Find and keep the thanksgiving that is within you, that you are here in these fine moments of the present to act, to learn, to love, and to laugh.

We have one other thing to say, but are having difficulty using this instrument. If you will be patient, we will condition this instrument. We shall be using one word at a time, for this instrument is not prepared to channel this part of the message. However, this instrument has challenged us and is aware that we are of Hatonn and accepts the communication. It is not earth-shaking.

We wish to say that we feel that it is good to say at this time, because we have a very small group, that those who are present may consider well those things with which they may be through, those things which they wish to begin. In a larger group we would need to be far more general. The birth and the death have much in common, that is, transformation. These transformations are painful, and a mother will tell you of the pain of birth and we have no need to tell you of the pain preceding dying. However, the moment of birth and death is always, when it is healthy, joyous; when it is hindered, it is not joyous. Therefore, if you sense a transformation, hinder it not and allow the joy of transformation to be experienced as is natural. First the pain that precedes, then the joy of the moment, and then much rejoicing at that which is near.

We thank this instrument for allowing itself to be put in a somewhat deeper state. It is not often that we find that we may speak generally and yet somewhat specifically. We ask you to understand that our opinion is only opinion and that you must not take us literally but allegorically, for we cannot be responsible for your actions; we only give you food for thought.

There are stages of maturity, spiritually speaking. Each stage involves transformation and initiation. The unhindered will still have pain. When change is resisted or muddied by worry, the process can become quite unnecessarily painful. We urge each of you to minister to each other and to love each other and to let love abound and grow and take root wherever it may. We encourage each relationship, encourage each new-found realization, and we encourage careful attention to and analysis of emotional and spiritual pain, for the powers of transformation are great and the rewards are enormous. Nevertheless, transformations occur well to those with courage and a great sense of love.

We thank each of you for asking us to be with you. Our comments are poor and we are most grateful that we are allowed to share them with you. We are with you at any time that you wish to meditate with our company. I am of Hatonn, and I leave you in the love and the light and the laughter of the infinite Creator. Adonai vasu borragus.

(Jim channeling)

I am Latwii, and I greet you, my friends, in love and light. We are pleased to be called to your group once again. We hope that we may be of some small service this evening by attempting to answer those queries which may be of interest to those present. May we begin, then, with the first query?

C: Latwii, several nights a week I play and sing to my son B prior to his going to sleep at night, and I have found that he has a definite favorite as far as music I play goes. And I was wondering if his particular favorite song—what it is about it that draws someone this young to it? Is it the particular arrangement of the various sounds and vibrations? Why would someone that young be totally engrossed in one particular piece of music?

I am Latwii, and am aware of your query, my brother. The young entity of which you speak is one like many who has brought certain sensitivities and abilities and experiences, shall we say, into this incarnation in order that they might become the means by which it learns, experiences, grows and serves the one Creator. The songs, and especially the one of which you speak, serve as a means for this young entity to recognize some of those abilities that lie before it, knowing that it wishes to travel in a certain manner and to utilize these abilities. The young entity is especially appreciative of the reminder, the means by which it becomes consciously aware of that which it made unconsciously available to its current self before the incarnation began. Certain phrases within this song and certain vibrational sequences of sound serve to remind this young entity of the great path which it has chosen to travel.

It may seem unusual that a certain song could have this effect upon any entity, but we remind each present that the illusion you inhabit is quite dense and filled with veils, yet each veil is permeable and will be penetrated by the action of the unconscious and conscious awarenesses attracting each other according to similarity. These words and vibrations have, shall we say, struck a chord within this young entity and the remembrance, though faint, is awakened.

May we answer you further, my brother?

C: No, thank you. There is another question that hit me today. In our foodstuffs we use a new sweetening agent, aspartame, or what is called Nutrasweet, and I know on me, personally, it has a physical effect. I was just wondering if that particular chemical combination has any kind of effect on your spiritual self as far as doing damage to it?

I am Latwii, and am aware of your query, my brother. We might suggest that the great Self which is your spirit, as you have called it, is quite indestructible. It is this center which has sent you out into this world of experience which you now inhabit. This world of experience has many factors and agents which will work upon the mind and the body of an entity. You may see your world as one which is full of, what might be called, experiential friction. This friction is the rubbing together of the entity and its surroundings, experiences and situation in general.

This rubbing effect is for the purpose of creating a smoothness of being where there was once roughness. It is for perfecting the shining surface of the jeweled facets which are potentially within each. Yet there are in each entity's experience those grains of sand, shall we say, which tend to scratch and mar the smooth surface. This surface, yet, is a portion of the mind and body and is subject to the greater Self, that which you have called the spirit. There are many agents within your illusion which may be taken within the body or mind complex and which will have what seems to have a deleterious effect. Yet each experience, however deleterious or efficacious, can be worked with by the entity and serve to glorify the one Creator which …

(Side one of tape ends.)

(Jim channeling)

I am Latwii, and am once again with this instrument. The response which we had hoped to be of service by sharing was at an end with the tape, and [we] shall now ask if there is a further way in which we may respond, my brother?

C: No. I have one more question that's been on my mind. It seems that here the last several years I've found that, well, it used to be I used to like be able to, say, go to different fairs and things and ride the rides, and enjoy everything in town, and be able to not have certain emotions bother me. But in the last few years just the act of spinning at all … I seem to be very susceptible to get sick or feel extremely drained almost to the point of passing out if I have anything to do with them. And I was just wondering if some particular imbalance within myself is causing this?

I am Latwii, and am aware of your query, my brother. We examine this phenomenon within your experiential being and can find no difficulty which it is a symptom of. We apologize for the preposition at the end of the sentence, but this instrument is somewhat fatigued and is not quite sure where to place such prepositions. To continue our response. Each entity upon this planet [is] quite unique, as you are aware, and may express certain symptoms as you have mentioned and yet be quite and whole and balanced within its mental and physical and spiritual being. We use the term balance in the sense that the entity has prescribed before the incarnation so that the phenomenon of which you speak can be said to be one which is not terribly unusual or of any deleterious nature. It is simply that which you experience as a portion of your being as many would experience other seemingly distracting phenomena.

May we answer you further, my brother?

C: No, thank you.

I am Latwii, and we are most grateful to you. We hope that our responses are somewhat helpful. Is there another query at this time?

Carla: Well, I didn't understand the last answer, and so I wondered if I could go into it more or just ask you to restate it. Reprise it for me, why dizziness would be acceptable and the guy is real healthy but he is dizzy as he gets older, but it's okay. That there's nothing wrong with him. So why is he dizzy? Could it be tension, stress, something like that? Bad eyesight? Should he get his eyes checked? I mean, when you're saying he isn't balanced, are you leaving out bad eyesight and stress, or are you just saying that that's programmed into the incarnation at this point?

I am Latwii, and am aware of your query, my sister. We shall attempt a more succinct answer, yet we do not wish to give too much emphasis to the small details of your daily existence, for the concentration upon detail is not that which you have come to expend energy upon.

Carla: No. The point that interested me was the suggestion that a seeming imbalance like being dizzy, if fixed before incarnation, would be part of what the spiritual being would consider being a balanced being. That was the suggestion that I think I heard, like a preincarnative choice.

I am Latwii, and am aware of your query, my sister. Let us put it this way. The entity before incarnation decides to provide itself with certain opportunities to learn and to serve. Certain capabilities are then programmed. It may be that in this programming there shall be certain side effects which shall be considered, shall we say, inconsequential. This, shall we say, dizziness is such a side effect. For the entity to have, perhaps, certain physical abilities it will be necessary for the musculature and the skeletal system and internal organs to function in such and such a way, coordinated by the central nervous system and the brain. And for these capabilities to be expressed, then there will be certain side effects which shall be basically inevitable within your third-density illusion, given the way that the illusion functions.

May we answer you further, my sister?

Carla: No, I give. I still don't understand exactly what you're trying to say.

C: And we've also now become confused.

I am Latwii, and we do apologize for the confusion which our response has generated.

Carla: I apologize for being stupid.

We shall attempt one small analogy. An engine is built of certain parts within your illusion. The purpose of the engine is such and such. It shall do certain work. As the work is accomplished there is friction here and there within the moving parts of the engine. Yet the engine accomplishes its task. The friction here and there may be attended to by one who is aware of it by the application of that which you call oil or perhaps the repositioning of a certain part. The friction is not of a major concern, yet is there. Just so is the effect of which was spoken. The dizzying effect is there, is within the engine of the entity's being, and may be attended to, not because it is of great concern and shall cause harm to the entity. It may be attended to by the avoidance of circular motion or by the ability to withstand the discomfort.

May we attempt further response?

Carla: Then, you're basically saying that people get older, their parts wear out and that's the way it goes. Is that what you're basically saying?

I am Latwii. Ah, my sister. We believe you are more succinct than we. Yes, indeed. As one grows older within your illusion you will find the furnace which fires the physical vehicle develops certain, shall we say, idiosyncrasies.

May we attempt further response or another query?

Carla: No, thank you. Of course, I've got Don on the brain but I don't know what to ask. If you would like to comment, you're welcome. Such questions as how can we help, how can he help himself, do people really get better on that medication, am I worrying too much, and other questions like that. You can pick any of those. What is the nature of depression? What causes one person to be hurt terribly by exactly the same circumstances that two other people go through bitching and moaning the whole time but retaining sanity?

I am Latwii, and believe we have queries enough to attempt a choice of one. We shall then choose the latter, which seems to have the greater degree of interest. The depression which is experienced by the one known as Don has the purpose, as all catalyst does, of allowing balance to be achieved. One may look at that called depression and see that the potential for its opposite is being created. For one to be in despair, to be pressed down by the weight of one's own fears, is an action which has as its balance the transformation of the fear and the self so that there shall be a rising up in joy and faith. The greater the pressing down, the greater the potential for the rising up.

This is a great transformative experience for any to attempt. Yet remember, my sister and my friends, that within your illusion truth is still the truth. The one Creator exists within each moment and being in full at all times. And this entity which now moves through the moment of the illusion of depression shall present to itself the opportunity to move into a moment in which it is fully realized that the one Creator has always been present, is present now, and shall always be present, and the rising up in joyful thanksgiving for this knowing is that which awaits the one which has pressed itself down with its own fears that it is alone and is not enough to meet the occasion which it feels must be met.

May we attempt further response, my sister?

Carla: No, thank you.

I am Latwii, and we thank you, my sister. Is there another query at this time?

(Pause)

I am Latwii, and we are grateful to have been asked to join your group this evening. We hope that we have not been overly wordy and have not confused those present overly much. A little confusion, perhaps, is helpful in the seeking, yet we do not mean to be too helpful.

We look forward to each gathering of this group, for we are greatly honored to be invited to each gathering. We remind you that we shall join you in your meditations at your request. We shall leave this group, or so it shall seem, but in truth are always one with you. We are of Latwii, and we leave you in the love and in the light of the one infinite Creator. Adonai, my friends. Adonai vasu borragus.

Sunday Meditation
June 3, 1984

(C channeling)

I am Laitos, and greet you, my friends, in the love and light of the one infinite Creator. It is indeed a privilege to be again with you. We have received a request for our conditioning and would at this time pass among you and be with each who requests. I am Laitos.

(Pause)

I am Laitos, and am once again with this instrument. We would at this time speak but briefly to you to remind you that this is indeed an illusion and that you now exist and you many times forget this and allow yourselves to feel stress pressures that need not necessarily be there. My friends, take your time. Allow yourself those few, quiet, precious moments. We will be with you at any time. You need but request ours or any of our brothers' and sisters' presence. I am Laitos.

(Carla channeling)

I am Laitos. We have not spoken through this instrument for a considerable amount of your time. We are attempting to gear to this instrument's requirements. We greet you in the love and in the light of the one infinite Creator and we are exceedingly happy to greet each of you and to be using this instrument, which is a rare pleasure for us since we normally listen to the confused perplexities of this instrument rather than speaking through the instrument using its unperplexed vocabulary.

We would speak to you this evening upon the subject of love. This is an old favorite, and we enjoy coming back to it again and again. In this particular application, my friends, we want you to consider love as work and work as movement and movement as initiation and initiation as transformation. It is quite common for those who are seeking upon the spiritual path to feel that they are going through transformations of one kind or another. Quite often these so-called transformations are surface ripples upon a very shallow pond, and the seeker, rather than being transformed, is entertaining himself, playing a sort of game which passes the time without motion being accomplished. This often can only be seen by the seeker in retrospect and sometimes cannot be seen at all.

Conversely, it is true that sometimes the deepest transformations are not immediately recognizable. However, the motion of a true transformation has certain characteristics. Among these characteristics are direction and speed, in other words, my friends, the components of motion. It is not well to judge yourself or another spiritually, but when you wish to understand as well as you can the nature of what some call initiation, and what we would prefer to call transformation, you may first look for the indications of movement. Do you see direction? Do you see a rate of speed in which motion in that direction is being accomplished? These practical considerations may well inform you as to whether your own transformation or another's about whom you are curious is apparent or real.

We encourage this rather practical consideration because it is well that all transformation be, shall we say, down to earth, with roots as well as wings. Otherwise, the transformation, as we have mentioned, is only apparent, only a ripple upon the face of the personality, and will not bring either the burial or the resurrection for which one hopes in any transformational experience.

Perhaps the greatest question is why should there be initiatory periods or experiences in one's incarnational measure of space/time? Is there not a steady state of progress, the process by which one learns the laws of love? This is often seen as the case, however, it is not. There are levels or portions of experience, kinds of understanding or knowledge of love which, once having been learned, open a plateau and mesa experience, and for some of your space/time there will seem to be a steady stream of learning, assimilating and manifesting that which you have learned.

However, the seeker who is hungry—and, my friends, all seekers if they are alive are hungry and thirsty for the truth—reach the end of that particular mesa or plane or level or portion of love. It is not a question of going onward. It is a question, rather, of breaking through into another portion, another understanding of knowledge, of love. It is [a] question of ever so subtly changing the illusion itself. The illusion in which you live is semi-permeable. In initiation you bring forth that which is new from that great well of wisdom which is within you, and as a beginner, young and green and inexperienced, you start to explore the territory that you have with so much difficulty spread out for yourself. Your geography is not simply onward or further than you have been before; your geography is that of a different plane of experience.

If you could learn a new language it would help you to understand the nature of initiation, because even if you go through transformation in one place, the next time you say "cloud," you will perceive cloud differently, as though you said cloud in a foreign tongue and perceived it as that culture perceives cloud, and not as you have in the past perceived.

Each portion of the laws of love has its own needs, its own difficulties and its own offerings to add to a bounty of experience which is in the end one. And it is infinitely more possible to choose initiation while incarnate as you are at this time in third time, in third density, than at any later, or as you would say, higher density, due to the fact that the illusion, as our brothers and sisters of Laitos have said, is so very excellently devised to be difficult to penetrate. You must in some way pierce the veil that separates you from your birthright as you move into initiation.

This would seem to suggest that you should hurry right out and get an initiation right away. But, my friends, you have planned this important an experience before this incarnation. If you are working on what this instrument would call indigo ray you have already reached the point where you are capable consciously of choosing your incarnational experience in a large sense, not, of course, in a day-to-day sense. Your initiation will visit you; you do not call it. You prepare by using the experience that you have in order to find the one transformation that all transformations are about. That, my friends, is the original Thought. That, my friends, is love.

If you are seeking in this moment to find love, you are ready for your initiation, whatever it may be. We cannot tell you and would not if we could. If you are not seeking love in this moment, you will not proceed with your initiation. We may comfort you with the knowledge that your initiation will break through and will appear when you are ready. We may assure each that that extremely difficult but rewarding state is available to each in this group, and, indeed, each in this group has at one time or another been offered and to one extent or another accepted the responsibility of transformation.

Your experience of time as a river is greatly muted by the illusion. Time is set up within your illusion as discrete moments; certain numbers of these moments are also discrete and form a kind of clock within which time/space is linked to your daily existence. The more that you are in touch with love, the more closely that you are able to tune to the moments of true time, and thereby move into time/space to do that work which, done while incarnate, will be the richest and the most rewarding.

We are aware that there have been many questions about initiation, mostly from this instrument. We surprised this instrument by speaking through it when it thought it was very perplexed. We assure this instrument that it is, indeed, very perplexed, however, it is a good channel and we thank this instrument. We encourage each of you to move ever closer to the tuning of love, the reaching, the finding, and the sharing of the one original Thought with yourself and with each other. To love one another is to be the Creator. On the other hand, my friends, you are stuck with the job anyway.

We again express our delight in speaking to you, and would at this time transfer the contact to the entity known as Jim. We transfer in love and in light. I am Latwii.

(Jim channeling)

I am Laitos. The one known as Carla was, indeed, somewhat perplexed at our speaking through it. We thank that entity for its graciousness in transmitting our thoughts to this group.

Carla: What was your name again?

We are those, as you know, of Laitos, and greet this group once again in love and light. It is our privilege to assume a service which we are seldom able to assume for this group. This evening it is appropriate that we do so, and that is that we attempt to answer those queries which may be upon the minds of those present. May we then begin with the first query?

Questioner: Yes, I have a question. It refers—something you said a moment ago prompted me to think of this. I read a long time ago or heard somewhere that any work done on this side of the veil, of physical existence, as versus work done on the other side, that anything done on this side is basically multiplied in its effect on our spiritual self simply because we have such adversity in the physical to overcome in order to accomplish anything. Could you comment on that?

I am Laitos, and would be happy to attempt this query. It is true, my brother, that each of you within your illusion labors under quite, as you would say, adverse conditions, for each of you is the Creator, yet that truth can only be felt to most of your peoples through faith, for that great veil of which you speak does indeed exist. That veil shields your knowing of your true identity from your conscious mind with great efficiency so that you are as the one who plays the game of cards. You do not know the rules, yet you hold the hand and on the other side of that veil could see clearly each card, each rule, each play, and would do what was most loving with each action and thought. Yet, in your present position, you struggle through a darkness of forgetting, searching for the card and perplexed at the game and learning the rules, shall we say, by trial and by error.

Yet, we say there are no errors, for each experience is a grand effort of the Creator to know Itself, and as you move through your illusion little by little the light of truth which you see illuminates more and more of your path. The great obstacles which stand before you due to your own ignorance of your identity allow you to achieve a spiritual strength which would not be possible should there be no veil and should you know that you are the Creator and should you know that without doubt.

May we answer you further, my brother?

Questioner: No, that's fine. Thank you.

We thank you, my brother, for allowing us this humble service. Is there another query?

Questioner: I have a question that's similar to his, that's related to his, and that is, are you saying that it's not a matter of learning to love so much as getting back in touch with love, that we already basically know it but that the veil hides us from our knowledge? Is that essentially what you're saying?

I am Laitos. That is correct, my sister. There are many ways in which this simple truth might be stated, and you have chosen two which are most clear.

May we attempt further response?

Questioner: Thank you very much, that's sufficient.

I am Laitos, and we thank you, my sister. May we attempt another query?

Carla: Are you sure you're Laitos?

I am Laitos, and am reasonably sure that we have used the same vibration for some period of time and timelessness. We speak to this group this evening concerning the basic vibration of love, for this particular group is vibrating in that mode, shall we say, with a great and deep frequency.

May we attempt another query?

Carla: No, I'm just getting the vibration of Latwii. Perhaps both of you are here.

I am Laitos, and we would affirm that those of Latwii have joined this group and have assisted us in conditioning this instrument, for Latwii is the usual contact for this instrument and is therefore most familiar with the requirements for blending vibrations, and it has been quite some time, as you call it, since we have used this instrument.

May we attempt another query?

Questioner: Yes, Laitos. I just received conditioning which is very similar to the conditioning I receive from Latwii, and wonder if that was Latwii or if that was you, and if so … well, I'll let you answer.

I am Laitos, and would suggest that the conditioning which you have just received was a gift from those of Latwii, for you as others within this group are quite well tuned to that particular vibration and are comforted by it.

May we attempt another query, my brother?

Questioner: I have another question. Several of us in this group have a good friend named Don and he appears to be very confused in his thinking, and we are having a great struggle supporting him to grow in a good way, and I was wondering if you had any comments or statements to make about our dilemma to help us?

I am Laitos, and would make a simple analogy concerning this entity's current condition. If you will look at any entity which is being born into the world from your own human species to those of your animal, as you call it, kingdom, the young of each species is a most pitiful and bedraggled creature as it enters your illusion, quite helpless, and in need of great succor and support from its parents, shall we say, and in need of nurturing from its environment. Yet, as it gains its strength, it becomes able to move with its own power, to walk on strengthening legs and limbs, and to find its own food. Yet, did not this entity at one time exist within another illusion, in a form quite whole and mature, and did it not then choose to wrap itself in what one might call the cocoon of the womb that it might be born into another illusion in order that it might continue its great evolutionary journey of unity with the one Creator?

So does the one known as Don now seek to break from its cocoon of confusion as that which is old begins to fall away. Yet, still being aware of the old portion of the self as a portion of the self, it is difficult for the new entity being born to let go of that which is no longer needed. Yet, as that process occurs in what you call time, the new is born within the confusion of the old and the love of those which surround is that which nurtures it, even though it may not understand the form of that love, and may not know that it hungers for the food which is placed before it.

May we attempt further response, my sister?

Questioner: I think that is very sufficient, and thank you very much. It really clears up a lot of questions.

We are most pleased to be of some small service. May we attempt another query?

Carla: If two people are going through initiation at the same time and they are in the same family, are those two initiations …

(Side one of tape ends.)

(Jim channeling)

I am Laitos, and am with this instrument once again. The condition of which you speak, my sister, is a condition which does, indeed, reflect a unity which is always present, yet is present to a much finer and fuller degree in the current situation. The process of initiation is one which is periodically made available to the conscious self by the preincarnative programming, shall we say, and the incarnative placement through time and space by the unconscious entity or mind, and it is this placement of opportunity which has now occurred within the entity known as Don and within your own being.

These initiations, as they have been called, have been placed simultaneously in order that there might be a greater opportunity for each to aid the other since each is, indeed, a great unified portion of the other in ways which are most difficult for us to enunciate using your words.

May we answer you further, my sister?

Carla: No, thank you.

I am Laitos, and we thank you, my sister. May we attempt another query?

S: Yes, Laitos. I think I'd like to jump on this conditioning bandwagon this evening. Were you attempting to get ahold of me? I felt my heart jump up to ninety miles a minute and I thought, "Well, who the heck is that?" And of course after you came,

I thought, "Well that's probably what it was," but would you confirm that for me?

I am Laitos, and would be happy to confirm that we have indeed attempted to blend our vibrations with yours, but found that there was some reservation upon your part concerning the speaking of our words, and therefore we retired to another instrument.

May we answer you further, my sister?

S: No, thank you. I'll keep a closer eye out for you. It's just been so long since you were with me, I didn't recognize you.

I am Laitos, and am most pleased to once again be able to speak to this group and to blend our vibrations with each present, and we hope that our great desire to share the concept of love and our perception of it might be a mark which is noted as ours and our service to you.

May we attempt another query?

(Pause)

I am Laitos. Those of Latwii and those of our group wish to express great appreciation to each for inviting our presence this evening. We are honored to share our humble service with you as each seeks the love and the light of the one Creator. We join you in the praise and in the thanksgiving which we find in each heart even through the difficulties which face many. Seek that love and light always, my friends, for it is the heart of your being and the heart of each moment through which you pass, and if you can but keep a glimmer within your consciousness, you will have a guidepost which shall not fail you, even though the world about you may seem to crumble into tears, into dust, and into confusion. All that shall pass away for it is but illusion, yet the love and light of the one Creator shall never leave you, for you are It.

We leave you in that love and light. Adonai my friends. Adonai vasu borragus.

www.ingramcontent.com/pod-product-compliance
Lightning Source LLC
Chambersburg PA
CBHW080420230426
43662CB00015B/2165